Cosmopolitanism in Hard Times

International Studies in Sociology and Social Anthropology

Series Editor

Alberto Martinelli (*University of Milan*)

Editorial Board

Vincenzo Cicchelli (*Ceped, Université Paris Descartes/*IRD)
Vittorio Cotesta (*Università degli Studi Roma Tre*)
Benjamin Gregg (*University of Texas at Austin*)
Leo Penta (*Katholische Hochschule für Sozialwesen Berlin*)
Elisa Reis (*Universidade Federal do Rio de Janeiro*)
Madalina Vartejanu-Joubert (*Institut National des Langues et Civilisations Orientales*, Paris)

VOLUME 136

The titles published in this series are listed at *brill.com/issa*

Cosmopolitanism in Hard Times

Edited by

Vincenzo Cicchelli and Sylvie Mesure

BRILL

LEIDEN | BOSTON

Cover illustration: Fushimi Inari-taisha, Kyoto, 2019. Photo courtesy of Vincenzo Cicchelli.

The Library of Congress Cataloging-in-Publication Data is available online at http://catalog.loc.gov
LC record available at http://lccn.loc.gov/9789004438019

Typeface for the Latin, Greek, and Cyrillic scripts: "Brill". See and download: brill.com/brill-typeface.

ISSN 0074-8684
ISBN 978-90-04-43801-9 (hardback)
ISBN 978-90-04-43802-6 (e-book)

Copyright 2021 by Koninklijke Brill NV, Leiden, The Netherlands.
Koninklijke Brill NV incorporates the imprints Brill, Brill Hes & De Graaf, Brill Nijhoff, Brill Rodopi, Brill Sense, Hotei Publishing, mentis Verlag, Verlag Ferdinand Schöningh and Wilhelm Fink Verlag.
All rights reserved. No part of this publication may be reproduced, translated, stored in a retrieval system, or transmitted in any form or by any means, electronic, mechanical, photocopying, recording or otherwise, without prior written permission from the publisher. Requests for re-use and/or translations must be addressed to Koninklijke Brill NV via brill.com or copyright.com.

This book is printed on acid-free paper and produced in a sustainable manner.

*In memory of
Robert Fine,
David H. Held,
Etienne Tassin*

ἐρωτηθείς πόθεν εἴη, κκοσμοπολλίίττηςς, ἔφη'
Asked where he came from, he answered: 'I am a citizen of the world'
DIOGENES LAËRTIUS, *Lives and Opinions of Eminent Philosophers*

Le patriotisme, c'est d'abord l'amour des siens, le nationalisme, c'est d'abord la haine des autres
ROMAN GARY, *Pour Sganarelle*

∴

Contents

Acknowledgments XI
List of Figures and Tables XII
List of Abbreviations XIII
Notes on Contributors XV

Introduction: Splendors and Miseries of Cosmopolitanism 1
Vincenzo Cicchelli and Sylvie Mesure

PART 1
Conceptualizing Cosmopolitanism

1 The First Axial Age and the Origin of Universalism 27
   Vittorio Cotesta

2 Kantian Cosmopolitanism 40
   Stéphane Chauvier

3 Cosmopolitanism and Classical Sociology 53
   David Inglis

4 Cosmopolitanism as a Siamese-Twin Global Concept 67
   Stéphane Dufoix

5 Ulrich Beck's Critical Cosmopolitan Sociology 82
   Estevão Bosco

6 Cosmopolitanism Is a Humanism 97
   Daniel Chernilo

7 Human Rights and Dignity 109
   Sylvie Mesure

8 From Subaltern Cosmopolitanism to Post-Western Sociology 121
   Laurence Roulleau-Berger

PART 2
Establishing Cosmopolitanism

9   Inequality and Global Justice   139
     David Held† and Pietro Maffettone

10 International Human Rights System   153
     Daniel J. Whelan

11 Cosmopolitan Democracy   167
     Daniele Archibugi

12 Cosmopolitanism and Multiculturalism   181
     Alain Policar

13 Cosmopolitan Cities   192
     Delphine Pagès-El Karoui

14 The Future That Europe Has Left Behind   205
     Massimo Pendenza

PART 3
Experiencing Cosmopolitanism

15 Unpacking Cosmopolitan Memory   221
     Hiro Saito

16 Hospitality, Cosmopolitanism, and Conviviality: On Relations with Others in Hostile Times   233
     Magdalena Nowicka

17 International Mobility and Cosmopolitanism in the Global Age   248
     Camille Schmoll

18 The Cosmopolitan Stranger   263
     Esperança Bielsa

19 Aesthetico-Cultural Cosmopolitanism   276
     Sylvie Octobre

20 The Cosmopolitan Individual in Tension   289
    Vincenzo Cicchelli

PART 4
Challenging Cosmopolitanism: a Fractured Cosmopolis

21 The Nation-State in a Global World   305
    John Agnew

22 Cosmopolitanism in an Age of Xenophobia and Ethnic Conflict   317
    Paul Bagguley and Yasmin Hussain

23 Cosmopolitanism and Religion   328
    Bryan S. Turner

24 The Dialectic of Populism and Cosmopolitanism   339
    Lauren Langman

25 Terrorism and Counterterrorism as Counter-cosmopolitanism   355
    Clive Walker

26 Competition for Global Hegemony   371
    Frédéric Ramel

27 Capitalism and Cosmopolitanism   383
    Robert Holton

    Index of Names and Notions   395

Acknowledgments

This book is the result of a long adventure that began in 2016. In these lines, we would like to warmly thank all those who have helped us. Our thoughts go to Massimo Pendenza, with whom Vincenzo Cicchelli organized in September 2016 (University of Salerno, Italy) the international symposium entitled 'Cosmopolitanism in Hard Times,' in which a number of the authors of this book participated, and who gave us his agreement to use this title. We would like to thank Alexandra Frénod for her invaluable help in the editorial work on the bibliographies. We would also like to express our gratitude to Jason Prevost (Brill) for his indefatigable support in this long-term project. Last but not least, three illustrious fellow travelers have unfortunately passed away, and we would like to pay tribute to their memory. This book is dedicated to Robert Fine, David H. Held, and Etienne Tassin, authors who have made a major contribution to the understanding of cosmopolitanism.

This book was supported by Gemass (Paris Sorbonne/CNRS) and by the IdEx Université de Paris, ANR-18-IDEX-0001.

Figures and Tables

Figures

4.1 Number of books and articles having *cosmopolitanism* in their title, 1970–2013 68
4.2 Yearly ratio of books and articles having *cosmopolitanism* in their title, 1970–2013 69
4.3 Number of books and articles having *cosmopolitanism* in their title, 1998–2011 69
5.1 The theory of world risk society and methodological cosmopolitanism 90
15.1 The variants of cosmopolitan memory 225

Table

21.1 Sovereignty regimes 311

Abbreviations

BLM	Black Lives Matter
CEDAW	Convention on the Elimination of All Forms of Discrimination Against Women
CERD	Convention on Racial Discrimination
CMIO	Chinese, Malays, Indians, and Others
COE	Council of Europe
CPED	Convention for the Protection of All Persons from Enforced Disappearance
CRC	Convention on the Rights of the Child
CRPD	Convention on the Rights of Persons with Disabilities
CTC	Counter-Terrorism Committee
EAC	East Asian Community
EASN	East Asian Sociologists Network
ECHR	European Convention on Human Rights
EU	European Union
FATF	Financial Action Task Force
GAFA	Google, Amazon, Facebook, Apple
GATT	General Agreement on Tariffs and Trade
GTD	Global Terrorism Database
ICC	International Criminal Court
ICISS	International Commission on Intervention and State Sovereignty
ICRMW	International Convention on the Protection of the Rights of All Migrant Workers and Members of their Families
ICTR	International Criminal Tribunal for Rwanda
ICTY	International Criminal Tribunal for the Former Yugoslavia
IMF	International Monetary Fund
IOM	International Organization for Migration
ISIL	Islamic State in Iraq and the Levant
LGBTQ	Lesbian, Gay, Bisexual, Transgender, or Questioning
LGBTQIA+	Lesbian, Gay, Bisexual, Transgender, Queer, Intersex, or Asexual
NGO	Non-governmental organization
OECD	Organisation for Economic Co-operation and Development
PPP	Purchasing power parity
R2P	Responsibility to Protect
TEU	Treaty on European Union
TfEU	Treaty on the Functioning of the European Union
UDHR	Universal Declaration of Human Rights
UN	United Nations

UNCAT	United Nations Convention against Torture
UNESCO	United Nations Educational, Scientific, and Cultural Organization
UNHCR	United Nations High Commissioner for Refugees
UNSCR	United Nations Security Council Resolution
UNTS	United Nations Treaty Series
UNWTO	United Nations World Tourism Organization
UPR	Universal Periodic Review
WIR	World Inequality Report
WTO	World Trade Organization

Notes on Contributors

John Agnew
is Distinguished Professor of Geography and Italian at the University of California, Los Angeles. He has taught at Syracuse University, the University of Chicago, the University of Siena, Queen's University Belfast, and the University of British Columbia, among other universities. He is a former President of the American Association of Geographers (2008–09) and founding Editor-in-Chief of *Territory, Politics, Governance*, a journal of the Regional Studies Association. He is the author of books and articles such as *Globalization and Sovereignty: Beyond the Territorial Trap* (Rowman & Littlefield, 2nd ed., 2018); *Hegemony: The New Shape of Global Power* (Temple University Press, 2005); *Geopolitics: Re-Visioning World Politics* (Routledge, 2nd ed., 2003); 'The Territorial Trap: The Geographical Assumptions of International Relations Theory,' *Review of International Political Economy* (1994); *Place and Politics: The Geographical Mediation of State and Society* (Routledge, 1989); (with Michael Shin) *Berlusconi's Italy* (Temple University Press, 2008); and (with Michael Shin) *Mapping Populism: Taking Politics to the People* (Rowman & Littlefield, 2019).

Daniele Archibugi
is a Research Director at the Italian National Research Council in Rome and Professor of Innovation, Governance, and Public Policy at Birkbeck, University of London. He works on the economics and policy of science, technology, and innovation, and on the political theory of international relations. He has worked at the Universities of Sussex, Cambridge, London School of Economics (LSE), Harvard, and Rome Libera Università Internazionale degli Studi Sociali 'Guido Carli' and gave courses at the Southwestern University of Finance and Economics Chengdu and at the Ritsumeikan University of Kyoto. In 2006 he was appointed Honorary Professor at Sussex University. In the field of international political theory, he has advocated a cosmopolitan democracy (coediting *Cosmopolitan Democracy: An Agenda for a New World Order* (Polity Press, 1995) and *Re-imagining Political Community: Studies in Cosmopolitan Democracy* (Polity Press, 1998); and authoring *The Global Commonwealth of Citizens* (Princeton University Press, 2008)). He has also worked on a greater involvement of transnational citizens to counterbalance the power of governments in world politics (editing *Debating Cosmopolitics* (Verso, 2003)). His latest books are a critical assessment of international criminal justice (with Alice Pease, *Crime and Global Justice: The Dynamics of International Punishment* (Polity Press, 2018)) and a plea to shape the European citizenship strategy (with Ali

Emre Benli, *Claiming Citizenship Rights in Europe: Emerging Challenges and Political Agents* (Routledge, 2017)).

Paul Bagguley
is a Reader in Sociology in the School of Sociology and Social Policy at the University of Leeds. His main interests are in the sociology of protest, social movements, racism and ethnicity, economic sociology, urban sociology, and sociological theory. In the fields of protest and racism and ethnicity studies he has worked on the 2001 riots in the UK, South Asian women and higher education, and the impacts of the 7/7 London bombings on different ethnic and religious groups in West Yorkshire, and super-diversity in traditional retail markets in the UK. His most recent books relevant to this collection include (with S. A. Tate, eds.) *Building the Anti-Racist University* (Routledge, 2018); and (with Y. Hussain) *Riotous Citizens: Ethnic Conflict in Multicultural Britain* (Routledge, 2018) and (*Moving on Up: South Asian Women and Higher Education* (Trentham Books, 2007). He is currently a co-investigator for the 'Northern Exposure: Examining the Implications of Brexit' project, funded by the UK's Economic and Social Research Council.

Esperança Bielsa
is an Associate Professor at the Department of Sociology of the Universitat Autònoma de Barcelona, Spain. She is the author of *Cosmopolitanism and Translation* (Routledge, 2016) and *The Latin American Urban Crónica* (Lexington Books, 2006), co-author, with Susan Bassnett, of *Translation in Global News* (Routledge, 2009), and coeditor, with Christopher Hughes, of *Globalization, Political Violence and Translation* (Palgrave Macmillan, 2009).

Estevão Bosco
is a postdoctoral researcher at the University of São Paulo and is currently a Visiting Research Fellow at the University of Sussex. He is a Fellow of the São Paulo Research Foundation, and a member of the Research Group in Political Geography and the Environment, University of São Paulo, and the Centre for the Philosophy of Social Sciences, Federal University of Rio de Janeiro. He sits on the editorial board of the journal *Sinais*. Previously, he was a research associate at the University of Campinas' Department of Sociology and the Research Group in Social Theory and the Environment; a São Paulo Research Fellow at the Free University of Berlin; and a member of the editorial board and editor of the journal *Ideias*. He is the author of several articles, chapters in edited collections, and the book *Risk Society: Introduction to the Cosmopolitan*

Sociology of Ulrich Beck (first published in Portuguese; Annablume & São Paulo Research Foundation, 2016).

Stéphane Chauvier

is Professor of Moral and Political Philosophy at Sorbonne University. Since his PhD dissertation devoted to Kant's cosmopolitan law, he has published various books and papers on global justice and migrations and, more recently, on the ethics of external effects. His academic works and publications also include many contributions on metaphysical and meta-ethical issues, especially on personal identity, first-person thought, and modalities.

Daniel Chernilo

has been a Lecturer in Sociology at Warwick, a Full Professor of Social and Political Thought at Loughborough University, and is now a Full Professor of Sociology at Universidad Adolfo Ibáñez in Santiago, Chile. He was written widely on the history of social thought, humanism, nationalism, and cosmopolitanism. His books include *Debating Humanity: Towards a Philosophical Sociology* (Cambridge University Press, 2017), *The Natural Law Foundations of Modern Social Theory* (Cambridge University Press, 2013), and *A Social Theory of the Nation-State* (Routledge, 2007).

Vincenzo Cicchelli

is an Associate Professor at Université de Paris and Research Fellow at Centre Population et Développement (Université de Paris/Institut de Recherche pour le Développement). He is the former General Secretary of the European Sociological Association (ESA); the former founder of the ESA research network 'Global, Transnational and Cosmopolitan Sociology'; and the former director of the multidisciplinary program 'Sociétés Plurielles' (Université Paris Sorbonne Paris Cité). He is currently the Director of International Relations at the Global Research Institute of Paris, University of Paris. He has been Visiting Professor at Roma Tre (Italy), the Universidad de la República (Montevideo, Uruguay), the Universidad de Santander (Spain), and the University of Salerno (Italy). At Brill, he is the Editor-in-Chief (with Sylvie Octobre) of the 'Global Youth Studies' suite (composed of the journals and the book series: 'Youth and Globalization'; 'Youth in a Globalizing World'; 'Brill Research Perspectives in Global Youth'): http://www2.brill.com/gys. He is the author of many books and articles, of which the latest are (with Sylvie Octobre and Viviane Riegel, eds.) *Aesthetic Cosmopolitanism and Global Culture* (Brill, 2019); (with Sylvie Octobre) *Aesthetico-Cultural Cosmopolitanism and French Youth: The Taste of the World* (Palgrave, 2018); *Plural and Shared: The Sociology of a Cosmopolitan*

World (Brill, 2018); and *L'esprit cosmopolite. Voyages de formation des jeunes en Europe* (Les Presses de Sciences Po, 2012).

Vittorio Cotesta

is a former Full Professor of Sociology, he has taught at the University of Roma Tre, the University of Salerno, the University of Rome La Sapienza, and the University of Naples, L'Orientale. He is a member of the Italian Association of Sociology, the Association Internationale des Sociologues de Langue Française, and the International Sociological Association. He has published numerous essays on sociology, in Italian and other languages, including: *Max Weber on China: Modernity and Capitalism in a Global Perspective* (Cambridge Scholars Publishing, 2018); *Kings into Gods: How Prostration Shaped Eurasian Civilizations* (Brill, 2015); *Global Society and Human Rights* (Brill, 2012); *Sociologia dello straniero* (Carocci, 2012); *Sociologia dei conflitti etnici* (2nd ed., Laterza, 2009); *Images du Monde et société globale. Grandes interprétations et débats actuels* (Les Presses de l'Université Laval, 2006).

Stéphane Dufoix

is Professor of Sociology at the University of Paris-Nanterre (Sophiapol Research Center) and teaches at Sciences Po. He is a senior member of the Institut Universitaire de France for the period 2018–23. His research focus includes globalization theory, historical sociology of social science, sociological and historical semantics of concepts, and political sociology of national identity discourses. His most recent publications include *La Dispersion. Une histoire du mot diaspora* (Editions Amsterdam, 2012; the English translation, published at Brill in 2017 under the title *The Dispersion*, was selected in 2018 by the magazine *Choice* as an Outstanding Academic Title for the year 2017). He coedited (with Alain Caillé, Philippe Chanial, and Frédéric Vandenberghe) *Des sciences sociales à la science sociale* (Le Bord de l'eau, 2018); (with Christian Laval) *Pierre Bourdieu dans l'espace des disciplines* (Presses Universitaires de Paris-Nanterre, 2018); and (with Alain Caillé) *Le Tournant global des sciences sociales* (La Découverte, 2013). He is currently working on an essay for *The World Sociological Archipelago* (forthcoming in 2020). In 2017, in coordination with Éric Macé (University of Bordeaux, France), he set up an international team of thirty sociologists to reflect upon the actual possibility of a non-hegemonic world sociology.

David Held†

was Master of University College, Durham, and Professor of Politics and International Relations at Durham University. At Durham, he was cofounder and Director of the Global Policy Institute and General Editor of the journal *Global*

Policy. He held a PhD in Political Science from the Massachusetts Institute of Technology. Before Durham, he was the Graham Wallace Professor of Political Science at the LSE. The author of over sixty books, he was the cofounder and Director of Polity Press. His major areas of research included globalization, democracy, cosmopolitanism, and critical theory.

Robert Holton
is Emeritus Professor of Sociology at Trinity College Dublin, and Adjunct Professor of Sociology in the Hawke EU Jean Monnet Centre of Excellence, University of South Australia. He is also editor of the Global Connections series published by Taylor and Francis. Robert Holton is author of many books and articles, including *Cosmopolitanisms* (Palgrave, 2009); *Globalization and the Nation-State* (2nd ed., Palgrave, 2011); *Global Finance* (Routledge, 2012); and *Global Inequalities* (Palgrave, 2014). He is also coeditor (with Bryan Turner), of the second edition of the *Routledge International Handbook of Globalization Studies* (Routledge, 2016). His most recent research on robotics and artificial intelligence is available (with co-author Ross Boyd) in the 2017 *Journal of Sociology* article 'Technology, Innovation, Employment and Power: Does Robotics and Artificial Intelligence Really Mean Social Transformation?'

Yasmin Hussain
is an Associate Professor in Ethnicity and Racism Studies in the School of Sociology and Social Policy at the University of Leeds. Her main interests are in ethnicity, gender, and terrorism. She has worked on the 2001 riots in the UK, South Asian women and higher education, and the impacts of the 7/7 London bombings on different ethnic and religious groups in West Yorkshire, South Asian migration to New Zealand, and super-diversity in traditional retail markets in the UK. Her most recent books relevant to this collection include (with Paul Bagguley) *Riotous Citizens: Ethnic Conflict in Multicultural Britain* (Routledge, 2012) and *Moving on Up: South Asian Women and Higher Education* (Trentham Books, 2007). She is currently a co-investigator for the 'Northern Exposure: Examining the Implications of Brexit' project, funded by the UK's Economic and Social Research Council.

David Inglis
is Professor of Sociology at the University of Helsinki. Before that, he was Professor of Sociology at the University of Exeter and the University of Aberdeen. He holds degrees in Sociology from the Universities of Cambridge and York. He writes in the areas of cultural sociology, the sociology of globalization, historical sociology, the sociology of food and drink, and social theory, both modern

and classical. He has written and edited various books in these areas, most recently *The Sage Handbook of Cultural Sociology* (Sage, 2016) and *The Routledge International Handbook of Veils and Veiling Practices* (Routledge, 2017; both with Anna-Mari Almila), and *An Invitation to Social Theory* (Polity Press, 2012). He is founding editor of the Sage/British Sociological Association (BSA) journal *Cultural Sociology*. His current research concerns the sociological analysis of wine and wine world globalization.

Lauren Langman

is a Professor of Sociology, Loyola University of Chicago. He has been Chairman of the Marxist section of the American Sociological Association and recipient of its lifetime achievement award. He is also been President of the Alienation Research and Theory Research Committee of the International Sociological Association twice, and remains on the board, as well as being on the board of the Social Movement Research Committee. His publications have included special volumes of *Critical Sociology* devoted to the Tea Party, as well as ideological domination (hegemony). His most recent books include (with George Lundskow) *God, Guns, Gold and Glory* (Brill, 2016), a psychocultural analysis of American character; and *Inequality in the 21st Century: Marx, Picketty and Beyond* (Brill, 2018). His next book is *Mobilization for Dignity or Ressentiment*, an analysis of the progressive as well as reactionary movements of the 21st century.

Pietro Maffettone

is Assistant Professor in Political Philosophy in the Political Science Department at the University of Napoli Federico II. He received his PhD from the LSE. Before joining Federico II he taught at the LSE and Durham University.

Sylvie Mesure

is a researcher at the Centre national de la recherche scientifique within the Groupe d'étude des Methodes de l'analyse sociologique de la Sorbonne. A member of the editorial board of the French journal *Sociologie* and Vice-President of the Société des Amis de Raymond Aron, she has focused, over the past few years, mainly on the history and epistemology of the social sciences. Through her collaboration with Vincenzo Cicchelli, she is returning here to a reflection initiated with Alain Renaut in their 1999 book: *Alter Ego: The Paradoxes of Democratic Identity* (Aubier).

Magdalena Nowicka

is a sociologist. She is a Head of Department Integration at the German Centre for Integration and Migration in Berlin and Professor for Migration and

Transnationalism at the Humboldt-Universität zu Berlin. Her research and teaching activities are in the field of transnational migration in Europe, cosmopolitanism and conviviality, social inequalities, diversity, racism, and qualitative research methods. She currently leads the project 'Revis(ualis)ing Intersectionality' (with Professor Elahe Haschemi-Yekani, HU Berlin). Previously, she led the project 'TRANSFORmIG. Transforming Migration—Transnational Transfer of Multicultural Habitus,' funded by the European Research Council (ERC) Starting Grant Scheme (2013–18) as well as various projects on Polish migration to Germany. Her most recent publications include *Transnationalism: Outline of a Paradigm* (in German; NOMOS, 2019); (with Mette Louise Berg) *Convivial Tools in Research and Practice* (UCL Press, 2019); and (coedited with Vojin Šerbedžija) *Migration and Social Remittances in a Global Europe* (Palgrave Macmillan, 2015).

Sylvie Octobre
is a researcher at Département des études, de la prospective et des statistiques, French Ministry of Culture, and Research Fellow at GEMASS/CNRS. At Brill, she is the Editor-in-Chief (with Vincenzo Cicchelli) of the 'Global Youth Studies' suite (composed of the journals and the book series: 'Youth and Globalization'; 'Youth in a Globalizing World'; 'Brill Research Perspectives in Global Youth'): http://www2.brill.com/gys. She is the author of many articles and books, of which the latest are (with Vincenzo Cicchelli and Viviane Riegel, eds.) *Aesthetic Cosmopolitanism and Global Culture* (Brill, 2019); *¿Qiéne teme a las culturas juveniles? Las culturas juveniles en la era digital* (Oceano Traverso, 2019); (with Frédérique Patureau) *Normes de genre dans les institutions culturelles* (Presses de Sciences Po, 2018); (with Vincenzo Cicchelli) *Aesthetico-Cultural Cosmopolitanism and French Youth: The Taste of the World* (Palgrave, 2018); and *Les techno-cultures juvéniles* (L'Harmattan, 2018).

Delphine Pagès-El Karoui
is an Associate Professor in Geography at Institut national des langues et civilisations orientales. Her research addresses Egyptian migrations (transnational networks and diasporas in Europe and the Gulf, imaginaries in literature and cinema); the spatial dimensions of Arab revolutions; and urban diversity and cosmopolitanism in Gulf cities. Since October 2017, she has been working part-time as a project officer for the General Directorate for Research and Innovation (DGRI) at the French Ministry of Higher Education. Delphine Pagès-El Karoui is author or co-author of three books, sixteen peer-reviewed journal articles, and nineteen book chapters. She has recently been invited to speak at several international conferences: at New York University Abu Dhabi,

Oslo University, Colegio de la Frontera Norte (and the Center of Mexican and Central American Studies (Tijuana), and Cairo University, among others. In the multidisciplinary program Sociétés Plurielles (Université Sorbonne Paris Cité, USPC), she heads one of the three research axis about migrations and cosmopolitanism in global cities. With Catherine Lejeune, Camille Schmoll, and Hélène Thiollet, she organizes the MAGMET (MigrAnts in Global Metropolises) seminar. It articulates urban change, migration, and globalization with a view to analyzing the fabric of world cities, in particular the diversity that emerges from large metropolises which are characterized by the growing presence of migrants and foreigners.

Massimo Pendenza
is Full Professor of Sociology at the University of Salerno (Italy), where he is the Director of the Centre for European Studies. His recent publications include the following articles: (with V. Lamattina) 'Rethinking Self-Responsibility: An Alternative Vision to the Neoliberal Concept of Freedom' (*American Behavioral Scientist*, 2019); (with D. Verderame) 'Young People in the Age of Crisis' (*Youth and Globalization*, 2019); 'Societal Cosmopolitanism: The Drift from Universalism towards Particularism' (*Distinktion*, 2017); 'Intimations of Methodological Nationalism in Classical Sociology' (*European Journal of Social Theory*, 2016); 'Cosmopolitan Nuances in Classical Sociology: Reshaping Conceptual Frameworks' (*Journal of Classical Sociology*, 2015); and the books: *Classical Sociology beyond Methodological Nationalism* (Brill, 2014) and *Radicare il cosmopolitismo* (Mimesis, 2017).

Alain Policar
is holder of the *agrégation* in Social Science and a Doctor of Political Science. Since 2008, he has been an associate researcher at the Political Research Centre of the Institute of Political Science. His main research themes are the issues of racism, cosmopolitism, and citizenship. His books deal with the history of sociological thinking: *Bouglé. Justice et solidarité* (Michalon, 2009); and with political philosophy: *La justice sociale. Les enjeux du pluralisme* (Armand Colin, 2006), *Le libéralisme politique et son avenir* (CNRS éditions, 2012), *Ronald Dworkin ou la valeur de l'égalité* (CNRS éditions, 2015), and *Comment peut-on être cosmopolite?* (Le Bord de l'eau, 2018). He has also contributed to numerous collective works, including to the *Dictionnaire historique et critique du racisme* (Presses Universitaires de France, 2013) as a member of the scientific committee and coordinator. He supervised the books *Ronald Dworkin, l'empire des valeurs* (Classiques Garnier, 2017) and *Le cosmopolitisme sauvera-t-il la démocratie?* (Classiques Garnier, forthcoming). He regularly contributes

to newspapers (particularly *Libération* and *Le Monde*). He also contributes to the online journals *La Vie des idées, Nonfiction.fr, The Conversation,* AOC, *En attendant Nadeau*, and is a member of the editorial board of the journal *Raison présente*.

Frédéric Ramel

is Full Professor of Political Science at Sciences Po Paris. Head of the Political Science Department since 2016 and member of Center for International Studies (CERI)-CNRS, he was the Scientific Director of the Strategic Institute of the Military School between 2009 and 2013 and also one of the founding members of the European International Studies Association. His research interests include strategic studies, intergovernmental organizations and international security, history of concepts in international relations (philosophy and sociology) and aesthetics in world politics, especially the role of music. He has published in English and French journals such as *Arts and International Affairs, International Peacekeeping, Etudes internationales, Journal of International Political Theory, Revue française de science politique*. Concerning his latest books, he is one of the coeditors of the *Dictionnaire de la guerre et de la paix* (Presses Universitaires de France, 2017) and *Music, Diplomacy. Sounds and Voices in the International Stage* (Palgrave Macmillan, 2018).

Laurence Roulleau-Berger

is Research Director at CNRS, Triangle, École Normale Supérieure de Lyon (ENS), PhD and Habilitation in Sociology. She was a Visiting Scholar at the University of Berkeley, at the Institute of Sociology in the Chinese Academy of Social Sciences, and a Visiting Professor at University of Lausanne (Switzerland) and University of Beijing. She has undertaken research in Europe and in China in urban sociology, economic sociology, and the sociology of migration for thirty years. Since 2006 she has been involved in the epistemological way on 'post-Western sociology.' She is the French Director of the International Associated Laboratory CNRS-ENS Lyon/CASS 'Post-Western Sociologies in Europe and in China.' She has written, edited, or coedited over twenty-five books and numerous articles and book chapters in French, English, and Chinese. Among her recent books are: *Post-Western Revolution in Sociology: From China to Europe* (Brill, 2016); (with Yan Jun) *Work and Migration: Chinese Youth in Shanghai and in Paris* (L'Aube, 2017); (with Xie Lizhong) *The Fabric of Sociological Knowledge* (in Chinese, Peking University Press, 2017); (with Li Peilin) *Post-Western Sociology: From China to Europe* (Routledge, 2018). She is Editor-in Chief of the series Post-Western Social Sciences and Global Knowledge (Brill) and of the series De l'Orient à l'Occident (ENS Publishers).

Hiro Saito

is Assistant Professor of Sociology at Singapore Management University. He is broadly interested in intersections between power and knowledge, and his research examines how interactions among government, experts, and citizens shape public policy. He is the author of *The History Problem: The Politics of War Commemoration in East Asia* (University of Hawaii Press, 2016/17), which illustrates how transnational controversies over Japan's past aggression evolved from 1945 through 2015, tracing interactions between the governments, historians, and non-governmental organizations (NGOs) in Japan, China, South Korea, and the United States. He is currently working on his second book (*The Horizon of Democracy: Fukushima and Okinawa as Method*), a case study of political struggles over the Fukushima Nuclear Disaster and the US military bases in Okinawa, aimed at intervening in the contemporary debates on populism, technocracy, nationalism, and globalization.

Camille Schmoll

completed a doctoral thesis at the University of Paris Nanterre (2004) and a Marie Curie post-doctorate at the European University Institute, Florence (2005–07). Currently a Junior Fellow of Institut Universitaire de France, she is an Associate Professor in Geography at University of Paris Diderot, member of the CNRS team 'Géographie-cités,' and a Fellow of Institut Convergences Migrations. In 2017 she was appointed a member of the scientific commission in charge of the new permanent exhibition of Musée National de l'Histoire de l'Immigration (Paris). Her research topics include migration policies, gender and space, urban approaches to migration patterns, cosmopolitanism, cities and borders in the EU, gender generation and the family in international migration, and qualitative methods. She has published several articles in the field, in journals such as *Identities: Global Studies in Culture and Power*; *Journal of Ethnic and Migration Studies*; *Revue Européenne des Migrations Internationales*; *Journal of Immigrant and Refugee Studies*; *Cambridge Journal of Regions, Economy and Society*; and *International Journal of Migration and Border Studies*. She coedited the following books: *Méditerranée. Frontières à la dérive* (Le Passager Clandestin, 2018); (with Catherine Wihtol de Wenden and Hélène Thiollet); *Migrations en Méditerranée* (CNRS, 2015); (with the Femmagh Group) *Expériences du genre* (Karthala, 2014); (with Eleonore Kofman, Albert Kraler, and Martin Kohli) *Gender Generations and the Family within International Migration* (Amsterdam University Press, 2011); (with Marzio Barbagli) *Stranieri in Italia. La generazione dopo* (Il Mulino, 2011). She is currently working on a book on *Gender and Migration in the Mediterranean* for French publisher La Découverte.

Bryan S. Turner

is Professor of Sociology at the Australian Catholic University, Emeritus Professor of Sociology at the Graduate Center City University of New York, Honorary Professor at Potsdam University Germany, and Honorary Fellow at the Edward Cadbury Centre for the Public Understanding of Religion, University of Birmingham, UK. He won the Max Planck Award in 2015. He is the Director of the Centre for Citizenship at Potsdam University and Director of the Institute for Religion Politics and Society at the Australian Catholic University. He is the series editor of the Anthem Companions to Sociology and the Routledge Religion in Contemporary Asia Series. He edited the *Wiley Blackwell Encyclopedia of Social Theory* (Wiley Blackwell, 2018) and wrote the 'Introduction' to Émile Durkheim's *Professional Ethics and Civic Morals* (Routledge, 2019).

Clive Walker

is Professor Emeritus of Criminal Justice Studies at the School of Law, University of Leeds, where he has served as the Director of the Centre for Criminal Justice Studies (1987–2000) and as Head of School (2000–05, 2010). He became a Queen's Counsel (Hon) in 2016. He has written extensively on constitutional, terrorism, and internet issues. In 2003, he was appointed as a special adviser to the UK Parliamentary Select Committee, which scrutinized what became the Civil Contingencies Act 2004, following which he published *The Civil Contingencies Act 2004: Risk, Resilience and the Law in the United Kingdom* (Oxford University Press, 2006). His books on terrorism are recognized and cited widely and include *Terrorism and the Law* (Oxford University Press, 2011); *The Anti-Terrorism Legislation* (3rd ed., Oxford University Press, 2014); *The Routledge Handbook of Law and Terrorism* (Routledge, 2015), and (with J. Gurulé and C. King) the *Palgrave Handbook of Criminal and Terrorism Financing Law* (Palgrave, 2018). In 2010, he was appointed by the Home Office as Senior Adviser to the Independent Reviewer of Terrorism Legislation. His research on the Internet produced the book (with Y. Akdeniz and D. Wall), *The Internet, Law and Society* (Pearson, 2001) as well as many papers on specialized aspects such as virtual democracy and cyberterrorism.

Daniel J. Whelan

is Professor of Politics and International Relations at Hendrix College in Conway, AR (USA) where he teaches courses in international law and history, political theory, normative political economy, and human rights and development. He currently holds the Dr. Brad P. Baltz and Rev. William B. Smith Odyssey Professorship, focusing on human rights. He is past Chair of the Human Rights Section of the International Studies Association, having served on its Executive

Committee between 2007 and 2009 and 2014 to 2019. He is also Faculty Affiliate of the Research Program on Economic and Social Rights of the Human Rights Institute at the University of Connecticut. He is co-author (with Jack Donnelly) of the fifth edition of *International Human Rights* (Routledge, 2017). His first book, *Indivisible Human Rights*, was published by the University of Pennsylvania Press in 2010. Professor Whelan has published articles appearing in *Human Rights Quarterly* and *Humanity: An International Journal of Human Rights, Humanitarianism and Development*, as well as several book chapters and contributions to reference works, such as the SAGE *Handbook of Human Rights*, the *Oxford Companion to International Relations*, and the *Oxford Companion to Comparative Politics*.

Introduction: Splendors and Miseries of Cosmopolitanism

Vincenzo Cicchelli and Sylvie Mesure

> It was the best of times,* it was the worst of times, it was the age of wisdom, it was the age of foolishness, it was the epoch of belief, it was the epoch of incredulity, it was the season of Light, it was the season of Darkness, it was the spring of hope, it was the winter of despair, we had everything before us, we had nothing before us, we were all going direct to Heaven, we were all going direct the other way.
>
> CHARLES DICKENS, *A Tale of Two Cities*, 1859

∴

1   Introduction

Anti-universalists, anti-humanists, anti-rationalists, and anti-democrats have reemerged onto the global stage after foundering since the Second World War to such an extent that we believed them to have been defeated once and for all. The return of counter-Enlightenment ideas (Sternhell, 2009) has been accompanied by anger, resentment, and fear that seem to have spread to countries all across the world, which are being confronted with an unprecedented wave of sovereignism, populism, and xenophobia. Both increasingly integrated, but also more fragmented, our global world, which seemed so open just a short time ago, nowadays seems to be giving in to the temptation of identity politics and 'exclusionary nationalism' (Mounk, 2018: 199). A Manichean vision is emerging that separates 'them' (the Other, which includes all those who are different from us regardless of cultural distance) from 'us' (a local, ethnic, religious, or national shared identity). This division has become the discursive matrix that justifies hostility and violence (Bauman, 2016: 127). Far from the optimistic predictions of Francis Fukuyama, and of those who once believed

---

* Edited by Cadenza Academic Translations.

they would witness the advent of a definitively open, free, and peaceful world after the collapse of the Berlin Wall, the contemporary era is rather gloomy and seems averse to the very idea of cosmopolitanism. In this age of increasing uncertainty and xenophobia, which has also been described as a 'great regression' (Geiselberger, 2017), publishing a book on cosmopolitanism is a challenge and seems alien to the spirit of the times.

Without neglecting this darker side of the global world, the aim of our work here is to evaluate the heuristics and solidity of a (neo)cosmopolitanism (Fine, 2007) capable of: (a) analyzing the 'cosmopolitanization' (Beck, 2006) of the world (*factual cosmopolitanism*); and (b) imagining alternatives and possible futures based on human rights, cosmopolitan citizenship, and democracy (*normative cosmopolitanism*). The aim of such a (neo)cosmopolitanism is therefore to *understand* as well as *judge* the contemporary world. Although this work cannot be considered a cosmopolitan manifesto, as we no longer live in a time of carefree enthusiasm, it is entirely motivated by the deep conviction that there is a moral community of humanity, according to which each person, as different as he or she can be, must be understood as the equal of oneself, as an individual who must be fully respected on the grounds of his or her dignity as a human being (Held and Maffettone, 2017). Considered in its normative aspect, cosmopolitanism represents 'ethics in a world of strangers,' to use Kwame Anthony Appiah's famous expression (2006). These ethics are undoubtedly less demanding than those associated with the figure of the 'saint,' driven by religious obligations based on an injunction to universal love, but they commit us no less in terms of the respect we owe each individual, in spite of all our differences—a respect requiring care, attention, and recognition.

By highlighting the factual and normative aspects of cosmopolitanism, this book brings together authors from different backgrounds who have agreed to share their reflections on contemporary cosmopolitanism, already developed in their previous works. This reflection is also intended to be clear-sighted, as we cannot ignore the rift between the ideal of normative cosmopolitanism and the challenges that globalization poses to contemporary societies. Therefore, in the vein of Charles Dickens' words in the epigraph to this chapter, we invite the reader into a discussion on the splendors, but also on the miseries, of cosmopolitanism.

Since the late 1980s, numerous studies have sought to lay the epistemological, theoretical, and methodological foundations of a cosmopolitan approach to contemporary societies.[1] Born at the very moment at which *global studies*

---

[1] To name a few: Held, 1995; Hannerz, 1996; Vertovec and Cohen, 2002; Archibugi and Koenig-Archibugi, 2003; Tassin, 2003; Appiah, 2005; Pogge, 2008; Delanty, 2009; Holton, 2009;

were beginning to emerge as a new paradigm for the social sciences (Appadurai, 1990; Hannerz, 1990; Robertson, 1992; Featherstone, 1995), the cosmopolitan approach played a part in the renewal of studies on modern societies, finding its inspiration in an idea that, while 2,500 years old, was duly reconceived and adapted to the contemporary historical context (Beck and Sznaider, 2006). These works are part of a vast international corpus of theories, concepts, and fields of research that explore the possible applications of cosmopolitanism. The term 'cosmopolitanism studies' has been coined (Delanty, 2018 [2012]) to characterize the scope and dynamism of an approach that has now proved its worth in sociology, anthropology, political science, law, geography, literature, and moral and political philosophy. We know that the social sciences have experienced a successive linguistic turn (Rorty, 1967), a cultural turn (Jameson, 1998; Bonnell and Hunt, 1999), a material turn (Bennett and Joyce, 2010), and finally a global turn (Caillé and Dufoix, 2013). What might a cosmopolitan turn (Beck, 2006; Beck and Grande, 2010; Delanty, 2018 [2012]) imply for the theoretical imagination and for methodological creativity (Cicchelli, Octobre, and Riegel, 2019)? To answer this question, by way of its relatively short but exhaustive and detailed chapters that welcome personal opinion, this book aims to enable scholars, students, and readers to consider the possible outcomes, discover the seminal authors, and review the controversies and achievements in this area of study, as well as providing access to definitions and research results.

2 *In Principio Erat* ... Globalization

Cosmopolitanism has many meanings in contemporary literature. It can be understood as: (a) a social fact and an epistemological principle of a science of the global world; (b) a prospect of belonging, beyond the allegiances bequeathed by birth, kinship, or ethnicity; (c) an everyday experience of others in a world where the possibilities of contact with all kinds of otherness are countless; and (d) the moral foundation of human rights and the normative foundation of national as well as supranational institutions. However, all studies on cosmopolitanism have one thing in common: they consider globalization as a *minimum* starting point, if not as a phenomenon that is historically necessary for the emergence of a de facto cosmopolitan world.

Nowicka and Rovisco, 2009; Rovisco and Nowicka, 2011;; Sznaider, 2011; Cotesta, 2012; Skrbiš and Woodward, 2013; Giri, 2018; and Cicchelli, 2018.

Like a mantra, scholars evoke globalization as the *deus ex machina* bringing about what has for millennia been a moral aspiration, an exercise in philosophical thought, an experience of the diversity of *mores* and the vastness of the world open to scholars, travelers, adventurers, soldiers, conquerors, missionaries, traders, sailors, and merchants (Chanda, 2007). Each of these ideal-typical figures could be illustrated by historical personalities, resulting in a gallery populated by individuals who are of different nationalities, historical inscriptions, and social conditions, but all of whom share a *cosmopolitan lifestyle*: Diogenes, Cicero, Seneca, Erasmus, Kant, Humboldt, Goethe, Paul Morand, Victor Segalen, Charles Montagu Doughty, T. E. Lawrence, Nicolas Bouvier, Bruce Chatwin, Alexander the Great, Marcus Aurelius, Marco Polo, Ibn Battuta, Hassan al-Wazzan, al-Idrisi, Giacomo Casanova, Lorenzo Da Ponte, Bartolomé de las Casas, Matteo Ricci, Domenico Zipoli, David Livingstone, and so on. To characterize the cosmopolitan individual, two indissolubly linked traits have always been mobilized.

First, an individual is ideally cosmopolitan if he or she wants to be open to others, expresses his or her inclination to enter into contact with other ways of life, and wants to visit other countries. The world is a limitless field of experimentation that the cosmopolitan crosses, explores, studies, travels through, and observes (Coulmas, 1995).

Second, a cosmopolitan individual advocates a form of community among all human beings, regardless of social and political affiliation (Kleingeld and Brown, 2006), and brings to the fore a strong concern for the fate of all humanity. Being cosmopolitan means to orient or aspire toward an ideal that transcends local boundaries. Cosmopolitan behavior is conspicuously based on considering the world as a sphere of action and fulfilment where all people are equal and related to one another. In claiming to be a 'citizen of the world' (a *kosmopolitês*), the philosopher Diogenes the Cynic (413–327 BC) invented the famous oxymoron that was to become one of the most enduring concepts in the history of Western thought, extending well beyond the Stoic philosophy upon which it was based (Coulmas, 1995). This affirmation must be understood as an expression of the will to surpass the enclosure of immediate and contingent belonging (the Greek *polis*) and project oneself toward a wider horizon (the *cosmos*), embracing the world known to the Greeks of the time, the *ecumene*. Indeed, Marcus Aurelius (AD 121–180) said exactly the same when, many centuries later, he wrote: 'My city and country, so far as I am Antoninus, is Rome, but so far as I am a man, it is the world.' One could argue that during the reign of this philosopher-emperor, the Roman Empire was still at its peak in terms of territorial extension—even if provinces annexed under Trajan (AD 53–117) a few decades earlier (especially the territories gained in the Parthian Empire) had proved to be ephemeral conquests. It extended from the northern border of Scotland to Mesopotamia, from the territories below the Danube to Libya, from Morocco to the Black Sea, from Brittany to Romania. Rome was a city that would be defined as global today, due to its size and infrastructure, the diversity of the populations that lived there, as well as its efficient and relatively safe road system and sea transport system, which supplied it with goods (including wheat from Egypt, wine from Gaul, minerals from Dacia, wild animals from sub-Saharan Africa, and amber from the Scandinavian countries) and quick links to the borders of the empire, to the best thinkers in the Greco-Roman intellectual who lived in the capital. In the Pantheon, all gods worshipped in the empire were prayed to, Latin was the language of reference and communication (as well as their own languages, the most common of which was undoubtedly Greek, in the East), and people were subject to the same laws.[2] From 212 onwards, thanks to the Edict of Caracalla (AD 188–217), any free man of the empire could aspire to Roman citizenship if he did not already possess it. Thus, through its ability to economically, politically, and culturally integrate the conquered territories, urban centers, allied and submissive populations (and not only their elites), the Roman Empire favored this opening up of the entire Mediterranean region (and beyond, to the borders of the Rhine, the Danube, and northern England) and the Near East. This unprecedented openness was manifested by the significant circulation of humans, culture, and goods, in short by the birth of what we would today call a multicultural, multiethnic, multiconfessional, polyglot society (Angela, 2016).

Yet, even if we can speak of an early globalization to characterize this powerful integration machine that was the imperial structure (Roman, 2016), only a part of the world was concerned, whereas the rest, much broader than the geographical limits of the ancient world, was only to be revealed over the passing of centuries to the consciousness of Europeans. With somewhat nostalgic accents, historians have referred to other historical periods in which cosmopolitanism flourished: famous examples are the cities of the Ottoman Empire, such as Istanbul, Alexandria, Smyrna, and Salonika (Braudel, 1990 [1949]; Mantran, 1996; Benveniste, 2002; Georgelin, 2003; Tapia, 2006), the cities of the Austro-Hungarian Empire, such as Vienna (Schorske, 1979), and, further afield, the Chinese Empire of the Tang Dynasty (Lewis, 2009).

In any case, this double matrix of cosmopolitanism (i.e., the projection of the individual into the *cosmos*—what Latin-language authors call *universum*)

---

2 A very famous example of this is Paul of Tarsus, who was protected from torture by his Roman citizenship, and stood proudly before the tribune, asking to be judged by the emperor and not by Jewish law. See Acts of the Apostles, 22: 24–30; 25: 8–12.

and the strength of curiosity toward others, seems able to flourish at particular historical moments: those that are conducive to the formation of supranational political structures and interconnection (hence the example of empires) and/or unified spiritual, religious, civilizational worlds. This was the case with Hellenism, medieval Christianity, the Republic of Letters from the Renaissance onwards, the Age of Enlightenment, and the *Mitteleuropa* in Europe, Islam at different stages of its existence, and Confucianism and Buddhism in East Asia. On the other hand, this matrix seems to vanish in periods of contraction and decline, as may have been the case during the Early Middle Ages and during the period when European nation-states were being constructed. As for the contemporary period, it has witnessed, as never before in the history of humanity, the greatest interconnection of realities that were once distant and separate, the greatest opening up of the peripheries, and the greatest speed in the diffusion of ideas, cultural and imaginary products, goods, and individuals (Giddens, 1990; Robertson, 1992; Urry, 1995; Castells, 2009).

In other words, in the past, this double matrix could only be conceived by the imagination, and concerned only a few individuals. It was geographically limited by the understanding of the world prior to the Age of Discovery, the creation of the colonial empires, the establishment of the modern transport system, and the new communication technologies that have led to the shrinking of the world. However, this double matrix is now linked to a more pervasive, factual, and global experience of the world (Cicchelli, 2018). Let us think of all the iconographies that make it possible to see the Earth from space (Cosgrove, 2001), for example, as a unified whole, as a single and fragile blue stone floating in interstellar space, as a homeland to those who, through this distance, free themselves from everything that separates them and appear simply as brothers and sisters. Let us also think of this vast reservoir of ancient and modern myths and imaginations (Appadurai, 1996; Steger, 2008; Cheah, 2012; Cicchelli and Octobre, 2018a), constantly reworked by the main global industries, sports events such as the football World Cup and the Olympic Games (Lechner and Boli, 2005; Szerszynski and Urry, 2006), experiences shared by a large proportion of humanity through the global media. The distribution and diffusion of cultural products provide individuals all around the globe with vast, complex repertoires of images and narratives, 'in which the world of commodities and the world of news and politics are profoundly mixed. What this means is that many audiences around the world experience the media themselves as a complicated and interconnected repertoire of print, celluloid, electronic screens, and billboards' (Appadurai, 1996: 35). While individuals continue to claim local and national belonging first (Kennedy, 2010; Pichler, 2012), they have developed a *vision* of the finiteness of the world, interconnections, and global risks (Beck, 2006). While the philosophical matrix of the inscription of the self within a common humanity remains a constant from any perspective of cosmopolitanism—as does its necessary complement, openness toward the *mores* of others—its actualization cannot be the same in different historical contexts. What has profoundly changed is therefore this 'cosmopolitanization' of the world (Beck, 2006), which makes the globe an immediate experience (Tomlinson, 2007). The condition of the contemporary individual is very global (Appadurai, 2013). Today, the *universum* of cosmopolitan thinkers is the entire world, the *cosmos* having expanded to encompass the globe, and in this book we argue that there are relevant, diffused elements of cosmopolitanism in the global world that may be able to inspire cosmopolitan studies (Inglis, 2012).

3   Between Cross-pollination and Specificity

Whether we understand cosmopolitanism as a normative principle for justice, democracy, supranational citizenship, and/or as a descriptive toolkit of the functioning of societies (Roudometof, 2005), a cosmopolitan approach cannot avoid confrontation with the challenges of globalization, such as economic crises, epidemics, social inequalities, migration, terrorism, global warming, the proliferation of weapons of mass destruction, and so on.

We will here mention three major issues that could open up a fruitful dialogue between *globalization studies* (Turner and Holton, 2016 [2012]) and *cosmopolitanism studies* (Delanty, 2018 [2012]). Indeed, the rapid acceleration of the processes of globalization (Held et al., 1999) raises three challenges that the cosmopolitan approach must address.

First, cosmopolitanism addresses the structural phenomena of globalization in order to base its investigations on the non-economic dimension of globalization. One of the main challenges that sociology and the social sciences face today is understanding how individuals, collective actors, and structures cope with the dilemmas, tensions, and ambivalences of modern societies embedded in supranational dynamics. The challenge is theoretical but maybe even more methodological (Cicchelli and Octobre, 2018b). As Nayan Chanda said, using an effective formula (2007: xi), 'the economic definition of globalization cannot explain why an electrician in New Haven cared about the Brazilian rain forest or how global awareness of such issues has arisen.' Thus, by working on cultural forms, identities, institutions, and *mores*, a cosmopolitan approach makes it possible to document, on a daily basis, the paradoxical nature of the impact of globalization on the individual experience in contemporary societies. Contemporary societies should be understood by their internal transformations, according to dynamics of integration/fragmentation, inclusion/exclusion, and dispersion/concentration of economic, institutional, political, and social realities, formerly contained within the borders of nation-states. As a kind of Janus Bifrons,[3] globalization poses a vast social challenge, as large-scale transnational processes provide those who are mobile and educated with a number of opportunities for empowerment, but can also generate new inequalities, frustrations, resentments, disillusions, or uproot among those who do not fulfill these criteria (Sassen, 2014; Milanovic, 2016; Stiglitz, 2019). Those who perceive themselves as 'losers' in global economic competition, because they are excluded from wealth distribution and/or feel that they are ethnically, culturally, or religiously discriminated against, are often tempted by identitarian closure. Faced with this dialectic, two approaches are possible. The first is to understand resistance to globalization as an attempt to contest a homogenizing, alienating, *and* alien ideology, which is also destructive of those protections guaranteed to lower classes by the welfare state, that once allowed them prosperity and social integration. In the second, an emphasis on the cultural dynamics of globalization, on their relative disjunction from economic dynamics (Appadurai, 1990), can make it possible to understand cosmopolitanism beyond the ideology of the global elite and global capitalism (Robinson, 2014).

Second, if globalization could once (and especially after the fall of the Berlin Wall and the attacks of September 11, 2001) be considered the synonym of American hegemony (Pieterse, 2017), the rapid growth of other countries and their presence in the global arena (the so-called 'rise of the Others'—Rubinovitz, 2015) makes contemporary geopolitical relations more uncertain and complex, leading to the emergence of a competition that can no longer be reduced to the opposition between a center (the North, the West) and a periphery (the South, the East), but between multiple centers and several peripheries. Globalization entails powerful competition between new global players (China, India, and Brazil, for example) and developed Western nations with a view to imposing a new international order, a new economic hierarchy, and a new cultural hegemony through the use of 'soft power' (Nye, 2004). In this multipolar world, new balances and rivalries are emerging, manifesting themselves at macro and micro levels, not only through geopolitical threats or difficulties of governance but also through new vulnerabilities, inequalities,

---

3   In the ancient Roman religion, Janus was the god of the beginnings, gates, transitions, time, duality, doorways, passages, and endings. He is usually depicted as having two faces, since he looks to the future and to the past.

imbalances, *and* opportunities, creativities, *empowerments*, and rebalances against formerly purely national powers.

Third, there is not a single work on institutional cosmopolitanism—probably the area where the normative dimension of the cosmopolitan approach is more obvious—that doesn't emphasize the need to humanize, to master globalization by developing cosmopolitan citizenship, democracy, and justice (Pogge, 2008). The advent of post-national governance is therefore considered a necessary response to global risks (Archibugi, Koenig-Archibugi, and Marchetti, 2011). This response is urgent because of the relative exhaustion of the national states' means of intervention—particularly in the military, security, health, and economic fields (Scholte, 2011). Globalization raises the question of cosmopolitan governance, defined as a set of norms that apply to the unique system that global society has become (Martinelli, 2005). There is a gap between the belief, at the root of political modernity, that states can determine the future of national societies and the relentless constraints of the global economy, international law, and military alliances that severely limit their room for maneuver (Held, 2004 [2000]). Besides the acceleration of interdependence, works on global institutions have been fueled by the intensification of ethno-religious conflicts and the global spread of unbridled financial capitalism (Kurasawa, 2004). While nation-states remain unavoidable political realities, global processes have led to their relative weakening, which can be seen in the multiplication of actors and supranational forms of governance put in place to counter the many global risks.

It therefore seems difficult to imagine a cosmopolitan approach that is free from dialogue with *global studies*, or cosmopolitanism as a social fact outside globalization. The novelty of globalization may have led to the idea that a *cosmopolis* could finally fulfill the dreams of cosmopolitan philosophers and thinkers, by achieving a unity of the world (Coulmas, 1995), this time embracing the entire globe and detaching itself from imperial structures and the great religions. Without believing in the spontaneous germination of cosmopolitanism emerging from a connected world (Castells, 2009), authors have imagined that conditions could be created for the advent of a cosmopolitan world. The analyses of David Held and Ulrich Beck are emblematic from this point of view. The former asserts that globalization has created 'a vast community of fate' (1995: 225), while for the German sociologist, any advent of political cosmopolitanism is the historically necessary outcome of the society of global risk that is its historical framework. After placing risk at the heart of the understanding of early modernity, Ulrich Beck (1992) has consistently taken into account the power of risk in structuring global society in order to give contemporary cosmopolitanism an empirical foundation and the political urgency that is lacking in the Kantian philosophical tradition (Beck, 2008, 2009, 2011).

4 Anti-Cosmopolitanism: the Return of Counter-Enlightenment Ideas

Without giving in to pessimism and despair, we must recognize that in these times of anxiety and uncertainty about the future, such an ideal appears tainted by reality. While the very concept of cosmopolitanism has been revived at a time when globalization could present a more radiant face and when the political situation seemed to create more favorable conditions than in the past (the fall of the Berlin Wall in 1989, the acceleration of the European integration process), in recent years it seems to be characterized by a current of 'counter-Enlightenment' (Sternhell, 2009) in the sense that its claimed anti-universalism is accompanied by a narrow parochialism. Should we conclude that we have abruptly gone from a 'cosmopolitan turn' to a 'populist turn' (Krastev, 2017: 74), to a 'post-human rights era' (Wuerth, 2016), to a 'sovereignist turn?' It is true that there are several elements that point us in this direction. To take only the case of France (of course, the examples could also include Orbán's Hungary, Salvini's Italy, and Bolsonaro's Brazil) Marine Le Pen's party has skillfully presented itself over the years as the defender not only—and as it might be expected—of the French nation, but also of the Republic. Le Pen's insistence on secularism and gender equality—rights guaranteed by the Republic and assimilated by this ideological operation to the nation's identity traits—leads to an ethnicity-based conception of citizenship that strongly contradicts the Republic's universal aims. The laws of the latter are not an expression of the values of a national community, but emanate from a social pact that allows individuals from different cultures to live together under said laws. Republican universalism has thus fallen back on national particularism. This deliberate superposition of the two planes increases the ethnicization of French society and the identarian closure it claims to combat, by splitting it into opposing, unassimilable groups. It is based on the declinist and reactionary theories of the end of the nation and of European civilization.

In the context of the global spread of far-right thinking in pursuit of cultural hegemony, one would be entitled to wonder whether we are witnessing a powerful rejection of the hopes that decolonization, civil rights movements, and feminism have embodied since the 1960s. Whether they are 'retrovolutions' (Amselle, 2010) or 'retrotopias' (Bauman, 2017), contemporary counter-Enlightenment phenomena have in common an attraction to the past, real or fantasized, which has traded faith in progress for a dystopic fear of the future (Boym, 2001). We are undoubtedly at a turning point, at a weighbridge, and in a historical phase of uncertainty, appearing to contemporaries in the form of a bifurcation. Will we give in to fear, anger, hatred, and democratic fatigue (Appadurai, 2017) in this world that is in the process of barricading itself? Or will we be able to make the necessary leap forward to take control of our destiny, to change and amend a global process that separates us as much as it unites us, so that we can face our common perils *together*?

Contrary to the dreams of the eulogists of a unified world, the anonymous forces of globalization are at the roots of the unfulfilled promise of the advent of cosmopolitanism. But this should not discourage us. Cosmopolitanism, this ancient dream of humanity, has, since its origins, preserved its distinctive and original matrices while adapting to different historical contexts, returning with strength after periods of partial eclipse and relative splendor. We might hope for the same in the world of tomorrow.

5 Presentation of the Book

Considering cosmopolitanism as a specific approach to globalization rather than as a subfield of *global studies*, this book focuses on all areas that we consider particularly relevant to the deployment of a cosmopolitan sociology: (a) the normative orientations and value structures that underpin and make possible a 'cosmopolitan *Weltanschauung*'; (b) global cultural dynamics and imaginaries; (c) mobility, migration, and the challenges of coexisting in multicultural and multiconfessional societies; and (d) the moral, legal, and institutional foundations of citizenship, democracy, and supranational governance.

Referring to the functioning of global society in its cultural, institutional, and political structure, we approach these topics with a strong awareness of the twofold need to: (a) participate in a tradition of ancient thought that continues to permeate and inspire contemporary thinking; and (b) test cosmopolitanism against the return of the counter-Enlightenment, as mentioned. By following in the footsteps of the works that have been carried out in the social sciences over the past thirty years, this collective work contributes to showing that cosmopolitanism can be improved and amended so as to remain a realistic approach to the study of global society (Beck, 2004). This book is split into four parts, each aiming to show the heuristic advantage of using the cosmopolitan perspective in understanding the contradictions and consequences of globalization, without however ignoring the difficulties encountered, both theoretically and methodologically.

Part 1 ('Conceptualizing Cosmopolitanism') is therefore devoted to the conceptualization of approaches in cosmopolitanism studies under the double aspect of genealogy and of the critical discussion of its fundamental components. It is therefore hardly surprising that Chapter 1, written by Vittorio Cotesta, deals with the origins of universalism. Starting his investigation by examining the very birth of civilizations during the axial revolution (Jaspers, 1953 [1952]; Eisenstadt, 2003), he shows the profound unity of Eurasian civilizations beyond strong cultural discontinuities, by expanding upon the notion of transcendence without which no notion of universalism can be established, and which has given rise to the idea of 'humanness,' at the very origin of that of cosmopolitanism. The following chapters examine the conceptual structure of contemporary cosmopolitanism in its dual theoretical and normative aspects.

Chapter 2, by Stéphane Chauvier, looks at the Kantian heritage. According to Chauvier, Kant holds a central position in the history of cosmopolitanism because his legal-political work was the first to shift the ancient ideal of a *cosmopolis* from a vague yearning to a precise and realistic organizational perspective, anchored in the logic of the historical development of human societies. Cosmopolitanism was considered possible by Kant because of the ineluctability of an integrated and complete organization of human society.

In Chapter 3, David Inglis starts with the assumption that many developments in the thought of Marx and Tönnies on the one hand, and Saint-Simon, Comte, and Durkheim on the other, arose from the cosmopolitan thinking of Kant. While these German authors focus on the ambivalently cosmopolitan nature of capitalism, embodied especially in the metropolis, and their French counterparts concentrate on intergroup solidarities and the emergence of transnational moral cultures, these major lines of cosmopolitan thinking and politics in classical sociology are still relevant today.

In Chapter 4, Stéphane Dufoix looks at the emergence of the current landscape of *cosmopolitan studies* by historicizing the semantic journey of cosmopolitanism: the latter should be understood against the backdrop of the emergence of other Janus-faced concepts like diaspora or globalization, in a new epistemic era characterized by the increasing visibility of new academic actors coming from non-Western countries.

Building on the heritage of the classics and the renewal of cosmopolitan studies, Chapter 5, written by Estevão Bosco, focuses on the work of Ulrich Beck, whose cosmopolitanism is of crucial importance as it discloses the conflictive and integrative dynamics at play in the actors' experience of the side effects of technological development and globalization, and subjects this to normative and political criticism while also querying said normative and political horizon.

After this first set of genealogical chapters, the next three focus on analyzing the normative structure of cosmopolitanism through a reflection on the axiological concepts of humanism and dignity on the one hand, and problematize the concept of universalism on the other. In Chapter 6, Daniel Chernilo's goal is twofold: it is reconstructive, as he reassesses the way in which a critique of humanism has become the standard position in contemporary debates. In order to do so, he focuses mostly on Martin Heidegger's *Letter on Humanism*. Chernilo also aims to offer a positive argument on the relationships between humanism and cosmopolitanism, taking his cue from Jean-Paul Sartre's lecture *Existentialism is a Humanism*.

Sylvie Mesure (Chapter 7) extends these reflections by focusing on human rights. After analyzing the axiological core of the Universal Declaration of Human Rights (UDHR), based on the concept of dignity, she shows how, despite its specific historical roots at the end of the Second World War and the onset of the Cold War, the Declaration still possesses normative resources that are pertinent for anyone who cannot in good faith resign themselves to the world's injustices.

To conclude Part 1, Laurence Roulleau-Berger (Chapter 8) proposes a 'post-Western sociology' to enable a dialogue on common concepts situated in European and Asian theories. From the production of epistemologies of the Souths and the Easternization of the Westernized East, she introduces the idea of the de-multiplication, complexification, and hierarchization of new epistemic autonomies vis-à-vis Western hegemonies in sociology and the new epistemic assemblages between European and Asian sociologies.

Part 2 of the book, 'Establishing Cosmopolitanism,' examines the conditions for the effective implementation of cosmopolitanism. In particular, it shows how, since the dignity of every human being requires rights, an institutional and political cosmopolitanism could emerge. This part is intended to test the imagination of researchers in proposing supranational legal, political, and institutional apparatuses. Taking advantage of the consequences of globalization means changing the scale of regulation and rethinking the functions of the state in the global context. It is questionable whether global systemic interdependencies necessarily lead to a sense of obligation of international solidarity on the one hand, and whether there are institutional actors capable of fulfilling this aspiration to global regulation and enacting universally accepted and shared legal norms on the other. We can also question the degree of control of globalization by contemporary states and institutional actors. While geopolitical relations between nation-states are still thought of in Westphalian terms, it is of the utmost urgency that 'the *international* community of states [develops] into a *cosmopolitan* community of states and world citizens'

(Habermas, 2012 [2011]: xi; original emphasis). It also aims to show how the ever-increasing cultural differentiation of our societies and the creation of global cities, by making a greater interaction possible, gives rise to the hope of an at least partial realization of cosmopolitanism, understood in the sense of openness to and respect for others.

In Chapter 9, David Held and Pietro Maffettone begin by stating that the current global economic order is deeply unjust, as it enables some to thrive in ways that would have been unimaginable in the past, but still allows too many to perish in ways that are preventable. Therefore, they claim a minimal conception of common standards of decency and argue that the equal moral standing of human beings requires that they have certain basic rights, including the right to subsistence.

Since respect for human rights is 'a kind of civil religion of modern cosmopolitanism' (Beck, 2002: 37), it is logical that Chapter 10 offers a reflection on how the international human rights regime developed from the 1948 UDHR. In this chapter, Daniel J. Whelan considers that while the expansion of the normative and institutional features and practices of human rights has been impressive, this expansion has made us ever more aware of the vulnerabilities of human populations and the continuing need for human rights. As we witness the continual expansion of human rights norms, treaties, and institutions, we also know that their violations continue apace.

Chapter 11, written by Daniele Archibugi, is based on the observation that transferring sovereignty from states to international bodies becomes necessary because of the systemic constraints of global society. The power of international organizations is increasing at the expense of the democratic process that legitimizes national states. Therefore, the only credible and viable alternative to the confiscation of national democracy by some supranational bodies is 'extending democratic procedures beyond national borders' (Habermas, 2012 [2011]: 16). Cosmopolitan democracy is a project of normative political theory that attempts to apply the core principles, values, and procedures of democracy to global politics. It is an effort to reform the current international organizations and create new ones, with the aim of expanding the practices of democratic systems.

The effort to build a cosmopolitan democracy is even more urgent due to the multicultural societies in which we live. Nevertheless, as Alain Policar points out (Chapter 12), while the question of social justice is the backdrop of the encounter of these two concepts, they each approach cultural difference in distinct and perhaps irreconcilable ways. While multiculturalism is associated with a strictly holistic ontology wherein individuals are pawns manipulated by collective forces, cosmopolitanism is understood as an option wherein individual autonomy may be constructed without the need of an encompassing social matrix. Multiculturalism as a fact—and not just as a political option—is particularly prevalent in global cities (Sassen, 1991).

But how can we define a cosmopolitan city? It is this question to which Chapter 13, written by Delphine Pagès-El Karoui, is dedicated. As it is quite challenging to find a precise conceptualization of what a cosmopolitan city actually is, the author explores multiple cosmopolitan urbanities in a short tour of cosmopolitan cities: utopian and real, ancient and contemporary, Western and non-Western, by questioning whether 'cosmopolitanism' is an appropriate analytical tool for describing urban diversity in all times and places.

In the final chapter of Part 2 (Chapter 14), Massimo Pendenza attempts to highlight the *normative cosmopolitan* features of the European Union (EU), the only cosmopolitan and supranational political organization in the world, which distinguishes Europe from other global geographical spaces and results mainly from its historical-cultural characteristics. But Pendenza's chapter also dwells on the current crisis gripping the European project and questions its longevity, its destiny, its deepest meaning, its ideals, and its history, facing the crude reality of events.

According to Kwame Anthony Appiah (2006), a cosmopolitan approach should start by considering individuals as the object of moral concern, which means it should also take the choices individual people make seriously, including those related to the culture in which they live, and to the global spread and hybridization of culture. The aim in Part 3 of this book is to locate cosmopolitan theories in social actors' experiences and move from cosmopolitanism as a theoretical perspective of global society to the study of the tangible mechanisms that construct the lives of individuals in contemporary societies. Research has investigated how the continuous exposure of individuals to transnational phenomena leads to the emergence of a cosmopolitan outlook on the world. The forms of identification with humanity and the globe are fractured by the boundaries of the self and others, threats and opportunities, and the value of things global and local, which means that most people are likely to be ambivalent cosmopolitans (Skrbiš and Woodward, 2007).

This tension inherent in the cosmopolitanism experienced by social actors is visible in the chapter written by Hiro Saito (Chapter 15) on cosmopolitan memory. Here the author shows how cosmopolitan and national memory interact with each other, given that both cosmopolitanism and nationalism are legitimated to constitute an institutional contradiction, as a focal point for both the collaboration and competition of collective memories across national borders. In this sense, cosmopolitanism and nationalism form an untranscendable dialectic of collective memory in a globalizing world.

Cosmopolitan memory is not the only aspect of everyday cosmopolitanism that needs to be reformulated. This is also the case with the reception of refugees, an issue of the utmost political relevance, particularly in Europe. In Chapter 16, Magdalena Nowicka discusses the heuristic capacity of cosmopolitanism to understand the dynamics of hospitality. For her, while cosmopolitanism assumes that every human is capable of humanism by virtue of being human, conviviality draws attention to how hospitality is embedded in power relations that enable and disable the practice of hospitality. In turn, through the lens of conviviality, she reformulates the tension between hospitality and hostility not as opposing positions, but as a dialectical relationship. By continuing to explore the heuristic gain of cosmopolitanism in the understanding of cosmopolitan agency, Camille Schmoll (Chapter 17) considers whether increasing mobility over ever greater distances necessarily leads to the development of a cosmopolitan competence or whether, conversely, spatial immobility entails a fatal inability to be interested in others and 'willing to engage with the Other.' She answers these questions through today's experiences of human mobility on an international scale, particularly its two currently prevailing forms: migration and tourism.

The cosmopolitan perspective has undoubtedly focused on understanding the place of others—the global Other (Beck and Grande, 2010)—in our societies. Esperança Bielsa (Chapter 18) starts with the idea that in developing perspectives for engaging with the needs and views of others in heterogeneous societies, cosmopolitanism has contributed to specifying the key social and political relevance of the stranger today. For this reason, her chapter aims to theorize the cosmopolitan stranger, whose skills are particularly important under the conditions of generalized societal otherness.

Can a cosmopolitan position stand today without an analysis of global cultural consumption? In her chapter (Chapter 19, written in collaboration with Vincenzo Cicchelli), Sylvie Octobre assumes that individuals are no longer just consumers but also agents of cultural globalization, since they take part in the production and diffusion of increasing volumes of cultural contents, from tutorials to self-published and collaborative creations. Therefore, the growing use of cultural resources to define one's identity has made aesthetico-cultural cosmopolitanism one of the most readily available and thus banal forms of cosmopolitanism.

Cosmopolitanism 'on the ground' is far from a coherent philosophy and it is thus inadequate as a descriptive term for ordinary people's imaginative and discursive interactions. Consequently, Vincenzo Cicchelli's chapter (Chapter 20, written in collaboration with Sylvie Octobre) proposes to move toward a cosmopolitan socialization aimed at understanding the long, tangled, and reversible paths that lead people to produce (or not) universalistic accounts and cosmopolitan repertoires, and to perform (or not) cosmopolitan cultures.

The idea that cosmopolitanism will emerge through an incoercible community-wide force of destiny does not seem plausible in the short term—the American subprime mortgage crisis and the Europe's Migration Crisis have proven this, in Europe at least (Beck and Grande, 2007 [2004]; Cicchelli and Pendenza, 2015). As the chapters of this book illustrate the reflections behind the idea of the need to confront cosmopolitanism with the contemporary historical realities around which it unfolds, it is therefore in Part 4 that anti-cosmopolitan trends are more carefully considered. In a global world, nation-states do not disappear at all. However, they are adapting to the constraints of globalization, in particular by reformulating their sovereignty. This is what John Agnew demonstrates in Chapter 21. For him, the assumption of a close match between sovereignty and territory in the idealized nation-state is problematic. In its place, he develops a relational typology of 'sovereignty regimes' that serves to acknowledge and explore the complexities of sovereignty in the global era.

However, the question of resistance to the cosmopolitanization of the world is not reflected in the resistance of institutional actors. Anti-cosmopolitan trends have grown even more evident with the return of nationalism, and with increasing xenophobia, Islamophobia, and racism. In Chapter 22, Paul Bagguley and Yasmin Hussain begin with a discussion of Beck's (2002) analysis of cosmopolitanism to heuristically assess recent developments in the UK in terms of moments of 'anti-cosmopolitanism.' They show that what we have witnessed is not so much the increased cosmopolitanization that Beck predicted, but increased resistance to these processes. For the UK, this will manifest in an epoch of structural economic, political, and social changes in its relationship with Europe.

Another example of the fact that the cosmopolitanization of the world is by no means an established and indisputable fact is the return of religious fundamentalism. Bryan S. Turner (Chapter 23) begins his analysis with the consensual statement that a common narrative in the social sciences claims how secularization ushered in a world of enlightenment and eventually a regime of individual rights that allowed cosmopolitanism to flourish. Yet contemporary reality is far more complex than this. In fact, in response to globalization and secular modernity, there has been a widespread growth in religious fundamentalism, revivalism, and conservative religious movements that are opposed to modernity and its dominant theory, namely liberalism. Long ago in the history of human existence, Axial Age religions shaped what we now take to be humanity. However, these open cosmopolitan regimes have been deeply threatened by political radicalism, the origins of which are partly explained by the failures of economic globalization to sustain the living conditions of the working class.

In line with Bryan S. Turner's considerations, but with other tools and references, Lauren Langman (Chapter 24) explores populism as a powerful anti-cosmopolitan force. In his view, populisms are compensatory reactions to the spread of cosmopolitan values and identities. This leads to virulent 'clashes of identities' between various modern, better-educated, urban cosmopolitans, and more traditional, rural, or exurban groups who embrace reactionary populism as a reaction to a rapidly changing world that challenges and undermines economic well-being as well as traditional values, lifestyles, and heretofore privileged inclusive identities of real people facing decline, if not extinction. This in turn has engendered fear, anxiety, anger, and resentment.

Can the generous precepts of cosmopolitanism hold fast in the face of contemporary terrorism, especially after 9/11? Clive Walker's Chapter 25 attempts to answer this delicate question. Terrorism certainly causes problems for cosmopolitanism. However, a 'weak' and 'moderate' version of cosmopolitanism (Tan, 2004: 10) is applied in this chapter. It is 'weak' in that it does not claim that cosmopolitanism equates to the wholly equal treatment of people, irrespective of borders, but it does demand an equality of treatment that is sufficient to satisfy international standards of treatment. The version is 'moderate,' as it does not claim that cosmopolitanism is the sole relevant normative value.

The core of the applicable morality within cosmopolitanism remains the universality of human rights. Chapter 26, written by Frédéric Ramel, illustrates how a search for hegemony and the cosmopolitan project do not make good bedfellows. Their horizons are different. Thus, tackling the relationship between hegemony and cosmopolitanism becomes a pivotal element of the universalization of the cosmopolitan project: How can the Other be integrated within it without denying the singularity of otherness, from ways of thinking to manners of designing polities?

Last but not least, the final chapter of the book (Chapter 27), written by Robert Holton, shows that there is no convincing general theory of connections between capitalism and cosmopolitanism. Capitalism and cosmopolitanism have such a diverse range of manifestations that there is no singular relationship between the two. Global inequality is a major destabilizing feature of the contemporary world, and capitalist corporations, labor markets, and elite political and cultural formations play a very significant role in promoting and reproducing economic inequalities. Yet cosmopolitanism does not appear either as an unambiguous promoter of social justice able to offset global inequality, nor as a cultural buttress to the operation of global capitalism.

References

Amselle, J. L. 2010. *Retrorévolutions. Essais sur les primitivismes contemporains*. Paris: Stock.

Angela, A. 2016. *Empire: un fabuleux voyage chez les Romains avec un sesterce en poche*. Paris: Payot.

Appadurai, A. 1990. 'Disjuncture and Difference in the Global Cultural Economy.' *Theory, Culture & Society* 7 (2–3): 295–310.

Appadurai, A. 1996. *Modernity at Large: Cultural Dimensions of Globalization*. Minneapolis: University of Minnesota Press.

Appadurai, A. 2013. *Future as a Cultural Fact: Essays on the Global Condition*. London; New York: Verso Books.

Appadurai, A. 2017. 'Democracy Fatigue.' In *The Great Regression*, edited by H. Geiselberger, 31–56. Cambridge, UK: Polity Press.

Appiah, K. A. 2005. *The Ethics of Identity*. Princeton, NJ: Princeton University Press.

Appiah, K. A. 2006. *Cosmopolitanism: Ethics in a World of Strangers*. New York; London: W. W. Norton & Co.

Archibugi, D. and M. Koenig-Archibugi (eds.). 2003. *Debating Cosmopolitics*. London; New York: Verso.

Archibugi, D., M. Koenig-Archibugi, and R. Marchetti (eds.). 2011. *Global Democracy: Normative and Empirical Perspectives*. New York: Cambridge University Press.

Bauman, Z. 2016. *Strangers are at Our Doors*. Cambridge, UK: Polity Press.

Bauman, Z. 2017. *Retrotopia*. Cambridge, UK: Polity Press.

Beck, U. 1992. *Risk Society: Towards a New Modernity*. London: Sage.

Beck, U. 2002. 'The Cosmopolitan Society and Its Enemies.' *Theory, culture & society* 19 (1–2): 17–43.

Beck, U. 2004. 'Cosmopolitical Realism: On the Distinction between Cosmopolitanism in Philosophy and the Social Sciences.' *Global Networks* 4 (2): 131–156.

Beck, U. 2006. *The Cosmopolitan Vision*. Cambridge, UK: Polity Press.

Beck, U. 2008. 'World at Risk: The New Task of Critical Theory.' *Development and Society* 37 (1): 1–21.

Beck, U. 2009. 'Critical Theory of World Risk Society: A Cosmopolitan Vision.' *Constellations* 16 (1): 3–22.

Beck, U. 2011. 'Cosmopolitanism as Imagined Communities of Global Risk.' *American Behavioral Scientist* 55(10): 1346–1361.

Beck, U. and E. Grande. 2007 [2004]. *Cosmopolitan Europe*. Cambridge, UK: Polity Press.

Beck, U. and N. Sznaider. 2006. 'Unpacking Cosmopolitanism for the Social Sciences: A Research Agenda.' *British Journal of Sociology* 57 (1): 1–23.

Beck, U. and E. Grande. 2010. 'Varieties of Second Modernity: The Cosmopolitan Turn in Social and Political Theory and Research.' *British Journal of Sociology* 61(3): 409–443.

Bennett, T. and P. Joyce (eds.). 2010. *Material Powers: Cultural Studies, History and the Material Turn*. London; New York: Routledge.

Benveniste, A. 2002. 'Salonique, ville cosmopolite au tournant du XIXe siècle.' *Cahiers de l'Urmis*. http://journals.openedition.org/urmis/18.

Bonnell, V. and L. Hunt (eds.). 1999. *Beyond the Cultural Turn: New Directions in the Study of Society and Culture*. Berkeley and Los Angeles: University of California Press.

Boym, S. 2001. *The Future of Nostalgia*. London. Basic Books.

Braudel, F. 1990 [1949]. *La Méditerranée et le monde méditerranéen à l'époque de Philippe II*. Paris: A. Colin.

Caillé, A. and S. Dufoix (eds.). 2013. *Le tournant global des sciences sociales*. Paris: La Découverte.

Castells, M. 2009. *Communication Power*. Oxford: Oxford University Press.

Chanda, N. 2007. *Bound Together: How Traders, Preachers, Adventurers and Warriors Shaped Globalization*. New Haven, CT: Yale University Press.

Cheah, P. 2012. 'What is a World? On World Literature as World-Making Activity.' In *Routledge Handbook of Cosmopolitan Studies*, edited by G. Delanty, 138–149. London: Routledge.

Cicchelli, V. 2018. *Plural and Shared: The Sociology of a Cosmopolitan World*. Leiden: Brill.

Cicchelli, V. and M. Pendenza. 2015. 'The Looming Shadows of the Walls: Is Cosmopolitan Europe still Possible?' *Participazione e Conflitto: The Open Journal of Sociopolitical Studies* 8 (3): 625–642.

Cicchelli, V. and S. Octobre. 2018a. *Aesthetico-Cultural Cosmopolitanism and French Youth*. Cham: Palgrave Macmillan.

Cicchelli, V. and S. Octobre. 2018b. 'Debating Cosmopolitanism: A New Appraisal of Globalization.' In *Globalization, Supranational Dynamics and Local Experiences*, edited by M. Caselli and G. Gilardoni, 43–63. London: Palgrave Macmillan.

Cicchelli, V., S. Octobre, and V. Riegel (eds.). 2019. *Aesthetic Cosmopolitanism and Global Culture*. Leiden; Boston, MA: Brill.

Cosgrove, D. E. 2001. *Appolo's Eye: Cartographic Genealogy of the Earth in the Western Imagination*. Baltimore, MD: John Hopkins University Press.

Cotesta, V. 2012. *Global Society and Human Rights*. Leiden: Brill.

Coulmas, P. 1995. *Les citoyens du monde. Histoire du cosmopolitisme*. Paris: Albin Michel.

Delanty, G. 2009. *Cosmopolitan Imagination: The Renewal of Critical Social Theory*. New York: Cambridge University Press.

Delanty G. (ed.). 2018 [2012]. *The Routledge Handbook of Cosmopolitanism*. London: Routledge.

Eisenstadt, S. N. 2003. *Comparative Civilizations and Multiple Modernities*. Leiden; Boston, MA: Brill.

Featherstone, M. 1995. *Undoing Culture: Globalization, Postmodernism and Identity*. London: Sage.

Fine, R. 2007. *Cosmopolitanism*. London: Routledge.
Geiselberger, H. (ed.). 2017. *The Great Regression*. Cambridge, UK: Polity Press.
Georgelin, R. 2003. 'Smyrne à la fin de l'empire ottoman: Un cosmopolitisme si voyant.' *Cahiers de la Méditerranée* 67: 125–147.
Giddens, A. 1990. *The Consequences of Modernity*. Cambridge, UK: Polity Press.
Giri, A. K. (ed.). 2018 *Beyond Cosmopolitanism: Towards Planetary Transformations*. New York; Basingstoke: Palgrave Macmillan.
Habermas, J. 2012 [2011]. *The Crisis of the European Union: A Response*. Cambridge, UK: Polity Press.
Hannerz, U. 1990. 'Cosmopolitans and Locals in World Culture.' *Theory, Culture & Society* 7 (2–3): 237–251.
Hannerz, U. 1996. *Transnational Connections: Culture, People, Places*. London; New York: Routledge.
Held, D. 1995. *Democracy and the Global Order: From the Modern State to the Cosmopolitan Governance*. Stanford, CA: Stanford University Press.
Held, D. (ed.). 2004 [2000]. *A Globalizing World? Culture, Economics, Politics*. London; New York: Routledge.
Held, D., McGrew, A. G., Goldblatt, D., and Perraton, J. 1999. *Global Transformations: Politics, Economies and Culture*. Cambridge, UK: Polity Press.
Held, D. and P. Maffettone. 2017. 'Moral Cosmopolitanism and Democratic Values.' *Global Policy* 8 (6): 54–63.
Holton, R. 2009. *Cosmopolitanisms: New Thinking and New Directions*. Basingstoke: Palgrave Macmillan.
Inglis, D. 2012. 'Alternative Histories of Cosmopolitanism: Reconfiguring Classical Legacies.' In *The Routledge Handbook of Cosmopolitanism*, edited by G. Delanty, 11–24. London: Routledge.
Jameson, F. 1998. *The Cultural Turn: Selected Writings on the Postmodern, 1983–1998*. London: Verso Books.
Jaspers, K. 1953 [1952]. *The Origin and Goal of History*. New Haven, CT; London: Yale University Press.
Kennedy, P. 2010. 'Mobility, Flexible Lifestyles and Cosmopolitanism: EU Postgraduates in Manchester.' *Journal of Ethnic and Migration Studies* 36 (1): 465–482.
Kleingeld, P. and E. Brown (2006). 'Cosmopolitanism.' In *Stanford Encyclopedia of Philosophy*, edited by E. N. Zalta. Stanford, CA: Stanford University Center for the Study of Language and Information, http://plato.stanford.edu/entries/cosmopolitanism/.
Krastev, I. 2017. 'Majoritarian Futures.' In *The Great Regression*, edited by H. Geiselberger, 65–77. Cambridge, UK: Polity Press.
Kurasawa, F. 2004. 'Cosmopolitanism from Below: Alternative Globalization and the Creation of a Solidarity without Bounds.' *European Journal of Sociology* 45 (2): 233–255.

Lechner, F. J. and J. Boli. 2005. *World Culture: Origins and Consequences.* Malden, MA: Wiley-Blackwell.

Lewis, M. A. 2009. *China's Cosmopolitan Empire: The Tang Dynasty.* Cambridge, MA: Belknap Press of Harvard University Press.

Mantran, R. 1996. *Histoire d'Istanbul.* Paris: Fayard.

Martinelli, A. 2005. *Global Modernization: Rethinking the Project of Modernity.* London; Thousand Oaks, CA: Sage.

Milanovic, B. 2016. *Global Inequality: A New Approach for the Age of Globalization.* Cambridge, MA: Harvard University Press.

Mounk, Y. 2018. *The People vs. Democracy: Why Our Freedom Is in Danger and How to Save It?* Cambridge, MA; London: Harvard University Press.

Nowicka, M. and M. Rovisco (eds.). 2009. *Cosmopolitanism in Practice.* Farnham; Burlington, VT: Ashgate Publishing.

Nye, J. S. 2004. *Soft Power: The Means to Success in World Politics.* New York: Public Affairs.

Pichler, F. 2012. 'Cosmopolitanism in a Global Perspective: An International Comparison of Open-Minded Orientations and Identity in Relation to Globalization.' *International Sociology* 27 (1): 21–50.

Pieterse, J. N. 2017. *Multipolar Globalization: Emerging Economies and Development.* London: Routledge.

Pogge, T. 2008. *World Poverty and Human Rights: Cosmopolitan Responsibilities and Reforms.* Cambridge, UK: Polity Press.

Robertson, R. 1992. *Globalization: Social Theory and Global Culture.* London: Sage.

Robinson, W. I. 2014. *Global Capitalism and the Crisis of Humanity.* New York: Cambridge University Press.

Roman, Y. 2016. *Rome, de Romulus à Constantin: histoire d'une première mondialisation, VIIIe s. av. J.-C – IVe s. apr. J.-C.* Paris: Payot.

Rorty, R. (ed.) 1967. *Linguistic Turn: Recent Essays in Philosophical Method.* Chicago: University of Chicago Press.

Rovisco, M. and M. Nowicka (eds.). 2011. *The Ashgate Research Companion to Cosmopolitanism.* Farnham: Ashgate Publishing.

Roudometof, V. 2005. 'Transnationalism, Cosmopolitanism and Glocalization.' *Current Sociology* 53 (1): 11–135.

Rubinovitz, Z. 2015. 'The Rise of the Others: Can the US Stay on Top?' In *Great Powers and Geopolitics: International Affairs in a Rebalancing World*, edited by A. Klieman, 31–64. Cham: Springer.

Sassen, S. 1991. *Global City: New York, London, Tokyo.* Princeton, NJ: Princeton University Press.

Sassen, S. 2014. *Expulsions: Brutality and Complexity in the Global Economy.* Cambridge, MA: Belknap Press of Harvard University Press.

Scholte, J. A. (ed.). 2011. *Global Democracy? Civil Society and Accountable Governance.* New York: Cambridge University Press.

Schorske, C. E. 1979. *Fin-de-Siècle Vienna: Politics and Culture.* New York: Alfred A. Knopf.

Skrbiš, Z. and I. Woodward. 2007. 'Ambivalence of Ordinary Cosmopolitanism: Investigating Cosmopolitan Openness.' *The Sociological Review* 55 (4): 730–147.

Skrbiš, Z. and I. Woodward. 2013. *Cosmopolitanism: Uses of the Idea.* Los Angeles, CA: Sage.

Steger, M. B. 2008. *The Rise of Global Imaginary: Political Ideologies from the French Revolution to the Global War on Terror.* Oxford; New York: Oxford University Press.

Sternhell, Z. 2009. *The Anti-Enlightenment Tradition.* New Haven, CT: Yale University Press.

Stiglitz, J. 2019. *People, Power and Profits: Progressive Capitalism for an Age of Discontent.* New York; London: W.W. Norton & Co.

Szerszynski, B. Z. and J. Urry. 2006. 'Mobility and the Cosmopolitan: Inhabiting the World from Afar.' *British Journal of Sociology* 57 (1): 113–131.

Sznaider, N. 2011. *Jewish Memory and the Cosmopolitan Order: Hannah Arendt and the Jewish Condition.* Cambridge, UK; Malden, MA: Polity Press.

Tan, K. C. 2004. *Justice without Borders: Cosmopolitanism, Nationalism, and Patriotism.* Cambridge, UK: Cambridge University Press.

Tapia de, S. 2006. 'Entre Europe et Asie: Istanbul, cité cosmopolite, carrefour des diasporas?' *Espace Populations Société* 1: 167–179.

Tassin, E. 2003. *Un monde commun: pour une cosmo-politique des conflits.* Paris: Seuil.

Tomlinson, J. 2007. *The Culture of Speed: The Coming of Immediacy.* London: Sage.

Turner, B. S. and R. J. Holton (eds.). 2016 [2012]. *The Routledge Handbook of Globalization Studies.* Abingdon; New York: Routledge.

Urry, J. 1995. *Consuming Places.* London; New York: Routledge.

Vertovec, S. and R. Cohen. 2002. *Conceiving Cosmopolitanism: Theory, Context and Practice.* New York: Oxford University Press.

Wuerth, I. 2016. 'International Law in the Post-Human Rights Era.' *Texas Law Review* 96: 279–349.

PART 1

Conceptualizing Cosmopolitanism

CHAPTER 1

The First Axial Age and the Origin of Universalism

Vittorio Cotesta

1   Introduction*

The Axial Age theory holds that, during the first millennium BC—in particular around the 6th and 5th centuries BC—a revolution, fundamental for the history of humanity, took place. That was when man as we know him today emerged: a being capable of reflexivity and universalization, capable of devising, singlehanded, a new conception of humanity and the universe, as well as of the social and political world. For the very first time, man sought to answer questions regarding his life, his destiny in both this and the next world, availing himself of reason alone and challenging the fantastic narratives of myth and religion (Jaspers, 1953).

This new conception of humanity, of society and the universe, seems to have been born *at the same time* within the Chinese, Indian, and Greek civilizations. Confucius, Buddha, and Socrates are considered the *symbols* of this spiritual revolution. Furthermore, this revolution seems to have taken place independently in each of these three Eurasian civilizations.

The Axial Revolution gave rise to a new conception of human history. Having established a *before* and an *after*, historical phenomena were collocated within a definitive common framework, making it possible to compare and contrast the various cultures. At the same time, this led to a number of problems. The first concerned the very idea of the *rationalization* of history itself. Were the myth and religion really to be discarded? Was it not possible that, alongside this *new* philosophy and the science of the universe and nature, religion and myth might go on playing their roles in competition with the scientific approach to the contemplation of reality? When all comes to all, considering matters from a *long-term* perspective (*longue durée* view), the old myths, as well as religion itself, changed (and this holds in particular for the Jewish viewpoint) so as to be able to respond to the spiritual needs of human beings. It was necessary, however, to take into account the birth of a new way of considering God, the universe, as well as the physical and social

---

* Translated by Catherine McCarthy.

worlds in a more complex, dialectical, and conflictual manner. From then on, religious, philosophical, and scientific perspectives regarding the world confronted each other and engaged in a challenge in search of responses to issues essential to people's lives.

The Axial Theory, as formulated by Karl Jaspers, excluded the civilizations of Ancient Egypt and Mesopotamia from the agenda of historical investigation. On the one hand, he relegated them to the realm of *prehistory*, on the other, he denied them membership of the processes of *rationalization* which he considered the prerogative of the civilizations of China, India, and Greece (Assmann, 2018).

Finally, if one considers the *Axial Revolution* as a shift in the cultural assumptions and premises of a civilization, then we need to hypothesize the possibility of the existence of several Axial revolutions, not just one. This is the conclusion Shmuel N. Eisenstadt (2003) reached, when he posited that the course of history over the last three thousand years had been characterized by *two Axial Revolutions*: that of the first millennium BC, having its peak in the 6th to 5th centuries BC, and that born in Europe between the 15th and 16th centuries AD. Jaspers, on the contrary, considered this second revolution simply as a worldwide diffusion of Western thought and technology.

Despite the ambiguities and the as yet unsolved speculative issues, the theory of the Axial society is an excellent tool to apply when seeking to understand the origins of specific traits of various civilizations. In order to do this, however, it is necessary to use the concept in a broader manner than Jaspers had in mind and return to Weber, in particular to his conception of *rationalization* and *constellation of factors*. This will help us comprehend the origin of historical-cultural phenomena as Eisenstadt did, partially in agreement and partially in disagreement with Weber (Cotesta, 2018). If we wish to grasp the origins of cosmopolitanism and human rights we need to refer to this new, ample view, created by the theory of the Axial Age. A conception of humans as universal beings may arise only within a *non-local world*, within a society internally complex and differentiated, whose life reference is a territorially vast habitat with broad horizons. The *empire* is the ambit within which a concept like that of man as a universal being, along with a practice of cosmopolitan life, may emerge. Jaspers was right on this score when he placed the turning point of the Axial Revolution in the first half of the first millennium BC. In the cases of all three civilizations taken into consideration by him, the territorial references of their political systems were actually expanding progressively at the time of the revolution, due both to internal dynamics and conflict from outside of their individual political boundaries. In China, for example, the long period of the so-called Warring States began when several kingdoms competed for cultural hegemony and political dominion. In Greece, the growth of the city-states, of Athens in particular, led to conflict with the empires of the Medes and the Persians. In India, too, unifying tendencies were born within the different local kingdoms. In China, in India, and later in Rome, all these new political tendencies were to lead to the creation of the empire.

These political setups needed to be thought out in their spatial, cultural, and institutional dimensions. Already, in previous cases, like those of Ancient Egypt and Persia, universal ideas of man and society had been conceived. This is how we should consider the *Hammurabi Code*, where we find a law common to all those belonging to the empire, as well as special laws for the different single populations comprising it. Existing historical documentation shows, however, how a *new kind* of social reflexivity unfolds completely during the Axial Age, as hypothesized by Karl Jaspers. In this sense, the grand personages considered as the *symbols of the Axial Revolution* may be seen as the founders of the universalist concept of man, of cosmopolitanism as a way of life (Confucius, Socrates, and Buddha), as well as of the possibility of a theory and practice of human rights (Socrates).

2   Man as a Universal Entity

At the root of the idea of human rights and the way of life we call cosmopolitanism lie both historical and cultural premises. These do not apply, however, to every historical case. There may exist a general universal concept of human beings that fails to imagine them as entitled to rights or a different concept of rights themselves. The historical basis of the emergence of universal conceptions of man—as mentioned—is the creation of political realities that are not local in size. These are complex, highly differentiated societies, with a marked division of labor and a strong differentiation between the center and the periphery. These are systems capable of reflexivity, of control of their own boundaries, of dealing with internal conflict. This does not mean that they are perfect, seeing that their duration in time was limited. Herodotus in *The Histories* already observed that the duration of empires—in reality he was thinking of the ancient Persian Empire—is inversely proportional to their territorial extension. The greater their extension, the higher the probability that the peripheries may try—and succeed—in emancipating themselves from their political centers. To keep political units of similar dimensions together, a system ensuring rapid communication between the various parts of the empire is mandatory. Written communication, with its secret modalities, known only to the correspondents, took over from the oral form, so fragile and imperfect. Written communication guaranteed the stability of new political systems and created a stable *bureaucracy* capable of administering the state. It may be that this transition took place before the first Axial Revolution—as occurred in Egypt or in the reign of Hammurabi. In any case, it is a trait of all the empires that existed prior to the first millennium. It is a phenomenon linked to the growth of political entities. Without a system of written communication it was impossible to institute a stable political setup or trace a history: a narration of the origins of a *kingdom* leading to the legitimization of present rulers.

To contemporary eyes, the issue of the legitimization of power may appear to be associated only with the liberal and liberal-democratic systems of the modern era. In actual fact, with modern types of legitimacy, their sources and the resources available to legitimize power changed, but not the need for legitimation itself. Every form of power aspires to legitimization. The forms—cultural, religious, or mythical means by which legitimization may be achieved—differ. No form of power lasts long unless it has a cultural basis of legitimation all its own.

The task of legitimizing a social structure belongs to an imposing group of professionals. Usually we think of intellectuals as theologians, philosophers, and scientists. This is true, but only in part. First, it is the functions that the political system performs that need to be able to guarantee its legitimacy. If a ruler—of whatever type—fails to guarantee the safety and well-being of his or her society when it is possible to provide this at a given historical moment, he/she will not last long. This is one of the primary functions to which all power systems need to attend. If they do not, other forms of power will take over. In a society—even in ancient times—there are different conceptions of life and power, of God and man, and varying ideas and sources of justice and human happiness. This cultural differentiation implies, however, that the society be structurally stable. Within a framework of this kind, complex forms of cultural legitimacy emerge alongside specialized forms of legitimization of society, of institutions and the legitimate exercise of power.

The regulation of a power system presupposes a differentiated society, with division of labor and roles, as well as competition between various views of life and of people in society. Finally, cosmopolitanism is possible only within global societies where diversity of cultures and lifestyles are added to territorial differences. Only in a complex context of that kind can a conception of universal man emerge, applicable to the whole world and allowing local differences to subsist, both geographically and culturally. Cosmopolitanism can exist only within ambits with vast horizons where the cultural unity of individuals goes hand in hand with the existence of differences in lifestyle. The cosmopolitan, from this point of view, is a 'transvestite,' capable of experiencing difference, of passing through it, while, at the same time, remaining the same person. He/she can live according to different lifestyles, while maintaining his/her general human traits.

Another matter is whether the Axial Revolution put the three civilizations (China, India, Greece) in contact with each other. Jaspers—as we hasten to recall—said that the Axial Revolution occurred independently in each of the three civilizations. It is certain, however, that communication between the Mediterranean area and China was mediated by the peoples of Central Asia, although direct contact began only during the period of the Roman Empire. At one point, each of them began to be certain of the existence of the other but direct relationships are not documented. It took another season of human history for these two worlds to begin talking to each other.

Now, let us see how the universal conceptions of man emerged under local geographical and cultural conditions and how universal modes of thinking arose within the various civilizations. For reasons of space we will limit our discussion here to two exemplary cases only: Ancient China and Ancient Greece.

3   *Tian xia* and *Agorà*: Two Pathways toward the Universal Conception of Man

The point of departure of our discourse is Confucius and Confucianism. Confucius' intellectual and political proposals were truly revolutionary. First of all he advocated paying attention to the rapport between *words and things*. In his *Analects* he stated that

> If things are not called by their proper names, one's argument cannot stand to reason. If one's argument cannot stand to reason, nothing can be accomplished. If nothing can be accomplished, regulations and rituals as well as music will not flourish; if these do not flourish, punishment for crimes will not be appropriate; if punishment for crimes is not appropriate, the common people will have nothing to go by.
> CONFUCIUS, *Analects*, 13.3

The Chinese society of the time was so *corrupt*, Confucius claims, that a *semantic* revolution was necessary to understand how certain things stood and what to do to reestablish social *order* and *harmony*. To achieve this goal it was mandatory that everyone should act according to what was foreseen and prescribed by their *function*. The first rule was to 'Let the sovereign be a sovereign, the subject a subject, the father a father, the son a son' (Confucius, *Analects*, 12.11). So that there might be good government, all had fulfill the role implicit in their names: the sovereign was a sovereign; the people, the people; and so on. This was the Way by which to reach and maintain *harmony*. The second rule was that all should pursue the aim for which they had been destined. The ruler should possess: (a) abundant food, so that they people might not suffer from hunger: 'When the people have plenty, the sovereign will not be in want; when the people are in want, how can the sovereign have plenty?' (Confucius, *Analects*, 12. 9); (b) many weapons; and (c) the trust of the people. 'After all—said the Master—, since the beginning of time, no one has been able to escape the fate of death. But without the trust of the common people, the government would have nothing to sustain itself.' (Confucius, *Analects*, 12.7).

Social *order* and *harmony* might be achieved, Confucius held, only *if* all remained within their social bounds, did what they were expected to do, and behaved according to their roles. Social order was placed within the framework of cosmic order. If the government of a given society betrayed the eternal norms dictated by Heaven, it became illegitimate and might be overturned. Its task was to provide for the well-being of the people, if it did not, it no longer had any validity.

This aspect of Confucian thought may be understood only if one also considers his concept of man and humanity/humaneness (*ren*). Everyone—the ruler or the ordinary person—he held, had to follow the Way (*Dao*). The Way was the highest point of human experience: 'If in the morning I have learned the Way, I would have no regret dying that same day' (Confucius, *Analects*, 4.8). The Way was not a being, an object, a given. The Way

> is the point of arrival of a long, laborious process, the noblest expression of ethical becoming, the quintessence of the activities and experiences accumulated down through the centuries thanks to the work of exceptionally talented people of very high moral stature who have contributed to the creation of the culture of people who lived in the States of the Centre (*zhongguo*), the Zhou Dynasty's seat of temporal and religious power, for centuries considered the cradle of civilization.
>
> SCARPARI, 2010: 93

Humaneness (*ren*) was not attributed to the individual, as in the case of the Western tradition, but was considered the outcome of a process of formation that each person might follow. The result was not guaranteed but all might strive to become virtuous, that is to say, 'humane.' Confucius taught not only those who could pay him but also poor young men endowed with the moral and intellectual stature necessary to undergo a lengthy training process (Confucius, *Analects*, 15.39). What needed to be done to become virtuous and humane?

The concept of humaneness was intrinsically akin to that of virtue and nobility. On the one hand, Confucius aimed at forming the sovereign and members of the noble feudal class, on the other, he also contemplated the idea of 'nobility' of spirit as something stemming from a person's actions and not related to social rank alone. On the contrary, he stated that, 'Humaneness is more vital to the common people than fire and water. I have seen people die in fire and water but I never seen anyone die by following the course of humaneness' (Confucius, *Analects*, 15.35). 'Only the humane knows how to love and how to hate' (Confucius, *Analects*, 4.3). 'Love your fellow men ... Promote the righteous and set them over the unrighteous. That can make the unrighteous righteous' (Confucius, *Analects*, 12.22). The golden rule of Confucian thinking was to love your neighbor and hate injustice. What was meant exactly can only be seen within particular social contexts because Confucius, on the one hand, addressed men of government, princes, nobles, in the social sense of the word; on the other, people in general. As to governors of all kinds (sovereigns, princes, executives) his thoughts may be summed up in his recommendations to Ji Kangzi, a minister of state belonging to the Lu family: 'Treat the common people with dignity, and they treat you with reverence; promote filial piety and humaneness and they will be loyal to you; promote the righteous and instruct the incompetent, and they will eagerly do their best' (Confucius, *Analects*, 2. 20). The sovereign needed to promote filial piety and humaneness before and above all else.

Much has been said about this aspect of Confucian thinking, in particular about the role of the people in social government. Anti-Confucian thinkers (Daoists, Legalists) have criticized this reference to the people as a fable (Legalists). Mozi (2003) proposed a more radical interpretation of the Confucian Way by saying that Mengzi had been obliged to reformulate the original thinking of Confucius. The question of the legitimacy of power implies the very notion of humanity. If, as Confucius maintained, one became humane only if one lived for others, then—said Mozi—love needed to be universal and could not be directed toward the limited circle to which one belonged. Mozi actually drew inspiration from what Confucius himself said. King Wu of the Zhou Dynasty is believed to have stated that: 'Although I have many relatives, I prefer the virtuous' (Confucius, *Analects*, 20.1). For Confucius, the clan was not the basis of the social bond. Along these lines it was possible to constitute universal brotherhood. This concept appears clear in the following dialogue:

> Sima Niu complained, 'Others have brothers, I alone have none.' Zixia said to him: 'I have heard it said that life and death are decided by fate; wealth and rank decreed by Heaven. The man of honour is dedicated to his work, does nothing wrong and is respectful and polite to others. Thus all people within the Four Seas are his brothers. Why, then, does he have to worry about not having any brothers?'
>
> CONFUCIUS, *Analects*, 12.5

Justice was the foundation of humaneness and brotherhood. Brotherhood did not rest on natural links but on correct action. The way to humaneness passed through relations with others. A series of thoughts define what it meant for Confucius to be or to act as a human/humane being: 'To restrain oneself and observe the rituals that constitute humaneness. Once you have done these, the world will consider you humane. However, the practice of humanness depends on no one but yourself' (Confucius, *Analects*, 12.1). One should neither look nor hear; everything had to be done according to prescribed ritual, both in public and in private.

> In public, act as if you were receiving an honoured guest. While employing the service of the common people, act as you were officiating a major ceremony. Do not do to others what you do not wish others do to you. In this way, you will incur no bitter feelings against you whether in state or family affairs.
>
> CONFUCIUS, *Analects*, 12.2; cf. also 5.12

This was to be the guiding principle for the whole of one's life: 'Do not do unto others what you would not others do unto you' (Confucius, *Analects*, 15.24). This imperative had a positive side to it too. It envisaged helping others to do what you wanted them to do. 'A humane person is one who helps others establish what he himself wishes to establish and to achieve what he himself wishes to achieve. To be able correlate one's own feelings with those of others may be the best way to approach humaneness' (Confucius, *Analects*, 6.30). One was never 'humane/human' once and for all. Being human/humane implied a *tension* toward the well-being of others, on the part both of rulers and the people.

According to Confucius, this tension, which aimed at realizing humanity/humaneness in oneself, was universal. It was up to the ruler and the people to try to realize human order by means of correct observance of rites. Each person was expected to fulfill his/her role. If this did not happen, the harmony of the human and social world, the harmony of the cosmos, was broken. For rulers this meant losing the favor of the Heavens; therefore the loss of power. For the people it meant the impossibility of reaching happiness.

This idea of humanity/humaneness led to one of cosmopolitanism. Confucius actually envisaged overcoming localism and introducing universality. He never saw particular bonds or ties as the basis of society, but saw instead a network of relationships among virtuous men. This *universal* society of his was not conceived, however, as being based on law, but upon people striving for virtue. Confucian thinking emancipated men from the clan system although it did nail them down to the particularism of their functions and the virtues associated with them.

The Axial Revolution in Greece gave rise to a different view of man and society. If the literal formulation of man as a *zoòn politikon* (political animal) belongs to Aristotle, the concept itself goes back some centuries before him. What made the Greek world different—along with its tradition of the *agorà*—from the Chinese *tian xia* (all there is below Heaven) was the *constitution* of its society, the idea that men all belonged to the same society and had equal rights and duties. Certainly, not everything existed already in the early Athenian constitutions, as Aristotle used to say, 'The people, having the power of the vote, become sovereign in the government' (Aristotle, *Athenian Constitution*, IX, 2). The constitutions changed but always with a view to enlarging the power of the people as far as collective decisions were concerned. When Solon established the fact that the poorer citizens might take part in the assemblies and express their will through the vote, he was actually setting up a community at the same time. If power *remained* the prerogative of the upper classes, so too did the moral obligation to behave well and religious condemnation of those who acted against the interests of the community, as well as the concrete possibility of being removed from power by the citizens if it was believed that the people had been harmed by the behavior of those who governed. This perspective coincided with the *tian xia* tradition when it came to the need to legitimize power. It was different as regards the source of legitimation and the role of the people. According to Confucius, the well-being of the people was the aim of government; without the people, the government was nothing. There is no mention of the possibility that the people might take part in public decisions. Each one—as we have already noted—was expected do his/her duty and this was established by the role each one was called upon to play: the sovereign was the sovereign; the people were the people. Nothing more. We are indebted to Mengzi for at attempt to clarify this issue. Mengzi claimed that

> The Son of Heaven can present a man to Heaven, but he cannot cause Heaven to give him the realm ... In antiquity Yao presented Shun to

> Heaven, and it was Heaven that accepted him. He displayed him to the people, and the people accepted him. This is why I said that 'Heaven does not speak.' This was manifested solely through his actions and his conduct of affairs ... I venture to ask how it was that Yao presented him to Heaven and Heaven accepted him, and he showed him to the people and the people accepted him?' 'He caused him to preside over the sacrifices, and the hundred spirits enjoyed them. This shows that Heaven accepted him. He put him in charge of affairs, and affairs were well ordered, and the hundred surnames were at peace. This shows that the people accepted him. Heaven gave it to him; the people gave it to him.'
> MENGZI, 5. A. 5

And so the people remained in the background; they were not protagonists according to the Confucian tradition. Even Confucius himself said that 'One can make the common people follow a course of action but not let them understand why they should do so' (Confucius, *Analects*, 8.9). The sovereign forfeited legitimacy—the favor of Heaven—if he failed to govern for the good of the people, but the people might not intervene when it came to collective issues. Mengzi's position too was the object of criticism. Popular confirmation of the emperor was only a myth, according to Xunzi (2003). In Daoism and Legalism, the role of the people in the government of society was not even mentioned. *Tian xia* philosophy created the need to legitimate power, yet it continued to entrust Heaven with the task of legitimating the sovereign or—as the Legalists held later—providing them with strength.

The philosophy of the *agorà* conceived of a community where the task of legitimating the government of the *polis* was the responsibility of its members. *Each one* here thought and acted on the basis of his own political and religious convictions or, more often than not, in his own interests. *Harmony*, when it did emerge, was the result of the conflict between differences, not of their peaceful conciliation.

The pathway toward the idea of a political community had been around for a long time, even in the ancient Greek world. In Plato and Aristotle we find the finest formulations of the Greek way of establishing the State. People's reciprocal need of each other was the basis of the political community.

> A State, I said, arises, as I conceive, out of the needs of mankind; no one is self-sufficing, but all of us have many wants ... Then, as we have many wants, and many persons are needed to supply them, one takes a helper for one purpose and another for another; and when these partners and

helpers are gathered together in one habitation the body of inhabitants is termed a State.

PLATO, *Republic*, II, 369, c

Aristotle generalized the idea, saying that man was a political, that is, a social animal (Aristotle, *Politics*, I, 1253a). Furthermore, relationships between people had to be based on justice. When it came down to it, all humans needed to pursue their own happiness.

Plato's conception of justice bears some resemblance to that of Confucius and that of Mengzi. For Plato too justice was possible for the whole community if the individual might find it there too. Aristotle's approach was quite different: here too the happiness of the individual might be achieved only within a positive moral context; the difference consisted, however, in the way the role of the individual is conceived. Pursuit of 'just means' was the way to achieve happiness. Plato, Mengzi, and Confucius all sought to change the moral environment, the society within which the individual acted; Aristotle placed greater emphasis on the action of the individual and his or her ability to deal with a complex moral environment where the general principle of justice did not always prevail.

The problem is that between Confucius and Aristotle there was a gap of over a century and that the processes of rationalization, in politics above all, advanced very quickly. To reconstruct an integrated society around traditional values as Confucius or Mengzi wished, or to set up *new one* as Plato would have liked to, seemed like utopia to Aristotle. It is true that he knew nothing of China, but he wished to avoid the Greek Constitution regarding the individual as irrelevant, as was the case in India. Aristotle followed a pluralist model and this shows how strongly his theories were rooted in the social, political, and cultural processes of his day.

The Aristotelian theory corresponds, actually, with the process of the construction of a global world in most of Eurasia. This is shown not only by the fact he had been the preceptor of Alexander the Great—the most determined builder of a global, multicultural society of the Axial Age—but, above all, by his pluralist theories of society and politics. During this phase of history, the *Greek* vision became global but, at the same time, it had to come to terms with other cultures like the Persian, Indian, Egyptian, Hebrew, and Roman (Momigliano, 1975). Greece, according to the Hellenistic perception of reality, was surrounded by a world of 'barbarians,' whose views on life, man, and society were different from those of the Greek model. The 'barbarians' the Chinese had to deal with were the Mongols. Here we are talking of two cultures which had reached vastly different levels of organization: Chinese society was already very refined while the Mongols were semi-nomadic warriors living along the northern borders of China. Greece had to deal with quite highly developed civilizations, like the Egyptians, although these were experiencing a state of crisis. Rome was still distant but capable of being integrated into Hellas because it availed itself of a constitutional element similar to that of Greece: the Plebs, who, although they occupied a subaltern position in society, had a say in matters regarding the Republic (Momigliano, 1975: 13).

Aristotle provided this world in the making with a vision of man that was both unitary and pluralistic. Only within a unitary prospective was it possible to integrate different peoples. Only if differences were not annulled but every group was allowed to find its own role was it possible to create a political community.

Not all is attributable, however, to Aristotle. The idea of universal citizenship was a specific contribution made by the Stoic philosophers (Pohlenz, 1959). It was along these lines that the Roman world built up its particular image of the citizen. The ability of the Romans to integrate into its imperial system of citizenship a myriad of different cultures is a well-known fact; to be able to say *civis romanus sum* (I am a Roman citizen) was the aspiration of the cultural and political elites in many of the empire's peripheries. The system grew so vast until it became a world; often erroneously conceived as *the* world. In any case, it appeared to be a world without limitations due to Rome's capacity for cultural and military conquest.

This world experienced very important forms of cosmopolitan life. On the one hand, Roman citizenship permitted the political, cultural, and military elites to play administrative roles throughout the empire; on the other, territorial and social mobility became the basis of a cosmopolitanism hitherto unknown in Eurasia. This political-cultural system possessed its own reflexivity: it was necessary to create juridical norms applicable to the entire domain, a system capable of attracting the peoples on the borders of the empire. The simplest and most elegant expression of this juridical system is to be found in Gaius' *Institutiones*, a text used to train Roman jurists and magistrates. This form of law was neither new nor original. In the Hammurabi Code we find a distinction between general laws and particular laws for the different peoples of the empire. In the Indian tradition, in a collection of sayings attributed to Emperor Aśoka, we find analogous references. In Gaius' *Institutiones* we find similar distinctions between general laws regarding the whole of humanity and particular laws for specific peoples: a kind of juridical recognition of cultural differences. The difference of the Roman system did not consist so much in its form as in the relationship between the law and the citizenry. The universal form of the law was one side of the coin; the rights of individuals were the other. The Roman juridical system comprised, on the one hand, recognition of the universality of the law, on the other, the rights of men, what we might call today 'subjective rights.'

A number of processes took place in the three civilizations affected by the Axial Revolution. In general, a process of *disenchantment* (Weber, 1988) and rationalization or abandonment or reformulation of the previous traditions within new boundaries occurred everywhere. A new communications network for the elite was set up. Only in the Greek and Roman world, however, was all of this associated with a conception and practice of citizenship, unknown to the other civilizations. Herein, when it comes down to it, lies the difference between the *Western* and other views of the world, between the tradition of *agorà* (public meeting place) and that of *tian xia* (all there is below Heaven).

References

Aristotle. 1887–1902. *Politics*, edited by W. L. Newman. Oxford: Clarendon Press.

Aristotle. 1935. *The Athenian Constitution*. London: William Heinemann; Cambridge, MA: Harvard University Press.

Assmann, J. 2018. *Achsenzeit. Eine Archäologie der Moderne*. Munich: C. H. Beck.

Cotesta, V. 2018. *Max Weber on China: Modernity and Capitalism in a Global Perspective*. Newcastle upon Tyne: Cambridge Scholars Publishing.

Eisenstadt, S. N. 2003. *Comparative Civilizations and Multiple Modernities*. Leiden and Boston, MA: Brill.

Gaius. 1995. *Institutiones*. Naples: Edizioni Simone.

Herodotus. 1996. *The Histories*. London: Penguin.

Jaspers, K. 1953. *The Origin and Goal of History*. New Haven, CT; London: Yale University Press.

Lau, D. C. (trans.) 2010. *Confucius: The Analects*. Beijing: Foreign Language Press.

Mengzi. 2009. *Mengzi*, translated by Irene Bloom; edited and introduced by Philip J. Ivanhoe. New York: Columbia University Press.

Momigliano, A. 1975. *Alien Wisdom: The Limits of Hellenization*. Cambridge: Cambridge University Press.

Mozi. 2003. *Basic Writings*, translated by Burton Watson. New York: Columbia University Press.

Plato. 2004. *Republic*. New York: Barnes & Noble Books.

Pohlenz, M. 1959. *Die Stoa. Geschichte einer geistigen Bewegung*. Göttingen: Vandenhoeck & Ruprecht.

Scarpari, M. 2010. *Il confucianesimo*. Turin: Einaudi.

Weber, M. 1988. *Gesammelte Aufsätze zur Religionssoziologie*, vol. 3. Tübingen: Mohr Siebeck.

Xunzi. 2003. *Basic Writings*, translated by Burton Watson. New York: Columbia University Press.

CHAPTER 2

Kantian Cosmopolitanism

Stéphane Chauvier

If Kant holds a central position in the history of cosmopolitanism, it is chiefly because his legal-political work was the first to shift the antique ideal of a *cosmopolis* from a vague yearning to a precise and realistic organizational perspective, anchored in the logic of the historical development of human societies.* In Kant's mind, cosmopolitanism was not the cheerful—albeit inaccessible—antithesis of a nasty and brutish reality to which man is condemned as a result of his egoism or malice. Cosmopolitanism was nothing other than the ineluctability of an integrated and complete organization of human society; an inevitable, exhaustive, and definitive exit from the state of nature. Although this perspective finds its bearings in the long view of human history, it nevertheless represents a natural and non-sacrificial development of this history. Kantian cosmopolitanism is thus a non-polemic form of cosmopolitanism: it is in opposition with nothing other than incomplete and unfinished organizational forms of human society and knows no true normative alternative.

1   Attitudinal and Institutional Cosmopolitanism

We shall start with something of a paradox: Kant is an important figure in the cosmopolitan tradition, yet the very notion of cosmopolitanism (*Kosmopolitismus*) itself is virtually absent from his writing.[1] Of course, we may in principle find that we have no difficulty mobilizing the substantive 'cosmopolitanism' to better come to terms with the content of Kant's work, nor even to speak of 'Kantian cosmopolitanism.' However, if we are to acknowledge Kant's

---

*   I thank Katherine Evans for her assistance in preparing the English version of this chapter.
1   Only once, in *Anthropology from a Pragmatic Point of View* (1798, AK, VII: 331) does Kant touch upon the notion of 'cosmopolitan society', writing the Latin *cosmopolitismus* in parentheses. (All our references to Kantian works are to *Kant's Gesammelte Schriften, herausgegeben von der Königlich Preußischen Akademie der Wissenschaften,* hereafter referred to as AK, followed by the volume and page number, available online at https://korpora.zim.uni-duisburg-essen.de/kant/verzeichnisse-gesamt.html.

contribution to the philosophy of cosmopolitanism with any hope of accuracy, it is paramount that we remain mindful of the way in which Kant himself categorizes what we are inclined to associate with the notion of cosmopolitanism. Indeed, we are hard-pressed to find an abstract and normative term like 'cosmopolitanism' in Kant's prose. Instead, we find a set of concrete and descriptive notions: twenty-odd occurrences of the adjectives *weltbürgerlich* or, less frequently, *kosmopolitisch*, which equate to 'cosmopolitan' in English, as well as just as many instances of the substantive 'citizen of the World,' *Weltbürger*, or, on occasion, *Erdbürger*, 'citizen of the Earth.'[2] Accordingly, if there is any sense to Kantian cosmopolitanism, we must seek it in the qualifications of these adjectives and in the type of behavior and prerogatives that the words 'citizen of the World' or 'citizen of the Earth' entail.

First, consider the adjectives *weltbürgerlich* and *kosmopolitisch*. Perfectly synonymous, they variably characterize a point of view, an orientation of the conscience, a sentiment: two notable examples are Kant's thoughts on a cosmopolitan view of history,[3] or a cosmopolitan position regarding education.[4] In other instances, these adjectives evince a legal or political construction: Kant speaks of a 'cosmopolitan whole' (1790, §83, AK, V: 432), a 'cosmopolitan society' (1798, AK, VII: 331), or a 'cosmopolitan constitution' (1795, AK, VIII: 358). What does 'cosmopolitan' signify in these two types of instance?

Let us begin with the most straightforward case, in which the word 'cosmopolitan' signifies a particular legal-political organization. In these types of occurrence, the context affords us little doubt concerning Kant's usage of the word 'cosmopolitan' as a perfect synonym for what we today call 'global'; a word which, in the language of his time, could not be employed to designate that which it designates today. Cosmopolitan constitutions, societies, or communities are simply *global* constitutions, societies, and communities; indicating various forms or organizations that connect all of the Earth's inhabitants, individuals, or peoples. 'Cosmopolitan' here refers to the antithesis of all that is local or national, or what is fragmented or plural, since a 'cosmopolitan whole' or a 'cosmopolitan constitution' is not only a *global* legal structure, but also a legal structure that is *common* to the ensemble of the world's inhabitants. We

---

2   See the online index which covers the ensemble of *Kant's Gesammelte Schriften*: https://korpora.zim.uni-duisburg-essen.de/kant/suche.html.
3   The very title of his 1784 essay: *Idea for a Universal History from a Cosmopolitan Point of View* [*Absicht*] AK, VIII: 15–31.
4   *Pedagogy*, edited by Fr. Th. Rink, 1803, AK, IX: 448: 'The attachment to an educative plan must be made cosmopolitan.'

would then undoubtedly reproduce the correct meaning of the word 'cosmopolitan' in the preceding examples if we intended to mean 'common to all the Earth' or 'common to all inhabitants of the Earth.'

However, the word 'cosmopolitan' gains in complexity when it indicates a sentiment (*Gesinnung*) or a point of view (*Absicht*). In these instances, it can still be associated with a certain 'globality': to consider history from a cosmopolitan point of view is to consider the 'world' history of mankind, not that of one population or another. Developing one's sociability with cosmopolitan intentions is to open one's self to the affairs of the world as a whole (1797b, §48, AK, VI: 473). However, in these cases, what is added to the notion of globality is the notion of humanity, understood both in terms of *Humanität*, or the collectivity of human beings, and as *Menschheit*, or the common essence of human beings, or more precisely still, their common rational destination. To regard history 'from a cosmopolitan point of view' is to regard it in terms of what it affords humanity as a whole (*Humanität*), or what it lends to the development of humanity (*Menschheit*) in each human being. Similarly, imparting a cosmopolitan orientation to the education of a child involves raising them to see her/himself in terms of her/his humanity, not in terms of her/his eventual social class, race, or profession. The most striking example of Kant's use of cosmopolitanism as an attitude or an outlook can be found in the following passage of his *Pedagogical Lessons*:

> There is something in our soul that makes us having interest 1) in our Self, 2) in our close relatives and we must next 3) take interest in the good of the world [*Weltbesten*]. We have to introduce children to this interest, so that it may warm their soul. They must be happy about the good of the world, even if it is not the advantage of their fatherland or their own profit. (1803, AK, IX: 499)

The sentiment that consists in taking an interest in the 'good of the world,' Kant calls, some few lines earlier, a cosmopolitan sentiment, *weltbürgerlichen Gesinnung*. In contrast with the love of humanity (*Menschenliebe*) or philanthropy, which Kant likewise mentions, this cosmopolitan sentiment cannot be understood as the passive faculty of being moved or touched by the fate of every man. Instead, it is an active disposition characterizing the *interest* that we have in humanity, in the two aforementioned senses: in the totality of humans and in humanity in itself. The child in which we strive to instill this cosmopolitan sentiment must come to take an interest, not only in all that concerns human beings, as foreign and distant as they may be, but also in all that is good for the fate of human beings, in everything that contributes to the improvement of humanity. In the *Doctrine of Virtue*, when regarding not only children but adults, Kant associates this cosmopolitan sentiment with the active interest that we must have for the commerce of all men, far beyond the familiar circle of those who surround us.

Thus, these uses of the adjective 'cosmopolitan' suggest that what we are inclined to call cosmopolitanism entertains a dual form in Kant's thought. On one level, which we might qualify as *attitudinal*, cosmopolitanism is an individual attitude that consists in the opening of the individual conscience to the totality of the world, by means of an active interest in humanity in and of itself. An individual is a citizen of the world, in this first sense, when she/he feels concerned and interested by the 'good of the world.' This neither amounts to the moral *obligation* we have to respect the humanity of each man nor to demonstrate a certain beneficence in his regard. Instead, it pertains to the *interest*, just as much theoretical as practical, that we must have for all that concerns mankind and all that encourages the development of its humanity. The world citizen, in this attitudinal interpretation, can therefore be concretely described as a 'globe-trotter,' traveling the world so as to get to know mankind, in its myriad cultural manifestations, and to enter into 'commerce' with them. Still, the world citizen can likewise be immobile: the philosopher, holed up in his chamber in Königsberg can feel himself to be a world citizen whenever he practices philosophy in its 'cosmic concepts' or its 'cosmopolitan sense' (1800, AK, IX: 25), in other words when he aims to answer the question 'what is man?' In all cases, cosmopolitanism, in the attitudinal sense of the term, denotes the capacity for a concern for the good of all men in and of themselves, a capacity that supersedes and trumps the spontaneous or natural interest one has for oneself and those that resemble or surround one.

From this cosmopolitanism of attitude, whose presence is scant in Kant's work, we must distinguish a second form of cosmopolitanism, of an *institutional* or *legal* character, which is explicitly thematized in all of the legal-political work of Kant.[5] Cosmopolitanism, under this interpretation, is no longer an individual attitude or a state of mind, but instead an organizational perspective embedded in the logic of the progress of human societies; the perspective of a sociability that is simultaneously *global* and *legal*, resulting in a 'cosmopolitan whole' or a 'cosmopolitan constitution.' If 'state of nature' implies an interactional setting stripped of any rule of equality, a setting in which the liberty of one man may stifle the liberty of another, *rule of law* or

---

5 Essentially, the 1784 essay *Idea for a Universal History*; the essay *On the Common Saying: That May Be True in Theory, but It Is of No Use in Practice* of 1793; the 1795 essay *Perpetual Peace*; and the last part of his *Doctrine of Right* of 1797.

legal condition (*rechtliche Zustand*), in contrast, denotes 'this relationship of men to each other, which contains the conditions under which only everyone can enjoy his right' (1797a, §41, AK, VI: 306–307).

This is to say that the liberty of one man can coexist with the liberty of another, according to the rule of equality. For Kant, the law is at the service of freedom, in so far as this freedom expands across society, thus naturally coming into conflict with the virtually oppressive freedom of other individuals. Institutional or legal cosmopolitanism is accordingly the perspective of a society that is concurrently global and juridical, a rule of law that is common to all of Earth's inhabitants (*ein allgemeiner weltbürgerlicher Zustand*; 1784, AK, VIII: 28). What is at play within legal cosmopolitanism is thus more than a move beyond the exclusive attachment to what is near to the detriment of what is far, it is an expansion of legality beyond the frontiers of the state, in other words, the globalization of law.

It follows, then, that 'Kantian cosmopolitanism,' if such a term can be used, denotes two very different theoretical positions. On the one hand, it entails the explicitly normative affirmation that it is good to take an interest in the welfare of the world: this is the normative cosmopolitanism of the educator or the moralist. On the other hand, Kantian cosmopolitanism can just as easily indicate a certain fusion of the normative and the predictive: the harbinger of an inextricable globalization of law and legal relations, an inevitability which is yet perceived as a benefit to humanity, and not as a loss or tragedy.

2 The Natural Expansion of Legal Relations

How do these two forms of cosmopolitanism connect? It is evident that the globalization of law presupposes a globalization of social interactions, which then presupposes that at least a handful of people individually decide to globetrot. After all, a world in which the frontiers of one's state coincide with the frontiers of one's world could not provide fertile ground for legal cosmopolitanism. Nevertheless, Kant's most significant thesis maintains that legal cosmopolitanism does not have a generalized cosmopolitan mentality among its preconditions. Even in a world in which the majority of individuals are interested only in those that surround them, a world where the familiar is worth more than the foreign in the eyes of each person, the law remains destined to steadily spread, eventually embracing the whole planet.

One reason for this—and the central theme of the preeminent 1784 essay— is that the law is *genetically* independent from morality. If it is morally better that men in their social interactions be placed under the rule of law rather than a state of nature, and if an organization that allows each individual to exercise his or her right is morally better than one in which an individual is exposed to the violence of others, it still does not require that individuals be motivated by moral dispositions to engage in legal relations. The legal organization of human interaction is an emergent process, which Kant regards as reminiscent not of a 'spontaneous order' as Hayek might qualify it, but as a process that is animated and driven by 'nature.' Nature 'asks' that mankind develop these dispositions, and to lead him or her toward this goal brings him or her to *prize* competition and rivalry with others:

> The means employed by Nature to bring about the development of all the capacities of men is their antagonism in society, so far as this is, in the end, the cause of a lawful order among men. By 'antagonism' I mean the unsocial sociability of men, i.e., their propensity to enter into society, bound together with a mutual opposition which constantly threatens to break up the society. (1784, AK, VIII: 20–21)

The emergence of law is then nothing other than the effect of self-interest, properly understood: as individuals come to understand the devastating consequences of lawless rivalry, the tension between rivalry and cooperation characteristic of the unsocial sociability of mankind resolves itself gradually, evolving toward an organization in which 'general antagonism' goes hand in hand with 'the most exact definition of freedom and fixing of its limits' for each man, so that 'it may be consistent with the freedom of others' (1784, AK, VIII: 22).

Yet Kantian legal cosmopolitanism does not lie in the thesis—altogether mundane since Hobbes—that man will inevitably come to take an interest in law so as to trade the absolute but fragile freedom of the state of nature for the tempered freedom of the civil state. Kant's originality and innovation hangs on the affirmation that if this process of the spontaneous *legalization* of human interaction first develops at the interindividual level and leads to the emergence of societies that administer law at the national or state level, it will continue on its irrepressible path until it encompasses the whole of humanity. Accordingly, there are in principle two very different ways to envisage this expansion.

Consider a world comprised of small, fragmented, and *closed* societies. In this world, the rule of law could be present across the entire Earth, and all human interaction extricated from the state of nature, because each of these small societies would administer law on a national basis and level.[6] Yet the rule of law, while ubiquitous, would not in itself be global, in so far as it would

---

6 The very perspective Fichte (1800) would come to develop in *The Closed Commercial State*.

not be *common* to all the Earth's inhabitants. For such a collective—and not distributive—global rule of law to appear, a world of small and closed societies cannot be envisaged. Instead, we must imagine a world comprised of a plurality of political societies, *open* to one another, gradually interacting across the expanse of the Earth. Similar to our first case, in such a world we would find a plurality of national legal spaces. However, over and above these spaces, a place would likewise exist for the emergence of *international* law, virtually global and common to all the national societies it entails.

Kantian cosmopolitanism finds its home in this delicate middle ground between national and international, between pluri-politanism and cosmopolitanism. Kant's far from trivial thesis is that 'the very same unsociability that compelled individuals [...] to enter a civil society governed by laws' holds between 'civil societies or bodies politic.' Just as the effects of freedom without law compel individuals to subject their freedom to law, the effects of wars between states must equally bring them to exit 'the anarchical condition of savagery to enter a Society of Nations' (1784, AK, VIII: 24). The emergence of this international legal space is what drove Kant to introduce the notion of a 'cosmopolitan rule of law,' a 'cosmopolitan constitution,' or a 'cosmopolitan whole.' What is cosmopolitan or virtually so, which is to say simultaneously global and common to all the Earth's inhabitants, is the international law collectively enacted by the Society of Nations. If the connection between the Society of Nations and the nations of which it is comprised was at times met with hesitation on the part of Kant—one example is his essay from 1793 in which he talks of a 'universal state of peoples,'[7] employing the word 'State' (*Staat*)—the texts from 1795 and 1797, in addition to that of 1784, insist on the fact that the Society of Nations does *not* necessarily spell the destruction of national states. For Kant, *multiple* national political orders exist and above them is an international order common to all peoples, which is alone constitutive of cosmopolitanism. An order, Kant affirms, whose emergence is as inevitable as that of national legal relations. The day will come, so Kant's prophecy goes, when 'partly by the most adequate establishment of the civil constitution on the domestic level, partly externally by a common convention and legislation, a state of affairs will be established which, like a universal civil community (*Bürgerlichen gemeinen Wesen*), can be maintained of itself as an automaton' (1784, AK, VIII: 25).

We have here, in its principle but not in its final form, what is peculiar to Kantian cosmopolitanism and is constitutive of its originality in the history

---

7 '*Allgemeiner Völkerstaat*,' see Kant, 1793, AK, VIII: 313.

of cosmopolitanism. First, the decoupling of moral cosmopolitanism and of institutional cosmopolitanism: the latter in no way presupposes that mankind show, throughout its behavior, an interest for the good or the welfare of the world. Institutional cosmopolitanism, understood as progressive globalization and piecemeal development of legal relations, proceeds through a mechanical or automatic process that depends solely on the self-interested but enlightened interests of international actors. The relationship of dependence is in actuality rather reversed: a cosmopolitan sentiment will spread as legal relations globalize. There will come a moment, as Kant writes in his essay on perpetual peace in 1795, when 'the social relations between peoples having spread universally, a violation of the right in one point is felt everywhere' (1795, AK, VIII: 360). The welfare of the world is then concurrent with the self-interest of each individual, feeding each individual's concern for the most distant or exotic of populations.

Yet the originality of Kantian cosmopolitanism is not limited to this decoupling of law and morality, which paints the globalization of law as the result of an unconscious mechanism. Its originality also resides in the essentially *dual* form that the legal organization of global society maintains. If the formation of national legal societies is genetically prior, if mankind first introduces rules of law into interactions with one's neighbors, forming together a society that administers law at the local level, then the extension of legal relations does not pass through a progressive broadening of national political societies until the emergence of a Kojevian *universal homogeneous state* (Kojève, 2000). It rather arrives through the emergence of a *second* legal order, this time international in character. Here, the originality of Kant's thought is to maintain that this second international legal order does not resemble natural law, nor conventional bilateral law, but that it must take the form of an international law, multilaterally or commonly enacted by all peoples assembled in a Society of Nations. Suddenly, the *cosmopolis* appears as a Society of Societies, where the law of the global society does not replace those of the composite national societies, but instead adds to or superposes them.

This idea is quite obviously crucial, since, in tandem with our first argument, it implies that institutional cosmopolitanism does not hold among its conditions the abolition, sacrifice, or surpassing of the natural sentiments that Kant describes in the preceding passages of his *Pedagogical Lessons*, namely, the interest one takes in one's own good and the good of one's surrounding community. In a world corresponding to this idea of a universal rule of law or a cosmopolitan community, it is not necessary that mankind be moved by the sentiment of universal fraternity, nor neglect the interest of their compatriots. Cosmopolitanism, in a Kantian sense, is not a species of political philanthropy but a reasonable expression of the entire gamut of human interests, in such a way as to allow each individual to exist in legal society with all others.

3 The Universal Society in Its Final Form: the Right of the Citizen of the World

The dual form of the *cosmopolis* that we have just described is a constant in Kant's legal-political thought: all of his texts underscore the assertion that the interactions among states are a potential source of oppression and misery for the lives of individuals. In effect, it may not suffice for an individual to shield her/himself with the laws of her/his state, so as to better develop her/his capacities and enjoy the benefits of social life. It must also be the case that the states themselves, throughout their reciprocal relations, subject themselves to laws which are decided in common.

Nonetheless, we should not consider this dual form of the *cosmopolis* to be Kant's final word on the subject. If the aforementioned texts of 1784 and 1793 only touch on this duality between national political law and international law or law of peoples, and if the *cosmopolis* appears as a Society of Societies which includes national legal systems and an international law that is commonly enacted within a *Völkerbund*, then our portrait remains unfinished. In effect, the 1795 text on perpetual peace and the *Doctrine of Right* in 1797 fortify these two dimensions of law with a *third* legal class which Kant calls '*Weltbürgerrecht*,' the 'right of citizens of the world.' This third legal class is an innovation on Kant's part: all previous legal treaties only recognized the duality of national political law and international law of peoples. At the same time, while entirely original, the mention of this third legal class is somewhat terse in the texts in which it figures: all in all, two paragraphs in the 1795 essay and a sole paragraph in the treatise of 1797a (§62). Kant defines the right of the citizen of the world as the 'right of any Foreigner not to be treated as an Enemy in the country where he arrives,' as a 'right to visit any foreign country,' which he distinguishes from a 'right of settlement or of establishment,' which he refuses to grant to foreign individuals who may only 'try to get in touch with the natives.' Kant goes on to maintain that the right of citizens of the world 'tends to a possible union of all the peoples through a set of universal laws regulating their mutual relationships' and that its development will inevitably be accompanied by the development of generalized commerce between peoples. This, in virtue of the fact that the Earth is round, thus forbidding the possibility of an infinite expansion into unpopulated territory.

These terse statements require delicate interpretation. Initially, there can be no doubt that in Kant's mind the right of the citizen of the world finds its principal setting within the period of European colonial expansion. This point is of no small significance. Kant in effect only accords this right of the world citizen to the respective rights of European cosmopolitans and the indigenous peoples they may happen to visit. The 'citizen of the world,' in Kant's examples, is characterized by the European colonizer, and Kant manifestly struggles to define under which conditions Europeans, and Asian or American aboriginals, could have, or still could, 'exercise their rights.' It is not, in effect, useless to remind ourselves that beyond being a theorist of cosmopolitanism, Kant was also one of the first theorists of the racial diversity of humanity,[8] alongside being an analyst of the psychological character of different peoples (1798, VII: 311 s). And, in his writings on races, just as much as in his ethno-anthropological writings, he insists on the *cosmopolitan* mission of the European people: rather than subjecting 'savage' or 'barbarous' peoples to their domination, they must, through their interactions with them, draw them out of their 'torpor' or savagery and encourage their development toward more humane dispositions. Let us mention a few significant passages: 'Eastern nations are unable of progress on their own. It is in the West that we must seek the continuous progress of the human race which, from here on, will extend to the entire Earth' (1770, AK, XV, 2: 788–789); 'Many people will not progress on their own. Greenlanders. Asians. It has to come from Europe' (1770, AK, XV, 2: 781); and:

> If the happy inhabitants of Tahiti had never been visited by more polished nations and were destined to live in their tranquil indolence for thousands of centuries, we would answer the question: what good is the existence of these people? and would it not be as much to have populated these islands with happy sheep and calves as with happy men in pure physical satisfaction?(1785b, AK, VIII: 65)

It would be fallacious indeed to suppress the portrait these passages paint of 'Kantian cosmopolitanism.' For Kant, the 'globalization' of sociability and law goes hand in hand with European expansion, in itself credited with the function of producing an 'awakening' among non-Europeans. In sum, the European expansion across the globe is the reason the Earth is becoming an integrated social space. However, it would be just as fallacious to *reduce* the

---

8   Kant maintains that humanity is composed of four original and persistent races (1785a, AK, VIII: 91–106).

right of the citizen of the world to the application Kant had envisaged. The concept of a right of the citizen of the world appears in Kant's texts from 1795 onwards, the moment at which he began to redact his *system* of law. One might remember that all systematic divisions in Kantian theory are tripartite, not out of some mystical connection to the number three, but simply because Kant exploited what he saw to be a serendipitous link between this trichotomous structure on the one hand, and the demands of exhaustivity and completeness that are inalienable to any system on the other (1790, introduction, final note, AK, V: 197). Thus, what Kant had truly discovered in his elaboration of legal categories is that the traditional division of political law and law of peoples did not exhaust all of the possible forms of legal relations among individuals. If we imagine a case where all the world's inhabitants are affiliated with national states, and these states together form a Society of Nations which administers the law of relations between states, there still exists another possible form of interaction not covered by these two kinds of law: the form of interaction that is born when *individual* members of one state engage in commerce with the individuals of another. Neither political law, nor the law of peoples, incorporate the necessary legal conditions that support such a concord of freedom between the non-native traveler and the natives of the land he intends to 'visit.'

It is therefore this *universal* dimension of human interaction that the right of the citizen of the world is meant to bring under the purview of law. As we have explained in greater detail elsewhere (Chauvier, 1996), it may incontestably have been the case that, for Kant, the right of the citizen of the world was primarily conceived as an explanatory vessel for the legally problematic 'visits' of his time, namely, those of the European colonizers. Yet the pure concept of the right of the citizen of the world which supports a 'right of visitation' for the foreigner, and a corollary right of the host community to decide his eventual 'installation,' has, at least in principle, universal import. It sketches the contours of a legal institution which we have sought, in vain, in the world of today: that of an *international* or *common law of migration*, which would articulate the rights of migrational candidates and their respective host communities within an international or multilateral framework, under the authority of the 'Society of Nations.' The right of the citizen of the world is the right of the individual who leaves his state, the law of individuals once they are, in a legal-political sense, *foreigners*. An individual becomes a citizen of the world in a legal and not attitudinal sense, when she or he can invoke, in any corner of the globe, a right that grants the freedom to 'cosmopolitize,' both to her/him and to those whom she/he is destined to meet.

4 Conclusion

If the word 'cosmopolitanism' was rarely penned by the hand of Kant, it is doubtless because he did not see the construction of a universal rule of law as a perspective to which one could be normatively opposed. A perspective that is at once rational and non-sacrificial, an inevitable and universal rule of law, unrivalled by any counter-ideal. The ignorance of mankind may hamper its arrival, but a universal rule of law such as this would not deprive humanity of anything valuable or worthwhile. Neither freedom, understood as autonomy or independence, nor security or prosperity would be in jeopardy in a world which satisfies the following three conditions: (1) each individual would be a citizen of a republican state, a state in which power is exercised solely in the service and declaration of the rights of its citizens; (2) each state would be a sort of citizen within a confederation of free states (*Völkerbund*), which would shoulder the responsibilities of 'declaring' the right of each state, and settling any disputes in accordance with the commonly accepted laws (law of peoples); and finally, (3) each individual would exercise, on foreign soil, his rights as a citizen of the world (*Weltbürgerrecht*).

An organization such as this—one that upholds the political separation of mankind and does not guarantee an individual the right to settle anywhere he pleases—may appear unsatisfactorily weak to some. They may long for a cosmopolitan Republic, or a world without borders. However, it would be difficult to confidently deny that a world which drew upon Kant's organizational perspective would not indeed be better than the world in which we currently live.

References

Chauvier, S. 1996. *Du droit d'être étranger: Essai sur le droit cosmopolitique kantien*. Paris: L'Harmattan.
Fichte, J. G. 1800. *The Closed Commercial State*. Tübingen: Cotta.
Kant, I. 1770. *Notes for the Course on Anthropology from 1770s*. In *Kant's Gesammelte Schriften*, vol. XV, 2: 657–798.
Kant, I. 1784. *Idea for a Universal History from a Cosmopolitan Point of View* [*Absicht*]. In *Kant's Gesammelte Schriften*, vol. VIII: 17–31.
Kant, I. 1785a. *Determination of the Concept of a Human Race*. In *Kant's Gesammelte Schriften*, vol. VIII: 91–106.
Kant, I. 1785b. *Recension of Herder's Ideas for a Philosophy of the History of Mankind*. In *Kant's Gesammelte Schriften*, vol. VIII: 45–66.
Kant, I. 1790. *Critique of Judgment*. In *Kant's Gesammelte Schriften*, vol. V: 167–485.

Kant, I. 1793. *On the Common Saying: That May Be True in Theory, but It Is of No Use in Practice*. In *Kant's Gesammelte Schriften*, vol. VIII: 275–313.

Kant, I. 1795. *On Perpetual Peace*. In *Kant's Gesammelte Schriften*, vol. VIII: 343–386.

Kant, I. 1797a. *Doctrine of Right*. In *Kant's Gesammelte Schriften*, vol. VI: 205–355.

Kant, I. 1797b. *Doctrine of Virtue*. In *Kant's Gesammelte Schriften*, vol. VI: 373–493.

Kant, I. 1798. *Anthropology from a Pragmatic Point of View*. In *Kant's Gesammelte Schriften*, vol. VII: 119–333.

Kant, I. 1800. *Logik*, edited by B. Jäsche. In *Kant's Gesammelte Schriften*, vol. IX: 1–150.

Kant, I. 1803. *Pedagogy*, edited by Fr. Th. Rink. In *Kant's Gesammelte Schriften*, vol. IX: 439–499.

Kant, I. 1900–. *Gesammelte Schriften, herausgegeben von der Königlich Preußische Akademie der Wissenschaften*. Berlin: G. Reimer; from 1922 W. de Gruyter.

Kojève, A. 2000. 'Tyranny and Wisdom.' In *On Tyranny*, edited by L. Strauss, 135–176. Chicago: Chicago University Press.

CHAPTER 3

Cosmopolitanism and Classical Sociology

David Inglis

1   Introduction

This chapter sets out the main relationships between the body of knowledge customarily referred to as 'classical sociology' and ideas about cosmopolitanism. Cosmopolitan currents run throughout the works of the major classical sociologists. One such current is primarily to be found among German classical sociologists, while another is discernible among French thinkers.

The chapter traces these developments in the thought of Marx and Tönnies on the one side, and Saint-Simon, Comte, and Durkheim on the other. Both currents in large part come out of the cosmopolitan thinking of Immanuel Kant.[1] The German focus was more on the ambivalently cosmopolitan nature of capitalism, especially embodied in the metropolis. The French focus was more on intergroup solidarities and the emergence of transnational moral cultures. Both foci can be said to be still relevant for understanding cosmopolitanism and globalization processes today.

2   Irrelevant Classics?

What are we today to make of the classical sociologists' cosmopolitan thinking? One possible answer is that all the major thinkers were insufficiently cosmopolitan, being far too rooted in nation-state-centric ways of thinking. In the early 2000s, Ulrich Beck (2002) set out the epistemological contours of a contemporary 'cosmopolitan sociology' able to grasp the complexities of transnational, globalizing processes. He contrasted this with the classical sociologists' alleged methodological nationalism. In the 19th century:

> the association between sociology and nation-state was so extensive that the image of 'modern,' organized individual societies—which became definitive with the national model of political organization—itself became

---

1   See Chapter 2 in this volume.

an absolutely necessary concept in and through the founding work of classical social scientists. Beyond all their differences, such theorists as Émile Durkheim, Max Weber and even Karl Marx shared a territorial definition of modern society, and thus a model of society centered on the national-state, which has today been shaken by globality and globalization.

BECK, 2000: 24

This viewpoint has met with much criticism since the late 1990s. Some scholars (Chernilo, 2006, 2007) have found the place of the nation-state in classical sociological thinking to be much more ambivalent than Beck alleged. The ideas of the classical sociologists tended to reflect and refract not only the territorial structures of nation-states, but also the emerging transnational contexts. While Marx sometimes emphasized the power of particular nation-state governments over the workers' movement, his analysis of that transnational movement, and of the globalizing capitalism that was its antagonist, very much emphasized the planetwide spread of both (Renton, 2001). Chernilo (2006, 2007) likewise acquits Max Weber of the charge of methodological nationalism, as Weber did not define the term 'society' in a national sense, nor did he focus on social relations which only operated within states' borders.

Much classical sociology, especially its Durkheimian variant, has been defended as possessing cosmopolitan visions which Turner (2006: 133; also 1990) argues were intended 'to challenge the nationalist assumptions' of the times (Fine, 2003a, 2003b). While Beck would exempt classical sociologists from the conceptual realm of contemporary cosmopolitan sociology, the scholars mentioned want to include them. The classical thinkers seem much more attuned to the emergence of cosmopolitan and globalizing phenomena in their own times than Beck admitted. Because at least some classical thinkers were much more sensitive to world-spanning complexification processes than Beck's account allowed for, they may still be of use today for thinking in cosmopolitan ways about real-world 'cosmopolitizing' processes.

3   Back to Kant

One ironic feature of Beck's attack on the classical sociologists for being insufficiently cosmopolitan is that both the thinkers he criticized and his version of cosmopolitan sociology are very much indebted to the thought of Immanuel Kant. Thinkers in 19th-century France and Germany took up Kant's legacy in differing ways. So too did Beck—so much so that some of his critics have alleged that his vision of a cosmopolitan world in our own times is insufficiently empirically grounded, in fact being a disguised Kantian political philosophy (Roudometof, 2005).

Beck seems not to have appreciated that some of the classical sociologists were also doing precisely what he was trying to do: to recalibrate Kantian cosmopolitan thinking for new times, and to develop a workable cosmopolitan sociology—or sociology of empirical cosmopolitan conditions—partly out of Kant's cosmopolitanism. Kant's cosmopolitan thinking has been the focus of much attention since the late 1990s, stimulated by Nussbaum's (1997) attempt to revivify it. Critics have also pointed to Kant's alleged racism, which seems to undermine his claim he was a truly cosmopolitan thinker (Papastephanou, 2002).

Nonetheless, Kant's cosmopolitanism was never located only in the realm of political philosophy, for it was also already a kind of sociology, aimed at understanding emergent empirical cosmopolitan conditions across the world (Inglis, 2014). Kant's analysis seeks to discern the emergence of cosmopolitan political and moral structures that come to affect every part of the world, and to understand the empirical global historical processes that have made these possible. Kant's writings encompass both a set of world-encompassing cosmopolitan norms and actually existing political structures, as well as empirical processes—that today we might call 'globalization'—which make possible and spread those structures and norms across the world.

Kant tells a very long-term historical story in this regard. Initial human dispersal across the habitable parts of the planet was followed by increasing interconnections among geographically disparate groups. By placing 'each people near another which presses upon it,' historical conditions compelled each group to 'form itself into a state in order to defend itself.' This provoked wars between states. Two cultural factors also impelled different states to be hostile to each other: 'differences of language and of religion ... involve a tendency to mutual hatred and pretexts for war' (Kant, 1963a: 111). It was the human propensity to discord which paradoxically eventually drove humans to peaceful forms of association, first within particular states (the social contract à la Hobbes and Locke), and then between states (i.e., cosmopolitan world conditions). Humans in the very long run learnt that the best means of meeting their interests, individual and collective, was to engage in peaceful 'national' and 'inter-national' association with each other. World history eventually brought about, among humans,

> that which reason could have told them at the beginning and with far less sad experience ... to step from the lawless condition of savages into a league of nations ... [where] even the smallest state could expect security

and justice ... a united power acting according to decisions reached under the laws of their united will.
>
> KANT, 1963b: 19

This is a 'cosmopolitan condition' that eventually will pertain throughout the whole world (Kant, 1963b: 20).

Kant adds that over time intergroup trade develops. Different states 'unite because of mutual interest. The spirit of commerce, which is incompatible with war, sooner or later gains the upper hand in every state ... states see themselves forced, without any moral urge, to promote honourable peace' (1963a: 114). Increasingly, world-level trading relations help to create 'understanding, conventions and peaceable relations [which are] established [even] among the most distant peoples' (1963a: 110). Kant's emphasis on the potentially peace-generating effects of world-level trade was a reflection of broader 18th-century liberal and radical sentiments, to be found in the work of figures like Adam Smith and Voltaire (Muller, 2003).

Kant discerned only the beginnings of a world-level cosmopolitan order in his own period. But he was confident that the current situation showed that 'there is a rising feeling which each [state] has for the preservation of the whole ... [and thus] a universal cosmopolitan condition ... will come into being' at some point (1963b: 23). He also discerned the first flourishing of a world-level moral community. Within this 'a violation of rights in [any] one place is felt *throughout the world*' (1963a: 105; emphasis added). This is an important early anticipation of later notions of a world-spanning moral culture, based around sentiments of revulsion for, and condemnation of, actions which undermine human rights. Regardless of where those actions might happen, the condemnation that follows is literally *global*: it comes from all over the world, and in effect is the moral response of the *whole world*, understood as a single moral entity (1963a: 103).

This view of the really existing nature of a global moral culture furnished Kant with the grounds to strongly criticize colonizing European states which had gone to 'terrifying lengths' to subjugate other peoples, stealing their lands from them (1963a: 103). If colonialism is a facet of globalization, so too is the very globe-spanning moral culture that provides grounds for colonialism's condemnation. Globalization simultaneously produces both colonialism, as well as the moral norms and means (e.g., newspapers of global reach) for condemning it.

4 The Cosmopolitan Features of Capitalism and *Gesellschaft*

In these reflections by Kant, one can see the beginnings of the dialectical accounts of world history in general, and of empirical globalization processes that would later be taken up by Hegel and then Marx (Buchwalter, 2011). Marx's views on the worldwide spread of capitalism, out from Europe to the rest of the world, betray the influence of Kant's account of cosmopolitan historical unfolding.

In the *Communist Manifesto*, Marx and Engels (1968 [1848]: 38) argued that 'the need of a constantly expanding market for its products chases the bourgeoisie over the whole surface of the globe.' Capitalism's dynamic nature compels it, in the constant search for profit, to expand its markets across the world. The capitalist class seeks to bring every single person on the planet under its sway, as both an exploited producer of goods and as a consumer of them. Increasingly, globe-spanning capitalism 'batters down all Chinese walls ... It compels all nations, on pain of extinction, to adopt the bourgeois mode of production ... [and] to introduce what it calls civilization into their midst, i.e., to become bourgeois themselves' (Marx and Engels, 1968 [1848]: 38).

Marx thought that all regions of the world would eventually be thoroughly transformed by capitalism, local cultures being swept away by a new world-encompassing order of production, profit, and exploitation. This socioeconomic set of affairs is understood by Marx as being quite as 'cosmopolitan' as the socio-moral cultural world condition envisaged by Kant. Marx's famous ambivalence about capitalism is clear in this regard. The development of European colonial expansion is recognized as bloody and vicious, but the arrival of Europeans in places like India is seen to pave the way for a global socialist revolution. Colonialism smashes older and more local structures of ruling-class power and ideology, creating the conditions for modernized industry and economic relations, and thus a new globe-spanning proletariat. Consequently, Marx has been criticized for his acceptance of the destruction of local cultures around the world, in the name of blindly Eurocentric notions of 'progress' (Howe, 2007).

Marx's influence—and more dimly that of Kant—can also be discerned in the ideas of another important German classical sociologist, Ferdinand Tönnies. Tönnies (1957 [1887]) introduced to sociology the famous distinction between *Gemeinschaft and Gesellschaft*. This describes a movement from situations where tightly bound, affectively based groups were the main sorts of social actors, to those where rationally calculating, selfish individuals occupied center-stage in the social order. One might also examine a particular society and possibly find within it elements both of *Gemeinschaft* and of *Gesellschaft*. Tönnies explicitly defines the *Gesellschaft* created by the merchants as 'modern, cultured, cosmopolitan,' for reasons explicated later in this section (ibid.: 134). These concepts are derived from two more fundamental notions, two different types of 'will'—that is, the ways in which an individual conceptualizes the world and acts upon it. These are *Wesenwille* (natural will) and *Kürwille* (rational will). The former involves a judgment as to the intrinsic value of an act rather than its practicality. The latter involves a conscious choice of specific means for the pursuit of a specific end. While *Wesenwille*—characterized by strong affectivity and group-oriented feelings—describes the typical psychological and social-relational dispositions that constitute *Gemeinschaft*, *Kürwille* describes dispositions—involving high levels of individualistic calculation—that constitute *Gesellschaft*.

An important rejoinder to Beck's criticism of classical sociology is that for Tönnies (a thinker whom Beck did not explicitly mention), neither *Gemeinschaft* nor *Gesellschaft* is seen to be contained within nation-state borders (Inglis, 2009). One could apply this mode of analysis to *any* configuration of social relations, including transnational ones. There is no reason why *Gemeinschaft or Gesellschaft*, or *Wesenwille* and *Kürwille*, have to refer to 'national' entities. Tönnies was *not* methodologically nationalist, but rather provided categories that could be used for cosmopolitan sociological purposes. Indeed, Tönnies explicitly states that 'the existence of ... [nation-]states is but a temporary limitation of the boundaryless *Gesellschaff*' (Tönnies (1957 [1887]: 221).

For Tönnies, the innate tendency of *Kürwille* forms of consciousness is to pull ever greater numbers of people into their orbit, such ways of thinking having a decontextualized character which allows them to spread anywhere and everywhere. The group that above all promotes these ways of thinking are the class of merchants, who for Tönnies are the real cosmopolitan revolutionaries of human history. *Gesellschaft* is defined by Tönnies (1957 [1887]: 76) as 'a condition in which, according to the expression of Adam Smith, 'Every man ... becomes in some measure a merchant.' The merchant class's embodiment of the spirit of *Kürwille,* as well as their capacity to transmit over large distances its characteristic modes of thought and interaction, give them a powerful capacity to transform social relations wherever their reach is felt. Tönnies approvingly cites Adam Smith: 'A merchant ... is not necessarily the citizen of any particular country' (ibid.: 81). The merchant is radically cosmopolitan because

> [he or she] is without home, a traveller, a connoisseur of foreign customs and arts without love or piety for those of any one country, a linguist speaking several languages. Flippant and double-tongued, adroit, adaptable ... [S]he moves about quickly and smoothly, changes his [or her] character and intellectual attitude (beliefs or opinions) as if they were fashions of dress, one to be worn here, another there.
> TÖNNIES, 1957 [1887]: 168

The merchant's exceptional freedom from the thought patterns of *Wesenwille,* and the social relations of *Gemeinschaft,* means that he is unburdened by any of the moral considerations of *Gemeinschaft*, such as ties of patriotism. While the home-loving peasant 'turns his [or her] attention inwardly towards the centre of the locality ... to which [s]he belongs ... the trading class lends its attention to the outside world; it is concerned only with the roads which connect towns and with the means of transit' (Tönnies, 1957 [1887]: 79).

Tönnies develops Marx's ideas by saying that the purest expressions of *Kürwille* forms of consciousness and *Gesellschaft* modes of action and interaction are capitalist forms of exchange and production. These are 'cosmopolitan and [potentially] unlimited in size' (Tönnies, 1957 [1887]: 258–259). The merchants' capitalist ways of thinking and acting reach out from the urban areas where they were originally concentrated, pulling ever more locales into their sphere of influence:

> The more extensive the trade area, the more probable it is that the pure laws of exchange trade prevail, and that those other non-commercial qualities which relate men [sic] and things may be ignored. Trade tends, finally, to concentrate on one main market, the world market, upon which all other markets become dependent.
>
> TÖNNIES, 1957 [1887]: 79

Just as *Gemeinschaft* is by definition about locality, *Gesellschaft*, its ideal-typical opposite, is by definition non-local (indeed anti-local) and always potentially global in scope. *Kürwille* involves modes of formal rationality that could be adopted anywhere and everywhere, precisely because they are not freighted with the weight of cultural particularities. The generalizability, transportability, and mobility of *Kürwille* is what makes this way of thinking always potentially global in reach and therefore profoundly cosmopolitan in nature (Ritzer, 2007).

The cosmopolitan nature of the urban metropolis is central in Tönnies' thinking. The 'more general the condition of *Gesellschaft* becomes in the nation or a group of nations, the more this entire "country" or the entire "world" begins to resemble one large city' (Tönnies, 1957 [1887] 227). Each particular metropolis, like Berlin or New York, is described thus:

> [It contains] representatives from a whole group of nations, i.e. of the [whole] world. In the metropolis, money and capital are unlimited and almighty. It is able to produce and supply goods and science for the entire earth as well as laws and public opinion for all nations. It represents the world market and world traffic; [and] world industries are concentrated. Its newspapers are world papers, its people come from all corners of the earth, being curious and hungry for money and pleasure.
>
> TÖNNIES, 1957 [1887]: 266–267

Echoing Kant's points about the emergence of global public opinion through the emergence of transnational media, the metropolis has media outlets that are 'not confined within natural [sic] borders, but, in its tendencies and potentialities, ... [are] definitely international' (Tönnies, 1957 [1887]: 221).

The *Gesellschaft* of the metropolis is also 'pervaded with haste, unrest, continual novelty, fluidity and a persistence only in incessant change' (Tönnies, 1957 [1887]: 135). These are themes that Marx had already pointed to about incessant change in the big cities of the capitalist world system. Such ideas were also taken up by Georg Simmel. Tönnies argues that in the huge urban agglomerations, 'the arts must make a living; they are exploited in a capitalistic way. Thoughts spread and change with astonishing rapidity. Speeches and books through mass distribution become stimuli of far-reaching importance' (Tönnies, 1957 [1887]: 227–228). Novel ideas, opinions, and styles are created, and are at first taken up by metropolitan elites. '[T]he views of the upper and ruling classes ... are formed outside of custom ... These views partially originate in deviant new usages and habits, and the latter are frequently based on an imitation of strangers' and foreigners more generally (Tönnies, 1961 [1909]: 114). Ideas and realities are therefore constantly being cosmopolitized. Through a series of what are nowadays called 'inventions of tradition' (Hobsbawm and Ranger, 1992), metropolitan elites try to construct forms of culture that are allegedly expressive of older forms of *Gemeinschaft*. The lower-middle and working classes eventually take up cultural forms, both (supposedly) native and more (explicitly) cosmopolitan, imported or invented by their social superiors (Tönnies, 1961 [1909]: 117). Over time, even the lowest social classes thus come to exist within increasingly cosmopolitized social realities. Tönnies' striking thoughts about the cosmopolitization of sociocultural conditions were, alas, almost completely ignored in Beck's critique of classical sociology.

5 Cosmopolitan Thematics in French Sociology

Just as Kant's cosmopolitan themes were taken up and developed in a German line of thought about capitalism and metropolises, so too were they adapted by thinkers in the French sociological tradition, most notably Durkheim. The latter's cosmopolitan sociology mediated the Kantian inheritance through France's distinctive intellectual and political culture.

Utopian socialism was an important influence on embryonic sociology in France. With an echo of Kant's optimism, Saint-Simon and his followers argued that the end point of human history was 'universal association ... the association of all men [sic] on the entire surface of the globe in all spheres of their relationships' (Iggers, 1958: 58). The ancient Greek cosmopolitan idea of universal brotherhood was recalibrated to become a product of the emerging global division of labor. Over time, 'the various nations, scattered over the face of the earth, shall appear only as members of one vast workshop, working under a common law for the accomplishment of one and the same destiny' (ibid.: 85). Similar sentiments were voiced by Auguste Comte. The likelihood of 'universal peace' is increased as 'labor becomes an instrument for humanity as a whole' (Boas, 1928: 151–152). What Durkheim would later call 'organic solidarity' was envisaged by Saint-Simon, Comte, and others as being both a cosmopolitan (world-spanning) phenomenon, and having cosmopolitan moral-political outcomes.

Durkheim's cosmopolitanism synthesizes Saint-Simonian and Comtean with Kantian themes. The political philosophy Durkheim adumbrated at the turn of the 20th century was clearly an attempt to update Kantian themes for new times. Turner (2006: 141) notes that 'in equating what he called "true patriotism" with cosmopolitanism, Durkheim anticipated the modern debate about republicanism, patriotism and cosmopolitanism by almost a century.' Durkheim sought to reconcile nation-state structures and national identities with cosmopolitan moral dispositions, in a like manner to present-day thinkers such as Appiah (1996). These themes were set out at the Paris Universal Exposition of 1900:

> Doubtless, we have towards the country in its present form, and of which we in fact form part, obligations that we do not have the right to cast off. But beyond this country, there is another in the process of formation, enveloping our national country: that of Europe, or humanity.
> Cited in LUKES, 1973: 350

Durkheim formulated these ideas further in lectures on morality and politics he gave in Bordeaux between 1890 and 1900, repeated at the Sorbonne in 1904 and 1912 (Durkheim, 1992). Durkheim here considered the apparently contradictory notion of 'world patriotism.' This does not involve modes of affiliation to a putative 'world state.' Like Kant, he notes that 'such an idea, while not altogether beyond realization, must be set in so distant a future that we can leave it out of our present reckoning' (Durkheim, 1992: 74).

He then develops the concept of 'world patriotism' from within what he takes to be the apparently rigid empirical realities of the contemporary international system, while attempting to raise this system to what he understands as a higher moral and ethical level, very much mirroring Kant's earlier efforts. Each state should, and in future would, encourage the highest moral sentiments among all its citizens. Each national government would endeavor 'not to expand, or to lengthen its borders, but to set its own house in order and to make the widest appeal to its members for a moral life on an ever higher level' (Durkheim, 1992: 74). If this were to happen, then 'civic duties would be only a particular form of the general obligations of humanity' (ibid.).

Durkheim here points toward some kind of 'world culture,' constituted of certain moral and ethical codes, which are contributed to by particular nation-states. When these codes have become part of an acknowledged 'world culture,' they are in turn taken on board by all of nation-states, albeit with specific national colorings, regarding the education of the actions and aspirations of the citizenry. Durkheim notes that the various European countries 'have not yet reached the point when this kind of patriotism could prevail without dissent' (Durkheim, 1992: 75). But Durkheim, again like Kant, wishes to root his cosmopolitical philosophy in an account of what he takes to be emerging world-level social conditions that could further foster the desired political outcome of cosmopolitan forms of citizenship.

Turner (1990: 347) has argued that for obvious pragmatic reasons compelled by the international political situation, at the outbreak of the First World War Durkheim partly turned away from such explicitly cosmopolitan reflections toward 'the idea of nationalism as a modern version of more traditional sources of the conscience collective.' This is partly true, but we must add that the onset of war did not see Durkheim relinquishing the cosmopolitan 'world patriotism' position entirely. Indeed, his cosmopolitan political position was repurposed as a crucial resource for dealing with challenging wartime conditions.

In the 1915 pamphlet entitled 'Germany Above All,' Durkheim shows the German state's aggressive behavior is driven by a narrow and chauvinistic nationalism that is antithetical to 'world patriotism.' It is morally condemnable because it goes against the norms of—the empirically existing, if rudimentary, contemporary version of—world patriotism and world moral culture. German elites of the 19th century were positive contributors to 'world culture,' as they were people 'who belonged without any reservation to the same moral community as we ourselves' in France and the Allied countries (Durkheim, 1915: 4). But the Germans' instigation of the war and their brutal treatment of both combatants and civilians alike signified a total denial of their moral responsibilities as members of the global 'moral community.' Germany had become a rogue state, far removed from the norms of world-level moral culture. Germany could be forcefully condemned on the basis of existing world-level norms, precisely because it had flouted these so flagrantly.

For Durkheim to be able to make a convincing case about the existence of such a world moral culture, he had to demonstrate the mechanisms whereby such a culture had come into existence, moving, like Kant, from the more abstract realm of political philosophy to the more concrete world of history and social conditions. This is exactly what *The Elementary Forms of the Religious Life* (Durkheim, 2001 [1912]) partly set out to achieve. An embryonic theory of globalization is contained in its later chapters, which underpins his views on world moral culture and political cosmopolitanism (Inglis and Robertson, 2008).

These later chapters depart quite considerably from the strong emphasis on 'society' understood as a bounded, territorial unit, with strong symbolic boundaries surrounding it, found in the earlier chapters. What comes into sight at the book's end is an account of the sociological reasons whereby a world-spanning moral culture develops over time. The Australian aboriginal ethnographic material is deployed to demonstrate that 'religious universalism'—a condition whereby a particular belief system claims to have authority over, and relevance for, more than one social group—is found not just in the 'world religions' but 'at the summit' of Australian aboriginal religion too. Durkheim argues that in Australia, particular gods are recognized by multiple tribes, and so 'their cult is, in a sense, international' (2001 [1912]: 321).

Echoing Kant's points about human dispersal across the planet, neighboring tribes are seen to be unable, over the long term, to avoid contact with each other, and progressively they become more systematically interlinked, primarily through the means of trade and group intermarriage. They enter into conditions whereby they become ever more conscious of what aspects of life they have in common, and 'mutual [cultural] borrowings ... serve to reinforce' this sense of 'international' commonality (Durkheim, 2001 [1912]: 321). With the increasing interpenetration of previously distinct tribal groups at the material level (a basic form of emergent organic solidarity), 'international gods' are born. Each tribe's idea of a god fuses with the ideas of the other tribes with whom they are in systematic contact. The resulting 'international god' is made manifest as an idea in the minds of all participants. The 'international gods' are therefore products of a 'hybridization' of distinct tribal (or in more modern terms, 'national') traditions.

The 'international gods' are, for Durkheim, above all gods of initiation ceremonies. As such, they are generated through the initiation rituals held at 'intertribal assemblies.' Durkheim argues that at these assemblies 'sacred beings were ... formed that were not fixed to any geographically fixed society.' The geography they correspond to, and in fact are produced by, is intertribal, that is to say 'inter-national' or 'inter-societal.' It does not have clear borders, and conceptually speaking is 'spread over an unlimited area.' The gods that correspond to this territory 'have the same character [as the territory itself]; their sphere of influence is not circumscribed; they glide above the particular tribes and above space. They are the great international gods' (Durkheim, 2001 [1912]: 321).

A territorially bounded 'society' produces a body of religious beliefs which express the structure of that society. We might therefore expect that 'international' or 'global' society produces a body of beliefs—about, and symbolized by, 'international gods'—which reflect its nature too. If 'national' religions are the necessary preconditions for effective social functioning within a given bounded 'society,' then the functioning of an international or global society would also seem to depend on its 'religious' expressions, both in the guiding of individuals' actions through norms and in the carving up of 'reality' through its cognitive lenses. An 'international' or 'global' religion does its conceptual carving up of reality in ways that are more 'cosmopolitan' than those of 'national' religions, especially given that the former is a hybrid and emergent entity.

Using these ideas about aboriginal international religion, Durkheim sought to analyze the emerging world-spanning social and cultural conditions of his day. He notes that in the present day,

> there is no people, no state, that is not involved with another society that is more or less unlimited and includes all peoples ... There is no national life that is not dominated by an inherently international collective life. As we go forward in history, these international groupings take on greater importance and scope ...' (2001 [1912]: 322)

The globalizing transformation of aboriginal life in the past revealed the essential mechanisms of growing organic solidarity, intergroup assembly, and cultural hybridization that have previously generated cosmopolitan moral cultures. For Durkheim, similar mechanisms are again producing the latter, in his present and in the future, but this time at a truly global level.

6 Conclusion

This chapter has examined two major lines of cosmopolitan thinking and politics in classical sociology, one which developed among German thinkers and another which was elaborated by French scholars. Both streams of thought derive from Kant's original formulations, and then were adapted to different national intellectual contexts and changing empirical conditions. Each stream of thought emphasizes a different articulation of cosmopolitanism and sociology, the German trend focusing more on capitalism and the metropolis, the French tradition more oriented to issues of culture, morality, and the civil sphere.

The blind spots of the one tradition can be partly overcome by consideration of the insights of the other. For example, the sometimes more harsh and pessimistic tenor of the Germanic version can be compensated for by the more optimistic and positive French dispositions, and vice versa. Putting both strands together indicates an overall trajectory in 19th- and early 20th-century European sociological thought which engaged, problematically but still fruitfully, with multiple issues to do with cosmopolitanism, nationalism, intergroup relations, and morality in a globalizing world context. The classical sociologists covered much of the same social, political, and moral terrains with which cosmopolitan sociologists nowadays seek to deal. Their analytic orientations are, despite their flaws, still worth attending to.

References

Appiah, A. 1996. 'Cosmopolitan Patriots.' In *For Love of Country: Debating the Limits of Patriotism*, edited by J. Cohen, 21–29. Cambridge, MA: Beacon.

Beck, U. 2000. *What Is Globalization?* Cambridge, UK: Polity Press.

Beck, U. 2002. 'The Cosmopolitan Society and Its Enemies.' *Theory, Culture and Society* 19 (1–2): 17–44.

Boas, F. 1928. *Anthropology in Modern Life*. New York: Norton.

Buchwalter, A. (ed.). 2011. *Hegel and Global Justice*. Amsterdam: Springer.

Chernilo, D. 2006. 'Social Theory's Methodological Nationalism: Myth and Reality.' *European Journal of Social Theory* 9 (5): 5–22.

Chernilo, D. 2007. 'A Quest for Universalism: Re-assessing the Nature of Classical Social Theory's Cosmopolitanism.' *European Journal of Social Theory* 10 (1): 17–35.

Durkheim, É. 1915. 'Germany Above All: German Mentality and War.' Paris: Librairie Armand Colin.

Durkheim, É. 1992. *Professional Ethics and Civic Morals*. London: Routledge.

Durkheim, É. 2001 [1912]. *The Elementary Forms of Religious Life*. Oxford: Oxford University Press.

Fine, R. 2003a. 'Kant's Theory of Cosmopolitanism and Hegel's Critique.' *Philosophy and Social Criticism* 29 (6): 609–630.

Fine, R. 2003b. 'Taking the "Ism" Out of Cosmopolitanism: An Essay in Reconstruction.' *European Journal of Social Theory* 6 (4): 451–470.

Hobsbawm, E. and T. Ranger (eds.). 1992. *The Invention of Tradition*. Cambridge, UK: Cambridge University Press.

Howe, S. 2007. 'Edward Said and Marxism: Anxieties of Influence.' *Cultural Critique* 67: 50–87.

Iggers, G. 1958. *The Doctrine of Saint-Simon: An Exposition*. Boston, MA: Beacon.

Inglis, D. 2009. 'Cosmopolitan Sociology and the Classical Canon: Ferdinand Tönnies and the Emergence of Global Gesellschaft.' *British Journal of Sociology* 96 (12): 813–832.

Inglis, D. 2014. 'Cosmopolitanism's Sociology and Sociology's Cosmopolitanism: Retelling the History of Cosmopolitan Theory from Stoicism to Durkheim and Beyond.' *Distinktion: Scandinavian Journal of Social Theory* 15 (1): 69–87.

Inglis, D. and R. Robertson. 2008. 'The Elementary Forms of Globality: Durkheim and the Emergence and Nature of Global Life.' *Journal of Classical Sociology* 8 (1): 5–25.

Kant, I. 1963a. 'Idea for a Universal History from a Cosmopolitan Point of View.' In *On History*, edited by L. White Beck. Indianapolis: Bobbs-Merrill.

Kant, I. 1963b. 'Perpetual Peace.' In *On History*, edited by L. White Beck. Indianapolis: Bobbs-Merrill.

Lukes, S. 1973. *Emile Durkheim: His Life and Work. A Historical and Critical Survey*. London: Allen Lane.

Marx, K. and F. Engels. 1968 [1848]. 'Manifesto of the Communist Party.' In *Marx–Engels Selected Works*. Moscow: Progress Publishers. 31–63.

Muller, J. 2003. *The Mind and the Market*. New York: Anchor.

Nussbaum, M. 1997. 'Kant and Stoic Cosmopolitanism.' *Journal of Political Philosophy* 5 (1): 1–25.

Papastephanou, M. 2002. 'Kant's Cosmopolitanism and Human History.' *History of the Human Sciences* 15 (1): 17–37.

Renton, D. 2001. *Marx on Globalization*. London: Verso.

Ritzer, G. 2007. *The Globalization of Nothing*. Newbury Park, CA: Pine Forge.

Roudometof, V. 2005. 'Transnationalism, Cosmopolitanism and Glocalization.' *Current Sociology* 53 (1): 113–115.

Tönnies, F. 1957 [1887]. *Community and Society*, edited and translated by C. D. Loomis. London: Routledge.

Tönnies, F. 1961 [1909]. *Custom: An Essay on Social Codes*. New York: Free Press.

Turner, B. S. 1990. 'The Two Faces of Sociology: Global or National.' *Theory, Culture & Society* 7 (3–4): 317–332.

Turner, B. S. 2006. 'Classical Sociology and Cosmopolitanism: A Critical Defence of the Social.' *British Journal of Sociology* 57 (1): 133–151.

CHAPTER 4

Cosmopolitanism as a Siamese-Twin Global Concept

Stéphane Dufoix

The current landscape of what has come to be called *cosmopolitan studies* has been very well described in a number of books that have been published since around the late 1990s (Vertovec and Cohen, 2002; Delanty, 2009, 2012; Nowicka and Rovisco, 2011; Skrbiš and Woodward, 2013; Cicchelli, 2018). They provide a wide presentation of the various—and sometimes contradictory—contents and applications that were recently given to the notion of cosmopolitanism. This chapter finds its rationale in the now classical statement, according to which a new round of cosmopolitanism began after 1989 (Delanty, 2012), but it intends to explore this hypothesis from a more uncommon perspective than usual, shifting the emphasis from either a normative or a conceptual use of *cosmopolitanism* to a historical-sociological approach of its uses in the social sciences. Relying on both sociology of ideas (Camic and Gross, 2001) and social-historical semantics (Dufoix, 2017), it aims at historicizing the academic trajectory of *cosmopolitanism* and understanding the connection between the concepts of cosmopolitanism and globalization. Because of the necessary short format of this chapter, but also because of the incredible diversity acquired by this concept of cosmopolitanism since the late 1980s, it will not aim at providing a comprehensive synthesis of how cosmopolitanism was used in the social sciences since that time, but rather will attempt to provide some sketch of how the semantic career of *cosmopolitanism* should be understood against the backdrop of the emergence of other Janus-faced concepts like *diaspora* or *globalization* in a new epistemic era—that roughly began in the second half of the 1980s—characterized by the increasing visibility of new academic actors coming from non-Western countries—even if mostly living and working in the North—who would challenge the classical understanding of some words and phenomena.

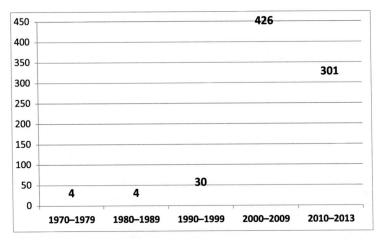

FIGURE 4.1 Number of books and articles having *cosmopolitanism* in their title, 1970–2013
SOURCE: INTERNATIONAL BIBLIOGRAPHY OF THE SOCIAL SCIENCES (ACCESSED JUNE 27, 2014)

1 From an Early Mertonian Matrix to the Global Explosion

Gerard Delanty (2012: 3) noted that the 'revival' of the interest in cosmopolitanism from the early 1990s onwards (also see Fine, 2007: 1ff.)—which he saw as the emergence of 'cosmopolitanism studies'—had to be understood against the backdrop of macro-geopolitical changes such as the fall of communism in the USSR and in Central and Eastern Europe, the democratization of the Arab world, and the end of apartheid; of intellectual thinking such as the bicentennial of Immanuel Kant's *Perpetual Peace* in 1995; and of the revolution in communication technologies that made it possible to gradually envision both instantaneity of communication and potential ubiquity.

These statements find a direct confirmation in the evolution of the number of books and articles having the word cosmopolitanism in their title (Figure 4.1). The evolution of the yearly ratio is perhaps even more impressing (Figure 4.2).

Figures 4.1 and 4.2 may give us an idea about the numbers and about the progression but they have to be more refined. For instance, a first glance at these two tables may give the impression that the 1990s is the decade when cosmopolitanism gains a new momentum. A closer look shows (Figure 4.3) that more than half of the notices (15 out of 30) were published in 1998 and 1999, which seems to make it clear that the actual editorial explosion of cosmopolitanism is more accurately linked to the late 1990s than to the early 1990s.

These data need to be completed by a more intellectual history of the uses of the word. The first element to emphasize is that an early career of

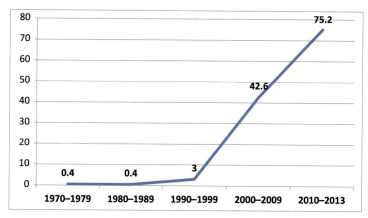

FIGURE 4.2 Yearly ratio of books and articles having *cosmopolitanism* in their title, 1970–2013
SOURCE: INTERNATIONAL BIBLIOGRAPHY OF THE SOCIAL SCIENCES (ACCESSED JUNE 27, 2014)

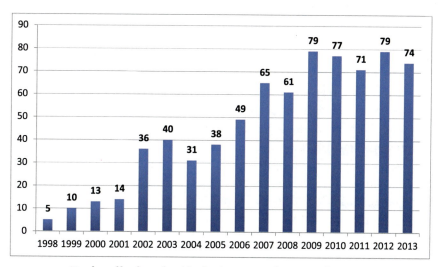

FIGURE 4.3 Number of books and articles having *cosmopolitanism* in their title, 1998–2011

cosmopolitanism in social science can be noticed. It goes back to a study entitled 'Patterns of Influence: Local and Cosmopolitan Influentials,' published in 1949 by the American sociologist Robert K. Merton (1949) after an earlier report for the Bureau of Applied Social Research in November 1943.[1] It was based

---

[1] The title of the initial study was 'Time Readership and the Influence Structure of Dover, N.J.'

on a research conducted in the town of Rovere (the pen name of Dover, New Jersey) from interviews with eighty-six men and women and more in-depth investigation with thirty 'influential people in the town.' After analyzing their answers to a question like 'Do you worry much about the news?,' he split these thirty people into two groups that he named 'local influentials' and 'cosmopolitan influentials,' depending on the orientation of their influence on other people with regard to the problems of the city for the 'locals' and to the problems of the world for the 'cosmopolitans.' The terms do not refer, of course, to the regions in which interpersonal influence is exercised, since both types of influentials are effective almost exclusively within the local community.

Merton's conceptual opposition between cosmopolitans and locals became a *locus classicus*, notably in American sociology, and it was frequently cited in sociological works using the cosmopolitan frame, and sometimes even expanded, as was the case with Alvin Gouldner's (1957 and 1958) use of the pattern for formal organizations, including bureaucracies, 'locals' being those 'high on loyalty to the employing organization, low on commitment to specialized role,' whereas the 'cosmopolitans' were those 'low on loyalty' and 'likely to use an outer reference group orientation' (Gouldner, 1957: 290). Yet, on the whole, it could be argued that was at stake in this pioneer study was less cosmopolitanism as we usually know it than *cosmopoliteness* as a resource, the world here being everything that is outside the local, but not necessarily as large as the planet, all the more so as sociology at that time was mostly nationally oriented.

A reappraisal of Merton's conceptual pattern was proposed by the Swedish anthropologist Ulf Hannerz in the second half of the 1980s, with a greater emphasis on world culture. His article, 'Cosmopolitans and Locals in World Culture,' published in the special issue of *Theory, Culture and Society* devoted to 'Explorations in Critical Social Science' in 1990, but the first version of it this article was presented at the First International Conference on the Olympics and East/West and South/North Cultural Exchanges in the World System, in Seoul in August 1987. This chronological precision is of importance because it replaces Hannerz's reflection on cosmopolitanism into the larger frame of his work on the world in creolization also published in 1987 (Hannerz, 1987). Considering Merton's seminal study, he writes: 'since then [the time when Merton wrote about locals and cosmopolitans], the scale of culture and social structure has grown, so that what was cosmopolitan in the early 1940s may be counted as a moderate form of localism by now' (Hannerz, 1990: 237). Hannerz's intention is both to show that the world has become more and more infused with 'transnational cultures,' with more and more people on the move, and that our gaze on what is a culture and how it can be territorially delineated has more than often proved to be wrong, since, according to him, 'culture, rather than being easily separated from one another as the hard-edged pieces in a mosaic, tend to overlap and mingle' (ibid.: 239). The necessity to change our representation of cultures in the world is therefore both epistemological and historical. Hannerz calls for a re-evaluation of who is a cosmopolitan and who is a local. Just as a cosmopolitan is not 'just anybody who moves about in the world' (ibid.: 238), but has to be an 'actor' in the diversity of culture, a local is not necessarily stuck since the media and the transnational networks loosen the possibility of only one culture at home as people come to be more and more involved, in different ways, with more than one culture. The keyword here is interrelation: if Hannerz believes in the existence of 'one world culture,' he sees it as the product of how 'all the variously distributed structures of meaning and expression are becoming interrelated, somehow, somewhere. And people like the cosmopolitans have a special part in bringing about a degree of coherence (...)' (ibid.: 249).

The vocabulary used by Hannerz has to be taken into consideration here. In this late 1980s article, words like 'transnational,' 'networks,' 'global homogenization' are part of a new lexicon that is slowly taking shape in the social sciences and that both sustains and is sustained by new uses of 'cosmopolitanism.'

2   Cosmopolitanism and Globalization

From the late 1980s, a move toward a 'global turn in the social sciences' (Caillé and Dufoix, 2013) can be noticed, with new concepts being stabilized even if they had been coined years or sometimes decades before: globalization, world or global culture, diaspora, network, flow, transnational, and so on. 'Cosmopolitanism' and its derivatives are part of this conceptual and theoretical evolution. Even if we saw that conceptual cosmopolitanism in the social sciences predates the end of the bipolar world, its re-elaboration against the backdrop of the proliferation of cultures made it enter in elective affinity with new conceptualization of the world in the making and with the gradual construction and adoption of the concept of globalization. However, a precise understanding of how these conceptual changes were made possible requires a closer analysis of the rise of globalization as a concept. As I recently showed it elsewhere (Dufoix, 2018; also see Dufoix, 2013), it was born in the late 1980s and very early 1990s as a twin concept, two completely distinct and almost contradictory versions of globalization being brandished: globalization as a continuity within the whole process of world-making and within the conceptual history of the social sciences, and globalization as a rupture within those same processes. The latter conception is best exemplified in the works of such authors as Stuart Hall, Arjun Appadurai, and Ulrich Beck, both in their analysis of the contemporary situation and of the epistemological challenges faced by social scientists in order to account of the changes of and in the world. In this respect, 'cosmopolitanism' finds a new and crucial place in the conceptual architecture of a new social science that needs to be properly distinguished from the outdated, classical, and national-oriented social science.

If the British sociologist Stuart Hall has become world famous for his works on culture and identity, his study of these two themes in the context of globalization are lesser known, despite the fact that they were among the very first ones on this topic in relation to the question of modernity, notably in courses he gave in association with David Held and Anthony McGrew at the Open University from the late 1980s (Hall, 1992). His vision of culture, ethnicity, diaspora, and identity cannot be dissociated with his perception of 'new times' (Hall, 1989b) bringing about new identities and ethnicities. In two talks delivered in spring 1989 (1991a, 1991b), he insisted on how globalization meant important transformations of the relationship between the local and the global, and thus important modifications of the meanings of identity and ethnicity, since those two could not be understood within the old stable and fixed traditional definition, but had to be analyzed across boundaries and across frontiers (Hall, 1991a: 38).

In this logic, the old academic conception of identity has to be replaced by a new one—less homogeneous and more hybrid—that might closely fit the transformations of identities themselves. He considers that 'the great collective social identities which we thought of as large-scale, all-encompassing, homogenous, as unified collective identities,' such as class, race, nation, gender, and the West, have indeed not disappeared, but 'none of them is, any longer, in either the social, historical or epistemological place where they were in our conceptualizations of the world in the recent past. They cannot any longer be thought in the same homogenous form' (Hall, 1991b: 44–45). For Hall, globalization is thus characterized by two ongoing processes, one that heads toward more homogenization, and another one that heads in the other direction, toward the production of more and differences. Reminiscent of the Siamese-twin emergence and existence of both globalization and cosmopolitanism, he later opposed, in an interview with Pnina Werbner, a 'cosmopolitanism of the above' to a 'cosmopolitanism from below,' the former being the promise of making the world more and more alike, while the latter drives people across borders and creates new identities and differences (Hall, 2008: 346).

At the same time, in the late 1980s, alone or with his anthropologist wife Carol Breckenridge, Arjun Appadurai worked in the same direction as Stuart Hall. In 1988, Breckenridge and he launched the journal *Public Culture*. Reading some of the editorials they wrote for the first issues is quite telling with regard to their vision of what cosmopolitanism means. If these texts are not among the most famous by either authors, they do give us an inestimable access to the making of a new way of thinking about the world, a new way that emphasizes a new lexicon as well, or that at least reconfigures an older lexicon, and not only about cosmopolitanism but also about *diaspora* or *modernity* (see Dufoix, 2017). The very first lines of their editorial in the first issue of *Public Culture* set the tone:

> Our principal goal in starting this journal is to create an intellectual forum for interaction among those concerned with global cultural flows. Such flows, by their nature, are reflected in the emergent public cultures of many nation-states. Furthermore, these public cultures constitute the centers of new forms of cosmopolitanism in many linguistic and cultural ecumenes.
> APPADURAI AND BRECKENRIDGE, 1988a: 1

Therefore, from this starting point, they emphasize the need to both relativize and situate forms of knowledge, while taking cosmopolitanism seriously and 'finding colleagues and voices in different parts of the world who can and do speak for themselves' (Appadurai and Breckenridge, 1988a: 1). The latter means that it has to be pluralized (*cosmopolitanisms*), thus dissociating cosmopolitanism and homogenization.

In the same issue, Breckenridge and Appadurai wrote a five-page statement about the journal, starting with the idea that 'the world of the late twentieth century is increasingly a cosmopolitan world' (1988b: 5). Yet the cosmopolitan cultural forms offer a paradox: if they are 'emerging everywhere,' it seems like every society brings 'its own special history and traditions, its own cultural stamp, its own quirks and idiosyncrasies' (ibid.) Exactly as it could be noticed with Stuart Hall's vision of globalization and identity, they're asking for a new conceptual vocabulary. This reframing of concepts was, for instance, once again just like Stuart Hall's ideas at the same time (Hall, 1989b)—directed at the concept of diaspora in a later editorial: 'Indeed, to speak of diasporas— if by diasporas we mean phenomena involving stable points of origin, clear and final destinations and coherent group identities—seems already part of a sociology for the world we have lost' (Hall, 1989a: i). In his own research, Arjun Appadurai came to the same conclusions, especially in a 1990 article in which he assumed that 'the central problem of today's global interactions is the tension between cultural homogenization and cultural heterogenization' (Appadurai, 1990: 295). The vocabulary-reconfiguring enterprise takes the shape of the five scapes (ethnoscapes, mediascapes, financescape, ideoscapes, and technoscapes) that are supposed to replace the older concepts of identity, ethnicity, territory, and so on.

As a matter of fact, for these authors, the capacity to accurately account for the transformations of the world entailed the necessity to dissociate themselves from the older concepts and to coin new ones that would constitute the architecture of a new social science. This idea was never so fully developed and displayed than by Ulrich Beck (see Chapter 5 in this volume) in his promotion of 'methodological cosmopolitanism' as the new paradigm for social science (see Beck, 2000, 2006, 2011). Taking up on the Portuguese sociologist Hermínio Martins' (1974) notion of 'methodological nationalism,' he made it the main characteristic of modern and classical sociology, with its emphasis on the nation-state, on territory, and on sovereignty. Conversely, the new methodological cosmopolitanism should pay much more attention to spatiality, alterity, inequalities, and differences.

This opposition between two antagonistic visions of sociology that also implied displaying different interpretations of its past, present, and future, has become, since the late 1980s, an important epistemological issue, whether it opposed promoters of a new cosmopolitan social science to defenders of a more classical one, or promoters of a critical 'Southern' sociology to defenders of the universality of Western sociology.

3   Cosmopolitanism, Methodological Nationalism, and Non-Western Thinking: How Many Sociologies?

We have seen that from the late 1980s onwards, classical sociology has been reproached by various authors for both not having the capacity to explain the complex process of globalization because of its historical focus on the nation-state. Yet the question of what 'national' or 'global' sociology is or should be like was raised some years before by Bryan S. Turner. Discussing in 1986 the problems of sociology as both a calling and a trade, he developed the idea that 'sociology is essentially a form of supranational consciousness' and that 'the form of consciousness promoted and required by sociology is wholly cosmopolitan,' even though institutionalized sociology had grown and expanded within national markets (Turner, 1986: 279). In the following years, Turner has been defending the same idea over and over again, while at the same time trying to reduce the gap that was said to inherently exist between classical sociology and global sociology. For instance, against the potential threats of particularism and anti-Westernism entailed by the postcolonial critique of Orientalism, he argues that 'sociology itself has to break out of its nationalistic and parochial concerns with particular nation-states from a society-centered perspective' and he calls for the advent of a 'genuinely global perspective' that was 'largely implicit' but was present in the sociological tradition (Turner, 1989: 636). The idea of classical sociology having to be reconsidered so that its genuine global ambition might be visible gradually appears as a way to both ensure the preservation of the sociological tradition and its possible move toward a sociology of the global without having to choose between both and therefore provoke a divide between sociologists. The 'two faces of sociology' (Turner, 1990) have to be understood as the two faces of the same coin and not as opposite projects. In this respect, Turner is certainly one of the very first authors to write about a 'cosmopolitan sociology,' this formula being used to qualify classical sociology (ibid.: 346). The link between the 19th century and the late 20th century is elaborated through the prism of globalism and humanity, the vocation of sociology being that of 'a global sociology of humanity' (ibid.: 356).

Turner's approach to cosmopolitan sociology and to the dangers or prospects of global sociology in the late 20th century is all the more interesting as it was presented at about the same time when Hall, Appadurai, and later on Beck, started launching their attacks at classical sociology. Some fifteen years later, after Beck encapsulated classical sociology under the name of methodological nationalism, Turner and other authors replied to the accusations directed at the pioneers of the discipline with the argument that they could not be suspected of methodological nationalism and also that their approach was thoroughly and already cosmopolitan. The last fifteen years (since the early 2000s) have seen a proliferation of studies advocating the 'cosmopolitanism' of Durkheim—who was quite often the main target of these attacks—and of other classical figures such as Tönnies, Simmel, Pareto, or Michels (among others, see Fine, 2003, 2007; Truc, 2005; Chernilo, 2006, 2007; Turner, 2006; Inglis and Robertson, 2008; Inglis, 2009; Pendenza, 2014; see also Chapter 3 in this volume). Actually proving that, historically, Durkheim or others had a cosmopolitan outlook or were not 'methodological nationalists' was not really at stake here. Even when they used the words *cosmopolitan, cosmopolitanism, universal,* or *universalism* in their own language, the meaning associated to these terms was not identical to their current meanings. The issue here does not concern an effective history of classical sociology; it has everything to do with the retrospective use of the past as a resource in an epistemic—and not only epistemological—controversy. The discussion about Durkheim being the epitome of methodological nationalism or the pioneer of globalization theory does not actually tell us anything about Durkheim but tells a lot about the current situation of social science, torn as it is between its past and its present.

This debate about the past is nothing but a debate about the present with the interpretation of classical sociology being used as the main mode of legitimation, thus making us remember that social scientists are the first—and more than often the only—historians of social science. Chernilo's statement that 'methodological nationalism needs to be rejected and transcended' (Chernilo, 2006: 5) is in itself a clue for a better understanding of the issue at stake.

The fundamental opposition between the modernist stance—with its focus on territory, state, boundaries—and the 'beyond the modern' one—insisting on transnationalism, diasporic relationships, deterritorialization—does not really ensure cosmopolitanism as a concept is strictly limited to one of those two camps. In a similar way to what happened to other concepts emerging or reemerging in the early 1990s, as, for instance, diaspora or globalization (Dufoix, 2017, 2018), most scholars agree on the importance of the concept per se as well as on its name—the main disagreement is on the definition and on the meaning. This very particular epistemological conjunction, in which the validity of the concept goes hand in hand with harsh disputes about the definition, creates the very condition of possibility for the diffusion and popularization of the word itself.

From what preceded, one may have the impression that social science from the early 1990s onwards became torn between, on the one hand, defenders of a single sociology who had as their core the ambition to understand the world as a whole and, on the other, promoters of a necessary shift from older, classical sociology to a new version of it that would be less associated with Western modernity and with the specific territorialization of the nation-state, and more prone to considering other forms of spatiality and social relations. This impression is not wrong, but it is only accurate when one looks at social science from the Western part of the world or with a Western gaze.

The current framework of uses of cosmopolitanism has to be understood against the backdrop of new developments in the word geoepistemics. The idea that cosmopolitanism belongs not to the history of thought as such but to the history of Northern thought, having been instrumentalized as the history of thought in general, has to be taken into consideration in this discussion.

A deep and effective genealogy of the history of social sciences—sociology (Bhambra, 2014), anthropology (Ribeiro and Escobar, 2006), and history (Goody, 2006)—shows how much non-Western traditions of thought were silenced or suppressed by Western colonialism and/or scientific hegemony, thus leading to what the Indian political scientist Rajeev Bhargava (2013) has named the 'epistemic injustice of colonialism' (see Chapter 8 in this volume). The existence of this structural inequality within the world production of social sciences was challenged quite early on—at least from the 1950s—in Asia,

Latin America, Africa, and the Arab world. However, the global invisibility of these early reactions to Western hegemony in the social sciences remained the rule until the 1990s,[2] when the 'indigenous' or 'autonomous' perspective on the one hand (Akiwowo, 1986; Alatas, 2006), and the 'decolonial' perspective on the other, saw their opposition to Western epistemic hegemony grow more and more visible in the global academic field. Since 2009, this multiform and plural counter-hegemonic movement has but amplified itself, notably through various individual or collective voices in books or articles advocating the necessity to take into consideration the diversity of traditions in the social sciences (in the case of sociology, see Patel, 2010; and Burawoy, Chang, and Hsieh, 2010). In a similar way to what could be noticed with the 'global' visions by Hall and Appadurai, the notion of cosmopolitanism was either criticized for its Western flavor or re-elaborated in order to make it fit a more 'subaltern' and 'Southern' agenda.

A few instances should suffice here. In 2011, the Indian sociologist Sujata Patel came to terms with Ulrich Beck's methodological cosmopolitanism on the ground that this notion, despite its ambition of moving toward a less 'modern' and more 'fluid' understanding of the world, took it for granted that the whole was moving from a national to a cosmopolitan lens. Defending the idea that 'unfortunately the terms "cosmopolitan"/"cosmopolitanism" and "global" have had a long history within European modernities and remain overburdened with these histories and thus their meanings' (Patel, 2011: 13), she actually emphasized the fact that the necessity for Southern sociologists to defend their particularity in relation to Western epistemic domination resulted in the valorization of national or localized sociologies that nevertheless did not renounce a connection with scientific universalism.

This emphasis on epistemic power relations is precisely at the core of the semantic re-elaboration recently undertaken by two social scientists, promoting the necessity to disconnect sociological thinking in the South from Northern sociological reflection in order to establish a better epistemic balance. The Portuguese sociologist Boaventura de Sousa Santos and the Argentinian semiologist Walter Mignolo have thus both advocated the importance of proposing a new version of cosmopolitanism. For the former, the neoliberal and top-down type of globalization has been challenged by the 'transnationally organized resistance against the unequal exchanges produced or intensified by globalized localisms and localized globalisms,' that he calls 'insurgent

---

2 Global invisibility refers here to the general absence of the main authors writing against this hegemony in the academic circles or publication venues considered as being the most legitimate.

cosmopolitanism' (Santos, 2006: 397). Characterized as it is by horizontal solidarities and the defense of 'alternative non-imperialist, counter-hegemonic cultural values,' it would have known its 'first eloquent demonstration' with the protests against the World Trade Organization summit in Seattle in 1999 (ibid.). As he put it later on, while using another adjective, 'subaltern, oppositional cosmopolitanism is the cultural and political form of counter-hegemonic globalization' (Santos, 2007: 63, note 39; 2014).

From the early 2000s onwards, in line with his recent shift from the postcolonial approach to the decolonial approach (Grosfoguel, 2007), Walter Mignolo insisted on the necessity to move from Eurocentrism and its 'global designs'—what he described as the 'darker side of modernity' (2009)—to a less universal and more 'pluriversal' conception of the world and of social science and humanities in general. As early as 2000, he pleaded for the urgency to 'reconceive cosmopolitanism from the perspective of coloniality,' calling this new perspective 'critical cosmopolitanism' (Mignolo, 2000: 723). Such a proposal presents two particularities that he further elaborated in a 2010 article. The older versions of cosmopolitanism were characterized by the fact that they 'were concocted and enacted in and from the "center" (that is, in the heart of Western imperial countries and histories), and functioned as a "universalization of Western Nativism/Localism"' (Mignolo, 2010: 125–126). On the contrary, critical or decolonial cosmopolitanism is a proposal from the margins, thus making Mignolo argue that it's the only possible way to maintain cosmopolitanism as a goal, albeit it would mean understanding it as coming from localism, from below, and not from the universal above.[3] As he puts it, '"cosmopolitan localism" is another expression for pluri-versality as a global project' (ibid.: 127).

Where does acknowledging the polysemy and quite often invisible ambiguity of the current uses of cosmopolitanism take us? Stating and showing it is one thing, but this does not really lead anywhere. The most important lesson of such a mapping, however incomplete it may be, concerns the necessity to shift the academic gaze from the notion per se to its various uses, in order to have a better understanding of its availability and of its usefulness within the academic field. Of course, such a statement does not intend to any way relativize the importance of more normative or analytical studies of cosmopolitanism. It only aims at opening a new pathway that would inscribe the uses of social science notions and concepts into a wider geoepistemic landscape while at the same time making it possible to see concepts not only as scientific

---

3   For a similar proposal, see Mendieta (2009).

designators of reality but also as semantic battlefields and as issues at stakes among social scientists.

References

Akiwowo, A. 1986. 'Contribution to the Sociology of Knowledge from an African Oral Poetry.' *International Sociology* 1 (4): 343–358.
Alatas, S. H. 2006. 'The Autonomous, the Universal and the Future of Sociology.' *Current Sociology* 54 (1): 7 –23.
Appadurai, A. 1990. 'Disjuncture and Difference in the Global Cultural Economy.' *Theory, Culture and Society* 7 (2): 295–310.
Appadurai, A. and C. Breckenridge. 1988a. 'Editors' Comments.' *Public Culture* 1 (1): 1–4.
Appadurai, A. and C. Breckenridge. 1988b. 'Why Public Culture?' *Public Culture* 1 (1): 5–9.
Beck, U. 2000. 'The Cosmopolitan Perspective: Sociology of the Second Age of Modernity.' *British Journal of Sociology* 51 (1): 79–105.
Beck, U. 2006. *The Cosmopolitan Vision*. Cambridge, UK: Polity Press.
Beck, U. 2011. 'Cosmopolitan Sociology: Outline of a Paradigm Shift.' In *The Ashgate Research Companion to Cosmopolitanism*, edited by M. Rovisco and M. Nowicka, 17–32. Farnham: Ashgate Publishing.
Bhambra, G. 2014. *Connected Sociologies*. London: Bloomsbury.
Bhargava, R. 2013. 'Pour en finir avec l'injustice épistémique du colonialisme.' *Socio* 1: 41–75.
Burawoy, M., M. K. Chang, and M. Fei-yu Hsieh (eds.). 2010. *Facing an Unequal World: Challenges for a Global Sociology*. Taipei: Academia Sinica.
Caillé, A. and S. Dufoix (eds.). 2013. *Le tournant global des sciences sociales*. Paris: La Découverte.
Camic, C. and N. Gross 2001. 'The New Sociology of Ideas.' In *The Blackwell Companion to Sociology*, edited by Judith Blau, 236–249. Malden, MA: Blackwell.
Chernilo D. 2006. 'Social Theory's Methodological Nationalism: Myth and Reality.' *European Journal of Social Theory* 9 (1): 5–22.
Chernilo, D. 2007. 'A Quest for Universalism: Re-assessing the Nature of Classical Social Theory's Cosmopolitanism.' *European Journal of Social Theory* 10 (1): 17–35.
Cicchelli, V. 2018. *Plural and Shared: The Sociology of a Cosmopolitan World*. Leiden: Brill (first French edition 2016).
Delanty, G. 2009. *The Cosmopolitan Imagination: The Renewal of Critical Social Theory*. Cambridge, UK: Cambridge University Press.
Delanty, G. 2012. 'The Emerging Field of Cosmopolitanism Studies.' In *The Routledge Handbook of Cosmopolitanism Studies*, edited by G. Delanty, 1–8. London: Routledge.

Dufoix, S. 2013. 'Les naissances académiques du global.' In *Le tournant global des sciences sociales*, edited by A. Caillé and S. Dufoix, 27–43. Paris: La Découverte.

Dufoix, S. 2017. *The Dispersion: A History of the Word Diaspora*. Leiden: Brill (first French edition 2012).

Dufoix, S. 2018. 'Premiers éléments pour une sociologie historique des théories de la globalisation.' In *Des sciences sociales à la science sociale*, edited by A. Caillé, P. Chanial, S. Dufoix, and F. Vandenberghe, 249–263. Paris: Le Bord de l'eau.

Fine, R. 2003. 'Taking the "Ism" Out of Cosmopolitanism: An Essay in Reconstruction.' *European Journal of Social Theory* 6 (4): 451–470.

Fine, R. 2007. *Cosmopolitanism*. Abingdon: Taylor & Francis.

Goody, J. 2006. *The Theft of History*. Cambridge, UK: Cambridge University Press.

Gouldner, A. 1957. 'Cosmopolitans and Locals: Toward an Analysis of Latent Social Roles. I.' *Administrative Science Quarterly* 2 (3): 281–306.

Gouldner, A. 1958. 'Cosmopolitans and Locals: Toward an Analysis of Latent Social Roles. II.' *Administrative Science Quarterly* 2 (4): 444–480.

Grosfoguel, R. 2007. 'The Epistemic Decolonial Turn: Beyond Political–Economy Paradigms.' *Cultural Studies* 21 (2–3): 211–222.

Hall, S. 1989a. 'Cultural Identity and Diaspora.' *Framework* 36: 68–81.

Hall, S. 1989b. 'The Meaning of New Times.' In *New Times*, edited by S. Hall and J. Martin, 116–133. London: Lawrence & Wishart.

Hall, S. 1991a. 'The Local and the Global: Globalization and Ethnicity.' In *Culture, Globalization and the World-System: Contemporary Conditions for the Representation of Identity*, edited by A. King, 19–39. Binghamton: State University of New York.

Hall, S. 1991b. 'Old and New Identities, Old and New Ethnicities.' In *Culture, Globalization and the World-System: Contemporary Conditions for the Representation of Identity*, edited by A. King, 14–68. Binghamton: State University of New York.

Hall, S. 1992. 'The Question of Cultural Identity.' In *Modernity and Its Futures*, edited by S. Stuart, D. Held, and A. McGrew, 273–316. Cambridge, UK: Polity Press/The Open University.

Hall, S. 2008. 'Cosmopolitanism, Globalisation and Diaspora: Stuart Hall in Conversation with Pnina Werbner, March 2006.' In *Anthropology and the New Cosmopolitanism: Rooted, Feminist and Vernacular Perspectives*, edited by P. Werbner, 345–360. Oxford: Berg.

Hannerz, U. 1987. 'The World in Creolisation.' *Africa: Journal of the International African Institute* 57 (4): 546–559.

Hannerz, U. 1990. 'Cosmopolitans and Locals in World Culture.' *Theory, Culture and Society* 7 (2): 237–251.

Inglis, D. 2009. 'Cosmopolitan Sociology and the Classical Canon: Ferdinand Tönnies and the Emergence of Global *Gesellschaft*.' *British Journal of Sociology* 60 (4): 813–832.

Inglis, D. and R. Robertson. 2008. 'The Elementary Forms of Globality: Durkheim and the Emergence and Nature of Global Life.' *Journal of Classical Sociology* 8 (1): 5–25.

Martins, H. 1974. 'Time and Theory in Sociology.' In *Approaches to Sociology*, edited by J. Rex, 246–294. London: Routledge & Kegan.

Mendieta, E. 2009. 'From Imperial to Dialogical Cosmopolitanism.' *Ethics & Global Politics* 2 (3): 241–258.

Merton, R. K. 1949. 'Patterns of Influence: A Study of Interpersonal Influence and of Communications Behavior in a Local Community.' In *Communications Research*, edited by P. Lazarsfeld and F. Stanton, 180–219. New York: Harper & Brothers.

Mignolo, W. 2000. 'The Many Faces of Cosmo-Polis: Border-Thinking and Critical Cosmopolitanism.' *Public Culture* 12 (3): 721–748.

Mignolo, W. 2009. 'Coloniality: The Darker Side of Modernity.' In *Modernologies: Contemporary Artists Researching Modernity and Modernism*, edited by S. Breitwisser, 39–49. Barcelona: Catalog of the Exhibit at the Museum of Modern Arts.

Mignolo, W. 2010. 'Cosmopolitanism and the De-colonial Option.' *Studies in Philosophy and Education* 29 (2): 111–127.

Nowicka, M. and M. Rovisco (eds.). 2011. *The Ashgate Research Companion to Cosmopolitanism*. Burlington, VT: Ashgate Publishing.

Patel, S. (ed.). 2010. *The ISA Handbook of Diverse Sociological Traditions*. London: Sage.

Patel, S. 2011. 'An International Sociology with Diverse Epistemes.' *Global Dialogue* 1 (4): 12–13.

Pendenza, M. (ed.). 2014. *Classical Sociology beyond Methodological Nationalism*. Leiden: Brill.

Ribeiro, G. L. and A. Escobar (eds.). 2006. *World Anthropologies: Disciplinary Transformations within Systems of Power*. Oxford: Berg.

Santos, B. de Sousa. 2006. 'Globalizations.' *Theory Culture Society* 23 (2–3): 393–399.

Santos, B. de Sousa. 2007. 'Beyond Abyssal Thinking: From Global Lines to Ecologies of Knowledge.' *Review* 30 (1): 45–89.

Santos, B. de Sousa. 2014. *Epistemologies of the South. Justice against Epistemicide*. London: Taylor & Francis.

Skrbiš, Z. and I. Woodward. 2013. *Cosmopolitanism: Uses of the Idea*. London: Sage.

Truc, G. 2005. 'Simmel, sociologue du cosmopolitisme.' *Tumultes* 24: 49–77.

Turner, B. S. 1986. 'Sociology as an Academic Trade: Some Reflections on Centre and Periphery in the Sociology Market.' *Journal of Sociology* 22 (2): 272–282.

Turner, B. S. 1989. 'From Orientalism to Global Sociology.' *Sociology* 23 (4): 629–638.

Turner, B. S. 1990. 'The Two Faces of Sociology: Global or National?,' *Theory, Culture & Society* 7 (2–3): 343–358.

Turner, B. S. 2006. 'Classical Sociology and Cosmopolitanism: A Critical Defence of the Social.' *British Journal of Sociology* 57 (1): 133–151.

Vertovec, S. and R. Cohen (eds.). 2002. *Conceiving Cosmopolitanism: Theory, Context, and Practice*. Oxford: Oxford University Press.

CHAPTER 5

Ulrich Beck's Critical Cosmopolitan Sociology

Estevão Bosco

One of the major changes provoked by recent globalization in the social sciences is the advent of the cosmopolitan sociology project.[1,2] Ulrich Beck was a pioneer in attempting to grasp the implications of globalization for the sociological imagination and justifying cosmopolitanism as a way for sociology to evolve with the changing trends of the social world. Witnessing a proliferation in research since the 1990s, cosmopolitanism is now a *studies* in its own right and is conceived in as diverse ways as the social sciences are in their approaches.

Beck's cosmopolitanism is critical in that it discloses the conflictive and integrative dynamics at play in the actors' experience of technological development and globalization's side effects, and subjects this to normative and political criticism while also querying said normative and political horizons. In Beck's formulation, critical cosmopolitan sociology comprehends three internally connected dimensions: he conceives cosmopolitanism as an empirical-analytical category, a normative and political category, and as an experimental, methodological foundation of sociology aiming at transcending the latter's national and disciplinary assumptions.

While Beck's sociological cosmopolitanism has not gone without criticism, as is usually and cheerfully the fate of concepts and theories in the social sciences, its contemporary relevance endures. In what follows, I first reconstruct Beck's critical cosmopolitan sociology, presenting next three criticisms it faces. In light of these criticisms, I draw out the pertinence of Beck's primary endeavor, which is to present the resources for a cosmopolitan spirit of critical inquiry.

1   World Risk Society and Cosmopolitanism

Beck's cosmopolitan sociology is based on the diagnosis of global risks and is justified by his twofold critique. The first is directed toward the

---

1 This chapter partially draws on and updates the reconstruction of Beck's work first presented in an article (Bosco and Giulio, 2015) and a book (Bosco, 2016) to appraise the author's contribution to cosmopolitan scholarship.
2 Thanks to Neal Harris for comments on an earlier draft.

hyper-specialization of knowledge, institutional functional differentiation, and the unleashing of unpredictable side effects (Beck, 1992: 26–34, 57–71, 170–176). The second critique targets sociology's methodological nationalism and questions the validity of established concepts and categories for understanding globalized society (Beck, 2006: 24–32). That is why he adopts an essayist discursive-analytical strategy, for he aims at averting, what he terms, 'the gravitational pull of old ways of thinking' (Beck, 1992: 9).

Beck's thought is dialectical, and instead of thinking of social actors from an external perspective, he attempts to, as Bruno Latour remarks, 'learn from the actors how he must think them' (Latour, 2001: 9). The dialectics which structures his whole edifice interplays modernization successes and the unpredicted, destructive side effects it produces, thereby unfolding opportunities for action. Therefore, to fully understand Beck's cosmopolitanism, one must first understand his theory of world risk society.

1.1 Cosmopolitan Realism: Risk, Cosmopolitanization, and Reflexivity

The author's realist claim does not mean he is refusing that reality holds meaning inasmuch it is socially construed. This is an 'anti-constructivist provocation' aiming at stressing, first, that reality itself has become cosmopolitan (Beck, 2006: 75); second, that there is a mismatch between our nationally conceived categories, concepts, and theories, and reality's cosmopolitanization.

Cosmopolitanization refers to existing daily practices which reject, combine, and mix diverse global elements changing, from within, the national patterns of the social world. The internalization of global elements goes along with increasing interdependence and the continuous and ambivalent refashioning of boundaries in a transnational direction. No clear lines can be traced between 'we' and 'them,' the internal and the external, the national and the international, the local and the global. This ambivalent redrawing of boundaries, Beck argues (2006: 4–7), requires us to move beyond national frames of reference and to reevaluate the relationship among experience, locality, and world.

As an experience, cosmopolitanization relates to mobility, whether physical, imaginative, or virtual; to the communicative infrastructure, making people reachable everywhere, at any time; to the local side effects of economic crises triggered elsewhere; to the differently lived ubiquity of environmental crisis; to media narratives on global events; to interstate legislation and governance. The biographical upshot is a 'polygamy of place,' one's belonging is no longer circumscribed to one place anymore, as in the example of the immigrants who have to 'defend their cross-border polygamy of place in a continual daily struggle against the intrusions of state control and power' (Beck, 2006: 44). The world's contradictions are not unevenly distributed 'out there' but have become constituent of one's own life. As commodities, pollution, information, knowledge, money, people, images circulate globally, pluralizing cultural belonging and loyalties as well as shaping a moral interdependence, worlds take form 'in-between-spaces' (or as 'disjunction' to quote Appadurai).

The sociological relevance of global risk to understand cosmopolitanization lies on its heuristic usage as a *medium*, steering public awareness on global threats and destructions within the interplay of local and global forces and structural interdependence: 'A system of "risk-cosmopolitanism" is developing in which an exceptional degree of cosmopolitan interdependence, itself a side effect of side effect global publics, is bringing transnational conflicts and commonalities into the everyday practices which necessitate political (state) and subpolitical (civil society) action' (Beck, 2006: 34). To grasp this risk-cosmopolitanism relationship, I shall first briefly present the three main theses of the world risk society. These are based on the critical conception of modernization as cognitive-technological rationalization and increasing functional differentiation, affecting personality and consciousness, identity and culture, ultimately changing the 'entire social structure' and the 'sources of certainty' (Beck, 2001: 50, note 1).

The first thesis sustains that the social production and distribution of wealth (labor, goods, welfare) are coupled with the social production and distribution of risks and destructions (pollution, economic crisis, terrorism, structural unemployment) (Beck, 1992: 19–50). Societal rationalization unleashed by modernization producing wealth and steering social differentiation by labor (the class situation) overlaps with societal rationalization unleashed by modernization producing risks and steering social differentiation by insecurity (the threat situation). In short, Beck is saying that modernizing forces are provoking a rationalization (triggered by risks) of rationalization (triggered by labor). The diagnosis can be summarized as follows: 'dangers are being produced by industry, externalized by economics, individualized by the legal system, legitimized by the sciences and made to appear harmless by politics' (Beck, 1998: 16). This thesis is developed further into environmental and economic global risks.

The second thesis demonstrates that the development of productive forces and scientific knowledge, and the construction of the welfare state, has transformed industrial society's living conditions (higher level of education, income increase, feminization of work, spatial mobility, and institutional standardization of biography). Structuring categories of the industrial society (nuclear family, labor, class) are replaced by others, more flexible, thus more 'risky' ones (Beck and Beck-Gernsheim, 2002). As a consequence of the welfare state standardization of biography, the individual sphere (career, education, kids) becomes the *locus* in which to solve structural side effects of modernization (unemployment, for instance). Thus, individualization becomes reflexive as life situation and trajectory are taken as the outcome of individual decisions, the result being the internalization of more uncertainties: social inequality is individualized (Beck, 1992: 87–150).[3]

The third thesis is an encompassing one and performs two generalizations. First, as a consequence of the central role scientific knowledge has taken in contemporary society—with its influence ranging from lifestyle to global governance—science and its controversies have generalized. Science becomes simultaneously the cause and medium of the definition of threats and catastrophes (Beck, 1992: 155–182). Second, politics accordingly also generalizes: everything becomes political, what medicine to take or not to take, what to eat or not to eat, the domestic division of tasks, the negotiation of careers within couples, identity, environment, scientific innovations (Beck, 1992: 183–236). A new form of the political then emerges, taking on daily life and not aiming at disputing state power. In a broad sense, subpolitics characterizes the politicization of the private sphere and everyday life. Engagement is driven toward specific issues and displays selective solidarities, thereby being a highly individualized form of the political.

Considering these three theses altogether, the upshot is that by attempting to prevent, mitigate, and remedy the risks and destructions produced by its modernization, society becomes a danger for itself (Beck, 1994). Hence, one can speak of a reflexive modernization. Modern institutions enter a reflexive dynamic as unpredicted side effects of modernization retroactively become themselves a source of modernization.

What distinguishes contemporary risks from erstwhile ones is not their destructive potential, but, first, that they are *institutionally manufactured* (by science, market, government, mass media) (Beck, 1999: 19–47). Second, their *invisibility* means that they are not perceptible by human senses (pesticides, GMO, etc.) (Beck, 1992: 24–27). Third, they have neither *spatial nor temporal borders* (radiation, for instance) (Beck, 1992: 27–28). Risk does not exist in itself; its objectivity is conditioned by the ambivalences inherent to its 'staging'

---

3 The reflexive individualization thesis relates to the global biographical risk. In his penultimate book, Beck states that he will '[decipher] the intermeshing (and opposition) of "individualization" and "cosmopolitanization"' in a 'later study' (Beck, 2009: 236), which, to the best of my knowledge, he never did. This is the reason I do not mention the biographical risk later in this chapter. I have nonetheless decided to present the reflexive individualization thesis, for it is an essential part of the risk society dynamics.

(Beck, 2009: 1–23). Risk becomes 'real,' and a social situation of threat is construed, through the entwining of relations of definition (among politicians, entrepreneurs, experts, activists, journalists, and so on) constituted as relations of domination (Beck, 2009: 24–46). The emergence of the world risk society then characterizes a broad anthropological condition: risks and destructions cannot be ascribed to external causes anymore (fate, gods), society itself manufactures them (*manufactured uncertainties*) (Beck, 1992: 72–74). Reflexively propelled, world risk society entails the need to rethink and reinvent the industrial design of the social, economic, and political systems.

In this society, issues over risk calculability and predictability gain prominence for institutional action, regulation, and legitimation. Hyperspecialization, Beck argues (1992: 170–176), is the cause of the uncontrollability of side effects. For scientific knowledge isolates results in the laboratory, which, once industrially applied, are no longer isolated and become more complex and unpredictable. 'Many decisions over major risks do not involve a choice between safe and risky alternatives, but one between different risky alternatives, and often a choice between alternatives whose risks concern qualitatively different dimensions which are scarcely commensurable' (Beck, 2009: 3–4). As experts cannot establish a clear relationship among cause, risk, and damage, a pluralization of controversial definitions of threats and an 'organized irresponsibility' take place, meaning that political and economic actors take decisions where no one can be accountable for any possible side effects (Beck, 2009: 27–34).

Since risks have neither spatial nor temporal borders, the staging of risks entails the reflexive cosmopolitanization of experience (Beck, 2006: 33–35, 40–45, 85–98). Experience gets 'cosmopolitanized,' as a catastrophic anticipated global future colonizes the present as a source of conflict and forces political and subpolitical transnational integration (Beck, 1999: 23–35, 201–229, 236–248). It is an industrially induced, scientifically anticipated, politically managed, socially perceived, and globally shared threatening future which forces the reflexive cosmopolitanization of experience.

Beck identifies environmental, economic, and terrorist global risks and distinguishes them reciprocally according to the binomial *purpose/chance* (Beck, 2009: 13–14, 199–204). Although qualitatively different, environmental and economic risks nonetheless share the characteristic that they both relate to action as chance, as unpredicted side effects of decisions taken during modernizing processes. Moreover, both share the dialectics of positives and negatives as constitutive of ambivalences in political decisions and economic activity. By coming into public awareness through their staging, they trigger legitimation issues of political decision and economic activity as regards to the commensurability of their destructive potential and accountability (Beck, 2009: 14–16, 27–39, 42–46, 193–195). To the extent that scientific controversies translate into non-evidence in the legal sphere, the uncertainty over side effects is lived as injustice in the social sphere.

In turn, with the risk posed by terrorism, purpose takes over chance. The anticipated catastrophe slips away from the rational principles of risk calculation as the latter is driven by the predictability over decisions' possible, non-intended outcomes (in short, accidents). Accordingly, institutional regulatory action fosters the security-driven imagination and tends to undermine the 'foundations of freedom and democracy': more security implies less freedom (Beck, 2009: 14; see also 10–11, 39–42, 67–69, 133–135).

None of these risks and the anticipated catastrophes they refer to are circumscribed to the national space—as the Fukushima nuclear disaster, the 2008 financial crisis, the war on terror illustrate. Risk then entails a cosmopolitanization from within as a forced transnational integration through contingencies: 'Debates over global ecological threats and technical economic global crises and their visibility for a global public have revealed the cosmopolitan significance of fear' (Beck, 2006: 72). This means that risk-steered (sub-)politicization has global scope (Beck, 2009: 47–66, 81–108). Global publics form amid the awareness arising from the experience of a trans-territorially shared situation of threat and endangered civilization (Beck, 2011). Cosmopolitan society then emerges as global threats progressively disrupt national societies.

As global risks and destructions provoke conflicts which disintegrate the national world, they show the empirical, cognitive, and normative limitations of a national outlook while connecting particular needs, aspirations, world horizons, and structures. Normatively, global risks cosmopolitanism brings on the necessity to think of relativism and universalism, difference and sameness, in their corrective reciprocity. To avoid the totalitarian trend of universal norms (as in national revolutions with global intentions), one must emphasize the immanent particularity of every perspective. Conversely, to avoid relativism's incommensurability of perspectives and the ethical and moral indifference toward the other stemming from it, one must emphasize the immanent sameness in being human. Therefore, '[cosmopolitanism], realistically understood, means the affirmation of the other as both different and the same' (Beck, 2006: 58).

Learning from the actors' experience of global risks, Beck advocates for a 'contextual universalism' based on a negative universalism (defending against evils threatening life and freedom) and procedural universalism (shared legal procedures; Habermas) (Beck, 2006: 58–61). For instance, the annihilative threat posed by the military use of nuclear fission (negative universalism) has forced global legislation to prevent its proliferation (procedural universalism), for whose implementation the International Atomic Energy Agency was created (institutionalized cosmopolitanism). The strength of Beck's diagnosis lies precisely on this empirical–normative–political risk–cosmopolitanism connection. Beck takes neither the cynical attitude of relativizing the other's perspective as incommensurably particular nor the authoritarian impetus of universal normative claims. He engages seriously with difference and the possibility to overcome conflicts and issues common to us all through knowledge and the work of political institutions.

To sum up, one understands that risk, cosmopolitanization, and reflexivity are key concepts: risk is the source of conflict/integration through which social reality is construed; cosmopolitanization is the broad phenomenon steering empirical, normative, and political changes; and reflexivity explains the dynamics of this reality. Risk–cosmopolitanization–reflexivity grasps the nonlinear, ambivalent, and contradictory coordination of action engendered by a self-overlapping modernization. In other words, cosmopolitanism is the unpredicted side effect of modernization's unpredicted side effects (global risks). As a result, a first, national, and simple modernity has transformed itself into a second, reflexive, and cosmopolitan modernity.

1.2   Methodological Cosmopolitanism

To the extent that cosmopolitanization discloses the relevance of global entanglements on the constitution of social life and politics, Beck argues that it shows the interpretive and explanatory limits of classical concepts and theories, the implication being the need to reestablish sociology from a cosmopolitan perspective. Methodological cosmopolitanism is based on the theoretical differentiation and interplay of the actor outlook (historical dimension) and the observer outlook (logical dimension) as well as on the methodological intertwining of spatial and temporal dimensions of experience.

Beck states that the theories of the first modernity are characterized by a methodological nationalism (observer outlook), which, in correspondence with the national outlook (actor outlook), formulates an 'empirically false' national 'metatheory of identity, society and politics' (Beck, 2006: 5), assimilating more or less tacitly the concept of society to the nation-state. Accordingly, classical thought would proceed through the 'either/or principle' and the logic of *exclusive* differentiation in building categories and concepts—German *or* Turk, social sciences *or* natural sciences, society *or* nature, and so on. As society becomes cosmopolitan (actor outlook), it would be necessary to think through the 'both/and principle' and the logic of *inclusive* differentiation (observer outlook)—German *and* Turks, social *and* natural sciences, society *and* nature (Beck, 2006: 57–71). Beck then advocates for a paradigm shift, from the exclusive to the inclusive, the simple to the reflexive, the national to the cosmopolitan. In other words, he pleads for an epistemological rupture.

Methodologically, this logic of inclusive differentiation implies a shift of direction at the spatial-temporal dimension of experience. Beck asks for replacing the primacy of local–national and national–national relations by 'translocal, local-global, transnational and global-global patterns of relations' (Beck, 2006: 77). This shift in orientation, he continues, must be connected to the temporal dimension as it would otherwise lead to 'a false *onedimensional* real-cosmopolitanism and the reification of an ahistorical global present' (Beck, 2006: 77). At the temporal dimension, empirical-analytical and normative questions arise as to the 'cosmopolitanization of society and politics, history and memory.' Translating this into a methodological question means asking, for instance, '[in] what sense does the globalization of risks and crises become "real" against the background of different contexts of historical experience, and how are they politically processed' (Beck, 2006: 77).

While methodological nationalism concerns future implications of a nationally shared past, methodological cosmopolitanism concerns present implications of a globally shared future which is not based on a shared past (Beck, 2009: 4–14; 1999: 137–138). One then understands that Beck's conception of cosmopolitanism does not oppose nationalism; it rather includes it into a broader perspective aiming at having the world society as a reference. Considering the two simultaneously, the spatial and temporal dimensions define the methodological orientation toward the normative and political implications of a sociologically situated transhistoricity (of risks).

Therefore, cosmopolitanism affords world risk society a conception of the subject/object relation and methodological orientation, as Figure 5.1 summarizes.

On the background of this formulation, one finds a relational and highly stratified conception of social reality. It is relational as Beck conceives social reality to be the ambivalent process steered by global mediums of action coordination (such as risk, power, money). This ambivalence is inherent to the actor's reflexivity and the dialectical tensions of social reality's contradictions. That our way in interacting with others and things in the world is reflexive and embedded in contradictions means that our world experience happens through a particular horizon permeated with uncertainties, potentially reaching the global within the interplay of ('cosmopolitanized') practices and structures and their unpredictable side effects. Social reality is thus conceived of as

	First Modernity	*Second Modernity*
World Risk Society	- National society - Labor society - Simple rationality - Simple modernization - Wealth production steers rationalization - Legitimation problems stems from wealth production-distribution	- Cosmopolitan society - Risk society - Reflexive rationality - Reflexive modernization - Risk production steers rationalization - Legitimation problems stems from global risk production-distribution
Methodological Cosmopolitanism	Actor's outlook: Experience and worldview circumscribed by the nation-state Observer's outlook: Methodological nationalism: - The concept of society assimilates to the nation-state; - Logic of exclusive differentiation; - Local-nation and national-national patterns of relations	Actor's outlook: Experience and worldview steered by cosmopolitanization Observer's outlook: Methodological cosmopolitanism: - The concept of society defined by transnational processes; - Logic of inclusive differentiation; - Trans-local, local-global, transnational and global-global patterns of relations

FIGURE 5.1 The theory of world risk society and methodological cosmopolitanism

local–global entanglements of diverse actors' finite horizons steering conflictive/integrative processes, which none of us can fully picture.

Beck's critical cosmopolitan sociology aims at transiting from the monological (exclusive differentiation) and mono-perspectival (either us or them) nationalism to a dialogic (inclusive differentiation) and multi-perspectival (both us and them) cosmopolitanism (Beck, 2006: 78–79, 81–83). 'The cosmopolitan outlook and sensibility open up a space of *dialogical imagination* in everyday practice and in the relevant sciences. Cosmopolitan competence, as a fact of everyday and of scientific experience, forces us to develop the art of translation and bridge-building' (Beck, 2006: 89). From this cosmopolitan approach, issues concerning legitimacy, existential aspirations, innovation, production and redistribution, and scientific imagination are not only mediated by the national institutions and outlook capability in creating certainties anymore but also, and foremost, by the ability to craft new forms of cosmopolitan and transdisciplinary cooperation; by our ability, in sum, in handling 'cosmopolitan-ly' uncertainties of an open future.

2   Three Criticisms

Among the many controversies Beck's work has ignited, I would like to highlight three criticisms which question his cosmopolitan outlook more broadly. The first one stresses that Beck's critique of methodological nationalism and his cosmopolitan alternative are characterized by a presentism (Fine, 2007: 9–14). Robert Fine argues that the conception of second cosmopolitan modernity succeeding first national modernity is simplistic as it disregards first modernity's non-national horizons and structures, such as revolutions with global aspiration, multinational empires, the League of Nations, inter alia. Accordingly, Beck's presentism in claiming first modernity's concepts and theories redundant by simply announcing the emergence of a new cosmopolitan era is based on a historical deficit. The implicit implication of this is that methodological nationalism would have been adequate in the first modernity era. Daniel Chernilo (2006) furthers this point and argues that Beck's critique prevents us from understanding that methodological nationalism was as misleading in the first modernity as it is in the second. Methodological nationalism, and the self-understanding it affords, leads to the false empirical conception of social transformation as a self-sufficient national process. Furthermore, both Fine (2007) and Chernilo (2007) demonstrate that Beck misrepresents social theory's non-national horizon and continuous, however ambivalent, critique of methodological nationalism. This is nothing but social theory mirroring the nation-state's historical ambivalences and trying to '"square the circle" of the project of modernity' (Chernilo, 2006: 17–18). In short, Fine and Chernilo draw into question Beck's purported epistemological rupture.

The two other criticisms come from the postcolonial scholarship and head for Beck's cosmopolitanism within modernization theory. Both Sergio Costa (2006) and Gurminder Bhambra (2011) question the theoretical, converted into an axiomatic supposition that Western Europe's self-sufficient modernization would linearly precede and teleologically determine the modernization of the rest of the world (coined as 'West and the 'Rest'). Costa argues that concepts such as risk and cosmopolitanization 'have an evident historical and historiographical deficit as well as disregard tensions between geographical levels of analysis' (Costa, 2006: 122–123). Beck's two-phase model of modernity 'possibly finds application in some European societies; however, in regions that integrated into the modern world as colonies and enslavement societies, the critical spirit came well before (modern) certainties. Somehow, these societies were already "reflexive" long before they industrialized' (Costa, 2006: 220).

Costa goes further and sustains that Beck's methodological critique replaces the empirically false world image composed by isolated nation-state societies by another, though geographically wider, divide between 'the West and the Rest.' Thus, Beck transposes the self-referred first modernity's European nationalism into the self-referred second modernity's Western cosmopolitanism. The analytical consequence is the reduction of global modernization, its various and entwined paths toward modernity, to what is relevant for the recent and particular experience of Western societies, namely risk and cosmopolitanization.

The third criticism also addresses the West/Rest dichotomy, but from a different standpoint and a much wider claim, encompassing classical sociology. Like classical concepts and theories, Bhambra (2011) argues, Beck's critique of methodological nationalism and the cosmopolitan alternative not only reduces world society to European self-understanding, but it is also blind to the imperialist structures which gave European modernization its global range in the first modernity period. This blindness remains in the methodological cosmopolitanism as regards to the reproduction of imperialist mechanisms in the postcolonial context. In short, Bhambra sustains that Beck's transition from nationalism to cosmopolitanism keeps intact culturally self-referred theoretical logic: from the first to the second modernity, one goes from a 'methodological eurocentrism,' which takes the sociopolitical organization of part of Western Europe (nation-state) as an analytical world model, to a 'methodological occidentalism,' which takes Western societies' sociopolitical organization (liberal democracy and the European Union (EU)) as an analytical world model.

Accordingly, Beck's cosmopolitan discourse of reflexive modernization puts forward, so to speak, an 'occidentalocentric' definition of what is, and is not, cosmopolitan. Bhambra's criticism acknowledges classical theories' explanatory limits, as identified by the critique of methodological nationalism, and brings the latter to the world level when analyzing the nation-state's logical implications beyond the centripetal force of European nationalist self-understanding, that is, including processes of imperialism and colonialism.

3   Final Considerations

Beck's provocative and relentless mind has fostered public debate and turned our attention to changing trends in contemporary societies and interpretive and explanatory limits of how we conventionally understand these. Despite their different approaches and implications, those three criticisms address a common methodological issue: the risk in taking a particular historical experience as a world reference. However, it is worth mentioning that, probably after listening to criticisms such as those outlined in this chapter, Beck attempted to further 'cosmopolitanize' his own work. This can be seen in the *British Journal of Sociology* special issue he coedited with Edgar Grande on the 'Varieties of Second Modernity' (Beck and Grande, 2010); as well as, more significantly, in his posthumously published conference paper given in Nagoya, Japan, in 2010, in which he acknowledges the still 'provincial' state of social theory in that 'it mistakenly absolutizes the trajectory, the historical experience and future expectation of Western, i.e., predominantly European or North American, modernization and thereby also fails to see its own particularity' (Beck, 2016: 258). Critical cosmopolitan sociology still has to fully grasp the relevance of diverse and entangled routes to modernity, of extra-European cultures for the formations of European modernity, and work through the reflexive wheel of the reproduction of world historical asymmetries.[4] Shalini Randeria's 'entangled modernities' thesis (Randeria, 1999, 2002; Conrad and Randeria, 2002), which Beck himself quotes (Beck, 2006: 166; Beck and Grande, 2010: 414), is illustrative of this when disclosing modernity's coproduction within an ambivalent dynamics of sharing, differentiation, and domination.

The onto-epistemological issue permeating Beck's cosmopolitan sociology as a whole is still relevant today: globalization has reasserted the immanent finitude of the sociological inquiry, that our embeddedness in culture shapes a particular world horizon previously and restrictively driving our imagination, despite what heroic positivists, with their faith in method's neutralizing force of the knowledge subject's subjectivity, may say. Beck's outlook can be summarized as the endeavor to handle the following open question: How can we know a globalized social world, 'cosmopolitan-ly'? Risk's transnationalism and complexity led him to conceive of 'cosmopolitan thinking' as the transcendence of

---

4   Gerard Delanty's (2009; Delanty and Harris, 2018) idea of critical cosmopolitanism advances significantly in this respect, when reasserting the relevance of immanent transcendence both for critical theory and to distinguish cosmopolitanism (and cosmopolitanization) from transnationalism, while connecting this to the multiple modernities thesis (Eisenstadt) and global history's understanding of the historical process as 'entangled histories.'

both the national outlook and of disciplinarity. He attempted to achieve this by, so to speak, going back to the 'things themselves' (to use the phenomenological guidance metaphorically), heuristically analyzing risk's action coordination effects within the local–global force field.

If we are to take the finitude of our understanding seriously,[5] it goes without saying that experiencing other cultures' worlds, preferably through their languages, is paramount, as intercultural experience—with its estrangement singular in its disruptiveness—potentially expands our world horizon and fosters imagination toward new directions. Second, from Beck's cosmopolitanism and the criticisms of it, it is apparent that, in addition to focusing on phenomena entangling different worlds (such as risks), an intercultural orientation would benefit critical cosmopolitan sociology. This involves translation, bridge-building, and opening us up to other intellectual traditions, not only, as it is usually the case, in the fashion of an argumentative battle, but also, and foremost, with the empathetic attitude of someone who is aware of his or her unfamiliarity with the infinite worlds of others and the finite understanding of which he or she is capable.

References

Beck, U. 1992. *Risk Society: Towards a New Modernity*. London: Sage.

Beck, U. 1994. 'The Reinvention of Politics: Towards a Theory of Reflexive Modernization.' In U. Beck, A. Giddens, and S. Lash, *Reflexive Modernization: Politics, Aesthetics and Traditions in the Modern Social World Order*, 1–55. Stanford, CA: Stanford University Press.

Beck, U. 1998. 'Politics of Risk Society.' In *Politics of Risk Society*, edited by J. Franklin, 9–22. London: Polity Press.

Beck, U. 1999. *World Risk Society*. London: Polity Press.

Beck, U. 2006. *Cosmopolitan Vision*. London: Polity Press.

Beck, U. 2009. *World at Risk*. London: Polity Press.

---

5 Here, I have in mind Gadamer's dialectics of finitude/infinitude and three preconditions of understanding (our previous embeddedness in a hermeneutical situation [Gadamer, 2004: 267–277, 290–298], the progressive structure of discourse, and the phenomenological situatedness of our world experience [435–468]). An in-text citation of Gadamer would require a digression which unfortunately I cannot offer here. On Gadamer and critique, see Habermas (1988: 143–170), Ricoeur (1986), and Kögler (1996). For considerations on the implications of Gadamer's hermeneutics for methodology and validity claims in the context of intercultural understanding, and in close dialogue with Habermas' theory of truth, see my work: Bosco (2016: 289–317).

Beck, U. 2011. 'Cosmopolitanism as Imagined Communities of Global Risk.' *American Behavioral Scientist* 55: 1346–1361.

Beck, U. 2016. 'Varieties of Second Modernity and the Cosmopolitan Vision.' *Theory, Culture & Society* 33 (7–8): 257–270.

Beck, U. and E. Beck-Gernsheim. 2002. *Individualization: Institutionalized Individualism and its Social and Political Consequences*. London: Sage Publications.

Beck, U. and E. Grande. 2010. 'Varieties of Second Modernity: The Cosmopolitan Turn in Social and Political Theory and Research.' *British Journal of Sociology* 61 (3): 409–443.

Bhambra, G. 2011. 'Cosmopolitanism and Post-Colonial Critique.' In *The Ashgate Companion to Cosmopolitanism*, edited by M. Rovisco and M. Nowicka, 313–328. Farnham: Ashgate.

Bosco, E. 2016. *Sociedade de risco: introdução à sociologia cosmopolita de Ulrich Beck*. São Paulo: Annablume and FAPESP.

Bosco, E. M. G. R. L. 2016. 'Por uma teoria social cosmopolita: modernização, mundialização/globalização e entendimento intercultural.' PhD, State University of Campinas, Brazil.

Bosco, E. and G. M. di Giulio. 2015. 'Ulrich Beck: considerações sobre sua contribuição para os estudos em Ambiente e Sociedade e desafios.' *Revista Ambiente e Sociedade* [online] 18 (2): 145-156.

Chernilo, D. 2006. 'Social Theory's Methodological Nationalism: Myth and Reality.' *European Journal of Social Theory* 9 (1): 5–22.

Chernilo, D. 2007. 'A Quest for Universalism: Re-assessing the Nature of Classical Social Theory's Cosmopolitanism.' *European Journal of Social Theory* 10 (1): 17–35.

Conrad, S. and S. Randeria. 2002. 'Einleitung: Geteilte Geschichten—Europa in einer postkolonialen Welt.' In *Jenseits von Eurozentrismus: postkolonialen Perspektiven in der Geschichts- und Kulturwissenschaften*, edited by S. Conrad and S. Randeria, 9–49. Frankfurt am Main: Campus.

Costa, S. 2006. *Dois Atlânticos: teoria social, anti-racismo, cosmopolitismo*. Belo Horizonte: Editora UFMG.

Delanty, G. 2009. *The Cosmopolitan Imagination: The Renewal of Critical Social Theory*. Cambridge, UK: Cambridge University Press.

Delanty, G. and N. Harris. 2018. 'The Idea of Critical Cosmopolitanism.' In *The Routledge Handbook of Cosmopolitanism Studies*, edited by G. Delanty, 91–101. London: Routledge.

Fine, R. 2007. *Cosmopolitanism*. London: Routledge.

Gadamer, H.-G. 2004. *Truth and Method*. London: Continuum.

Habermas, J. 1988. *On the Logic of the Social Sciences*. London: Polity Press.

Kögler, H.-H. 1996. *The Power of Dialogue: Critical Hermeneutics after Gadamer and Foucault*. Cambridge, MA: MIT Press.

Latour, B. 2001. 'Préface: Beck ou comment refaire son outillage intellectuel.' In U. Beck, *La société du risque. Sur la voie d'une autre modernité*, 7–11. Paris: Flammarion.

Randeria, S. 1999. 'Jenseits von Soziologie und soziokulturelle Anthropologie: zur Verortung der nichtwestlichen Welt in einer zukünftigen Sozialtheorie.' *Soziale Welt* 50 (4): 373–382.

Randeria, S. 2002. 'Entangled Histories of Uneven Modernities: Civil Society, Caste Solidarities and Legal Pluralism in Post-Colonial India.' In *Unraveling Ties: From Social Cohesion to New Practices of Connectedness*, edited by Y. Elkana, I. Krastov, E. Macamo, and S. Randeria, 284–311. Frankfurt am Main: Campus.

Ricoeur, P. 1986. 'Herméneutique et Critique des Idéologies.' In P. Ricœur, *Du texte à l'action. Essais d'herméneutique II*, 333–361. Paris: Seuil/Esprit.

CHAPTER 6

Cosmopolitanism Is a Humanism

Daniel Chernilo

These are bad times for both key terms in the title of my chapter. Always a contentious term, the idea of cosmopolitanism gained some renewed traction toward the turn of the century as the more normatively oriented side of globalization debates that focused primarily on the economy and technological transformations (Habermas, 1998; Fine, 2007; Delanty, 2009). Best represented in human rights that were to be conceived through independence from interstate relations, a cosmopolitan ideal points to a global legal order that was to treat human beings always as ends and never as pure means: the rejection of colonial and expansionist wars, a universal commitment to hospitality for those fleeing persecution at home, an end to all kinds of slavery and human trafficking (Kant, 1991). Historically, its origins can be traced back to the *cosmopolite* dissenters of classical Greece—that is, those who were not prepared to surrender their moral and political judgment to the particularism of *their* polis and whose primary allegiance remained that of being citizens of the world (Hammond, 1951). Since the 18th century, the modern trajectory of cosmopolitanism has seen it all: at the same time that it was central to Immanuel Kant's idea of perpetual peace, it has also been a term of opprobrium, most famously in the anti-Semitic trope of the 'rootless cosmopolitan Jew' during the 19th century and beyond (Deutscher, 1981; Fine and Spencer, 2017). It has equally been criticized for its allegedly Eurocentric origins, its elitist bias, and its idealistic outlook (Calhoun, 2002).

Humanism has followed a different trajectory but has not necessarily fared much better. A concept that gained visibility in relation to a break with medieval education, the so-called Italian *quattrocento* (the 1400s) is usually seen as the precursor of the Renaissance and the revival of its *humanist* culture (Bullock, 1985). The movement that ensued became known for the development of novel trends in modern art, science and philosophy that gave rise to a more secular kind of education and engagement with the world. Here, its practical and intellectual emphasis was anti- or at least a-religious (Davies, 1997). By the late 19th century, humanism had undergone a critical transformation through which it also became universalistic—all humans without exception belong to the same species—as well as anthropocentric—humans are the makers and thus measure of all things in the world. By the middle of the

20th century, however, a revisionist account of the causes of the world wars slowly but surely started eroding humanist convictions and shifted the blame for recent massacres and monstrosities. Humanism was now being held as an hypocritical façade, an unfettered ideology of material progress and technical advancements whose anthropocentric bias was responsible for a process of dehumanization that was nonetheless based on humanist grounds (Soper, 1986). From Levi-Strauss to Althusser, Foucault, Luhmann, or Derrida, many if not most of the best-known writers of the past half a century share very little in their outlooks but do hold in common the default position that most of what is wrong in modern times can be encapsulated in the universalistic and anthropocentric underpinnings of humanism. Since the late 1990s, humanism's 'definitive' demise has also become apparent through cyborgs who challenge conventional ideas of human nature, animal lovers who challenge conventional ideas of human rights, and green campaigners who challenge conventional ideas of human sustainability. Post- or indeed anti-humanist positions, we are told, are to be preferred.

Within this context, my goal in this short chapter is twofold. The first one is reconstructive, as I should like to succinctly reassess the way in which a *critique of humanism* has become the standard position in contemporary debates. In order to do so, I will focus mostly on Martin Heidegger's 'Letter on Humanism,' which was composed very soon after the end of the Second World War, in 1946. This text can be credited with having laid the foundations for the normative inversion of humanism I have just mentioned. My second aim is to offer a positive argument on the relationships between humanism and cosmopolitanism that is also able to counter some of these criticisms. Here, and not without some reservations, I take my cue from Jean Paul Sartre's lecture 'Existentialism is a Humanism,' which was first delivered in October 1945. Needless to say, my title is a nod to Sartre's lecture.

1 The Mainstream Critique of Humanism: Heidegger and Beyond

In a recent discussion of Heidegger's 'Letter on Humanism,' Peter Sloterdijk makes the following assessment: 'Why should humanism and its general philosophical self-presentation be seen as the solution for humanity, when *the catastrophe of the present clearly shows* that it is man himself, along with his system of metaphysical self-improvement and self-clarification, that is the problem?' (Sloterdijk, 2009: 17; emphasis added).

There are three issues worth highlighting from this initial quotation. First, humanism is defined as a 'metaphysical' system for 'self-improvement and self-clarification.' In other words, humanism means here two of modernity's most significant values: *progress* and *autonomy*. Humanism belongs within a *system of metaphysics* because there is nothing rational about it as a set of beliefs: it is little but the dogmatic assertion that humans are peaceful, caring, and intelligent by nature—whereas history clearly demonstrates that this is just not the case. Second, Sloterdijk contends that an inversion has taken place, whereby 'man' and 'humanity' are not seen as a promise toward a *better future* but as the source of *past and current ills*. We ought to turn the humanism upside down because the belief in humanity's autonomy and self-improvement has had such pernicious effects. Finally, there is the sentence that I highlighted in the middle of the quotation: the *catastrophe of the present* that 'clearly' shows that humanism is always the wrong answer to whatever normative question. That catastrophe surely includes the Nazis, but it refers also to a longer-term, and for Sloterdijk at least also more profound, cultural crisis: the collapse of men's faith in their own ability to control themselves and learn from their mistakes.

In order to understand this inversion fully, we need to go back to the period in between the two world wars. A critique of modern technology was already a common trope in social and cultural debates by the middle of the 19th century and, by the 1930s, it had become a major issue for both left and right. Their radically different politics notwithstanding, these are themes that we find in Ernst Jünger and Carl Schmitt as much as we do it in Theodor Adorno and Walter Benjamin: the troubled relationships between the promises of emancipation and the realities of mechanization are central to epochal diagnostics of the current crisis. The critical role given to mechanization has to do with the fact that technology has a pride of place in the organization of modern societies: technology—from electricity to automobiles and gramophones—has become the face of material progress that made life more tolerable and even enjoyable to wider segments of the population than ever before. My argument is not that right- and left-wing critiques of technology were at the time based on *the same* presuppositions—even less that they pointed in the same normative direction toward the future. Yet, there is an elitism that contaminates this critique of technology insofar as mass industrial society—soulless, beauty-less, disenchanted—is the offspring of modern technology. Modern technology expresses the most fundamental but also dangerous constructivism of modernity: a world that can be transformed—indeed created—at man's will.

Heidegger's critique of humanism contributed to articulate further this elitist view of technology. The success it has enjoyed ever since lies precisely in the fact that it was able to locate humanism—with its rather vague but mostly positive normative appeal toward democracy and progress, with its semantic dependence on the human—as the one term with the help of which we can assess the project of modernity as a whole. Heidegger offers a critique of the *modern* understanding of *modern* technology because technology has become the key expression of the materialism and anthropocentrism of modern culture as a whole. But rather than being a mere instrument, technology is a 'form of truth' which 'is grounded in the history of metaphysics' (Heidegger, 1993a: 243–244). Technology triggers an inauthentic relationship among being, man, and the world: 'because the essence of technology is nothing technological, essential reflection upon technology and decisive conformation with it must happen in a realm that is, on the one hand, akin to the essence of technology and, on the other hand, fundamentally different from it' (Heidegger, 1993b: 340). The radical inauthenticity of modernity obtains from the 'monstrousness' of modern technology itself (Heidegger, 1993b: 321). Heidegger's dislike of technology has then to do with its intrinsically *cosmopolitan* qualities: technology uproots and transforms the world within which it is applied, technology no longer allows for an essential relationship between what is authentic and what is not, between natives and strangers.

The main argument in Heidegger's 'Letter on Humanism' is that we can only understand 'man' if we relate it to the higher question of 'being'; we must break free from the humanist illusions of autonomy and self-determination. Heidegger composed his text in 1946, partially at least in order to respond to Sartre's 'Existentialism is a Humanism' lecture that had been delivered the year before in Paris.[1] Heidegger rejects humanism as the consummate expression of modern egalitarianism, rationalism, and subjectivity; indeed, humanism centers on the very values that we associate with a cosmopolitan outlook: autonomy, universal jurisdiction of the rule of law, democracy, self-determination. These are the *same* values that, for Heidegger, were to *blame* as the main causes of the war. In Heidegger's account, the Second World War had nothing to do with racism, nationalism, anti-Semitism, irrationalism, mob rule; it was not characterized by the total suspension of the rule of law (both at home and abroad), aggressive propaganda, militarization, and ubiquitous images of war. This was exactly how Heidegger inaugurated the argument we just saw replicated now in Sloterdijk: the humanism of Western metaphysics is responsible for the crisis of modern society: 'is the *damage* caused by all such terms [as humanism] still not sufficiently obvious?' (Heidegger, 1993a: 219; emphasis added). Now

---

1 For the general context in which Heidegger composed *Letter*, see Kleinberg (2003: 162–168). I have discussed this extensively in Chernilo (2017: 23–63).

that this kind of humanism is well and truly dead, the philosopher's task is to make sure it can never be revived.[2]

To Heidegger, humanism is subjectivism because it focuses on the narrow, particularistic of point of view of 'man' and, in so doing, it renounces grasping the ultimate essence of being: humanism sides with the subjectivity of the *anthropos* and, in so doing, it rejects the pursuit of what is genuinely essential. Humanism is also a form of relativism and even nihilism because it gives humans an authorization to do as they please. This radical constructivism of humanism is to blame for the self-destructive nature of modernity: it allows human to act *as if* they can think for themselves, rule themselves, and create their own institutions. This farewell to humanism must also mean the rejection of anthropocentrism; that is, the notion that 'man' is the ultimate measure of all things.

The anti-cosmopolitan nature of this critique is apparent at three levels. First, humanism fails to deliver on its promise of a genuinely strong sense of the human; it offers instead only subjectivism and nihilism. Second, while humanism claims to be self-positing, in actual fact it requires the external justifications that nature, history, or gods can provide. The egalitarianism that is central to modern humanism flattens all transcendental commitments and understands only the abstract and formal recommendations of instrumental rationality. Because of this, third, humanism makes it impossible to grasp the more general questions of being as the genuine source of dignity of all forms of human experience: the near experience of death, an original relation to language, the essential rootedness of communal life, a permanent attachment to the nation as a *Volk*. Elitism is to be preferred in order to avoid the repetition of the massacres caused by egalitarian humanism and this is construed around a whole range of anti-cosmopolitan tropes: irrationalism is more sober and less authoritarian than rationality, authenticity and simplicity more genuine than emancipation and self-determination, only poetry and contemplation touch on the essential in a manner that science and above all modern technology are merely able to manipulate. Domesticity, authenticity, and rootedness are the only options for a pristine and unpolluted existence in a world that,

---

2 It is now clear that the authoritarian, nationalistic, anti-Semitic, and irrationalist dimensions of Heidegger's philosophy made his political support of the Nazi regime a fact that is both biographically *and* philosophically significant (Safranski, 1998; Faye, 2009; Rockmore, 2009; di Cesare, 2018). Credit must then be given to Karl Löwith, who saw it all quite clearly even in 1946: 'Heidegger did not "misunderstand himself" when he supported Hitler; on the contrary, anyone who did not comprehend how he could do this did not understand him' (Löwith, 1995: 223).

through technology, state bureaucracy, and mass democracy, has nearly destroyed itself. The real danger of inhumanity lays dormant underneath modern institutions and the humanistic hubris of emancipation, social change, and self-determination.

Humanism blocks our ability to ask *ultimate* questions and, in dogmatically asserting a purely metaphysical idea of man, it *contributes* to the devaluation of humanity; because it only concentrates on the subjectivity of the *anthropos*, it becomes *responsible* for humans' inability to see beyond themselves. It is within this context, for instance, that Heidegger criticizes the traditional conception of the *animal rationale*, which still conceives our humanity in terms of what we share with beasts: 'Animal means beast. Man is the beast endowed with reason' (Heidegger, 2004: 61). Heidegger offers instead an idea of *humanitas* that he recovers from the Romans. Heidegger rejects conventional metaphysics 'because it does not set the *humanitas* of man high enough' (1993a: 233–234). The fact that humans share an organic constitution with other living creatures blocks our ability to accept the uniqueness of their humanity; this is too base a ground to establish what is essential in our humanity. This is a form of anthropocentrism that reproduces the traditional dualisms of the metaphysical tradition—the mind and the organism, the body and the soul—and thus everything that is wrong with current attempts at understanding the human. Heidegger's critique of humanism is then construed through a dual negation: first, the notion of 'being' is to be preferred over against that of 'the human,' which means that there is little to be concerned about undermining its normative status (e.g., humanity equals bestiality in Carl Schmitt's famous formulation); second, within humanity itself, higher forms of *humanitas* are to be cared for at the expense of *animale* rational. By rejecting the egalitarianism of mass society, Heidegger now made humanism the true totalitarian ideology of modern times. The humanity of human beings is to be defined through an essential notion of being because only thus may man be able to raise genuinely fundamental questions. A full-blown elitism is one key normative pillar of Heidegger's particular version of humanism.

2   A Cosmopolitan Humanism: J.-P. Sartre

Jean Paul Sartre's (2007) *Existentialism is a Humanism* was originally delivered to a full lecture hall in October 1945 and remains his most popular piece. This is a rare text in which Sartre explicitly tries to articulate an optimistic type of politics that was to serve France for its reconstruction after the war (Levy, 2002). Sartre did not make an explicit connection with cosmopolitanism in his piece, but my argument is precisely that there are at least three ways in which his ideas point in the direction of what we may call a *cosmopolitan humanism*: (1) a principle of subjective responsibility that is not individualistic; (2) a critique of essentialism in the form of group thinking; and (3) a notion of universal empathy that works as a regulative Idea.

Let me start with subjective responsibility. Sartre sought an idea of the individual that was not, however, individualistic; he used the notion of *subjectivity* in order to highlight the centrality of intersubjective relations in the human condition: rightly understood, subjectivity always implies relationships with others. There is a positive dimension in the notion of the modern individual because of its relation to the idea of *freedom*: 'I cannot discover any truth whatsoever about myself except through the mediation of another. The other is essential to my existence [...] intimate discovery of myself is at the same time a revelation of the other as a freedom that confronts my own' (Sartre, 2007: 41–42). There is a Kantian echo here, as Sartre connects the particular and the universal insofar as human responsibility is 'much greater than we might have supposed, because it concerns all mankind' (Sartre, 2007: 24). This is a cosmopolitan and humanist idea of freedom as it builds on an insight that is altogether alien to Heidegger: 'freedom wills itself *and the freedom of others*' (Sartre, 2007: 49; emphasis added).

This is a cosmopolitan argument because individual freedom, indeed individuality itself, is *inseparable* from a generalized version of the human species as a whole: 'man finds himself in a complex social situation in which he himself is committed and by his choices commits all mankind' (Sartre, 2007: 45). Given that intersubjectivity is the condition that makes a human world possible, then an adequate notion of it must include two, rather different, reference points. On the one hand, intersubjectivity is directly constituted through an individual's interactions with all those significant others with whom s/he actually interacts in daily life—parents, partners, friends, and colleagues. On the other hand, these contextual and particular references are increasingly framed within the notion of a general subject that encompasses humanity as a whole. Sartre's idea of intersubjectivity requires both moments: the one that is concretely located and necessarily corresponds to the here and now of our specific contexts and the generalized notion of humanity that includes all possible others, most of whom are not here with us and never will be.

Given the humanist premise that humans are free and responsible beings, Sartre cannot but reject the essentialism of resorting to ahistorical ideas of human nature. Sartre (1995: 82) equally warns us against the perils of 'group error' in modernity; that is, attempts that seek to draw substantive traits from treating 'the Germans,' 'the French,' and indeed 'the Jews' as homogenous units.

These collective nouns may be common in everyday language and do possess a sociocultural locus (e.g., nation-states), but they are not substantive wholes or self-contained entities: instead, our commitment must remain with the individuals who belong to these groups. To Sartre, the worst problem with group thinking is the fact that it assumes that it can do without subjectivity and individuality. A dialectics between individual freedom and the general freedom of the human species as a whole frames his approach: we 'will freedom for freedom's sake through our individual circumstances. And in thus willing freedom, we discover that it depends entirely on the freedom of others, and that the freedom of others depends on our own' (Sartre, 2007: 48).

What makes Sartre's position a *cosmopolitan humanism* is the combined argument that only human beings create values for themselves, that all humans are equally able to create values and the values achieve their normative purchase in relation to their appeal to the human species as a whole (Chernilo, 2017, 2018). In making this claim, Sartre explicitly based his position on the very egalitarianism that later critiques of humanism have sought to undermine. This is most apparent in Sartre's distinction between two meanings of the term humanism. The first type of humanism, which he rejects, is a humanism that takes pride in the collective accomplishments of the human species—for instance, its works of art or technological innovations—and then invites *individual* human beings to partake in this admiration for what *the best* humans have been able to achieve. To Sartre, this is a 'cult of humanity,' which he rejects as a form of reification: one can 'never consider man as an end, because man is constantly in the making' (2007: 52). But the main reason for Sartre to reject this type of humanism *lies in its elitism*: the glorification of the accomplishments of the few cannot be used to justify passive admiration on behalf of the many, because this opens the door for the ultimate devaluation of those who are not deemed capable of reaching such heights. This is the racism, mysogyny, ableism that underpins mistreatment of women, Roma, the ill. This is not a cosmopolitan humanism because it is based on the notion that we must rank certain groups of people or indeed individuals as better than others. This is a false humanism because it 'leads ultimately (…) to Fascism' (Sartre, 2007: 52).[3]

Having rejected the elitist option, Sartre then delineates the humanism to which he is positively committed. He uses the notion of *human transcendence* in this context: 'man is always outside of himself, and it is in projecting and losing himself beyond himself that man is realised (…) it is in pursuing

---

3   Incidentally, Sartre's own interpretation of Heidegger was that of a humanist philosopher. To this generation of writers, Heidegger could not have been a Nazi sympathizer *because* he was an existentialist (Blackham, 1962; Goldmann, 1969).

transcendental goals that he is able to exist' (Sartre, 2007: 52). This appeal to transcendental goals, however, requires no external cosmology but points to the 'liberation' of human beings' own *internal transcendence*: 'man is nothing other than what he makes of himself (...) there is no other legislator than himself' (Sartre, 2007: 22, 53). Sartre's humanism then focuses on the human capacity for self-legislation, which in turn is defined as the *creative capacity* of imagining a different world and of making the world a different place. This type of humanism demands a form of realism that gives humans no place to hide, for instance, from their own selfish motivations: this is a humanism that requires humans to take full responsibility for who they are, for the way they behave, and for the decisions they make.

3   The Idea of Universal Empathy

The final dimension of Sartre's cosmopolitan humanism is his universalistic commitment to the notion that humans have the ability to develop a generalized sense of empathy. This capacity of placing oneself in somebody else's position is possible because there are some conditions or experiences that people do *not* share. The very definition of empathy is that, being situated in our particular contexts, we are able to reach across most of our differences in order to see the world with different eyes. Whilst, since the 1990s, it has become more common to define empathy by looking the experiences people *share*, Sartre made it clear that he was committed to a strong, universal, notion of empathy:

> Human universality exists, but it is not a given; it is in perpetual construction (...) I construct it by understanding every other man's project, regardless of the era in which he lives (...) The fundamental aim of existentialism is to reveal the link between the absolute character of the free commitment, by which every man realizes himself in realizing a type of humanity—and a commitment that is always understandable, by anyone in any era—and the relativity of the culture ensemble that may result from such a choice.
>
> SARTRE, 2007: 43

An idea of universal empathy is something that ought to be refined and retained; this is essential if genuine sociocultural and normative dialogue is to remain open. Sartre (1995: 43) makes this point explicitly as a critique of Eurocentrism when he refers to our mutual understanding with a 'Chinese, Indian or black African: There is universality in every project, inasmuch as any man is capable of understanding any human project.' The idea of universal empathy works because, as members of the same human species, there are some needs and capabilities that apply to us all: we can and indeed do experience intercultural and transcultural sympathy on such key experiences as grief, pain, love, fear, joy, admiration, and happiness. This universalism is incompatible with elitism or cultural essentialism and only makes sense on the basis of a strong commitment to the egalitarianism of universal membership of all individuals.

Sartre was wrong when he claimed that humans are nothing but what they make of themselves; this anthropocentrism misses the extent to which humans also live as members of the natural world, that they are in possession of a human body that they cannot fully control, and there are social, cultural, and technological structures that present themselves as alien to humans themselves. There is a conflation between humanism and anthropocentrism in his argument that threatens some of his own best insights. But this is also why a cosmopolitan rendition of some of them may offer a way forward for both humanism *and* cosmopolitanism.

Within contemporary debates, posthumanist positions are incapable of renewing a normative outlook that is fit for the global world we live in. Their original thrust was to make apparent the limitations and contradictions of modernity. The ways in which they are currently construed are, of course, not responsible for the hypocrisy of Heidegger's original critique of humanism and yet they remain fundamentally contaminated by it. In Heidegger's argument, making humanism responsible for the widespread destruction of the war was strategically devised to hide his own support for the Nazi regime, politically, and for authoritarian, elitist, irrationalist politics, philosophically. Subsequent posthumanist arguments do not necessarily share or are even fully aware of this original motif. Yet they have also contributed to the critique of modern values and principles: this tradition remains vitiated by this initial diagnostic that rationalism rather than irrationalism, democracy rather than authoritarianism, cosmopolitanism rather than nationalism are the most dangerous of modern illusions.

By recasting Sartre's argument (with a twist!), my main claim in this contribution has been that cosmopolitanism offers the best fit for the renewal of humanism as a normative outlook.

- Cosmopolitanism is a humanism because of its commitment to a universalist egalitarianism. Our common membership to the same species is the most fundamental normative fact of the human condition.
- Cosmopolitanism is a humanism because its normative commitment is not derived from nature nor is it founded on religious beliefs. It is instead a result of social relations themselves.

- Cosmopolitanism is a humanism because subjective autonomy is seen as result of, and fully compatible with, our ability to take others into account. A genuinely cosmopolitan idea of freedom presupposes others who are equally free.
- Cosmopolitanism is a humanism because humans create legal orders within which they are able to recognize themselves as members of the same species and treat one another with mutual respect.
- Cosmopolitanism is a humanism because it understands the significance of individual belonging to social groups. And it understands also how our particular identities are a fundamental resource to see each other as members of the same species.
- Cosmopolitanism is a humanism because of the ways in which it seeks to construe a human understanding of what makes us different as much as of our shared human predicament.

References

Blackham, H. J. 1962. *Six Existentialist Thinkers*. London: Routledge.
Bullock, A. 1985. *The Humanist Tradition in the West*. Wisbech: Thames & Hudson.
Calhoun, C. 2002. 'The Class Consciousness of Frequent Travellers: Towards a Critique of Actually Existing Cosmopolitanism.' In *Conceiving Cosmopolitanism: Theory, Context, and Practice*, edited by S. Vertovec and R. Cohen, 86–109. Oxford: Oxford University Press.
Chernilo, D. 2017. *Debating Humanity: Towards a Philosophical Sociology*. Cambridge, UK: Cambridge University Press.
Chernilo, D. 2018. 'There is No Cosmopolitanism without Universalism.' In *The Routledge Handbook of Cosmopolitanism Studies*, 2nd ed., edited by G. Delanty, 30–41. London: Routledge.
Davies, T. 1997. *Humanism*. London: Routledge.
Delanty, G. 2009. *The Cosmopolitan Imagination: The Renewal of Critical Social Theory*. Cambridge, UK: Cambridge University Press.
Deutscher, I. 1981. *The Non-Jewish Jew and Other Essays*. London: Merlin.
di Cesare, D. 2018. *Heidegger and the Jews: The Black Notebooks*. Cambridge, UK: Polity Press.
Faye, E. 2009. *Heidegger: The Introduction of Nazism into Philosophy*. New Haven, CT: Yale University Press.
Fine, R. 2007. *Cosmopolitanism*. London: Routledge.
Fine, R. and P. Spencer. 2017. *Antisemitism and the Left: On the Return of the Jewish Question*. Manchester: Manchester University Press.

Goldmann, L. 1969. *The Human Sciences and Philosophy*. London: Cape.
Habermas, J. 1998. 'Kant's Idea of Perpetual Peace: At Two Hundred Years' Historical Remove.' In *The Inclusion of the Other: Studies in Political Theory*, edited by C. Cronin and P. De Greiff, 165–202. Cambridge, MA: MIT Press.
Hammond, M. 1951. *City-State and World State in Greek and Roman Political Theory until Augustus*. Cambridge, MA: Harvard University Press.
Heidegger, M. 1993a. 'Letter on Humanism.' In M. Heidegger, *Basic Writings*, 217–265. London: Routledge.
Heidegger, M. 1993b. 'The Question concerning Technology.' In M. Heidegger, *Basic Writings*, 307–341. London: Routledge.
Heidegger, M. 2004. *What Is Called Thinking?* New York: HarperCollins.
Kant, I. 1991. *Political Writings*, 2nd ed. Cambridge, UK: Cambridge University Press.
Kleinberg, E. 2003. *Generation Existential: Heidegger's Philosophy in France 1927–1961*. Ithaca, NY: Cornell University Press.
Levy, N. 2002. *Sartre*. Oxford: Oneworld.
Löwith, K. 1995. *Heidegger and European Nihilism*. New York: Columbia University Press.
Rockmore, T. 2009. 'Foreword to the English Edition.' In *Heidegger: The Introduction of Nazism into Philosophy*, edited by E. Faye, vii–xxviii. New Haven, CT: Yale University Press.
Safranski, R. 1998. *Martin Heidegger: Between Good and Evil*. Cambridge, MA: Harvard University Press.
Sartre, J.-P. 1995. *Anti-Semite and Jew: An Exploration of the Etiology of Hate*. New York: Shocken.
Sartre, J.-P. 2007. *Existentialism is a Humanism*. New Haven, CT: Yale University Press.
Sloterdijk, P. 2009. 'Rules for the Human Zoo: A Response to the Letter on Humanism.' *Environment and Planning D: Society and Space* 27: 12–28.
Soper, K. 1986. *Humanism and Anti-Humanism*. La Salle, IL: Open Court.

CHAPTER 7

Human Rights and Dignity

Sylvie Mesure

December 2018 was the seventieth anniversary of the Universal Declaration of Human Rights (UDHR).*,1 Marking the culmination of international efforts to lay the groundwork for a new ethico-legal world order in the wake of the Second World War, the Declaration was adopted by an overwhelming majority in the United Nations General Assembly on December 10, 1948; no fewer than forty-eight of the fifty-eight contemporary member states voted in favor.[2] The UDHR represents a veritable turning point in the history of political and moral ideas: by basing human rights on the principle of human dignity and thus establishing that a legal form of cosmopolitanism must rest on the basis of moral cosmopolitanism, it would come to embody the normative core of the international legal human rights system as we know it today. In fact, after the Second World War, the universalist principle of dignity came to the fore in human rights discourse (Kretzner and Klein, 2002), with the result that what has been called the 'Age of Human Rights' (Henkin, 1990) has also been considered as the 'Age of Dignity' by some (Dupré, 2015). And yet we are forced to observe that 'the human rights revolution'—a period which is commonly seen as lasting until the 1990s, when many still naively believed that with the fall of the Berlin Wall democratic principles would finally be able to prevail throughout the world—is now a relic of the past. We must also admit that today human rights are no longer at the center of most intergovernmental negotiations. On the occasion of the Declaration's seventieth anniversary, results are mixed. The UDHR was the product of an ethical reaction to the horrors of the Holocaust. Despite the important steps taken toward the institutionalization of human rights and the activism of countless non-governmental organizations, however, many genocides and other forms of ethnic cleansing have continued to take place: during the 1990s, the Rwandan genocide and ethnic cleansing in Kosovo (ex-Yugoslavia); since 2010, large-scale killings in the Democratic Republic of

---

* Translated by Sarah-Louise Raillard.
1 See also Valentine Zuber (2018).
2 Two states were absent, eight abstained, and none voted against. On this point, see Morsink (2009: 72–77).

the Congo; since 2014, the violence inflicted against the Yazidis in Iraq; since the summer of 2018, the massacre of Houthis in Yemen; and the ongoing persecution of the Rohingya in Myanmar, just to list a few instances of genocidal violence in recent history. Nor have human rights helped to significantly reduce poverty and injustice throughout the world, despite the stated goal of the Declaration to combine the achievement of economic and social rights with civil and political rights. In fact, our era marks a return to Spinoza's 'sad passions,' impulses which do little to foster the respect of human rights: proud or defensive nationalism, populism (Alston, 2017), fundamentalism, intolerance, identitarian closure, and the rise of a will to power (economic and/or political) that oversteps or ignores all normative guidelines. The euphoria provoked by the triumphal declaration that human rights had been recognized the world over was followed by the sobering up of a disillusioned world, one that is now uncertain of its fate. Must we therefore conclude that we have entered a 'post-human rights era' (Wuerth, 2016: 279)? Only if we capitulate to fatalism and inertia. In this chapter, after analyzing the axiological heart of the UDHR based on the concept of dignity, we shall demonstrate how, despite its specific historical roots at the end of the Second World War and the onset of the Cold War, the Declaration still possesses normative resources that are pertinent for anyone who cannot in good faith resign themselves to the world's injustices.

1 The UDHR, a Pivotal Moment

The UDHR (1948) marked a veritable turning point in the history of political and legal ideas, as it was the first time that the concept of dignity was linked to the idea of human rights in a legal text with international scope.[3] No such connection had been established between the two concepts in early texts such as the 1789 Declaration of the Rights of Man and of the Citizen, where the term 'dignity' only appears in its pre-modern meaning of *dignitas*. In its Article VI, the 1789 Declaration stipulates that '[a]ll citizens, being equal in the eyes of the law, are equally eligible to all dignities and to all public positions and occupations, according to their abilities, and without distinction except that of their virtues and talents.' The word dignity, used in the plural, has a very different meaning here than when it is used in the 1948 Declaration to refer to the universal dignity that belongs to every human being by virtue of being human,

---

3 It should be pointed out that this is a possible retrospective reading of the 1948 Declaration, even if the real history of the installation of dignity at the basis of human rights is in reality much more complex, as Samuel Moyn (2015) has shown.

and as the *moral grounds* for any rights-based demands. As it is presented in the 1948 Declaration, the connection between inherent dignity and universal rights was in fact the result of a long historical trajectory, as shown by Donnelly (2015) and Waldron (2012), which culminated in the universalization and the democratization of a principle that had hitherto been seen as an aristocratic notion serving to establish a hierarchical division between the elite and everyone else—and which was more often called 'honor.'[4] From this perspective, the Declaration can be seen as a pivotal moment, given that it helped to universalize and democratize the principle of dignity that would hitherto reside at the heart of all human rights discourse. In fact, the conclusion that dignity represented the foundation of all human rights would never subsequently be challenged: it was reaffirmed in the 1966 covenants and in all subsequent major legal instruments, including the 1993 Vienna Declaration and Programme of Action, ratified by 171 states, which reaffirmed in its preamble 'that all human rights derive from the dignity and worth inherent in the human person, and that the human person is the central subject of human rights and fundamental freedoms, and consequently should be the principal beneficiary and should participate actively in the realization of these rights and freedoms.'

But while the Declaration represents the end point of a historical evolution that led to the universalization of the principle of dignity, it was simultaneously the starting point for the lengthy process of the politicization, juridification, and institutionalization of human rights (McCrudden, 2008), which could only be interpreted in the Declaration as moral rights, given that they had no binding institutional strength. In fact, it was only starting in 1966 and after much prevarication that the two documents which gave the Declaration binding power—the International Covenant on Civil and Political Rights and the International Covenant on Economic, Social and Cultural Rights—were adopted by the United Nations General Assembly. Thanks to these legal instruments, the Declaration could be legally implemented and become the normative framework for the protection and promotion of human rights at international, regional, and national levels alike.

By basing human rights on the principle of human dignity, the UDHR thus performed an act with significant normative scope. But this act was not

---

4 On this point, it is useful to refer to a work by Peter Berger (1970), which, despite being itself somewhat dated, still constitutes an obligatory reference point on the subject, given that it accurately pinpoints the logic of modernity at work in the universalization of the concept of dignity. According to Berger, the shift from the traditional societies of the *ancien régime* to modern societies also heralded the transition from aristocratic honor to democratic dignity as the key concept in play.

self-evident for all and gave rise to much criticism. Some have thus questioned the legitimacy of any research into the philosophical grounds of human rights, from either a 'pragmatic' (Rorty, 1993) or a 'political' (Beitz, 2009) conception of these rights, which examine human rights only from the angle of their positivity.[5] Given that this concept seems so ambiguous, some have rejected the proposition that human dignity forms the moral basis of human rights. This last argument is the one we shall focus on here in order to understand the normative logic of the UDHR, as well as the essential ethical consequences of choosing human dignity as the basis for such rights.

2   Dignity, a Debated Topic

Before we examine why the drafters of the UDHR believed it was their duty to base human rights on the principle of dignity, we must concede the following point: despite numerous contemporary attempts to deconstruct the notion of the 'subject' or 'person,' attempts that are often grouped together under the theme of 'the death of man,'[6] the concept of dignity has returned to the forefront of the intellectual scene—at least if we are to believe the numerous works devoted to its study since the early 2000s.[7] Even outside of academia, the concept of dignity seems to have invaded our democratic existence. It is omnipresent in the public sphere, as equally relevant for debates on bioethics and the end of life as for a plethora of religious, cultural, or identity-based movements clamoring for recognition. The concept of dignity is mobilized in the fight waged by LGBTQIA+ (lesbian, gay, bisexual, transgender, queer, intersex, or asexual) groups to obtain new rights, as well as by feminist activists. More generally, the call for dignity seems to constitute the common thread running through all contemporary protest movements: from New York's Occupy Wall Street to the Spanish Indignados. It was embodied by the watchwords shouted on Egypt's Tahrir Square and on Tunisia's Bourguiba Avenue during what has been called, rightly or wrongly, the 'Arab Spring' (starting in

---

5   Anti-foundationalism, as advocated by Richard Rorty (1993) and Charles Beitz (2009), is justified by its effectiveness. According to Rorty and Beitz, it is of no use to engage in interminable disputes regarding the foundation of human rights when it is simply a question of ensuring respect for human rights in international politics and as they are enshrined in recognized international legal practices and texts. However, it is uncertain whether such an approach is sufficient—in the name of what would these rights be respected in such a scenario?
6   See Chapter 6 in this volume.
7   See in particular Georg Kateb (2011), Michael Rosen (2012), Christopher McCrudden (2014), and Marcus Düwell et al. (2014).

December 2010): the demand for 'bread, freedom, social justice and dignity' similarly constituted an appeal to the *normative concept* of dignity across a wide variety of contexts.[8] Moreover, the concept of dignity seems to have become part and parcel of our contemporary consciousness: dignity for women, dignity for patients, dignity for persons with disabilities, dignity for the dying, dignity for the elderly, dignity for children, and so on; attempts to obtain recognition and respect for these various groups appear to be inexorably tied to a democratic evolution toward ever greater equality.

And yet the widespread deployment of a concept that seemed otherwise to have been rendered obsolete by French Theory's radical critique of the subject during the 1960s and 1970s is not without its challenges. In fact, there is profound disagreement on what constitutes human dignity, and regarding the argument that all individuals are granted dignity by sheer virtue of being human. The detractors of dignity are numerous and the virulence of their critiques is only matched by the intensity with which this term is brandished by their opponents. Some have argued that the concept of dignity is ambiguous and vague (Bargaric and Allan, 2006). Others claim that dignity is often used as a 'knock-out argument' to settle ethical debates and silence dissenting outliers. It has been argued that dignity is a 'reactionary concept' (Moyn, 2015: 129). Some critics have even condemned the 'stupidity of dignity' (Pinker, 2008). The reason for all this criticism is that dignity is not a descriptive concept, in the sense that it is not possible to describe, using empirical observation or by intuiting their essence, the attributes that would allow us to conclusively establish the basis of human dignity. Rather, the concept entails an axiological value judgment; like all normative concepts, dignity should be considered as an *interpretive concept*, as rightly emphasized by Ronald Dworkin in his work, *Justice for Hedgehogs* (2011). The drafters of the UDHR were in fact quite conscious of this fact during their preparations (Morsink, 1999), as evidenced by their numerous discussions regarding the meaning that was to be attributed to human dignity. They were nonetheless able to reach consensus regarding the fact that the dignity in question was the dignity that befalls every human being as a moral subject to whom a certain respect is owed. Some have viewed this agreement as the product of a Rawlsian 'overlapping consensus,' because the foundation of human rights presented in the Declaration can be understood as a 'minimalist' or 'thin' foundation, since it disregards all comprehensive doctrines and religious traditions that could

---

[8] The events that took place in Tunisia between 2010 and 2011 were described by Tunisians themselves as the 'Dignity Revolution.' On this subject, see Rainer Grote and Tilmann J. Röder (2018: 5).

otherwise have provided legal grounds or 'thickness' (Kohen, 2012). While the drafters of the Declaration, who came from different cultural backgrounds, were able to agree on human dignity as the foundation of human rights, the Declaration provides no definition of 'human nature,' nor does it offer an interpretation of what constitutes the dignity that must be attributed to each and every human being. In the spirit of reaching a consensus, the drafters of the 1948 Declaration were careful to eliminate any references to theology or metaphysics, which might have allowed for conclusions to be drawn regarding the ontological status of human beings.[9] By agreeing that human rights must be based on the dignity of the moral subject, the writers of the Declaration decided in favor of ethical subjectivism, or a kind of moral individualism stemming from a conception of humanity as an 'ethical community'—consequently developing a legal form of cosmopolitanism on the basis of moral cosmopolitanism.

3   The Principle of Dignity in the UDHR: from Moral Cosmopolitanism to Legal Cosmopolitanism

In the Declaration, the concept of dignity appears to have three different statuses: (1) as an attribute that is inherent to all human beings *qua* human beings; (2) as the moral foundation of human rights; and (3) as an ideal to be protected and promoted through the allocation of rights.[10]

Dignity is first and foremost construed as an attribute that is inherent to all human beings, regardless of their social status, performance, or abilities. Article 1 of the UDHR reminds us that we all possess this dignity, as we are human beings represented as such: 'All human beings are born free and equal in dignity and rights. They are endowed with reason and conscience and should act towards one another in a spirit of brotherhood.' In the framework of the Declaration, since we are 'endowed with reason and conscience,' it logically follows that we possess dignity, which must be respected through the allocation of rights. This is precisely why the Declaration makes human dignity the moral foundation for all human rights.

---

[9] The Declaration has been described as embodying a kind of 'benign secularism': rather than being anti-clerical or anti-religious, the document studiously avoids any reference to religion (Morsink, 2017: 17).

[10] Our aim here is that of a normative reconstruction and not the accurate restitution of what the drafters of the declaration actually thought when the installed the principle of dignity as the foundation of human rights. On this last point, see Morsink (1999).

Even in 1948, it was evident that enshrining the principle of dignity in the Declaration would have significant ethical and political implications:

First of all, by establishing the principle of dignity as the foundation of human rights, the UDHR stipulates that the subject of these rights must be considered as a *moral subject*, that is, as a person defined by his or her capacity for autonomy, reflection, and choice. Human beings are 'endowed with reason and conscience,' as stated in Article 1, and this is why they possess a form of dignity that warrants consideration.

Second, by emphasizing the fact that all human beings possess inherent dignity by virtue of being human beings, the Declaration also postulates the *moral equality* of all individuals when considered as normative subjects whose dignity must be respected by means of the allocation of rights. According to the logic of what was 'declared' in 1948, human rights must be seen as *social forms of respect*.

Finally, by defining the subject of rights as a moral subject, the UDHR also claimed that all subjects must be granted rights by reason of their very 'nature' rather than out of charity or benevolence.[11] The moral subject thus becomes a being who 'has the right to have rights,' to use Hannah Arendt's expression (1979 [1951]: 296). It follows logically from the reasoning introduced in the 1948 Declaration that the moral equality of individuals should stem from an *equality of rights*, since equal dignity entails equal rights. Consequently, in its Article 2, the Declaration in fact stipulates that '[e]veryone is entitled to all the rights and freedoms set forth in this Declaration, without distinction of any kind, such as race, colour, sex, language, religion, political or other opinion, national or social origin, property, birth or other status.'

Understood as the moral foundation of human rights, the concept of dignity reappears in multiple different articles of the Declaration, in particular Articles 22 and 23, where it is no longer seen as being *inherent* to human beings, but as an *ideal* that should be promoted through the allocation of rights—as though it were necessary to emphasize the gap between the autonomy that characterizes the moral subject and the everyday reality of attempting to act autonomously.[12] More specifically, according to the 1948 Declaration, autonomy is simultaneously an ability with which every human being is endowed and an ideal to be attained, given that we are far from behaving as purely autonomous subjects. Social science research demonstrates just how many elements can determine our behavior, revealing that our self-determination is always more

---

11   See Chapter 9 in this volume.
12   See also Glenn Hugues (2011).

or less 'hindered,' depending on the circumstances. As Amartya Sen (2004) has argued, individuals may be 'disempowered' and 'disenfranchised,' in the process losing many of their freedoms. In reality, we always operate at some (greater or lesser) distance from the ideal of autonomy, the notion of which is nonetheless essential for us to understand our behaviors and our choices as stemming from our freedoms, and for us to feel responsibility for them. Some individuals are, of course, further from this ideal than others, especially if they are subject to conditions of extreme poverty and vulnerability that obstruct their autonomy and threaten their dignity. This point, surprisingly often overlooked, is precisely what the UDHR was addressing when it stipulated that economic and social rights were necessary for 'an existence worthy of human dignity.'[13]

By basing human rights on the idea of universal dignity, the UDHR was simultaneously basing a legal form of cosmopolitanism on a moral cosmopolitanism (or universalism) that was not dissociated from the ideal of achieving peace and justice throughout the world. From the beginning, however, the Declaration was accused of Occidentalism, ethnocentrism, and even parochialism.[14] Some wondered whether the normative heart of the UDHR was grounded in a flawed universalism.

4   'Hypocritical' Universality? A Rebuttal

Today, these are still the criticisms levied against the idea that human rights are universal (Mutua, 2016: 252). This is evidenced by the fact that in the 1990s, human rights doctrine was criticized via culturalist and differentialist arguments in the name of 'Asian values.' Similarly, the drafting of the Universal Islamic Declaration of Human Rights began in 1981. The document was presented as an Islamic alternative to the UDHR that reflects Islamic principles. For many non-Western countries, human rights doctrine remains a contentious topic.

Despite its manifest universalism, the UDHR was quite careful *not* to mention colonial territories in its Article 2, which might have threatened the interests of contemporary colonial empires, in particular France and Great Britain.[15] It is also true that Western politics has sometimes sought to unilaterally

---

13   Which can also be linked to demands for a 'decent society,' to use the expression coined by Avishai Margalit (1996).
14   See in particular Maxwell O. Chibundu (2012).
15   On the colonial debates that took place during the drafting of the UDHR, see Morsink (1999).

instrumentalize human rights doctrine. For example, the United States unquestioningly supported a number of dictatorships during the Cold War and continued to make similarly dubious choices when invading Iraq and Afghanistan. Or what about Guantánamo? We could come up with a lengthy list of double standards for every Western country (France's role in Rwanda comes to mind). We must also admit that such policies have sometimes been deployed with a certain degree of arrogance by Western leaders, who are often eager to preach and point the finger.[16] For all that, is it reasonable to argue that the Universal Declaration is a 'deeply communitarian text' (Moyn, 2015: 206)? Is it reasonable to insist that human rights are purely a tool wielded in the service of Western ideological and political domination? It is always surprising when some Western intellectuals, who enjoy all the advantages of a democratic society, end up making these kinds of assertions, thus disregarding the plight of so many people around the world who currently invoke human rights in their attempt to fight against the truly 'inhuman' conditions under which they live. The implication is that respect for human rights, despite legitimizing the Western democratic system and protecting Western freedoms, remains a purely ideological matter when applied to other parts of the world, according to the mirror argument produced by advocates of non-Western culturalism ('human rights are good for me, but are inaccessible and even perhaps harmful for you, given their dominant ethnocentrism which threatens your cultural values'). However, as if rebutting such separatisms and cultural essentialisms, the UDHR provides us with normative resources that can transcend all kinds of identity cleavages. By founding human rights on the dignity that is owed to all moral subjects, the Declaration suggests that all individuals, regardless of their culture, should have the same moral value, and that this moral equality must necessarily lead to equal rights. This ideal enshrined within the UDHR allows us to transcend the document's particular limitations,[17] since it can still be mobilized today to counter the deadly dynamics of identitarian closure and cultural retreat.

Objections to this argument can only be made by those for whom individual lives have no value in light of other objectives, or by those who consider that the rights of God take precedence over human rights, the former denying the very status of human beings as moral subjects capable of making choices

---

16   In this regard, see Costas Douzinas (2007).
17   The Declaration on the Granting of Independence to Colonial Countries and Peoples adopted by the United Nations General Assembly on December 14, 1960 can in fact be seen as an attempt to transcend the limits of the UDHR in the name of the ideal that it had itself first expressed. On this subject, see Roland Burke (2010).

freely and thus assuming responsibility. Objections can also be made by those who divide the world into a binary and bellicose 'us' and 'them,' reducing the individual to an interchangeable exemplar of the group to which s/he belongs. Without denying the importance of cultural traditions, we argue that individuals are not reducible to the former: human beings can retain their individuality and their ability to train a critical eye on their own culture. The mention of cultural traditions is a good excuse, but should be seen for what it is: namely, an alibi. This is because, on the one hand, cultures are not homogenous entities and are likely to be subject to numerous interpretations and reinterpretations, only some of which run diametrically counter to human rights (much like human rights, culture can also be instrumentalized). And because, on the other hand, the reasons given for refusing human rights that have been outlined here are not inherently associated with a specific culture.

As a rebuttal to such identitarian excesses, it therefore seems that the ideal expressed by the Universal Declaration remains incredibly pertinent today. More broadly, when human rights are taken seriously—from the universalist perspective of the Declaration—then they go beyond being merely humanitarian rights and express an ideal of justice that can hardly be rejected, given the plight of millions around the world. The fight for dignity is a fight for rights and for their implementation. And this fight is never over.

More concerning than the ongoing debate regarding the universality of human rights is the fact that today human rights discourse is no longer—or scarcely—part of negotiations between states. It appears as if the logic of power, growth, and economic competition had removed it from the political agenda of many countries around the world, including Western countries. In this regard, the withdrawal of the United States from the Human Rights Council in June 2018 is highly significant, as is the rise of intolerant and oppressive regimes in the very heart of Europe. From this perspective, it seems that the golden age of human rights has indeed come to a close. And yet the idea that human rights should be universally respected remains deeply embedded in our modern conscience. Let us hope that the voice of this conscience is never drowned out by the ill winds that seem to be blowing in all directions.

References

Alston, P. 2017. 'The Populist Challenge to Human Rights.' *Journal of Human Rights Practice* 9: 1–15.

Arendt, H. 1979 [1951]. *The Origins of Totalitarianism*. New York; London: Harcourt Brace. Schocken Books.

Bargaric, M. and J. Allan. 2006. 'The Vacuous Concept of Dignity.' *Journal of Human Rights* 5 (2): 257–270.

Beitz, C. 2009. *The Idea of Human Rights*. Oxford; New York: Oxford University Press.

Berger, P. 1970. 'On the Obsolescence of the Concept of Honor.' *European Journal of Sociology* 11 (2): 339–347.

Burke, R. 2010. *Decolonization and the Evolution of International Human Rights*. Philadelphia: University of Pennsylvania Press.

Chibundu, M. O. 2012. 'The Parochial Foundations of Cosmopolitan Rights.' In *Parochialism, Cosmopolitanism and the Foundations of International Laws*, edited by M. N. S. Sellers, 172–211. Cambridge, UK; New York: Cambridge University Press.

Donnelly, J. 2015. 'Normative versus Taxonomic Humanity: Varieties of Human Dignity in the Western Tradition.' *Journal of Human Rights* 14 (1): 1–22.

Douzinas, C. 2007. *Human Rights and Empire: The Political Philosophy of Cosmopolitanism*. Abington; Oxford; New York: Routledge-Cavendish.

Dupré, C. 2015. *The Age of Dignity: Human Rights and Constitutionalism in Europe*. Oxford; Portland, OR: Hart Publishing.

Düwell, M., J. Braarvig, R. Brownsword, and M. Dietmar (eds.). 2014. *The Cambridge Handbook of Human Dignity: Interdisciplinary Perspectives*. Cambridge, UK: Cambridge University Press.

Dworkin, R. 2011. *Justice for Hedgehogs*. Cambridge, MA: Harvard University Press.

Grote, R. and R. Tilmann. 2018. *Constitutionalism, Human Rights and Islam after the Arab Spring*. New York: Oxford University Press.

Henkin, L. 1990. *The Age of Rights*. New York: Columbia University Press.

Hugues, G. 2011. 'The Concept of Dignity in the Universal Declaration of Human Rights.' *Journal of Religious Ethics* 39 (1): 1–24.

Kateb, G. 2011. *Human Dignity*. Cambridge, MA; London: Harvard University Press.

Kohen, A. 2012. 'A Non-Religious Basis of the Idea of Human Rights: The Universal Declaration of Human Rights as Overlapping Consensus.' In *The Handbook of Human Rights*, edited by T. Cushman, 266–274. London; New York: Routledge.

Kretzner, D. and E. Klein. 2002. *The Concept of Dignity in Human Rights Discourse*. The Hague; London; New York: Kluwer Law International.

Margalit, A. 1996. *The Decent Society*. Cambridge, MA: Harvard University Press.

McCrudden, C. 2008. 'Human Dignity and Judicial Interpretation of Human Rights.' *European Journal of International Law* 19 (4): 655–724.

McCrudden, C. (ed.). 2014. *Understanding Human Dignity*. Oxford: Oxford University Press.

Morsink, J. 1999. *The Universal Declaration of Human Rights. Origins, Drafting and Intents*. Philadelphia: University of Pennsylvania Press.

Morsink, J. 2009. *Inherent Human Rights: Philosophical Roots of the Universal Declaration*. Philadelphia: University of Pennsylvania Press.

Morsink, J. 2017. *The Universal Declaration of Human Rights and the Challenge of Religion*. Columbia: University of Missouri Press.

Moyn, S. 2015. *Christian Human Rights*. Philadelphia: University of Pennsylvania Press.

Mutua, M. 2016. 'Is the Age of Human Rights Over?' In *The Routledge Companion to Literature and Human Rights*, edited by S. A. McClennen and A. Schultheis Moore, 450–457. London; New York: Routledge.

Pinker, S. 2008. 'The Stupidity of Dignity.' *The New Republic*, May 28: 28–41.

Rorty, R. 1993. 'Human Rights, Rationality and Sentimentality.' In *On Human Rights: The Oxford Amnesty Lectures 1993*, edited by S. Shute and S. Hurley, 112–134. New York: Basic Books.

Rosen, M. 2012. *Dignity: Its History and Meaning*. Cambridge, MA: Harvard University Press.

Sen, A. 2004. 'Elements of a Theory of Human Rights.' *Philosophy and Public Affairs* 32 (4): 315–356.

Waldron, J. J. 2012. *Dignity, Rank and Rights*. New York: Oxford University Press.

Wuerth, I. 2016. 'International Law in the Post-Human Rights Era.' *Texas Law Review* 96: 279–349.

Zuber, V. 2018. 'Les soixante-dix ans de la Déclaration Universelle des Droits de l'Homme. Un anniversaire en demi-teinte.' *Le Débat* 201: 106–121.

CHAPTER 8

From Subaltern Cosmopolitanism to Post-Western Sociology

Laurence Roulleau-Berger

From the production of an epistemology shared with Chinese, Korean, and Japanese sociologists, we propose a *Post-Western Sociology* to enable a dialogue—on a level footing—on common concepts and concepts situated in European and Asian theories, to consider the modes of creation of continuities and discontinuities, the conjunctions and disjunctions between knowledge spaces situated in different social contexts, to work on the gaps between them. From the production of epistemologies of the Souths and the easternization of the westernized East, we will introduce the idea of the demultiplication, the complexification, and the hierarchization of new epistemic autonomies vis-à-vis Western hegemonies in sociology and the new epistemic assemblages between European and Asian sociologies (Roulleau-Berger, 2016; Roulleau-Berger and Li, 2018). In fact, epistemic autonomies become plural and diversify, even hierarchize among themselves, without this dynamic of recomposition of the geographies of knowledge in the social sciences being really perceived on the side of the Western worlds. The question of Western hegemonies continues to arise through the process of recognition, visibility, and legitimacy of this plurality of epistemic autonomies. Then we will identify some transnational theory, theoretical discontinuities and continuities, located and common knowledge in Western and non-Western contexts.[1]

1   From the Cosmopolitan Turn to Non-Western West

The criticism of Eurocentrism—already initiated by Edward Saïd, Dipesh Chakrabarty, Gayatri Chakravorty Spivak, Homi Bhabha, and Syed Farid Alatas among others—has gained momentum. The situation in which, in various parts of the world, analytical categories are derived from the Western

---

[1] This chapter is a modified version of Laurence Roulleau-Berger, 'Post-Western Sociology and the Global Revolution,' in *Post-Western Sociology: From China to Europe*, edited by L. Roulleau-Berger and L. Peilin, 19–38. London and New York: Routledge.

experience, and are argued in favor of putting an end to 'the epistemic injustice produced by the West' (Barghava, 2013).

After deconstructing the de-provincialization of European universalism, Ulrich Beck and Edgar Grande (2010) introduced the notion of a 'cosmopolitan turn' opening a conceptual space to the possibility of a variety of different and autonomous interlinked modernities between the First and the Second Modernities. Today we can perceive a diversity of westernisms—some more Eurocentric, others more Americanocentric—either merging or in tension; as there is a diversity of westernisms there is also a plurality of easternisms situated in different epistemic spaces and constructed and ordered into hierarchies according to differentiated political, historical, and civilizational processes. The diversity of knowledge is organized in conceptual spaces linked to paradigms and programs, which in turn are linked to ethnocentric knowledge processes. As important as the phenomena and issues of the domination and overlapping of non-Western theories by Western theories might be, the issue of the blurring of boundaries is of greater importance, particularly the blurring of the boundaries between Western and non-Western sociologies. This blurring contains non-declared competition and struggles for the recognition of ignored or forgotten scientific cultures. The construction of a *decentered and de-westernized sociology* enables us to gain access to a plurality of narratives told by societies about themselves and the analysis of modes of legitimization and/or disqualification of narratives. This approach enables the undoing of intellectual dissymmetries constructed by westernisms and easternisms from determined places and temporalities.

More recently, we have to take in account the construction of a non-Western West by different Western scholars in social sciences (Roulleau-Berger, 2011, 2016; Dufoix, 2013; Bhambra, 2014; Santos, 2014; Brandel, Das, and Randeria, 2018; Koleva, 2018). Epistemologies of the South have been produced by social scientists based in the Global South but also in the Global North, looking for recognition of the epistemic and cultural diversity of the world. Epistemic injustice also invites us to an epistemology of absent knowledges and absent intellectual figures. It means to have 'a decolonial break' from Eurocentric epistemologies, to consider a plurality of knowledge spaces (Savransky, 2017) and called 'subaltern modernity as a process of epistemological-spatial/temporal/ agential-coalescence constituting a transverse solidarity politics,' (Raman, 2017: 93) in demonstrating how resisting subjects are producing livelihood-environmental resistance. In another closed way, Bonelli and Mattar (2017) have purposed a 'sociology of equivocal connections' between a plurality of sensory worlds. Santos (2014) purposed to develop epistemologies of the South, which concerns the production of ecologies of knowledge anchored in the experiences of resistance as the anti-imperial South. For him, the North-centric and Western-centric thinking is abyssal and he distinguished abyssal exclusions and non-abyssal exclusions. Santos considered the return of the colonial and the return of the colonizer and called on subaltern insurgent cosmopolitism to describe the global resistance against abyssal thinking. He invites us to move from an epistemology of blindness to the epistemology of seeing based on the creation of solidarity as a form of knowledge and the mutual recognition of others as equal; three epistemological demarches are purposed to produce a new constellation of knowledge and the transformation of the mystified conservative common sense into a new emancipatory common sense, and to open a space for a non-colonial or decolonial order: the epistemology of absent knowledges, the epistemology of absent agents, and the revisitation of representations and limits. So it means to define an anti-imperial South space where a plurality of epistemological Souths were structured around counter-knowledges born in experiences of resistance (Bhambra and Santos, 2017). Bhambra (2014) purposed 'connected sociologies' in arguing for recognition of the historical connections generated by scientific hegemonies, colonialism, dispossession, and appropriation. It means using connected histories for a revision of sociology and social sciences; 'connected sociologies' are a way to reconstruct theoretical categories and create new understandings that incorporate and transform previous ones. Both Santos and Bhambra question the need for a singular global sociology or several alternative global sociologies. Andrew Brandel, Veena Das, and Shalini Randeria (2018) propose to unravel the concept of 'world anthropology' and to deconstruct the category of the 'global South' in demonstrating that different regions of the world have not carried the same value for the making of cosmopolitan disciplinary traditions. For these authors, in anthropology and in sociology the theme of American hegemony resonates in different locations in different ways, and they advocate being attentive to the multiple contestations and employments of concepts within transnational circulations, the plurality of traditions and styles of thought to move behind the cliché binaries of Eurocentrism and Orientalism. This means producing sociological knowledge in a pluricentric world and asking whether a secular and democratic nation could be built on concepts and institutions of colonial provenance. Regarding the dynamics of de-territorialization and re-territorialization of non-indigenous anthropological and sociological knowledge, they are showing that, on the one hand, Indian scholars are contributing to Western sociological and anthropological theory and, on the other hand, like Chinese sociologists they take concepts generated in their society and apply Western theory in dialogue with other non-Western regions.

In Eastern and Central Europe, Svetla Koleva (2018) has developed a non-hegemonic sociology in reestablishing continuities with the past of the discipline, and she argues the view of an existing unity of totalitarian experiences of Eastern European sociologies, a unity that is due to the 'community of shared destinies' formed by the Central and Eastern European countries after the Second World War; then she questions the diversity of knowledge productions both within the separate national sociologies and across them. In Central and Eastern Europe, the entire postwar history of sociology in communist countries shows that, despite the hostile conditions in which it was practiced, it succeeded in maintaining the scientific tradition of production of knowledge.

2 Easternization of the Westernized East and Plurality of Epistemic Autonomies

Epistemological Souths are constructed in a process of easternization of the westernized East, which looks like a kind of matrix of epistemic autonomies today in non-Western countries. The question of Western hegemonies continues to arise through the process of recognition, visibility, and legitimacy of this plurality of epistemic autonomies. In East Asia, the creation of the East Asian Sociologists Network (EASN) in 1992 by Chinese, Japanese, and Korean sociologists to produce connected sociologies represented a major challenge. In their preface to *A Quest for East Asian Sociologies*, published in 2014, Kim Seung Kuk, Li Peilin, and Shujiro Yazawa affirm that the EASN was an initiative to transcend the effects of the variety of conflicts in this region of the world, to construct a new East Asia and a radically reflexive sociology, calling into question the concept of Western modernity. Today in Asian regional forums, intellectuals from China, Korea, and Japan continually discuss the modes of producing epistemic autonomies in a context of non-Western hegemony. The challenge is to develop a diversity of epistemic autonomies in a critical global sociology.

3 Sinicization of Chinese Sociology and Plural Epistemic Autonomies

In China, the question of epistemic autonomy vis-à-vis Western sociology was first posed in the 1930s by Sun Benwen. Indeed, he would develop a sociology of the individual from a subtle distance from historical materialism; it would play a decisive role in the process of sinicization of Chinese sociology. We can then speak here of affirming an epistemic autonomy when Sun Benwen, President of the Chinese Society of Sociology, launched the movement of indigenization of the sociology, which means to produce a proper thought while mobilizing Western methods and theories. In 1979, at the time of the recreation of the discipline, rests the question of the sinicization of the discipline, which is rebuilt *next*, *with*, or *against* Western thoughts by affirming the refusal of hegemonic postures, seeking anchors in moments of the Chinese civilization of yesterday and today, and also in filiations, displacements, hybridizations with European and American ideas (Roulleau-Berger, 2008). The question of the epistemic autonomy of sociology via its sinicization in China has always been present in the idea of producing sociological knowledge emancipated from the hegemonic thoughts related to 'Western' sociologies.

Today in Chinese sociology we could distinguish three forms of epistemic autonomy: *historic epistemic autonomy, relative epistemic autonomy, strong epistemic autonomy*.

What about an *historic epistemic autonomy*? It means the reestablishment of continuities with epistemic frameworks which had been constructed before 1949 then forgotten. In Europe most intellectuals ignore renowned pre-1949 Chinese sociology; for example, Li Peilin and Qu Jingdong (2016) have demonstrated how Chinese sociology in the first half of the 20th century flourished in a context of intellectual blooming comparable to the first half of the Eastern Zhou period in Chinese history.

Xie Lizhong and He Yijin are participating in the production of a *relative epistemic autonomy*. Xie Lizhong (2012) has defined post-sociology as a pluralistic discourse analysis constructed in a new perspective in China, based on the abandon of 'given realism,' 'representationalism,' 'essentialism,' 'fundamentalism,' and so on, to open an epistemological space on a plurality of theoretical paradigms and to establish theoretical assemblages beyond Western and non-Western theory. Then He Yijin (2018) has used the concept of 'captive mind' from Syed Hussein Alatas (1974) to analyze the lack of autonomous social sciences in Asia and to explain why the monopoly of social sciences remain intact in a context of abandon of Eurocentrism in social sciences. In the continuity of a long history of sinicization, Chinese sociology could produce epistemic autonomy walking through the 'postcolonial fog.' He Yijin purposed the notion of *alternative autonomy* in analyzing the self-adaptations of Chinese sociology in the 1950s.

Qu Jingdong (2017) proposes there is a *strong epistemic autonomy* in coming back to historical views, reconstructing the sociological imagination to understand the reality of Chinese society and the context of modern transformation of Chinese social thoughts. According to Qu Jingdong, by reinterpretation of Kang Youwei's theory of the Three Eras—'Era of War,' an 'Era of

Good Governance,' and an 'Era of Peace'—from the classics, 'The inspiration of classic sociology made us realize that the structure and transitions of modern Western society have different traditions, structural conditions, and senses of real-life experiences' (Qu Jingdong, 2017: 140).

4   Partial Epistemic Autonomy and Eastern/Western Knowledge in Korea

In South Korea, the necessity of an epistemic autonomy affirmed itself rather early. In political science, Kang Jung In (2006) analyzed the dependence of the Korean academic world with regard to American political science, which led to the marginalization of the Korean experience through Western ethnocentrism. Shin Kwang Yeong (2013) identified three modes of hegemonic social sciences constructed in a double indigenization of social sciences: the development of paradigms in the West; the dominance of located concepts and theories associated with institutional power; and the contested hegemony that refers to unavailable alternative theories.

Kim Seung Kuk (2014) spoke of an 'East Asian Community (EAC)' and introduced the idea of the invention of an 'East Asianism' to propose the reinitialization of an East Asia westernized from hybridizations of 'Western' and 'non-Western' knowledge, and to move toward a cosmopolitan society by constructing transnational regional identities. In an in-depth dialogue with Ulrich Beck, Han and Shim (2010) also supported a 'bottom-up' methodological cosmopolitanism, by using East Asian identity, history, and culture to overcome the 'risk society' and develop the idea of reflexive modernization; that is, to reappropriate Confucianism in working out this new vision as an alternative to the Western theory of hegemonic instrumental rationality (Han, 2019). In the same way, Chang Kyung-Sup (2017) developed the theories of 'compressed modernities' and of 'internalized reflexive cosmopolitization.'

5   Unstable Epistemic Autonomy in Japan

In Japanese sociology, the development of an epistemic autonomy is being constructed in different terms. Kazuhiko Yatabe (2015) recalls that the Japanese intellectual history for 150 years has been organized around a double process of pendulum oscillation between the passion of the West and exaltation of the Japanese and/or Asian spirit on the one hand, and of going beyond modernity, on the other. For Shujiro Yazawa (2014), Western sociology was shifted to Japan in the context of a process of cultural translation adapted to the Japanese academic field. Until the 1960s, in the context of the development of capitalism, Japanese sociologists were subjected to the influence of American positivism, then to that of Parsons and Marx. Shujiro Yazawa then explains that, after 1980, a postmodern Japanese sociology developed, with the reappearance of forgotten prewar authors such as Takada, Ariga, Suzuki, and an indigenous sociological theory began to form, key elements of which were Takeshi's critical theory, Torigoe's sociology of the environment, and Hoshikawa's take in the 2000s on the public space. Recently, the theory of individualization has also mobilized many scholars in sociology. If Masakazu Yamasaki (1984) distinguished the 'hard individualism' in the industrial society, the 'soft individualism' in the post-industrial society, and the 'individualization of misfortune' during the decline of the nation-state, Masataka Katagiri (2013) describes three selves in different periods of Japanese society: individualized self, private self, and psychological self. Shujiro Yazawa (2014) revealed how a reflexive sociology organized around the production of a transcendental subject.

In this unstable epistemic autonomy, the Great East Japan Earthquake and tsunami has changed the vision of sociology and anthropology in redefining the subjects' status in public and political space. Takakura (2016) has suggested disaster salvage anthropology should be conducted among many stakeholders (anthropologists, government, non-governmental organizations, and the people affected) from the perspective of an intangible cultural heritage.

Materially, these forms of epistemic autonomies join up in the context of networks of forums, of colloquiums. In China, Japan, Korea, different forms of cosmopolitan imaginations are developing, translating differences and diversities of traditions and cultural influences. The political, historical, social, and economic contexts affect the production of intellectual epistemic autonomies that defend positions, sensibilities, relationships to different worlds in the scientific field, and that depend on margins of action and liberty that vary from one country to another.

6   What Is Post-Western Sociology?

Saïd's work *Orientalism* (1978) represented a very important moment in the history of postcolonial thought. Orientalism signified the establishment of systems that would intercept, capture, and orient gestures, discourses, and viewpoints. This process of interception was particularly selective; by making active knowledge invisible, by seizing 'inert' knowledge—like the knowledge associated with ancient philosophies—in order to incorporate and contain it in subfields. The postcolonial discourse based itself on the idea of provincializing Europe (Chakrabarty, 2000), to consider the 'subaltern histories' according to their own value, and played a key role over the last thirty years in the international debate on the 'global turn' and the end of Western hegemonies. However, as stated by Achille Mbembe (2006), postcolonial studies are characterized by their heterogeneity but not their originality, thus it is difficult to talk of postcolonial theory. Although, in the context of postcolonial studies, the 'post' does not mean 'after' but 'beyond' (Kilani, 2009)—if the concept of a third space was proposed by Bhabha (2007) to enable heterotopian thoughts to appear—a significant challenge for today's sociologists is to invest in different types of third spaces, both situated and globalized, by creating epistemological conjunctions and disjunctions.

How to define Post-Western Sociology? Post-Western Sociology does not only mean encouraging a multiplicity of non-Western narrative voices but also, and above all, identifying the theories they contain and seeing how these can assist us in revisiting and reexamining Western theories. Post-Western Sociology proceeds from the decentering and the renewing of universalisms originating in different Eastern and Western spaces. Post-Western Sociology is, above all, relational, dialogue-based, and multi-situated. Contrary to global sociology and similarly to 'connected sociology' (Bhambra, 2014), Post-Western Sociology refuses term-for-term structural comparisons and favors intersecting viewpoints concerning registers of understanding, agreement, and disagreement as well as the scientific practices of the co-present actors. Post-Western sociology can also be defined as a global critical sociology. However, in order to progress toward a global critical sociology, we must open knowledge spaces which have not all been rendered visible in academic spaces. Being fully aware of a strong lack of symmetry in the visibility of knowledge produced in Europe and in China, we have opened a space for active dialogue between Western and non-Western sociologies to show that contemporary sociology can only be the result of intellectual dynamics between the various centers of the West and the East (Roulleau-Berger and Li, 2012).

Post-Western sociology relies on different knowledge processes (Roulleau-Berger, 2015): 'knowledge niches' which appear to be specifically European or Asian and do not signify a transferability of knowledge; intermediary epistemological processes which encourage the partial transfer of sociological knowledge from Europe to Asia and from Asia to Europe; and transnational epistemological spaces in which European knowledge and Asian knowledge are placed in equivalence. Post-Western sociology is elaborated from the connections between field practices and the intersecting exploration of what individuals in different situations do, say, and think. It utilizes not the differences but the *intervals* between the perspectives, practices, and concepts of Chinese and European sociologies to coproduce new knowledge. This is the starting point of the construction process of Post-Western sociology, and as such, it precedes the conception of theoretical and methodological combinations and assemblages. International sociology and global sociology do not imply this erasing of epistemological boundaries: this is precisely where the distinction among post-Western sociology, international sociology, and global sociology lies (Roulleau-Berger and Li, 2018; Xie and Roulleau-Berger, 2017).

How to produce decolonial, non-hegemonic, Post-Western knowledge? In post-Western sociology, *doing with or doing together* still looks central in the fabric of sociological knowledge, taking account of an alternative political economy of knowledge and an *anti-piratic way* (Tilley, 2017). Finally, in accordance with Vincenzo Cicchelli (2018), new tools are necessary to develop sociological studies of cosmopolitanism in different fields and to define the matrices of singularity and the place of the plurality.

7   Epistemic Discontinuities and Common Space

7.1   *Epistemic Discontinuities and Located Knowledge*

From epistemic autonomies and theoretical discontinuities, we can find *located knowledge* in European and in Chinese sociology. Here, we will introduce the topics of the Individual, the State, and subjectivation in Chinese and French sociology, drawing some theoretical discontinuities between them.

Chinese sociologists now speak about the paradox of autonomy, which characterizes a process of individuation that cuts through Chinese society, in which the least well-endowed in social, economic, and symbolic capital lose a barely acquired autonomy. Li Youmei (2012) has stressed the collision effect between individual autonomy and the autonomy of social groups which were formed after 1978. The notion of autonomy is seen as independence in terms of determination and self-government, and is thought of as individual but also capable of evolving into collective autonomy. The concept of 'collective individualism' produced by Alexis de Tocqueville is often used in Chinese sociology to understand how social groups with divergent interests form and how different types of social conflict are born.

In China, processes of individuation, linked to regimes of premodernity, modernity, and postmodernity, also intermingle to hybridize and produce forms of individuation that are both localized and globalized. Individuals remain heavily dependent on the authoritarian state and continue to think of themselves as part of the state, even while developing strategies of individual or collective emancipation. Shi Yunqing (2018) defines the *compressibility* between tradition and modernity, the coexistence of socialism and capitalism, the social and political emancipation of individuals subjected to an authoritarian state. From studying the collective litigation of persons pursuing a local government for violations of their property and social rights, activists would introduce an egalitarian state–individual relationship to relations with the authoritarian state. What is at stake here is the question of the production of an 'Eastern-style' individuation linked to an authoritative state. A process of partial individuation (Yan, 2010) is defined by Chinese sociologists under the control of the central state, when individual/local government/central government relationships are part of circles linked to interpersonal networks, of which the boundaries are more or less permeable and more or less enable the self-empowerment of individuals. By exploring *Suku*—a singular Chinese concept which refers to a political technique used by the Chinese Communist Party and a practice of confessing individual suffering in a collective public forum—Sun Feiyu (Sun, 2013) has combined power, identity, and subjectivity to open a new theoretical sociological approach, really situated in the Chinese context, to understand subjective meaning through narratives of suffering from the perspective of political identity.

Li Youmei, Shi Yunqing, and Sun Feiyu have introduced a situated problematic about the concepts of the individual, state, and subjectivity quite different from the European conception, especially the French one, of the individual. In Western European sociology, autonomy has been defined as a largely shared aspiration and a very binding norm before which individuals are unequal. Since the late 1990s, particularly in France, sociology has taken a subjectivist turn (Ehrenberg, 2010) that confirms the very socio-centered way European societies examine themselves, particularly with regard to the process of 'self-totemization.' Issues of autonomy and subjectivity have assumed an important status in sociological research. This status varies according to paradigms, but has provided impetus to a certain number of researchers focusing on processes of individuation, or, more precisely, on the work of societies and work on oneself. On the European, and particularly French, sociological scene, the contemporary individual who appears uncertain, introspective, self-sufficient, and so on, is at the heart of sociological reflection.

In European—especially French—sociology, in the process of subjectivation, the place of the *self* is first situated within a process of individuation before being linked to the *We*. In Chinese sociology, the *self* has not appeared dissociated from the *we*; the *narrative self* has a superior status to the *reflexive self*, whereas in French sociological theory the *reflexive self* is superior in status to the *narrative self*. Among French authors, the work of Paul Ricoeur (2004) on the narrative identity has been and still is a major influence in the definition of what enables a plurality of *selves* to cohabit. Whereas in Western theories, the *me*, the *I*, and the *others* are seen as distinct moments in a discontinuous process of the *self*, in Chinese thinking these separate steps are not so clearly delineated, as the process itself is much more continuous.

7.2 Transnational Knowledge and Common Space

Here we deal with some continuities of sociological knowledge and transnational concepts of some major theoretical issues in European and Chinese sociologies. This approach, although not exhaustive, is rather eloquent regarding what remains of common knowledge. We will deal with the topic of collective action and social movements as an illustration of shared theoretical space.

Since the late 2000s, the sociology of collective action has largely developed in China in the academic field (Huang, Wen, and Yong, 2016). Among the most significant studies figure environmental protests and demonstrations (Sun and Zhao, 2007), peasants' protests (Ying, 2007), workers' protests (Tong, 2008), owners' protests (Zhang, 2005; Shen, 2012), and anti-demolition protests (Lü, 2012). These works focus on the analysis of theories of social movements, then study the organization, the mobilization, and the strategy of diverse actors, beginning with the theory of the mobilization of resources, of political opportunities, and of frameworks of action. More recently, the works of Chen Tao and Xie Jiabiao (2016) have started from the question of the environmental resistance of peasants and collective mobilizations in China of 'weak actors.' In these different works on the new forms of collective action, Chinese sociologists highlight the production of new citizens' demand for public recognition and respect, which are formulated in a diversity of spaces and intermediary places, distancing them from the state.

In Europe in the 1980s, sociologists began to study urban violence in working-class suburbs in France, where situations of alarm and inequality were multiplying, thus making the sufferings, racial discrimination, social segregation, and discontent in these areas visible, as well as highlighting the capacities for citizen mobilization and action. In European cities today sociologists are analyzing how the descendants of immigrants, asylum seekers, refugees, the unemployed, and so on strongly demand their rights in the public space by affirming their sentiment of injustice, of being distrusted, of being treated as 'gullible.' A new political sociology has developed in France from the analysis of riots in working-class suburbs (Lapeyronnie and Kokoreff, 2013), to the new forms of political mobilization of those without a voice. Progressively, a sociology of recognition has established itself at the heart of a sociology of collective action.

We can see some discontinuous continuities between the Chinese sociology of collective action and the European one, so we can understand how they produce and circulate transnational theory, and located and common knowledge.

8 Conclusion

Post-Western Sociology has become simultaneously a local and global critical conception, challenging the established boundaries of certain scientific territories while also taking into consideration new forms of competition and the domination of certain conceptions and ways of thinking over others. If, in the new geography of non-hegemonic conceptions a non-westernization of the West and an easternization of the westernized East have simultaneously emerged, it means the plurality of epistemic injustices and autonomies are demultiplicated in new assemblages of local and de-localized epistemologies of Souths and Norths. A post-Western sociology is coproduced between epistemologies of Souths and Norths, blurring the boundaries between Western and non-Western sociologies, using a cosmopolitan sociological imagination to create a new future of social sciences and revise Western knowledge.

References

Alatas, S. H. 1974. 'The Captive Mind and Creative Development.' *International Social Science Journal* 24 (4): 691–700.

Beck, U. and E. Grande. 2010. 'Varieties of Second Modernity: The Cosmopolitan Turn in Social and Political Theory and Research.' *British Journal of Sociology* 61 (3): 409–444.

Bhabha, H. K. 2007. *Les lieux de la culture: une théorie postcoloniale*. Paris: Payot.

Bhambra, G. K. 2014. *Connected Sociologies*. London; New York: Bloomsbury.

Bhambra, G. K. and B. de Sousa Santos. 2017. 'Introduction: Global Challenges for Sociology.' *Sociology* 1: 3–10.

Bhargava, R. 2013. 'Pour en finir avec l'injustice épistémique du colonialisme.' *Socio* 1: 41–77.

Bonelli, C. and D. V. Mattar. 2017. 'Towards a Sociology of Equivocal Connections.' *Sociology* 51 (1): 60–75.

Brandel, A., V. Das, and S. Randeria. 2018. 'Locations and Locutions: Unravelling the Concept of World Anthropology.' In *Post-Western Sociology: From China to Europe*, edited by L. Roulleau-Berger and Li P., 88–105. London and New York: Routledge.

Chakrabarty, D. 2000. *Provincializing Europe: Postcolonial Thought and Historical Difference*. Princeton, NJ: Princeton University Press.

Chang, K. S., 2017. 'China as a Complex Risk Society.' *Temporalités* 26, https://journals.openedition.org/temporalites/3810.

Chen, T. and Xie, J. 2016. 'Hunhe xing kangzheng-dangqian nongmin huanjing kangzheng de yige jieshi kuangjia' [The mixed resistance: Analysis of environmental struggle by peasants]. *Shehuixue yanjiu* [Sociological Research] 3.

Cicchelli, V. 2018. *Plural and Shared: The Sociology of a Cosmopolitan World*. Leiden; Boston, MA: Brill.

Dufoix, S. 2013. 'Les naissances académiques du global.' In *Le tournant global des sciences sociales*, edited by A. Caillé and S. Dufoix, 27–44. Paris: La Découverte.

Ehrenberg, A. 2010, *La société du malaise*. Paris: Odile Jacob.

Han, S.-J. and Y.-H. Shim. 2010. 'Redefining Second Modernity for East Asia: A Critical Assessment.' *British Journal of Sociology* 61 (3): 465–488.

Han, Sang-Jin. 2019. *Confucianism and Reflexive Modernity: Bringing Community back to Human Rights in the Age of Global Risk Society*. Leiden/Boston: Brill.

He, Y. 2018. 'An Alternative Autonomy: The Self-Adaptations of Chinese Sociology in the 1950s.' In *Post-Western Sociology: From China to Europe*, edited by L. Roulleau-Berger and Li P., 288–299. New York: Routledge.

Huang, R., Wen Z., and Yong G. 2016. 'Multi-Channelled Forceful Intervention, Frames and Protest Success: A Fuzzy-Set Qualitative Comparative Study of 40 Anti-Demolition Protests in China.' *Journal of Chinese Sociology* 3: 23.

Kang, J. I. 2006. 'Academic Dependency: Western-Centrism in Korean Political Science.' *Korean Journal* 46 (4): 115–135.

Katagiri, M. 2013. 'The three selves in Japanese society: individualized, privatized, and psychological selves in Japanese Social Theory.' In *Routledge Companion to Japanese Social Theory*, edited by A. Elliott, M. Katagiri, and A. Sawai, 139–158. New York: Routledge.

Kilani, M. 2009. *Anthropologie. Du local au global*. Paris: Armand Colin.

Kim, S. K. 2014. 'East Asian Community as Hybridization: A Quest for East Asianism.' In *A Quest for East Asian Sociologies*, edited by S. L. Kim, Li P., and S. Yazawa, 3–31. Seoul: Seoul University Press.

Kim, S. K, Li P., and S. Yazawa (eds.). 2014. *A Quest of East Asian Sociologies*. Seoul: Seoul National University Press.

Koleva, S. 2018. *Totalitarian Experience and Knowledge Production Sociology in Central and Eastern Europe 1945–1989*. Leiden: Brill.

Lapeyronnie, D. and M. Kokoreff. 2013. *Refaire la cité*. Paris: Seuil.

Li, P. and Qu J. 2016. *La sociologie chinoise avant la Révolution*. Paris: Editions FMSH.

Li, Y. 2012. *The Transition of Social Life in China*. Beijing: Encyclopedia of China Publishing House.

Lü, D. 2012. 'Meijie yunyuan, dingzi hu yu kangzhen zhengzhi: Yihuang shijian zai fenxi' [Media Mobilization, Holdouts, and Struggle Politics: Reanalysis of the Event of Yihuang]. *Shehui* 3, *Chinese Journal of Sociology* 32 (3): 129–117.

Mbembe, A. 2006. 'Qu'est-ce que la pensée postcoloniale?' *Esprit* 330: 117–133.

Qu, J. 2017. 'Back to Historical Views, Reconstructing the Sociological Imagination: The New Tradition of Classical and Historical Studies in the Modern Chinese Transformation.' *Chinese Journal of Sociology* 3: 135–166.

Raman, R. K. 2017. 'Subaltern Modernity: Keral, the Eastern Theatre of Resistance in the Global South.' *Sociology* 51 (1): 91–110.

Ricoeur, P. 2004. *Parcours de la reconnaissance*. Paris: Stock.

Roulleau-Berger, L. 2008. 'Pluralité et identité de la sociologie chinoise contemporaine.' In *La nouvelle sociologie chinoise*, edited by L. Roulleau-Berger, Guo Yuhua, Li P, and S. Liu, 13–81. Paris: Editions du CNRS.

Roulleau-Berger, L. 2011. *Désoccidentalisation de la sociologie. L'Europe au miroir de la Chine*. La Tour d'Aigues: L'Aube.

Roulleau-Berger, L. 2015. 'Sciences sociales post-occidentales: de l'Asie à l'Europe.' *Socio* 5: 9–17.

Roulleau-Berger, L. 2016. *Post-Western Revolution in Sociology: From China to Europe*. Leiden; Boston, MA: Brill.

Roulleau-Berger, L. 2018. 'Post-Western Sociology and the Global Revolution.' In *Post-Western Sociology: From China to Europe*, edited by L. Roulleau-Berger and L. Peilin, 19–39. London; New York: Routledge.

Roulleau-Berger, L. and Li. P. (eds.). 2012. *European and Chinese Sociologies: A New Dialogue*. Leiden and Boston, MA: Brill.

Roulleau-Berger, L. and Li, P (eds.). 2018. *Post-Western Sociology: -From China to Europe*. London and New York: Routledge.

Said, E. W. 1978. *Orientalism*. London: Routledge.

Santos, B. S. 2014. *Epistemologies of the South: Justice against Epistemicide*. New York: Routledge.

Santos, B. S. and Bhambra, G. K., 2017. 'Introduction: Global Challenges for Sociology,' *Sociology* 51 (1) 3–10.

Savransky, M. 2017. 'A Decolonial Imagination: Sociology, Anthropology and the Politics of Reality.' *Sociology* 51 (1): 91–110.

Shen, Y. 2012. 'Housing Transforms China: The Homeowners' Rights Campaign in B. City.' In *European and Chinese Sociologies: A New Dialogue*, edited by L. Roulleau-Berger and L. Peilin, 245–255. Leiden: Brill.

Shin, K. Y, 2013. 'The Emergence of Hegemonic Social Sciences and Strategies of Non (Counter) Hegemonic Social Sciences.' In *A Quest for East Asian Sociologies*, edited by S. K. Kim, Li. P., and S. Yazawa, 225–257. Seoul: Seoul National University Press.

Shi, Y. 2018. 'Individualization in China under Compressed and Contradictory Modernity: A Selection Mechanism of State–Individual Relations in Urban Movements.' *Temporalités* 26, https://journals.openedition.org/temporalites/3853.

Sun, F. 2013. *Social Suffering and Political Confession*. Singapore: World Scientific Publishers.

Sun, Y. and N. Zha. 2007. 'Multifaceted State and Fragmented Society: Dynamics of Environmental Movement in China.' In *Discontented Miracle: Growth, Conflict, and Institutional Adaptations in China*, edited by D. L. Yang, 111–159. Singapore: World Scientific Publishers.

Takakura, H. 2016. 'Lessons from Anthropological Projects Related to the Great East Japan Earthquake and Tsunami: Intangible Culture Heritage Survey and Disaster Salvage Anthropology.' In *World Anthropologies in Practice: Situated Perspectives, Global Knowledge*, edited by J. Gledhill, 211–224. London; New York: Bloomsbury.

Tilley, L. 2017. 'Resisting Piratic Method by Doing Research Otherwise.' *Sociology* 51 (1): 27–42.

Tong, X. 2008. 'Continuité de la tradition culturelle socialiste: action collective et résistance dans les entreprises d'Etat.' In *La nouvelle sociologie chinoise*, edited by L. Roulleau-Berger, Y. Guo, Li P., and S. Liu, 217–237. Paris: Editions du CNRS.

Xie, L. 2012. *Postsociology*. Beijing: Social Science Academic Press.

Xie, L. and L. Roulleau-Berger. 2017, 社会学知识的建构.后西方社会学的探索, [The Fabric of Sociological Knowledge. Explorations in Post-Western Sociology]. Peking: Peking University Press.

Yamasaki, M. 1984. *Yawarakai Kojinshugi no Tanjo* [The Birth of Soft Individualism]. Tokyo: Chuo-Koron.

Yan, Y. 2010. 'The Chinese Path to Individualization.' *British Journal of Sociology* 6 (3): 489–451.

Yatabe, K. 2015. 'Le dépassement de la modernité japonaise.' *Socio* 5: 115–138.

Yazawa, S. 2014. 'Civilizational Encounter, Cultural Translation and Social Reflexivity: A Note on History of Sociology in Japan.' In *A Quest of East Asian Sociologies*, edited by S. K. Kim, Li P., and S. Yazawa, 131–167. Seoul: Seoul National University Press.

Yatabe, K. 2015. 'Le dépassement de la modernité japonaise.' *Socio* 5: 115–138.

Yan, Y. 2010. 'The Chinese Path to Individualization.' *The British Journal of Sociology* 6 (3): 489–451.

Ying, X. 2007. 'The Grassroots Mobilization and the Mechanism of Interest Expression of the Peasants Group.' *Sociological Studies* 1: 1–23.

Zhang, L. 2005. 'Beijing House Owners' Rights Protection Movement: Reasons of Breakout and Mobilization Mechanism.' *Sociological Studies* 6: 1–3.

PART 2

Establishing Cosmopolitanism

CHAPTER 9

Inequality and Global Justice

David Held† and Pietro Maffettone

1   Introduction

We live in a world where poverty is still a widespread source of misery, broken lives, and ultimately death. Yet we also live in a very unequal world—one in which income and wealth disparities are staggering. If we take seriously the defining feature of all cosmopolitan thinking in Western culture, that is, a universal concern for the equal moral standing of human beings, then we can conclude that the current global economic order is deeply unjust. It enables some to thrive in ways that would have been unimaginable in the past, but still allows too many to perish in ways that are preventable.

These are, in our view, the basic elements of a minimalist and yet compelling account of global political morality—one that can be subscribed to from across a wide range of political perspectives. This chapter starts by offering a clear moral foundation: it is grounded in a cosmopolitan commitment to the equal moral standing of all human beings. It then highlights that universal moral standing translates, at a minimum, into a concern for the basic human rights of individuals. Such basic rights include rights to subsistence, understood as rights to the stable and secure satisfaction of basic needs. Yet global poverty figures, if properly interpreted, suggest that a large part of humankind is far from having such rights fulfilled. Furthermore, such figures suggest that the goal of reaching a minimally decent standard of living for all human beings is not out of reach, at the very least insofar as it would not impose unbearable sacrifices on those who have more.

One caveat before the argument develops. What we offer here is not, strictly speaking, a conception of global justice. Or at least, it is not a conception of global justice if by 'justice' we refer to an overarching normative ideal. Instead, our view is closer to what we can call a minimal conception of common standards of 'decency'; that is, a conception of what kinds of features the global order should display when it comes to the way it treats human beings for us to be able to live with it, morally speaking. A world in which every human being's basic rights are guaranteed is not a just world. Political injustice and human suffering are compatible with a merely decent global order. And yet at least the most severe forms of disregard for our fellow human beings would be eliminated if global common standards were met. This order would still be unjust but it would, we submit, be much less callous and would restore some hope concerning the possibility of human progress.

2   Moral Foundations: the Cosmopolitan Plateau

Ronald Dworkin once famously wrote that all contemporary political philosophy rested on egalitarian foundations (1986: 296–267). Libertarianism, utilitarianism, and liberal egalitarianism, the most influential approaches to moral and political philosophy, can all be seen as providing different interpretations of what it means to treat persons with equal respect and concern. The idea of moral equality, in Dworkin's own words, provided 'a kind of plateau in political argument' (1983: 25). Something similar can be said about the debate in global political theory. Here we can say that we have reached a cosmopolitan plateau (see Blake, 2013). Of course, the term 'cosmopolitan' can be interpreted in many different ways (Brown and Held, 2010; Held and Maffettone, 2016a, 2016b). However, the most influential contemporary account relates to our understanding of the moral status of human beings.

Thomas Pogge (1992) has provided the most influential definition of moral cosmopolitanism. According to Pogge:

> Three elements are shared by all cosmopolitan positions. First, *individualism*: the ultimate units of moral concern are *human beings*, or *persons*—rather than, say, family lines, tribes, ethnic, cultural, or religious communities, nations, or states. The latter may be units of concern only indirectly, in virtue of their individual members or citizens. Second, *universality*: the status of ultimate unit of moral concern attaches to *every* living human being *equally*—not merely to some subset, such as men, aristocrats, Aryans, whites, or Muslims. Third, *generality*: this special status has global force. Persons are ultimate units of moral concern *for everyone*—not only for their compatriots, fellow religionists, or suchlike.
> POGGE, 1992: 48–49; original emphasis

Pogge's definition reminds us of what it means to assign a certain status to human beings as moral agents. Most importantly, it provides a framework for our political discussions; and it is a framework that is accepted by all those who participate in the conversation of global political theory. It is important to stress the latter point. Some will inevitably complain that a term or label that includes all participants in a given debate may not be particularly useful

(Blake, 2013: 35–37), since it fails to identify any form of serious disagreement. To the contrary, we think that the terminology, and the concept that underlies it, still have something admirable to contribute; namely, that they help us delineate the boundaries of reasonable disagreement within our moral debates in a way that is philosophically consistent. They act as a screen to filter the range of plausible moral approaches to the moral understanding of the global political domain. The filter is basic and morally capacious. It tells us that moral and political theories that deny the basic moral equality of human beings are wrong and cannot offer a credible starting point for global political theory. Accordingly, the cosmopolitan plateau tells us that to subscribe to forms of value collectivism, or to deny the equal moral status of all human beings, implies that one's views are beyond the boundaries of reasonable disagreement and thus have no standing in the debate about the moral bases of global politics.

3   The Implications of the Cosmopolitan Plateau

Of course, to be committed to moral cosmopolitanism is to be committed to a very abstract moral outlook. What are the political and distributive implications, if any, of such an outlook? The most important political implication of the cosmopolitan plateau is, we contend, the commitment to basic human rights. Basic human rights have come to articulate the normative focal point of global political theory. They constitute the most important benchmark (though, of course, not the only one) for the evaluation both of internal and external state conduct, for the actions of global governance institutions, for the norms and principles that constitute international and transnational regimes, for the policies of multinational corporations, and for the behavior of political leaders and public officials. Or, in Henry Shue's words, they articulate what he calls the 'moral minimum,' '[t]he lower limits on tolerable conduct, individual and institutional' (1996: xi). Our position resonates with this notion.

Why should the acceptance of moral cosmopolitanism entail the acceptance of certain basic rights? The simple answer, in our view, is that moral cosmopolitanism is an articulation, or a codification, of the recognition of human dignity. But human dignity is, if not impossible, at least severely damaged if rights are not attached to it. Dignity, understood as a peculiar kind of standing, requires that we are able to demand respect for our most basic interests, not simply accept that their fulfilment may be the result of luck or benevolence. Or, in Feinberg's eloquent words:

> Legal claim-rights are indispensably valuable possessions. A world without claim-rights, no matter how full of benevolence and devotion to duty, would suffer an immense moral impoverishment. Persons would no longer hope for decent treatment from others on the ground of desert or rightful claim. Indeed, they would come to think of themselves as having no special claim to kindness or consideration from others, so that whenever even minimally decent treatment is forthcoming they would think themselves lucky rather than inherently deserving, and their benefactors extraordinarily virtuous and worthy of great gratitude. The harm to individual self-esteem and character development would be incalculable.
>
> FEINBERG, 1973, quoted in SHUE, 1996: 113

Human dignity, we have just claimed, is connected to rights. What are rights? Following a widely accepted account, X has a right if there are sufficient reasons to hold another agent, Y, under a duty to deliver that right (Raz, 1986: 166). Put differently, X has a right to something if an aspect of X's well-being, X's interest, would be furthered by other agents being under a duty, and we can offer a clear justification for Y having such a duty. An interest is thus part of the grounds of a right. However, interests alone cannot justify the existence of rights. I certainly have an interest that my daughter receives an Ivy League education, but I have no right to it. I have an interest in winning the lottery, but have no right to it. This holds even in non-trivial cases. I have a fundamental interest in a kidney transplant if I suffer kidney failure, but have no right to a kidney transplant just because a key aspect of my well-being would be furthered by receiving one. And one could go on *ab libitum*. Interests are an important ground for rights, but they cannot be a conclusive argument in their favor, no matter how strong they are. The reason, starkly illustrated by the kidney example, is that, in the world as we know it, human interests conflict with one another. My interest in a kidney is strong, but so might be yours and someone else's. The presence of the interest, by itself, cannot resolve the conflict of interests. Nonetheless, interests are crucial. Without the existence of an interest, it seems difficult to talk about rights (but cf. Wenar, 2008). Accordingly, any analysis of basic human rights will have to start with an account of a special class of interests.

If dignity requires rights, and if rights are partly grounded in human interests, which interests should we focus on? What is the special class of human interest that we should concentrate on? Clearly, the expression 'human interests' is, at least in some respects, controversial, since it implicitly builds on a conception of the person. As Rawls (1996) famously taught us, in a morally diverse political domain, and global politics certainly is one, metaphysical or ontological ideas about the nature of human beings are bound to be reasonably rejected by some. Thus, what persons are, and what their interests are as persons, should not, as far as possible, be determined by metaphysical or ontological claims. Instead, it seems wiser to proceed in what we can call a normatively parsimonious way. Some human interests, whatever one's conception of human persons, are central simply because their fulfilment is the precondition for the realization of any account of what a human being is. Put differently, the best way to proceed is 'negatively.' What does it mean to proceed 'negatively'? Paraphrasing the Italian poet and Nobel laureate Eugenio Montale, it is far easier to start from what we are not and what we do not want. Different outlooks on life will deliver different comprehensive accounts of human interests given that such interests will, ultimately, depend on what it means, according to those accounts, to be fully human. This being the case, it is, in our view, not philosophically wise to start the elaboration and defense of something so morally and politically urgent as basic human rights by referring to controversial accounts of human interests based on a thick conception of the person. How else can one proceed then? The negative answer, as we have called it, simply tells us that we should look for that subset of fundamental interests that any reasonable conception of the person will need to include. In other words, the human interests we should focus on are those interests that, when they are not securely guaranteed, imply the impossibility of realizing any reasonable conception of what a human being is at all.

So, what are those interests? Offering a detailed list would, we believe, be neither interesting nor possible in the present context (Held, 1995). Rather, the focus should be on what they must include; that is, on the secure and stable satisfaction of basic needs. In turn, the secure and stable satisfaction of basic needs creates the preconditions for achieving a minimally decent standard of living. Without shelter, health care, clothing, nourishment, and so on human life simply does not last very long, let alone flourish. And this is irrespective of one's conception of human flourishing.

Clearly enough, there is much more to human beings than their needs and how we make sense of them. To mention just one example, most human beings live in political societies, and thus some of their interests will be connected to how those societies are organized and how their rules of distribution function. One can even reasonably claim that human needs cannot be precisely determined in the abstract given that their specification must rely on a thicker cultural understanding of how persons are situated in a social world. We are happy to concede both points. Yet whatever human life 'can be,' whatever telos or ways of flourishment one can conceive, these are, simply put, impossible if persons' most basic needs are not securely met. Even conceding that a full articulation of basic needs is culturally situated, it is clearly not implausible to think that the basic needs we have just referred to should be understood as parameters: their exact value, rather than their general meaning and importance, varying according to context.

Moral cosmopolitanism requires rights. Rights are (at least in part) grounded in human interests. And while it is controversial to state what a human person is or should be, there are certain aspects of a person's well-being that simply cannot be ignored. Yet, following Henry Shue, it is also important to stress that to enjoy a right it is not enough that one contingently, or occasionally, enjoys the substance of the right. If I have an interest in my subsistence, and if this interest of mine supports sufficient reasons to put other agents under a duty, I then have a right to subsistence. Yet this right cannot be enjoyed if, for example, my ability to purchase or consume food is hostage to the vagaries of market transactions or dependent on weather patterns or luck. As Henry Shue convincingly argued, to really enjoy a right means to be protected against the standard social threats against its enjoyment (1996). The latter is not a trivial point. If people have a right to subsistence, then they have a right to a secure provision of the means to their subsistence.

In the section of the chapter that follows we survey some basic evidence about global poverty and suggest the best way to interpret this data. The focus is on how the global economic order does not securely guarantee the basic rights of a large part of humanity. This is for two reasons. First, because even taken at face value, global poverty numbers are bleak. Second, because if we are interested in the enjoyment of certain rights, the data offers no reassurance that a much wider number of people other than those deemed to live in 'severe poverty' are protected against standard threats to the enjoyment of the substance of their basic rights.

4 Global Poverty

According to recent World Bank figures (World Bank, 2015), roughly 10 percent of the global population live in severe poverty. More specifically, the data suggests that around 736 million people globally live below the $1.90 a day international poverty line, characterized by the World Bank as extreme poverty. The geographical and demographic features of the data are worth highlighting. For the most part, the global poor are rural (80 percent), very young (44 percent are fourteen or younger), lack education (39 percent of the global poorer lack any kind of formal educational experience), work in the agricultural sector (65 percent according to World Bank figures; working in the agricultural sector makes a person four times more likely to be poor), and are members of larger than average households (i.e., households with a higher than average number of children).

When it comes to the geographical location of the global poor, and taking official figures at face value, sub-Saharan Africa hosted more than half of the world's poor in 2013—a share that goes well beyond the region's proportion of the global population. East Asia accounts for roughly 10 percent of global poverty, while South Asia still contains about 33 percent (World Bank, 2013). These figures are largely the result of the differences in economic performance in China, India, and West Africa since the late 1980s.

It is also interesting to observe the relative magnitude of the so-called poverty gap in different regions. The poverty gap 'represents the average distance to the poverty line among all the poor' (World Bank, 2016: 36). The general global poverty gap is relatively small at 3.2 percent, and yet it is roughly five times larger in sub-Saharan Africa, at 15.9 percent. This suggests that sub-Saharan Africa is not simply the region that hosts a disproportionate number of the global poor but also that it is the region where the poor are furthest away, on average, from the international poverty line set by the World Bank.

Even taking this data at face value, one is bound to be struck by the sheer magnitude of the implied human suffering. Yet, thinking about what the data means for a moment longer makes for an even more morally depressing experience, for three reasons. First, consider what the international poverty line set by the World Bank actually means. The $1.90/day poverty line is not an exchange rate value. The Bank is not suggesting that a person is among the global poor if he or she fails to secure 1.90 US dollars each day. In fact, the figure refers to purchasing power parity values (PPP values); that is to say, $1.90/day refers to the equivalent basket of goods one could buy in the USA with $1.90. The reason for using PPP values is that we are typically interested in what people can actually consume through their income. The PPP exchange rate is the exchange rate which allows for approximately the same bundle of goods and services to be purchased in all countries of the world. For poor countries, PPP exchange rates will tend to be smaller than the market exchange rates, reflecting lower price levels in those countries. Note that the correction implied by differences in price levels can be substantial. For example, in 2011, the exchange rate between Indian rupees and US dollars was 46/1, yet the estimated PPP exchange rate was 15/1, and this suggests that the price level in India was about 1/3 of the price level in the USA at that time (Milanovic, 2016: 15).

In short, the relevant question one needs to ask is: How would I live on what $1.90 could buy in the contemporary USA (or some other developed country with a similar price level) on any given day? The answer is, to put it mildly, not very well. The amount of $1.90 is less than the price of a coffee at Costa in the

UK or Starbucks in the USA, less than what the average person would spend on a sandwich bought during their lunch break, less than the cost of a single metro ride in most European capitals, and constitutes a tiny fraction (in fact an order of magnitude less) of the income one could earn by working at the minimum wage in any Organisation for Economic Co-operation and Development (OECD) country. The list could go on. And what is more, the global poor have to find a way to survive in a context where infrastructure and public goods are, on average, far less developed than in richer countries.

Second, the international poverty line set by the World Bank is far from uncontroversial (see Pogge and Reddy, 2010). It is specified by reference to some of the poorest countries in the world. It does not, by design, count every individual who is considered poor in each and every country. The alleged reason for this is that, as mean consumption levels in a country go up, poverty measures exhibit what economists call an 'economic gradient.' In poor countries, poverty lines tend to be more stable (that is, anchored to a minimum level of potential consumption), while in richer countries they tend to vary more with mean consumption. This entails that while poverty lines in poor countries tend to refer to absolute poverty, they generally refer to relative levels of potential consumption as a country becomes richer (see Ravallion, Chen, and Sangraula, 2009). Nonetheless, although it seems reasonable to concede that moral priority should be given to those who are poor in a poorer country, given that the notion of poverty involved is closer to an absolute level of destitution, this is far from a conclusive reason to argue that *only* those who are poor in the poorest countries are to be considered among the poor at the global level. The difference is conceptually subtle but worth emphasizing. Global poverty as measured by the World Bank offers a 'one world' picture where poverty is meant to designate the worst-off members of any society anywhere in the world. And this is clearly different from considering poverty as a condition that persons experience differently in different social contexts. What is certain is that global poverty statistics (as opposed to poverty numbers at the global level) provide a very conservative estimate of how many people are poor in the world and do not, furthermore, seem to match our considered convictions about the meaning of poverty. Such statistics would basically entail, for example, that hardly anyone is poor in Western countries, a conclusion, we think, that is palpably absurd.

Third, consider what the international poverty line and the related headcount of the world's poor cannot tell us. The data we highlight are, in some sense, static. They offer a snapshot of how many people are poor at any given point in time. Even when the World Bank provides trends concerning the evolution of global poverty numbers over several years, it simply offers a comparison between two static pictures. Yet what the data simply cannot tell us is how many people have been poor as a percentage of the global population at any point in time over the course of their lives. This is important as it clearly would affect our judgment of the problem to know that, for example, while 10 percent of the global population lives in absolute poverty today, 20 percent as opposed to 30 percent or 50 percent of the world's population is likely to have experienced severe poverty over the course of their lives. And this is because, in the end, when we judge the global economic order, we care not only about how many people can be lifted out of poverty at a certain point in time, but also about how precarious their lives are and what their chances are of experiencing poverty. Put differently, not being deprived, in our judgment, does not simply entail being able to consume certain things at a certain point in time, but also to feel secure over the life cycle.

5   Global Inequality

When it comes to rights—and to claiming that someone has a right to something—two normative tasks can be distinguished. The first is to argue for the importance of the interests that form part of the ground of the right. The second is to offer a defense of the implications of claiming that some other subjects should be burdened with duties connected to the alleged right. Are there sufficient reasons to put a given agent under a duty to do (or refrain from doing) something? In part, the answer to the latter question depends on the amount or kind of sacrifice that the duty in question would require of the agent. For example, we all have an interest in being loved. Many would add that, in fact, without being loved, it seems impossible to lead a decent life. And yet, few (but see Liao, 2015) believe that persons have a right to be loved. To put other agents under a duty to love us would not be reasonable, among other reasons, because it would entail the imposition of an unreasonable sacrifice of some of the basic interests of those agents. As we have seen, human interests conflict, and thus to have an interest in something, even a fundamental interest, is not to have right to the protection of that interest, since other agents may be required to sacrifice too much of their own interests to comply with the duty.

There is often a tendency, at least among those who support human rights, to focus exclusively on the first normative task. This is understandable: to focus on the specification of fundamental human interests, at least in the context of global politics, is to focus on the plight of those who are worse off. Certain basic human interests, such as physical integrity and the means of subsistence, are worth protecting in any outlook that gives universal importance to the moral standing of persons. Nonetheless, what also matters is the 'amount of sacrifice' of their own interests that duty bearers are required to accept if the rights in question are to be considered acceptable.

Who are the duty bearers when it comes to basic rights (see O'Neill, 2005)? And how can we judge if the sacrifice that is demanded of them is reasonable? There is ongoing disagreement about the answer to the first question. Basic rights are rights that human beings have in virtue of their dignity and standing. Yet this does not tell us who should be held accountable in the event of breaches. According to many, it is first and foremost states and governments that should be tasked to protect basic rights (see Beitz, 2010, for a discussion). Others would add that by contributing to the promulgation and enforcement of the rules of a global economic order that 'foreseeably and avoidably' violates the basic rights of millions, the citizens of Western countries also acquire specific negative duties toward the global poor (Pogge, 2008). These are important questions, but we cannot settle them here. A reasonable and relatively standard answer (see Rawls, 1999), is that the basic rights of all human beings should be secured by the states and governments under which they happen to live and that only when this proves to be impossible (or, when states and governments are unwilling to do so) should the task be passed on to the wider international community. Yet to assign *primary* responsibilities to states for the protection of basic rights is not to limit the scope and moral significance of those rights to national jurisdictions and procedures.

What remains to be seen is whether the international community can be reasonably asked, directly or indirectly, to be under a duty to protect the basic rights of all human beings. In the first instance, there is a precedent for this position, set by the 'Responsibility to Protect' (R2P) doctrine (Hale, Held, and Young, 2013: 79–80). Second, how far basic human rights can be upheld will depend, in our view, on whether the global economic order is affluent enough to make the protection of these rights against standard social threats a plausible endeavor. Global inequality data offer ample empirical reassurance that, bluntly put, humanity can afford to save and protect the insecure and destitute. According to the 2018 World Inequality Report (WIR, 2018), the income share of the global top 1 percent has risen from 16 percent of global income to over 20 percent of global income since 1980. Within the same time frame, the income share of the poorest 50 percent of the global income distribution has remained stable at about 9 percent (WIR, 2018: 7). The figures are even starker when it comes to global wealth distribution, given that 'the world's top 1% wealthiest people increased from 28% to 33%, while the share commanded by the bottom 75% oscillated around 10% between 1980 and 2016' (WIR, 2018: 13). And, if recent trends continue, the '[t]op 1% global wealth share would reach 39% by 2050, while the top 0.1% wealth owners would own nearly as much wealth (26%) as the middle class (27%)' (WIR, 2018: figure 9).

The fact that there is significant income and wealth inequality, some will inevitably object, does not tell us much concerning the real prospects for redistribution. That there are enough resources to be redistributed does not entail that redistribution is possible. This is due to the simple reason that redistribution might alter the incentives people have to accumulate economic resources and thus might prove to be self-defeating. This is certainly a point worth bearing in mind. To illustrate, Arthur Laffer famously argued that the relationship between tax rates and total tax revenue will have the shape of an 'inverted U,' precisely because of incentive mechanisms (for an overview see Canto, Joines, and Laffer, 1983). As tax rates go up, persons might respond by working less. There are two points worth making here. First, as we will see in the final section of the chapter, 'Concluding remarks,' to claim that there is a moral duty to redistribute because we can afford to do so does not tell us how redistribution needs to be achieved. Changing the rules of the game—that is, affecting institutional processes—might be the most effective way to proceed and yet it might not have the same impact on incentives than simply altering the distribution of economic resources. Second, and even accepting the general point made by supply-side economists, the crucial bit of information we lack is precisely at which level of redistribution persons will start to react to the incentives. Put differently, and sticking to Laffer's argument for the sake of simplicity, even if tax revenue goes down after a given level of tax rates, we still need to offer an empirical specification of the level in question. If this level is higher than the current level of tax rates, then this implies that higher taxes would indeed lead to higher tax revenues. The same holds, *ceteris paribus*, for redistribution at the global level. If the current level of redistribution is lower than the one at which more redistribution would affect incentives, then more redistribution would not be self-defeating.

Let us go back to global inequality figures: What do they tell us, concretely? The figures we have summarized highlight the staggering inequalities that permeate the global economic order. Some find these inequalities to be problematic in and of themselves. According to many egalitarians, persons should not be penalized for the result of brute bad luck (see, for example, Cohen, 2008). Given that country of birth (as opposed to social class) is today by far the most important factor in explaining a person's prospects in life (Milanovic, 2016), then global income and wealth inequalities will strike many as morally arbitrary and thus intrinsically unjust.

However convincing, the latter argument does not, in our view, capture what is morally most urgent about the global economic order and about global inequality in wealth and income. Inequalities are often troubling for non-egalitarian reasons. According to Thomas Scanlon '[e]galitarian reasons [...] are reasons for objecting to the difference between what some have and what others have, and for reducing this difference' (2017:1). Egalitarian reasons to care about inequality find something intrinsically, or non-instrumentally, wrong with inequality (see O'Neill, 2008, for the distinction). By contrast, non-egalitarian or purely instrumental concerns disclose many of the brutal consequences of inequality, which are deeply concerning.

In recent years, a substantial and increasing corpus of academic literature has drawn attention to the negative effects of high levels of income and wealth inequality on such issues as life expectancy and infant mortality, obesity rates, children's educational performance, teenage births, homicide levels, incarceration rates, social trust, mental health, social mobility, and political participation (see Held, 2006; Wilkinson and Pickett, 2009; O'Neill, 2010; Stiglitz, 2012). What these results tell us is that income and wealth inequalities can have important negative consequences for some of the central welfare indicators and social trends. Instrumental concerns with high levels of inequality thus abound within modern social systems. The reduction of severe poverty is, thus, the *primus inter pares* of the instrumental reasons to care about inequality. Inequality is morally troublesome, first and foremost, in a context where those who have less have weak and highly vulnerable life chances. The proper moral sequencing of caring about inequality, the aforementioned literature might suggest, is that inequality should be considered wrong first and foremost for reasons that are not egalitarian in nature. And that the most urgent of these instrumental reasons, in turn, is given by the condition in which the worst-off members of humanity find themselves.

Furthermore, it is important to consider the 'magnitude of the gap' between rich and poor. If we consider the size of this gap as a function of how 'rich' the global rich actually are, then it tells us that the relative costs, in terms of welfare and opportunities (both important aspects of their well-being), affecting redistribution are bound to be contained. From a formal perspective, and assuming that the utility that income and wealth generate for persons are subject to diminishing marginal returns, the fact that the rich are enormously wealthier (broadly defined) than the poor is important. It can tell us something morally relevant about the extent that the rich are asked to sacrifice their interests for the poor. Looking at the data we have just highlighted in this section, the global economic order is a clear case in point: a case where the welfare of the rich, especially of the very rich, would not greatly be affected by forms of redistribution that would improve the condition of those who live in severe poverty at the global level.

6   Concluding Remarks

We have argued that the equal moral standing of human beings requires that they have certain basic rights, including rights to subsistence. We have also argued that, looking at recent empirical trends in the world economy, the basic rights of a large part of humankind are not securely protected. These basic rights are genuine rights since the duties they impose on the global rich do not imply unreasonable sacrifices. Furthermore, the redistribution or the instrumental reduction of global inequalities in wealth and income for the sake of the global poor is, we contend, both required and justified.

While the argument in this chapter falls short, as indicated, of offering a full theory of global justice, its implications are nonetheless radical. If poverty and destitution were a thing of the past, global politics could begin to claim a progressive mantle. The moral cosmopolitan position is both simple and elegant in its form, but, if taken seriously, can be seen to lay out a pathway of highly significant change. Establishing common standards of decency provides the means to specify the elements that the global order must display if all human beings are to be free of the appalling conditions that, all too often today, rob them of their basic rights and, ultimately, of their lives.

References

Beitz, C. 2010. *The Idea of Human Rights*. Oxford: Oxford University Press.

Blake, M. 2013. 'We Are All Cosmopolitans Now.' In *Cosmopolitanism versus Non-Cosmopolitanism*, edited by G. Brock, 35–54. Oxford: Oxford University Press.

Brown, G. and D. Held (eds.). 2010. *The Cosmopolitanism Reader*. Cambridge, UK: Polity Press.

Canto, V. A., H. D. Joines, and A. B. Laffer. 1983. *Foundations of Supply-Side Economics*. New York: Academic Press.

Cohen, G. A. 2008. *Rescuing Justice and Equality*. Cambridge, MA: Harvard University Press.

Dworkin, R. 1983. 'Comment on Narveson: In Defense of Equality.' *Social Philosophy and Policy* 1: 24–40.

Dworkin, R. 1986. *Law's Empire*. Cambridge, UK: Cambridge University Press.

Feinberg, J. 1973. *Social Philosophy*. London: Pearson.

Hale, T., D. Held, and K. Young. 2013. *Gridlock: Why Global Cooperation Is Failing When We Need It Most*. Cambridge, UK: Polity Press.

Held, D. 1995. *Democracy and the Global Order*. Cambridge, UK: Polity Press.

Held, D. 2006. *Models of Democracy*, 3rd ed. Cambridge, UK: Polity Press.

Held, D. and P. Maffettone. 2016a. *Global Political Theory*. Cambridge, UK: Polity Press.

Held, D. and P. Maffettone. 2016b. 'Legitimacy and Global Governance.' In *Global Political Theory*, edited by D. Held and P. Maffettone, 117–142. Cambridge, UK: Polity Press.

Liao, S. M. 2015. *The Right to be Loved*. Oxford: Oxford University Press.

Milanovic, B. 2016. *Global Inequality*. Cambridge, MA: Harvard University Press.

O'Neill, M. 2008. 'What Should Egalitarians Believe?' *Philosophy & Public Affairs* 36 (2): 119–156.

O'Neill, M. 2010. 'The Facts of Inequality.' *Journal of Moral Philosophy* 7 (3): 397–409.

O'Neill, O. 2005. 'The Dark Side of Human Rights.' *International Affairs* 81 (2): 427–439.

Pogge, T. 1992. 'Cosmopolitanism and Sovereignty.' *Ethics* 103 (1): 48–75.

Pogge, T. 2008. *World Poverty and Human Rights*. Cambridge, UK: Polity Press.

Pogge, T. and S. G. Reddy. 2010. 'How Not to Count the Poor.' In *Debates on the Measurement of Global Poverty*, edited by S. Anand, P. Segal, and J. Stiglitz, 42–85. Oxford: Oxford University Press.

Ravallion, M., S. Chen, and P. Sangraula. 2009. 'Dollar a Day Revisited (English).' *World Bank Economic Review* 23(2): 163–184, http://documents.worldbank.org/curated/en/403331468147538738/Dollar-a-day-revisited.

Rawls, J. 1996. *Political Liberalism*. New York: Columbia University Press.

Rawls, J. 1999. *The Law of Peoples*. Cambridge, MA: Harvard University Press.

Raz, J. 1986. *The Morality of Freedom*. Oxford: Clarendon Press.

Scanlon, T. M. 2017. *Why Does Inequality Matter?* Oxford: Oxford University Press.

Shue, H. 1996. *Basic Rights*. Oxford: Oxford University Press.

Stiglitz, J. 2012. *The Price of Inequality*. New York: W.W. Norton & Co.

Wenar, L. 2008. 'Property Rights and the Resource Curse.' *Philosophy & Public Affairs* 36 (1): 2–32.

Wilkinson, R. and K. Pickett. 2009. *The Spirit Level: Why More Equal Societies Almost Always Do Better*. London: Allen Lane.

WIR (World Inequality Report). 2018. *World Inequality Report 2018*, https://wir2018.wid.world/files/download/wir2018-full-report-english.pdf.

World Bank. 2013. 'Shared Prosperity: A New Goal for a Changing World,' May 8, http://www.worldbank.org/en/news/feature/2013/05/08/shared-prosperity-goal-for-changing-world.

World Bank. 2015. 'Annual Report 2015,' http://www.worldbank.org/en/about/annual-report-2015.

World Bank. 2016. *Poverty and Shared Prosperity 2016: Taking on Inequality*. Washington, DC: World Bank, https://openknowledge.worldbank.org/bitstream/handle/10986/25078/9781464809583.pdf.

CHAPTER 10

International Human Rights System

Daniel J. Whelan

In 1942, anticipating the eventual victory of the Allies over the Axis powers, Winston Churchill remarked that the Second World War would end with the 'enthronement of human rights.'* Since the founding of the United Nations (UN) and the adoption of the Universal Declaration of Human Rights (UDHR) in 1948, the security and welfare of all human beings has become a legitimate concern of international society and a core responsibility of the UN itself. Since the end of the Second World War, the idea that human rights are universal holds great purchase.[1] The coin of universality has two sides, however: first, all human beings—no matter their station in life, where they live, their ages or genders, or any other differentiating circumstances—have human rights. The other side of the coin is more problematic, but equally important: all states—no matter their levels of development, history, or particular cultural or religious ways of life—are obligated to respect and protect core minimum standards of human rights for all.

While expansion of the normative and institutional features and practices of human rights has been impressive—especially considering the long history of human suffering at the hands of governments and other powerful actors—this expansion has made us ever more aware of the vulnerabilities of human populations and the continuing need for human rights. The loss of civilian lives to famines, war, civil strife, genocide, and other crimes against humanity represents the most severe violation of human rights. Even more widespread, however, are the economic and social vulnerabilities that result from globalization, because people's livelihoods are ever more dependent on the forces of globalization and modernization that strain many societies. Here, human rights can play a protective role as well. As the sometimes disparate developments of the 'Arab Spring' of 2011 demonstrated, there are millions around the world for whom the language and support networks of human rights have been enormously powerful in their struggle for political self-determination and democratic governance.

---

* This chapter is derived from Donnelly and Whelan (2017) and Whelan (2012).
1 See Chapter 7 in this volume.

The contemporary era of human rights represents a paradox—that as we witness the continual expansion of human rights norms, treaties, and institutions, we are also aware that violations continue apace. This paradox should not overshadow the critical shift in international relations that has occurred as a result of the expansion of human rights since 1948. Whereas the survival and security of the nation-state itself was the central concern of international relations from the mid-17th century until the end of the Cold War, the human rights revolution has led us to embrace the notion that it is the protection of *human* security that is the most pressing concern to international society. It is ever more widely recognized that instabilities within the international system stem from significant 'unfreedoms' that exist within societies, exemplified by failed systems of rulership that lead to failed states. Increasingly, human rights frameworks and global and regional institutions continue to reshape our understanding of international politics and the challenges facing international society in the 21st century.

1 Historical Background

Since the onset of the 21st century, an emerging literature has engaged with historical accounts of the origins and development of human rights. Some (Lauren, 2003; Ishay, 2008) have attempted to trace the idea back to antiquity. Others (Hunt, 2008; Moyn, 2010) start much later. Some suspect that such a search for origins is futile: the best one can hope to find are numerous genealogical roots of contemporary human rights norms and institutions or the numerous logical spaces within which today's 'overlapping consensus' about human rights was able to emerge from a variety of traditions and histories.

Nevertheless, these recent meta-histories tend to focus on the emergence of human rights as part and parcel of the historical universality of political struggle, rooted in timeless disputes about the nature of justice. Some reject arguments that conclude that no history of truly *human* rights can extend much further back than the Enlightenment and its notion of natural law, which posits that, by nature, rights *inhere* in individuals by virtue of their naturally endowed reason, rather than as a result of social ascription, group membership, or divine donation.

Most histories of human rights, however, tend to see the development of human rights ideas as part and parcel of the concomitant development of market economies, the modern state, the modernization of warfare, and the globalization of these trends and institutions. Thus, the first truly *international* human rights movement arose in the early 1800s, to abolish the slave trade. The rise of journalism and the mobilization of public opinion in the 1850s and 1860s led the Swiss businessman and social activist Henri Dunant to found the International Committee of the Red Cross in response to the inhumanity he witnessed on the battlefields of Solferino in 1859. His efforts led to the adoption of the first Geneva Convention, for the protection of wounded soldiers, in 1864.

These historical accounts focus on the development of humanitarian law and institutions through which states have agreed to certain limitations on their freedom of action, or have agreed on certain principles that are similar in form to contemporary human rights commitments. Therefore, one often sees reference made to the 'minorities clauses' that were included in each of the five peace treaties that ended the First World War, in which the successor states to the multiethnic Ottoman and Austro-Hungarian empires were obligated to protect the rights of their religious and linguistic minority populations. The origins of the protection of minority rights and liberties, however, can be traced back to the recognition of Serbia in 1878 (contingent upon the protection of religious liberty), the recognition of territories annexed by the Netherlands in 1814, and, indeed, the protection of certain forms of religious liberty as part of the overall Westphalian settlement of 1648. Therefore, in many respects, the genealogical roots of contemporary human rights ideas can be found at the beginnings of the contemporary nation-state system itself.

These more recent meta-histories notwithstanding, most of the literature uses the Second World War and the founding of the UN in 1945 as the logical starting point for discussing the development and evolution of contemporary international human rights norms and institutions. In the early days of the war, public officials and scholars alike had acknowledged that the global depression, violations of international legal and diplomatic obligations, and the rise of fascist and Nazi totalitarianism had led to the war, and that Allied war aims must be guided by a commitment to upholding certain moral principles. These begin with Franklin Roosevelt's early 1941 articulation of a postwar world order founded upon four 'fundamental freedoms' (freedom of speech, freedom of religion, freedom from want, and freedom from fear). Later that year, Roosevelt and British Prime Minister Winston Churchill met to formulate the Atlantic Charter, which pledged a postwar order based on self-determination, a free and open global economy, disarmament, and international cooperation in the pursuit of national, personal, economic, and social security. The 1942 'Declaration by United Nations' pledged those nations that joined the wartime alliance against the Axis to uphold the principles of the Atlantic Charter.

Some early drafts of the United Nations Charter included specific references to human rights. The first US State Department draft (1943) included a 'Bill of

Human Rights' as an annex to the Charter. While these provisions disappeared from the 1944 Dumbarton Oaks drafts, the efforts of many Latin American states and individual American non-governmental advocates at the San Francisco Conference in 1945 ensured they would be included in the final version of the United Nations Charter. As its Article 1 states quite unequivocally, international peace and cooperation is wholly dependent upon respect for and protection of human rights and fundamental freedoms 'for all.' The Charter created the Economic and Social Council, which immediately established the UN Commission on Human Rights in early 1946. The first task assigned to it was the drafting of an International Bill of Human Rights.

2   The Universal Declaration and the Covenants

The first part of the bill, the UDHR, was adopted without a single dissenting vote by the UN General Assembly on December 10, 1948. The Universal Declaration includes thirty articles, most of which enumerate specific civil, political, economic, and social rights—without drawing any sharp lines between these different categories of rights. Also included is the entitlement of everyone to a social and international order in which human rights can be fully realized (Article 28). This entitlement suggests that it is the obligation of the international community to continue to develop the standards and mechanisms for the protection and promotion of human rights.

While it was widely understood that the adoption of the Universal Declaration was a historic achievement, the document itself was not legally binding. The second and third parts of the International Bill of Rights were to outline specific duties of states and obligations for monitoring and enforcement. In early 1949, the Commission returned to its work on the original draft Covenant on Human Rights (first proposed in 1947), which at the time enumerated only civil rights. During the 1950 session of the Commission on Human Rights, some delegations raised the question of whether economic and social rights should be included in the covenant. Later that year, the UN General Assembly adopted a resolution instructing the Commission to include 'a clear expression' of economic and social rights.

The debate over this question led to a great deal of controversy over the nature of civil and political rights relative to economic and social rights, and the relationships between the two categories of rights in the covenant. While many scholars attributed these debates to the ideological rivalries of the Cold War, there was a much greater and deeper divide between the West and some (but not all) of the newly emerging states of the postcolonial world. After the

Commission had drafted and included economic and social rights in the covenant, the General Assembly was asked to reconsider its decision for one covenant with both sets of rights, due to the fact that there were distinct sets of state obligations and separate procedures for monitoring and implementation of the two sets of rights. After long and acrimonious debate, in early 1952 the General Assembly voted for separate covenants.

Owing to the rapid growth of UN membership in the 1950s and especially in the early 1960s, the place of the covenants on the General Assembly's social, cultural, and humanitarian agenda was quickly overshadowed with concerns over decolonization and racial discrimination, including the problem of apartheid. In December 1966, the General Assembly finally adopted the International Covenant on Economic, Social and Cultural Rights, and the International Covenant on Civil and Political Rights. Both treaties entered into force ten years later, in 1976.

3   Core International Instruments and Institutions

Following the work of former UN High Commissioner for Human Rights, Bertrand Ramcharan (2011), we can identify four key institutional human rights pillars within the UN system. All four pillars aim at greater protection and promotion of human rights: securing justice against those responsible for crimes under international human rights and humanitarian law, collecting data and investigating human rights issues, supporting the work of a variety of UN and other international agencies and offices, and assisting member states in capacity- and institution-building at the national and local levels.

The first pillar is constituted by the major human rights treaties, their reporting procedures, and their monitoring committees, all of which place legal obligations and duties upon member states. The first of these core instruments to be adopted by the UN was the Convention on Racial Discrimination (CERD) in 1965. The International Covenants on Economic, Social and Cultural Rights, and on Civil and Political Rights, were adopted in 1966. Subsequent treaties include the Convention on the Elimination of All Forms of Discrimination Against Women (CEDAW, 1979), the UN Convention Against Torture (UNCAT, 1984), the Convention on the Rights of the Child (CRC, 1984), the International Convention on the Protection of the Rights of All Migrant Workers and Members of their Families (ICRMW, 1990), the Convention for the Protection of All Persons from Enforced Disappearance (CPED, 2006), and the Convention on the Rights of Persons with Disabilities (CRPD, 2006). In 2017, the average ratification rate of these instruments (excluding the ICRMW and

CPED) is 175 states-parties each—nearly 90 percent. Each of these treaty regimes includes a list of enumerated rights, limitations, and general or specific state duties and obligations. Each establishes a system of periodic reporting by states-parties and establishes a committee of independent experts to review these reports. Most of the core instruments also include procedures for handling state-to-state complaints, although these have never been used. Most of the core instruments—either in the convention itself or as part of an optional protocol—also allow the monitoring committees to receive individual or group complaints against states-parties and give committees limited powers of investigation.

The second pillar consists of the Charter-based organs: the UN General Assembly, the Security Council, the Human Rights Council (which replaced the Commission on Human Rights in 2006), the Office of the High Commissioner for Human Rights, and the Office of the Secretary-General of the UN. The Office of the High Commissioner and the Human Rights Council are the most important of these institutions, insofar as they set international standards (through the drafting of legal instruments), oversee the special procedures, and carry out the ever-ongoing Universal Periodic Review (UPR) of UN member states' human rights records. The UPR, which in early 2020 is in its third round, is significant in terms of its universal scope (all members must submit to the process) and interactive process of review between member states.

The system of special procedures created by the Commission and continued by the Human Rights Council comprises the third pillar of human rights at the UN. Special procedure mandate holders (dubbed 'special rapporteurs' or 'independent experts') are empowered to investigate and publish information about gross and systematic human rights violations within specific countries or regions. Other mandates focus on specific human rights problems (such as violence against women or forced disappearances) in broad comparative perspectives. This pillar serves a vital function to the credibility of the UN as a watchdog for protecting human rights.

The fourth pillar comprises ad hoc criminal tribunals established by the Security Council (for Yugoslavia in 1991 and for Rwanda in 1994), special courts and tribunals established by the UN (e.g., for Sierra Leone in 2002 and Cambodia in 2003), and the International Criminal Court (ICC), which was established by the Rome Statute in 2002. The establishment of the ICC was meant to replace the ad hoc arrangements represented by the International Criminal Tribunal for the Former Yugoslavia (ICTY) and the International Criminal Tribunal for Rwanda (ICTR), and to settle the jurisdictional boundaries of international humanitarian criminal law, the mandate of the court, and its procedures. The Special Court for Sierra Leone, the Special Court for Lebanon, and the Extraordinary Chambers in the Courts of Cambodia are cases in which the UN is working in partnership with the governments in question to assist in the indictment and trial of those accused of grave violations of international humanitarian law—in the case of Cambodia, for the genocide carried out under the Khmer Rouge government in the late 1970s.

4 Evolution of Human Rights Standards and Law

In addition to these core instruments, there are a number of other conventions, declarations, programs of action, and statements of principle covering a wide array of specific human rights concerns or focusing on discrete vulnerable populations. While UN Declarations—such as the Declaration on the Right to Development (1986) and the Declaration on the Rights of Indigenous Peoples (2007)—do not have the binding force of treaty law,[2] they are nevertheless important normative signposts in the development of human rights norms and institutions, demonstrating the ways in which the international community continues to acknowledge how an increasingly globalized world creates new vulnerabilities.

In the years since 1948, the concept of human rights and the institutionalization of the human rights norms have grown and evolved in many ways. We can identify four major shifts here. The first is the expansion of human rights instruments to address the unique vulnerabilities of specific populations—for example, racial minorities, women, children, migrant workers, and the disabled. While more widespread recognition of the needs of vulnerable populations, and the role that human rights can play in protecting them, is welcomed by many observers, others see in this an unnecessary proliferation of human rights instruments. This, they argue, has the effective of diluting the normative value of core human rights. Particularly controversial in this respect are new rights that are not about specific populations but are third- and fourth-generation 'solidarity' rights, such as the right to self-determination (which is enumerated as a human right in both covenants, yet evades efforts to pin down precise duties and obligations), the right to development, the right of peoples to peace, and any number of so-called group rights.

Concomitant with the first trend is the growth in the robustness of human rights institutions at the national, regional, and international levels. The

---

[2] The UN has just recently begun the process of drafting a Convention on the Right to Development, which would be legally binding on those states that ratify it.

committees that monitor the core human rights treaties already mentioned now have several decades' worth of jurisprudential activity from which to further elaborate the content and reach of human rights. Human rights norms are further embedded by overlapping institutions at the international and regional levels, with systems of monitoring under the Council of Europe (COE), the Organization of American States, and the African Union (less robust regional arrangements are found in Southeast Asia and the Middle East). Of these, Europe has the most comprehensive system of protection, wherein all forty-seven member states of the COE have accepted the jurisdiction of the European Court of Human Rights, whose decisions are binding.

The third development is the diffusion of human rights stakeholders. In the early days, human rights were the province only of governments, civil servants, and a few international lawyers. Since the 1970s, and especially after the end of the Cold War and the watershed Vienna Conference on Human Rights in 1993, the number of non-governmental organizations (NGOs) and other advocacy organizations working in the area of human rights has exploded. These organizations with transnational reach (such as Human Rights Watch and Amnesty International) have fostered crucial networks with local advocates—networks that have contributed to greater internalization of human rights norms at the national level. In the academy, human rights have become a subject of inquiry in departments of anthropology, sociology, and economics, adding to traditional interests in human rights from departments of political science and international relations and schools of law.

All three of these developments point to the fourth: the simultaneous broadening and deepening of human rights discourses and practices in international politics. Most observers would contend that human rights norms are now fairly embedded in the practices of international society, such that no government actively rejects the idea of human rights outright. While the expansion of human rights norms and institutions may continue apace, however, we are constantly reminded of the great divides that continue to persist between the norms and people's actual enjoyment of their rights and freedoms.

5   Human Rights and Sovereignty

That the protection and promotion of human rights is now a central concern of the international community is significant in two major and interrelated ways. The first is that individuals and their rights have become subjects of international law. Second, the philosophy, ethics, and law of human rights have significantly influenced the meanings and practices of sovereignty itself, which is, of course, one of the central organizing principles of international law. Within international relations scholarship, there are three broad schools of thought about the impact that human rights have had on the institution of sovereignty.

For realists, adherence to human rights law supposes a loss of sovereignty on the part of states. Because traditional realism views sovereignty in zero-sum terms—that states would never voluntarily agree to allow external actors, such as other states or the UN, to make judgments about their activities, or give them the power to enforce sanctions against them—then human rights 'law' is 'soft,' more akin to goals and values than solid, enforceable promises. A less strident form of realism might agree that while states-parties to a variety of regional or international institutions may allow themselves to be bound to certain commitments and requirements, these are substantively weak provisions (that is, that states are obligated to submit periodic reports to a monitoring body) which do not erode sovereignty in any meaningful way.

The second broad strand of thinking about this question comes from the liberal-institutional perspective. In this view, states have indeed ceded some portion of their sovereignty (meaning absolute freedom of action) to international or regional institutions, but because they have chosen to commit themselves to a common course of action that may yield larger benefits in other areas of international affairs, the trade-offs are worth whatever loss of sovereignty they incur. Another, related liberal-institutional argument (or, perhaps, an international-society approach) would posit that participating in human rights institutions is part and parcel of a broader commitment to acting in international society. Participation becomes an expectation of membership in that society, and over time, norms surrounding human rights become embedded in state behaviors and practices. In other words, while states at first may have been reluctant to join institutions, they intentionally designed those institutions to have fairly weak norms and levels of commitment. As membership has grown, so has the potential for more robust institutional designs and expectations.

Whereas, for many decades, debates among scholars about the relationship between sovereignty and human rights fell along this broad realist/liberal-institutionalist divide, recently, constructivist approaches have sought to accommodate both views by exploring the ways in which the rise of human rights and placement of individual security and well-being actually constitute sovereignty itself. For the constructivist, the 'ideal' type of sovereignty, such as the Weberian modern bureaucratic state with a monopoly on the use of force, has never really existed. Accordingly, the idea that human rights have somehow 'eroded' the 'hard shell' of state sovereignty is not nearly as useful a theoretical model as the idea that by the mid-20th century, in the aftermath of the horrors of two world wars and a global economic depression, sovereignty was redefined to make space for human rights.

This reading of sovereignty sits at the core of the recently emergent notion of the 'responsibility to protect' (ICISS, 2001). It posits that when states claim sovereignty, they are claiming a domain of exclusivity and freedom of action—sovereignty accords rights of non-interference from other states. The legitimacy of these rights, however, is *contingent* upon the fulfillment of certain responsibilities and duties. That some of these responsibilities are to other states—such as prohibitions against aggressive war—is well understood. The 'responsibility to protect' (R2P) adds to that the duties upon governments to protect the rights of those living under their jurisdiction. When a state cannot (because of lack of capacity) or will not (active refusal) protect the rights and welfare of its citizens, the R2P people falls elsewhere—to other states or to the international community as a whole.

While this notion of 'sovereignty as responsibility' is fairly recent, it is a powerful reading of the significance that the emergence of human rights norms, institutions, and law have had on the very meanings and practices of sovereignty. It is significant that the 2011 UN-authorized intervention in Libya specifically cited the norm as conferring significant legitimacy upon the Security Council authorization. On the other hand, charges by major powers such as China and Russia that the R2P norm was invoked as a thin veil for 'regime change' quickly hobbled the Security Council during the ongoing crisis in Syria, where the same norm has repeatedly been rejected by Russian and Chinese vetoes.

6   Assessment and the Future

The human rights record of the first decade and a half of the 21st century has been decidedly mixed. In many countries, the human rights progress of the 1980s and 1990s was maintained or even extended. This has been especially striking in Latin America. In sub-Saharan Africa as well, steady if limited and often fitful progress has been most typical, although the Congo, Sudan, and Somalia continue to suffer under decades-long humanitarian crises, and new crises have emerged in Mali, Nigeria, and the Central African Republic. Elsewhere, however, efforts to improve human rights conditions, such as the various 'color revolutions' in the 2000s (Georgia, Ukraine, Iran) either failed or were ultimately reversed. Although the Arab Spring popular uprisings of 2011 resulted in the removal of long-entrenched dictators in Tunisia, Egypt, and Libya, human rights conditions in these countries (and across the Arab world more generally) remain discouraging—and Syria has descended into barbarous war waged by the Assad government against the bulk of its population.

The 'global war on terror' initiated in the aftermath of the September 11, 2001, terrorist attacks against the United States led many to fear that human rights would once again be pushed into the background in international politics, as had occurred during the Cold War. The reality has been much more complex. In a few instances, rights-abusive regimes (e.g., Pakistan) have been able to parlay anti-terrorism into protection from international human rights pressures. In others, such as the Philippines and Russia, anti-terrorism has added to existing rights-abusive practices. In many liberal democracies, some human rights have been subjected to limited infringements. And US abuses of (often illegally held) prisoners in Iraq, Afghanistan, and Guantánamo, as well as the kidnapping and international transport (extraordinary rendition) of suspects, provoked widespread national and international criticism. But there has not been the same kind of systemic negative impact as was seen in the Cold War. International human rights policies in general seem about as robust as at the turn of the millennium, and, at worst, the war on terror has produced only a modest downturn in global respect for some civil and political rights.

Globalization poses a much more serious new challenge to human rights—and is the most significant factor that has led to the rise of a illiberal, populist backlashes in states as diverse as Poland, Hungary, the Philippines, Brazil, Italy, the United States, and the United Kingdom. States are the central mechanism for implementing and enforcing internationally recognized human rights. Even if the threat to states posed by globalization is exaggerated, the relative capabilities of states are declining, especially when it comes to being able to extract revenues to support social welfare programs that realize economic and social rights. No alternative source of provision, however, seems to be emerging to fill the resulting gap. Global markets are likely to be a much greater threat to human rights in the coming decades than either terrorists or the war against them.

Thus, while we have seen the development of an extensive and substantively admirable body of international human rights law, it is not matched by comparably strong international implementation procedures. States have largely reserved for themselves the right to interpret the meaning of their international human rights obligations and to implement them in their own territories. While it is true that international human rights norms have been fully internationalized, the implementation of those obligations remains almost entirely national.

There is, of course, an immense amount of national and international human rights advocacy. States, international organizations, NGOs, and private individuals promote human rights every day in every country of the world. Their efforts, however, are focused ultimately on states, which still hold not only the duty but also the right to implement human rights in their own territories.

The shortcomings of this system of national implementation of international human rights has been the focus of a great deal of attention recently, with a variety of pessimistic appraisals and assessments emerging from many quarters (see, e.g., Hafner Burton, 2013; Hopgood, 2013; Posner, 2014; Moyn, 2018). This has spurred a number of sober yet optimistic counterpoints (Sikkink, 2017; Brysk, 2018; Howard-Hassmann, 2018). A recent exchange in the pages of the *Journal of Human Rights Practice* was precipitated by a clear-eyed stocktaking of the 'populist challenge' to human rights by renowned UN human rights expert Philip Alston (2017a, 2017b; see also Dudai, 2017; Nagaraj, 2017). Clearly, there are significant challenges facing the international human rights system of protection, and ongoing economic, political, and social pressures continue to expose the many shortcomings of that system—as well as the protection of human rights by states themselves.

However, it remains my view that these challenges do not diminish the significant independent contribution of international human rights norms, law, and institutions to the well-being of humanity. International human rights law has been so widely endorsed because its normative force is seemingly inescapable in the contemporary world. Even states like North Korea and Belarus, which have never given any serious attention to implementing internationally recognized human rights, are parties to at least some core human rights treaties. And even cynical endorsements of these norms are of real practical significance for national and international human rights advocates.

Without an internationally agreed-upon understanding of what constitutes the core of human rights, national human rights advocates would be subject to charges of political or cultural bias, inauthenticity, and even treason. But when repressive governments today level such charges at their critics, those critics can reply that all they are doing is advocating rights that the government itself has repeatedly endorsed, including by accepting binding international legal obligations. This decisively shifts the burden of persuasion from the advocates of human rights to the governments that are violating those rights. Of course, might regularly triumphs over right, especially in the short run. But national human rights advocates are supported by international human rights norms. This makes a real practical difference in all but the most closed and repressive countries. And in countries with even merely not-too-bad human rights records, these protections are of immense day-to-day value to advocates and activists.

Similarly, when transnational human rights NGOs, foreign states, and regional and international organizations raise concerns about a state's human rights record, those states cannot credibly respond that it is none of their business. *All* states in the contemporary world have accepted that human rights are a legitimate subject of international politics, much as they hate to have their shortcomings brought to the attention of national and international audiences. And all states have agreed that the UDHR and the International Human Rights Covenants provide an authoritative set of international human rights norms. All member states of the UN are compelled to have their records examined through the UPR. And there is a widespread consensus among states that, at the most basic level, sovereignty cannot be invoked as a shield against criticism for the most serious of human rights violations: sovereignty is *conditional* rather than *absolute*.

International human rights law has taken off the table debates over whether human rights are real and what belongs on a list of human rights. The scarce resources of human rights advocates thus can be focused on the real work of implementing internationally recognized human rights. Thus, for all its shortcomings, the body of international human rights law rooted in the UDHR has both armed human rights advocates and disarmed their opponents, at least normatively. This fundamental redefinition of the terms of national and international political legitimacy is the principal legacy of the global human rights regime.

References

Alston, P. 2017a. 'The Populist Challenge to Human Rights.' *Journal of Human Rights Practice* 9 (1): 1–15.

Alston, P. 2017b. 'Reply to Dudai and Nagaraj.' *Journal of Human Rights Practice* 9 (1): 25–28.

Brysk, A. 2018. *The Future of Human Rights*. Medford, MA: Polity Press.

Cardenas, S. 2017. 'Human Rights and the State.' *Oxford Research Encyclopedia of International Studies*, https://oxfordre.com/internationalstudies/view/10.1093/acrefore/9780190846626.001.0001/acrefore-9780190846626-e-52.

Dudai, R. 2017. 'Human Right in the Populist Era: Mourn then (Re)Organize.' *Journal of Human Rights Practice* 9 (1): 16–21.

Donnelly, J. and D. J. Whelan. 2017. *International Human Rights*, 5th ed. New York: Routledge.

Hafner-Burton, E. 2013. *Making Human Rights a Reality*. Princeton, NJ: Princeton University Press.

Hopgood, S. 2013. *The Endtimes of Human Rights*. Ithaca, NY: Cornell University Press.

Howard-Hassmann, R. E. 2018. *In Defense of Universal Human Rights*. Medford, MA: Polity Press.

Hunt, L. 2008. *Inventing Human Rights: A History*. New York: W.W. Norton.

ICISS (International Commission on Intervention and State Sovereignty). 2001. T*he Responsibility to Protect*. Ottawa: ICISS.

Ishay, M. R. 2008. *The History of Human Rights: From Ancient Times to the Globalization Era*. Berkeley: University of California Press.

Lauren, P. G. 2003. *Evolution of International Human Rights: Visions Seen*, 2nd ed. Philadelphia: University of Pennsylvania Press.

Moyn, S. 2010. *The Last Utopia: Human Rights in History*. Cambridge, MA: Harvard University Press.

Moyn, S. 2018. *Not Enough: Human Rights in an Unequal World*. Cambridge MA: Belknap/Harvard University Press.

Nagaraj, V. K. 2017. 'Human Rights and Populism: Some More Questions in Response to Philip Alston.' *Journal of Human Rights Practice* 9: 22–24.

Posner, E. 2014. *The Twilight of Human Rights Law*. New York: Oxford University Press.

Ramcharan, B. 2011. *The UN Human Rights Council*. New York: Routledge.

Sikkink, K. 2017. *Evidence for Hope: Making Human Rights Work in the 21st Century*. Princeton, NJ: Princeton University Press.

Whelan, D. J. 2010. *Indivisible Human Rights: A History*. Philadelphia: University of Pennsylvania Press.

Whelan, D. J. 2012. 'Human Rights.' In *The Oxford Companion to International Relations*. Oxford: Oxford University Press.

CHAPTER 11

Cosmopolitan Democracy

Daniele Archibugi

1   Introduction*

Cosmopolitan democracy is a project of normative political theory that attempts to apply the core principles, values, and procedures of democracy to global politics. Born in the aftermath of the fall of the Berlin Wall (Archibugi and Held, 1995; Archibugi, Held, and Koehler, 1998), it was developed by scholars who had already worked on democratic theory and practices, such as David Held (1995), thinkers that actively participated in the East–West dialogue in the 1980s, such as Mary Kaldor (1999) and myself (Archibugi, 2008), and human rights and anti-war legal theorists such as Richard Falk (1995). From the very beginning, cosmopolitan democracy was not an intellectual exercise only, but an attempt to link theoretical arguments to social and political activism.

Cosmopolitan democracy has been an effort to reform the current international organizations and create new ones, with the aim of expanding practices of democratic systems such as:
- transparency in decision-making;
- accountability of decision-makers;
- involvement of citizens and non-governmental bodies in world politics;
- political equality across individuals of different political communities;
- implementation of the rule of law in international affairs; and
- enforcement of human rights.

This is a very ambitious program, based on the hope that some of the conquests that democratic practice has achieved within nations could also be capitalized in world politics. Besides envisaging reformed and renewed international organizations, cosmopolitan democracy is also an attempt to review the standard practice of democracy within states. It aims to empower citizens to self-government, creating new forms of participation for trans-border polities, minority groups, and epistemic communities. The guiding

---

* I wish to thank Ali Emre Benli, Nicole Bogott, Marco Cellini, Stefano Degli Uberti, and the editors for their comments on a previous version.

principle is that all those affected by decision-making should be consulted and involved.

The next section, 'Cosmopolitanism and international integration,' discusses the feasibility of the cosmopolitan project in the current political landscape when nationalistic feelings are on the rise. The subsequent one presents the genealogy of cosmopolitan democracy, followed by a discussion on the content of cosmopolitan democracy for global politics. Finally, the ways in which cosmopolitan democracy could reinvigorate democracy at the local and national level are also explored.

2   Cosmopolitanism and International Integration

The cosmopolitan ideal is so old, and so unaccomplished, that it cannot be assessed against contingent political events. But precisely because cosmopolitanism has such a long history (Fine, 2007; Brown and Held, 2010) it is worth admitting that, at the dawn of the 21st century, its enemies appear stronger than ever. Xenophobic and racist parties are increasing their consensus in almost all European countries and also outside Europe. The most palpable enemy of cosmopolitanism—namely nationalism—is becoming more and more powerful.

It is true that several of the cosmopolitan aspirations have never been fulfilled and often not even addressed in the dominant political setting. But the Second World War clearly indicated that nationalism could easily lead to violence, war, and catastrophes. The winners of the war partially tried to prevent future scourges increasing international integration, and this led to several treaties and covenants. The creation of the United Nations (UN) and the making and reinforcement of many other international organizations were the most visible outcomes of this. International integration, especially when carried out through intergovernmental consensus, is not necessarily a synonym of cosmopolitanism, but in principle it paves the way to more advanced forms of amalgamation that do not limit themselves to governmental diplomacy but also allow citizens to become active players of a global community.

The first four decades of the post-Second World War period were not those of institutional cosmopolitanism, but rather made up the age of the Cold War. The overall international organization was functional enough to regulate the East–West rivalry, sometimes successfully, sometimes unsuccessfully. Inside each of the blocs there were strong nationalistic feelings but, at the same time, both of them had also an international aim, in the form of 'Third World emancipation' in the Soviet bloc and 'political and economic liberalism' on the Western side. In a planet dominated not by sovereign nations, but by militarily opposed alliances, many of these international aims were contained and repressed. When the Cold War ended, there were strong hopes that the decent internationalist spirit of each bloc could prevail and lead to a new era of world politics. A season genuinely inspired by cosmopolitanism was advocated, leading to the hope that bottom-up ventures could flourish and change standard intergovernmental rules in Europe (Kaldor, 1991) and in throughout the world (Falk, 1993).

Since the 1990s, proposals for disarmament, new human rights regimes, economic cooperation, monetary unions, and world parliaments have flourished. Many of these proposals originated through grassroots movements and civil society organizations, which genuinely hoped to be finally heard by statesmen. In many occasions, new social groups attempted to directly take care of their destiny by producing and delivering public goods and services. Policy-makers, policy advisers, and pundits also attempted to expand some of the values and norms of democracy globally, including rule of law, transparency and accountability of public decisions, equality among citizens, and majority rule. Cosmopolitan democracy is one of several ideas that blossomed in this season (Archibugi and Held, 1995). Unfortunately, a fundamental historical occasion was lost and not much has been achieved to reform the world order. However, we should not to forget that the post-1989 era also led to fundamental changes in world affairs.

International trade, foreign direct investment, migration, and tourism, to name just a few areas for which quantitative indicators are available, have steadily grown, and not even the 2008 economic crisis has managed to dramatically revert these long-term trends, clearly indicating that 'globalization' really has become a core trend of our epoch. States have tried to match economic and social globalization by increasing their cooperation and international organizations have become bigger and more influential. The European Union (EU) expanded to the East, and several European countries gave up their monetary sovereignty, creating the euro, the most important post-national currency. Other regional organizations started to flourish in Asia, Latin America, North America, and Africa. Trade began to be regulated by international organizations such as the newly created World Trade Organization (WTO). International crimes, that had been for long been left unpursued, began to be investigated and prosecuted by a new generation of international tribunals, including the International Criminal Court (ICC). In other words, some steps were taken, and even if highly insufficient, there were at least some attempts to match, through public international cooperation, the pace of financial, economic, and social globalization.

But if we look at the years since the beginning of the economic crisis, it seems that a U-turn has occurred in world politics. Brexit, the outcome of almost all referendums on the EU, the election of a nationalistic president in the United States, the US withdrawal from the Paris Agreement on Climate Change, the rise to government of anti-European political forces in so many countries, do indicate that something is changing. Has the triumphal march of economic and social globalization come to a halt today? International commitments are no longer increasing: they are either in a steady state or even reducing. Some commentators have even wondered if this is the end of the liberal international order (Ikenberry, 2018). To find an historical analogy we need to go back many decades, namely to the dark 1930s, when Germany withdrew from the League of Nations in 1933 and Soviet Union was expelled in 1939. These cases sadly remind us that when international cooperation is reversed, it can lead to tragedy and devastation.

Hopefully, the current season of global disintegration will be short and will not lead to the disasters experienced in the past. The trends toward social, economic, and cultural globalization are strong and it is unlikely that they can be reversed by political decisions. Nonetheless, we have to take the current nationalistic reaction as a serious signal and understand its origin: globalization has distributed its fruits very unevenly with a few winners and too many losers (Milanovic, 2016).[1] This has generated resentments that have already exploded in anti-politics. Nationalistic or even xenophobic sentiments are often the wrong reactions toward issues that have not been properly addressed by dominant political powers. Too many people felt lost in a global arena which gave no hope of also becoming a global society.

For this reason, it is crucial to clearly outline the basic difference between *globalization*, led by uncontrolled social and economic forces, and *cosmopolitanism*, which implies the active civic participation of individuals in world politics. Globalization has too often not respected local heritages, the working of local businesses, the well-being of specific communities, leading to brutal reorganizations of economic and social life which were no longer controlled by citizens. The underdogs were left without a voice: they could lose their jobs or see their communities depopulated without even knowing to whom to address their protests. Cosmopolitanism, on the contrary, is an attempt to empower individuals, including in global affairs, allowing them to participate in choices affecting their lives and preventing them being passively affected by decisions taken elsewhere (Beck, 2006; Cicchelli and Octobre, 2018). Cosmopolitan

---

[1] See Chapter 9 in this volume.

democracy, in particular, has, since the beginning, been an attempt to specify the forms according to which citizens can effectively participate in world politics. In the new international landscape, cosmopolitan democracy can hopefully be an intellectual impetus to resist the current nationalistic drift, suggesting forms of accountable global governance on the one hand, and inclusive methods of domestic political participation on the other.

3 The Origin and Sources of Cosmopolitan Democracy

Cosmopolitan democracy is a revival and development of ancient peace projects. In particular, it is an attempt to refine and apply to the current political landscape some of the insights of institutional pacifism. An international system dominated by wars and/or by the fear of war is often the best way of allowing tyranny within nations. External threats are traditionally used by authoritarian states to justify repression, human rights violations, and lack of accountability. A peaceful international system is often the ideal environment to expand participation, enforce human rights, and keep rulers accountable.

Peace can be achieved through a variety of methods and one of them is strengthening international norms, covenants, and organizations. Several peace projects of the past, including those of William Penn, the Abbé of Saint-Pierre, Jeremy Bentham, Immanuel Kant, and Claude-Henri de Saint-Simon, already envisaged international organizations able to manage conflicts through peaceful means rather than through war. This body of thought had a crucial role in the creation of modern international organizations, including the League of Nations, the UN, and the EU. Developing this noble tradition, cosmopolitan democracy has also tried to explore how existing international organizations could increase their powers and to create new ones in areas where they are needed.

To become more authoritative vis-à-vis demanding public opinion, international organizations should try to apply several principles, values, and procedures of democracy. Rule of law, transparency, accountability, and participation should be the guiding principles of reformed international organizations. These, in turn, require that international organizations should be more than just intergovernmental associations, giving voice and political representation also to other players of each political community. So far, international organizations have been mostly intergovernmental and they have not managed to satisfactorily guarantee participation to minorities, opposition political parties, trade unions, or non-governmental organizations (NGOs).

Cosmopolitan democracy does not aim to substitute existing states with a world political power. It is therefore different from several world federalist projects, even if it has acquired considerable inputs from this virtuous tradition (Marchetti, 2008). Rather than being an attempt to concentrate force in a single source, it aims to subjugate coercive powers by developing more advanced constitutional rules.

But there is also an internal component of cosmopolitan democracy that needs to be further developed: each modern political community is heterogeneous and has to accommodate individuals with different values, heritage, faith, and language. Through migrations, tourism, and business exchanges, our political communities have become more and more diverse, and often this is an asset, increasing well-being and enriching cultures. Nonetheless, most states have not yet been able to respond positively to these historical transformations. Cosmopolitan democracy is therefore also an attempt to develop national democratic systems with the aim of minimizing political exclusion and increasing participation.

4 The Global Dimension of Cosmopolitan Democracy

Since the 1990s, democratic regimes have spread across the East and the South. For the first time in history, elected governments administer the majority of the world's population (Marshall and Elzinga-Marshall, 2017). Although not all of these regimes are equally respectful of basic human rights, there is significant pressure to achieve representative, accountable, and lawful administration. Democracy has become, both in theory and in practice, the principal source of legitimate authority and power. Why then have democratic forces not seriously tried to reach a process of democratization in international institutions?

Cosmopolitan democracy is based on the empirical observation that, while states are legally sovereign, they are in practice non-autonomous. Environmental threats, contagious diseases, trade, terrorism, and migration make it more and more difficult for states to be truly independent (Held, 1995). Each political community has to cope with phenomena that take place outside its territorial jurisdiction and for which it has no direct accountability and control (for a discussion, see Koenig-Archibugi, 2018). In these circumstances, it is becoming increasingly difficult to preserve meaningful democratic decision-making within states. If the democratic principle of involvement and equality of all members affected by decision-making is to be preserved, the participation of individual states in world politics needs to be reconsidered.

It is certainly true that the contemporary world is composed of highly heterogeneous regimes. In spite of the democratic wave of the last quarter of a century, too many nations are still under authoritarian governments. Moreover, the quality of democracy is very different across nations as diverse as, say, Sweden and Mongolia (for an attempt to identify democratic regimes and their quality, see Morlino, 2012). Democratic regimes could be unwilling to create political bonds with countries that have authoritarian rule or that have rather rudimentary democratic institutions. Even in the case of the EU, composed by nations that already satisfy a threshold of democratic level, it is often difficult to engage in greater integration because of internal differences in political practices. These objective difficulties should generate fresh energies able to improve the practices of internal regimes as well as the procedures of international organizations, with the explicit aim to increase the quantity of democratic nations *and* the quality of democracy within each state. This, in turn, could be a key factor in increasing the responsiveness of international organizations to the problems of its members.

For many years, it has been assumed (both explicitly and, more often, implicitly) that liberal and democratic states are less likely to commit international crimes or to become involved in aggressive wars. Many of those that consider liberal democracy a desirable internal regime also implied that they were honorable members of the international community. Cosmopolitan democracy challenges the view that the foreign policy of democratic states is more virtuous than that of non-democratic states. Even the most democratic states can be aggressive, selfish, and prepared to defend their vital interests by any means. History provides evidence that many aggressive wars have been perpetuated by democratic regimes.

The hypothesis according to which 'democracies do not fight each other' (the so-called democratic peace) is widely debated in international relations (Russett, 1993). According to this hypothesis, even if democracies are often war-prone, there have never been wars among consolidated democracies. Not everybody agrees with this fact, but those that do agree also claim that if all states of the world were democratic, war may disappear. The normative implication is that to achieve the goal of peace it is necessary to promote muscularly internal democratization. Some policy-makers, such as George W. Bush, misunderstood the implications of this hypothesis and went so far to wage war against despotic regimes with the aim of forcing a regime change and inducing these countries to become democratic.

Cosmopolitan democracy has an opposite view: although it shares the desire to increase both the quantity of democratic states and the quality of their democratic procedures, it does not assume that the goal of peace can be achieved through regime change obtained by military invasions. Moreover, it argues that 'exporting' democracy through war is contradicting the very nature of the democratic process, since this has to be built from below and not from above. For these reasons, cosmopolitan democracy suggests that an international system based on cooperation and dialogue is a fundamental condition to foster democratic progress inside individual countries and also to allow peoples living under dictatorships to endogenously change their own regime. Strong democracies are the outcome of bottom-up impetus, not of top-down imposition. While the 'peace among democracies' hypothesis tends to stress the causal link from internal democracy → to international peace, cosmopolitan democracy points out at an equally important link: from international peace and cooperation → to internal democracy (Archibugi and Cellini, 2017).

A more active and participative international organization can, in fact, have a fundamental effect in helping individual nations to move toward democratic regimes and in consolidating existing ones. The case of the EU is certainly instructive: it managed to facilitate democratic transition in Southern Europe in the 1980s and in Eastern Europe in the 1990s. In both occasions, it gave to new and young democratic nations the same rights and dignity as established member states. It can be argued that Western European countries used their overwhelming economic power to force the Eastern nations to replicate their political and also social and economic model (Ingram, 2013), and this may even explain why today some Eastern Europeans are distancing themselves from the standard EU doctrine. Nevertheless, the EU played a vital role of supporting and nurturing already existing endogenous democratic forces both in the South and in the East.

Can similar strategies be attempted also in other continents, and be empowered by the UN and other regional organizations? This depends very much on the incentives that the most powerful and affluent members of these international organizations, in particular Western democracies, can offer to foster democratic transition and consolidation. If democratic nations are really willing to extend democratic regimes worldwide, they should increase the resources devoted to cooperation and integration policies. This, in turn, will facilitate releasing the internal energies which are so often repressed by authoritarian regimes.

There have been authoritative attempts to apply democracy also to the international arena, including those of two secretary-generals of the UN (Boutros-Ghali, 1996; Annan, 2002) and a director-general of the WTO (Lamy, 2005). Unfortunately, these suggestions have not been implemented. As a consequence, international organizations continue to represent mostly governments, and core issues concerning war and security are still in the hands of national governments that, as in the past, can take decisions autonomously.

Cosmopolitan democracy is therefore concerned with democratizing international organizations. In particular, it actively participates to campaign for the creation of a parliamentary assembly within the UN (Leinen and Bummel, 2018), to limit the veto power within the UN Security Council, to enlarge the jurisdiction of the ICC (Archibugi and Pease, 2018), to strengthen the power and functions of judicial institutions such as the International Court of Justice, and to strengthen the international human rights regime (Cabrera, 2010; for an analysis of several international organizations, see Levi, Finizio, and Vallinoto, 2014).

5 Democratic Practice in a Globalizing Planet

The scope of cosmopolitan democracy is not limited to the realm of international relations. Each political community has to deal with a certain degree of heterogeneity: this applies to multi-language or multi-faith communities, to areas riven by conflicts and civil wars, to self-determination claims. Democratic theory and practice has tried to address these problems for many years (Held, 2006). In particular, to activate the procedures of democracy, each political community needs to predefine its members and, in most cases, also its boundaries: Which citizens are entitled to participate to decision-making and who could be appointed as decision-makers? But when we have 'overlapping communities of fate' (Held, 1995: 225) rigid constituencies might be the wrong answer.

Democracy has progressively increased the number of participants: from the restricted community of male citizens of the Athenian polis[2] to contemporary universal suffrage. But even universal suffrage is limited to those living inside an established community. The outcome has led to painful exclusions (such as those of migrants) and arbitrary definitions of borders and boundaries. These exclusions are often highly controversial and might even transform a sophisticated democratic polity into a xenophobic community (Mann, 2005). Democracies still have to learn how to deal with those perceived by a large part of the population as outsiders: migrants, ethnic minorities, indigenous populations, or refugees. This is a conundrum that has accompanied democratic theory and

---

2   It is well known that in Athens ancient democracy many residents were not considered citizens, including women, slaves, and foreigners, making the total share of citizens to not more than a quarter of the total resident population. See Jones (1958).

practice since its inception: on the one hand, there is the assumption that some core democratic creeds—such as participation, equality, and accountability—work better in culturally and linguistically homogeneous communities. On the other hand, the democratic principle according to which all those affected by decision-making should not just be rule-takers but also rule-makers, implies that the boundaries of the political community need to be continuously reassessed. For example, if a state decides to locate a hazardous nuclear power plant close to its borders with other states, should the neighboring citizens be consulted? Which form of consultation should be undertaken? There is therefore an implicit tension between the *kratos* of the *demos* on the one hand, and the *polis* of the *cosmos* on the other. Can this tension be reconciled?

States have, so far, been the main institutions called upon to assess how political communities should be defined and limited. It is a fact that, so far, democracy has managed to flourish within states: we do not (yet?) have examples of sophisticated democratic systems working outside clearly defined states. In order to achieve self-government, states have also promoted a certain 'homogeneity' within the community, reinforcing common identity, language, values, shared history, and tradition. Democratic states have done something more, namely attempted to guarantee that all their citizens, including minorities, enjoy equal political and civil rights.

But to be able to respond adequately to the challenges of increasing multicultural and interdependent communities, some basic principles of democratic practice and organization should be revisited. Until now democracy has been developed in relation to territorially delimited communities. In this situation, an individual belongs to community A or to community B, but not to both, and therefore can participate in the democratic process of either A or B, but not both. Is it possible to reimagine the boundaries of political communities in order to make them inclusive toward 'others'? Others can be aliens such as migrants or refugees living or seeking to live in an established political community. But they might also simply be citizens living in community B who are directly affected by facts or decisions taken in a community A.

Unfortunately, democratic states are not yet prepared to deal with the preferences and needs of individuals of other political communities in the same way they deal with those of their own citizens. Something more is needed to safeguard the basic democratic principles of equality and participation, namely the willingness of states to undertake agreements that enshrine procedures of democracy among and across states. These agreements do not solely involve states, as in the case of international organizations discussed, but involve local governments, epistemic communities, or focus groups willing to create appropriate forms of consultation or decision-making across borders.

There are more and more political communities that are no longer territorially based. For the first time it has become possible to generate virtual communities among citizens who share similar problems across the world, for example because they heavily rely on a common therapy to cure their disease, they share the same faith, they speak an endangered language, they belong to an ethnic group scattered across different states, or simply share the same hobby (Gould, 2014). New information and communication technologies are opening the gates to a genuine global public sphere, and it has become technically feasible for communities living in remote parts of the world to take part in the same deliberative process, either for specific or general purposes. Such deliberations are already happening in elite circles such as professional associations. But they can also involve the global *demos* as a whole, especially when issues that affect the destiny of all humanity (such as environmental and security issues) are at stake. These are typical cases in which members will need to be both citizens of a state *and* citizens of the world.

In many cases, communities involved in specific issues could be self-organizing. There are growing examples of transnational communities that have even started to directly deliver public goods and services that for many years were exclusively provided by the state. More often, and even when stakeholders are willing to participate, some forms of international organizations are needed, as in the case of the International Commission for the Protection of Lake Constance. Indigenous people still need to be protected vis-à-vis the state they belong from international covenants. Refugees are still in need of international protection since so many states are reluctant to implement international covenants (Benhabib, 2004). The distinctive aspect of cosmopolitan democracy, which complements many valuable initiatives to protect human rights, is that it insists in considering individuals not only as rights-holders, but also as potential participants to the decision-making process. This requires that at all levels of political participation new channels should be opened to make participation possible.

6   Cosmopolitan Democracy as an Alternative to Nationalism

The democratic wave that started in 1989 gave to the people in the East and in the South the hope that a new season of human rights and prosperity would be coming and, in turn, that global affairs could be managed through cooperation. Economic and social globalization has continuously progressed. It cannot be simply judged as 'good' or 'bad' since it obviously includes both positive and negative aspects. But something can be said: it has been a typical case in which the economic base has proceeded at a certain speed while the institutional superstructure had serious difficulties keeping up. Global governance has been mapped (Koenig-Archibugi, 2002), scrutinized (Zürn, 2018), and invoked, but so far it has not managed to deliver what citizens in many parts of the world expected: civil wars continue in spite of the so-called responsibility to protect (R2P), migration flows are not managed through international cooperation, poverty has not decreased. And certainly the global governance actually applied has not been inspired by the democratic principles preached by liberalism: more powerful groups, economic lobbies, and stronger states have managed to get the lion's share, abandoning marginal groups and peripheral locations.

The predictable outcome has been that a large part of the discarded populations has perceived, often with good reason, external intrusions to be detrimental to their welfare. This has led them to reinforce their own identities and be concerned about further uncontrolled integration. This explains why nationalistic and even xenophobic political parties and groups have managed to increase their consensus in spite of the fact that communications, media, tourism, and foreign direct investment have increased. While the current so-called populist wave is an explicable reaction, it is not able to deliver any meaningful outcome. Can states really, without any international agreement, regulate migration, the Internet, or trade flows? To exercise absolute power will imply so many costs that they will jeopardize long-term prosperity.

Cosmopolitan democracy offers an alternative: it is an attempt to subjugate globalization to democratic control, recognizing individuals do not only fulfill the passive roles of 'workers', 'consumers,' or simply the 'dispossessed.' It aims to give to individuals the dignity of being citizens of the world, namely active participants of the community where they live. This should imply a minimal list of rights and duties that existing political institutions, including international organizations, states, and local authorities, should guarantee and expand (Cabrera, 2010). It is often argued that there are no political subjects willing to fight for a cosmopolitan democracy, but this is inaccurate. There are already key areas in which important practices of cosmopolitanism actually exist (Beck, 2006). The interests and the political actions carried out to prevent an uncontrolled globalization are more extensive than is generally thought (Archibugi and Held, 2011). Even weak and marginal groups can act to defend their rights, as asylum-seekers have done in Europe (Benli, 2018). Besides the many and valuable actions that are taken every day, there is also a need to envisage the world community that we would like to build. Cosmopolitan democracy is just an ambitious attempt to contribute to this vision.

References

Annan, K. A. 2002. 'Democracy as an International Issue.' *Global Governance* 8 (2): 135–142.
Archibugi, D. 2008. *The Global Commonwealth of Citizens: Toward Cosmopolitan Democracy*. Princeton, NJ: Princeton University Press.
Archibugi, D. and M. Cellini. 2017. 'The Internal and External Levers to Achieve Global Democracy.' *Journal of Global Policy* 8 (S6): 65–77.
Archibugi, D. and D. Held (eds.). 1995. *Cosmopolitan Democracy: An Agenda for a New World Order*. Cambridge, UK: Polity Press.
Archibugi, D. and D. Held. 2011. 'Cosmopolitan Democracy: Paths and Agents.' *Ethics and International Affairs* 25 (4): 433–461.
Archibugi, D., D. Held, and M. Koehler (eds.). 1998. *Re-imagining Political Community: Studies in Cosmopolitan Democracy*. Cambridge, UK: Polity Press.
Archibugi, D. and A. Pease. 2018. *Crime and Global Justice: The Dynamics of International Punishment*. Cambridge, UK: Polity Press.
Beck, U. 2006. *The Cosmopolitan Vision*. Cambridge, UK: Polity Press.
Benhabib, S. 2004. *The Rights of Others: Aliens, Citizens and Residents*. Cambridge, UK: Cambridge University Press.
Benli, A. E. 2018. 'March of Refugees, Cosmopolitanism and Avant-Garde Political Agency.' In *Migration, Protest Movements and the Politics of Resistance: A Radical Political Philosophy of Cosmopolitanism*, edited by T. Caraus and E. Paris, 121–139. New York: Routledge.
Boutros-Ghali, B. 1996. *An Agenda for Democratization*. New York: United Nations.
Brown, G. W. and D. Held (eds.). 2010. *The Cosmopolitan Reader*. Cambridge, UK: Polity Press.
Cabrera, L. 2010. *The Practice of Global Citizenship*. Cambridge, UK: Cambridge University Press.
Cabrera, L. (ed.). 2018. *Institutional Cosmopolitanism*. Oxford: Oxford University Press.
Caraus, T. and E. Paris (eds.). 2018. *Migration, Protest Movements and the Politics of Resistance: A Radical Political Philosophy of Cosmopolitanism*. London: Routledge.
Caselli, M. and G. Gilardoni (eds.). 2018. Globalization, Supranational Dynamics and Local Experiences. London: Palgrave Macmillan.
Cicchelli, V. and S. Octobre. 2018. 'Debating Cosmopolitanism: A New Appraisal of Globalization.' In *Globalization, Supranational Dynamics and Local Experiences*, edited by M. Caselli and G. Gilardoni, 43–63. London: Palgrave Macmillan.
Falk, R. 1993. *Explorations at the Edge of Time: The Prospects for World Order*. Philadelphia, PA: Temple University Press.
Falk, R. 1995. *On Humane Governance: Towards a New Global Politics*. University Park: Pennsylvania State University Press.

Fine, R. 2007. *Cosmopolitanism*. London: Routledge.

Gould, C. 2014. *Interactive Democracy: The Social Roots of Global Justice*. Cambridge, UK: Cambridge University Press.

Held, D. 1995. *Democracy and the Global Order*. Cambridge, UK: Polity Press.

Held, D. 2006. *Models of Democracy*, 3rd ed. Cambridge, UK: Polity Press.

Held, D. and A. McGrew (eds.). 2002. *Governing Globalisation*. Cambridge, UK: Polity Press.

Ikenberry, J. 2018. 'The End of Liberal International Order?' *International Affairs* 94 (1): 7–23.

Ingram, J. 2013. *Radical Cosmopolitanism*. New York: Columbia University Press.

Jones, A.H.M. 1958. *Athenian Democracy*. New York: Praeger.

Kaldor, M. (ed.). 1991. *Europe from Below: An East–West Dialogue*. London: Verso.

Kaldor, M. 1999. *New and Old Wars*. Cambridge, UK: Polity Press.

Koenig-Archibugi, M. 2002. 'Mapping Global Governance.' In *Governing Globalisation*, edited by D. Held and A. McGrew, 46–69. Cambridge, UK: Polity Press.

Koenig-Archibugi, M. 2018. 'International Organizations and Democracy: An Assessment.' In *Institutional Cosmopolitanism*, edited by L. Cabrera, 180–195. Oxford: Oxford University Press.

Lamy, P. 2005. *Towards World Democracy*. London: Policy Network.

Leinen, J. and A. Bummel. 2018. *A World Parliament: Governance and Democracy in the 21st Century*. New York: Democracy without Borders.

Levi, L., G. Finizio, and N. Vallinoto (eds.). 2014. *The Democratization of International Institutions: First International Democracy Report*. London; New York: Routledge.

Mann, M. 2005. *The Dark Side of Democracy: Explaining Ethnic Cleansing*. Cambridge, UK: Cambridge University Press.

Marchetti, R. 2008. *Global Democracy*. London: Routledge.

Marshall, M. G. and G. Elzinga-Marshall. 2017. *Global Report 2017: Conflict, Governance and State Fragility*. Vienna, VA: Center for Systemic Peace.

Milanovic, B. 2016. *Global Inequality: A New Approach for the Age of Globalization*. Cambridge, MA: Harvard University Press.

Morlino, L. 2012. *Changes for Democracy: Actors, Structures, Processes*. Cambridge, UK: Cambridge University Press.

Russett, B. 1993. *Grasping the Democratic Peace: Principles for a Post-Cold War World*. Princeton, NJ: Princeton University Press.

Zürn, M. 2018. *A Theory of Global Governance: Authority, Legitimacy, and Contestation*. Oxford: Oxford University Press.

CHAPTER 12

Cosmopolitanism and Multiculturalism

Alain Policar

There can be no doubt that some instances of the two political-philosophical currents, multiculturalism and cosmopolitanism, make it difficult if not impossible to compare the two.* If multiculturalism is associated with a strictly holistic ontology wherein individuals are pawns manipulated by collective forces while cosmopolitanism is understood as an option wherein individual autonomy may be constructed without the need of an encompassing social matrix, an option that celebrates a disincarnated subject who fails to acknowledge the importance of shared practices and values, then there can be no encounter between the two. It is therefore incumbent on me to attend to incarnations of cosmopolitanism and multiculturalism that will allow for fruitful assessment. Most importantly, it seems to me, they share a concern about how liberal democratic societies handle otherness. If we agree that custom and lifestyle diversity and relativity in no way dissolve the universal in a mosaic of differences but on the contrary bring to light the cosmopolitan character of all human beings, then the conditions of compatibility coalesce around assessing the value of diversity. It is precisely that value that is at the center of critiques leveled by normative multiculturalism against liberal modernity—critiques that furnish cosmopolitanism with precious theoretical resources. I shall therefore emphasize convergences between the two without dissimulating possible tensions. While the question of social justice is the backdrop of the encounter, we shall see that the ways in which the two approach cultural difference are quite distinct and perhaps irreconcilable.

1 Egalitarian Dynamics and Diversity

In an oft-cited typology, Steven Lukes distinguishes between 'communitarians' in a broad sense and 'communitarians' in a narrow sense on the one hand, 'High' and 'Low' 'communitarians' on the other (Lukes, 1995). The first distinction concerns attitudes toward liberalism. Narrow communitarians are

---

* Translated by Amy Jacobs-Colas.

anti-liberal; in other words, they are communitarianists in the strongly pejorative sense of the term, whose aim is to create and protect communities that are founded on strictly defined cultures of recognition. Broad communitarians, meanwhile, stress that liberal societies, like all others, need ties to hold them together and that this in turn produces self-restraint, mutual commitment, and public virtue. The second distinction is more objective: High communitarians are intellectuals concerned about possible philosophical deficiencies in liberalism whereas Low communitarians want to implement policies on the ground. Lukes' conclusion is that communitarians who have gotten liberalism into what may be called family quarrels are all of the broad and High variety, concerned about such problems as the social development of the subject and the incarnate, substantive status of the person. In other words, they are proponents of normative multiculturalism. In many respects, the type of integration that normative multiculturalism proposes is different from the notion of assimilating people in order to make them equal. It is therefore inaccurate to take normative multiculturalism to be an ethno-cultural vision of the political tie. These multiculturalists' project is rather to restore to equals their difference. Their aim is to make greater progress in instating equality than the classic republican solution has been capable of doing.

2 Diversity as a Value

Political cosmopolitanism cannot be indifferent to this project, as its fundamental aim is to establish a different relationship to otherness than that generally put forward by the nation-state. Both multiculturalism and cosmopolitanism are moved to ask what principles our societies should choose for treating the diversity through which the human condition manifests itself. In many ways, the history of the last two decades (the late 1990s to 2019) recounts a shift from the issue of identity to the issue of diversity, from demands based on collective membership to demands for recognition of the primacy of the individual as a rights-endowed subject. *Diversity*, then, and not *identity*, can correctly translate the respective inflections of cosmopolitanism and multiculturalism while suggesting a way in which the first may be able to surpass the second. The best the multiculturalist project has to offer—though this does not necessarily represent its natural inclination—is its contribution to what Alain Renaut (2009) has called the 'decolonization of identities,' a process that presupposes reconciling adherence to the principles of political liberalism with genuine attention to cosmopolitanism; a reconciliation that the crimes of colonization have made very difficult.

Successfully decolonizing identities does not mean trying to 'subject the diverse to the identical' (Renaut, 2009: 250). On the contrary, it means simultaneously encompassing diversity promotion and the perception of our shared humanity—similar but diverse, diverse but similar, as Renaut writes. He was already endorsing this project in 1999, in a major work written with Sylvie Mesure. The point was to 'test the type of diversification by which "fellow" human beings—what all human beings are—find a marker or mark of dignity in the way they appear to each other as "different"' (Renaut and Mesure, 1999: 257). Édouard Glissant's distinction between creoleness (*créolité*) and creolization (*créolisation*) helps us perceive how the diversity paradigm breaks with the identity problem:

> I am entirely against the term *créolité*. ... I think the idea of *créolisation* corresponds better to the situation of the world. It's the idea of a continuous process that can produce both the identical and the different. It seems to me that *créolité* turns multilingualism or multi-ethnicism into a dogma or model. I'm against models, so I prefer the open term of *créolisation* to the space of essence or state suggested by the term *créolité*.
> Quoted by RENAUT, 2009: 326; original emphasis

This crucial distinction enables us to formulate a version of universalism that would be open to diversity while avoiding the pitfall of differentialism. For *créolité* as essence we need to substitute a non-substantialized identity that is also a relation. As soon as this is done, cultural mix appears, 'one condition of a Same-and-Different combinatory that does not dissolve diversity' (Renaut, 2009: 339). Furthermore, how could individuals be treated in a way that recognizes their dignity while bracketing 'that which makes them non-interchangeable' (ibid.: 372)? Renaut's perspective holds normative multiculturalism at bay while also distancing itself from a kind of French republicanism that has been incapable of understanding that differentialist demands are often only a response (a bad one, obviously) to a perverse process of identity ascription, a process through which 'the majority tends to erect certain differences as signs of objective otherness, thereby transforming them into sources of domination over minorities' (Guérard de Latour, 2009: 52).

3   An Ethics of Coexistence

It has been wrongfully claimed that affirmative actions go against the fundamental principles of political liberalism. That claim elides the fact that since the aim of such measures is to foster equality they can be defended on the grounds of distributive justice. We therefore must be careful not to confuse compensatory policy actions, which are supported by many multiculturalist philosophers, with recognition politics, wherein cultural difference is an essential way of expressing individual identity. Compensatory policies work to efface disadvantageous differences; that is, to ensure that inherited collective traits do not hamper individual opportunity, and later to reestablish a policy of indifference to difference. In recognition politics, the focus is not on differences that need to be eliminated but their opposite: differences as features to be promoted. While compensatory measures are compatible with cosmopolitanism, recognition politics is entirely alien to it.

Whereas recognition logic leads to essentializing identities, the egalitarian concern of liberal multiculturalism works, like cosmopolitanism, to promote the art of conversation between individuals from different sociocultural worlds. Conversation transcends identity borders, simply in that it 'helps people get used to one another' (Appiah, 2006: 85). It also makes possible an ethics of coexistence, one that does not demand that we understand each other, only that we hear each other. In this connection, Kwame Anthony Appiah speaks of cosmopolitan *curiosity*: on the basis of a few points in common, we can discover different ways of thinking or action. This is how he arrives at what he calls 'the great lesson of anthropology: when the stranger is no longer imaginary, but real and present, sharing a human social life …. [I]f it is what you both want, then you can make sense of each other in the end' (ibid.: 151). That assertion is moral cosmopolitanism's point of departure. Need it be specified that it does not require us to have the same feelings for all the world's inhabitants as we have for those closest to us?

4   On the Status of Otherness

Cosmopolitanism obviously cannot deny otherness since in some respects it is, like multiculturalism, a politics of difference. But more importantly, as Louis Lourme points out:

> Feeling oneself to be citizen of the world does mean one is … claiming an otherness within a given political community. Saying one is a citizen of the world means referring to something other than self or one's own citizenship. It means introducing all other people into the heart of a particular community. Cosmopolitans are signs of otherness within their

communities, just as any cosmopolitical project necessarily guarantees protection for otherness at the level of the world.
LOURME, 2008

We still need to determine what conditions are required to accomplish this, and it is here that multiculturalism and cosmopolitanism become increasingly distinct.

5   Culture: a Booby-trap Category

While the cosmopolitan perspective is attentive to difference, its primary preoccupation is to ensure that individuals are distinguished from each other. The first subject of cosmopolitical justice is the individual, regardless of the group to which that individual belongs (Couture, 2010: 23). In its very essence, moral cosmopolitanism is an individualist doctrine in that it is concerned above all about the interests of individuals.

This does not mean that it slights the importance of families, communities, and countries. But it treats their value as derivative: they are of value exactly to the extent that they contribute to the welfare of individuals—both those within the group and those outside it, weighting their interests equally (Barry, 1998).

This takes us some distance from multiculturalism, which has rightly been criticized for essentializing cultural membership. As Anne Philipps (2007: 14) has pointed out:

> Much recent literature claims that [multiculturalism] exaggerates the internal unity of cultures, solidifies differences that are currently more fluid, and makes people from other cultures seem more exotic and distinct than they really are. Multiculturalism then appears as not as a cultural liberator but as a cultural straitjacket, forcing those described as members of a minority cultural group into a regime of authenticity, denying them the chance to cross cultural borders, borrow cultural influences, define and redefine themselves.

For Philipps, then, the culture category can be a trap. This is undoubtedly one of the most powerful arguments against multiculturalist logic.

It should be noted, however, that studies seeking to isolate the differential effect of multicultural policies find that they have had positive effects in terms of political participation, social capital, prejudice reduction, psychological well-being, and academic performance. Despite the risks they create for individual freedoms, rights that aim to protect what the Canadian philosopher Will Kymlicka called 'societal cultures' seem to work as external protections that reestablish equality among groups rather than as internal restrictions that limit minority members' freedom. Above all, they seem to reduce minority member vulnerability to majority decisions and do not at all seem to be used by minority groups to suppress civic and political liberties internally. In fact, active individual autonomy seems to drive change within societal cultures, an effect that greatly relativizes the reproach of essentialism.

So we need not believe that the liberating dynamic of multiculturalism has been subverted by culture and identity essentialization. And yet it would seem that the positive effects observed have occurred *despite* existing essentialist tendencies. However that may be, culture does not seem the relevant dimension. For both Appiah (2007) and Seyla Benhabib (2007), what really needs to be pursued is civic equality rather than cultural preservation. That position neatly sums up the opposition between multiculturalist logic and the type of thinking promoted by cosmopolitanism. We can agree to protect a minority language for political reasons, reasons related to accomplishing the duties of citizenship. We no longer have to advocate for a relatively substantialist conception of culture, one that would, in addition, be in conflict with the fundamental principles of political liberalism—the very principles that multiculturalism claims to enrich rather than reject.

6   Domination as a Heuristic Notion

Rather than reformulate liberal multiculturalism so as to clarify the principles cited by multiculturalists in their demands for cultural rights, it would be more judicious to grant a nodal position to the notion of *agency*. Given that this notion emphasizes individual autonomy, it should enable us to do without the vague signifier 'culture,' whose theoretical substance is highly uncertain. It cannot be denied that 'culture' is used to designate extremely heterogeneous entities, including ethnic groups (Latinos in the United States), religious groups (Jews or Muslims), lifestyle or mores-defined groups (homosexuals), sex groups (women), 'racial' groups (blacks), and even language groups or social classes. In fact, such entities are only turned into cultures by granting primacy to one characteristic to the detriment of all others. The danger of reifying and therefore naturalizing a single characteristic is real and present.

Cosmopolitanism, meanwhile, though it cannot accommodate a version of multiculturalism that is primarily concerned with maintaining existing cultures and ensuring compliance with traditions, is in no way opposed to multiculturalism that would agree to value individuals' hybridity and cultural creativity, their ability to reinterpret and reinvent cultural schemata.

It is precisely the task of public reason to make reciprocity among citizens possible despite the weight of cultural and religious differences. The aim of integrating minority groups into existing institutions and thereby enabling them to achieve cultural recognition—the demand that drives multiculturalism—should be understood as an integral part of a wider citizenship program: 'the fight against all forms of domination—political, ethno-racial, economic and social' (Laborde, 2013, quoted in Guérard de Latour, 2013: 228–229). Defined as an arbitrary balance of power, the notion of *domination* offers the advantage of stressing issues of *power* rather than *identity*. This in turn suggests that the concept of culture may distract attention from injustices that demand other analytic tools. How could we not perceive, for example, that the difference between blacks and whites in the United States is not a matter of distinct cultures but of race-differentiated treatment? It seems to me that most of the authors who identify themselves as multiculturalist do not properly understand that obvious fact. As Magali Bessone judiciously points out, 'racial justice has much more to gain from being grounded in a discourse on justification formulated in terms of discrimination and the need to combat it than a discourse on cultures and the need to respect them' (Bessone, 2013, quoted in Guérard de Latour, 2013: 134).

I fully endorse that conclusion, especially because it relativizes collective identities, a move that seems to me fundamental to cosmopolitics, which is by nature attentive to sources of injustice against minorities as they relate to national political construction processes. It is undeniable that majority collective decisions weigh, unequally, on different cultural minorities. But cosmopolitanism rejects rule-and-exception as a political model; that is, it stands opposed to any measure likely to foster differentiated citizenship. The main reason for that stance is surely its view of the notion of collective identity.

7 Collective Identities and Cosmopolitanism

Normative multiculturalism has a strong propensity to politicize identity, and indeed to naturalize politics by positing a natural right to culture. Consistent cosmopolitans, conscious of the fragility of collective identities, cannot take that path. But adopting a radically critical perspective on our *collective identities* in no way means opting for an entirely non-material perspective. Following Appiah, we can reasonably hope that a 'rooted' cosmopolitanism is possible; that is, a cosmopolitan identity conscious of its local preferences.

8   Identity as a Philosophic Fable

In many respects, identity is a 'philosophic fable,' to cite Benmakhlouf (2011). Though it is often jealously or resentfully laid claim to, it has been shown by philosophers—first and foremost David Hume—to be a fiction. Linguistic conventions are what lead us see some kind of permanence behind identities. In doing so we take 'ethereal beings' for tangible realities. 'These shadowy companions of the substantives,' wrote Wittgenstein (quoted by Benmakhlouf, 2011: 27), give us the equivalent of 'mental cramps': 'we think there is something that remains identical to itself over time, and instead of thinking of proper names as convenient abbreviations of descriptions we take them for the very emblem of an identity's invariability' (ibid.: 27–28). But, as Hume insisted, identity is necessarily ascribed: our thought 'confounds the succession with the identity' (Hume, 1995: 288).

I now turn to the question of individual identity because it seems to me this is at least implicitly linked to that of cultural identity. For many of us, belonging to a given group has strong meaning for personal identity. Moreover, classic examinations of individual identity such as Locke's are not irrelevant to understanding the investigative thinking that membership in a given group—particularly a given nation—may elicit. Which of a person's characteristics should be considered essential in ensuring that he or she remains fundamentally the same over time? Likewise, on what bases can a nation (or a culture) recognize itself as being essentially what it has always been?

We can better measure the difficulty if we find ourselves 'belonging' to two or more cultural groups that have ended up fundamentally opposed to each other due to the contingencies of history. Think of children born to immigrant parents, of people who become members of a totally different community than the one in which they grew up, of people who thought they belonged to a nation and then discover that in the oppressor's view of them they are first and foremost Jews, Tutsis, or Bosnians, for example, rather than members of that nation. What happens then to the supposedly essential components of their collective identity?

In fact, 'when we identify someone as being from a particular country, a particular region of the world,' we have said very little about her/him. 'Everything about her/him as a singular being, different from all others, including those she/he resembles, is yet to be discovered' (Guenancia, 2017: 77). This is obviously not what racists think; as far as they are concerned, once you know where a person comes from you have said it all: racists 'perceive identities, not singular beings' (ibid.: 77). I am allowed to be black as others are white without that detail defining me as a person. However, to change that natural characteristic into 'négritude' and make it the very framework of my personal existence is to deprive me of my singularity (Guenancia, 1995: 620). In fact,

> a person only exists as such if he can conceive of himself/herself as distinct from all passive or received marks of identity, even if he appropriates those marks to himself/herself in a spirit of solidarity in cases where they correspond to an oppressed or persecuted people. … As long as a person has not completely renounced her/his freedom, she/he cannot entirely and adequately coincide with herself/himself, much less coincide with the figures that chance and perhaps also a sense of duty have led her/him to assume.
> GUENANCIA, 1995: 620

We see the inanity of the move to reduce individuals to their color (for example), a desire that leads to claiming that people should stick to their 'own kind' and, ultimately, to defending apartheid. On the contrary, we need to encourage 'imaginaries of encounters, interstices, Creolization' (Noudelmann, 2016); we need to make sociocultural mix an essential political principle. We see how distant this perspective inherent in any cosmopolitics is from multiculturalism and the vague and generally shallow identity-based memberships with which it encumbers itself.

9   Rooted Cosmopolitanism

Let us return to Appiah's 'rooted cosmopolitanism.' While it is perfectly acceptable to feel that one belongs to a nation, a religion, or any other collective, we need to be able to imagine other memberships in time and space. As Pierre Guenancia explains (1995), it is variation of this sort, variation of which we are capable thanks to our intelligence, that will enable us to escape our destructive, hate-fueled passions; to get free of oneself in order to

> isolate the absolute invariant in one's being: the simple fact of being a human being, and sharing that identity equally with all other human beings, universally considered, so that one can say with Montaigne, 'I consider all men my compatriots, and embrace a Pole as I would a Frenchman, setting this national bond after the common and universal one.'
> GUENANCIA, 1995: 621

To find the universal in self, then, we need to disencumber ourselves of ourselves. Doing so makes us realize that what is specifically human is reason: 'identical reason in every person is the only thing that constrains us to recognize a human identity, and therefore the presence of total humanity in each human being' (Guenancia, 1995: 623).

I have just put forward what seems the fundamental requisite for developing a political cosmopolitanism around the figure of the stranger. For as Étienne Tassin understood so well, 'the most acute sense of politics, its highest value, is experienced in the ability to make a "common world" with strangers and their worlds when the two most often meet in conflict mode' (Tassin, 2017: 101). It follows that any authentic politics is a cosmopolitics.

While multiculturalism is a necessary moment, enabling us to take into account the demands of minorities within the nation-state, its latent ontology grants considerable importance to collective categories such as identity and culture. Cosmopolitanism is rightly concerned to give individual autonomy the decisive place that multiculturalism refuses to grant it. Moreover, the cosmopolitical vision goes beyond demanding justice within national borders. It maintains that it is our responsibility to combat all morally arbitrary privileges; that is, privileges due to circumstances rather than choices. A theory of global justice is therefore a necessary component of that vision. And such a theory implies a renewed concept of citizenship that will recognize that rights follow simply from belonging to the world. We now see why it is justified to claim from a resolutely egalitarian perspective that cosmopolitanism definitively surpasses multiculturalism. And this in turn indicates that the democracy of the future will be democracy in a shared world where everyone has rights. 'The common life' to borrow Achille Mbembe's excellent expression (Mbembe, 2016), presupposes sharing in a world we all only pass through. A worthy political community therefore must include those negatively impacted by the arbitrariness of birth.

References

Appiah, K. A. 2006. *Cosmopolitanism: Ethics in a World of Strangers*. New York: W. W. Norton & Co.

Appiah, K. A. 2007. 'Ethics in a World of Strangers: W.E.B. Du Bois and the Spirit of Cosmopolitanism.' In *A Transnational World*, edited by K. A. Appiah, S. Benhabib, I. M. Young, and N. Fraser, 15–44. Berlin: Humboldt University.

Barry, B. 1998. 'International Society from a Cosmopolitan Perspective.' In *International Society: Diverse Ethical Perspectives*, edited by D. R. Mapel and T. Nardin, 144–163. Princeton, NJ: Princeton University Press.

Benhabib, S. 2007. 'Crises of the Republic: Transformations of State Sovereignty and the Prospects of Democratic Citizenship.' In *Justice, Governance, Cosmopolitanism, and* the Politics of Difference, Reconfigurations in a Transnational World, edited by K. A. Appiah, S. Benhabib, I. M. Young, and N. Fraser, 45–78. Berlin: Humboldt University.

Benmakhlouf, A. 2011. *L'identité. Une fable philosophique*. Paris: Presses Universitaires de France.

Bessone, M. 2013. 'Réaliser la justice raciale: multiculturalisme ou théorie critique des races?' In *Le multiculturalisme a-t-il un avenir?* edited by S. Guérard de Latour, 105–134. Paris: Hermann.

Couture, J. 2010. 'Qu'est-ce que le cosmopolitisme?' In *Le cosmopolitisme: Enjeux et débats contemporains*, edited by R. Chung and G. Nootens, 15–35. Montreal: Presses de l'Université de Montréal.

Guenancia, P. 1995. 'L'identité.' In *Notions de philosophie II*, edited by D. Kambouchner, 563–635. Paris: Gallimard.

Guenancia, P. 2013. 'Le citoyen du monde. Prolégomènes à une philosophie du cosmopolitisme.' *Bulletin de la Société Française de Philosophie* 107 (2).

Guenancia, P. 2017. 'Identité et cosmopolitisme.' *Raison présente* 201, issue edited by A. Policar: 75–86.

Guérard de Latour, S. 2009. 'Le multiculturalisme, un projet républicain?' *Les Ateliers de l'Éthique* 4 (2): 43–54.

Hume, D. (1738), *Traité de la nature humaine*, trad. fr., Paris, Flammarion, 1995.

Laborde, C. 2013. 'Républicanisme critique et multiculturalisme libéral.' In *Le multiculturalisme a-t-il un avenir?* edited by S. Guérard de Latour, 227–242. Paris: Hermann.

Lourme, L. 2008. 'Cosmopolitisme.' In *DicoPo, Dictionnaire de théorie politique*, edited by B. Vincent and R. Merrill, entry 111, http://www.dicopo.fr/spip.php.

Lukes, S. 1995. 'L'arrachement social et ses mythes: sur la querelle entre libéralisme et communautarisme.' *Le Banquet* 7: 174–190.

Mbembe, A. 2016. *Politiques de l'inimitié*. Paris: La Découverte.

Noudelmann, F. 2016. 'L'inquiétante racialisation du discours de gauche.' *Le Monde*, May 12.

Philipps, A. 2007. *Multiculturalism without Culture*. Princeton, NJ: Princeton University Press.

Renaut, A. 2009. *Un humanisme de la diversité. Essai sur la décolonisation des identités*. Paris: Flammarion.

Renaut, A. and S. Mesure. 1999. *Alter ego. Les paradoxes de l'identité démocratique*. Paris: Grasset.

Tassin, E. 2017. 'Cosmopolitique et xénopolitique.' *Raison présente* 201, issue edited by A. Policar: 99–107.

CHAPTER 13

Cosmopolitan Cities

Delphine Pagès-El Karoui

1   Introduction

What is a cosmopolitan city? One spontaneously thinks of people from a wide range of countries, 'the world in a city' involving a slight shift from the term's Greek etymology 'the citizen of the world', alongside vibrant urban landscapes, 'ethnic' shops, restaurants, and clubs, and neighborhoods strongly associated with a single community (Chinatown, Little Italy, etc.) or combining several. New York and London are usually the first metropolises that come to mind. When a more quantitative indicator is chosen—the percentage of foreign-born population, used by several websites ranking the ten most cosmopolitan cities in the world—Dubai usually overtakes New York and London to take first place thanks to its 92 percent foreign population. Because 'cosmopolitanism' has multiple and sometimes contradictory definitions, 'a cosmopolitan city' can mean several things. When Latham (2006) speaks of cosmopolitan landscapes in Auckland, he applies the term to bars, cafés, and restaurants that are becoming more diverse, more international, and more worldly by imitating French or Italian cafés to differentiate themselves from traditional local pubs, for example. Here, 'cosmopolitan' means an environment that is glamorous thanks to the influence of ideas, products, or consumption practices from elsewhere. This sense of the word is embedded in the story of cultural globalization, unrelated to migrant or ethnic diversity. The scope of this chapter is more focused on the former meaning. Even with this restriction, however, it is still a complex task to theoretically define 'the cosmopolitan city.'

It is challenging to find a precise conceptualization of what a cosmopolitan city actually is, which is all the more surprising considering the vast literature on cosmopolitanism that has resurged since the 1990s, in connection with global and migration studies. There are two main reasons for this. First, scholarship remains largely theoretical and often adopts a normative perspective. Cosmopolitanism is conceived as an ideology, a philosophical and political project of global citizenry or solidarity, thinking beyond the nation and the local (Beck, 2006) and implying a democratic horizon (Harvey, 2000). The city is not central in these formulations, but the world as a new scale of analysis is.

Second, a more descriptive perspective embedded in sociology and anthropology usually uses cosmopolitanism to refer to the orientations and dispositions of individuals, their familiarity and comfort with diversity, and their 'willingness to engage with the other' (Hannerz, 1996: 103). Scholars of this approach are thus interested in distinguishing 'cosmopolitans' from 'non-cosmopolitans' and describing experiences of encounters with alterity in urban environments. Despite calls for more empirical work on 'grounded cosmopolitanism,' cosmopolitanism is rarely studied in its spatial applications. Cities are thus still seen as the preferred setting for analyzing the cosmopolitan orientations, dispositions, and practices of cosmopolitan individuals, but they are more of a backdrop than the focus of their analysis. There is, however, some scholarship tackling interactions between cosmopolitanism and cities (Binnie et al., 2006; Yeoh and Lin, 2012).

Building upon a multidisciplinary literature and my own experience in Middle East studies, I will explore multiple cosmopolitan urbanities in the following short tour of cosmopolitan cities: utopian and real, ancient and contemporary, Western and non-Western. During the voyage, I will question whether 'cosmopolitanism' is an appropriate analytical tool for describing urban diversity in all times and places. After scouting for the 'truly cosmopolitan city,' I will make stops in six cosmopolitan cities, presented in pairs: New York and London—both global cities, both models of cosmopolitan metropolises in the Western world with democratic systems and policies for migrant integration; Alexandria and Istanbul—evoking a past cosmopolitanism under the multiethnic Ottoman Empire; and Dubai and Singapore, two non-Western wannabe-global cities with highly diverse populations and non-integrative policies.

2   Desperately Seeking the 'Truly' Cosmopolitan City

Although the question of the 'stranger' is at the heart of the definition of urbanity as Simmel and urban academics have always celebrated cities as sites of difference, many scholars working on urban diversity are wary of 'cosmopolitanism' and use it cautiously or avoid it in favor of other terms such as 'multicultural,' 'multiethnic,' or 'super-diverse,' the latter coined by Vertovec (2007) and popular since the late 2000s.[1] The explanation is likely found in the diverse critiques of cosmopolitanism, accused of being a catch-all concept,

---

1   See Chapter 12 in this volume.

overly Eurocentric for its universalism and its ties to colonialism, limited to elites, and containing numerous tensions and contradictions.

But regardless of the words they use, scholars usually converge on a recurrent question: To what extent are multicultural cities 'truly' cosmopolitan? In other words, a demographically diverse population does not ensure that people's attitudes and practices will open up to and tolerate this diversity or that they will engage in deep interactions with the other. Sennett (1994) has deplored that co-existence or co-presence in Greenwich Village, in New York, is based more on indifference than real interactions. And according to Calhoun (2002), we need not only tolerance, but also solidarity.

This obsession of the 'truly' cosmopolitan city reminds us of cosmopolitanism's strong normative dimension and the positive, democratic values it inherited from Kant and the Enlightenment, which presupposes the inclusion of the migrant in this instance. This leads to the very challenging question of whether a multicultural city is capable of sharing a common destiny. While Sennett would answer that 'a multicultural city cannot have a common civic culture' (1994: 358), others are less pessimistic. Safier (1996), for one, is an urbanist studying how to produce a general sense of a civic 'cosmopolitan' culture, while distancing himself from assimilationist theory. Based on his professional experience with the reconstruction of cities after war and destruction in Sarajevo and Jerusalem, he proposes several elements: reinforcing the shared sense of civil society, advancing status equality, promoting communal cooperation, and being inclusive of migrants. His arguments echo Sandercock, whose central question is 'how can "we" (all of us), in all of our differences, be "at home" in increasingly multicultural cities?' (2006: 38). She sees cosmopolitan urbanism as a political project that responds to the normative imperative to engage in meaningful intercultural (rather than multicultural) interactions.

Douglass, another urbanist, elaborates a dichotomy opposing two ideal-types, *cosmopolis/globopolis*, one attractive and the other repulsive but both flowing from the same obsession with the truly cosmopolitan city: 'global cities are perhaps becoming more descriptively cosmopolitan, [but] they are not become more substantively so' (2009: 69). So the *cosmopolis* describes a convivial, tolerant, inclusive city inhabited by people from all around the world, with many levels of citizenship. In a context of democratization and strong civil participation in governance, the *cosmopolis* is oriented toward neighborliness, and vibrant common and public spaces fostering chance encounters and social gathering. It also implies the participation of all residents in the making of the city, and their ability to mark their own identities in the cityscape. In contrast, the *globopolis* represents the cosmopolis' antithesis in a neoliberal setting: an unequal, increasingly privatized and consumer-driven city where urban space is transformed in response to global competition for markets and investment. Relying on the disposable labor of marginalized populations who will never become citizens, the globopolis is also characterized by mega-scale projects realized by star architects, a dearth or absence of public and civic spaces, the inability of residents and neighborhoods to engage in place-making, and the destruction of vernacular architecture. Mobility is also contrasted, since the *globopolis* favors a car-based urban fabric while the *cosmopolis* tends to be more walkable.

If Gulf cities like Dubai, Abu Dhabi, and Doha seem to correspond well to the *globopolis* type, it is more difficult to identify any existing city with the cosmopolis. Douglass is vague himself, briefly mentioning San Francisco but providing little support. As seductive as it may be, the *cosmopolis/globopolis* dichotomy is not focused on ethnic diversity and is concerned instead with rejecting the model of globalized urban modernity and vaunting a more convivial urbanity in which cosmopolitanism is imagined as an idealized version of globalization. With so many narratives about what the ideal cosmopolitan city ought to be, the next question is whether the authentic cosmopolitan city has ever really existed. To escape the axiological debate, let's confront theory with empirical case studies.

3 'Cosmopolitan' Tales of Two Global Cities

According to Sassen (2001 [1991]), New York, London, and Tokyo are the top global cities, meaning major centers of the command and control of economic globalization. Although global cities do not automatically have diverse immigrant populations (Tokyo is a good example), the top-ranking metropolises in the world are more likely to host a large and diverse population of migrants. They are usually strategic nodes of transnational capital and thus attract international flows of labor migration, which provide the cheap and flexible labor crucial to capital accumulation.

New York is often named as the quintessential cosmopolitan city. In the *Cambridge English Dictionary*, the definition of 'cosmopolitan' comes with the example, 'New York is a highly cosmopolitan city.' With about one third of its population foreign-born, the city hosts the largest number of immigrants in the world. Once a major port of entry for migrants (as celebrated at the Ellis Island immigration museum), it has a long history of successive arrivals of ethnic groups and immigrant inclusion. New York's patterns of immigration are different from other American cities. First, the city has an extraordinary diverse array of migrants. A variety of minority groups came in waves of immigration—Jewish, Italian, African American, Puerto Rican, West Indian, those from the former Soviet Union, Asian—with none permanently dominant. Scholars call it a 'no majority' city. Second, there is a relative balance between high-skilled and low-skilled immigrants, while migrants in other American cities are predominantly low skilled. This directly influences the positive image of migrants in New York. Third, the city officially promotes cultural pluralism and glorifies its multiethnic character, allowing ethnic festivals and parades such as the West Indian American Parade in Brooklyn on Labor Day. New York is seen as an immigrant-friendly city, developing public programs to welcome newcomers and help them settle into the city and distancing itself from federal immigration authorities and the Trump administration, which is deporting increasing numbers of undocumented migrants.

Although discrimination is still widespread, class and racial inequalities remain strong, tensions between racial and ethnic groups (especially Latinos and native blacks) persist, and residential segregation between whites and blacks is still high, peaceful coexistence is still the rule, and the forces encouraging ethno-racial mixing and mingling are more influential in New York than elsewhere else in the United States. If not a perfect model of inclusion, New York provides a 'positive model of creative multiculturalism and inclusion' in which hybrids and fluid exchanges are possible across group boundaries (Kasinitz, Mollenkopf, and Waters, 2004: 17). Even though primary sociability may be centered on the community of origin (same race, ethnicity, and/or class), friendships occur in schools, playgrounds, and workplaces, intermarriage is increasing, and cultural hybrids are emerging, especially in music. The second generation see themselves as 'New Yorkers' rather than Americans, evidence of the city's powerful capacity to generate identities. This description seems to be a perfect fit with the idea of cosmopolitan city, but American scholars rarely use the word. They prefer to use 'immigrant gateway city' to refer to the diversity of the population, and 'multiculturalism' to evoke the coexistence of multiple cultures or cultural diversity (Foner, 2007).

As for London, which concentrates 41.6 percent of the UK migrant population and hosts representatives of 229 nationalities (the largest groups being Indian, Polish, and Irish), 'super-diversity' and 'multiculturalism' are preferred to 'cosmopolitanism.' Wessendorf (2013) conducted ethnographic research in the borough of Hackney, one of the most ethnically diverse tracts of Britain, with people coming from more than a hundred countries and, like New York, no dominant ethnic group in terms of numbers, culture, or politics. She argues that Hackney's super-diverse setting increases acceptance of alterity, at least superficially. People are used to diversity, which thus becomes normal to them. Many residents develop what she calls an 'ethos of mixing,' and they expect everyone to play along and mix in public spaces. They have trouble understanding those who seem unwilling to mix (Orthodox Jews and hipsters). To a lesser extent this is reminiscent of the 'cosmopolitan canopy' Anderson (2011) coined to describe the American context based on observations in the Philadelphia Terminal Market. It refers to certain spaces that act as islands of interracial civility in a world of palpable tensions dominated by segregated living. The 'cosmopolitan canopy' offers a chance for strangers to come together, providing a place where people can feel safe, engage in 'folk ethnography,' and challenge their stereotypes and prejudices about each other.

Coming back to the UK, Amin also questions the 'daily negotiation of ethnic difference.' He argues that neighborhood-scale ethnic residential mixing is not the necessary solution and that public spaces are not 'natural servants of multicultural engagement' (2002: 11). Instead, he introduces 'micro-publics' as more efficient sites of intercultural interaction. Places such as workplaces, schools, sports clubs, and community centers require dialogue and negotiation and create spaces of interdependence and mundane engagement. Another way of exploring the modalities of spatialization of ethnic diversity is to conduct analysis at the street level. Building upon Glick Schiller and Çağlar (2009), Hall brings space back into the globalization debate, demonstrating how migrants engage in practices of city-making and contribute significantly to urban change, thus countering narratives of de-territorialization. She conducted ethnography research on Rye Lane in central Peckham, South London, which is one of the most ethnically diverse and most impoverished places in the UK. Instead of studying gentrification, which has already been the focus of a considerable body of literature, she focuses on the agency of shop owners from twenty countries who were drawn there by the low rent. She analyses the internal subdivision of their shops, which may be sublet to others, to demonstrate how they create diverse forms of 'mutualism' and 'arrangements of economic and cultural coexistence' (Hall, 2014: 32).

These ethnographies embedded in the local scale of neighborhoods, streets, public spaces, and 'micro-publics' are interesting responses to calls for studying 'everyday' and 'grounded' cosmopolitanism, even if they do not use the term. It is paradoxical that the scholars studying urban diversity in Western global cities do not use such a central concept, at least in European social sciences. Historians of the Ottoman Empire are less reluctant to use the concept of cosmopolitan cities, even if they usually express reservations about it.

4   'Bygone' Cosmopolitan Cities of the Ottoman Empire

Alexandria is frequently presented as the model par excellence of the cosmopolitan city, its conviviality magnified in European literature (Lawrence Durrell, Constantine Cavafy), and celebrated by the Egyptian director Youssef Chahine. With its renaissance under Muhammad Ali at the beginning of 19th century, the Egyptian city became one of the biggest ports of the Mediterranean Sea, and, with the cotton boom, turned into a major commercial and financial center, attracting Greek, Armenian, Italian, and French migrants. Ilbert and Yannakakis (1997) have aptly described these powerful foreign and minority communities that managed to obtain to a degree of autonomy through their elites, who founded one of the first municipalities in Egypt. These notables were linked by common interests, and shared a lifestyle and socialized together in coffee houses and sport clubs. They created hospitals and schools for their own community, providing services that the state could not offer. They managed the social lives of individuals within their own community. Instead of a melting pot, Alexandria's unity came from the existence of horizontal relations (solidarity) at the top between the notables of each community and vertical relations (loyalty) within each community. Behind the myth of 'conviviality' lies a range of situations spanning peaceful coexistence, tolerance, cooperation, indifference, and downright hostility and pogroms, as during the anti-European riot of 1882.

From the Alexandrian example, we can learn three lessons. First, cosmopolitanism has to be understood as only lasting for a period of a city's history: Alexandria's cosmopolitan page was turned in 1956 with the nationalization of the Suez Canal by Nasser, declaring the effective decolonization of Egypt. Second, the narratives of cosmopolitan Alexandria have been deeply criticized for their colonialist and elitist timbre, overshadowing the vast and silent majority of colonial rule, the semi-colonial character of their society is undeniable. But at the same time, can we suspect Youssef Chahine of nostalgia for colonial rule because he celebrated Alexandria's model of conviviality and tolerance in his tetralogy of the city? Even today there is fierce debate, among academics and Alexandrian civil society alike, between those nostalgic for 'cosmopolitan Alexandria' and those who deny it. Third, Driessen (2005) objected to labeling entire cities as cosmopolitan, and advocated shifting the term's application to individuals. But his argument collapses if you acknowledge (paraphrasing the old adage) that the air of a cosmopolitan city does not a cosmopolitan make. Cosmopolitanism is thus considered as cultural and social praxis, arising from a diverse environment and unequally distributed across time, space, and the social spectrum (although not reserved for the elite).

If Alexandria was often presented as an enclave *beside* (and not *in*) Egypt, Istanbul offers another case study of a city in which minorities were not exactly the same as foreigners. The capital of the Ottoman Empire was not a colonized city but the showcase of a profound modernization process emulating the European model. It had developed various forms of cosmopolitanism at different social levels throughout its history, under the *millet* system. Rooted in the inequality between Muslims and non-Muslims, this allowed the coexistence of various religious and ethnic minorities but maintained strict barriers to keep them from mixing (Eldem, 2013). In 1900, 15 percent of Istanbul's population were foreign, more than the native Jewish and Armenian communities together. They were concentrated in the neighborhoods of Galata and Pera, which were considered 'European' districts and had supplanted the then marginalized ancient city center. Eldem describes the 'hybrid identities of half-Westernized local non-Muslims and of Westerners who had "gone native" as a result of several generations of residence in the Ottoman land' as 'Levantine cosmopolitanism' (Eldem, 2013: 222). This fragile and marginal form of cosmopolitanism was destroyed by Turkish nationalism, built on the eradication of cultural diversity. In the 1990s, Istanbul (in becoming a globalized city) rediscovered its cosmopolitan past. Nostalgic references to its partly reimagined cosmopolitanism were highly influential in the gentrification of Beyoğlu (Pera). Eldem proposes an appealing definition of cosmopolitanism: 'a social environment can be qualified as truly cosmopolitan only as long as it is shaped by the diversity of its constituents, while they, in turn, are also transformed by the cosmopolitan cultural milieu they had contributed to form.' (Eldem, 2013: 218) He indicates two prerequisites for cosmopolitanism: the existence of political intent to promote exchange and interaction among subjects, and the capacity of an urban setting to produce its own culture distinct from the simple juxtaposition of several differing cultures.

So although historians have helped us to refine the definition of cosmopolitanism, it still brings us back to the 'truly cosmopolitan city,' and we are once again facing the endless question: Are people really mixing, or are they simply living side by side?

5   Cosmopolitanism and Segregation in Wannabe Global City-States

Singapore, a center of trade in the 19th century, is now a prosperous city-state that became a major world financial and commercial hub after gaining its independence. At first sight, Singapore presents the two prerequisites of a truly cosmopolitan city. Nicknamed a 'child of diaspora,' Singapore's ethnically and racially diverse national population is not only very visible in urban landscapes, but also acknowledged in collective representations and official discourses under the motto of 'separate but equal.' The city celebrates and stages its cosmopolitanism and the production of hybrid identities in several museums, including the Peranakan Museum. It is also sustained through public policy, such as that ensuring the equal distribution of each ethno-racial group (CMIO: Chinese, Malays, Indians, and Others) in public housing (Yeoh, 2004). Upon several occasions, starting in the 1990s, the government has celebrated the city's capacity to welcome people of different origins and has asserted its intention to 'cosmopolitanize' both places and people (that is, making those seen as 'heartlanders' more cosmopolitan). The objective is to transform Singapore into a real *cosmopolis* that can attract and retain new tourists, investors, and 'foreign talent,' as they call highly skilled workers. This cosmopolitan branding is a way for Singapore to prove its standing as a global city and provide world-class consumption and cultural infrastructures, allowing global lifestyles. Singapore is a pioneer of urban marketing in the wake of the success of Florida's concept of 'creative city,' which gauges the attractiveness of a city on its ability to welcome diversity. Cosmopolitan aspirations are used to forge a state-led national identity in Singapore, which is a reminder that the cosmopolitan should not be systematically opposed to the national level and is strongly associated with global modes of consumption.

Since the late 1980s, Singapore's urban life has been strongly transformed by massive fluxes of international migrations, both skilled and unskilled, coming from various parts of the world to offer cheap labor and overcome the limitations of local resources. Super-diverse communities have emerged, but they are marked by transience due to non-integrative migration policies with very restrictive access to citizenship, adding complex layers to the legacy of the city-state's cosmopolitan colonial past. So cosmopolitanism in Singapore is organized into very strongly racialized categories (the CMIO system): people belonging to these are supposed to live together in the urban space but are not obliged to mix. Attitudes toward newcomers are extremely unequal, since a complex work-permit system differentiates between low wage migrants (who cannot marry Singaporeans or request family reunification) and high wage migrants (who can bring spouses and children and have easier access to permanent residency and even citizenship). The will to keep poor migrants invisible and transient is accompanied by strong segregation practices.

An interesting parallel can be drawn with Dubai, another young 'quasi' city-state in a federation of emirates, under an authoritarian regime. Its economic development was sparked by inspired branding, as a global city that succeeded in putting its name in the map of world cities, through global forms of consumption. This was achieved through mega-projects led by star architects, flaunted with a fierce sense of excess (boasting of the biggest mall, tower, and airport in the world) but based on the massive exploitation of cheap labor from South Asia. Dubai's minority/majority balance is inversed, since nationals represents less than 10 percent of the total population, which partly explains the current very restrictive access to citizenship. Being a citizen includes numerous benefits from a generous welfare state, based first on the redistribution of oil revenues, and now on more diversified sources. Foreigners from all over the world, both skilled and unskilled, are transient residents who may have to leave as soon as they lose their job, without any hope of integration. Although Dubai does not go as far as Singapore in presenting itself as cosmopolitan, it is branding itself with an image of a multicultural city that is tolerant and open to diversity, to differentiate itself from the surrounding region, which is strongly associated in the international imagination with conflicts, fundamentalist Islam, and terrorism. In a city with very fragmented urbanism, and in an Emirati society highly stratified along racial, ethnic, and social lines, the forces for segregation are strong, epitomized by their most extreme landscapes: labor camps scattered along the periphery where poor migrants (primarily from South Asia) live in insecure conditions and luxurious gated communities for the privileged elite. In one of the most masculine cities in the world (only 30 percent of residents are women), over twenty of the neighborhoods (mainly dedicated to housing foreign labor) have male residency rates over 90 percent, and not a single woman has been counted in five of them. But patterns of segregation are more complex and some forms of ethnic (but not really social, except for living maids) mixing are present in apartment towers (Pagès-El Karoui, 2018). Cosmopolitan cities in non-Western and non-inclusive contexts still have much to teach us, and can help us to more accurately document the tensions between various forms of cosmopolitanism and the ways in which they exclude, especially at a time when immigration and integration policies are increasingly challenged in Western countries.

6 Conclusion

During this short journey through cities marked by ethnic diversity around the world, we encountered several difficulties in defining cosmopolitan urbanity, which is too often stranded in a mythicized cosmopolitanism positing the romanticized peaceful coexistence of people of diverse origins living in relative harmony. We have learned that in order to use cosmopolitanism as an analytical tool in urban studies, it must not be put in opposition to the national, and should not be used synonymously with globalization, even if it is to celebrate its positive side. To be heuristic, it has to be separated from the Kantian ideal and its normative dimension. We must accept the need to account for its tensions and contradictions and consider it as a social praxis that is unequally distributed across space, time, and social groups (while not limited to elites), inherited from *situations* where heterogeneous populations are the norm.

Do we have to abandon the term to qualify a city? That is an option, but why? No real competitor (multicultural or super-diverse) seems to do the same job. Another option is to opt for a very broad meaning, calling every diverse urban environment cosmopolitan. A third option, more demanding, is to choose to restrict this label to cities where real interactions take place, where a variety of cosmopolitan situations can occur. Not every form of diversity is cosmopolitanism. For these reasons, some scholars prefer to distinguish between 'pluralist cities,' where separate communities live side by side, and 'cosmopolitan cities,' implying more interactions between communities, where migrants, foreigners, or minority groups visibly mark the city and help create a specific, hybrid culture, distinct from the sum of the diverse cultures. In that sense, to be cosmopolitan, a city must be shaped by diversity and produce a specific identity, something new in common. And there should be a will or awareness of the necessity of promoting exchange and interactions. If we choose this last option, we could also study gradients and forms of cosmopolitanism, since we have experience with many types of cosmopolitan urbanity. Typologies are hard to establish, since each configuration seems to be specific and embedded in a particular space and history, but such an undertaking could set the research agenda for the coming years and ultimately make an excellent contribution to the understanding of cosmopolitan spaces.

References

Amin, A. 2002. 'Ethnicity and the Multicultural City: Living with Diversity.' *Environment and Planning A: Economy and Space* 34 (6): 959–80, https://doi.org/10.1068/a3537.

Anderson, E. 2011. *The Cosmopolitan Canopy: Race and Civility in Everyday Life*. New York: W. W. Norton & Co.

Beck, U. 2006. *The Cosmopolitan Vision*. Cambridge, UK: Polity Press.

Binnie, J., J. Holloway, S. Millington, and Y. Craig. 2006. *Cosmopolitan Urbanism*. London; New York: Routledge.

Calhoun, C. 2002. 'The Class Consciousness of Frequent Travelers: Towards a Critique of Actually Existing Cosmopolitanism.' *South Atlantic Quarterly* 101 (4): 869–897, https://doi.org/10.1215/00382876-101-4-869.

Douglass, M. 2009. 'Globopolis or Cosmopolis? Alternative Futures of City Life in East Asia.' *Journal of Urban Humanities* 2: 67–115.

Driessen, H. 2005. 'Mediterranean Port Cities: Cosmopolitanism Reconsidered.' *History and Anthropology* 16 (1): 129–141.

Eldem, E. 2013. 'Istanbul as a Cosmopolitan City: Myths and Realities.' In *A Companion to Diaspora and Transnationalism*, edited by A. Quaysib and G. Daswani, 212–230. Hoboken, NJ: Wiley Blackwell.

Foner, N. 2007. 'How Exceptional Is New York? Migration and Multiculturalism in the Empire City.' *Ethnic and Racial Studies* 30: 999–1023.

Glick Schiller, N. and A. Çağlar. 2009. 'Towards a Comparative Theory of Locality in Migration Studies: Migrant Incorporation and City Scale.' *Journal of Ethnic and Migration Studies* 35 (2): 177–202.

Hall, S. 2014. 'Super-Diverse Street: A "Trans-Ethnography" across Migrant Localities.' *Ethnic and Racial Studies* 38 (1): 1–14.

Hannerz, U. 1996. *Transnational Connections*. London: Routledge.

Harvey, D. 2000. 'Cosmopolitanism and the Banality of Geographical Evils.' *Public Culture* 12 (2): 529–564.

Ilbert, R. and I. Yannakakis. 1997. *Alexandria 1860–1960: The Brief Life of a Cosmopolitan Community*. Alexandria: Harpocrates Publishing.

Kasinitz, P., J. Mollenkopf, and M. Waters. 2004. 'Worlds of the Second Generation.' In *Becoming New Yorkers: Ethnographies of the New Second Generation*, edited by P. Kasinitz, J. Mollenkopf, and M. Waters, 1–19. New York: Russell Sage Foundation.

Latham, A. 2006. 'Sociality and the Cosmopolitan Imagination: National, Cosmopolitan and Local Imaginaries in Auckland, New Zealand.' In *Cosmopolitan Urbanism*, edited by J. Binnie, J. Holloway, S. Millington, and Y. Craig, 89–111. London: Routledge.

Pagès-El Karoui, D. 2018. 'Cosmopolitisme et ségrégation à Dubai.' *Urbanisme* 409: 64–67.

Safier, M. 1996. 'The Cosmopolitan Challenge in Cities on the Edge of the Millennium.' *City* 1 (3–4): 12–29.

Sandercock, L. 2006. 'Cosmopolitan Urbanism: A Love Song to Our Mongrel Cities.' In *Cosmopolitan Urbanism*, edited by J. Binnie, J. Holloway, S. Millington, and Y. Craig, 37–52. London: Routledge.

Sassen, S. 2001 [1991]. *The Global City: New York, London, Tokyo*, 2nd ed. Princeton, NJ: Princeton University Press.

Sennett, R. 1994. *Flesh and Stone: The Body and the City in Western Civilization*. New York: W. W. Norton.

Vertovec, S. 2007. 'Super-Diversity and Its Implications.' *Ethnic and Racial Studies* 30 (6): 1024–1054.

Wessendorf, S. 2013. 'Commonplace Diversity and the "Ethos of Mixing": Perceptions of Difference in a London Neighbourhood.' *Identities* 20 (4): 407–422.

Yeoh, B. 2004. 'Cosmopolitanism and its Exclusions in Singapore.' *Urban Studies* 41 (12): 2431–2445.

Yeoh, B. and W. Lin. 2012. 'Cosmopolitanism in Cities and Beyond.' In *The Routledge Handbook of Cosmopolitanism Studies*, edited by G. Delanty, 208–219. Abingdon: Routledge.

CHAPTER 14

The Future That Europe Has Left Behind

Massimo Pendenza

1   Introduction

In this chapter we attempt to highlight the *cosmopolitan normative* features of Europe—which, for us, should also be the purpose of the European Union's (EU's) constitutive project—and dwell on the current crisis gripping it. We will delineate these traits, not embedding them within a philosophical concept, but searching for them in the history of Europe and in the articles of the EU's constitutional charters, of whose *finalité* they represent the political-institutional essence. As we shall see, despite their great ideals, the treaties and the Charter of Fundamental Rights contain a minimum of cosmopolitan normative language. This distinguishes Europe from other global geographical spaces and results mainly from its historical-cultural traits. The history of Europe is indeed 'particular' in terms of principles and respect for the dignity of individual and of peoples, elements that lead us to support the thesis of a Europe envisaged as a *potential* place for normative cosmopolitanism and which have induced others to speak of the *European* as opposed to the *American dream* (Rifkin, 2004). However, revealing that the European documents use a minimum of cosmopolitan language and that particular traits of Europe's history are laudable as regards cosmopolitanism does not at all prove that Europe already constituted a well-defined cosmopolitan space. On the contrary, what is happening now, before our eyes—with the governance of refugees and the sovereign debt crises in some EU member states—is confirmation of this. Such events do not reveal a practical application of European ideals, either within the borders of Europe or outside them. Rather, they highlight *betrayal*, that is, a gap between the historical experience of a cosmopolitan normative Europe and the intrinsic intention in its official papers, and the crude reality of events. This seriously questions the endurance of Europe, its destiny, its deepest meaning, its ideals, and its history.

Our reflections are developed in three stages: first we offer evidence to support the thesis of a Europe as the expression of a historical space with the potential for affirming *normative cosmopolitanism*, specifically different from the United States; we then extrapolate such evidential traits from the articles of the constitutional treaties and the EU Charter of Fundamental

Rights; finally, we illustrate the betrayal of such ideals, as well as the relentless emergence of an alternative project, which, by contrast, we call *market cosmopolitanism*.

2 Europe as a 'Privileged Space for Human Hope'

Why does Europe, in our view, represent a historical space for the affirmation of normative cosmopolitanism, particularly as compared to the United States? It is undeniable that the cultural roots of these two areas of the world are the same and that the West has provided the lifeblood of both, it is equally evident that Europe and the United States are expressions of two variants of modernity and that there are elements in the European political space that are not present in that of the USA (Rifkin, 2004; Martinelli, 2007). Such elements, depending on history and political and cultural choices, characterize this part of the world, including in regard to 'cosmopolitanism.' Ferrara (2008) identifies at least three elements, from which he derives the impression of Europe as an 'exemplary force' of a cosmopolitan cast.

The first element deals with the different capacity for 'building peace.' For cultural and territorial reasons, if we exclude the American Civil War, the USA has never been obliged to fight endogenous enemies. This has determined a 'border culture' which disseminates, even today, a widespread sense of justification of suppression of the enemy, and of an unlimited physical-geographical expandability of the American way of life that leads to the negation of the rights of others and arbitrarily impacts on their fate. The war against Nazism, the Cold War against the dangers of communism in the USSR, and, currently, the war against Da'esh (also known as ISIL: Islamic State in Iraq and the Levant) and global terrorism, are pertinent examples of this mind-set. In contrast, the historical experiences of wars in Europe have highlighted, above all, the changing face of the enemy, as well as the impossibility of totally eliminating it—in other words, Europe must always reckon with the expression of diversity rather than an abstract enemy. Leaving aside Europe's imperialistic and colonialist wars (not to mention the Holocaust), which would seem to refute a substantial difference in this respect between the USA and Europe, the internal conflicts among European countries, albeit cruel and fratricidal, have always resulted in a definitive conclusion. The EU is itself an example of this, especially if we consider the former impossibility of even imagining a new Franco-German axis, which only a few years before the Second World War represented the greatest obstacle to peace and to the building of a united Europe. Moreover, after centuries of fratricidal devastation, Europe, as an institution, has been able to put a 'perpetual' brake on war within its territories,[1] even receiving the 2012 Nobel Peace Prize. From this perspective, the EU is the first political entity in history whose *raison d'être* is 'peace-building.' These considerations lead inevitably to a question: If we extend this difference between the EU and the USA to a global scale, where borders tend to expand and blend globally (while at the same time interaction between states becomes more complex due to global competition), given the American stance—aiming to expand and overcome its borders—and the European position—transforming borders into boundaries to cross (*limen*)—we might ask which of the two is closer to the cosmopolitan ideal in relation to others, whether they be rivals or enemies?

Ferrara's second element links the history of Europe to its particular relationship with capitalism, democracy, and welfare. This link is quite different from that present in the USA. As is well known, except at its beginning, the spread of European democracy has never been based merely on free trade and a market economy. In Europe, at least since the end of the Second World War, the regulation of free trade superimposed itself on the self-regulation of the marketplace. The outcome has been more a kind of capitalism under surveillance and kept 'under control'—linked to a system of redistribution of wealth (i.e., the welfare state)—rather than a capitalistic system that puts free enterprise before solidarity or deregulation before the normalizing of utilitarianism. In other words, while in Europe the relationship between democracy and capitalism has always been distinguished by tensions, at times giving rise to open conflict, in America it has generally been translated into coexistence. From the social doctrine of the Church to socialism and social democracy, Europe has always considered capitalism more as a price to pay for the stability of democracy than as an element, unequivocally taken for granted, of human development—though not to the extent of undermining the human and social rights so laboriously gained through revolutions and social struggle. In other words, European models of social status are more independent of the market than are American models. Economic regulation by public authorities in Europe has been designed to prevent the negative consequences of market mechanisms rather than to intervene *ex post facto*. From these brief considerations we derive the unequivocal inference that Europe, more than the USA or any other country in the world, is the most favorable place to achieve that political space for human dignity and overall development; in Europe, more so than anywhere else, resides the spirit of cosmopolitanism.

---

1   It must be said, however, that the EU has not included any article in its treaties with a specific reference to the 'repudiation of war.'

The third element compares the two political orders and their respective modes of institutional government. The American politico-institutional system, crystallized in a constitution that sets out precise goals, has an institutional architecture that assigns functions and remits specific to government bodies. The European system, on the contrary, is an ongoing project, subject to constant change and with unspecified goals. In other words, while the American Constitution is an institutive act of an already defined, political reality, the European Constitution is still in the making. Furthermore, as many political commentators rightly point out, the biggest difference is that marked by the presence or otherwise of an institutive *demos* (Grimm, 1995; Habermas, 1995; Weiler, 1999). Since the EU is not a state, at least not in the sense defined during the 20th century, nobody knows where its territorial boundaries lie. For many, the EU is, rather, an intellectual notion, the result of a shared past and a common destiny. Europe still has much work to do to achieve the *modus operandi* characterizing world constitutions. However, what we consider the limits of its constitution are also its strengths. With its constitution *in fieri*, Europe's efforts are addressed toward bringing together national particularities, norms, and supranational identities. Before Europe, which areas of the world have succeeded in such a project, except through annexation? The EU, Beck and Grande (2007: 121) have said, is 'an open project' whose borders have not yet been defined. This means welcoming anyone who wishes to become part of the great European family, sharing its values, and, above all, accepting participation in the unequaled cosmopolitan project of governance and voluntary inclusion.

In light of these three elements, we should ascertain what kind of power Europe has with which to play an active, accountable, and capable role in the world arena. Not being a state in the classic sense of the term—that is, an organism with a single centralized political body—means the EU is an institutional system *sui generis*, founded on the dynamic and multifactorial balance of its elements and open to new inclusions. In contrast to the USA, Europe's power is certainly not military. However, its economic power is immense, given its weight in trade and global exchanges. The truth is that the EU, because of the three mentioned elements, but also because of awareness of 20th-century horrors, has developed its political system and international role well away from the model of classical power—an initiative for which the term 'civil power' was specially coined (Duchêne, 1972; Bull, 1982; Manners, 2002; Padoa-Schioppa, 2004; Telò, 2006)—along a path quite unknown to realistic and state-centric thought, which continues dominant and unchallenged in the USA. If these three elements encourage such a *viaticum* offering solid political and ethical roots, two concepts also require verification: (a) that in the content of the EU constitutional documents, traces of such ideals exist; and (b) that there is coherence between profoundly cosmopolitan ideals and the effective actions and political choices made by the EU.

3   The Cosmopolitan Normative Identity of Europe

For European political and bureaucratic elites, the EU is not seen as a cosmopolitan project, as it is a fact that the word 'cosmopolitanism' does not appear among its official documents, nor is it ever mentioned in official public speeches. On the other hand, we do not risk denial if we say that the EU has long maintained a crucial role in the promotion of human rights and democracy—within (Alston, 1999) and outside of its borders (Manners, 2002)—and that signs of a 'subconscious cosmopolitanism' can be found in many of its acts. The trend that the EU has developed over time represents its 'normative' as well as its social and political cosmopolitan identity (Habermas, 2003; Delanty, 2005; Beck and Grande, 2007; Rumford, 2007; Robertson and Krossa, 2012).

It is well known that the European Community has always underwritten democracy and human rights as basic criteria for accession. Portugal, Spain, and Greece were not admitted before they abolished totalitarianism and changed their form of government. Turkey has not yet been accepted, despite the EU's political avalanche in defense of democratization and human rights—in particular since 2002—given that Turkey lacks a substantially democratic constitution and does not respect the principles of human rights. Furthermore, recently, the EU Parliament has approved the procedural *iter* for sanctions against Hungary, in compliance with Article 7.2 of the Treaty on European Union (TEU) for its violation of fundamental rights as set out in Article 2. Concerning trade and international cooperation in general, there has always been EU commitment to democracy and human rights. Since 1989, the 'human rights clause' has been incorporated into all cooperation and association agreements (Bartels, 2005). In fact, the EU has cut direct support to the budget of many states in cases of their violation of fundamental human rights. In 1998, the EU launched an initiative on combatting the death penalty and torture, and, through the United Nations (UN), raised the issue bilaterally and multilaterally throughout the world. The number of countries that have abolished capital punishment as a result of EU pressure is impressive. As Eriksen (2006: 226) rightly points out, these conditions can be 'ambivalent' and the mechanisms to achieve them incoherent, as in the cases of China, Israel, and ultimately Russia, only marginally sanctioned for its war against Ukraine and for its forced annexation of Crimea. But in spite of this, it is undeniable that human rights and, more generally, respect for human dignity, are at the basis of the principles of the EU.

As concerns the aspects linked to Europe's cosmopolitan *normative* identity, these are more effectively captured in the EU constitutional papers: the TEU and the Treaty on the Functioning of the European Union (TfEU), including the Charter of Fundamental Rights of the European Union. In many of the articles, the cosmopolitan imprint of the EU can be found, and indicates, as Manners (2008) suggests, a 'normative power' or 'civil power' inherent in its relations with the rest of the world. Although, after the 2005 French and Dutch referenda, the document that was approved in Lisbon lost some of its cosmopolitan spirit,[2] many of the references to human dignity and the values that underpin the peaceful and regulated coexistence of European citizens have remained. Principles of great ideals, which are not expressed in high-sounding words and not fixed in the collective imagination, give rise, however, to an ideal dialogue that brings to mind all the most significant European principles and values. In the TEU Preamble we find, for example, that the signatories are *inspired* by 'the cultural, religious and humanist inheritance of Europe, from which have developed the universal values of the inviolable and inalienable rights of the human person, freedom, democracy, equality and the rule of law.' (The same concepts are repeated in the TfEU Preamble, albeit with a more economic and political-institutional nature.) The principles explicitly expressed in the subsequent Article 2 of the TEU, emblematic of the true purpose of the EU, sum up well what we mean by the presence of traces of an implicit normative cosmopolitanism: 'The Union is founded on the values of respect for human dignity, freedom, democracy, equality, the rule of law and respect for human rights, including the rights of persons belonging to minorities […].' These fundamental principles that the EU makes its own are repeated several times in the TEU. In substance, however, as Article 6 reminds us, they derive from diverse sources: the Charter of Fundamental Rights of the European Union (Article 6.1), the European Convention on Human Rights (ECHR) (Article 6.2), and the constitutional traditions common to the member states (Article 6.3).

Besides the principles delineated in Article 2, which we have no difficulty in defining as cosmopolitan, others are to be found later in the document: defense of the environment, sustainable development, full employment, the fight against social exclusion, elimination of poverty, equal rights between men and women, solidarity between generations, consumer protection, and

---

2 In the Preamble, for example, the meaningful and eloquent phrase indicating the spirit of Europe, as being a 'privileged space of human hope,' was removed.

so on (Article 3.3). At a specifically social level, the treaties declare that the EU is working for the welfare of its citizens by taking 'measures to ensure co-ordination of the employment policies of the Member States' (Article 5.2 of the TfEU). This means providing consistency, and eventually rendering widespread in the world, the great conquest of civilization, that is, the EU social model of solidarity, mentioned as one of the cosmopolitan traits of Europe as compared to the rest of the world.

Among the values included in Article 2, however, we do not find the cosmopolitan principle par excellence—'peace'—one of the most important and probably the oldest of European principles. The reason is that the whole of Article 3.1 is dedicated to peace: 'The Union's aim is to promote peace, its values and the well-being of its peoples.' In addition to 'peace' (for the determination of which the EU was awarded the Nobel Prize in December 2012), 'freedom' is certainly another founding principle of the Union—a principle, however, which, by virtue of its ambivalent character (Foucault, 2008), in part distances itself from the normative dimension of cosmopolitanism, bringing it closer to a mercantile approach. While it is true that in Articles 3.2 and 67 of the TfEU the Union is described as intending to 'constitute an area of freedom, security and justice with respect for fundamental rights' (Title V), it is equally true that the EU tends to translate this commitment mostly into terms of free movement of goods, people, services, and capital (Title IV and Article 26.2 of the TfEU). Finally, the cosmopolitan normative principles of the EU emerge as 'democracy' and 'defence of human rights,' as mentioned in Article 2. In this context, the TEU states that the Union 'consolidate(s) and support(s) democracy' (Article 21.2.b) through Parliament, the parties, and associations (Title II, Articles 9–11), and defends human rights first of all, by adhering to the charters mentioned in Article 6.

Besides the treaties, and annexed to them, the Union has mainly promulgated its own Bill of Rights: the Charter of Fundamental Rights of the European Union, which, as stated in Article 6.1 of the TEU, 'shall have the same legal value as the Treaties.' Already in the Preamble, its aims are declared, the first of which is to 'respect the diversity of the cultures and traditions of the peoples of Europe.' The Charter then lists and defines, one by one, the six foundation rights: dignity, freedom, equality, solidarity, citizenship, and justice—essential principles that highlight the EU's will to propose to its citizens, and to the rest of the world, a cosmopolitan space in which the dignity of the human person, not only as a citizen, is protected in the most complete way. It is unfortunate that the Charter has been *excluded* from the treaties when, prior to Lisbon, it had been conceived as the pillar upon which to base the *constituenda* institutional integration of the European peoples. Was this perhaps already a sign of the inverted tendency toward anti-cosmopolitanism in Europe? Could it be considered an incipient (a)moral and institutional wedge, by means of which the subsequent economic austerity policies and the walls erected by proto-nationalist states have prospered by perpetuating the betrayal of the cosmopolitan normative project inscribed in the history and in the institutional papers of the EU?

4   The Blurred Lines of EU Normative Cosmopolitanism

Unfortunately, the blurred lines of Europe's cosmopolitan regulatory project are several, and trends, following the British referendum of June 2016, are even more disturbing. Furthermore, it is no wonder that after the first enlightening decade of this millennium, there is almost no mention of cosmopolitan Europe or even of how the semantics of the project has changed. How can we evaluate Europe today after the return of traditional rivalries and the emergence of new ones, and renewed xenophobia? Judgment is conflicting. How many traces of normative cosmopolitanism can we still find in the EU's political responses to the various crises that assail it? Recent events linked to the economic-financial crisis and that of political asylum seekers would prompt a negative answer, seen in terms of a betrayal—by specific elites, perpetrated against the cosmopolitan ideals inscribed in the history of Europe and in the institutional documents of the EU—rather than as an inevitable outcome.

The first instance of betrayal relates to the EU response to the financial crisis and the sovereign debts to which some member states have been subject—a response made by the technocratic and neoliberal elites and put in place by virtue of the 'European emergency legislation,' which Balibar (2013) described, in no uncertain terms, as effectively a 'top-down revolution,' and which Habermas (2012) defined as 'executive federalism.' Such legislation, demanded above all by Germany and its allies, envisaged measures designed by those who love the neoclassical 'monetarist' economy and are convinced that debt crises can be overcome only by drastic cuts in public spending and wages. This has resulted in the creation of new economic emergency tools and the approval of increasingly stringent rules for the control of national budgets and the rebalancing of the most exposed ones (Two Packs, Six Packs, Fiscal Compact, European Stability Mechanism). The management of an economic-financial crisis—deriving from the irresponsibility of banks and disguised as a public debt crisis—has been managed in a way that has reduced the EU's 'internal' positive solidarity and expanded negative solidarity through the freedom of the market, elevated to the status of a panacea of all ills (Fazi and Iodice, 2014). What has occurred is a massive lack of internal cohesion, solidarity, and the sharing of economic difficulties among the member states. The inevitable consequence has been millions of unemployed individuals who have less and less protection. This has initiated a course of events that have ended up revealing the cracks within the Union and among its member states (now distinguished between 'virtuous' and 'spendthrift,' 'innocent' and 'guilty,' North and South), rather than the transnational destinies of different classes winning or losing out through the crisis (Offe, 2014)—even to the paradoxical outcome of punishment being meted out to the countries rescued by drastic EU economic measures, light years away from European law and EU principles. This is clearly in violation of the provisions set out in the treaties relative to the social sphere (Nruun, Lörcher, and Schömann, 2012) or, worse, of the human rights enshrined in the numerous articles (e.g., Article 9 of the TfEU, which advocates the 'guarantee of adequate social protection') and the dozens of conventions or pacts in force to which Europe or individual states adhere (Salomon, 2015). The pressure brought to bear in the management of the financial crisis reflects a betrayal of the process of continental cosmopolitan integration, which is not in tune with the intention of 'constitutionalizing' the Union, the great promise at the beginning of the third millennium. Moreover, the EU's response to the crisis has produced—evidently—a partial or total restructuring of European economies and societies in a neoliberal vein (Duménil and Lévy, 2002: 12; Inglis, 2015: 739; Ferrera, 2016: 97), manouvered by a cosmopolitan market orientation, compatible with liberal rights. Rights that, in particular, promote, support, and defend freedom from the government and free enterprise in the economic field (Parker, 2012: 199; Parker and Rosamond, 2013: 241; Inglis, 2015: 775) against those rights (mentioned earlier in this chapter) which represent the distinctive features of the 'normative cosmopolitanism' of the European project (Felski, 2012; Parker, 2012): a clash of cosmopolitanisms (Inglis, 2015) present from the beginning and always in tension.

A second instance of betrayal concerns the deception of the post-Westphalian nature of Europe, the consequences of which—following the current immigration crisis—are directly linked to the EU's 'external' integration process. Clearly the EU has channeled itself toward the definitive overcoming of the sovereignty of national states and thereby the overcoming of the logic of international relations;[3] however, what is most evident is that, while it has worked to 'tame' its internal/international domains, it reneges when it

---

3 Although Brexit has made deep cracks in the post-Westphalian EU project, it has now been exploited by the many anti-European forces widespread among its member states.

raises barriers and is ambiguous with respect to its internal cosmopolitan project. Obviously, we are referring to the immigration crisis and asylum-seeking of peoples who disembark on the coasts of Southern Europe, and the subsequent rejection of or controlled quotas imposed on immigrants through intergovernmental policies. While, on the one hand, the EU promotes its internal 'market cosmopolitanism' by eliminating borders to facilitate the free movement of people, goods, and services, on the other, it erects—or allows states to erect—wider barriers around its external borders (Baban, 2013). If, internally, the EU has always worked to endow itself with cosmopolitan Kantian hospitality rights—encouraging the mobility of travelers, workers, entrepreneurs, and traders—now, by closing its borders against the outside, in terms of protection and treatment of people who are not Europeans citizens (Van Houtum and Pijpers, 2007; Geddes, 2008), it reveals an identity that separates the EU from the rest of the world (Eriksen, 2006), further fueled by a dawning 'European nationalism' (Bruter, 2005).

Political governance of the refugee crisis, therefore, seems to directly refute the legitimate application of Kant's third definitive 'Perpetual Peace' article (Kant, 1970), which states that not only must the federated members commit to maintaining the basic laws of domestic cosmopolitan hospitality, but also that such laws are to be applied beyond federal boundaries (Eriksen, 2006: 262; Brown, 2014: 686). The article claims that members of the federation must show their status of belonging, respecting the principle that the 'Cosmopolitan Right shalt be limited to Conditions of Universal Hospitality'—in other words, 'the right of a stranger not to be treated with hostility when he first arrives on someone else's territory' (Kant, 1970: 105). This is all the more significant if one considers how strongly Kant criticizes the European economic and political policy addressed to the New World. For Kant, well-rooted cosmopolitanism is that where the federated members harmonize their relations with non-federated peoples in the light of peaceful and mutually beneficial relations, eventually to create a potential universal 'civil constitution' (see Article 21 of the TEU). In our opinion, the lack on the part of the EU to achieve such a goal does not denote its incapacity to position itself as a cosmopolitan force in the world, but emerges rather as a betrayal of its great potential.

5 Conclusion

Despite the idealism emerging from the treaties and the resolutions on human rights, the two mentioned crises distance the Union from the Kantian cosmopolitan project, sought after by many (Archibugi, Held, and Köhler,

1998; Habermas, 2003; Beck and Grande, 2007; Rumford, 2007; Robertson and Krossa, 2012). Europe's management of the crises highlights its self-betrayal and also shows how debate on Europe is currently focused on its ambiguities. In the name of a *market cosmopolitanism*, Europe, on the one hand, defends and promotes economic and market freedoms, and, on the other, refutes its *normative cosmopolitanism*, depreciating and humiliating social principles of solidarity—a 'clash of cosmopolitanisms' (Inglis, 2015) that scholars have represented in various ways: 'Europe as a normative power' v. 'Europe as a market power' (Manners, 2002; Damro, 2012); 'a Kantian constitutional mindset v. a managerial mindset' (Brunkhorst, 2014); or 'a market-correcting Europe' v. 'a market-making Europe' (Ferrera, 2016)—all in an attempt to better grasp the *future that Europe has left behind.*

References

Alston, P. 1999. *The EU and Human Rights.* Oxford: Oxford University Press.

Archibugi, D., D. Held, and M. Köhler (eds.). 1998. *Re-imagining Political Community: Studies in Cosmopolitan Democracy.* Cambridge, UK: Polity Press.

Baban, F. 2013. 'Cosmopolitan Europe: Border Crossing and Transnationalism in Europe.' *Global Society* 27 (2): 217–235.

Balibar, É. 2013. 'A New Europe Can Only Come from the Bottom Up.' *Open Democracy*, May 6, https://www.opendemocracy.net/en/new-europe-can-only-come-from-bottom-up/.

Bartels, L. 2005. *Human Rights Conditionality in the EU's International Agreements.* Oxford: Oxford University Press.

Beck, U. and E. Grande. 2007. *Cosmopolitan Europe.* Cambridge, UK: Polity Press.

Brown, G. W. 2014. 'The European Union and Kant's Idea of Cosmopolitan Right: Why the EU is Not Cosmopolitan.' *European Journal of International Relations* 20 (3): 671–693.

Brunkhorst, H. 2014. *Das doppelte Gesicht Europas.* Berlin: Suhrkamp Verlag.

Bruter, M. 2005. *Citizens of Europe? The Emergence of Mass European Identity.* Basingstoke: Palgrave Macmillan.

Bull, H. 1982. 'Civilian Power Europe: A Contradiction in Terms?' *Journal of Common Market Studies* 21 (2): 149–164.

Damro, C. 2012. 'Market Power Europe.' *Journal of European Public Policy* 19 (5): 682–699.

Delanty, G. 2005. 'The Idea of a Cosmopolitan Europe: On the Cultural Significance of Europeanization.' *International Review of Sociology* 15 (3): 405–421.

Duchêne, F. 1972. 'Europe's Role in World Peace.' In *Europe Tomorrow: Sixteen Europeans Look Ahead*, edited by R. Mayne, 32–47. London: Fontana.

Duménil, G. and D. Lévy. 2002. 'The Neoliberal (Counter-)Revolution.' In *Neoliberalism: A Critical Reader*, edited by A. Saad-Filho and D. Johnston, 9–19. London: Pluto Press.

Eriksen, E. O. 2006. 'The EU: A Cosmopolitan Polity?' *Journal of European Public Policy* 13 (2): 252–269.

Fazi, T. and G. Iodice. 2014. *The Battle for Europe*. London: Pluto Press.

Felski, R. 2012. 'A New Europe: Introduction.' *New Literary History* 43 (4): v–xv.

Ferrara, A. 2008. *The Force of the Example: Explorations in the Paradigm of Judgment*. New York: Columbia University Press.

Ferrera, M. 2016. *Rotta di collisione. Euro contro welfare*. Rome and Bari: Laterza.

Foucault, M. 2008. *The Birth of Biopolitics: Lectures at the Collège de France, 1978–1979*. New York: Palgrave Macmillan.

Geddes, A. 2008. *Immigration and European Integration: Towards Fortress Europe*. Manchester: Manchester University Press.

Grimm, D. 1995. 'Does Europe Need a Constitution?' *European Law Journal* 1 (3): 282–303.

Habermas, J. 1995. 'Remarks on Dieter Grimm's "Does Europe Need a Constitution?"' *European Law Journal* 1 (3): 303–307.

Habermas, J. 2003. 'Towards a Cosmopolitan Europe.' *Journal of Democracy* 14 (4): 86–100.

Habermas, J. 2012. *The Crisis of the European Union: A Response*. Cambridge, UK: Polity Press.

Kant, I. 1970. 'Perpetual Peace.' In *Kant's Political Writings*, edited by H. Reiss, 93–130. Cambridge, UK: Cambridge University Press.

Inglis, D. 2015. 'The Clash of Cosmopolitanisms: The European Union from Cosmopolitization to Neo-Liberalization.' *Partecipazione & Conflitto* 8 (3): 736–760.

Manners, I. 2002. 'Normative Power Europe: A Contradiction in Terms?' *Journal of Common Market Studies* 40 (2): 235–258.

Manners, I. 2008. 'The Normative Ethics of the European Union.' *International Affairs* 84 (1): 45–60.

Martinelli, A. (ed.). 2007. *Transatlantic Divide: Comparing American and European Society*. Oxford: Oxford University Press.

Nruun, N., K. Lörcher, and I. Schömann (eds.). 2012. *The Lisbon Treaty and Social Europe*. Oxford: Hart Publishing.

Offe, C. 2014. *Europe Entrapped*. Cambridge, UK: Polity Press.

Padoa-Schioppa, T. 2004. *Europe, a Civil Power: Lessons from EU Experience*. London: Federal Trust for Education and Research.

Parker, O. 2012. 'The Ethics of an Ambiguous Cosmopolitics: Citizens and Entrepreneurs in the European Project.' *International Theory* 4 (2): 198–232.

Parker, O. and B. Rosamond. 2013. ' "Normative Power Europe" Meets Economic Liberalism: Complicating Cosmopolitanism Inside/Outside the EU.' *Cooperation and Conflict* 48 (2): 229–246.

Rifkin, J. 2004. *The European Dream*. Cambridge, UK: Polity Press.

Robertson, R. and A. Krossa. 2012. *European Cosmopolitanism in Question*. Basingstoke: Palgrave.

Rumford, C. (ed.). 2007. *Cosmopolitanism and Europe*. Liverpool: Liverpool University Press.

Salomon, M. E. 2015. 'Of Austerity, Human Rights and International Institutions.' *European Law Journal* 21 (4): 521–545.

Telò, M. 2006. *Europe: A Civilian Power?* New York: Palgrave Macmillan.

Van Houtum, H. and R. Pijpers. 2007. 'The European Union as a Gated Community: The Two-Faced Border and Immigration Regime of the EU.' *Antipode* 39 (2): 291–309.

Weiler, J. H. H. 1999. *The Constitution of Europe*. Cambridge, MA: Harvard University Press.

PART 3

Experiencing Cosmopolitanism

CHAPTER 15

Unpacking Cosmopolitan Memory

Hiro Saito

Cosmopolitanism is here to stay despite rising nationalist sentiments and movements against the forces of globalization. To be sure, some groups are suspicious of, and even hostile to, the increasing numbers of foreigners and foreign products coming into their countries, but other groups accept and embrace more opportunities to interact with foreign others and cultures. Similarly, while policies and laws continue to take the nation-state as a primary frame of reference, they have also incorporated the idea of humanity to expand rights for both citizens and foreign residents. A globalizing world is full of these contradictory forces of cosmopolitanism and nationalism. In this sense, cosmopolitanism and nationalism form a central dialectic of globalization.

This dialectic also operates as a focal point for the construction of 'collective memory' today. Since the early 1800s, collective memory has been integral to the formation of national identity to the extent that Max Weber (1978: 903) defined the nation as a 'community of memories.' At the beginning of the 21st century, however, nationalism is no longer the only logic of collective memory. As Ulrich Beck, Daniel Levy, and Natan Sznaider (2009) argued, the logic of cosmopolitanism is now increasingly found in a variety of mnemonic practices, thanks to the globalization of human rights discourse and the growing sociocultural interactions across national borders.

But exactly what does 'cosmopolitan memory' (Levy and Sznaider, 2006) look like? Is it the same as 'transnational memory' (De Cesari and Rigney, 2014) or 'multidirectional memory' (Rothberg, 2009)? Does cosmopolitan memory facilitate the creation of 'global identity' (Smith, 1990) and 'global solidarity' (Misztal, 2010), and, if so, how? After all, how does emerging cosmopolitan memory interact with existing national memory (Saito and Wang, 2014), and how does this dialectic unfold in a globalizing world? These are important questions concerning the nature of cosmopolitan memory, but they have yet to be systematically answered, partly because there has been much confusion over the concept of collective memory itself (Bell, 2003) and partly because cosmopolitanism studies is still a relatively new field that needs further conceptual refinement and empirical research (Delanty, 2012).

In this brief chapter, then, I prepare the ground for answering the important questions about cosmopolitan memory in three steps. To begin with, I elaborate on the concept of collective memory in terms of how mnemonic practices, especially commemorations, articulate mnemonic schemas and objects as the basis of collective autobiography vis-à-vis group identity. Given this clearer conceptualization of collective memory, I proceed to unpack the working of cosmopolitan memory—how it comes about and how it differs from, as well as overlaps with, transnational and multidirectional memories. Finally, I illuminate the dialectic of cosmopolitanism and nationalism in terms of the concept of 'institutional contradiction' (Friedland and Alford, 1991) and illustrate how this dialectic shapes the dynamics of collective memory in a globalizing world.

1 What Is 'Collective Memory'?

To have 'memory' of a past event, people have to experience it themselves. Learning of an event secondhand, individuals acquire knowledge, but not memory. Yet, when researchers speak of 'collective memory,' they routinely include as agents of memory those who do not have firsthand experience (Halbwachs, 1992; Assmann, 1995). But in what sense can these agents be said to have memory of a past event of which they lack firsthand experience? This conceptual clarification is worthwhile because more than a few researchers have used collective memory metaphorically as a category of analysis, obscuring its underlying causal mechanisms (Bell, 2003).

Simply put, collective memory emerges when those without firsthand experience of a past event identify with those who have such an experience, establishing both sets of actors as sharing membership in the same group. The creation of this affect-laden, first-person orientation to the past is at the crux of commemoration, one of the emotionally most powerful mnemonic practices available in society (Saito, 2018). Commemoration typically positions those who have firsthand experience center stage, whether in person or as images and symbols. This setup tends to lead those who lack firsthand experience to fix their attention on those with firsthand experience and induce the former to experience a past event vicariously from the imaginary first-person perspective of the latter. Commemoration also structures this vicarious experience in terms of mnemonic schemas—patterns of feeling and thinking about an event—to be shared by those without firsthand experience. In short, the concept of collective memory is meant to capture the misrecognition of secondhand knowledge as living memory by virtue of identifications on the part of those who lack firsthand experience.

Put another way, just as autobiographical memory is crucial to generating and maintaining personal identity, collective memory provides people with autobiographical narratives of their purportedly shared past as the basis of their group identity. People are then induced to accept such narratives as authentic through mnemonic practices like commemoration that mobilize strong emotion. This is why social life is marked by an array of commemorations organized around anniversaries—the existence of any social group, be it a family, a company, or a nation, depends on constant reaffirmation of its collective autobiography, homogenizing mnemonic schemes among group members.

However, mnemonic schemas constitute only one dimension of collective memory. Mnemonic schemas can be stabilized and shared across time and space only when they are accompanied by mnemonic objects that include, but are not limited to, archives, memorials, museum exhibits, and history textbooks (Nora, 1989). In fact, the built environment as a whole can be seen as a gigantic set of multiple mnemonic objects enveloping people. Creatively rethinking the phrase 'out of sight, out of mind' as 'out of site, out of mind' nicely captures this constitutive role of mnemonic objects in the construction of collective memory. In this regard, collective memory is best understood as being 'distributed' partly in the internal world of mnemonic schemas and partly in the external world of mnemonic objects (Olick, 1999; Wertsch, 2002). Collective memory is then reproduced when mnemonic practices articulate the same sets of schemas and objects, whereas it is destabilized and even transformed when mnemonic practices rearticulate schemas and objects newly and differently.

Since the early 1800s, this process of production, reproduction, and transformation of collective memory has been dominated by the logic of nationalism to the extent that much of collective memory studies assumed the nation as a unit of analysis (Olick, 2003). By using the nationalist logic of collective memory, people focused on what happened to their conationals, whether heroes or victims, without sufficient regard for foreign others. This exclusive focus on conationals has manifested most clearly in the collective memory of an armed conflict, which often elevates fallen soldiers to immortal heroes of the nation while disregarding what these soldiers might have done to foreign others—the moment when one's own nation becomes sacred above all else, as Benedict Anderson (1991) pointed out. Moreover, nationalism excludes foreign others from commemoration in another sense: the principle of national sovereignty prohibits foreign others from participating in the process of shaping the content of commemoration. When a government plans a memorial ceremony for war dead at a national cemetery, for example, it typically does not allow foreign governments to influence the content of the ceremony. Thus, given the dominance of nationalism in both societies and social sciences (Wimmer and

Glick Schiller, 2002), collective memory has been often equated with national memory.

2 Which Collective Memory Is 'Cosmopolitan'?

Nevertheless, nationalism is no longer the only logic of collective memory available today. As Ulrich Beck and his colleagues (Beck, Levy, and Sznaider, 2009; Levy and Sznaider, 2006, 2010) argued, cosmopolitanism, an orientation of openness to foreign others and cultures, is increasingly institutionalized in a variety of mnemonic practices in the contemporary world, thanks to the globalization of human rights discourse and the growing sociocultural interactions across national borders. Cosmopolitanism here presents an alternative logic of feeling and thinking that takes humanity, rather than nationality, as a primary frame of collective memory. Drawing on the logic of cosmopolitanism, people remember what happened to foreign others as members of humanity, but they also invite those others to contribute to shaping the content of collective memory. As Beck put it, cosmopolitan memory involves

> acknowledging the history (and the memories) of the 'other' and integrating them into one's own history, … where the national monologues of victimization that are celebrated as national memory are systematically replaced by transnational forms and forums of memory and dialogue, which also enable the innermost aspects of the national realm—the founding of myths—to be opened up to and for one another.
> BECK, 2005: 43

Cosmopolitanism thus allows people to extend identifications beyond national borders and engage in transformative dialogues with foreign others, steering their collective autobiographies away from the logic of nationalism.

To be sure, 'cosmopolitan memory' is an important conceptual innovation capable of sensitizing researchers to the changing nature of collective memory in a globalizing world; however, it has also created some conceptual confusion since researchers in collective memory studies began to use similar concepts (Assmann and Conrad, 2010). For example, some researchers introduced the concept of 'transnational memory' (Erll, 2010; De Cesari and Rigney, 2014) to understand how and why memories travel across countries and regions, whereas others developed the concept of 'multidirectional memory' (Rothberg, 2009) to illuminate how the globalization of human rights discourse allows people to connect memories of multiple events from different times and places. But how do transnational and multidirectional memories differ from, and overlap with, cosmopolitan memory?

I argue that this conceptual confusion is actually productive because it presents an opportunity to elaborate exactly what is distinct about cosmopolitan memory vis-à-vis similar concepts. Here, the case of Holocaust remembrance, often seen as a quintessential example of cosmopolitan memory (e.g., Levy and Sznaider, 2006, 2010), offers a useful point of departure. Suppose only people in Israel remember the Holocaust as an important event for the Jewish nation. This would be a case of national memory of the Holocaust. But, if people in other countries begin to remember the Holocaust as something relevant to them as members of humanity, collective memory of the Holocaust will become cosmopolitan. In other words, the degree of cosmopolitanness of collective memory can vary on the transnational dimension—the more nationalities remember the past event, the more cosmopolitan its memory becomes (see x-axis in Figure 15.1). Along this transnational dimension, memory of a single past event like the Holocaust can become 'singularly cosmopolitan.'

The transnational dimension alone, however, cannot capture all variants of cosmopolitan memory because transnational and cosmopolitan memories are not identical. Suppose, this time, only people in Israel remember the Holocaust, but they remember it in conjunction with slavery, genocides, and other

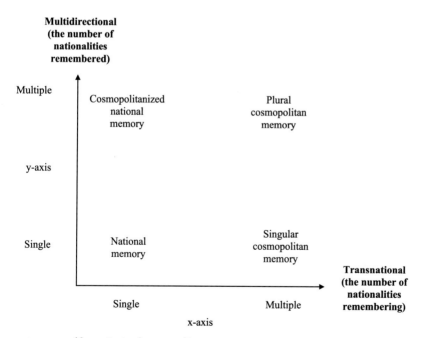

FIGURE 15.1 The variants of cosmopolitan memory

episodes of large-scale violence that happened around the world. Their collective memory exists within national borders, but it encompasses victims of multiple past events irrespective of their nationalities. I propose to call such collective memory 'cosmopolitanized national memory': even though this memory is still centered on conationals, it is also extended with openness to and inclusion of foreign others. In this regard, the degree of cosmopolitanness of collective memory varies on the multidirectional dimension—the more nationalities are remembered, the more cosmopolitan this act of remembering becomes (see y-axis in Figure 15.1).

Such conceptual formalization of 'cosmopolitan memory' is anything but a mere intellectual exercise, for it effectively facilitates empirical investigation. Take, for example, collective memory of the atomic bombing of Hiroshima (Saito, 2015). On the one hand, as more and more people outside Japan came to learn the damages of the atomic bombing against the backdrop of the worldwide antinuclear movement in the 1950s, collective memory of the event became more cosmopolitan on the transnational dimension, similar to the aforementioned 'singular cosmopolitan memory' of the Holocaust. On the other hand, as more and more people in Japan began to remember victims of the atomic bombing in conjunction with victims of other armed conflicts—eventually including Asian victims of Japan's own past aggression—the Japanese memory of the event became more cosmopolitan on the multidirectional dimension in the sense of 'cosmopolitanized national memory.'

Moreover, this conceptual formalization helps identify empirical cases where maximal transnationality combines with maximal multidirectionality to produce the highest degree of cosmopolitanness in collective memory, that is, 'plural cosmopolitan memory,' wherein people around the world remember multiple past events as relevant to their common humanity. Construction of such 'truly' cosmopolitan memory has been promoted by the United Nations Educational, Scientific and Cultural Organization (UNESCO). Currently, UNESCO runs the World Heritage site program. Launched in 1972, the program aims to preserve natural and cultural sites around the world as shared heritage for humanity as a whole. While cultural sites consist mostly of ancient castles, temples, and monuments, they also include sites related to slavery, the Holocaust, the atomic bombing, and other forms of extreme human suffering. UNESCO also established the Memory of the World Programme in 1992 to protect historic documents, relics, and works of art as focal points for remembering world history. This program also includes projects to preserve historical documents related to negative aspects of world history, such as the Holocaust. These two UNESCO programs encourage people around the world to remember various events that happened to foreign others as fellow human beings—hence their potential to produce plural cosmopolitan memory as the basis of 'global solidarity' and 'global identity' (Misztal, 2010).

3   What Is the Relationship between Cosmopolitan and National Memories?

As Anthony Smith (1990: 180) recognized, however, 'The central difficulty in any project to construct a global identity and hence a global culture, is that collective identity, like imagery and culture, is always historically specific because it is based on shared memories and a sense of continuity between generations.' Even if people around the world begin to remember the same set of past events as relevant to their common humanity according to the UNESCO programs, they will also continue to have memories of other past events that are relevant to their national identities. This is why the most common form of cosmopolitan memory today is likely to be 'cosmopolitanized national memory,' wherein people remember past events constitutive of their national identity together with similar events that happened to foreign others—in the sense that Holocaust memory 'does not replace national collective memories but exist as their horizon' (Levy and Sznaider, 2006: 13). By the same token, 'singular cosmopolitan memory' is likely to have significant regional variations: European countries are more likely to remember the Holocaust than countries in other regions, and even those European countries remember the Holocaust very differently given their diverse national histories (Chirot, Shin, and Sneider, 2014).

Thus, the relationship between cosmopolitan and national memories is not zero-sum but symbiotic, as Ulrich Beck and Natan Sznaider (2006: 20) observed '[c]osmopolitanism does not only negate nationalism but also presupposes it.' While United Nations (UN) organizations promote human rights, national governments are still responsible for implementing them in education systems and other societal institutions (Meyer, 2000). Similarly, even though membership in humanity is emphasized, national citizenship continues to structure access to socioeconomic resources and political rights (Soysal, 1994). This is why researchers need to keep in mind that 'even in a so-called postnational age, the "national" as a framework for identity and memory-making is still a powerful one' (De Cesari and Rigney, 2014: 19).

Since both cosmopolitanism and nationalism are legitimated as logics of collective memory, this creates an 'institutional contradiction,' wherein contradictory but equally legitimate logics clash with each other (Friedland and Alford, 1991). This institutional contradiction serves as a focal point of political struggles for the legitimate memory, and these struggles are likely to be intense and protracted because all sides, subscribing to cosmopolitanism and nationalism differently, have reasonable claims to legitimacy (Saito and Wang, 2014). Take, for example, the so-called history problem in East Asia, where Japan is embroiled in intense controversies with South Korea and China over how to commemorate the Asia-Pacific War that ended in 1945 (Saito, 2016). To name but a few, points of contention include interpretations of the Tokyo War Crimes Trial, apologies and compensation for foreign victims of Japan's past aggression, prime ministers' visits to the Yasukuni Shrine, and history textbooks.[1] In essence, the history problem in East Asia is a clash of incompatible national memories in Japan, South Korea, and China—and even the United States—that developed transnational feedback loops reinforcing nationalism in each country involved (Yoneyama, 2016), precisely when the human rights discourse, associated with cosmopolitanism, came to be increasingly institutionalized around the world. The East Asian case thus demonstrates the open-ended interplay between cosmopolitan and national memories in a globalizing world.

Put another way, how collective memory of a past event maps onto the transnational and multidirectional dimensions (Figure 15.1) depends fundamentally on political struggles among relevant actors. Collective memory of the atomic bombing, for example, did not become as cosmopolitan as that of the Holocaust despite the worldwide antinuclear movement in the 1950s, partly because the United States, one of the superpowers during the Cold War, suppressed it (Levy and Sznaider, 2006: 40). In turn, Japanese memory of the atomic bombing came to be considerably cosmopolitanized in the early 1990s because the transnational network of non-governmental organizations (NGO s) inside and outside Japan advocated for former 'comfort women' and other victims of Japan's past aggression (Saito, 2015).[2] The politics of collective memory thus simultaneously divides and unites relevant actors: although

---

1 Prior to the end of the Asia-Pacific War, the Yasukuni Shrine had been managed by the government to enshrine war dead. Although it lost government sponsorship after the war, it has remained the most important site of Japan's nationalist commemoration. Especially because Yasukuni enshrines fourteen wartime leaders who had been prosecuted as Class A war criminals at the International Military Tribunal for the Far East, the governments and people in South Korea and China regard Japanese prime ministers' visits to the shrine as an unrepentant justification of Japan's past aggression.
2 'Comfort women' were those who had provided 'sexual services' to the Japanese military during the Asia-Pacific War. Comfort women had been recruited from both Japan and its colonies, such as Korea and Taiwan. Some women had agreed to work at 'comfort stations,' whereas others had been forced by deception or coercion. After Japan had started war with the Allied powers in December 1941 and occupied Southeast Asia, the military had increased its involvement in recruitment, with methods that became increasingly coercive.

political struggles may lead one group of actors to dominate others to prevent the emergence of cosmopolitan memory, it may also lead previously disparate groups to form a coalition that will expand the scope of collective memory and identity in a cosmopolitan direction.

In short, the dialectic of cosmopolitanism and nationalism reinforces the dual nature of collective memory as a focal point of both group solidarity and intergroup conflict on an increasingly global scale. On the one hand, the growing transnational circulation of collective memories vis-à-vis the globalization of human rights discourse allows people to remember all kinds of victims equally within the horizon of common humanity to express global solidarity and forge global identity. On the other hand, such transnational collaboration of collective memories, according to the cosmopolitan logic, will not eliminate competition between national memories. In fact, the cosmopolitan logic itself can reinforce international competition of memories when it is appropriated by nationalists demanding their national tragedies be remembered by people of other nationalities (Nakano, 2018). And yet such competition can also facilitate the growth of cosmopolitan memory because it publicizes previously little-known past events to global audiences and hence expands the coverage of nationalities to be remembered worldwide. Thus, collective memories in a globalizing world will continue to evolve in a complex manner, revolving around the institutional contradiction between cosmopolitanism and nationalism.

4 Conclusion

In this brief chapter, I have unpacked the concept of cosmopolitan memory to lay the groundwork for fully understanding the changing nature of collective memory in the contemporary world. First, I have cleared up some confusion over the concept of collective memory—this conceptual clarification is a necessary first step for identifying which collective memory is cosmopolitan. Specifically, I have proposed conceptualizing collective memory as a set of mnemonic schemas and objects that articulates a collective autobiography, which in turn serves as the basis of group identity among people with and without firsthand experience of past events. Then, I have proceeded to theorize how and why some collective memories become cosmopolitan in three different ways—singular cosmopolitan memory, cosmopolitanized cosmopolitan memory, and plural cosmopolitan memory—depending on where these memories map onto the dimensions of transnationality and multidirectionality. Such theorization of cosmopolitan memory is important because it helps empirically identify variants of cosmopolitan memory in the world. Finally, I have illustrated how cosmopolitan and national memories interact with each other, given that both cosmopolitanism and nationalism are legitimated to constitute an institutional contradiction as a focal point for both collaboration and competition of collective memories across national borders. In this sense, cosmopolitanism and nationalism form an untrancendable dialectic of collective memory in a globalizing world.

In conclusion, I suggest two lines of further research for fully understanding the working of cosmopolitan memory. The first pertains to cross-national and cross-regional comparisons, because cosmopolitan memory is fundamentally perspectival, as indicated by the pioneering case studies of the cosmopolitanization of Holocaust memory (Levy and Sznaider, 2006, 2010; Beck, Levy, and Sznaider, 2009). In effect, this research has focused on North American and Western European perspectives on the Holocaust—and more generally, the field of collective memory studies itself is 'West-centric' (Olick, Sierp, and Wüstenberg, 2017). The Holocaust, however, looks very different from African, Latin American, and Asian perspectives (Rothberg, 2009). Similarly, past events that drive the cosmopolitanization of national memories differ across countries—the atomic bombing of Hiroshima and Nagasaki in the case of Japan, the tragedy of 'comfort women' in the case of South Korea, and so on (Saito, 2016). Given the conceptual unpacking of cosmopolitan memory in this chapter, cross-national and cross-regional comparisons will shed light on a wide variety of cosmopolitan memories that are emerging around the world today.

In addition, the second line of further research can critically probe into the relationship between cosmopolitan memory and historical justice. This is not only because justice by definition presupposes memory as well as other documentations of past wrongs, but also because the globalization of human rights discourse has prompted more and more people around the world to confront historical injustices of slavery, colonialism, and other legacies of violence that happened on a transnational scale (Neumann and Thompson, 2015), including the tragedy of 'comfort women.' Transnational dialogues on these historical injustices, however, are often obstructed by nationalist memories that discount the suffering of foreign others. In this regard, the pursuit of historical justice on a transnational scale is coterminous with the problem of cosmopolitan memory: how to remember what happened to foreign others. Thus, further research on cosmopolitan memory has the potential to generate important implications for the larger debate on how to obtain historical justice in a globalizing world.

References

Anderson, B. 1991. *Imagined Communities*. London: Verso.

Assmann, A. and S. Conrad (eds.). 2010. *Memory in a Global Age: Discourses, Practices and Trajectories*. London: Palgrave Macmillan.

Assmann, J. 1995. 'Collective Memory and Cultural Identity.' *New German Critique* 65: 125–133.

Beck, U. 2005. *Power in the Global Age: A New Global Political Economy*. Cambridge, UK: Polity Press.

Beck, U., D. Levy, and N. Sznaider. 2009. 'Cosmopolitanization of Memory: The Politics of Forgiveness and Restitution.' In *Cosmopolitanism in Practice*, edited by M. Nowicka and M. Rovisco, 111–128. Farnham: Ashgate Publishing.

Beck, U. and N. Sznaider. 2006. 'Unpacking Cosmopolitanism for the Social Sciences: A Research Agenda.' *British Journal of Sociology* 57 (1): 1–23.

Bell, D. 2003. 'Mythscapes: Memory, Mythology, and National Identity.' *British Journal of Sociology* 54 (1): 63–81.

Chirot, D., Gi-Wook Shin, and D. Sneider (eds.). 2014. *Confronting Memories of World War II: European and Asian Legacies*. Seattle: University of Washington Press.

De Cesari, C. and A. Rigney (eds.). 2014. *Transnational Memory: Circulation, Articulation, Scales*. Berlin: De Gruyter.

Delanty, G. (ed.). 2012. *Routledge Handbook of Cosmopolitanism Studies*. London: Routledge.

Erll, A. 2010. 'Regional Integration and (Trans) Cultural Memory.' *Asia Europe Journal* 8 (3): 305–315.

Friedland, R. and R. R. Alford. 1991. 'Bringing Society Back In: Symbols, Practices, and Institutional Contradictions.' In *The New Institutionalism in Organizational Analysis*, edited by W. W. Powell and P. J. DiMaggio, 232–263. Chicago: University of Chicago Press.

Halbwachs, M. 1992. *On Collective Memory*. Chicago: University of Chicago Press.

Levy, D. and N. Sznaider. 2006. *The Holocaust and Memory in the Global Age*. Philadelphia, PA: Temple University Press.

Levy, D. and N. Sznaider. 2010. *Human Rights and Memory*. University Park: Pennsylvania State University Press.

Meyer, J. W. 2000. 'Globalization: Sources and Effects on National States and Societies.' *International Sociology* 15 (2): 233–248.

Misztal, B. A. 2010. 'Collective Memory in a Global Age: Learning How and What to Remember.' *Current Sociology* 58 (1): 24–44.

Nakano, R. 2018. 'A Failure of Global Documentary Heritage? UNESCO's "Memory of the World" and Heritage Dissonance in East Asia.' *Contemporary Politics* 24 (4): 1–16.

Neumann, K. and J. Thompson (eds.). 2015. *Historical Justice and Memory*. Madison: University of Wisconsin Press.

Nora, P. 1989. 'Between Memory and History: Les Lieux de Mémoire.' *Representations* 26: 7–24.

Olick, J. K. 1999. 'Collective Memory: The Two Cultures.' *Sociological Theory* 17 (3): 333–348.

Olick, J. K. (ed.). 2003. *States of Memory: Continuities, Conflicts, and Transformations in National Retrospection*. Durham, NC: Duke University Press.

Olick, J. K., A. Sierp, and J. Wüstenberg. 2017. 'The Memory Studies Association: Ambitions and an Invitation.' *Memory Studies* 10 (4): 490–494.

Rothberg, M. 2009. *Multidirectional Memory: Remembering the Holocaust in the Age of Decolonization*. Stanford, CA: Stanford University Press.

Saito, H. 2015. 'The A-bomb Victims' Plea for Cosmopolitan Commemoration: Toward Reconciliation and World Peace.' *Thesis Eleven* 129 (1): 72–88.

Saito, H. 2016. *The History Problem: The Politics of War Commemoration in East Asia*. Honolulu: University of Hawaii Press.

Saito, H. 2018. 'The Changing Culture and Politics of Commemoration.' In *The Handbook of Cultural Sociology: Second Edition*, edited by J. R. Hall, L. Grindstaff, and Ming-Cheng Lo, 648–656. New York: Routledge.

Saito, H. and Y. Wang. 2014. 'Competing Logics of Commemoration: Cosmopolitanism an Nationalism in East Asia's History Problem.' *Sociological Perspectives* 57 (2): 167–185.

Smith, A. D. 1990. 'Towards a Global Culture?' *Theory, Culture & Society* 7 (2/3): 171–191.

Soysal, Y. N. 1994. *Limits of Citizenship: Migrants and Postnational Membership in Europe*. Chicago: University of Chicago Press.

Weber, M. 1978. *Economy and Society*, vol. 1. Berkeley: University of California Press.

Wertsch, J. V. 2002. *Voices of Collective Remembering*. Cambridge, UK: Cambridge University Press.

Wimmer, A. and N. Glick Schiller. 2002. 'Methodological Nationalism and Beyond: Nation-State Building, Migration and the Social Sciences. *Global Networks* 2 (4): 301–334.

Yoneyama, L. 2016. *Cold War Ruins: Transpacific Critique of American Justice and Japanese War Crimes*. Durham, NC: Duke University Press.

CHAPTER 16

Hospitality, Cosmopolitanism, and Conviviality
On Relations with Others in Hostile Times

Magdalena Nowicka

1   Europe's Refugee Drama

Since the late 1990s, the population of forcibly displaced people has doubled. The United Nations High Commissioner for Refugees (UNHCR) counted 65.6 million people worldwide who had to flee their homes due to armed conflict or fear of persecution. Ten million people are now stateless, and 22.5 million are refugees under international mandate. Seventeen percent of the world's displaced people are being hosted in Europe (UNHCR, 2017). On average, no more than one-quarter of all asylum seekers are granted refugee status, allowing them to settle in one of the European Union (EU) member states (Eurostat, 2017). Regulations prohibiting family reunification certifies the temporary status of those who are granted subsidiary protection only (COE, 2017).

The very idea of the EU as open to the inside and protected from the outside is an uneasy fit to the EU's commitment to human rights vis-à-vis continuous flows of voluntary and involuntary migrants. This challenge has never been adequately addressed (Scipioni, 2017). The already tense situation escalated in late summer of 2015. The International Organization for Migration (IOM) recorded 1,046,599 arrivals to Europe in 2015; the majority of the refugees were from Syria and entered the EU via Turkey and Greece, heading north through the Central Balkans, Hungary, and Austria (IOM, 2015). The condition of refugees became dramatic in mid-July 2015 when Hungary began building a razor-wire fence along its border with Serbia to decrease migrant arrivals. In the early days of September, Hungarian police sealed off Keleti railway station in Budapest to stop the refugees moving on. The sustained media coverage of the drama triggered Europe-wide compassion and a sense of moral obligation toward these people. Many saw this moral duty realized in Chancellor Angela Merkel's decision, announced on September 4, 2015, to allow the refugees to enter Germany and register there as asylum seekers; this decision was lauded internationally as 'a spectacular manifestation of humanitarianism' (Takis, 2015).

Controversial in Europe, Merkel's politics has also polarized public opinion in Germany (Holmes and Castañeda, 2016). The tendencies toward nativism, xenophobia, and racism, mobilized by right-wing populists, were countered by a growing number of volunteers willing to help the refugees (Hamann and Karakayali, 2016; Fleischmann and Steinhilper, 2017). These volunteers were motivated to show solidarity by various factors ranging from biographical and professional aims to political and religious norms and values. Humanitarian and cosmopolitan ideals drove many of them to engage in creating non-national, alternative urban spaces in which refugees would feel welcomed and encounter non-migrants on equal terms (Turinsky and Nowicka, 2019).

The arguments of the domestic opponents of Germany's refugee politics did not question the moral obligation to allow entry to the refugees; instead, they raised concerns with the post-arrival integration of the refugees (Berry, Garcia-Blanco, and Moore, 2015). Angela Merkel's assertion 'we can make it' was soon rephrased into a skepticism on 'how we could manage' this crisis. This 'capacity' debate focused on a lack of adequate housing opportunities, a potential increase in crime, doubts surrounding the successful labor market integration of the refugees, capacities of schools to accommodate new children in light of the existing shortages of teachers, insufficient investments in infrastructure, and a lack of resources necessary to meet the particular health demands of refugees. Further concerns included refugees' supposed lack of shared values, whether they would show respect for the rule of law, the potential for anti-Semitism among Muslim refugees, threats of Islamic radicalization and terrorism, or misuse of asylum by 'labor migrants' or 'welfare tourists.' The backlash surrounding the 'culture of welcome' crystallized around reception quotas and upper limits to asylum claims (Conrad and Aðalsteinsdóttir, 2017). In consequence, it was argued, humanitarian aid should be increased to help refugees outside of Europe rather than inside, in their country of origin or in other areas where these people find shelter. The aim would be to make their homes livable spaces again, or the shelters good enough to lessen the pressure to migrate to Europe. This shifting narrative mirrors a more general reframing of the treatment of refugees, from questions of hospitality to questions of humanitarian policy (Blitz, 2017).

This 'war of positions' (Gramsci, 2005: 291) surrounding the appearance of refugees in Germany is, for me, an instructive case which can be used to discuss cosmopolitanism and its limits. The debate demonstrates that while it is a consensus that refugees should not be rejected upon arrival when their lives are in danger, this kind of hospitality remains, for many, a somewhat abstract ideal, for the arrival of refugees carries with it the potential for settlement, and this is linked to a number of concrete issues. For the debate, the highly contested differentiation between the 'other' who remains an outsider and the 'other' who becomes the 'other within' is thus central. The current case is thus useful when thinking of the place of the other in our world. I look at this issue from the vantage point of hospitality.

The debate as I perceive it thus includes three aspects that relate to the temporal dimension of hospitality. Accordingly, I structure my contribution to discuss: (1) the acceptance of the newly arrived in a territory; (2) modalities of treatment of these guests; and (3) the question of treatment of those 'guests' who stop being outsiders and become 'the others within.' I consider it productive to disentangle these aspects exactly because they are merged in public debates. Thereby, I distinguish two perspectives on the 'other.' The first one is cosmopolitanism, which I locate as relating primarily to the first and second aspects. The second perspective is conviviality, which concerns the third aspect. I attempt thus to sketch the contours of convivial hospitality in contrast to cosmopolitan hospitality.

2   Hospitality, Cosmopolitanism, and the External Other

Hospitality is a concept that carries a complex meaning, which makes it particularly useful as a lens for addressing our relations with others in the context of voluntary and involuntary migrations. It evokes openness and giving one's space to another; as an ethical stance, it governs relations between locals and newcomers; as a practice of sociability it enables people to cohabitate peacefully (Germann Molz and Gibson, 2007; Lashley, 2016). It is widely accepted that the term 'hospitality' is highly ambivalent. As its linguistic roots in Latin ('hospes' derived from 'hostis') indicate, hospitality refers to host and guest, as well as to stranger, enemy. Following this definition, scholars point to a particular affective geography of hospitality: any act of hospitality, a conscious invitation or acceptance of the arrival of the 'stranger' in one's home, reasserts the spatial duality of inside and outside (Bulley, 2015). While this geographical lens is worth keeping in mind, I rather draw attention to temporal aspects of hospitality.

The cosmopolitan dimension of hospitality that relies on respectful treatment of other natives as human beings can be traced back from the Roman Stoics and Greek Sophists to the colonialism of the 16th century (Brown, 2010). Kant's cosmopolitan right is restricted to the right to hospitality; it is rooted in the idea that relations between states and those between peoples (nations) are not the same. Accordingly, people can relate to states of which they are not members, and to other individuals who are members of other states. Belonging to a community of humans thus has primacy over citizenship. As all people share a limited space for living, they must share spaces of interaction with one another. Kant's hospitality is not goodwill, but a right to visit granted to foreigners, although they must behave peaceably and hospitably themselves (Kleingeld, 1999). This proposal is limited for it requires a further pact between visitors and those being visited for more extensive entitlements (Cavallar, 2002). Settlement is thus another matter entirely. Kant was critical of European colonization and saw the need for an uncoerced informed contract governing settlement (Flikschuh and Ypi, 2015).

The modern international order embraces Kant's idea of hospitality (Cavallar, 2002). Yet this is perhaps more a source of the problem than an adequate solution to today's challenges. Kant's right to hospitality was oriented toward the needs of Europeans engaged in exploration and trade, and this situation is incomparable with the global challenges of refugee and migration movements. Despite the hopes that the United Nations' (UN's) system is a right step toward a world order offering possibility for more justice and equality (Archibugi and Held, 1995), and the implementation of the cosmopolitan ideals in Article 33 of the UN Convention on Refugee Status, various commentators stress the substantial shortage of cosmopolitan hospitality. The differentiation between the right to visit and the right to settle legitimizes the exclusionary character of granting citizenship to selected individuals (Benhabib, 2006). Thus, as Kate Nash argues, cosmopolitanization of law does not result in greater equality and justice (Nash, 2009). The UN Convention, moreover, does not extend the prohibition of expulsion or return to the obligation of hospitality understood as a certain practice, nor does it rule the modalities of hosting (Knowles, 2017). There is not only an outrageous disparity between European countries' commitment to this convention when rejecting refugees (Bhambra, 2017), but also a basic flaw in the very concept of cosmopolitan hospitality.

Derrida (2010) addresses this tension between ideal and practice in how he differentiates between the unconditional law of hospitality and conditional laws of hospitality. The unconditional law of hospitality is absolute: it requires admitting a newcomer without any identification, thus irrespective of her or his status or a reason for arrival, and Derrida opposes it to Kant's right to hospitality. The conditional laws of hospitality set restrictions on the right of entry and stay and obligations on the foreigner. Unconditional hospitality is an ethical stance, and its unconditionality ends with the question 'who are you?' for it renders the moral obligation conditional and results in violence at the borders (Still, 2010; Kakoliris, 2015). This is not to say that Derrida values unconditional hospitality higher than conditional laws. Unconditional hospitality necessarily requires a regulatory framework; otherwise, it remains abstract, utopian.

Unconditional hospitality inherits, on the other hand, the possibility to rethink the other, by transcending the other's difference and undertaking the other's position (Baker, 2009), although this move leads to a rejection of the Kantian legacy of cosmopolitanism. Such a vision of hospitality requires a stance that rejects the idea of total sovereignty and thus the power of the host over the guest. Consequently, if we follow Derrida in accepting that the moral obligation to hospitality requires conditional laws of hospitality, then we need to critically engage with how conditional hospitality reinforces the congruity of a symbolic home and a (nation-)state (Bulley, 2015).

This is an important point, as it directs us to the tension between an individual's moral obligations toward strangers and laws of hospitality made by (nation-)states, for they define themselves against others. In Kantian and Derrida's approaches to hospitality there is an implicit tension between humanistic ethics of (unconditional) hospitality as the relationship between individuals and the regulative authority of (nation-)states (and international bodies). The first tends to be idealized as 'pure' and 'true,' if opposed to state and international law. It is because one tends to forget that hospitality as social relations (between individuals) also carries potential for violence. To invite someone home means both to remind him/her that this home is ours, and not his/hers. Having a home is prerequisite of hospitality, but it also enhances unequal power relations (Derrida, 2010). Hospitality as a practice includes socially prescribed roles for those who administer the visit and those who receive hospitality (Visser, 1991). Beliefs about hospitality are located in views and visions of the nature of society and the 'natural order' of things. A failure to act appropriately is treated with social condemnation (Lynch et al., 2011; Lashley, 2016). Acts of hospitality thus have social and political implications.

Also, we also not ought to forget that people are not necessarily altruistic when being hospitable (Nikunen, 2014). Ethico-political motivations for readiness to provide shelter and help to refugees, as various studies demonstrate, are intertwined with biographical motivations, ranging from gaining a sense of purpose and community belonging, to acquiring skills and networks helpful in finding employment (Turinsky and Nowicka, 2019). The practice of hospitality reflects thus the normative idea of a certain relationship with others who are in need of help, as much as it mirrors the ideal of value in meeting people from other places and cultures (Skrbiš and Woodward, 2011). As much as hospitality is a basic human feature, hospitality is also highly demanding: it prerequires a particular cultural setting in which a guest is considered not only someone to be helped, but also someone who is worth a prolonged encounter.

3 Hospitality, Conviviality, and the Other Within

So far, the limits of cosmopolitan hospitality have been discussed without reference to time or to debates that explicitly focus on the 'open borders' option (Paasi et al., 2018). But hospitality has a temporal dimension—it relies on the assumption that guests are nothing more than this because they will leave (soon). This does not match the reality now. Refugees stay a long time, longer than anybody could have imagined. When the first Somali refugees arrived at the Dadaab refugee camp in Kenya in 1991, nobody could foresee that in 2020, almost thirty years later, the third generation is being born in this quasi-city. The refugee flows from Afghanistan have not stopped since the Soviet invasion in 1979; more than 200,000 Afghans fled their homes in 2017 alone. The number of internally displaced people is at its highest in decades (UNHCR, 2017); these people are not a subject to international or national protection, but they are seeking new homes as well (McKinley, 2009). The scale of such involuntary movements is likely to increase due to climate change, and the new climate refugees might not return to their old homes either.

By bringing time into the discussion, we see that the challenge of hospitality is not limited to restrictions on access or practice of first reception (DeBono, 2018); central to this challenge is the question of cohabitation with this other who does not leave, as a guest would do, or remains distant as a stranger. As Derrida argued, letting the guest in is dangerous, for we do not know if the guest will turn out to be a friend or an enemy. Therefore, nation-states develop a complex, repressive apparatus of first reception which should effectively distinguish guests from settlers and minimize the danger that a guest stops being a guest and become a settler (or a 'bad guest' to be deported) (Fassin, 2005; Chouliaraki and Georgiou, 2017). Anticipation of a guest's transformation into a settler confines unconditional hospitality, as Derrida argued. It invokes a 'politics of naming' (Long, 2013; Sigona, 2017): labeling people as refugees or as migrants implies that we have a moral obligation toward refugees but not toward migrants (Zetter, 2007). This politics, on the other hand, turns the vulnerable into productive subjects in anticipation of them staying longer than a 'guest' would. This is the case in Germany where the public discourse shifted to view Syrians not as 'just refugees' but as 'skilled individuals,' equaling their symbolic status to that of labor migrants. Such narratives are highly ambivalent, for they create positive atmospheres around otherwise 'suspicious' groups; they do, however, act along ethnic and racial lines and thus reinforce the unbridgeable difference between valuable workers and mediocre others.

Unconditional hospitality does not assure peaceful cohabitation, nor does it eliminate violence (Lawlor, 2006). Are different rules thus necessary, as Kant insisted, to guide the reception of strangers and cohabitation with others, to at least attempt protection from those already within who might turn into enemies? Alternatively, is it possible and even necessary to reject the Kantian legacy in this respect?

Extending the rule of warm and generous treatment of guests, which defines hospitality, to cohabitation with others, which relies on a receptive and open manner of encountering others, lies at the heart of the idea of conviviality (Noble, 2009; Nowicka and Vertovec, 2013; Wise and Noble, 2016). With the term conviviality, many authors draw attention to everyday ways people relate to each other, aligning along common interests and shared passions rather than difference related to origin in another country. Yet the concept offers more than a description of situation as peaceful and people as accepting foreigners as quasi-equals. Conviviality, in order to be productive, needs to be understood as an alternative to autonomy, to a (Western) modern understanding of humans (or system) as self-standing, nondependent, non-need entities (Boisvert, 2010: 58–59). As Nyamnjoh (2017: 262) puts it, conviviality is the recognition of the fact of being incomplete, and thus it 'encourages us to reach out, encounter and explore ways of enhancing or complementing ourselves with the added possibilities [...] of others.' Conviviality as a way of thinking helps us see individuals through the meanings of their interrelatedness, their deeply rooted interdependency. Conviviality thus emerges both as an ethical and analytical project, which guides one's relations with others and ensures scholarly analyses do justice to others.

Through the lens of conviviality, hospitality concerns practical aspects of social relations with others. At least three elements could build a foundation of convivial hospitality: a mode of engagement with difference which relies on the will to adjust to difference; a mode of interaction which acknowledges silence, absence, and withdrawal as productive gestures; a sense of collective sharing of responsibility and risks beyond state and society as instances providing moral guidelines.

3.1   *Engagements with Difference*

Conviviality serves as a reminder that difference is nothing that people simply 'have' as individuals but it is social and thus fundamentally relational and comparative. If difference is 'becoming different' in particular spaces and times then it is illusionary to distinguish a friend from an enemy, as every relationship can be a source of antagonism or of amity. Proving one or the other empirically is not only a tedious exercise, but also a part of the politics reasserting the essential difference altogether. Cosmopolitanism disappoints the expectation of hospitality, for it necessitates a stranger. Without a stranger, it dissolves into humanism, which prioritizes humanity before the particular sociality of others (Ossewaarde, 2007). Yet if reduced to moral obligation to humanity, and disentangled from the questions of power relations and their normative framing, cosmopolitan hospitality is in danger of remaining an abstract ideal which neglects the propensity and capacity of humans for indifferent, malevolent, and violent forms of relating to each other (Kunneman and Suransky, 2011).

Conviviality should be thus critical of a dominant normative order in Europe that encloses tolerance and openness as well as nativism, xenophobia, and racism. This normative order is visible in Europe's endless debates about borders, immigration, and cultural assimilation; it results in a culture in which responding to others matters a great deal and calls for a responsible response: offering hospitality or assessing hostility (Kearney and Semonovitch, 2011). Convivial hospitality requires us to understand which difference of the other is relevant, how it is relevant, and what consequences it brings about. For example, why does it matter that a refugee comes from Kenya or Syria, is Christian or Muslim, man or woman, and does why origin, religion, or gender matter more than other kinds of differences.

In some urban settings in Europe, cohabitation seems to be based on 'indifference to [categorical] difference' (Amin 2012: 72; also Gilroy, 2006). But because we are humans, we are different, and this difference does matter, though not always in the same way for all. An inquiry into *tacit difference*—that which remains inexplicated by speech—shows how these differences can be translated into ethnic categories (Lisiak and Nowicka, 2018). When we dismantle these categories, we arrive at a set of familiarities and understandings shaped by upbringings in a particular place, group, and time that make people different from each other. It is the sense of what is proper and improper, desired or not worth a struggle, correct or wrong, valuable or worthless, a sense of one's right place in the world that we gain through socialization; and while many 'rights' and 'wrongs' are common to all of us, some elusive aspects of being make a difference. It could be the pace of work or time investments in child-rearing (Lisiak and Nowicka, 2018) or views of child's personal autonomy or what it means to be a good woman (Eriksen, 2015) that, if different due to the different contexts of one's socialization, cause irritations in daily interactions between strangers.

Cosmopolitanism in multicultural, liberal democracies accepts these differences to enable hospitality. Yet convivial hospitality needs to be more radical: in order to rebalance the power involved in host–guest relations, the host ought to use the encounter with the stranger to deconstruct own norms and values (which does not mean to reject them) in order to accept own incompleteness. So far, Western modern culture constructs the 'other' as incomplete: migrants are as they are, and do what they do, because they are part of the group, the practice rooted in their community. But it is blind to own incompleteness. The Western modern 'I' is as (s)he is because (s)he is an individual, a complete entity on my own (Hernando, 2017). To recognize that I and the migrants are in relationship with each other means to accept own incompleteness, as Nyamnjoh (2017) postulates.

3.2 *Interactions*

If cosmopolitan hospitality relies on actively providing support to those in need, irrespective of their belonging, performing convivial hospitality might instead be nested in a respectful withdrawal. Cosmopolitan bridging across difference is a quest for commonality and similarity, but, as noted, it is full of flaws. What if we renounce this desire? Baker (2009: 88) follows a similar trail in his call for an alternative cosmopolitan hospitality. Recalling Derrida, he asks how it might be possible to 'respond to the call of the Other without turning the Other into the Same.' Undecidability is his answer. Drawing on the ethnographic studies on gestures of conviviality (Laurier, 2008), I rather speak of hesitation, which allows for creating more time and space for the other to emerge, become as she or he wants to be. Post-phenomenological and ethnomethodological works on social interactions in urban spaces draw our attention to silence, to non-verbal communication, but also to distance between the bodies, to gestures which 'make room' for the unfamiliar body to share the space. Often, convivial interactions are compared to dancing, as bodies attune to each other in how they inhabit a space. I think convivial hospitality depends on such gestures, for they enable encounters to unfold, they allow for time in which people can negotiate the terms of the encounter.

Refraining from questioning or photographing those who disembark a rescue boat in an port where first reception center is located—a merely human ethical behavior when people are most vulnerable, hungry, thirsty, and dirty—contains a grain of this kind of convivial hospitality. It gives people the time necessary to get into the condition when they regain at least some control over how they want to present themselves in the encounter with the hosts. Refraining from active help in this very moment allows avoiding invasive and oppressive politeness (Goh Hui Jun, 2017), but also signals that we indeed see people and not refugees in this moment. This also means to make an effort not to see people just as members of a category (migrant, refugee, Christian, Muslim, man, woman, etc.), which entraps hospitality in multicultural imaginary of togetherness inherent in the current world migration and asylum regime. Such hesitations are also opening moments in the sense that they enable developing a sense of place for living by newcomers and the hosts together.

As Kymlicka (2016) rightly reminds us, though, neither hospitality or conviviality (in his understanding, equal to peaceful togetherness in multicultural settings) is sufficient to reduce pressing inequalities and reduce the disadvantage of immigrants and refugees in hosting societies. In other words, peaceful togetherness is simply not enough, and therefore Kymlicka argues for the necessity of a stronger commitment to social justice that must encompass state policies.

3.3   Beyond Society and State

So far, the research into urban diversity constructed a vision of conviviality, solidarity, and hospitality beyond the state. It idealized urban spaces as 'state-less,' or at least as such which evade the direct influence of state (Neal et al., 2015). In such 'state-less space' people might feel free to exercise solidarity that is at odds with a state's approaches to immigration. Yet these interpretations remain in the Kantian legacy as they depart from a conflictual relationship between people and states. They rely on an idealized idea of an individual capable of social contract (and thus also rejecting the state as ultimate moral instance) typical to European Enlightenment (Hernando, 2017).

Empirically it is not true that urban spaces of interactions across categorial differences are state-free; nevertheless it is interesting to consider why whenever people do not feel the presence of the state they are more likely to engage meaningfully with others, and why they solidarize with refugees when they sense the state has failed in this respect (Turinsky and Nowicka, 2019). What surfaces here is an understanding of the state as a quasi-organism, largely independent from civil society, and thus put in opposition to bottom-up civic initiatives that aim at engagement with refugees. Conviviality achieved in this context draws inspirations from postcolonial, anti-capitalist, and anti-state struggles. Yet it is still deeply embedded in either liberalism or communitarianism, and doomed to fail in the long run. As Turinsky and Nowicka (2019) showed, the local initiatives for refugees that flourished in Germany were aimed at building up a convivial space in which the 'hosts' and the refugees met on equal terms. Yet they were soon confronted with the rules of the liberal democracy and its redistributive system, which requires a formal registration as an association in order to obtain state's funding for various activities. Such an association needs to have a status, a president and a vice-president, and a treasurer, and this structure conflicts with the idea of an open equal space the initiatives want to achieve. It reasserts the imbalance of power between the 'hosts' and the refugees, and at least symbolically excludes the last from the decision-making process.

Nonetheless, such initiatives have a political dimension insofar they question the state (and society) as a moral instance assuring that conflicting individual interests are balanced (Nyamnjoh, 2017). This kind of disobedience needs to be considered not in terms of individuals simply opposing a state, but within the normative order that produces individuals as moral subjects. Thus, a strategic engagement of conviviality needs to both value the opening of a space for radical imaginaries and politics beyond the state (Callahan, 2012), but at the same time critically address who is capable of such disobedience. Who is in a position to be hospitable and who is deemed evil for being hostile to refugees? The research points to how the field of refugee support is fragmented along the lines of gender, age, and education (Karakayali, 2018).

While cosmopolitanism assumes that every human is capable of humanism by the virtue of being human, conviviality draws attention to how hospitality is embedded in power relations that enable and disable the practice of hospitality. In turn, through the lens of conviviality we may reformulate the tension between hospitality and hostility so they are regarded not as opposing positions but as in a dialectical relationship. But at the same time, convivial hospitality needs to reject both the modes of treating the other embedded in liberalism and in communitarianism to unfold its transformative potential.

References

Amin, A. 2012. *Land of Strangers*. Cambridge, UK: Polity Press.
Archibugi, D. and D. Held (eds.). 1995. *Cosmopolitan Democracy: An Agenda for a New World Order*. Cambridge, UK: Polity Press.
Baker, G. 2009. 'Cosmopolitanism as Hospitality: Revisiting Identity and Difference in Cosmopolitanism.' *Alternatives: Global, Local, Political* 34 (2): 107–128.
Benhabib, S. 2006. *The Rights of Others: Aliens, Residents, and Citizens*. Cambridge, UK: Cambridge University Press.
Berry, M., I. Garcia-Blanco, and K. Moore. 2015. 'Press Coverage of the Refugee and Migrant Crisis in the EU: A Content Analysis of Five European Countries.' Report prepared for the United Nations High Commission for Refugees, http://orca.cf.ac.uk/87078/1/UNHCR-%20FINAL%20REPORT.pdf.
Bhambra, G. K. 2017. 'The Current Crisis of Europe. Refugees, Colonialism, and the Limits of Cosmopolitanism.' *European Law Journal* 23 (5): 395–405.
Blitz, B. 2017. 'Another Story: What Public Opinion Data Tell Us About Refugee and Humanitarian Policy.' *Journal on Migration and Human Security* 5 (2): 379–400.
Boisvert, R. 2010. 'Convivialism: A Philosophical Manifesto.' *The Pluralis* 5 (2): 57–68.

Brown, G. W. 2010. 'The Laws of Hospitality, Asylum Seekers and Cosmopolitan Right.' *European Journal of Political Theory*, 9 (3): 308–327.

Bulley, D. 2015. 'Ethics, Power and Space: International Hospitality beyond Derrida.' *Hospitality & Society* 5 (2): 185–201.

Callahan, M. 2012. 'In Defense of Conviviality and the Collective Subject.' *Polis* 33, http://polis.revues.org/8432.

Cavallar, G. 2002. *The Rights of Strangers: Theories of International Hospitality, the Global Community, and Political Justice since Vitoria*. Aldershot: Ashgate Publishing.

Chouliaraki, L. and M. Georgiou. 2017. 'Hospitability: The Communicative Architecture of Humanitarian Securitization at Europe's Borders.' *Journal of Communication* 67 (2): 159–180.

COE (Council of Europe). 2017. 'Realising the Right to Family Reunification of Refugees in Europe.' Issue Paper, https://rm.coe.int/prems-052917-gbr-1700-realising-refugees-160x240-web/1680724bao.

Conrad, M. and H. Aðalsteinsdóttir. 2017. 'Understanding Germany's Short-Lived "Culture of Welcome": Images of Refugees in Three Leading German Quality Newspapers.' *German Politics and Society* 125 (35): 1–21.

DeBono, D. 2018. 'Plastic Hospitality: The Empty Signifier of the EU's First Reception System in the Mediterranean.' EUI Working Paper RSCAS 2018/22, www.eui.eu/RSCAS/Publications/.

Derrida, J. 2010. 'Hospitality.' *Angelaki* 5 (3): 3–18.

Eriksen, T. H. 2015. 'Rebuilding the Ship at Sea: Super-Diversity, Person and Conduct in Eastern Oslo.' *Global Networks* 15 (1): 1–20.

Eurostat. 2017. 'First Instance Decisions on Applications by Citizenship, Age and Sex.' Annual aggregated data, http://appsso.eurostat.ec.europa.eu/nui/show.do?dataset=migr_asydcfsta&lang=en.

Fassin, D. 2005. 'Compassion and Repression: The Moral Economy of Immigration Policies in France.' *Cultural Anthropology* 20 (3): 362–387.

Fleischmann, L. and E. Steinhilper. 2017. 'The Myth of Apolitical Volunteering for Refugees: German Welcome Culture and a New Dispositif of Helping.' *Social Inclusion* 5 (3): 17–17.

Flikschuh, K. and Ypi, L. (eds.). 2015. *Kant and Colonialism: Historical and Critical Perspectives*. Oxford: Oxford University Press, http://dx.doi.org/10.1093/acprof:oso/9780199669622.001.0001.

Germann Molz, J. and S. Gibson (eds.). 2007. *Mobilizing Hospitality: The Ethics of Social Relations in a Mobile World*. Aldershot: Ashgate Publishing.

Gilroy, P. 2006. 'Multiculture in Times of War: An Inaugural Lecture Given at the London School of Economics.' *Critical Quarterly* 48 (4): 27–45.

Goh Hui Jun, D. 2017. 'Welcoming Possibility: Hospitality and the Rohingya Refugee.' *Berfrois*, May 26.

Gramsci, A. 2005. *Selections from the Prison Notebooks of Antonio Gramsci*. London: Lawrence & Wishart.

Hamann, U. and S. Karakayali. 2016. 'Practicing Willkommenskultur: Migration and Solidarity in Germany.' *Intersections* 2 (4): 69–86.

Hernando, A. 2017. *The Fantasy of Individuality: On the Sociohistorical Construction of the Modern Subject*. Cham: Springer, http://dx.doi.org/10.1007/978-3-319-60720-7.

Holmes, S. M. and H. Castañeda. 2016. 'Representing the "European Refugee Crisis" in Germany and Beyond: Deservingness and Difference, Life and Death.' *American Ethnologist* 43 (1): 12–24.

IOM. 2015. *Mixed Migration Flows in the Mediterranean and Beyond*, https://www.iom.int/sites/default/files/situation_reports/file/Mixed-Flows-Mediterranean-and-Beyond-Compilation-Overview-2015.pdf.

Kakoliris, G. 2015. 'Jacques Derrida on the Ethics of Hospitality.' In *The Ethics of Subjectivity: Perspectives since the Dawn of Modernity*, edited by E. Imafidon, 144–156. New York: Palgrave Macmillan.

Karakayali, S. 2018. 'Volunteers.' *South Atlantic Quarterly* 117 (2): 313–331.

Kearney, R. and K. Semonovitch. 2011. 'At the Threshold: Foreigners, Strangers, Others.' In *Phenomenologies of the Stranger: Between Hostility and Hospitality*, edited by K. Semonovitch and R. Kearney, 3–29. New York: Fordham University Press.

Kleingeld, P. 1999. 'Six Varieties of Cosmopolitanism in Late Eighteenth-Century Germany.' *Journal of the History of Ideas* 60 (3): 505–524.

Knowles, C. 2017. 'Hospitality's Downfall: Kant, Cosmopolitanism, and Refugees.' *Journal of Speculative Philosophy* 31 (3): 347–347.

Kunneman, H. and C. Suransky. 2011. 'Cosmopolitanism and the Humanist Myopia.' In *The Ashgate Research Companion to Cosmopolitanism*, edited by M. Rovisco and M. Nowicka, 387–402. Farnham: Ashgate Publishing.

Kymlicka, W. 2016. 'Rejoinder from Sociability to Solidarity: Reply to Commentators.' *Comparative Migration Studies* 4 (1): 9–9.

Lashley, C. (ed.). 2016. *The Routledge Handbook of Hospitality Studies*. London; New York: Routledge Taylor & Francis Group.

Laurier, E. 2008. 'How Breakfast Happens in the Café.' *Time & Society* 17 (1): 119–134.

Lawlor, L. 2006. 'Jacques Derrida.' In *Stanford Encyclopedia of Biography*, July 30, https://plato.stanford.edu/entries/derrida/#ElaBasArgWorHos.

Lisiak, A. and M. Nowicka. 2018. 'Tacit Differences, Ethnicity and Neoliberalism: Polish Migrant Mothers in German Cities.' *Gender, Place & Culture* 25 (6): 899–915.

Long, K. 2013. 'When Refugees Stopped Being Migrants: Movement, Labour and Humanitarian Protection.' *Migration Studies* 1 (1): 4–26.

Lynch, P., J. Germann Molz, A. Mcintosh, P. Lugosi, and C. Lashley. 2011. 'Theorizing Hospitality.' *Hospitality & Society* 1 (1): 3–24.

McKinley, M. A. 2009. 'Conviviality, Cosmopolitan Citizenship and Hospitality.' *Unbound* 5 (55): 55–87.

Nash, K. 2009. 'Between Citizenship and Human Rights.' *Sociology* 43 (6): 1067–1083.

Neal, S., K. Bennett, H. Jones, A. Cochrane, and G. Mohan. 2015. 'Multiculture and Public Parks: Researching Super-Diversity and Attachment in Public Green Space.' *Population, Space and Place* 21 (5): 463–475.

Nikunen, K. 2014. 'Hopes of Hospitality: Media, Refugee Crisis and the Politics of a Place.' *International Journal of Cultural Studies* 19 (2): 161–176.

Noble, G. 2009. 'Everyday Cosmopolitanism and the Labour of Intercultural Community.' In *Everyday Multiculturalism*, edited by A. Wise and S. Velayutham, 46–65. London: Palgrave Macmillan.

Nowicka, M. and S. Vertovec. 2013. 'Comparing Convivialities: Dreams and Realities of Living-with-Difference.' *European Journal of Cultural Studies* 17 (4): 341–356.

Nyamnjoh, F. B. 2017. 'Incompleteness: Frontier Africa and the Currency of Conviviality.' *Journal of Asian and African Studies* 52 (3): 253–270.

Ossewaarde, M. 2007. 'Cosmopolitanism and the Society of Strangers.' *Current Sociology* 55 (3): 367–388.

Paasi, A., E.-K. Prokkola, J. Saarinen, and K. Zimmerbauer. 2018. *Borderless Worlds for Whom? Ethics, Moralities and Mobilities*. Abingdon: Routledge.

Scipioni, M. 2017. 'Failing Forward in EU Migration Policy? EU Integration after the 2015 Asylum and Migration Crisis.' *Journal of European Public Policy* 53 (3): 1–19.

Sigona, N. 2017. 'The Contested Politics of Naming in Europe's "Refugee Crisis."' *Ethnic and Racial Studies* 41 (3): 456–460.

Skrbiš, Z. and I. Woodward. 2011. 'Cosmopolitan Openness.' In *The Ashgate Research Companion to Cosmopolitanism*, edited by M. Rovisco and M. Nowicka, 53–68. Farnham: Ashgate Publishing.

Still, J. 2010. *Derrida and Hospitality: Theory and Practice*. Edinburgh: Edinburgh University Press.

Takis, A. 2015. 'Refugee Crisis 2015: Chronicle of a Foretold Crisis.' Heinrich Böll Stiftung, December 7, https://gr.boell.org/en/2015/12/07/refugee-crisis-2015-chronicle-foretold-crisis.

Turinsky, T. and M. Nowicka. 2019. 'Volunteer, Citizen, Human: Volunteer Work between Cosmopolitan Ideal and Institutional Routine.' In *Refugee Protection and Civil Society in Europe*, edited by M. Feischmidt, L. Pries, and C. Cantat, 243–268. London: Palgrave.

UNHCR (United Nations High Commissioner for Refugees). 2017. 'Global Trends: Forced Displacement in 2016.' Geneva, http://www.unhcr.org/5943e8a34.pdf.

Visser, M. 1991. *The Rituals of Dinner: The Origins, Evolution, Eccentricities and Meaning of Table Manners*. New York: Grove Weidenfeld.

Wise, A. and G. Noble. 2016. 'Convivialities: An Orientation.' *Journal of Intercultural Studies* 37 (5): 423–431.

Zetter, R. 2007. 'More Labels, Fewer Refugees: Remaking the Refugee Label in an Era of Globalization.' *Journal of Refugee Studies* 20 (2): 172–192.

CHAPTER 17

International Mobility and Cosmopolitanism in the Global Age

Camille Schmoll

Mobility and cosmopolitanism are two inseparably related concepts. The very idea of cosmopolitanism, if taken as a desire or a capacity to engage with diversity or otherness, seems to be deeply conditioned by mobility, travel, and circulation—be it virtual or real, material or immaterial. The latest stage of globalization has witnessed an unprecedented intensification of human and non-human mobility, so that, since the late 1990s, attempts to theorize that process have resulted in the emergence of a whole field of interdisciplinary research—*mobility studies*. When coupled with globalization studies, the latter brings acutely into question the connection between mobility and cosmopolitanism: does increasing mobility, over ever greater distances, necessarily lead to the development of a cosmopolitan competence? Conversely, does spatial immobility entail a fatal inability to be interested in others and 'willing to engage with the Other'? Does immobility, or a sedentary life, nullify one's reflective ability to conceive of common places and/or a 'shared world' (Agier, 2011, 2016)?

These questions will be investigated in light of today's experiences of human mobility on an international scale, especially its two currently prevailing forms: migration and tourism. While a change in the place of residence is a feature common to these two types of mobility, their main difference lies with the duration of this change: whereas the tourist only travels for a relatively short period of time, the migrant's change of residence lasts at least a year according to international organization definitions. These two phenomena also differ in geographical scope: travelers still mostly originate from the most developed countries, although there has been a steep increase in global outbound tourism, notably from emerging countries whose share of international tourism flows has grown from 35 percent to 45 percent between 1995 and 2017 (UNWTO, 2018). Tourism destinations, in turn, remain largely located in Northern countries (France, Spain, and the United States ranking at the world's top destinations). On the other hand, migrants hail from and head for every region of the world. Finally, these two processes have not undergone the same evolution: migration has not increased significantly in relative terms, as international migrants make up the same proportion of these global flows today as in the 1920s, that is, around 3 percent (only the share of refugees has recorded a dramatic rise). By contrast, tourism flows have shown tremendous growth, from 420 million international tourist arrivals in 1990 to more than 1.3 billion in 2017 (UNWTO, 2018). It is thus fair to say that today the great mobility phenomenon is that of tourism. It may nevertheless be interesting to compare these two experiences of residential mobility on an international scale. First, both these mobility experiences bring together mobile individuals and people, both mobile and immobile. Among the people that these individuals may encounter, one can mention the case of residents (for instance, gentrifiers, as well as residents of areas being reshaped under the impact of tourism, which can spark tensions), as well as the case of communities being 'toured' by international travelers. Furthermore, these two experiences, that of the migrant and that of the tourist, often arise as a result of asymmetrical situations, in the sense that destination countries do not necessarily enjoy the same level of wealth and/or development as source countries do: it can therefore be assumed that inequality, which is a dimension constitutive of many mobility experiences, is not inevitably inconsistent with the cosmopolitan experience, in spite of the ways in which the latter has sometimes been romanticized.

This chapter draws mainly on the findings of ethnographic research, attuned to the performative, contextual, or routine aspects of cosmopolitanism in everyday life, as both an attitude and a capacity to '[represent] variously complex repertoires of allegiances, identity and interest' (Vertovec and Cohen, 2002: 4). Accordingly, among the multiplicity of possible understandings of cosmopolitanism, the definition emphasized here is one that conceives cosmopolitanism as an 'attitudinal or dispositional orientation' and 'a mode of practice or competence' (Vertovec and Cohen, 2002: 10). The notion of ordinary, or everyday, cosmopolitanism is critical: it denotes the way in which, from day to day, 'men and women from different origins create a society where diversity is accepted and rendered ordinary' (Hiebert, 2002: 212; Schmoll, 2003).

1 The Stranger as a Figure of Cosmopolitanism

As early as the first works of sociological scholarship, migration and cosmopolitanism have been intimately related notions. This connection could probably be dated back to Georg Simmel's 1908 excursus about the stranger (Simmel, 2011). According to Simmel, it was precisely by dint of the tension between proximity and distance, copresence and mobility, that the stranger was, by definition, cosmopolitan. It is important to recall Georg Simmel's work from the outset, for it provides a safeguard against the idea of cosmopolitanism as something wholly new stemming from globalization or the so-called 'second modernity.' At the same time, tracing this discussion back to Georg Simmel means starting with the assumption that there is indeed a connection between cosmopolitanism and modernity: the cosmopolitan is that new figure of man (women do not appear much in such writing), that figure of urbanization and industrialization which arose at the turn of the 20th century and which was thrown into contact with places, groups, and communities of different origins. Today this figure of cosmopolitanism needs to be reexamined in the light of more recent developments of globalization, which have seen both the growth of human mobility and the attendant rise of manifold circulations (financial transfers, virtual data and images, etc.).

Following on from Georg Simmel, and often in keeping with the Chicago School, several scholars have expanded on the figure of the stranger as a cosmopolitan. According to Robert E. Park, a disciple of Georg Simmel, he is 'the marginal man,' whose condition as a stranger is predicated on a sharp break with his background and on being thrust into close contact with another way of thinking and another way of life (Park, 1928). Park's approach is noteworthy in that mobility does not necessarily generate cosmopolitanism, since the latter presupposes an encounter with a different way of thinking and way of life. '"*Nomadic*" people, be they gypsies, vagrants or permanent hotel-dwellers, do not experience such a break, and, as such, their culture is not challenged' (Raphael, 2008: 82). Accordingly, Park's approach complicates the relation between mobility and cosmopolitanism.

2 Cosmopolitanism: a Blind Spot in Migration Studies until the 2000s

After Simmel and Park, the notion of cosmopolitanism mostly lost its relevance to migration scholarship, although, from the 1960s and 1970s, 'migration studies' coalesced into a field of interdisciplinary studies. How could that paradox be accounted for? A deliberate emphasis on the ethnic, the community, the 'in-group,' which to a great extent has characterized the English-language literature on migrations, has likely helped disregard this aspect of the migrant experience. Indeed, since the late 1960s, migration studies have often featured research focusing on a specific group, and thus have yielded a wealth of monographs on Italians, Koreans, Mexicans, and so on. An approach starting with ethnic groups as the analytical unit, the notorious 'ethnic lens,' obfuscates those processes occurring at the margins of these groups, in their modes of interaction and coexistence with other communities (Glick-Schiller, Çağlar, and Guldbrandsen, 2006). Consequently, a large part of the literature on migration has neglected cosmopolitanism. This methodological blindness, which Glick-Schiller and Çağlar (2008) have termed 'methodological ethnicity,' was particularly salient in one field of migration studies—concerned with ethnic entrepreneurship—that was especially prominent until the 1990s. Ethnic business literature was based on an interactive framework correlating cultural resources and group solidarity, on the one hand, and opportunity and constraint structures enabling (or not) migrants to develop ethnic economic activities, on the other hand (Aldrich, Ward, and Waldinger, 1990; Gold and Light, 2000). This ethnic lens was also typical of early research into transnational communities, which took shape in the early 1990s.

It was only in the 2000s that, owing to the development of socio-anthropological studies of globalization, the potential for a positive relationship between transnationalism and cosmopolitanism was eventually suggested and investigated (Werbner, 1999; Beck, 2000, 2002, 2006; Vertovec and Cohen, 2002; Mau, Mewes, and Zimmerman, 2008; Glick-Schiller, Darieva, and Gruner-Domic, 2011; for a quite opposite viewpoint, see Hiebert, 2002). In the early 2000s, Vertovec and Cohen, in order to stress the relationship obtaining between cosmopolitanism and transnationalism, thus wrote: 'Many individuals now seem to be, more than ever, prone to articulate complex affiliations, meaningful attachments and multiple allegiances to issues, people, places and traditions that lie beyond the boundaries of their resident nation-states. This holds especially for migrants, ethnic diasporas and transnational communities' (2002: 2). Their work establishes that ethnicity is not an exclusive component of identity, and that the latter is not one-dimensional. They describe the ways in which migrants are able to articulate singularity and universality in their everyday practices, as well as cosmopolitanism and forms of ethnic organization or identification. Recent scholarship on the potential common world conjured up by the World Wide Web is in keeping with such findings: research carried out on 'connected migrants' and virtual circulation bears out the ways in which the virtual space of migrants welds together forms of 'encapsulated' ethnic and diasporic affiliations on the one hand, and forms of cosmopolitanism on the other (Leurs and Ponzanesi, 2018).

3 The Migrant-trader: a Central Figure of Cosmopolitanism

To consider again the figure of the migrant entrepreneur, and in particular that of the trader: in the 1990s, a dynamic field of studies developed around the connection between migrant economic activities and cosmopolitanism and, coming mainly, as it did, from Francophone scholars, it usefully counterbalanced English-language theories about 'ethnic business,' which remained excessively committed to the ethnicity paradigm and hence unable to bring the cosmopolitan competences of migrants to light (Schmoll and Semi, 2013). At the time in France, Alain Tarrius' (1992) seminal work, in particular, radically challenged a number of preconceptions about migration, beginning with the assimilationist assumption underlying them. Building on his ethnography of the Marseilles marketplace, Tarrius recounts the rise of the 'suitcase trade,' especially along the Algiers–Marseilles route. It derived as much from the economic crisis in France, which drove migrants to seek alternative sources of income outside of wage labor, as from the introduction of a socialist economy in Algeria which was concomitant with the growth of informal trade practices (the *trabendo*). 'Europe's ants' (*Les fourmis d'Europe*, 1992), portrayed by Tarrius in his ethnography of suitcase trade, move from North to South items as varied as textile, linen, leathers and shoes, car spare parts and bicycles, and furniture—all goods subsequently sold off in the streets and markets of Algeria. As a result, the Belsunce area in Marseilles has become a central place for trade: since the late 1990s, it has acted as a vital commercial hub and the main nexus of shopping and circulation for tens of thousands of migrants, as part of a markedly cosmopolitan economy bringing Jewish and Armenian wholesalers together with sellers and customers from northern and Sub-Saharan Africa. Such a cosmopolitan economy was based on the ability of different ethnic groups to deal one with the other. Tarrius specifies that, in the course of the 1980s, business in Belsunce shops was supplied by 700,000 suitcase traders. There is no discernible contradiction in Tarrius' work between the cosmopolitan resources and the ethnic resources deployed by the traders of the Marseilles marketplace; in fact the opposite is true (Tarrius, 1992, 2000; see also Péraldi, 2001).

In the same vein, at the end of the 1990s, researchers embarked on North African trade circulation in cities such as Naples. In Naples then, as in Marseille, modes of entrepreneurship relied on a variety of resources, and on generating interactions and collaborations among actors of diverse provenance (Amato, 2000; Schmoll, 2003, 2004, 2011). Research showed how an economy geared toward the production and marketing of counterfeits (*o' fals'* in Neapolitan dialect) has flourished in the area surrounding Naples' railway station by dint of the presence of various actors: Chinese traders importing from Zhejiang products to be tagged with the 'fake brand'; Neapolitan seamstresses and Tunisian tailors, located in buildings of the 'Duchesca' underclass neighborhood; North African wholesalers tasked with storing and marketing these goods; a multifarious clientele (Senegalese door-to-door salesmen, Algerian and Tunisian suitcase traders, Italian merchants) selling the items across all European and Mediterranean commercial areas. The economic complementarity obtaining between these various actors has sustained the cosmopolitan operations of the marketplace, and, at the same time, it has not prevented each of these actors from starting his own business on the basis of his respective ethnic, often regional, networks. Research conducted in Naples has thus highlighted the use of cosmopolitanism as a resource in trade exchanges and led to the argument that, 'far from a Kantian political project of harmonious cohabitation, cosmopolitanism on the marketplace is rather a pragmatic and ordinary openness towards otherness' (Schmoll, 2011: 12). This ordinary cosmopolitanism in the marketplace could be observed, in a micro-interactionist fashion, through the strategic use of symbols and languages referring to different cultures. For instance, in the spatial organization of the shops, symbols referring to the cultural origins of the clientele—such as verses of the Koran—were often put in a prominent place, in proximity with Christian symbols such as Padre Pio's pictures.

In a similar vein, Antoine Pécoud's work on German-Turkish entrepreneurs in Berlin has also brought out cosmopolitanism as a resource in trade relations. Underlining the pragmatic nature of this form of cosmopolitanism, he has shown it to be embedded in everyday interactions taking place in shops (2004). Such scholarship on the cosmopolitanism of migrant traders or entrepreneurs has stimulated a debate on working-class cosmopolitanism (Werbner, 1999; Pécoud, 2004): it has suggested that, contrary to the propositions advanced by Ulf Hannerz or others, cosmopolitanism is not the preserve of the elite but, rather, a kind of resource which is complementary to ethnic or cultural resources for immigrants in the global era (Hannerz, 1990, 2004; Werbner, 1999; Pécoud, 2004). Although it has significantly broadened our thinking on the cosmopolitan competence of the working class, it comes with a fundamental problem. Can such research, exclusively concerned as it is with migrant entrepreneurs or traders and their attendant relationships with the clientele or the local community, speak to mobility?

That this scholarship should primarily revolve around trading communities is not inconsequential: the linkage between trade and cosmopolitanism was underscored early on by Simmel, who argued that economic activities, and the dealings of the stranger first and foremost, fostered the diversification of social relations. As a matter of fact, the relationship between trade and cosmopolitanism dates back, at the very least, to Montesquieu, who championed the notion that trade was conducive to peace.[1] The analytical entry point for understanding whether other connections can be established between migration,

---

1 Montesquieu (1748).

(im)mobilities, and cosmopolitanism must therefore be broader than the specific economic category of trade. An urban approach can help us to broaden our scope.

4   Cities: Mobility Crossroads, Cosmopolitan Crossroads?

Cities, and global cities in particular, are ideally suited to an analysis of the connection between mobility and cosmopolitanism, for they are both the place in which the neoliberal economy originates and the site where people of all origins and backgrounds coexist and cross paths. Cities also attract, in an especially strong manner, a wide array of internationally mobile people, ranging from tourists to businessmen, from migrants to students, as shown by urban scholars. Guido Martinotti, for instance, talked about 'second generation metropolis' when referring to the various modes of mobility constitutive of the modern city and how they had to be taken into account in discussions about 'the right to the city' (Martinotti, 1999). In other words, one needs to escape the confines of the methodological localism that has been pervasive in much of urban studies.

Urban studies also offer evidence that an inquiry into specific areas requires that we break away from 'methodological ethnicity' (Wimmer, Glick-Schiller, 2002; Berg and Sigona, 2013). The notion of super-diversity put forth by Steve Vertovec is undoubtedly useful, in that it strives to overcome the 'ethnic lens' by introducing other variables that are essential in order to gauge and raise awareness about diversity on an urban scale: language, gender, age, legal status, religion, migration record, and so on (Vertovec, 2007). In methodological terms, interesting innovations have also been brought forward to shed light on the forms of cosmopolitanism arising at the micro-local level in a super-diverse urban setting. For instance, Susanne Hall has offered modes of survey and mapping that testify to the widely diverse origins, as well as intercultural proficiencies, of the proprietors of Rye Lane, a street in the South London district of Peckham (Hall, 2015).[2] Alex Rhys-Taylor, on the other hand, has undertaken a sensory exploration of cosmopolitanism—especially through taste and smell—in order to show how sense-scapes involve processes of gendered, class-based, and racialized stratification, yet can also produce novel subjectivities and transcultural affinities that work toward more cosmopolitan senses of place (Rhys-Taylor, 2017).

---

2   See also Chapter 13 in this volume.

Two critical dimensions stand out in the urban studies literature: first, the role of 'micro-publics,' that is, the urban routine and the 'everyday negotiations of ethnic difference' in contact zones (Amin, 2002: 960). In particular, public spaces are construed as a potential breeding ground for cosmopolitanism. They epitomize the density and diversity performed by the city with all its potential for cosmopolitanism. Annick Germain's and Martha Radice's research on modes of sociability in the public spaces of Montreal multiethnic neighborhoods demonstrates that they are characterized by a kind of friendly and peaceful distance, enabling coexistence, and are referred to as 'cosmopolitan consensus' (2006: 125). Drawing on the concept of super-diversity, Susanne Wessendorf (2013) describes how people negotiate difference in a place where almost everybody comes from elsewhere. She suggests the twin notions of 'commonplace diversity' (which dovetails with the idea of the making of a shared world championed by theorists of cosmopolitanism; see Agier, 2016) and 'ethos of mixing' to elucidate these practices. These various approaches conjure up yet another concept, the 'cosmopolitan canopy' devised by Elijah Anderson to account for these places of consumption that foster convivial encounters and, in the process, offer a momentary respite from otherwise grim realities (Anderson, 2004).

5 Plural Mobilities and Urban Tensions: Cosmopolitan Logics under Siege in Gentrified and Touristic Neighborhoods

There may nevertheless be a risk attendant on these discourses about the urban engineering of cosmopolitanism: 'The danger is that contemporary discourses about cosmopolitanism and new urban citizenship, by celebrating the potential of everyday encounters to produce social transformations, potentially allow the knotty issue of inequalities to slip out of the debate' (Valentine, 2008: 333). Therefore, another way of addressing the linkage between cosmopolitanism and mobility in the urban setting is through the lens of social change, which provides a sharper assessment of the frictions inherent in specific cosmopolitan processes. For instance, gentrification, which is tantamount to a form of residential mobility of the upper class toward working-class areas, has dramatically reshaped the urban landscape. Such change may be coeval with greater diversity, at least outwardly, but this remains a consumer-oriented diversity designed for an educated middle class with access to the amenities offered by the city (Butler, 2003; Ley, 2004). The scholarship on gentrification brings out the paradoxical relationship among the cosmopolitan aspirations of gentrifiers, their role in the emergence of self-segregation, and the displacement of migrants from the inner-city neighborhoods they previously inhabited. Such writing serves as a useful reminder that a cosmopolitan lifestyle is by no means exclusive of relations of power and domination. Indeed, Tim Butler (2003) refers to gentrification as a form of exclusionary cosmopolitanism, a sort of cosmopolitan façade which may sometimes be violently at odds with the potential for truly cosmopolitan encounters. It is worth noting that many of these gentrifiers may themselves be of immigrant origin, although this specific aspect remains understudied in the gentrification literature (for an exception see De Verteuil, 2018).

Such issues bear a striking similarity to those that arise when specific areas are turned into tourist destinations. Indeed, the aesthetic cosmopolitanism of some sites has been foregrounded as a key rationale for tourism, in the manner of a 'cosmopolitan tale' (Chapuis and Jacquot, 2014: 75). Yet these aesthetic claims are at variance with the actual hollowing out of neighborhoods drained of their migrant communities as a result of the gentrification of inner cities initiated by tourism. The production of tourist areas in Paris is a case in point: while the city council's official discourse has tended to emphasize the cosmopolitan appeal of Paris neighborhoods, in practice the working class themselves, especially low-income migrant communities, have largely been priced out of these very neighborhoods as a result of skyrocketing housing costs.

Ultimately, the two aforementioned examples of urban change, whether the gentrification or the 'touristification' of inner cities, are evidence that various forms of mobility can conflict with one another and be irreconcilable. Although some mobilities may be congruent with an aesthetics of diversity, in practice they are no less likely to produce social exclusivity and separation.

6   Tourism and the Cosmopolitan Gaze

Travel is a key aspect of mobility (Clifford, 1997) and tourism can be conducive to cosmopolitanism insofar as it disseminates knowledge about other worlds (Urry and Larsen, 2011). Some anthropologists go as far as seeing tourism as the main vehicle for cosmopolitan orientations: 'Tourist performances and experiences are an important part of the ways people position themselves in and as part of the world. Tourism is an important part of what has been called "banal cosmopolitanism",' claims Haldrup (2016). For some, this 'aestheticocultural cosmopolitanism' (Cicchelli and Octobre, 2018) by way of tourism only amounts to an 'easy cosmopolitanism,' all the more so as it is short-lived and does not involve extensive and prolonged modes of coexistence. 'Food, tourism, music, literature and clothes are all easy faces of cosmopolitanism.

They are indeed broadening, after a fashion, but they are not hard tests for the relationship between local solidarity and international civil society,' argues Craig Calhoun (2002: 105).

In that respect, it is worth mentioning that the development of the Internet, as well as enhanced access to the world and its amenities thanks to communication technologies, have not had an adverse effect on the growth of tourist mobility, far from it: indeed, several scholars have stressed the localized, embodied, and sensory nature of the cosmopolitan tourist experience (Stock, 2008). This experience is multisensory: it is obviously that of the selfie (D'Eramo, 2017), the visual imprint of the experience that is circulated across social networks. But other senses are also involved. Jennie Germann Molz has thus shown how Western tourists 'cosmopolitanized' food through their performances and how such experiences ultimately amounted to 'consuming the Other' (2007: 81–82).

But is this truly cosmopolitanism, understood as openness to others? What do tourists seek through travel—an encounter with other people or with other places? And in the latter case, is tourism anything more than exoticism? Naturally, this question is a tricky one, especially as the tourist is always the Other (Mee, 2007; see also Urbain, 2002). While pondering the connection between cosmopolitanism and tourism, Ulf Hannerz (2004) has expressed doubts about the cosmopolitan abilities of tourists; but it is common knowledge that Hannerz holds a very narrow—and classed—view of cosmopolitanism. Again, a discussion of cosmopolitanism in relation to tourism is contingent on an approach cognizant of the power relations underpinning intercourse between tourists and locals. Precisely along such lines, a whole strand of critical literature has taken shape within the field of tourism studies.

For some scholars, it is not so much tourists that evince genuine cosmopolitan competences as those—immobile—people who guide and host them, namely tourism workers. Salazar, in particular, has carried out fieldwork on guides in central Java's Yogyakarta (Indonesia) and around East Africa's 'safari capital,' Arusha (Tanzania). For guides,

> cosmopolitan comprehension is vital to their work and resembles that of stereotypical cosmopolites, experienced travellers. In other words, guides do not physically need to wander around the world to develop a cosmopolitan attitude; the world simply comes to them. This confirms that 'sheer mobility (in and of itself) does not automatically entail cosmopolitanism' [Swain, 2009: 513]. Many successful local guides are conceived of as prototype cosmopolites. Of course, not all of them necessarily have cosmopolitan aspirations. Furthermore, not all guide settings

and professional roles are equally conducive to enacting cosmopolitan values. But for many guides, the tourism encounter is the liminal setting par excellence in which they can build up their cosmopolitan abilities. Paradoxically, contemporary global tourism is structured in such a way that tourists seem to lose out in the quest for cosmopolitan status.
SALAZAR, 2010: 61–62

These cosmopolitan guides could probably not travel to the home countries of the tourists that they are escorting: access to mobility, whether it is migration or tourism, is deeply stratified in geographical terms—the ability to obtain a passport or to travel without a visa, or even to be granted a visa, being contingent on one's country of origin and wealth level (Migreurop, 2019). Ultimately, a parallel can be drawn between the position of these tour guides and the eminently cosmopolitan, albeit equally subaltern and marginal, predicament of those who today live 'within the border.' Michel Agier, in his exploration of the situation of migrants 'stranded at the border,' has brought to light the remarkable cosmopolitan competences that they demonstrate as part of the development of a shared borderworld (Agier, 2011). Through stories and description of connections and exploitation, settlement, and displacement, Agier investigates the existence of an everyday or ordinary cosmopolitism experienced by Sudanese, Eritrean, Sri Lankan, Afghan, or German dwellers of Beirut, Paris, Patras, New York. It describes the cosmopolitan *condition* in the sense of a lived experience, an experience of sharing the world, no matter how inegalitarian and violent this may be.

7 Conclusion: Cosmopolitanism and Mobility, an Obvious Relationship?

The purpose of this chapter has been to suggest a few ways in which to rethink the connection between cosmopolitanism and mobility in the context of the intensification of mobility on a global scale. There seem to be two especially salient points. First, the cosmopolitan and the local cannot be set in opposition to each other: some people have never moved and hardly travel and yet remain genuinely cosmopolitan, whereas others have a merely superficial relationship to cosmopolitanism. The linkage between cosmopolitanism and mobility ought to be systematically investigated. Moreover, although cosmopolitanism is not the preserve of the elite, the issue of cosmopolitanism nevertheless cannot be considered in isolation from the power and inequality relations in which it is embedded. As mentioned, cosmopolitan relationships may be inegalitarian, subaltern, or even dominant. They are often expressed through forms of economic relations (trade and consumption, for instance) but also by located social change (the case of gentrification and 'touristification' of spaces). They are embodied and partake of intersectional relations in terms of gender, race, and class, as well as geographical position (Glick-Schiller, Darieva, and Gruner-Domic, 2011). A discussion of the connection between cosmopolitanism and mobility cannot dispense with such a critical perspective.

References

Agier, M. 2011. *Le couloir des exilés. Etre étranger dans un monde commun.* Paris: Editions du Croquant.

Agier, M. 2016. *Borderlands: Towards an Anthropology of the Cosmopolitan Condition.* Cambridge, UK: Polity Press.

Aldrich, H., R. Waldinger, and R. Ward. 1990. *Ethnic Entrepreneurs: Immigrant Business in Industrial Societies.* London: Sage.

Amato, F. 2000. 'La circolarità commerciale degli immigrati nel Napoletano.' *Afriche e Orienti* 2 (3/4): 53–57.

Amin, A. 2002. 'Ethnicity and the Multicultural City: Living with Diversity.' *Environment and Planning A* 34 (6): 959–980.

Anderson, E. 2004. 'The Cosmopolitan Canopy.' *Annals of the American Academy of Political and Social Science* 595 (1): 14–31.

Beck, U. 2000. 'The Cosmopolitan Perspective: Sociology of the Second Age of Modernity.' *British Journal of Sociology* 51 (1): 79–105.

Beck, U. 2002. 'The Cosmopolitan Perspective: Sociology in the Second Age of Modernity.' In *Conceiving Cosmopolitanism: Theory, Context and Practice*, edited by S. Vertovec and R. Cohen, 61–84. Oxford: Oxford University Press.

Beck, U. 2006. *Cosmopolitan Vision.* Cambridge, UK: Polity Press.

Berg, M. L. and S. Nando. 2013. 'Ethnography, Diversity and Urban Space.' *Identities* 20 (4): 347–360.

Butler, T. 2003. 'Living in the Bubble: Gentrification and its "Others" in North London.' *Urban Studies* 40 (12): 2469–2486.

Calhoun, C. 2002. 'The Class Consciousness of Frequent Travellers: Towards a Critique of Actually Existing Cosmopolitanism.' In *Conceiving Cosmopolitanism: Theory, Context, Practice*, edited by S. Vertovec and R. Cohen, 86–109. Oxford: Oxford University Press.

Chapuis, A. and S. Jacquot. 2014. 'Le touriste, le migrant et la fable cosmopolite. Mettre en tourisme les présences migratoires à Paris.' *Hommes et Migrations* 1308: 75–84.

Cicchelli, V. and S. Octobre. 2018. *Aesthetico-Cultural Cosmopolitanism and French Youth: The Taste of the World*. London: Palgrave.

Clifford, J. 1997. *Routes: Travel and Translation in the Late Twentieth Century*. Cambridge, MA: Harvard University Press.

D'Eramo, M. 2017. *Il selfie del mondo*. Milan: Feltrinelli.

De Verteuil, G. 2018. 'Immigration and Gentrification.' In *Handbook of Gentrification Studies*, edited by L. Lees and M. Phillips, 428–443. Northampton: Edward Elgar Publishing.

Germain, A. and M. Radice. 2006. 'Cosmopolitanism by Default: Public Sociability in Montreal.' In *Cosmopolitan Urbanism*, edited by J. Binnie, J. Holloway, S. Millington, and C. Young, 124–141. London: Routledge.

Germann Molz, J. 2007. 'Eating Difference: The Cosmopolitan Mobilities of Culinary Tourism.' *Space and Culture* 10 (1): 77–93.

Glick-Schiller, N., A. Çağlar, and T. C. Guldbrandsen. 2006. 'Beyond the Ethnic Lens: Locality, Globality, and Born-Again Incorporation.' *American Ethnologist* 33 (4): 612–633.

Glick-Schiller, N., A. Çağlar 2008. 'Beyond Methodological Ethnicity and Towards City Scale: An Alternative Approach to Local and Transnational Pathways of Migration Incorporation.' In *Rethinking Transnationalism*, edited by L. Pries, 52–73. London: Routledge.

Glick-Schiller, N., T. Darieva, and S. Gruner-Domic. 2011. 'Defining Cosmopolitan Sociability in a Transnational Age: An Introduction.' *Ethnic and Racial Studies* 34 (3): 399–418.

Gold, S. J. and I. Light. 2000. *Ethnic Economies*. San Diego, CA: Academic Press.

Haldrup, M. 2016. 'Banal Tourism? Between Cosmopolitanism and Orientalism.' In *Cultures of Mass Tourism: Doing the Mediterranean in the Age of Banal Mobilities*, edited by P. Obrador Pons, M. Crang, and P. Traviou, 63–84. London: Routledge.

Hall, S. M. 2015. 'Super-Diverse Street: A "Trans-Ethnography" across Migrant Localities.' *Ethnic and Racial Studies* 38 (1): 22–37.

Hannerz, U. 1990. 'Cosmopolitanism and Locals in World Culture.' *Theory, Culture and Society* 7 (2–3): 237–251.

Hannerz, U. 2004. 'Cosmopolitanism.' In *A Companion to the Anthropology of Politics*, edited by D. Nugent and J. Vincent, 69–85. Hoboken, NJ: Wiley Blackwell.

Hiebert, D. 2002. 'Cosmopolitanism at the Local Level: The Development of Transnational Neighbourhoods.' In *Conceiving Cosmopolitanism: Theory, Context and Practice*, edited by S. Vertovec and R. Cohen, 209–223. Oxford: Oxford University Press.

Leurs, K. and S. Ponzanesi. 2018. 'Connected Migrants: Encapsulation and Cosmopolitanization.' *Popular Communication* 16 (1): 4–20.

Ley, D. 2004. 'Transnational Spaces and Everyday Lives.' *Transactions of the Institute of British Geographers* 29 (2): 151–164.

Martinotti, G. 1999. 'A City for Whom? Transients and Public Life in the Second-Generation Metropolis.' In *The Urban Moment: Cosmopolitan Essays on the Late-20th-Century City*, edited by R. A. Beauregard and S. Body-Gendrot, 155–184. London: Sage.

Mau, S., J. Mewes, and A. Zimmermann. 2008. 'Cosmopolitan Attitudes through Transnational Social Practices?' *Global Networks* 8 (1): 1–24.

Mee, C. 2007. '"Che Brutta Invenzione il Turismo!": Tourism and Anti-Tourism in Current French and Italian Travel Writing.' *Comparative Critical Studies* 4 (2): 269–282.

Migreurop. 2019. *The Atlas of Migration in Europe*. London: Taylor & Francis.

Montesquieu. 1748. *The Spirit of the Laws*.

Park, R. E. 1928. 'Human Migration and the Marginal Man.' *American Journal of Sociology* 33 (6): 881–893.

Pécoud, A. 2004. 'Entrepreneurship and Identity: Cosmopolitanism and Cultural Competencies among German-Turkish Business People in Berlin.' *Journal of Ethnic and Migration Studies* 30 (1): 3–20.

Péraldi, M. 2001. *Cabas et containers. Activités marchandes informelles et réseaux migrants transfrontaliers*. Paris: Maisonneuve et Larose.

Raphael, F. 2008. 'Le Juif comme paradigme de l'étranger dans l'oeuvre de G. Simmel.' *Sociétés* 101 (3): 81–90.

Rhys-Taylor, A. 2017. *Food and Multiculture: A Sensory Ethnography of East London*. London: Bloomsbury Academic.

Salazar, N. B. 2010. 'Tourism and Cosmopolitanism: A View from Below.' *International Journal of Tourism Anthropology* 1 (1): 55–69.

Schmoll, C. 2003. 'Cosmopolitisme au quotidien et circulations commerciales à Naples.' *Cahiers de la Méditerranée* 67: 345–360.

Schmoll, C. 2004. 'Une place marchande cosmopolite. Circulations commerciales et dynamiques migratoires à Naples.' PhD thesis, University of Paris Nanterre.

Schmoll, C. 2011. 'The Making of a Transnational Marketplace: Naples and the Impact of Mediterranean Cross-Border Trade on Regional Economies.' *Cambridge Journal of Regions, Economy and Society* 5 (2): 221–238.

Schmoll, C. and G. Semi. 2013. 'Shadow Circuits: Urban Spaces and Mobilities across the Mediterranean.' *Identities, Global Studies in Culture and Power* 20 (4): 377–392.

Simmel, G. 2011. 'The Stranger.' In *The Sociology of Georg Simmel*, edited by K. H. Wolff, 402–208. Glencoe, IL: Free Press.

Stock, M. 2008. 'Il mondo è mobile.' In *L'invention du monde. Une géographie de la mondialisation*, edited by J. Lévy, 132–159. Paris: Presses de Sciences Po.

Swain, M. B. 2009. 'The Cosmopolitan Hope of Tourism: Critical Action and Worldmaking Vistas.' *Tourism Geographies* 11 (4): 505–525.

Tarrius, A. 1992. *Les fourmis d'Europe. Migrants riches, migrants pauvres et nouvelles villes internationales*. Paris: L'Harmattan.

Tarrius, A. 2000. *Les nouveaux cosmopolitismes*. La Tour d'Aigues: Editions de l'Aube.

UNWTO (United Nations World Tourism Organization). 2018. *Tourism Highlights*.

Urbain, J. D. 2002. *L'idiot du voyage. Histoires de touristes*. Paris: Payot & Rivages.

Urry, J. and J. Larsen. 2011. *The Tourist Gaze 3.0*. London: Sage.

Valentine, G. 2008. 'Living with Difference: Reflections on Geographies of Encounter.' *Progress in Human Geography* 32 (3): 323–337.

Vertovec, S. 2007. 'Super-Diversity and its Implications.' *Ethnic and Racial Studies* 30 (6): 1024–1054.

Vertovec, S. and R. Cohen. 2002. 'Introduction: "Conceiving Cosmopolitanism."' In *Conceiving Cosmopolitanism: Theory, Context and Practice*, edited by S. Vertovec and R. Cohen, 1–22. Oxford: Oxford University Press.

Werbner, P. 1999. 'Global Pathways: Working Class Cosmopolitans and the Creation of Transnational Ethnic Worlds.' *Social Anthropology* 7 (1): 17–35.

Wessendorf, S. 2013. 'Commonplace Diversity and the "Ethos of Mixing": Perceptions of Difference in a London Neighbourhood.' *Identities* 20 (4): 407–422.

Wimmer, A. and Glick Schiller, N. 2002. 'Methodological nationalism and beyond: nation–state building, migration and the social sciences.' *Global Networks* 2(4): 301–334.

CHAPTER 18

The Cosmopolitan Stranger

Esperança Bielsa

1   Introduction

In elaborating perspectives for engaging with the needs and views of others in heterogeneous societies, cosmopolitanism has contributed to specifying the key social and political relevance of the stranger today. In this context, democracy has been defined as a politics among strangers (Honig, 2001: 39–40, 72), while the rights of migrants (Benhabib, 2004) and the 'inclusion of the other' have led to a rethinking of the boundaries of a political community that is open to all (Habermas, 1998). More generally, philosophical and psychoanalytical insights have been deployed to formulate an ethics shaped by otherness (Levinas, 1991), to show how we all carry strangers within us (Kristeva, 1991), and to describe how the trace of the other and the opacity of translation challenge the assumed stability of both individual and collective identities (Sakai, 1997; Derrida, 1998; Ivekovic, 2005). Sociological approaches, on their part, have sought to reappraise classical definitions of the stranger as a key figure of modernity in light of what has been approached as the cosmopolitanization of reality, as well as the proliferation of social uncertainty and risk and the blurring of the once taken-for-granted boundaries of groups and communities.

This chapter theorizes the cosmopolitan stranger, whose skills are especially important under conditions of generalized societal strangeness, when familiar reference points are eroded. The next section introduces Simmel's classical characterization of the stranger and examines the main reasons for specifying the social significance of this figure in relation to contemporary cosmopolitanism. After that, the main contemporary approaches to the stranger are analyzed and a conceptualization of the cosmopolitan stranger is offered.

2   Strangers in the Context of Generalized Strangeness

In 1908 Georg Simmel defined the 'sociological form' of the stranger as the unity between wandering and fixation as its conceptual opposite: the stranger was a potential wanderer whose presence in the social group is basically determined by the fact that he or she brings qualities into it that cannot stem from the group itself (Simmel, 1950 [1908]: 402). In his classical essay, which is still very much the starting point for most contemporary formulations on the stranger, Simmel distinguishes between distance and strangeness as constitutive of the social experience of the stranger. Distance refers not to spatial but primarily to cultural distance: to the fact that 'he, who is close by, is far' (1950 [1908]: 402). More cryptically, strangeness 'means that he, who is also far, is actually near' (1950 [1908]: 402). According to Simmel, strangeness is due to the generality that lurks even in the most singular relationships, rather than the product of difference and incomprehensibility. There is a kind of strangeness that disallows the stranger's specificity and humanity in the name of generality, thus signaling a non-relation: as a group member, the stranger 'is near and far *at the same time*' (1950 [1908]: 407, original emphasis). Even if strangers become meaningful to us when they enter our social circle, we are led to ignore their singularity and specificity by the general attributes that accentuate everything that differentiates them from ourselves. Stressing the non-common element of the stranger—a strangeness of origins—means, as Simmel notes, that strangers are conceived not as individuals, but as strangers of a particular type. For Simmel, it is strangeness rather than distance that is the key to the stranger's ambivalence, because whereas cultural distance can also be attributed to a world of inert objects, strangeness exclusively refers to relationships between subjects.[1]

Simmel lived in central Berlin at the time of the capital's most accelerated period of growth. His stranger literally embodies the very qualities that were coming to define city life, above all, the social and political diversity that led to a fragmentation of narratives and challenged clarity of vision (Fritzsche, 1996), as well as the fugitiveness and ephemerality that define metropolitan modernity more generally (Baudelaire, 1964; Benjamin, 2006). Simmel, who was himself '[a]n alien in his native land' and a 'stranger in the academy' (Coser, cited in Frisby, 2002: 8–9; see also Bauman, 1991: 160–169, 185–190), emphasized freedom as a basic characteristic of the stranger, approaching this as both a freedom of movement and a freedom of thought, linked to the capacity for thinking outside the confines of the habits of social groups that become second nature. Significantly, Simmel also remarked on the active fostering of a certain strangeness or reserve as a negative means of

---

1 In its categorical distinction between subject and object, Simmel's approach can be used to identify the key difference between a banal cosmopolitanism as the product of an ossified objective culture (e.g., Indian cuisine or world music) and the vitality of a subjective culture that is entrapped by the former, embodied in the lived experience of the cosmopolitan stranger, as will be elaborated in this chapter.

self-preservation induced by the city's constant stimuli, perceived as an attack to the autonomy and individuality of their inhabitants. Thus, he maintains in his seminal essay on the metropolis that an attitude of reserve is characteristic of urbanites, often perceived by small-town people as cold and heartless, and that

> the inner aspect of this outer reserve is not only indifference but, more often than we are aware, it is a slight aversion, a mutual strangeness and repulsion, which will break into hatred and fight at the moment of a closer contact, however caused.
> SIMMEL, 1997: 179

If the stranger is a social figure who combines nearness and remoteness, strangeness introduces social distance in an urban context of extreme physical closeness, while disassociation is, for Simmel, an elemental form of socialization in the metropolis (1997: 180). Strangeness is both a form of guarding individuality in the face of overwhelming social forces (in Simmel's view antipathy protects from both indifference and indiscriminate suggestibility) and a condition that makes it possible for a wide variety of people to live together by avoiding the conflicts that closer contact with others would generate.

It is Simmel's merit to have grasped the centrality of strangeness to social relations in modernity, even if he left his intuitive account of its role largely unexplored. Contemporary authors are faced with the challenge of reconceptualizing the stranger in the context of what can be approached as the universalization of strangeness, when the closed boundaries of the communities against which the stranger was traditionally defined can no longer be maintained. The most sustained attempt to develop an analysis of contemporary strangeness is that of Chris Rumford. Strangeness already appears in his book *Cosmopolitan Spaces* (2008), but becomes the central reflection in *The Globalization of Strangeness* (2013). In his earlier work, Rumford argues that processes of globalization have led to an increased sense of strangeness, particularly with reference to political spaces, in relation to the undermining of the familiar territoriality of a world of nation-states. Strangeness refers to social spaces or political domains 'which have an unsettling, destabilizing, or disorienting effect in the sense that they are difficult to comprehend or assimilate' (2008: 69). In this account, global connectivity generates not simply the idea of a smaller world, but also leads to realizing its potential dangers, accounting for growing trends toward the reinforcement of borders and the securitization of everyday life. The author thus focuses on the proliferation of unfamiliar spaces in a world that is increasingly perceived as uncertain and threatening, and the blurring and reconfiguration of borders on a national as well as on a global scale.

The subject of Rumford's 2013 book, *The Globalization of Strangeness*, is no longer the increasingly unfamiliar spatiality that emerges as a product of globalization, but sociality itself. It approaches social theories of the stranger in the light of contemporary developments, while also centrally addressing current trends toward the universalization of strangeness. The author argues that

> Strangeness is encountered when there exists the realization that the social world is unrecognizable in many ways, and where familiar reference points no longer exist (or are far from reliable) … In other words, strangeness is a type of social disorientation (resulting from an experience of globalization) as a result of which we are no longer sure who 'we' are, and we find it difficult to say who belongs to 'our' group and who comes from outside.
> RUMFORD, 2013: xi–xii

In a context of mobile and increasingly ambiguous borders, Rumford highlights how it has become impossible to identify who the strangers are with reference to a clearly defined cohesive community, thus making the conventional sociological figure of the stranger impossible. Moreover, strangeness becomes unavoidable, but also a matter of perspective: 'it is no longer possible to stand outside of societal strangeness; everyone is a stranger to someone else' (Rumford, 2013: 48). Strangeness is viewed essentially as a form of dis-connectivity as familiar reference points are eroded (2013: 34), pointing to a significant experience of globalization that is often neglected in the literature. Therein also lies the fundamental link between cosmopolitanism and strangeness: cosmopolitanism is a political strategy that mobilizes subjective experience to open up new possibilities for human sociality under the constraints imposed by strangeness (2013: 107).

In addition to Rumford's compelling account of the link between cosmopolitanism and strangeness, there are at least three important reasons for examining the significance of the stranger in relation to contemporary cosmopolitanism. These relate to the need to consider individual lived experience, an aspect of cosmopolitanism that has not yet received sufficient attention in the literature, to the prominent role of the stranger—rather than the cosmopolitan—in the cosmopolitanism debate, and to the possibility of viewing strangers as a test for the degree of cosmopolitan openness in society. Each is briefly commented upon here.

First, by putting individual experience at the center (in addition to Rumford, 2013, see also Agier, 2016; Bielsa, 2016), the notion of the stranger allows for a concretization of cosmopolitan themes in the lives of individuals who, because of their particular circumstances, are forced to turn their ordinary experiences of incongruity and displacement into a source of cosmopolitan learning. Perhaps more significantly, the relevance of lived experience in responding to generalized societal strangeness should also be emphasized, as the latter is precisely characterized by the fact that it increasingly jeopardizes meaningful individual experience. The experiences, learning processes, and skills of the cosmopolitan stranger can be used as an antidote or a protection against social conditions that threaten the individual's capacity for meaningful experience itself, much in the same way as Walter Benjamin sought to describe in Baudelaire's experience of shock a combative response to the atrophy of experience in modernity (Benjamin, 2006).

Second, it is the stranger, rather than the cosmopolitan, who is at the center of contemporary debates about cosmopolitanism. The main reason for this is that the concept of the cosmopolitan has remained rather narrow and linked to traditional definitions that alluded to the perspective of an upper-class (mostly male) individual who traveled frequently and possessed as a result personal knowledge and experience of the diversity of the world. Even if this notion of the cosmopolitan is questioned and an alternative definition that contemplates not just knowledge but especially engagement with diversity and otherness is proposed, the concept remains far too restricted to refer to all of those who are today living cosmopolitan lives.[2] Arguably, an openness that is primarily conceived in aesthetic terms is, in our society, not available to all, but only to those who are freed from necessity, thus excluding the majority of the population (Bourdieu, 1986). If the figure of the cosmopolitan cannot get rid of an elitist cosmopolitanism primarily based on the aesthetic attitude, the stranger speaks to us about the lived experience of foreignness in our daily, ordinary lives. Here, we are attending not just to those of privileged backgrounds who have learnt to appreciate and live with cultural difference, but also to the vast numbers of migrants who become skilled cosmopolitans (Sennett, 2009), who may not be fully convinced cosmopolitans but perhaps unwilling or unconscious ones, but whose complex, creative, and often contradictory experience of the foreign can nevertheless be used in a cosmopolitan direction.

---

2 This was the path followed by Ulf Hannerz, who underlined 'intellectual and aesthetic openness toward divergent cultural experience' (1996: 103). More recently, it can also be found in Skrbiš and Woodward's (2013) approach.

A third reason for paying attention to the stranger is that strangers are a test for the degree of cosmopolitan openness in society. The significance of this aspect is clearly perceivable in Jacques Derrida's approach to cosmopolitan openness as unconditional hospitality to the foreigner, an absolute hospitality that does not ask for reciprocity or even for the stranger's name (Derrida and Dufourmantelle, 2000: 25). Absolute hospitality may be unattainable, or even undesirable, because it can recklessly put our lifeworld in danger (Bielsa and Aguilera, 2017), but it points in a very different direction to approaches based on recognition (Taylor, 1994; Honneth, 1995), which are often at the center of multiculturalist debates. Recognition always implies a degree of previous comprehension, an apprehension of others in terms of their relation to ourselves, which is inevitably a reduction. Hospitality is a more radical practice, preserving an existence of and creating an involvement with something we still do not understand. Recognition is not the key to the cosmopolitan challenge posed by the stranger, but rather hospitality and respect in the face of incomprehensible, unrecognizable difference (Aguilera, 2015). Strangeness is at the center of Europe's current refusal of solidarity with refugees, or of growing authoritarian responses to migration flows, most visible in Trump and Brexit. Very much in Simmel's sense of a rejection of the stranger's specificity and humanity in the name of generality, strangeness leads to fostering a non-relationship in an increasingly small world. Strangers, chosen to epitomize strangeness, offer a scapegoat for the anxieties provoked by rising uncertainty, unfamiliarity, and opacity (Bauman, 2007: 85). However, the incapacity to acknowledge and deal with strangeness can only lead to its further proliferation. Cosmopolitan strangers represent an alternative strategy that finds in an experience of the foreign the resources to productively engage with the constraints imposed by strangeness.

3   Conceptualizing the Cosmopolitan Stranger

What are the features of the cosmopolitan stranger? In which ways does he or she differ from the prototypical stranger, once described by Simmel as 'the person who comes today and stays tomorrow' (1950 [1908]: 402), a *potential* wanderer who retains the freedom to come and go, a person who 'is near and far *at the same time*' (1950 [1908]: 407)? Simmel's essay was written at a time when strangers elicited a reaction they no longer produce today, when they were still felt as an extraordinary presence, and in part his work derives its penetrating force from this fact. The stranger confronted a group with well-defined boundaries by being at a distance from it, and it is this aspect of Simmel's approach that requires most rethinking in the contemporary context, even if we preserve a notion of cultural distance as fundamental for a definition of the cosmopolitan stranger.

As Zygmunt Bauman maintained, 'all societies produce strangers; but each kind of society produces its own kind of strangers, and produces them in its own inimitable way' (Bauman, 1997: 17). On these grounds alone, an exploration of the figure of the cosmopolitan stranger is already justified. However, this chapter seeks to articulate a stronger claim for the social and cultural significance of cosmopolitan strangers concerning their privileged experience of the foreign, which can be put to work politically toward cosmopolitan ends. In this approach, the cosmopolitan stranger's self-reflexive journey can serve as an exemplary instance of the cosmopolitan imagination, of a cosmopolitan openness concerning 'shifts in self-understanding and self-problematization in light of the encounter with the Other' (Delanty, 2009: 83). Thus, cosmopolitan strangers are bearers of key forms of ethical and political learning of a cosmopolitan potential that can be generalized and transmitted to others.

Bauman himself, who conceived strangerhood as a central aspect of his sociology of modernity, identified key social developments that directly contribute to a characterization of the stranger in the contemporary context. Bauman's stranger is fundamentally defined by ambivalence, rather than distance, expressing both the inherent contradictions of assimilatory attempts in the liberal tradition, where strangers are called to individually resolve a strangeness that is always collectively defined, and the experience of the Holocaust as the most sustained attempt to eliminate ambivalence from social life. Thus, Bauman approached strangers as 'the true hybrids, the monsters—not just *unclassified*, but *unclassifiable*' (1991: 58; original emphasis), representing 'an incongruous and hence resented "synthesis of nearness and remoteness"' (1991: 60). He also crucially pointed to the universalization of the social experience of strangerhood from the Jews as prototypical strangers to the rest of society. This has to be taken not only in the sense that we must now all be confronted with the ambiguity and relativism that once marked the social experience of the Jews, but also as putting in doubt that coherent, well-defined home group that classical authors such as Simmel and Schutz could still take for granted.

Ulrich Beck (1998: 127) has noted that strangers are 'neighbours of whom it is said that they are not like "us,"' particularly referring to second-generation migrants. Beck, who shares Bauman's view of the stranger as ambivalence personified, places the emphasis on the effects of cosmopolitanization of reality on individual lives. He also explicitly breaks away from traditional views of the stranger that assume the relative clarity of the local world against which the stranger is defined, particularly by pointing to generalized mobile individual existence and to the universalization of the place polygamy that was once characteristic of the stranger. More and more of us are married to several places at the same time. Thus, Beck approaches processes of globalization of biography (Beck and Beck-Gernsheim, 2002: 25) and of cosmopolitanization of biography in the context of an experiential space in which local, national, and global influences interpenetrate (Beck, 2006: 43) and where cultural difference and the coexistence of rival lifestyles are internalized. He also explicitly refers to the average migrant, who becomes 'an acrobat in the manipulation of boundaries,' and who can be approached as 'the model of an experimental cosmopolitanism of the powerless in which the capacity to change perspectives, dialogical imagination and creative handling of contradictions are indispensable survival skills' (2006: 104).

For Rumford, as I have already indicated, a conceptualization of the cosmopolitan stranger must attend not only to the universalization of the social experience of strangerhood, but also to the generalization of societal strangeness in the contemporary context. In the midst of generalized strangeness, it is more appropriate to see the stranger as one who can pop out anywhere, anytime, not previously observed arriving (2013: 43). Thus, the cosmopolitan stranger is defined as a person who is 'here today and gone tomorrow'—in opposition to Simmel's stranger, who 'comes today and stays tomorrow.' The cosmopolitan stranger is made possible by modern technology, which offers the capability to connect globally without leaving home: 'whereas the cosmopolitan is a figure considered ... to be at home everywhere, the cosmopolitan stranger is "everywhere, at home"' (2013: 121). Rumford's examples of cosmopolitan strangers (which include the superhero Phoenix Jones, public artists, as well as collective actors such as the flash mob; see 2013: 124–135) underline their role in generating new forms of social solidarity through connecting people with distant others, thus opening up possibilities under the restrictive conditions of strangeness.

It is precisely when the universalization of strangerhood would seem to indicate that strangers have lost the social distinctiveness they once possessed because, as Bauman observed, 'if everyone is a stranger, no one is' (1991: 97), that the social experience and skills of the cosmopolitan stranger become more relevant to us all in the conduct of our ordinary lives in conditions of generalized strangeness. This is what makes the cosmopolitan stranger the paradigmatic stranger figure of the current age. Cosmopolitan strangers' particular biographical trajectories and existential conditions, particularly what Edward Said once described as a profound and painful 'discontinuous state of being' that marks the experiences of all migrants (2002: 140), have led them to embrace a self-reflexivity toward their own views and most ingrained beliefs.

Such a notion of the cosmopolitan stranger actualizes Simmel's prototypical stranger with a view to preserving Simmel's objective of capturing the modes of experiencing modern life (Frisby, 1988; 2002: 27). However, it differs from accounts based on Simmel in that it emphasizes openness, rather than non-belonging, as the basis of the stranger's experience of the foreign.

In this light, the following basic features of the cosmopolitan stranger can be distinguished:

1. The cosmopolitan stranger must be theorized somewhere in between the cosmopolitan, who is at home everywhere in the world, and the contemporary stranger as an eternal wanderer, 'homeless always and everywhere, without hope of ever "arriving" ' (Bauman, 1991: 79). I propose a focus on the cosmopolitan sociability of migrants that stresses simultaneous rootedness and openness, as well as cultural difference as the source of individual creativity for adapting and building a new home in a different environment (cf. Beck, 2006: 104; Sennett, 2009; Glick Schiller, Darieva, and Gruner-Domic, 2011; Agier, 2016). In this approach, the stress falls on displacement and cultural hybridity rather than on homelessness or detachment, pointing not to the dissolution of local bonds and forms of belonging but rather to the existence of various, sometimes conflicting, attachments and a certain degree of in-betweenness.[3]

2. The cosmopolitan stranger is an excellent translator between cultures. This is a key aspect in order to consider the stranger as an active agent of cosmopolitanism from below that often tends to be either underestimated or simply forgotten. It is related to how the stranger adapts to a new cultural context in a way that is meaningful and relevant not only to him or herself but also to locals. The emphasis lies here not on what is lost in translation, but on what is gained, relying on an understanding of translation not as transfer or communication of meaning, but on a much wider notion of translation as an experience of the foreign that is intimately related to our self-identity (Bielsa, 2014, 2016). Although the sociological literature has paid little attention to this significant aspect, Alfred Schütz explicitly identified how, to the stranger, 'the cultural pattern no longer functions as a system of tested recipes at hand' (1976: 96) as it does for the locals; strangers thus have to undertake a translation of the terms of the cultural pattern of the approached group into those of the home group. However, I propose to

---

3 On the in-between stranger see Marotta (2010); but see also Rumford's justified critique of the assumption that this leads to a privileged perspective. As Rumford argues, cosmopolitanism seeks to encourage multiperspectivalism rather than 'high point' thinking (2013: 116–118).

reverse Schütz's insights in considering this fact not a source of inadequacy that makes the stranger uncertain and socially handicapped, but mostly a source of creativity that can be used in a cosmopolitan direction—by successfully translating some elements from the cultural pattern of the home group into the terms of the approached group.

3. The cosmopolitan stranger is a mediated stranger, increasingly relevant not just with reference to face-to-face interaction with an approached group but to wide and heterogeneous mass publics that no longer belong to clearly defined communities with an inside/outside divide. Thus, a discussion of the cosmopolitan stranger needs to address the significance of the mediated public space, in which, as Roger Silverstone indicates, 'the mediated images of strangers increasingly define what actually constitutes the world' (2007: 4). Successful cosmopolitan strangers can become relevant and inspiring to international audiences across linguistic and cultural divides. They are not just the ubiquitous face of the other that is made visible but seldom heard (or even less understood), but rather prominent characters who have been able to communicate through the media to different publics in remarkable ways. Renowned foreign correspondents like John Carlin or Tiziano Terzani, who excel in their task as interpreters of the foreign and become appreciated in different national contexts, thus overcoming the domestic/foreign dichotomy, are exemplary stranger figures of this kind.

4. The cosmopolitan stranger is not the only, or even the most prevalent, kind of stranger today. Flawed consumers (Bauman, 1997: 14) and refugees, whom Bauman sees as outcasts and outlaws of a novel kind who 'lose their place on earth and are catapulted into a nowhere' (Bauman, 2007: 45; see also Bauman 2016), abound. Instead, I seek to identify a particularly relevant type of stranger: strangers whose survival skills are improved precisely because they have learned to communicate with strangers. These strangers not only manage to make themselves heard, but also challenge a world that has become second nature, leading to self-reflexivity and change in the light of the difference of the other. Precisely because of this, this type of stranger can make an important contribution in a cosmopolitan direction.

4 Conclusion

Contemporary globalization has witnessed the apparent overcoming of distance and a concomitant generalization of strangeness, which calls for a reappraisal of the figure of the stranger as a peculiar unity of nearness and remoteness. It is cosmopolitan openness, rather than non-belonging, that distinguishes the cosmopolitan stranger from other stranger figures, both past and present, and that is also the key to an experience of the foreign that can be transmitted to others and put to use toward cosmopolitan ends.

Such an approximation does not renounce a focus on cultural distance, which has not disappeared as a consequence of the significant transcendence of spatial distance. Like all strangers, cosmopolitan strangers face multiple conflicts and inadequacies that are precisely a product of distance—of the fact that, in spite of being close, they are far—and find original and creative ways of dealing with their often conflicting attachments. It is precisely this uncertain confrontation with and displacement of what since childhood has sedimented in our most inner self that is the key element of the stranger's freedom. Herein lies the source of the cosmopolitan stranger's emblematic character and also of the stranger's objectivity, celebrated by Simmel as a mixture of indifference and involvement, as a freedom from prejudice and from habit that can be put to use towards cosmopolitan ends. This is also why the cosmopolitan stranger belies the assumptions underlying notions of an abstract universal citizen, or of a cosmopolitan who feels at home in the world, or of a global elite of frequent travelers as phantasmagoric presences of unattached individuals; 'individuals without an anchorage, without borders, colorless, stateless, rootless, a body of angels' (Fanon, 2004: 155).

Simmel also identified the significance of strangeness in social relationships with strangers and in modern urban life. Since Simmel's time, strangeness has been generalized, destabilizing a familiar world of nation-states and challenging human sociality itself. We have all been turned into strangers who need to relate to one another in an increasingly unfamiliar world. Cosmopolitan strangers productively confront strangeness and turn it into a source of reflexive self-examination and cosmopolitan learning, thus mobilizing the qualities of human experience and sociality that are increasingly threatened by it in new meaningful ways.

References

Agier, M. 2016. *Borderlands*. Cambridge, UK: Polity Press.
Aguilera, A. 2015. 'Insuficiencias del reconocimiento para una apertura cosmopolita al otro.' *Papers. Revista de Sociologia* 100 (3): 325–344.
Baudelaire, C. 1964. *The Painter of Modern Life and Other Essays*. London: Phaidon Press.
Bauman, Z. 1991. *Modernity and Ambivalence*. Cambridge, UK: Polity Press.

Bauman, Z. 1997. *Postmodernity and its Discontents*. Cambridge, UK: Polity Press.
Bauman, Z. 2007. *Liquid Times*. Cambridge, UK: Polity Press.
Bauman, Z. 2016. *Strangers at Our Door*. Cambridge, UK: Polity Press.
Beck, U. 1998. 'How Neighbours become Jews: The Political Construction of the Stranger in the Age of Reflexive Modernity.' In *Democracy without Enemies*, edited by U. Beck, 122–140. Cambridge, UK: Polity Press.
Beck, U. 2006. *The Cosmopolitan Vision*. Cambridge, UK: Polity Press.
Beck, U. and E. Beck-Gernsheim. 2002. *Individualization: Institutionalized Individualism and its Social and Political Consequences*. London: Sage.
Benhabib, S. 2004. *The Rights of Others*. Cambridge, UK: Cambridge University Press.
Benjamin, W. 2006. *The Writer of Modern Life: Essays on Charles Baudelaire*. Cambridge, MA; London: Belknap Press.
Bielsa, E. 2014. 'Cosmopolitanism as Translation.' *Cultural Sociology* 8 (4): 392–406.
Bielsa, E. 2016. *Cosmopolitanism and Translation: Investigations into the Experience of the Foreign*. London; New York: Routledge.
Bielsa, E. and A. Aguilera. 2017. 'Politics of Translation: A Cosmopolitan Approach.' *European Journal of Cultural and Political Sociology* 4 (1): 7–24.
Bourdieu, P. 1986. *Distinction: A Social Critique of the Judgment of Taste*. London: Routledge.
Delanty, G. 2009. *The Cosmopolitan Imagination*. Cambridge, UK: Cambridge University Press.
Derrida, J. 1998. *Monolingualism of the Other*. Stanford, CA: Stanford University Press.
Derrida, J. and A. Dufourmantelle. 2000. *Of Hospitality*. Stanford, CA: Stanford University Press.
Fanon, F. 2004. *The Wretched of the Earth*. New York: Grove Press.
Frisby, D. 1988. *Fragments of Modernity*. Cambridge, UK: Polity Press.
Frisby, D. 2002. *Georg Simmel*. London; New York: Routledge.
Fritzsche, P. 1996. *Reading Berlin 1900*. Cambridge, MA; London: Harvard University Press.
Glick Schiller, N., T. Darieva, and S. Gruner-Domic. 2011. 'Defining Cosmopolitan Sociability in a Transnational Age: An Introduction.' *Ethnic and Racial Studies* 34 (3): 399–418.
Habermas, J. 1998. *The Inclusion of the Other: Studies in Political Theory*, edited by C. Cronin and P. De Greiff. Cambridge, MA: MIT Press.
Hannerz, U. 1996. *Transnational Connections*. London; New York: Routledge.
Honig, B. 2001. *Democracy and the Foreigner*. Princeton, NJ; Oxford: Princeton University Press.
Honneth, A. 1995. *The Struggle for Recognition*. Cambridge, UK: Polity Press.
Ivekovic, R. 2005. 'Transborder Translating.' *Eurozine*, 1–10, https://www.eurozine.com/transborder-translating/.

Kristeva, J. 1991. *Strangers to Ourselves*. New York: Columbia University Press.
Levinas, E. 1991. *Totality and Infinity: An Essay on Exteriority*. Dordrecht: Kluwer Academic Publishers.
Marotta, V. P. 2010. 'The Cosmopolitan Stranger.' In *Questioning Cosmopolitanism*, edited by S. Van Hoofdt and W. Vandekerckhove, 105–120. Dordrecht: Springer.
Rumford, C. 2008. *Cosmopolitan Spaces*. London; New York: Routledge.
Rumford, C. 2013. *The Globalization of Strangeness*. London: Palgrave Macmillan.
Said, E. W. 2002. *Reflections on Exile and Other Essays*. Cambridge MA: Harvard University Press.
Sakai, N. 1997. *Translation and Subjectivity*. Minneapolis; London: University of Minnesota Press.
Schütz, A. 1976. 'The Stranger.' In A. Brodersen (ed) *Collected Papers II: Studies in Social Theory*, 91–105. The Hague: Martinus Nijhoff.
Sennett, R. 2009. *The Public Realm*, https://www.richardsennett.com/site/senn/templates/general2.aspx?pageid=16&cc=gb.
Silverstone, R. 2007. *Media and Morality*. Cambridge, UK: Polity Press.
Simmel, G. 1950 [1908]. 'The Stranger.' In K. H. Wolff (ed.), *The Sociology of Georg Simmel*, 402–408. New York: Free Press.
Simmel, G. 1997. *Simmel on Culture*, edited by D. Frisby and M. Featherstone. London: Sage.
Skrbiš, Z. and I. Woodward. 2013. *Cosmopolitanism: Uses of the Idea*. London: Sage.
Taylor, C. 1994. 'The Politics of Recognition.' In *Multiculturalism: Examining the Politics of Recognition*, edited by A. Gutmann, 25–73. Princeton, NJ: Princeton University Press.

CHAPTER 19

Aesthetico-Cultural Cosmopolitanism

Sylvie Octobre

The consumption of globalized goods and services allows individuals to have immediate, widespread contact with cultural difference.* Some authors have argued that culture is in fact the most significant aspect of globalization, both in terms of the volume of financial trade and in the capacity for these exchanges to shape cultural imaginaries and representations of the world. These transactions are especially powerful, given that cultural consumption practices are leisure activities in which individuals can freely engage. Of the five global flows that Arjun Appadurai (1996) identifies as 'scapes,' three are cultural in nature: *mediascapes, ethnoscapes,* and *ideoscapes*. From a more radical perspective, Lechner and Boli (2005) argue that all of the elements that help to unify the world, including in terms of infrastructure, are profoundly cultural in nature. As a result, the global expansion of capitalism has granted greater significance to cultural matters (Robertson and White, 2007), with some scholars even going so far as to characterize contemporary capitalism as 'artistic' (Lipovetsky and Serroy, 2013).

Some scholars have established a link between the globalization of culture and the emergence of so-called aesthetic cosmopolitanism, both in terms of the cultural offering and how it is received and interpreted (Papastergiadis, 2012; Regev, 2013). Digital cultural industries, which are more global than ever, mean that individuals are no longer just consumers but also agents of cultural globalization, since they participate in the production and diffusion of increasing volumes of cultural content, from tutorials to self-published and collaborative creations (Octobre, 2018). In addition, the growing use of cultural resources to define one's identity has made aesthetico-cultural cosmopolitanism one of the most easily available and thus banal forms of cosmopolitanism, as illustrated by Mica Nava in her study of London women and fashion at the beginning of the 20th century. Her concept of 'visceral cosmopolitanism' expresses 'a diffuse cosmopolitan conscience (a cosmopolitan structure of feeling)' (Nava, 2007: 160). Finally, by marketing cultural

---

* This chapter was written in collaboration with Vincenzo Cicchelli. We thank Sarah-Louise Raillard for her assistance in preparing the English version of this chapter.

difference, contemporary consumerism identifies exoticism as an engine of desire for further consumption (Holt, 1998; Woodward and Emontspool, 2018). It is therefore essential to analyze cultural phenomena if we wish to understand globalization, since, as Malcom Waters has argued, 'material exchanges localize, political exchanges internationalize and symbolic exchanges globalize' (2001 [1995]: 20).

1 Competing for Global Cultural Imaginaries

Exchanges of cultural goods and services account for a significant portion of all global transactions, with cultural trade having reached a worldwide total of almost $213 billion in 2013—close to double the amount recorded in 2004. These exchanges are a reflection of the shifting geopolitical terrain: while the United States dominated cultural globalization until very recently—a phenomenon that was consequently sometimes called 'Americanization' (Kuisel, 1991; Norris and Inglehart, 2012)—since 2013, China has arisen as the leading exporter of cultural goods and services, accounting for more than $60 billion, or twice the total of American exports. Although the United States remain the leading importer of cultural goods (it should be noted that generally speaking, developed countries export less than they import), new producers such as Turkey and India have appeared on the scene and now feature among the top ten exporters worldwide. Production centers have proliferated across the globe: even if Western countries remain the primary consumers, what they consume now comes from many different regions of the world. In 1996, Arjun Appadurai observed that the United States had already become just one of many different producers of the global system of images, a highly complex landscape where transnational imaginaries proliferate and compete for dominance.

The globalization of culture has only become more pronounced since the mid-1990s, and a number of new transformations have occurred. First of all, cultural globalization has shifted toward a plurality of influences. Today, we can now assume that the globalization of culture serves a number of different functions for countries who wish for their cultural hegemony to appear unchallenged and for their narratives of the world to be so convincing that consumers embrace them without any kind of critical distance whatsoever. Amid the proliferation of cultural flows, many different world narratives exist side by side: Japanese manga; American comics; Hollywood, Bollywood, and Nollywood movies; Norwegian and English crime novels; and so on. This proliferation has do to with the shift from the logic of snobbery (associated with cultural legitimacy), toward the logic of eclecticism (Donnat, 1994) or omnivorism (Peterson and Kern, 1996)—that is, the logic of achieving distinction through cultural consumption—in a cultural landscape dominated by cultural industries, as studied by the sociologists of cultural practices since the 1990s. Second, analyses have highlighted the role played by imaginaries with regard to social behaviors, given that the mediated relationships to otherness provided by cultural products can help to mitigate the unfortunately still quite tangible limitations to our physical mobility. As a result, the role of the media and the audiovisual content that they disseminate is key, since they provide the narrative resources necessary for individuals to establish their worldview. Cinematographic production and consumption thus play a crucial role in the creation of cultural identities and the development of feelings of belonging: American blockbusters have audiences in the millions and are regularly among the top ten box-office hits everywhere in the world. In her analysis of American cinema, Diana Crane has shown how this sector plays a crucial role in the shaping of transnational imaginaries. In that regard, she has observed that 'The global domination of the American film industry exemplifies one of the major criticisms of cultural globalization, the potentially homogenizing effect of global culture, which constitutes a threat to the distinctiveness of national cultures' (Crane, 2014: 365). But Crane also highlights that the face of globalization has changed, and that a certain hegemonic logic has given way to a multipolar production landscape. 'Globalization cannot be easily described anymore as having a "distinctly American face." There is more and more evidence for competing centres of multiple globalization' (ibid.: 365–366). And it is, of course, with regard to imaginaries that this competition has increased. In addition to competition between older centers of production and their peripheries, we now see the resurgence of imperial ambitions, as evidenced by the recent success of the Chinese-American film *The Great Wall*,[1] as well as by the hubbub surrounding a number of Turkish television series broadcast around the world (*The Last Emperor*, which started airing in September 2017, and *The Magnificent Century*, which aired from 2011 to 2014). These productions all attest to hegemonic ambitions founded on nostalgia for the empires of yesteryear.

The competition for global imaginaries is nothing new. The use of soft power (Nye, 2004), which characterized the post-Second World War landscape,

---

[1] A 2016 monster film directed by Zhang Yimou, featuring Chinese and American stars (Jing Tian and Matt Damon), that grossed $334 million worldwide, against its $150 million production budget.

was in fact a political and social Trojan Horse.² As Wagnleitner (1993) demonstrates in his analysis of 'Coca-Colonization,' this competition was designed to help the United States fight the spread of communism while promoting the American (materialistic, individualistic, and consumerist) way of life. In the digital era, this cultural soft power has become unprecedented in scope: the Big Four tech companies (sometimes collectively called GAFA—Google, Amazon, Facebook, Apple) can, more than any of the pre-digital industries that preceded them, rapidly disseminate cultural content at the global level that promotes, whether implicitly or explicitly, social and political values such as individualism, heroism, consumerism, and feminism. These values are more easily appropriated by individuals when they are embedded inside popular products that are widely accessible, both economically or materially and cognitively, or when they are coproduced with/by consumers. But the soft power of transnational digital cultural industries can also take a different form, since it is less likely today that a state, or group of states, can preside over the production of cultural imaginaries that are in turn instrumentalized for political ends. The Big Four in fact promote values that cannot be reduced to a single ethno-national origin, given their global embedding (a fact which we recently witnessed in protests led by Google employees against the company's policy of using facial recognition technology to help the Trump administration track down illegal migrants). In reality, the Big Four tech companies have invented a kind of political soft power that goes beyond the state (see the sensation caused by a number of different data leaks), and which derives both its strength and its legitimacy from the participatory nature of cultural democracy, in an effort to mitigate the malfunctioning of democratic systems.

2   A Cultural Mosaic

In this competition, the globalization of culture has a number of different effects. On the one hand, it encourages the propagation of policies that react to the fear of homogenization and support cultural diversity, such as the French 'cultural exception' policy implemented within the General Agreement on

---

2   Nye defines soft power as follows: 'Soft power is not merely the same as influence. After all, influence can also rest on the hard power of threats or payments. And soft power is more than just persuasion or the ability to move people by argument, though that is an important part of it. It is also the ability to attract, and attraction often leads to acquiescence. Simply put, in behavioural terms, soft power is attractive power. Soft power resources are the assets that produce such attraction' (2004: 6).

Tariffs and Trade (GATT) in 1993, various measures to promote local cultures modeled on policies designed in the realm of environmental preservation, and efforts to expand the scope and application of heritage policies (see the United Nations (UN) Blue Helmets, for instance). These three aspects contribute to the diversity of global culture (Curran and Park, 2000). As a result, Hollywood enters into competition with Bollywood and Nollywood in certain geographical regions; many countries, such as Brazil, South Korea, and Turkey, have become major producers of television series; and certain cultural forms that had hitherto been purely national in their area of distribution are now widely exported (such as Northern European crime novels, Japanese manga, and K-pop). At the same time, the world has become increasingly concerned with the fate of various war-imperiled sites of cultural heritage (Palmyra comes to mind as a recent example).

On the other hand, the circulation of cultural products and services has hastened the advent of a 'global mélange' (Pieterse, 2009): namely, the rise of hybridization, combining universal elements with local ones and thus allowing distinct populations to identify as members of an ethno-national community while still also seeing themselves in a broader collective group. Although hybridization is a process as old as time,[3] it has become one of the main drivers of globalization, since 'the pace of mixing accelerates and its scope widens in the wake of major structural changes, such as new technologies that enable new phases of intercultural contact' (Pieterse, 2009: 98). In his studies of pop-rock music, Motti Regev (2013) has likewise highlighted that certain international elements (rhythm, the choice of instruments) are mobilized to support other elements that are considered to be purely national (voices, melodies, themes), ultimately creating a form of rock that is interpreted as the expression of a national genius, from Israel to Argentina. By speaking to a local public and providing it with local content, the songs produced in this manner are presented as the expression of a unified national culture. And yet these cultural products are part and parcel of the global aesthetic of the pop-rock genre, from their electric and electronic instrumentation to their sophisticated studio production techniques.

The world can therefore be understood as a cultural mosaic, both in terms of the cultural traits that are ostensibly specific to each nation, community, or geographical area and the interplay of cultural comparisons that these entail, and the emphasis that is placed on cross-cutting and/or hybrid cultural characteristics. This perception in terms of a global cultural mosaic is further

---

3   The process of hybridization can be defined as 'the ways in which forms become separated from existing practices and recombined with new forms in new practices' (Rowe and Schelling, 1991: 231).

supported by two complementary mechanisms: the first being the universalization of the particular—attested to by the diffusion of products made by global brands (Bookman, 2013; Bookman and Hall, 2019)—and the second being the particularization of the universal—a movement which has at times been called creolization (Tomlinson, 1999), indigenization (Appadurai, 1996), and even 'glocalization' (Robertson, 1995). Borrowing from the work of Boltanski and Chiapello (2005 [1999]), we can say that the aesthetico-cultural genius of America has precisely been its ability to embed the contradiction of Americanization within American cultural products. As Illouz (2007) would say: its ability to create transnational emotions that are sufficiently adaptable to be appropriated by all, but remained linked to a specific vision of the individual.

3 Cultural Odorlessness and Cultural Discount

Seen from this perspective, the globalization of culture is vigorously disparaged by the champions of cultural authenticity. Such criticisms usually follow one of two lines of reasoning. The first line of reasoning targets the cultural contents and their inherent qualities, arguing that the capacity for cultural contents to be appropriated by different individuals is maximized at the expense of their cultural value, resulting in what Iwabuchi calls 'cultural odorlessness' (2002). Consequently, if American movies are well liked, that is because they depict deculturalized and delocalized elements, and they simplify the cultural complexity of the elements that they *do* portray (Liebes and Katz, 1990). In fact, sometimes cultural products are even 'drained' of their cultural values to offer a variety of different meanings depending on the audience in question. It is therefore the process of deculturizing (and departicularizing) American culture that allows the country's cultural products to become global. Hollywood copies and recycles countless ideas, themes, cultural frameworks, and forms of expression from other cultures—especially Asian cultures—and forges a new identity composed of transnational influences that are reflected in products that can easily be appropriated by individuals, given that cultural particularities are reduced to mere details or exotic flourishes (such as décor) that blend into an otherwise predominantly American landscape. For example, Disney revamped the story of Mulan to transform the timid and unhappy young girl of the original Chinese tale into an emancipated, Western-style heroine (Pang, 2005). Wasser (1995) describes global products, whose hallmark is cultural recycling, as 'rootless,' and argues that fewer and fewer are truly addressed to a specific cultural community in particular. Higbee and Lim (2010) likewise conclude that transnational products are hybrid by nature and must therefore eliminate all overly specific traits. Pop culture, like all cultures which traffic in recycling, would therefore be seen as the mark of globalized culture, which is characterized by the permanent reappropriation of sources that are extremely varied in nature (Jenkins, 2004; Memeteau, 2014).

The second type of criticism targets the reception of cultural products, arguing that the appropriation of a given cultural content can only become possible when its cultural complexity is discounted, in turn lowering its value. Consequently, the concept of a cultural discount 'suggests that foreign media have limited appeal because audiences lack the background knowledge, linguistic competence, and other forms of cultural capital to appreciate them' (Lee, 2008: 118). Recent studies on the appropriation of global cultural products (Cicchelli and Octobre, 2018) have nonetheless illustrated that the latter *can* be appropriated in a myriad of different ways depending on social conditions, and may or may not 'speak' of their culture of origin, less in terms of authenticity than the dialectical distance between the 'near' and the 'far' (or the exotic) and one's capacity for self-reflection by means of this dialectic. As a result, an approach that focuses on global cultural contents and products does not so much deal with representativeness, or even veracity, with regard to what might considered as the culture of origin, but rather with the audience's ability to establish linkages between cultural contents and cultural elements such as norms, values, and behaviors. Moreover, criticisms of 'poor' reception are based on the notion that, in order to achieve a high-quality reception, it is necessary to possess prior skills and knowledge. Here again, many studies have looked at the reception of cultural products and shown that significant interest can develop, even despite an objective lack of competencies for appropriation (whether cultural, linguistic, or other). Research has also demonstrated that reception always involves the co-creation of meaning (Cicchelli and Octobre, 2018): individuals do not merely receive preexisting meanings nestled within cultural products. We cannot understand the popularity of Japanese manga and South Korean K-pop in France unless we concede that curiosity toward others can transcend the limits of preexisting cultural proximity (ostensibly reducing the distance between the self and the other). The accusation of cultural discount (which resurrects the specter of cultural legitimacy), assumes that the 'banal' forms of appropriation in a globalized context are of poor quality, and ultimately reestablishes a certain distance (this time, in terms of cultural legitimacy). France is not home to particularly large or prominent Japanese or Korean communities, as is the case in a country like Brazil, for instance. Nor does its history explain any specific ties to these two countries, unlike that of the United States, for example. And yet France is the second-largest consumer of Japanese manga, and has been since the 1990s.

4   Aesthetico-cultural Cosmopolitanism as an Innovative Approach to Cultural Globalization

Any analysis of cultural globalization thus requires a specific approach, one that takes into account what individuals *do* with globalized cultural products. What we have termed aesthetico-cultural cosmopolitanism is an orientation toward others that presupposes a certain degree of familiarity with aesthetic standards and cultural codes that fall outside of one's immediate sphere of belonging, a familiarity which can be developed through the consumption of globalized cultural products and contents (Cicchelli and Octobre, 2018). At the individual level, aesthetico-cultural cosmopolitanism is 'a cultural disposition involving an intellectual and aesthetic stance of "openness" towards peoples, places and experiences from different cultures, especially those from different "nations"' (Szerszynski and Urry, 2002: 468). This form of socialization to otherness through the consumption of global cultural products has both aesthetic and cultural facets, and helps individuals to elaborate imaginaries in a globalized context where cultural industries dominate free time and leisure activities (Baudrillard, 1968), especially since the advent of the digital age. Wherever you are, you can watch South Korean television series for their aesthetics or to learn more about the lifestyle of South Koreans; you can similarly admire the architectural perfection of the Giza pyramids or see them as the reflection of a social and religious structure imbued with a particular theological view of the world.

The skills and competencies developed by mediated encounters with cultural alterity are made possible thanks to one key mechanism—aesthetico-cultural *mise en genre*, or the categorization of cultural products according to their (alleged) national origins and their attributed aesthetic characteristics (Cicchelli and Octobre, 2018). As a result, individuals do not escape a kind of 'methodological nationalism' in terms of cultural reception, even when the characteristics seen as 'national' are in fact hybrid in nature and do not adhere to strictly ethno-national cultural forms (as might be classified by an anthropologist for example).

The process of *mise en genre* is accompanied by the identification of what is near and far, a kind of compass to orient oneself in a highly culturalized and aestheticized world, using a certain back-and-forth between direct and mediated contacts; the former being used to verify the latter, while the latter often helps to shape the imaginaries that motivate the former. In both cases, curiosity is the central motor: it feeds into desires to move beyond one's immediate circle, to be surprised, to experience wonder, discovery, and novelty. Through a process of self-reflection, curiosity and the desires that stem from it deliver the narrative resources that individuals need to establish their sense of belonging to a community or communities (be these ethno-national, ethno-racial, gender, social, generational or age-related communities, or even just loose affiliations based around shared taste preferences). It thus becomes crucially important to know how to establish the 'right amount of distance' to maintain the spark of curiosity and make moving away from one's center of reference (decentering oneself) possible (Cicchelli, 2018). Ultimately, such adjustments are the responsibility of the individual: while an individual's general social conditions (his or her economic, social, cultural, and linguistic capital, as well as potential for mobility) can inform some personal stances, other attitudes are more explicitly defined by an individual's resources (biography, desires, personal aspirations, etc.) (Cicchelli and Octobre, 2017).

A second mechanism then comes into play, which, instead of localizing the content of cultural products or the experiences encountered while traveling, serves to universalize the former. The process of universalization can take two different paths: either the path of cultural de-particularization, when a cultural product is treated as universal (works are then seen as belonging to a shared human heritage, part of the universal canon of beauty and meaning, which is implicitly founded on a certain hierarchy of tastes and knowledge); or the path of cultural re-particularization (for example, the exposition of primitive and indigenous arts or ethnographic museums). Such art forms represent a cultural and aesthetic enigma, based on the presumption of aesthetic and cultural relativism, and attest to the diversity of human production. As a result, these skills allow individuals to elaborate narratives about the world which continuously establish linkages between the particular and the universal.

Ultimately, many different skills can be developed in this way: the ability to establish connections between information, perception and emotions; the ability to compare different aesthetic values and cultural norms; the ability to suspend judgment, to develop interpretations and to express feelings, and so on. These attitudes cannot be reduced to the mere acquisition and application of 'global skills,' which are the purview of the globalized elite, who wield them to obtain profitable social positions for themselves (Cicchelli et al., 2018).

5   Conclusion: toward a Cosmopolitan Education

A whole swath of studies bitterly dissects this banal, consumerist cosmopolitanism of the masses, usually taking one of two stances. The first argument is that since this form of cosmopolitanism was born out of contemporary—artistic and aestheticized—capitalism, it is a merely cosmetic approach to alterity. In this virulent takedown of globalized consumerism (Binnie and Skeggs, 2004), the virtues of openness and curiosity are viewed as injunctions necessary to maintain the functioning of an economic system whose trademark is the exaltation of cultural diversity. The second stance posits that aesthetico-cultural cosmopolitanism may be the breeding ground for a new cosmopolitan humanism, one that is able to deal with the tensions, conflicts, and contractions engendered by globalization all over the world (Germann Molz, 2011; Papastergiadis, 2012; Cicchelli, Octobre, and Riegel, 2019).

Aligning ourselves with this latter interpretation, we argue that aesthetico-cultural cosmopolitanism can act as a gateway toward other forms of cosmopolitanism that are more ethical or political in nature.[4] However, this form of cosmopolitanism is unique in that it is neither governed nor supported by any institutional or educational structures. Most of the time, cosmopolitan individuals are left to their own devices to draw up their mental maps of the world, a process by which they successively combine and connect cultural contents to achieve a number of (sometimes contradictory) interpretations. The playful tinkering of aesthetico-cultural cosmopolitanism is in fact a form of generalized amateurism (Jenkins, 1992; Flichy, 2010; Octobre, 2018): it promotes the skills acquired by appropriating cultural products for oneself and transforming them, a process which is facilitated by global digital technologies and stimulated by the growing use of cultural resources to define one's identity. Observing the skills that are developed in this way, we are forced to note a unique characteristic: skills are developed and added to one's personal arsenal depending on one's individual passions and biographical trajectories, but never form part of an educational curriculum.

This cosmopolitan auto-didacticism, which favors the aesthetic and cultural dimensions, is also unique because it takes place on the margins of all educational institutions (schools, museums, libraries, etc.). In fact, most of these institutions generally close their doors to the products of cultural industries and do not provide any kind of tools or discourse to help individuals interpret such products as part of their cosmopolitan education, *Bildung*, or journey of personal empowerment. Most of the time, cultural auto-didacticism and institutional forms of education are pitted against each other, rather than being used in a complementary fashion. This likely means that we are underestimating the potential of self-education for aesthetico-cultural cosmopolitanism, both in terms of the characteristics of globalized cultural contents and their ability to 'tell stories' about the world, and in terms of the power of individual acts

---

4   See Chapter 20 in this volume.

of appropriation and their ability to create connections. We should therefore include auto-didacticism within a broader educational framework, establishing linkages between the cultural imaginaries that are the result of globalized industries with other elements such as heritage and science, while preserving, in these techno-cultures, precisely what frees individuals from their particularities and helps them to obtain a political education that encompasses global citizenship and allows them to find their place in a shared world, to refine their judgment, and to regulate their emotions. In short, to live in our global world.

References

Appadurai, A. 1996. *Modernity at Large: Cultural Dimensions of Globalization*. Minneapolis, MN: University of Minneapolis.

Baudrillard, J. 1968. *Le système des objets: la consommation des signes*. Paris: Gallimard.

Binnie, J. and B. Skeggs. 2004. 'Cosmopolitan Knowledge and the Production and Consumption of Sexualized Space: Manchester's Gay Village.' *The Sociological Review* 52 (1): 39–61.

Boltanski, L. and E. Chiapello. 2005 [1999]. *The New Spirit of Capitalism*. London; New York: Verso.

Bookman, S. 2013. 'Branded Cosmopolitanisms: "Global" Coffee Brands and the Co-creation of "Cosmopolitan Cool."' *Cultural Sociology* 7 (1): 56–72.

Bookman, S. and T. Hall. 2019. 'Global Brands, Youth, and Cosmopolitan Consumption: Instagram Performances of Branded Moral Cosmopolitanism.' *Youth and Globalization* 1 (1): 107–137.

Cicchelli, V. 2018. *Plural and Shared: The Sociology of a Cosmopolitan World*. Leiden; Boston, MA: Brill.

Cicchelli, V. and S. Octobre. 2017. 'Aesthetico-Cultural Cosmopolitanism among French Young People. Beyond Social Stratification: The Role of Aspirations and Competences.' *Cultural Sociology* 11 (4): 416–437.

Cicchelli, V. and S. Octobre. 2018. *Aesthetico-Cultural Cosmopolitanism among French Youth: The Taste of the World*. London: Palgrave.

Cicchelli, V., S. Octobre, and V. Riegel (eds.). 2019. *Aesthetic Cosmopolitanism and Global Culture*. Leiden; Boston, MA: Brill.

Cicchelli, V., S. Octobre, V. Riegel, T. Katz-Gerro, and F. Handy. 2018. 'A Tale of Three Cities: Aesthetico-Cultural Cosmopolitanism as a New Capital among Youth in Paris, São Paulo, and Seoul.' *Journal of Consumer Culture* 16 (3): 852–869.

Crane, D. 2014. 'Cultural Globalization and the Dominance of the American Film Industry: Cultural Policies, National Film Industries and Transnational Film.' *International Journal of Cultural Policy* 20 (4): 365–382.

Curran, J. and M.-J. Park. 2000. 'Beyond Globalization Theory.' In *De-westernizing Media Studies*, edited by J. Curran and M.-J. Park, 3–18. London: Routledge.

Donnat, O. 1994. *Les français face à la culture. De l'exclusion à l'éclectisme.* Paris: La Découverte.

Flichy, P. 2010. *Le sacre de l'amateur. Sociologie des passions ordinaires à l'ère numérique.* Paris: Seuil.

Germann Molz, J. 2011. 'Cosmopolitanism and Consumption.' In *The Ashgate Research Companion to Cosmopolitanism*, edited by M. Rovisco and M. Nowicka, 33–52. Farnham: Ashgate Publishing.

Higbee, W. and S. H. Lim. 2010. 'Concepts of Transnational Cinema: Towards a Critical Transnationalism in Film Studies.' *Transnational Cinemas* 1 (1): 7–21.

Holt, D. 1998. 'Does Cultural Consumption Structure American Consumption?' *Journal of Consumer Research* 25 (1): 1–25.

Illouz, E. 2007. *Cold Intimacies: The Making of Emotional Capitalism.* London: Polity Press.

Iwabuchi, K. 2002. 'From Western Gaze to Global Gaze: Japanese Cultural Presence in Asia.' In *Global Culture: Media, Arts, Policy and Globalization*, edited by D. Crane, N. Kawashima, and K. Kawasaki, 256–273. New York: Routledge.

Jenkins, H. 1992. *Textual Poacher: Television Fans and Participatory Culture.* London: Routledge.

Jenkins, H. 2004. 'Pop Cosmopolitanism: Mapping Cultural Flows in an Age of Media Convergence.' In *Globalization, Culture and Education in the New Millennium*, edited by M. M. Suarez-Orozco and D. B. Qin-Hilliard, 114–140. Berkeley: University of California Press.

Kuisel, R. F. 1991. 'Coca-Cola and the Cold War: The French Face Americanization, 1948–1953.' *French Historical Studies* 17 (1): 96–116.

Lechner, F. J. and J. Boli. 2005. *World Culture: Origins and Consequences.* Oxford: Blackwell.

Lee, F. L. F. 2008. 'Hollywood Movies in East Asia: Examining Cultural Discount and Performance Predictability at the Box Office.' *Asian Journal of Communication* 18 (2): 117–136.

Liebes, T. and E. Katz. 1990. *The Export of Meaning: Cross-Cultural Readings of Dallas.* New York: Oxford University Press.

Lipovetsky, G. and J. Serroy. 2013. *L'esthétisation du monde. Vivre à l'âge du capitalisme artiste.* Paris: Gallimard.

Memeteau, R. 2014. *Pop culture: réflexions sur les industries du rêve et l'invention des identités.* Paris: La Découverte.

Nava, M. 2007. *Visceral Cosmopolitanism: Gender, Culture and the Normalization of Difference.* Oxford: Berg.

Norris, P. and R. Ingelhart. 2012. 'The Persistence of Cultural Diversity despite Cosmopolitanism.' In *Routledge Handbook of Cosmopolitanism Studies*, edited by G. Delanty, 166–177. London; New York: Routledge.

Nye, J. S. 2004. *Soft Power: The Means to Success in World Politics*. New York: Public Affairs.
Octobre, S. 2018. *Les technocultures juvéniles: du culturel au politique*. Paris: L'Harmattan.
Pang, L. 2005. 'Copying Kill Bill.' *Social Text* 23 (2): 133–153.
Papastergiadis, N. 2012. *Cosmopolitanism and Culture*. Cambridge, UK: Polity Press.
Peterson, R. A. and R. Kern. 1996. 'Changing Highbrow Taste: From Snob to Omnivore.' *American Sociological Review* 61 (5): 900–907.
Pieterse, J. N. 2009. *Globalization and Culture: Global Mélange*. New York: Rowman & Littlefield.
Regev, M. 2013. *Pop-Rock Music: Aesthetic Cosmopolitanism in Late Modernity*. Cambridge, UK: Polity Press.
Robertson, R. 1995. 'Glocalisation: Time-Space and Homogeneity-Heterogeity.' In *Global Modernities*, edited by M. Featherston, L. Scott, and R. Robertson, 23–44. London: Sage.
Robertson, R. and K. A. White. 2007. 'What is Globalization?' In *The Blackwell Companion to Globalization*, edited by G. Ritzer, 54–66. London: Blackwell.
Rowe, W. and V. Schelling. 1991. *Memory and Modernity: Popular Culture in Latin America*. London; New York: Verso.
Szerszynski, B. and Y. Urry. 2002. 'Cultures of Cosmopolitanism.' *The Sociological Review* 50 (4): 461–481.
Tomlinson, J. 1999. *Globalization and Culture*. Chicago: University of Chicago Press.
Wagnleitner, R. 1993. *Coca-Colonization and the Cold War: The Cultural Mission of the United States in Austria after the Second World War*. Cambridge, MA: University of North Carolina Press.
Wasser, F. 1995. 'Is Hollywood America? The Trans-Nationalization of the American Film Industry.' *Critical Studies in Mass Communication* 12 (4): 423–437.
Waters, M. 2001 [1995]. *Globalization*. London: Routledge.
Woodward, I. and J. Emontspool (eds.). 2018. *Cosmopolitanism, Markets and Consumption: A Critical Global Perspective*. London: Palgrave Macmillan.

CHAPTER 20

The Cosmopolitan Individual in Tension

Vincenzo Cicchelli

1   Introduction*

In international academic literature, the adjective 'cosmopolitan' has been used in myriad different ways since the emergence of cosmopolitan studies as a viable theoretical approach (Delanty, 2012)—and according to some, as a truly new paradigm—and an empirical field of research in the social sciences. While we shall not attempt to provide a comprehensive overview of the word's many different applications (Vertovec and Cohen, 2002; Skrbiš and Woodward, 2013), we shall focus on trying to understand how individuals who are defined as 'cosmopolitans' develop a relationship to the world in our contemporary societies, characterized by globalization. Contemporary usage of the term cosmopolitan has somewhat distanced the term from its historical roots: for the first time, the possibility of cosmopolitanism is not tied to an imperial political structure, but is the result of a truly global historical and social configuration, whose primary drivers are not military conquests, but rather the spread of capitalism as well as certain Western lifestyles and aspirations. Contemporary cosmopolitanism is no longer just the transcendental utopian dream cherished by Stoic philosophers, Christian clerics, and intellectuals in the Republic of Letters, nor is it a lifestyle reserved for the most educated and international social classes, who are able to experience a number of shared worlds thanks to their refined artistic and literary taste preferences, their mastery of vehicular languages, and their penchant for formative travel experiences. Cosmopolitanism must now be seen as a concrete lifestyle that countless individuals can achieve through a plethora of points of contact with cultural difference, offered by global capital flows, as well as the circulation of norms, aspirations, imaginaries, products, services (especially in the media and cultural sphere), and persons. Nevertheless, we should not overlook the fact that at the very moment in history when highly multicultural and even hybridized societies are developing and a new exoticism is threatening to become the dominant

---

* This chapter was written in collaboration with Sylvie Octobre. We thank Sarah-Louise Raillard for her assistance in preparing the English version of this chapter.

standard of good taste among certain social classes and age cohorts (Cicchelli and Octobre, 2018), we are also witnessing the quasi-obsessional focus of public and political debate on fears linked to globalization. Countless pundits have discussed the potential threats of globalization on identity, language, and culture, designating as internal enemies a number of foreign communities that allegedly refuse integration—a problematic situation for coexistence, given that today's societies claim to be open and democratic. Anyone who analyses the current transformations of contemporary societies is sooner or later confronted with this significant difficulty. It is therefore necessary to examine the tensions inherent to (co)existence in our cosmopolitan world, both in terms of belonging and interpersonal relations. What sociology needs is a detailed analysis of the different dynamics of post-national socialization, one which takes into account how individuals open up *and* close off to the enormous global diversity of lifestyles and worldviews, develop the skills to move with ease through different multicultural societies, *or*, on the contrary, cultivate fears that discourage any acts of solidarity or hospitality, instead pushing individuals to withdraw into a world of familiar faces.

2   The Cosmopolitan Legacy and New Sociological Tools

This chapter builds on the cosmopolitan legacy (Cicchelli, 2018): namely, the key components that characterize cosmopolitanism as a worldview. We shall nonetheless translate these matrix elements into innovative sociological tools. It is important to ground the normative ideal of the cosmopolitan in the reality of personal experiences, by studying how such individuals are socialized to otherness—via a number of processes which simultaneously presuppose and enable the development of the skills needed to establish connections with the world—and how they use imaginaries, emotions, and knowledge to claim different shared identities for themselves. The concepts that are needed to understand the cosmopolitan experience stem inevitably from two of cosmopolitanism's fundamental tenets: openness to others and a belief in our shared humanity.

It has been observed that a 'symbiotic relationship' exists between cosmopolitanism and the idea of openness, as 'beyond openness lies a sphere of all things un-cosmopolitan' (Skrbiš and Woodward, 2013: 53). And yet this openness toward others is deeply ambivalent, fragile, and easily reversible; it can even exist alongside cultural withdrawal and even outright rejection of the other (Cicchelli and Octobre, 2018). As for belonging, the now canonical definition of the cosmopolitan proposed by Martha Nussbaum (1996)—someone 'who puts right before country, and universal reason before the symbols of national belonging'—relies on the deeper meaning of the word cosmopolitan, composed of *cosmos* (universe) and *polites* (citizen) (Lourme, 2012). However, such a definition opens itself up to virulent criticisms, with some critics even calling it a social situation where 'little weight' is attributed to belonging (Calhoun, 2003).

By overlooking the shortcomings of both of these matrix elements, some authors have emphasized the dialectical relationship between universalism and particularism in order to better define the cosmopolitan individual. The latter is better understood as a twofold insistence on the recognition of the other *and* on its non-dissolution in the universal (Beck, 2006): as the sum of our shared humanity plus the habits, traditions, customs, and creations of people in specific historical contexts (Appiah, 2006). Still, in spite of such programmatic assertions that reveal how established authors are massively and enthusiastically in favor of a cosmopolitan approach that encompasses the dialectics of the universal and the particular, we must recognize that this attempt, though laudatory, is far from being a self-evident endeavor. More than is commonly admitted perhaps, cosmopolitanism is far from being able to explain complex attitudes toward the world and toward otherness. It remains to be seen whether these two key elements conserve their heuristic potential in the global configuration that forms the backdrop of contemporary cosmopolitanism, since globalization can potentially, but does not necessarily, produce cosmopolitan individuals.

3   Globalization as Janus Bifrons

Although global mobility and flows of all kinds are creating shared worlds, while allowing for the expression of ever greater specificity, nation-states are simultaneously experiencing new forms of cultural retreat and isolationism. This can be seen in the resurgence of unchecked sovereignty, the implementation of protectionist policies, and the imposition of stricter and more effective measures to control immigration at national borders. Globalization moreover poses a vast social challenge, as large-scale transnational processes provide those who are mobile and educated with many opportunities for empowerment, while also generating new inequalities, frustrations, and forms of disillusionment, or uprooting, among those who are not (Sassen, 2014). Those who perceive themselves as 'losers' in the global economic competition, either because they are excluded from wealth distribution and/or they feel that they are ethnically, culturally, or religiously discriminated against, are often tempted by identitarian closure as a fallback position. If we abandon this simplistic lens, globalization is better understood as the simultaneous opening up and closing off of cultural, political, social, and symbolic boundaries that both unite and divide social institutions, human communities, and individuals. This is the deeply paradoxical nature of globalization and its repercussions. As a kind of Janus Bifrons, this twofold process leads to the emergence of a global world which is both more inclusive and exclusive, more integrated and more fragmented, more promising and more frightening (Cicchelli, 2018).

In Europe—and beyond—we have recently witnessed the appearance of a number of convergent phenomena that seem to contradict the cosmopolitan prerequisite of openness. In the political sphere: Brexit, the rise in power of far-right parties, the emergence out of the shadows of neofascist and neo-Nazi militant groups; in the social sphere, the resurgence of anti-Semitism, the rise of Islamophobia, and public reluctance to allocate funds for refugees. From a historical perspective, our era has brought revisionism and the denial of various horrific events in our past; and in terms of social mores, the undermining of certain fundamental freedoms that we believed to be protected by the law, such as women's bodily autonomy and their right to work, divorce, abort. Is it possible to imagine openness to others and an affiliation with universal ideals at this historical juncture, which appears to be dominated by the powerful resurgence of ethno-national movements and identity-related tensions and by an inherent distrust of all things universal? A specter is haunting Europe and the West as a whole: the specter of the anti-Enlightenment.[1]

Nevertheless, globalization cannot be seen exclusively as a Leviathan, a monster that swallows identities and traditions whole and regurgitates an amorphous, hybrid mass, what globalization's detractors call 'cosmopolitan culture,' and which creates or exacerbates inequalities across generations, genders, social classes, countries, and regions. However, globalization is also at the root of different forms of proximity that can lay the groundwork for a new cosmopolitan vision of the world: for example, the circulation of cultural goods and services and the rise of cultural tourism, which create new opportunities to experience different ways of thinking and living (Robertson, 1992). Our world is characterized by a great number of paradoxes, not the least of which is that we have still preserved highly national political structures, while our cultural repertoires are rapidly globalizing. The narratives, iconographies, and imaginaries produced by large global cultural industries and disseminated

---

[1] Zeev Sternhell (2009) defines the anti-Enlightenment as the various intellectual efforts undertaken to staunch the tide of universalism with a view to rejecting the notion that salvation could be found in the communal rather than the individual.

through movies, TV series, web videos, and the media more broadly can provide individuals with the resources they need to establish their identity, as well as their relationship to the wider world (Cicchelli and Octobre, 2018; Octobre, 2018). At the same time as a rhetoric of fear is spreading like wildfire, an unprecedented number of cultural interlinkages is shaping the world into a cultural mosaic, thanks to the juxtaposition of authentic and hybrid creations (Appadurai, 1996).

4 The Cosmopolitan Spirit: Building a Relationship with the World

In this regard, it is necessary to adopt a realistic perspective on the cosmopolitan individual operating in a global world by: (a) envisioning cosmopolitanism as an approach whose main concern is how the transnational processes intertwining individuals beyond national borders reflect, magnify, and alter our relationship with the other and the world at large; (b) and by exploring the mechanisms through which otherness *and* sameness, plurality *and* universality, openness *and* closure are handled by individuals. More precisely, the process of building a cosmopolitan relationship to the world—in other words, the development of a cosmopolitan spirit—requires examining the place of the other in contemporary identities, as well as how plurality and cultural diversity are managed, by considering cosmopolitanism as both a theory and praxis of alterity based on a 'hermeneutics of otherness' (Turner, 2006: 135). It also requires analyzing what characterizes the process of learning about the relation between the self and the other in a plural world by looking at the different orientations to alterity that can be adopted by the ego. Finally, developing a cosmopolitan relationship to the world entails inscribing one's own belonging into a broader horizon and recognizing one's common humanity.

If cosmopolitanism is ostensibly concerned with the process of learning how to be in the world (Delanty, 2009), then the key issue facing individuals in the era of globalization is learning 'how to live with alterity, daily and permanently' (Bauman, 1997: 30). Focusing on this issue alone is not enough, however, especially since studies on cosmopolitanism have largely overlooked the definition of the other and the impact of contact with alterity, despite the fact that these topics should logically figure among their primary concerns. The pervasiveness of alterity—one of the main themes of globalization—means that the primary topic of cosmopolitanism is the complex mechanism by which the other is included (or not). In Beck's view (2006), the internalization of the other is a major sociological asset, used to describe what he calls the cosmopolitanization of the world. In fact, given that the inclusion of the other is a daunting challenge, sociologists should investigate the processes by which a cosmopolitan spirit can be cultivated. This approach looks not for 'fixed or stable attributes, but to the performative, situational and accomplished dimensions of being cosmopolitan' (Woodward and Skrbiš, 2012: 129).

5   The Hermeneutics of Otherness

We propose distinguishing three registers of the representation of the self and the other: the *nomothetic*, the *idiosyncratic*, and the *empathetic* (Cicchelli, 2018). These registers entail different mechanisms used to gain knowledge of the other, as well as an understanding of how interactions with alterity are structured in terms of *symmetry*, *asymmetry*, and *power*. In a *nomothetic* relationship to otherness, the ego views the other as a particular case of a universal order that was established with the goal of allowing said other to access a shared symbolic order, but nonetheless established without the other's consent and with which s/he is forced to comply. Consideration of the other is designed so that the latter must conform to expectations that mitigate, perhaps even negate, his or her difference and uniqueness. This kind of representation of the other stems from a version of universalism that renders the other subordinate to the demands of the ego and establishes a de facto asymmetry between the two entities. In an *idiosyncratic* relationship to the other, the ego sees itself as a particular, *sui generis* case, and demands that others treat him or her as such. The ego may appreciate the symbolic order imposed by the other, so long as this order respects his or her individuality. Others are viewed through the lens of their capacity to infringe (or not) upon the ego's territory or trample his or her rights. Here lies a fundamental difference with the nomothetic relationship to otherness: here, the ego asks the other to comply with his or her particular characteristics and not with a set of universal traits of which the ego is merely a representative. While the first two ways of relating to alterity can explain why misunderstandings, antagonisms, or conflicts sometimes occur, the third, *empathetic* relation, expresses reciprocal understanding and the creation of a symmetrical relationship. In such cases, the ego views the other as a fully-fledged individual (and vice versa) that is worthy of dignity. In this kind of relationship, through mutual recognition of each other's humanity, both parties meet the expectations of the shared symbolic order to which they both belong. While the first two kinds of relationships are unilateral, the third is relational. The ego draws closer to the other (and vice versa) by fully accepting the other's individuality and by striving to understand his or her difference without seeking to erase or classify it. Drawing on a shared definition of what is desirable and what is just, the ego and the other go beyond the coercive universalism of the nomothetic relation and the fragmented particularism of the idiosyncratic relation, culminating instead in a symmetrical and reflexive universalism.

6 An Orientation toward Others

In general, there has been no definition of what socialization to otherness is—or should be—beyond the boundaries of the nation-state. Cosmopolitan socialization can be defined as a learning process, undergone by individuals with regard to the transnational dimensions of the world that surrounds them. It is a process during which people learn (or refuse to learn) how to permanently or even just occasionally engage in various forms of sociocultural proximity to others. It is a long, sinuous, and potentially reversible process—rather than a disposition or property—that is sometimes contradictory and incoherent, and which allows for the development of a cosmopolitan spirit through contact and/or encounters—whether imagined, virtual, or real—with otherness. The reflexive process of engaging with otherness has four major variants: the *cosmo-aesthetic*, *cosmo-culturalist*, *cosmo-ethical*, and *cosmo-political* orientations. These four orientations are distinguished in order to understand the conditions under which individuals do or do not espouse universalistic ideas, do or do not draw on cosmopolitan repertoires, and do or do not contribute to the performance of transnational cultures and imaginaries in the aesthetic, cultural, ethical, and/or political realm (Cicchelli, 2018).

The cosmo-aesthetic orientation manifests itself by curiosity and attraction toward the products and practices of cultures whose codes are situated outside of one's national aesthetic canon. While the cosmo-culturalist orientation shares the dimensions of curiosity and pleasure with the former, it is more explicitly concerned with learning the different codes associated with encountering specific cultures. In addition to exhibiting a certain degree of exotic escapism, this orientation is also interested in understanding others. The main trait of the cosmo-ethical orientation, based on the ideal of transnational solidarity, is concern for others. Beyond its association with an urban lifestyle and its veneration of cultural difference, ethico-national cosmopolitanism also entails an ethical imperative, that of shouldering one's responsibility with regard to the world's problems. What is at play with the cosmo-political orientation, on the other hand, is how individuals view: (a) living with cultural plurality, which requires the expression of tolerance and the display of hospitality toward individuals from different cultures; and (b) national immigration policies, transnational political regulations, and global governance. The modus operandi of the cosmo-political approach to coexistence is hospitality.

For the cosmo-aesthetic and cosmo-culturalist orientations, the particular is the starting point of a cosmopolitan outlook on the world, with universality being attained through the encounter between different cultures, which are all imbued with equal dignity. The cosmo-ethical and cosmo-political orientations, on the other hand, are based on a kind of a priori universalism. They stem from a feeling of belonging to a shared humanity and the aspiration of transcending cultural differences. This mechanism can even be applied to cosmopolitan citizenship, in which individuals are expected to transcend their own culture.

7   Cosmopolitan Belongings

Since the seminal study conducted by Robert K. Merton (1968 [1949]) on influential people in the American town of 'Rovere' (a pseudonym for Dover, New Jersey), the figure of the cosmopolitan has generally been identified through his or her different affiliations and belongings.[2] In the interviews they gave to Merton, Rovere inhabitants did not all have the same relationship to the local world in which they existed. 'The localite largely confines his interests to this community. Rovere is essentially his world. Devoting little thought or energy to the Great Society, he is preoccupied with local problems [...]. He is, strictly speaking, parochial' (ibid., 447). On the other hand, however, the cosmopolitan 'is [...] oriented significantly to the world outside Rovere and regards himself as an integral part of that world. He resides in Rovere but lives in the Great Society' (ibid.). The distinction proposed by Merton was tremendously popular for a number of years following the publication of his work. And even though Merton's work was published well before the rise of global studies and interest in cosmopolitanism more specifically, a number of authors have preserved his original local-cosmopolitan distinction in their recent work.[3] Consequently, the obligatory reference to Merton has allowed a number of empirical studies seeking legitimacy to introduce two elements (by cross-pollination with works drawing on globalization and new cosmopolitan theories) which now guide research in this field: the concept of scales to understand the phenomenon of belonging; and the opposition between two visions of the world: a 'top-down' vision, which involves identifying with a shared humanity, and a 'bottom-up'

---

2   See Chapter 4 in this volume.
3   For instance, Roudometof (2005), Thomson and Taylor (2005), Ossewaarde (2007).

vision, which entails ties to a local community. Victor Roudometof (2005) emphasizes the gap between locals and cosmopolitans and uses a minimal definition of these two types, essentially based on the criterion of attachment. These two human types are allegedly distinguished by: (a) their degree of attachment to a specific city, state, or country; (b) their degree of attachment to local culture and amount of support provided to the former; and (c) their degree of economic, cultural, and institutional protectionism. Cosmopolitans, who are generally much rarer than their local counterparts (Pichler, 2012), are usually unwed and well-educated young people; they are more likely to be students or employed than their local counterparts (Roudometof and Haller, 2007).

A cosmopolitan orientation entails the recognition that all individuals are insiders and outsiders at the same time (Rumford, 2013). Social actors can likewise be capable of ascribing to multiple identities and combining different scales of belonging depending on the situation or context at hand. Given that this orientation presumes an interpretation of the local and the global, its followers must be able to preserve a certain allegiance to particular groups, such as their family, friends, and community, while striking a balance between universalist and particularist concerns and demands (Hopper, 2007). By resisting the temptation to pit locals against cosmopolitans, and ultimately demonstrating that these attitudes are in fact two sides of the same coin (Thomson and Taylor, 2005), several studies have highlighted the complementarity of national and European dimensions of belonging. While the cosmopolitanism of young people who move throughout Europe and who live for at least six months in a foreign country can indeed be characterized by strong attachments to a national or subnational culture, it must also be noted that by confronting this culture with a universal horizon young people are able to encounter the different lifestyles and mind-sets of other Europeans. 'Attempting to transcend national belonging while still feeling strongly connected to one's country: such is the undertaking of the cosmopolitan individual' (Cicchelli, 2012: 252). Immersion in neighboring European societies can activate a feeling of closeness, leading young people to self-identify with larger cultural groups.

8   A Splintered Socialization

Taking into account the ubiquity of alterity can help us to understand the ambivalent relationships that individuals have to openness. Moreover, one's sense of belonging to a shared humanity is often challenged by the existence of symbolic borders between ethnic and social groups, the perceived threats and opportunities associated with globalization, and the degree of importance attributed to local affiliations (Skrbiš and Woodward, 2007). While individuals today generally appear to be increasingly favorable to intercultural contact, they can also declare their deep-seated hostility toward living in multicultural societies. Moreover, there is a disconnect between openness to the consumption of globalized cultural experiences—which provides individuals with exotic resources, thanks to which they can enrich and diversify their lifestyles and understanding of others—and the willingness of consumers to take responsibility for individuals who are physically and/or cultural distant (Kennedy, 2010). One's appetite for cultural diversity and one's attraction toward openness to others can therefore conflict with one's duty to express solidarity and exhibit hospitality. Given these elements, we can thus consider (Skrbiš and Woodward, 2007) that the ambivalence of openness to others is a defining characteristic of ordinary cosmopolitanism, one that manifests itself when individuals formulate self-reflective and decisive opinions about the impact of globalization on their lives. This is why cosmopolitanism cannot be seen as an ideal-type elaboration of a relationship to alterity, but rather as a frame of reference for that process. It is less important to ask whether individuals become more or less open and more or less cosmopolitan than it is to examine the reservations that they voice when developing their relationship to cultural difference. By accepting the ambivalence therein, we can therefore glean how individuals take advantage (or not) of the everyday opportunities offered to them in an increasingly open and interconnected world.

The analysis of the cosmopolitan spirit proposed herein is based on the assumption that when the ego is open to others, exchanges unfold in a peaceful, symmetrical, and reciprocal fashion. Moreover, this assumption also posits that intentional openness, with all its attendant virtues and positive emotions (empathy, benevolence, solidarity, hospitality, etc.) stems from the ego's efforts to establish a fulfilling relationship with the other. Such openness has, however, been sorely challenged by these recent counter-Enlightenment tendencies, illustrating just to what extent parochialism and isolationism may thwart openness to alterity—a phenomenon that cannot be explained by economic factors alone. In this context, we need to rethink the issue of living together. Hospitality toward those who no longer have a home, whether fleeing from wars, massacres, or other horrors, is the fundamental value of cosmopolitan humanism.[4] At the same time, everyone has the right to enjoy a decent society: this implies shared institutional rules and a certain degree of political courage to prevent the creation of a zero-sum game. As David Hollinger once wrote, 'cosmopolitanism respects the honest difficulties than even the most

---

4   See Chapter 6 in this volume.

human and generous people have in achieving solidarity with persons they perceive as very different from themselves' (Hollinger, 2006: xviii–xix).

Concerning the issue of belonging, the research is unequivocal: national belonging remains one of the strongest forms of individual attachment (Laczko, 2005). In international values surveys, nothing proves that cosmopolitan attitudes are on the rise, nor that a global community is slowly emerging (Pichler, 2012). This means that cosmopolitanism as a lifestyle and cosmopolitanism as a mind-set do not necessarily coincide. The 'cosmopolitan' citizen of the world overlaps with the 'national' citizen. In short, it is possible to live in a global society without sharing in the cosmopolitan spirit that pervades it. In other words, the structural and cultural aspects of the global society do not both necessarily move in the same direction (Cotesta, Cicchelli, and Nocenzi, 2013: xix).

9   Conclusion

The resurgence of counter-Enlightenment rhetoric in general, and nationalism in particular, poses a serious challenge to cosmopolitan openness. Indeed, without some sort of supranational cosmopolitan policy, aesthetico-cultural and ethico-political orientations tend to drift further and further apart,[5] with the former generally overtaking the latter. In order to be formed, a cosmopolitan individual needs a specific set of cultural, social, and institutional conditions: the cosmopolitan spirit does not just blow willy-nilly, as millennia of historical cycles clearly illustrate. How can we build a shared world if individuals frequently embrace cosmopolitan perspectives without feeling like they belong to the global community of humanity? Given the persistence of local and national forms of belonging in the contemporary world, what role does the nation-state continue to occupy with regard to the production of identities? Studies on cosmopolitan socialization must therefore analyze this apparent paradox, by exploring in depth what is at stake in the socialization of individuals in societies shaped by powerful transnational phenomena.

References

Appadurai, A. 1996. *Modernity at Large: Cultural Dimensions of Globalization*. Minneapolis: University of Minnesota Press.

---

5   See Chapter 19 in this volume; also Cicchelli, Octobre, and Riegel (2019).

Appiah, A. K. 2006. *Cosmopolitanism: Ethics in a World of Strangers*. New York: W. W. Norton & Co.

Bauman, Z. 1997. *Postmodernity and its Discontents*. Cambridge, UK: Polity Press.

Beck, U. 2006. 'Living in the World Risk Society: A Hobhouse Memorial Public Lecture Given on Wednesday 15 February 2006 at the London School of Economics.' *Economy and Society* 35 (3): 329–345.

Calhoun, C. 2003. '"Belonging" in the Cosmopolitan Imaginary.' *Ethnicities* 3 (4): 531–568.

Cicchelli, V. 2012. *L'esprit cosmopolite. Voyages de formation des jeunes en Europe*. Paris: Presses de Sciences Po.

Cicchelli, V. 2018. *Plural and Shared: The Sociology of a Cosmopolitan World*. Leiden; Boston, MA: Brill.

Cicchelli, V. and S. Octobre. 2018. *Aesthetico-Cultural Cosmopolitanism and French Youth: The Taste of the World*. London: Palgrave Macmillan.

Cicchelli, V., S. Octobre, and V. Riegel (eds.). 2019. *Aesthetic Cosmopolitanism and Global Culture*. Leiden; Boston, MA: Brill.

Cotesta, V., V. Cicchelli, and M. Nocenzi (eds.) 2013. *Global Society, Cosmopolitanism and Human Rights*. Newcastle-upon-Tyne: Cambridge Scholars Publishing.

Delanty, G. 2009. *The Cosmopolitan Imagination: The Renewal of Critical Social Theory*. Cambridge, UK: Cambridge University Press.

Delanty, G. (ed.). 2012. *Routledge Handbook of Cosmopolitan Studies*. London: Routledge.

Hollinger, D. A. 2006. *Cosmopolitanism and Solidarity: Studies in Ethnoracial, Religious, and Professional Affiliation in the United States*. Madison: University of Wisconsin Press.

Hopper, P. 2007. *Understanding Cultural Globalization*. Cambridge, UK: Polity Press.

Kennedy, P. 2010. *Local Lives and Global Transformation: Towards World Society*. New York: Palgrave Macmillan.

Laczko, L. S. 2005. 'National and Local Attachments in a Changing World System: Evidence from an International Survey.' *International Review of Sociology/Revue internationale de sociologie* 15 (3): 517–528.

Lourme, L. 2012. *Qu'est-ce que le cosmopolitisme?* Paris: Vrin.

Merton, R. K. 1968 [1949]. *Social Theory and Social Structure*. New York: Simon & Schuster.

Nussbaum, M. 1996. *For Love of Country?* Boston, MA: Beacon Press.

Octobre, S. 2018. *Les techno-cultures juvéniles. Du culturel au politique*. Paris: L'Harmattan.

Ossewaarde, M. 2007. 'Cosmopolitanism and the Society of Strangers.' *Current Sociology* 55 (3): 367–388.

Pichler, F. 2012. 'Cosmopolitanism in a Global Perspective: An International Comparison of Open-Minded Orientation and Identity in Relation to Globalization.' *International Sociology* 27 (1): 21–50.

Robertson, R. 1992. *Globalization: Social Theory and Global Culture*. London: Sage.
Roudometof, V. 2005. 'Transnationalism, Cosmopolitanism and Glocalization.' *Current Sociology* 53 (1): 113–135.
Roudometof, V. and W. Haller. 2007. 'Social Indicators of Cosmopolitanism and Localism in Eastern and Western Europe: An Exploratory Analysis.' In *Cosmopolitanism and Europe*, edited by C. Rumford, 181–201. Liverpool: Liverpool University Press.
Rumford, C. 2013. *The Globalization of Strangeness*. London: Palgrave.
Sassen, S. 2014. *Expulsions: Brutality and Complexity in the Global Economy*. Cambridge, MA: Belknap Press.
Skrbiš, Z. and I. Woodward. 2007. 'The Ambivalence of Ordinary Cosmopolitanism: Investigating the Limits of Cosmopolitan Openness.' *The Sociological Review* 55 (4): 730–747.
Skrbiš, Z. and I. Woodward. 2013. *Cosmopolitanism: Uses of the Idea*. London: Sage.
Sternhell, Z. 2009. *The Anti-Enlightenment Tradition*. New Haven, CT: Yale University Press.
Thomson, R. and R. Taylor. 2005. 'Between Cosmopolitanism and the Locals: Mobility as a Resource in the Transition to Adulthood.' *Young* 13 (4): 327–342i.
Turner, B. S. 2006. 'Classical Sociology and Cosmopolitanism: A Critical Defence of the Social.' *British Journal of Sociology* 57 (1): 133–151.
Vertovec, S. and R. Cohen. 2002. 'Editors' Introduction.' In *Conceiving Cosmopolitanism: Theory, Context and Practice*, edited by S. Vertovec and R. Cohen, 1–22. Oxford: Oxford University Press.
Woodward, I. and Z. Skrbiš. 2012. 'Performing Cosmopolitanism.' In *Routledge Handbook of Cosmopolitan Studies*, edited by G. Delanty, 127–137. London: Routledge.

PART 4

Challenging Cosmopolitanism
A Fractured Cosmopolis

CHAPTER 21

The Nation-State in a Global World

John Agnew

The nation-hyphen-state, as the clear and coherent mapping of a relatively culturally homogeneous group of people onto a territory with a singular and organized state apparatus of rule, has long been the structural underpinning of most claims about political legitimacy and democratic participation. The people should rule. But who exactly is 'the people'? As we look around the world, many of us see more exceptions to the clear and coherent mapping than we do of cases where there is any fit whatsoever. The contradictions loom ever larger. Rather than doubling down on creating ever more nation-states as the presumed solution to this impasse, we perhaps need to own up to its tragedy (Debarbieux, 2017). The failure to live up to its billing, without ethnic cleansing, population exchanges, suppression of minority rights, and so on, reveals that the model itself is essentially flawed. Consider the recent genocide against the Rohingya in the 'democratizing' Myanmar (Kesavan, 2018). Sadly this is an all-too-common feature of all statist regimes turning themselves into 'nation-states.' At the same time, the obsession with the so-called nation-state as the fundamental political unit of modernity misses the extent to which effective (as opposed to formal) political sovereignty has historically been shared across a wide range of actors, many of which, including many powerful states, operate beyond and across borders in ways that completely violate the rule of 'one territory, one sovereign' central to the nation-state model.

Conventional thinking about sovereignty in the academic fields of political theory and international relations sees the world as divided into neat blocs of space or territories over which states exercise mutually exclusive control and authority (Agnew, 2018). The historical basis to this claim of territorial exclusivity is relatively recent, going back only to the 18th century and reflecting, in one convincing account, the colonial claim to exclusive occupancy brought homeward to Europe and then used to challenge existing complex multi-jurisdictional and feudal arrangements involving empires (such as the Holy Roman Empire), fragmented dynastic polities, city-states, and the Church (Branch, 2010). Within the broad conception of sovereignty as invariably territorial, two more specific understandings can be distinguished: a Hobbesian account, that defines a state by its borders and the obligations of its subjects to it because of the protection it affords them; and a Lockean account, that gives a state's citizens a stronger role in terms of the state's obligations to them, particularly with respect to the provision and enforcement of private property rights. Neither account has ever accounted for the fact that sovereignty has never pooled up neatly in territorial spaces, states have long shared sovereignty with one another and outsourced it to other agencies both private and public, or that formal legal sovereignty (recognition by other putative states) is not the same as effective domestic sovereignty (delivering the goods to a population) or the Westphalian sovereignty that implies an ability to be effectively autonomous in interstate relations (Krasner, 1999, 2001).

1 States and Sovereignty

In practice, we all know that states are not equally sovereign in terms of their control over their borders, effective central bureaucracy to achieve collective ends, recognition by other states, capacity to influence and coerce others, or domestic legitimacy in the eyes of their populations (Agnew, 1999, 2018). The term sovereignty is used in all of these various ways to express the relationship between states, on the one hand, and people, considered as subjects or citizens, on the other. Yet the world political map and some international organizations, such as the United Nations (UN), are based on the fiction that each territory claimed by a given state is equally sovereign to all others. This is obviously problematic if we consider for a moment how many of the world's putative states are in fact completely ineffective, absent, lacking in control over large chunks of the state's territory, and faced with significant legitimacy deficits. Think, for example, of cases such as Somalia, Syria, Afghanistan, the Democratic Republic of the Congo, Iraq, Pakistan, Mexico, Venezuela, and Greece. Of course, these are all distinctive cases with various degrees of depleted or absent sovereignty. To paraphrase Leo Tolstoy on families, happy states may all be alike, but unhappy ones are all unhappy in their own ways.

Many of these states have never had much effective sovereignty. They emerged from colonialism and never achieved real independence (Berger and Miller, 2008; Breuilly, 2017). Their borders match neither any sort of cultural entity (such as a nation) nor a meaningful economic unit (such as a settlement network or a resource base). Others have become dependents of other states, fractured by organized criminal gangs or secessionist movements, or reliant on debt servicing and remittances from external sources. Finally, some, including many economically developed states, have become subject to policing by various public and private agencies such as credit-rating agencies, law firms and courts, human rights organizations, and charities, that have become sovereigns in their own right as a result of licensing by states because of their superior knowledge, expertise, and claims to neutrality. These agencies and more dominant states exercise their sovereignty through geographical networks rather than by territorial control. Thus, immigration enforcement now takes place away from state borders both inside and outside of states, credit-rating agencies based in world cities such as New York rank the sovereign bonds of even the most powerful states, such as the United States, and London-based law firms and English courts increasingly adjudicate on cases brought by parties resident in or with assets in long-distant jurisdictions.

Three examples of these 'sovereignty dilemmas' can be used to illustrate aspects of my argument. One involves the remarkable degree to which contractual disputes between Russian businessmen are now brought to court in London rather than in Russia. Estimates that as much as 60 percent of the London High Court's commercial and chancery divisions' work is devoted to Russian and East European cases are typical (Croft, 2012). London is favored because of the weakness of the rule of law in Russia, the fact that many of the assets at stake, though often looted or exported from Russia, are now in scattered bank accounts well beyond Russian shores, major London law firms specialize in cross-jurisdictional and international disputes, and the plaintiffs in question often live in London, an increasingly popular destination for nomadic billionaires sheltering their wealth. In a globalized economy legal jurisdiction is no longer neatly territorialized. In this context, corporate law, already increasingly working for managers and firms more than the publics to which law classically bears responsibility (Greenfield, 2006), is no longer clearly associated with any specific territorialized public which can hold it to account.

A second example concerns the role of private credit-rating agencies in providing ratings to the bonds used by governments to cover their debts (Sinclair, 2005). During the so-called Eurozone debt crisis since 2009, the three major agencies, Moody's, Standard & Poor's, and Fitch, have been major actors in mediating between states, on the one hand, and investors, on the other. In the case of countries such as Ireland and Greece, whose bonds suffered major rating declines in the 2008–12 period, it has become common to speak of a loss of sovereignty to the credit-rating agencies. In fact, the loss is to investors but the process has undoubtedly been facilitated by the agencies. But the role of the credit-rating agencies itself has become so important because states have become so reliant on international bond markets to finance their budgets. Before the 1970s this role was of minor importance. The credit-rating agencies are a good example of the privatization of sovereign authority across the world as licensed by states, such as the United States, that has empowered this role. Consider the consequences of this for the 'sovereignty' of Greece during the

Eurozone crisis, notwithstanding the domestic sources of the crisis in bureaucratic sclerosis and upper-class tax evasion (Angelos, 2015).

Finally, my third example relates to the de facto sovereignty exercised by the US government over the US naval base at Guantanamo Bay, Cuba (Sparrow, 2006), where so-called enemy combatants from the 'war on terror' in the aftermath of the terrorist attacks of 9/11 have been held without trial. The claim has been that this base, leased from Cuba when the government of that island was allied to the USA, is beyond the jurisdiction of US federal courts and thus is not subject to writs of habeas corpus (the right to a speedy trial) guaranteed by the US Constitution to all those within US jurisdiction. Though questioned in a major decision by the US Supreme Court—*Boumediene v Bush* (2008)—the in-between jurisdictional status of the base still continues to serve to deny the de jure obligations that would have faced the US government if the prisoners at Guantanamo had been incarcerated within the territory of the USA proper (Comaroff, 2007). While the effective sovereignty exercised by the USA over Guantanamo, therefore, is clear for all to see, notwithstanding the claim under international legal sovereignty made by successive US governments that it is *really* still part of Cuba, US courts remain confused in their decisions concerning the geographical scope of the basic right to speedy trial for those denied the status of prisoners of war, on the one hand, and ordinary criminal defendants, on the other (Ghosh, 2012). This example raises the issue of whether habeas corpus is safe 'at home' if it is so easily called into question 'abroad.'

In the contemporary world, as illustrated by these cases, but also historically, people's interests and identities are not readily and neatly associated with a clear state–territorial address. Flows of people, capital, regulatory authority, and security threats are not easily tied to specific territorial locations. In turn, multiple sources of effective authority suggest that sovereignty is no longer usefully thought of in terms of the conventional wisdom of a close territorial matching between functional area and geographical scope of sovereign control and authority.

More particularly, the very term 'nation-state' reflects Woodrow Wilson's old confusion of national self-determination with democratic popular sovereignty. One does not entail the other. Nationalism and democracy did start out together in the American and French Revolutions but the connection soon proved tenuous. As we know from European history, the association between 'nation' and 'democracy' (in the weakest sense of popular representation and the rule of law) has not always been close. Given that most states today are multinational and few have much history of democracy until recently, the claim weakens even further. States can *claim* to represent nations but making the two terms coterminous, as if they invariably go together everywhere, is more often than not either a work of anthropological fiction or has involved successful efforts at ethnic cleansing (from Scotland in the 18th century to Myanmar in the 21st). Murderous majorities have had their way but usually at the expense of humanity as well as of democracy.

Concurrently, it is also far from clear that states offer much by way of democratic accountability over the main economic actors located within their jurisdictions. World economic history is largely one of extractive or despotic elites extorting rents from populations rather than guiding economic development in the collective-territorial interest (Acemoglu and Robinson, 2012). Even in those states where, as a result of popular struggles, populations have achieved some degree of popular control over economic transactions that affect their lives, such as the social democracies of Northern Europe, a wide range of regulatory institutions are subject to capture by private interests or are beyond popular control.

2 Sovereignty Regimes

What has been lacking in understanding the range of practices that constitute sovereignty is a means of identifying the covariation between the effectiveness of central state authority, on the one hand, and its relative reliance on state territoriality, on the other (Agnew, 2018: 102–147). One useful approach comes from writing on the historical sociology of power. In distinguishing despotic from infrastructural power, Michael Mann (1984) identifies two different ways in which a state acquires and uses centralized power. These words refer to two different functions that states perform for populations and that jointly underpin their claim to sovereignty: respectively, the struggle among elites within and between states and the provision of public goods by states as a result of placating various social groups and pursuing and legitimizing despotic power. In Mann's words:

> Let us clearly distinguish these two types of state power. The first sense [despotic power] denotes power by the state elite itself over civil society. The second [infrastructural power] denotes the power of the state to penetrate and centrally co-ordinate the activities of civil society through its own infrastructure.
> MANN, 1984: 188

Before the 18th century infrastructural power was relatively less important than it is today. This is because elites have been forced by political struggles to be more responsive to their populations through providing more public goods. But economic development has also mandated increased provision of roads, weights and measures, elementary education, and so on, that will always be absent or underprovided with reliance on private provision. This boosted the territorialization of sovereignty because demand was defined in terms of territorial populations and provision was oriented to satisfying that demand. Technological change, the increased intensity of all kinds of flows across borders, and the vulnerability of state populations to increased global economic competition threatening to public good provision when foreign competitors provide fewer public goods have conspired to make infrastructural power increasingly networked. City regions and supranational entities (such as the European Union (EU)) challenge the state monopoly over public goods. International organizations, both public and private, have the capacity to deliver regulatory, financial, and legal services hitherto usually associated with states.

At much the same time, despotic power has come to rely much more on popular legitimacy. At one time, and this is at the root of Western territorialized conceptions of sovereignty, the ruler relied on the claim to stand in apostolic succession to God, as in the Divine Right of Kings. This eventually translated into the idea of the 'body politic' as a territorialized people/nation (Agnew, 2018: 51–101). Rulers needed to establish at least a modicum of popular authority before they could pursue their goals. Such legitimacy as they have, however, is increasingly fragile. As interests and identities cease to conform to territorial norms, rulers must adjust likewise. This can involve pursuing increased influence elsewhere (as in an imperium) or ceding authority to other parties in order to manage dissent and resistance. There is no necessary correlation, therefore, between despotic power and central state authority. Elites can be globalized with respect both to pursuing their goals through expanded statehood beyond home shores (as in empire-building) and in terms of alliances with multinational companies, banks, and other agents of a more networked world.

The main theoretical conundrum in terms of the relative location of sovereignty is the relative balance between the strength of continued central state authority (despotic power) on the one hand, and the degree to which public goods are provided and regulated on a territorialized basis (infrastructural power) on the other. The former involves judgment as to the extent a state has acquired and maintains an effective and legitimate apparatus of rule. The latter refers to the extent to which the provision and regulation of public goods is heavily state regulated and bounded territorially. In different terminology, the question becomes one of the relative balances between territory and networks in the operational scope of the sovereignty of states and the agents they license (Agnew, 2005: 102–147; Painter, 2009). The two dimensions of sovereignty define the degree of state autonomy and the extent to which it is territorial. From these, four extreme or ideal-type categories, or what I term 'sovereignty regimes,' can be identified. These are relational in character. They refer to the character of sovereignty as manifested by differing combinations of central state authority and territorialized provision of public goods in different places.

They are not best thought of as characterizing particular states in all their aspects; no particular state fits exactly into any of the boxes in question for all time. But they do provide a heuristic basis for identifying the relative complexity of sovereignty around the world today. This is a patchwork of more-and-less sovereign spaces and flows, not a rigidly territorial order, with some states and organizations more sovereign (in terms of their effectiveness) than others. In Table 21.1, the simplified relational categories are seen as representing stronger and weaker central state authority and consolidated and open territoriality. The purpose of thinking relationally about sovereignty is to move away from trapping thinking in absolute as opposed to relative distinctions (Allen, 1999). From this viewpoint, there is no simple 'either/or' to sovereignty when it is, on the one hand, either completely territorialized or, on the other, is not manifested territorially and therefore ceases to exist. This has been the trap into which much writing about sovereignty has fallen.

Of the four ideal types, the first one, the *classic*, comes closest to the conventional story about the bonding of sovereignty with national territory. Both despotic power and infrastructural power are largely territorialized and central state authority remains effective. Contemporary China perhaps best fits this case. But increasingly its dependence on the US dollar monetary standard, desire to achieve Great Power status, and the ambitions of its capitalist businesses well beyond China's shores suggest a future in which commitment to a

TABLE 21.1 Sovereignty regimes

		State Territoriality	
		Consolidated	Open
Central State Authority	Stronger	Classic	Globalist
	Weaker	Integrative	Imperialist

narrowly territorial sovereignty will no longer be possible. The second case, the *imperialist*, represents best the case of hierarchy in world politics but with networked as well as territorialized reach. It is the complete opposite of the classic case. Central state authority is seriously in question, often exercised by outsiders if in collusion with local elites, and infrastructural power is weak or reliant on external support. This was historically the case with European colonialism, the displacement of indigenous peoples by settler-colonialists worldwide, and economic subjugation even in the case of *prima facie* political independence (as in Latin America following independence from Spain and Portugal). Much of the Middle East and sub-Saharan Africa falls under this regime, with external powers such as France, Russia, and the United States regularly intervening in various ways.

The other two regimes are more complicated. The first, the *integrative*, is a regime where authority has migrated to both higher and lower tiers of government as a result of a sharing of sovereignty among states and where infrastructural power takes both territorialized and networked forms. Various sorts of unions or confederations of states take this form. The fullest contemporary example would be the EU from the perspective of its member states. The second of the two more complex sovereignty regimes is the *globalist*. This regime is closely associated today with the globalization of the world brought about since the 1960s under US auspices. In this construction, the world city system, particularly the cities at the top of it, such as New York and London, provide the geographical nodes for the agents who are central to this regime. They exercise sovereignty wherever states have ceded authority to external agents because of debt dependence or regulatory oversight. This regime has a potentially worldwide reach but its effects are particularly strong in those parts of the world most integrated into the world economy and without the limits set on integration by, for example, managed exchange rates and capital controls, by states with greater effective central state authority (such as China). The historic basis of this regime in US hegemony means that at least until recently US governments were able to use this regime as an alternative to the imperialist one. It relies much more on rule-based consensus, multilateral institutions (like the International Monetary Fund (IMF) and the World Trade Organization (WTO)) as well as on the spread of cultural norms about the benefits of free trade and open borders. But as central authority has slowly seeped out of US governmental hands, other agencies, including many private as well as public organizations, have picked up the slack from the credit-rating agencies and corporate lawyers to product-standard conventions and non-governmental organizations (NGOs) (Büthe and Mattli, 2011).

3   Taking Back Control?

Recent world events, from Brexit in Britain and the election of Trump to the US presidency to the crisis of the EU over the future of the euro and the spread of resurgent nationalism far and wide from China and Germany to Catalonia and Scotland, might suggest that the nation-state is once more on the march. The urge to make the world economy more responsive to local needs is certainly understandable. Local communities have distinctive needs that require close attention in a world in which they are increasingly subjected to pressures from well beyond national boundaries. Whether the nation-state is the best vehicle for achieving this, however, is open to considerable question (Wahman et al., 2017).

For one thing, increasingly global problems call for global solutions. Problems such as climate change can be ignored but cannot be adequately addressed simply on a one-country-at-a-time basis. Even if much world trade is still clustered regionally, financial markets and foreign investment flows have worldwide footprints. Worldwide there is a massive deficit of *global* public goods and democratic accountability that cannot be addressed solely at the state scale. The spatial scope of the problems and the spatial scope of governments do not match. Of course, current international organizations fall short in the job of managing global failures in regulation and provision of public goods (on, for example, refugees, tax evasion and money laundering, environmental standards, etc.). But there is no reason for thinking that after the recent round of 'taking back control' shows limited returns governments will not once again turn to cooperative projects to manage complex financial markets and so on. In the interim, global authority is increasingly privatized, as with credit-rating agencies, and beyond popular accountability. Absent increased surveillance over economic and financial flows at supra-regional and global levels we can expect little real democratic accountability over such transactions. The idealized nation-state simply cannot cut it alone (Stiglitz, 2017).

At the same time, as noted, nations do not map neatly onto states, so it is often not clear 'whose' interests are best served by 'taking back control' (is it people in post-industrial hinterlands whose jobs have gone largely because of automation rather than because of immigrants or foreign competition or large cities reliant on global financial flows?). The borders of most states have long been penetrated by more powerful states and companies that always manage to escape much local state-scale regulation (Agnew, 2018). Pretending that an ideal-type nation-state offers the way out of the conundrum of capitalism versus democracy is no solution to this dilemma (Morefield, 2005). It has never worked very well anywhere except perhaps for some small countries in

Northern Europe and for those states at the top of the global hierarchy, for a time. There seems little chance that it will work well anywhere ever again.

4 Conclusions

We still tend to think of sovereignty in the classic terms inherited from the theorists and monarchies of 17th-century Europe. Yet that tradition, based as it was in all sorts of cultural assumptions about the 'body politic' and the political theology of early modern Europe, is not very useful in understanding the workings of state sovereignty today. As I hope to have made clear, sovereignty, in combining control and authority, is not best thought of in the exclusively territorialized form that has typically been the case. In examining the relative location of sovereignty my intent has been to show that the assumption of a close match between sovereignty and territory in the idealized 'nation-state' is problematic. In its place I have developed a relational typology of 'sovereignty regimes' that serve to acknowledge and explore the complexities of sovereignty without being overwhelmed by them. That is the purpose of ideal types. Cosmopolitan challenges to much of what goes for democratic theory will have to take off from this point (Trepanier and Habib, 2011).[1]

The approach developed here raises several normative questions relating to constitutional law and human rights that I can do no more than mention by way of conclusion. One is whether legal jurisdiction can continue to be defined in such strong territorial terms as it has in recent judicial thinking, in the context of a world that progressively escapes its grasp. Increasingly, the hierarchy of states and the explosion of global financial transactions make a mockery of that 18th-century constitutionalism, particularly prevalent in the United States, which is locked into an absolutist territorial definition of sovereignty. At the same time, of course, US governments have long been the main protagonists of the world that no knows no boundaries. That contradiction stands in particular need of emphasis. The second is that state sovereignty is often used as an 'excuse' or hypocritical defense by governments trying to exclude external critique or intervention in their 'internal' persecution of minorities or stigmatized groups. On the relational view of sovereignty expressed in this chapter, such a claim can no longer bear close examination. The Hobbesian excuse that we can do what we want around here because you do what you want over there, justified amazingly in terms of protecting those persecuted

---

1 See Chapter 11 in this volume.

internally from their 'real' external enemies, never was anything other than a nasty ploy. It is past time that 'nation-states' which use it were recognized for their unconscionable hypocrisy.

References

Acemoglu, D. and J. Robinson. 2012. *Why Nations Fail: The Origins of Power, Prosperity, and Poverty*. New York: Crown.

Agnew, J. 1999. 'Mapping Political Power beyond State Boundaries.' *Millennium* 28: 499–521.

Agnew, J. 2005. *Hegemony: The New Shape of Global Power*. Philadelphia, PA: Temple University Press.

Agnew, J. 2018. *Globalization and Sovereignty: Beyond the Territorial Trap*, 2nd ed. Lanham, MD: Rowman & Littlefield.

Allen, J. 1999. 'Afterword: Open Geographies.' In *Human Geography Today*, edited by D. Massey, J. Allen and Ph. Sarre, 323–328. Cambridge, UK: Polity Press.

Angelos, J. 2015. *The Full Catastrophe: Travels among the New Greek Ruins*. New York: Crown.

Berger, S. and A. Miller. 2008. 'Nation-Building and Regional Integration, c. 1800–1914: The Role of Empires.' *European Review of History* 15 (3): 317–330.

Branch, J. 2010. '"Colonial Reflection" and Territoriality: The Peripheral Origins of Sovereign Statehood.' *European Journal of International Relations* 18 (2): 277–297.

Breuilly, J. 2017. 'Modern Empires and Nation-States.' *Thesis Eleven*, 139 (1): 11–29.

Büthe, T. and W. Mattli. 2011. *The New Global Rulers: The Privatization of Regulation in the World Economy*. Princeton, NJ: Princeton University Press.

Comaroff, J. 2007. 'Terror and Territory: Guantánamo and the Space of Contradiction.' *Public Culture* 19 (2): 381–405.

Croft, J. 2012. 'London Provides Fertile Ground for Lawsuits.' *Financial Times*, July 9.

Debarbieux, B. 2017. 'Hannah Arendt's Spatial Thinking: An Introduction.' *Territory, Politics, Governance* 5 (4): 351–367.

Ghosh, S. 2012. '*Boumediene* Applied Badly: The Extraterritorial Constitution after *Al Maqaleh v. Gates*.' *Stanford Law Review* 64 (507): 507–534.

Greenfield, K. 2006. *The Failure of Corporate Law: Fundamental Flaws and Progressive Possibilities*. Chicago: University of Chicago Press.

Kesavan, M. 2018. 'Murderous Majorities.' *New York Review of Books*, 65 (1): 37–40.

Krasner, S. D. 1999. *Sovereignty: Organized Hypocrisy*. Princeton, NJ: Princeton University Press.

Krasner, S. D. (ed.). 2001. *Problematic Sovereignty: Contested Rules and Political Possibilities*. New York: Columbia University Press.

Mann, M. 1984. 'The Autonomous Power of the State: Its Origins, Mechanisms and Results.' *European Journal of Sociology* 25: 185–213.

Morefield, J. 2005. 'States are Not People: Harold Laski on Unsettling Sovereignty, Rediscovering Democracy.' *Political Research Quarterly* 58 (4): 659–669.

Painter, J. 2009. 'Territoire et réseau: une fausse dichotomie?' In *Territoires, territorialité, territorialisation: controverses et perspective*, edited by M. Vanier, 57–66. Rennes: Presses Universitaires de Rennes.

Sinclair, T. J. 2005. *The New Masters of Capital: American Bond Rating Agencies and the Politics of Creditworthiness*. Ithaca, NY: Cornell University Press.

Sparrow, B. H. 2006. *The Insular Cases and the Emergence of American Empire*. Lawrence: University Press of Kansas.

Stiglitz, J. 2017. *Globalization and Its Discontents Revisited*. New York: Norton.

Trepanier, L. and K. M. Habib (eds.). 2011. *Cosmopolitanism in the Age of Globalization: Citizens without States*. Lexington: University Press of Kentucky.

Wahman, J., J. M. Medina, and J. J. Stuhr (eds.). 2017. *Cosmopolitanism and Place*. Bloomington: Indiana University Press.

CHAPTER 22

Cosmopolitanism in an Age of Xenophobia and Ethnic Conflict

Paul Bagguley and Yasmin Hussain

1   Introduction

In this chapter we evaluate the idea of cosmopolitanism in relation to some recent forces that appear to be reversing its existence, as in the return of nationalism in the United Kingdom (UK); the rise of populism in the West (Ashbee, 2017); counterterrorism discourse and practices; and increasing xenophobia, Islamophobia, and racism. This trend is taking place in the context of increasing social inequalities (Piketty, 2014) and global economic and political competition between nations. We begin with a discussion of Beck's (2002) analysis of cosmopolitanism, using this heuristically to assess recent developments in the UK in terms of three moments of 'anti-cosmopolitanism.' They are all characterized to some degree by a form of populism, transformed public discourses, and a shift in state institutions and practices.[1] Each of these moments signaled an anti-cosmopolitan movement in different fields. First, we look at the field of internal relationships between ethnic groups within the UK and how these are managed by the state. For example, the state's response to the 2001 ethnic riots in the UK (Bagguley and Hussain, 2008) was distinctly anti-cosmopolitan, being focused upon encouraging the assimilation of British South Asians. Second, in terms of international relations and internal securitization, the state's responses to the 9/11 attacks on the USA, but especially the 7/7 terrorist attacks in London, can only be read as being contrary to the process of cosmpolitanization identified by authors such as Beck (2006). Third, and most recently, the vote in the UK's referendum to leave the European Union (EU) (Clarke et al., 2017) popularly known as Brexit, also demonstrates both a popular- and state-level anti-cosmopolitanism.

---

1   See Chapter 24 in this volume.

2 Cosmopolitanism: between Normative Political Philosophy and Sociological Realism

Ulrich Beck stands as perhaps the most stridently optimistic social theorist in his view of the cosmopolitan present. The main thrust of his analysis was to take the idea of cosmopolitanism from the discourse of political theory toward a more sociological perspective. He argued that the idea of cosmopolitanism has

> left the realm of philosophical castles in the air and has entered reality. Indeed it has become the defining feature of a new era, the era of reflexive modernity, in which national borders and differences are dissolving ...
> BECK, 2006: 2

He conceived of cosmopolitanism in terms of national differences, while others would relate it to imaginary racial differences, ethnicity, or religion. Beck goes on to describe cosmopolitan thought and action as a 'vital theme of European civilisation and European consciousness ...' (Beck, 2006: 2). A key question for him is whether cosmopolitanism can 'include other modernities and civilisations' (Beck, 2002: 19), which is suggestive of a strategy of incorporation of the 'other' into 'the West.' Furthermore, Beck suggests that cosmopolitan ideas have gathered support recently because these are a reflection of cosmopolitan realities. This is related to his analysis of globalization, which he sees occurring within nation-states, so that the resulting cosmopolitan social reality characterizes people's everyday experiences and daily life. Although Beck was critical of 'methodological nationalism,' it might be argued that his approach risks being Eurocentric (Bhambra, 2014: 73). For example Turner (2002: 52) notes that cosmopolitanism in practice is not the monopoly of the contemporary West and that trading centers in early Islam enabled peaceful encounters between ethnically, religiously, and tribally diverse groups. Finally, Beck's discussion is not just located in the West, but, within that configuration, in the EU.

Harrington (2016: 352) has also pointed to the inherent circularity of Beck's argument whereby one has to accept the emergence of cosmopolitanism in order to be in a position to analyze and appreciate it. In addition, Martell (2008: 131) has suggested that Beck 'does not recognize the agency of actors in making cosmopolitanism and who can also reverse it.' In many respects it may be argued that this is precisely what has happened in the first two decades of this century in certain Western countries such as the UK. What Beck refers to as anti-cosmopolitanization has become dominant, contrary to his rather dismissive view of it as 'superfluous and absurd' (Beck, 2006: 110) and 'tantamount as to a clinical loss of reality' (Beck, 2006: 117). He suggests that anti-cosmopolitanism can only 're-erect the old boundaries only in theory, not in reality' (Beck, 2006: 117). This perspective has left Beck's analysis unable to properly understand and explain the anti-cosmopolitan developments that we discuss in this chapter. The Brexit vote in Britain may be seen as an attempt at the re-erection of old national boundaries in reality. Furthermore, Martell (2009) has pointed out that Beck sees American military power as humanitarian and cosmopolitan, which in effect legitimates global inequalities and the USA's routine negligence of international law. It could also be suggested that it overlooks the crisis of US hegemony (Bergesen and Lizardo, 2004) and why the 'war on terror' has become the dominant discourse of contemporary international politics as understood from the perspective of the West (Sayyid, 2013).

There are grounds for thinking of cosmopolitanism as being the cultural, philosophical, and social mirror of global capitalism. Within this perspective, those in the middle classes are seen by some as the strategic cosmopolitans of contemporary capitalism who serve as 'a nodal agent in the expanding networks of the global economy. He or she is the new, superior footsoldier of global capitalism' (Mitchell, 2003: 400). However, as Harrington (2016: 352–353) has noted, increased global mobility need not produce greater global sensitivity. Szerzynski and Urry (2002) see the spread of cosmopolitanism as the localized effects of globalization, and they give a central role to globalized media resulting in a 'banal globalism.' They usefully treat cosmopolitanism as an 'empty signifier' (Szerzynski and Urry, 2002: 469), and write of a 'ideal-typical' cosmopolitan individual who is characterized by extensive mobility, consumption of diverse places, curiosity of different peoples and places, risk-taking in encounters with others, able to make aesthetic judgments about different places, and is possessed of semiotic skills of interpretation together with an openness to other peoples and their cultures (Szerzynski and Urry, 2002: 470). Contrary to this analysis, it can be suggested that years since the late 1990s have seen a reversal of this trend at multiple levels in the UK in terms of state practices toward, political discourses about, and everyday experiences of those considered 'other.'

More recently there has been a resurgence of studies of everyday cosmopolitanism; while often critical of the prescriptive moral character of cosmopolitanism as political philosophy, it may be argued that they still retain a certain degree of optimism. This is despite often noting the racist or othering friction that sometimes occurs in cosmopolitan encounters in the UK for example (Hall, 2012: 67–68; Andreouli and Howarth, 2018: 14; Neal et al., 2018: 27). We feel that this approach overlooks or downplays three important issues. First, as studies of micro interactions between relatively powerless groups it does not fully take account of the wider structural context of racism. Second, it fails to consider the possibility of what Houts-Picca and Feagin (2007), in a US context, have theorized as 'two-faced racism.' This requires the recognition that otherwise convivial everyday interactions may be 'front-stage' performances in public settings, while 'backstage,' in a more private context where only white people are present, racism may reemerge. Third, it does not look at the ways in which public events give rise to many micro events of racist hostility; we shall discuss an example of this using the UK's vote to leave the EU. If we were truly on the path toward a cosmopolitan utopia, as implied by some, such as Beck (2006), then such events would be less likely, or least managed more effectively, by social and political elites.

3   Three Instances of Anti-cosmopolitanism in the UK

This section examines three instances of anti-cosmopolitanism in the UK. The first of these are the ethnic riots in the North of England in the summer of 2001 (Bagguley and Hussain, 2008). It then moves on to examine how responses to terrorist attacks in the UK and the Brexit vote may be seen as instances of anti-cosmopolitanism.

The spring and summer of 2001 was marked in the UK by a series of riots in the North of England in Oldham (May 26–29), Burnley (June 24–26), and, most seriously, in Bradford (July 7–9) (Bagguley and Hussain, 2008). In response, the government commissioned a report that became known as the Cantle report on 'Community Cohesion' (Cantle, 2002). What is striking about the Cantle report is how strongly anti-cosmopolitan its arguments were, and how its central ideas and policy prescriptions around 'community cohesion' came to dominate public political discourse and policy-making in the UK around matters of ethnic identity and racism. The idea of community cohesion was closely linked to the influence of communitarian thinking on the Labour government of Tony Blair (Bagguley and Hussain, 2008).

The Cantle report represented South Asian Muslim communities as self-segregating—not just geographically, but also socially and culturally. It saw South Asian Muslim communities in the North of England as in a state of self-generated crisis. They were seen as reproducing 'dysfunctional practices,' such as not speaking English at home, organizing arranged marriages, and becoming involved in intergenerational conflict. Muslim communities were 'required to integrate' under the Cantle report's recommendations (Bagguley and Hussain, 2008). The Cantle report and the subsequent translation of its ideas into local policies of community cohesion represent a clear example of anti-cosmopolitanism as a state practice.

The 9/11 attacks on the USA, the 7/7 bombings in London, and other attempted terrorist attacks have occurred at the height of academic debates around cosmopolitanism. Popular reactions to terrorist attacks, public discourse, and state policies are all aspects of the process of securitization of British Muslims (Hussain and Bagguley, 2012). All of these can be seen as anti-cosmopolitan. Securitization is the process by which an issue or group is defined as a security threat, so that governmental and societal resources are mobilized to counter it. Through this process, political leaders build public support—through political statements and the media—for exceptional and new legislation and state initiatives to counter the threat. The security 'threat' becomes 'common sense' in political debate, the media, and among the public. It becomes impossible to speak of that group without implying they are a 'threat' to security (Buzan, Waever, and de Wilde, 1998). In the UK, the Terrorism Act 2000 the Anti-Terrorism Crime and Security Act 2001 are examples of the exceptional powers taken on by the state as part of this process. These bestow additional powers to police—to search, arrest, and detain. In practice, these powers are applied in excess to the issues that they ostensibly address, as illustrated by the fact that of the 1,228 people arrested under anti-terrorism legislation between September 2001 and March 2007, only forty-one—or under 4 percent—of those arrested were convicted of a terrorist offence (Hewitt, 2007).

Even prior to 9/11 the main themes of news coverage of Muslims in the UK were overwhelmingly negative. Muslims have for several decades now been represented as a threat to UK security because they are seemingly involved in deviant activities of various kinds. Muslims are perceived as a threat to British values and therefore a threat to social integration. It is widely assumed that there are inherent cultural differences between Muslims and the British, which creates interpersonal tensions. At the same time, Muslims are seen as increasingly agitating for their interests in politics, education, and against discrimination (Poole, 2006).

Similar negative themes have continued in media reporting, but are now organized around one main theme: 'Islamic terrorism' (Poole, 2006). Islam is presented as anti-modern, politically unstable, undemocratic, barbaric, and chaotic. The representation of Muslims in the UK is dominated by this framework (Nickels et al., 2010). Islam is seen by journalists as a threat to British values, alongside ambiguous representations of Muslims as either moderate or extremist. Moderate Muslims are regarded as having a responsibility for bringing extremists under control—preventing 'radicalization.' The securitization of everyday encounters (Hussain and Bagguley, 2013) has meant that individual and collective experiences of verbal abuse and physical attacks on Muslims increased after terrorist attacks. Certain symbols seem to provoke such reactions, such as the carrying of a backpack or wearing clothing perceived as Islamic. Airports are routinely identified by British Muslims as locations of humiliating encounters with authority. What is humiliating about such experiences is the denial of taken-for-granted national identity and the challenge to 'respectability'—many who had such encounters were lawful, highly educated, and middle class—that these practices entail. Muslim identity is routinely regarded as threatening by UK airport authorities. Furthermore, markers of religious purity, for example, the hijab, are treated as signs of danger, as a reason to be suspicious (Blackwood, Hopkins, and Reicher, 2013).

The 'Prevent' strategy developed since the 2005 terrorist attacks on London seeks to challenge the ideology behind terrorism. It aims to disrupt those who promote terrorism, while supporting those who are seen as vulnerable to recruitment into terrorism. One of its main goals is to increase the resilience of communities to terrorism; however, the focus is almost entirely upon Muslim communities. The Prevent strategy is delivered locally through local councils and the police, schools, universities, and the health service, where frontline teachers, and healthcare and social-care workers are given short training courses on how to recognize the signs of terrorism among their clients.

Section 44 of the Terrorism Act allowed police to stop and search anyone anywhere anytime without reasonable grounds for suspicion that they were engaged in terrorist or terrorist-related activities. In 2009 more than 100,000 section 44 searches were carried out but none resulted in an arrest for a terrorism-related offence. A few hundred people were given warnings about alcohol use and possession of cannabis, so that it is evident that the legislation was being used to police petty crime. Evidence suggests that the legislation was disproportionately used against those of South Asian or other ethnic origins. Interviews with those stopped and searched revealed that those of ethnic origin felt they were stopped because 'they were Asian, Black or looked Muslim,' unlike white people who were stopped who felt that the stops were random (Parmar, 2011). What this also signifies is a breakdown of the boundary between counterterrorism policing and ordinary policing. Further interviews with the police revealed that they thought 'It's a really useful piece of legislation ...' Section 44 searches had the effect of 'reassuring the public' (Parmar, 2011: 370). This example of policing to reassure the public is a good example of securitization. However, the overall response to terrorism may be seen to exemplify anti-cosmopolitan tendencies. Rather than the features of cosmopolitanism identified by Beck (2006), such as openness and tolerance of national and ethnic differences, these very differences have become signs of a threat to a Britishness which is understood as traditional ethnically homogenous 'whiteness.'

The final example of an instance of anti-cosmopolitanism that is discussed here concerns the vote in the UK in a referendum to leave the EU—popularly known as the Brexit vote. First, the principal features of the leave campaign and how it was suffused with anti-cosmopolitan themes are outlined. Then the discussion moves on to consider the wave of racist attacks that occurred immediately after the vote. This wave of attacks is conceptualized as a form of 'celebratory racism.' By 'celebratory racism' is meant a form of public racist behavior that often expresses either 'anger' or 'fun.' It is performed for public audiences of other white British people, whether friends or even strangers. It reinforces a sense of white British superiority and 'victory' over the 'threat' from racialized minorities. This was especially important in the context of the Brexit campaign. It often occurs in contexts where there is a feeling that 'normal constraints' on behavior in public have been removed, so that racist performances that would normally be seen as 'deviant' are suddenly felt to be acceptable. What was previously expressed privately 'backstage' becomes expressed 'front stage' for a public audience.

Central to understanding how this celebratory racism suddenly emerged after the Brexit vote is how far immigration was the central issue underlying the campaign for Britain to leave the EU. Rather than the actual numbers and character of migration to the UK from Europe being the key factor, it was how politicians' concerns with immigration generated a series of myths about the numbers and categories of migrants that principally constructed the public response (Favell and Barbulescu, 2018). More generally it has been suggested that the Brexit vote reflected long-term deep-seated racism across the UK population and not just among a 'left-behind' working class (Virdee and McGeever, 2018).

The broader politics of Brexit were also a reflection of a divided ruling elite, especially within the ruling Conservative Party; a crisis of the party system within both major parties, but especially the Conservatives, who feared losing support to the anti-European UK Independence Party; and a crisis of legitimacy of the dominant neoliberal strategies for the country (Jessop, 2017: 134). The result was the cross-class character of the support for leaving the EU in the referendum of 2016. While two thirds of the traditionally defined manual working class voted in favor of leaving the EU, this made up only 24 percent of the overall vote in favor of leaving. Most of the votes in favor of leaving the EU came from the middle classes (Antonucci et al., 2017) and the South of England (Dorling, 2016). Furthermore, 66 percent of those aged sixty-six and over voted in favor of leave, with 53 percent identifying as 'white British' compared to only 23 percent from minority ethnic groups (Clarke et al., 2017: 155). Consequently, the leave vote was a cross-class coalition of older and middle sections of the population. This was mobilized partly in terms of a nostalgia for the British Empire, but also in terms of a British isolationism. The first of these was connected to the idea of returning democratic control of the country to the UK so that it could reestablish trading relations with the former empire. After the Brexit vote this economic strategy was referred to by UK government officials as 'Empire 2.0' (Virdee and McGeever, 2018: 1805). This reflects a postcolonial melancholia (Gilroy, 2004) rooted in the loss of empire and the decline of Britain's former imperial prestige, and in part explains the support for the leave campaign among the older sections of the population. The second aspect revolves around the longer-run constructions of the migrant as an economic threat (Virdee and McGeever, 2018: 1806) to the 'indigenous white working class,' as well as Muslims constructed as a security threat to the British nation (Hussain and Bagguley, 2012). This interpretation is also confirmed by statistical analyses of surveys after the vote, which showed that concerns about controlling the economy, immigration, and terrorism were strongly associated with voting leave, and that these were views solidly in place before the referendum (Clarke et al., 2017: 161).

The outpouring of interpersonal racism immediately after the vote to leave was announced was just as shocking and surprising as the leave vote itself. This involved not just verbal racism, but physical attacks on people and property. The number of hate crimes recorded for the last two weeks in June increased by 42 percent compared to the previous year. A total of 3,076 incidents were recorded across the country between June 16 and 30—compared to the 915 reports recorded over the same period in 2015.[2] Celebratory racism was apparent 'almost instantly,' but not spontaneously. It reflected the enduring nature of racism as a macro phenomenon, alongside the reproduction of racism 'privately' in 'backstage' safe spaces for racism. The racist character of the 'leave campaign' had effectively legitimated public expressions of racism, resulting in its normalization. What was also striking was the generic character of Brexit celebratory racism: all visible ethnic minorities were targeted not just Europeans. All ethnic and racialized minorities became represented during the Brexit campaign as 'immigrants' who would no longer be 'allowed in' or were to be 'sent home.' These performances of 'celebratory racism' were often expressed as either 'anger' or 'fun.' They were performed for public audiences of other white British people be they friends or strangers. They had the effect of reinforcing a sense of white British superiority and 'victory' over the

---

2 See https://www.theguardian.com/politics/2016/jun/29/frenzy-hatred-brexit-racism-abuse-referendum-celebratory-lasting-damage.

'threat' from 'immigrant' racialized minorities. These performances emerged from the feeling that 'normal constraints' on behavior in public had been removed by the Brexit campaign. Although racist incidents had been experienced before the Brexit votes by recent migrants to the UK (Rzepnikowska, 2018), what was new after the Brexit vote was both their scale and scope, and the ways in which they reflected the dominant discourse of the leave campaign (Burnett, 2017).

4   Conclusion: after the Cosmopolitan Revolution Just Racism as Usual?

Beck described the resurgence of interest in cosmopolitanism almost two decades ago as a 'revolution in the social sciences' (2002: 17). What we have seen since then is not so much the increased cosmopolitanization (Beck, 2002: 17) that he predicted, but increased resistance to these processes. In the case of the UK this will lead to epoch-making structural economic, political, and social changes in its relationship with Europe.

In one of this last public lectures, Zygmunt Bauman reflected upon Britain's Brexit vote and the wider global context of increasing populism, nationalism, and xenophobia as a situation which was already cosmopolitan but that popular belief was such: 'as if nothing had happened' (Bauman, 2016). What he was suggesting here was that people's cultural frameworks of action had been inherited from a more nation-state-bound past and were no longer congruent with a more globalized present. In one of his final books he developed the concept of 'retrotopia' as a form of nostalgia that reconciled security and freedom based on a highly selective memory of the past (Bauman, 2017). The past of the UK and Europe was, of course, always global to some degree, marked by colonialism, imperialism, migration, and trade, but that is not how most people remember it. The past that people recall is more nation-state bound and ethnically homogenous, and is captured by how Bauman conceives of retrotopia, where 'you feel free to fantasize, to imagine … how nice it was to live in the past, how much better there were the ways of life which our parents, or ourselves even, in our naivity abandoned' (Bauman, 2017: 3). Most strikingly in the case of the leave campaign for Brexit, but also in the case of the other examples that we have discussed here, the motivations and processes involved exemplify a particular form of retrotopia. Rather than living in an age of cosmopolitanism as conceptualized by Beck, we live in an age of retrotopia that has emerged as a form of reaction against the forces of cosmopolitanization.

References

Andreouli, E. and C. Howarth. 2018. 'Everyday Cosmopolitanism in Representations of Europe among Young Romanians in Britain.' *Sociology* 53 (2): 280–296.

Antonucci, L., Horvath, L., Kutiyski, Y., and Krouwel, A. 2017. 'The Malaise of the Squeezed Middle: Challenging the Narrative of the "Left Behind" Brexiter.' *Competition and Change* 21 (3): 211–229.

Ashbee, E. 2017. *The Trump Revolt*. Manchester: Manchester University Press.

Bagguley, P. and Y. Hussain. 2008. *Riotous Citizens: Ethnic Conflict in Multicultural Britain*. Aldershot: Ashgate Publishing.

Bauman, Z. 2016. 'Europe's Adventure? Still Unfinished.' Lecture at the University of Leeds, October 5.

Bauman, Z. 2017. *Retrotopia*. Cambridge, UK: Polity Press.

Beck, U. 2002. 'The Cosmopolitan Society and Its Enemies.' *Theory, Culture and Society* 19 (1): 17–44.

Beck, U. 2006. *The Cosmopolitan Vision*. Cambridge, UK: Polity Press.

Bergesen, A. J. and O. Lizardo. 2004. 'International Terrorism and the World-System.' *Sociological Theory* 22 (1): 38–52.

Bhambra, G. 2014. *Connected Sociologies*. London: Bloomsbury.

Blackwood, L., N. Hopkins, and S. Reicher. 2013. 'I Know Who I Am, But Who Do They Think I Am? Muslim Perspectives on Encounters with Airport Authorities.' *Ethnic and Racial Studies* 36 (6): 1090–1108.

Burnett, J. 2017. 'Racial Violence and the Brexit State.' *Race and Class* 58 (4): 85–97.

Buzan, B., O. Waever, and J. de Wilde. 1998. *Security: A New Framework for Analysis*. Boulder, CO: Lynne Rienner Publications.

Cantle, T. 2002. *Community Cohesion: A Report of the Independent Review Team*. London: Home Office.

Clarke, H. D., M. Goodwin, and P. Whiteley. 2017. *Brexit: Why Britain Voted to Leave the European Union*. Cambridge, UK: Cambridge University Press.

Dorling, D. 2016. 'Brexit: The Decision of a Divided Country.' *British Medical Journal* 354: 36–97.

Favell, A. and R. Barbulescu. 2018. 'Brexit, "Immigration" and Anti-Discrimination.' In *The Routledge Handbook of the Politics of Brexit*, edited by P. Diamond, 118–133. London: Routledge.

Gilroy, P. 2004. *After Empire: Melancholia or Convivial Culture?* London: Routledge.

Hall, S. 2012. *City, Street and Citizen: The Measure of the Ordinary*. London: Routledge.

Harrington, A. 2016. *German Cosmopolitan Social Thought and the Idea of the West: Voices from Weimar*. Cambridge, UK: Cambridge University Press.

Hewitt, S. 2007. *The British War on Terror: Terrorism and Counterterrorism on the Home Front since 9-11*. London: Continuum.

Houts-Picca, L. and J. R. Feagin. 2007. *Two-Faced Racism: Whites in the Backstage and Frontstage.* London: Routledge.

Hussain, Y. and P. Bagguley. 2012. 'Securitised Citizens: Islamophobia, Racism and the 7/7 London Bombings.' *The Sociological Review* 60 (4): 714–733.

Hussain, Y. and P. Bagguley. 2013. 'Funny Looks: British Pakistanis' Experiences after 7th July 2005.' *Ethnic and Racial Studies* 36 (1): 28–46.

Jessop, B. 2017. 'The Organic Crisis of the British State: Putting Brexit in its Place.' *Globalizations* 14 (1): 133–141.

Martell, L. 2008. 'Beck's Cosmopolitan Politics.' *Contemporary Politics* 14 (2): 129–143.

Martell, L. 2009. 'Global Inequality, Human Rights and Power: A Critique of Ulrich Beck's Cosmopolitanism.' *Critical Sociology* 35 (2): 253–272.

Mitchell, K. 2003. 'Educating the National Citizen in Neoliberal Times: From the Multicultural Self to the Strategic Cosmopolitan.' *Transactions of Institute of British Geographers* 28 (4): 387–403.

Neal, S., Bennett, K., Cochrane, A., and Mohan, G. 2018. *Lived Experiences of Multiculture: The New Social and Spatial Relations of Diversity.* London: Routledge.

Nickels, H. C., Thomas, L., Hickman, M. J., and Silvestri, S. 2010. *A Comparative Study of the Representations of 'Suspect' Communities in Multi-Ethnic Britain and their Impact on Irish Communities and Muslim Communities: Mapping Newspaper Content.* London: City University.

Parmar, A. 2011. 'Stop and Search in London: Counter-Terrorist or Counter-Productive?' *Policing and Society* 21 (4): 369–382.

Piketty, T. 2014. *Capital in the Twenty-First Century.* Cambridge, MA: Harvard University Press.

Poole, E. 2006. 'The Effects of September 11 and the War in Iraq on British Newspaper Coverage.' In *Muslims and the News Media*, edited by E. Poole and J. E. Richardson, 89–102. London: I.B. Tauris.

Rzepnikowska, A. 2018. 'Racism and Xenophobia Experienced by Polish Migrants in the UK Before and After the Brexit Vote.' *Journal of Ethnic and Migration Studies* 45 (1): 61–77.

Sayyid, S. 2013. 'The Dynamics of a Postcolonial War.' *Defence Studies* 13 (3): 277–292.

Szerzynski, B. and J. Urry. 2002. 'Cultures of Cosmopolitanism.' *The Sociological Review* 50 (4): 461–481.

Turner, B. S. 2002. 'Cosmopolitan Virtue, Globalisation and Patriotism.' *Theory, Culture and Society* 19 (1–2): 45–63.

Virdee S. and B. McGeever. 2018. 'Racism, Crisis, Brexit.' *Ethnic and Racial Studies* 41 (10): 1802–1819.

CHAPTER 23

Cosmopolitanism and Religion

Bryan S. Turner

1   Introduction

There is now a familiar narrative in the social sciences about how secularization ushered in a world of enlightenment and eventually a regime of individual rights that allowed cosmopolitanism to flourish. Thus it is argued that in the 20th century the majority of intellectuals welcomed secularization as the foundation of an expanding cosmopolitanism which was understood to be the humanistic culture of the city. Religion was seen to be the carrier of values and traditions that were contrary to the cosmopolitanism of the Enlightenment and to the promise of secular modernity. As the narrow world of religious traditionalism was being eroded by the steady march of secular modernity, new opportunities arose for a more universal humanistic culture to replace the sterile world of religion. Modernity was increasingly hitched to globalization that experienced an upturn as a capitalist economic system spread worldwide with the consumer boom of postwar reconstruction. The preeminent cosmopolitan development was the mid-century growth of human rights. In response to civilian casualties, displaced persons, and economic depression, the concept of human dignity became the basis of the Declaration of Human Rights in 1948. As Samuel Moyn (2015) has shown, the Declaration was not in the first instance a response to the Holocaust, recognition of which came later as international law was increasingly developed within a rights framework. The acceptance of human rights was delayed by the growth of postcolonial nationalism in Asia and Africa, where human rights were often regarded as Western interference in the development of national sovereignty. However, after the 1970s, human rights became a global response to human suffering as recognition of the true enormity of the Holocaust became widely accepted. Although it can be disputed, the legal notion of genocide can no longer be exclusively identified with the destruction of Europe's Jews. Large-scale genocidal conflicts have taken place in Bosnia, Rwanda, the Sudan, and Myanmar.

Of course, the 'rights revolution' was never the outcome of some smooth linear evolutionary process. More importantly, by the end of the century secularization, as an aspect of the theory of modernization, was widely criticized by historians and sociologists. Against the idea of secularization, sociologists recognized the vitality of religion in the whole of Africa, the global spread of Pentecostalism, and the growth and reform of Islam. In the 1970s there was an eruption of what José Casanova (1994) has called 'public religions' in Poland, the United States, Latin America, and Iran. With the exception of the Moral Majority in the USA, public religions could play a positive role in political movements to remove authoritarian regimes. Vatican II had a significant cosmopolitan message in offering some recognition to the value of other religions. It also recognized the legitimacy of political modernization by accepting democratic politics. Liberation theology was a progressive move in Latin America as the Catholic Church sought to distance itself from authoritarian military regimes. In Iran, mass protests inspired by an ideology that combined Marxism and radical Shia notions of martyrdom and sacrifice eventually brought down the Shah. However, while Michel Foucault had welcomed the Shia Revolution as an example of 'political spirituality,' most observers saw the emergence of an authoritarian theocracy as a betrayal of the revolution.

In response to globalization and secular modernity, there has been a widespread growth in religious fundamentalism, revivalism, and conservative religious movements that are opposed to modernity and its dominant theory—namely liberalism. While radical Islam has emerged in public debate as the religion that brings into question the cosmopolitan liberalism of the West, there are in fact significant struggles within Muslim societies between conservatives and reformers. Although the Western media typically portray Muslim women as the passive victims of religious fundamentalism, sociological research shows us a very different picture in which such women, often through changes in constitutional law, continue to struggle, often successfully, for social and legal improvements in their status (Cesari and Casanova, 2017). In addition, the Arab Spring was welcomed as the uprising of youth against political corruption and conservative authoritarian states. Although many of these movements either failed or were suppressed, in some societies, such as Tunisia and Indonesia, the movement for democratization continues. There were similar social movements in Asia such as the Umbrella Movement. In the United States, Occupy Wall Street was a protest against finance capitalism, unemployment, and inequality. However, these many uprisings were generally contained and strongman politics has been reasserted.

2   The Rise of Populism

This narrative is what we might call the optimistic narrative of the steady march of history toward more open, inclusive, and cosmopolitan societies.

There have, as we can all now appreciate, been major setbacks confounding inclusive, democratic, multicultural civil societies. Hence the prospects for cosmopolitanism have been deeply challenged since the attack on the Twin Towers in 2001 by austerity economic strategies and, more recently, by the growth of right-wing populism in the United States and Europe. While populist politics have in fact been around since the 19th century—for example, the People's Party in the United States—they have only recently emerged as the dominant protest movement against globalization, migration, multicultural policies, and cosmopolitan values. There has been a corresponding decline in trust toward liberal governments and their political elites, who, following the Paradise Papers—the disclosure of offshore investments in November 2017 exposing the hidden wealth of elites—are seen to be cynically indifferent to the plight of 'the people.' Populism is difficult to define because it has both strong left-wing and right-wing tendencies.[1] In fact, populism exposes a fundamental contradiction inside our modern notion of 'democracy.' Thus, Michael Mann notes that

> Democracy means rule by the people. But in modern times *the people* has come to mean two things. The first is what the Greek meant by their word *demos*. This means the ordinary people, the mass of the population. So democracy is rule by the ordinary people, the mass of the population. But in our civilization the people also means 'nation' or another Greek term, *ethnos*, an ethnic group—a people that shares a common culture and sense of heritage, distinct from other peoples. But if the people is to rule in its own nation-state, and if the people is defined in ethnic terms, then its ethnic unity may outweigh the kind of citizen diversity that is central to democracy.
> MANN, 2005: 3; original emphasis

The peculiar mixture of left and right political ideologies and policies is perhaps sharply illustrated by the rise of Podemos in contemporary Spanish politics. The political leadership of Podemos, in being critical of the austerity policies of the European Union (EU) and their terrible consequences for youth unemployment in Europe's periphery, has adopted a classic socialist response in their criticism of the dominance of Germany and finance capitalism. They have also been critical of what they see as the unresolved legacy of Franco's fascism, but ironically they draw heavily on the legacy of the fascist jurist Carl

---

1 See Chapter 24 in this volume.

Schmitt, especially his notions of 'exception' and 'decisionism.' This connection suggests a troublesome analogy between the fate of Weimar Germany and modern-day Spain, and an even more troublesome scenario for the EU where similar populist movements are challenging the postwar ascendancy of free markets, open borders, and liberal politics as the foundation for a peaceful and prosperous Europe (Booth and Baert, 2017).

Populism is notoriously difficult to define (Canovan, 1981; Mudde, 2007). However, what populism, in dividing the world in terms of 'us' and 'them,' has as a common denominator is a general animosity to migration, especially to migrants from the Middle East or more generally the Muslim world. Migrants are generally held responsible for stealing jobs from the host population by driving down the cost of labor. However, Muslims are also associated with violence and terrorism and are thought to be opposed to Western values. Throughout the West, the spread of Islamophobia has been a general characteristic of populist politics. The term 'Islamophobia' was first given wide currency in Britain in 1997 with the publication of the Runnymede Trust Report on Islamophobia (Conway, 1997). In fact the idea that Islam is a specific political threat to the West might be traced back to the Iranian Revolution of 1997 (Nasr, 2006) when Shia radicalism was described as 'Islamofascism' (Podhoretz, 2007), as the regime in Tehran evolved toward theocratic totalitarianism.

3   Populism and Religion

It is perhaps a characteristic of secular social science to think of religion as generally conservative and hence associated with reactionary politics. Religious institutions are seen to be promoting exclusive not inclusive membership. Unsurprisingly, European populism has been identified with Christian conservatism. It has been claimed that religion has been 'hijacked' by populist radicalism in its ideological contrast between Islam and Christendom (Marzouki, McDonnell, and Roy, 2016). Of course, the policies on refugees and asylum seekers of the various member states vary greatly. In Germany, an open-door policy was first endorsed by the government, whose aim was to integrate immigrants into German society. This inclusive policy was modified after the 2016 Berlin attack and in response to widespread criticism. Denmark and Sweden, normally regarded as bastions of positive socialist values, have implemented restrictive migratory measures. In 2015, the government of Poland decided to select refugees from the Middle East on the basis of their Christian faith. Countries situated on the main route of migration—such as Slovakia, Hungary, Slovenia, and Macedonia—have erected fences or have closed their borders to defend themselves and Europe from what they perceive as a civilizational threat. The conservative and nationalist Hungarian Prime Minister Viktor Orbán has regularly warned that Islam can potentially destroy Europe's Christian roots and values. In general terms, as it has been argued, far-right politics use Christianity as an identity marker rather than as a faith, putting Christendom above Christianity and defending Christian spaces rather than 'actual Christian values' (McDonnell, 2016: 21). On occasion, far-right movements have described the defense of European religious values with some degree of ambiguity as the 'Judeo-Christian heritage.' In the United States, populism has been a driving force behind President Donald Trump's election victory and his promise to build a wall along the Mexican border to resolve the political debate over illegal migration. Because these illegal migrants are predominantly Catholic, there is an implicit project to protect the white Protestant foundations of colonial America. We have, however, to recognize the diversity of Trump's base. The racist slogans of Charlottesville in 2017 included 'We shall not be subordinated to the Jew.' Looking across these examples, religious ideas and values are the driving force behind much political violence and social exclusiveness, from the Middle East, South Asia, and the southern states of North America, to sub-Saharan Africa.

The critical issue here, which is important for understanding religion and cosmopolitanism, is that far-right parties have typically found themselves at odds with the official teaching of the Catholic or other churches, or with other religious groups which have welcomed migrants in terms of religious values such as fraternity and compassion. In particular the global role of Pope Francis in promoting the universal values that underpin Christian compassion has divided the Catholic Church and Christianity more generally between a theology of brotherhood and fear of the other, especially Islam as the principal challenge to Christendom. Anticipating my conclusion, this tension will determine the future of cosmopolitanism as a challenge between nationalism and national sovereignty, with its religious borders and religious universalism as embedded in the Sermon on the Mount.

4   The Axial Age and Its Religions

To understand the relationship between religion and cosmopolitanism we need to take a much longer historical view. In particular we need to consider some of the issues raised by the contemporary interest in the so-called 'Axial Age religions.' The contemporary debate about the Axial Age is directed at issues raised by Karl Jaspers in his *The Origin and Goal of History*, which was published in Germany in 1949.² The moral purpose behind the text was a reflection on the causes of the Second World War, its destructive long-term consequences, and the postwar European crisis. His work may also be regarded as a critique of what we have come to know as 'Orientalism'; that is, the presumption that only Western thought is of significance and lasting importance. To correct that narrow and prejudicial presupposition Jaspers (1953) explored the ideas of Socrates, the Buddha, and Confucius. In looking at the Axial Age, he was critical of the legacy of Hegelian notions of history that excluded the Orient as static and thus unhistorical. Jaspers claimed, in exploring traditions outside Europe, that criticism, transcendence, and humanity were already highly developed in the Axial Age long before the rise of what is conventionally understood to be the modern world. According to Axial Age theories, 'modernity' has a much longer history than commonly assumed, and in this regard Jaspers offered a cosmopolitan reinterpretation of world literature and its religious roots. In a recent work Eugene Halton (2014) has claimed that the idea of an Axial Age was in fact explored much earlier by John Stuart Stuart-Glennie, in 1879 in his study of the history of ideas about morality. Stuart-Glennie developed the idea of a 'moral revolution' occurring well before the modern era; similar ideas were developed independently by Lewis Mumford in the 1950s. Perhaps one reason why Jaspers stands out in this context is that his view of the Orient was based on his view that Western civilization had collapsed with the rise of fascism and a devastating world war. By contrast Stuart-Glennie appears to have taken for granted the superiority of Western culture.

Against the background of the destruction of much of Europe by modern warfare, Jaspers' analysis of history explored the remarkable conjunction of prophets, poets, and philosophers in the period 800 to 200 BC and argued that this period came to define what we continue to regard as 'humanity.' These Axial Age figures included the Hebrew prophets, the Buddha, Socrates, Plato, Zoroaster, Confucius, Lao-Tse, and others, whose ideas offered, in Jaspers' moral vision, a basis for assumptions about the unity and not the irreducible diversity of mankind. Through the idea of revelation, the charismatic prophets constructed a vision of a different and superior world beyond the immediate empirical reality of the here and now. Through reason and revelation, these religious figures created ethical codes of conduct that established norms of virtuous conduct which constituted a breakthrough in human history. These charismatic prophets and philosopher-poets created 'the age of criticism' in understanding this world to be a place of corruption that must be countered

---

2   See Chapter 1 in this volume.

by critique on the basis of a morally superior vision of reality (Momigliano, 1975: 9). The age of criticism established a systematic tension between the political and the religious, and between earthly constraints and the possibilities for personal development established by these critical ethical norms. This critical response was based on a profound sense that everyday reality is deeply unsatisfactory—or *dukkha* in Buddhist teaching. More importantly, this world-to-come was available to all human beings and hence can be regarded as an Ur-cosmopolitan vision.

The underlying issue in this debate is that ethical behavior includes hospitality or an openness to others whom we recognize as not only part of our world but intrinsic to it. The rights of others grow out of a personal sense of vulnerability and life remains unsatisfactory without our transformative work on it (Turner, 2006). It is reasonable to claim that the ancient religions were the root of cosmopolitanism. Human vulnerability is shared by various religious and philosophical traditions. In the 20th century it was the Roman Catholic notion of human dignity and personhood that contributed significantly to the modern notion of human rights as the principal juridical framework of cosmopolitan values. However, this historical root is not somehow exclusively part of the Judeo-Christian-Muslim legacy, but, in Jasper's terms, a legacy that embraced diverse figures from the Axial Age. Religious traditions have generally promoted globalization, thereby laying some foundations for respect of other cultures and notions of common decency. Christian campaigns against slavery, building a global advocacy system, are an obvious example (Stamatov, 2013).

5 Does Cosmopolitanism Have a Future?

It is difficult to be optimistic about the prospects for cosmopolitanism. Grounds for optimism over a cosmopolitan future have been eroded by the growth of right-wing populism; by the referendum to take the United Kingdom out of the EU; by the resurgence of nationalist movements across Europe; by genocide in the Middle East; by the rise of strongman politics in China, Russia, and the Philippines; and by the strategies of President Donald Trump to make 'America Great Again' by embracing protectionism, promising to build a wall along the Mexican–American border, and by withdrawing from international trade and environmental agreements.

It is now widely assumed that the rise of right-wing populism is a response of the 'left behind' (such as unemployed men in the blue-collar sector of the labor market) and that the plight of marginalized communities is associated with the globalization of the economy. Popular anger directed at elites has been driven in part by the erosion of job security, by the decline in real wages, and by the increase in income inequality. The proletariat is now described as a 'precariat' and there is a general sentiment in the West that citizens are merely denizens. Resentment is now widespread in the United States and not simply among the 'left behind' but among the middle class, whose position in society has also been weakened. If the Tea Party was a protest of mainly white seniors fearful of their pensions and health-care entitlements, then Occupy Wall Street was mainly a protest by white, educated, young white-collar workers.

What are the communal bonds that might hold societies together as inclusive communities? Historically, religion (including civil religions) have been such a bond, but in contemporary political conflicts conservative religious movements have added to social and political divisions over gay marriage, abortion, and national identity. Islamophobia is an important element in populist rhetoric. Religion (or more specifically Christianity) has emerged in populist opposition to Islam insofar as Muslim migrants are uniformly regarded as actual or potential jihadists.

Although this mixture of politics and religion may strike many observers as a new development, in the United States, religion, especially since the creation of the Moral Majority, is never that far removed from politics. While religion played some role in the rise of the Tea Party, it was overtly absent from the election contest between Donald Trump and Hillary Clinton. However, it was explicitly present in the conflict over the legal decision that sanctioned abortion. It was also implicit in the references to the criminality of illegal Latin American (primarily Mexican) migrants to the USA. In the post-election period, religious issues and identities have become more prominent. Trump is enjoying support for his anti-abortion stand (from both Catholics and evangelical Protestants), for his pro-Israeli stance, and from 'Tender Warriors' (evangelical Protestants embracing masculinity and conventional gender roles). He enjoys the benefit of a spiritual guide in the televangelist Paula White who affirms that he has a 'hunger for God.' Finally, the President, at the yearly event National Prayer Breakfast, promised to 'destroy' the Johnson Amendment that separated politics and pulpit for churches classified as tax-exempt charities. It appears that religion is extending Trump's base and increasingly acts as a dimension of American populism.

These developments have exposed a major division within the Roman Catholic Church. Pope Francis has emerged as a major figure in the defense of the universal message of the Christian gospel in his welcome to migrants and refugees fleeing persecution in the Middle East and North Africa. His message, alongside the stance of Angela Merkel, has been a shining example of cosmopolitan virtue grounded in Catholic notions of justice and human dignity. Conservative cardinals within the Church are reluctant to openly challenge the authority of the Pope, whose message is a major underpinning of religious cosmopolitanism. Nevertheless, posters appeared in Rome in February 2017 that were critical of his inclusive agenda. His cosmopolitanism has divided the Church between conservatives such as the American Cardinal Raymond Burke and Catholic liberals who defend the Pope's embrace of outsiders. The conservative position of Burke has received support from Stephen K. Bannon who sees the Pope as closer to socialism than to Christianity. Burke and Bannon agree on the view that the West is dangerously weakened by European societies that have departed from the Christian foundations of the West and that the political elite is remote from and indifferent to the crisis of Western civilization.

The other underpinning of cosmopolitanism has been the rule of law. One can interpret laws relating to hate speech, gender equality, just treatment of minorities, and freedom of religion as a significant juridical wall against prejudice, discrimination, intercommunal violence, and injustice. Broadly speaking, the rule of law is a major guardian of social justice, the protection of the individual, and a conduit of shared values. Legal conditions can act in defense of the recognition of 'common necessity' in international law such as protection of the environment, open sea-lanes, regulation of nuclear power, and respect for the dignity of the individual.

However, it is clear, especially during the presidency of Barak Obama, that the law has been deeply politicized. Conservatives argue that the law has replaced democratic processes in decision-making and liberals fear the appointment of conservative judges to the Supreme Court. This battle around the Supreme Court was manifest in the career of Judge Antonin Scalia—an ardent Catholic and a defender of 'Originalism,' namely that interpretation of the meaning of the constitution must abide by the clear wording and intentions of the men who created it and that an evolutionary approach to the interpretation of the constitution to suit modern values has to be challenged. Inevitably this leads to conservative interpretations that would reject laws supporting recognition of abortion, same-sex marriage, and homosexuality. Scalia objected that his Catholicism did not influence his decisions as a lawyer, but his critics have suggested that the 'textualism' of Originalist methodology is a form of Catholic epistemology (Biskupic, 2009). The political struggle over the construction and role of the Supreme Court has continued unabated under the Trump presidency, thereby further eroding the rule of law as a component of a juridical defense of inclusive values.

6 Conclusion

In conclusion, I have argued that values of universalism and hospitality, the rule of law, and democratic procedures offer an important defense of cosmopolitan virtue against narrow prejudice against outsiders. While cosmopolitanism is typically understood in secular terms, we cannot avoid recognizing its religious roots. Many of these secular values and systems that define modernity had their origins in religious traditions and especially in Christianity, which paradoxically prepared the way into modern secularity (Gauchet, 1999). Over a longer history of human existence, Axial Age religions have shaped what we take to be 'humanity.' However, these open cosmopolitan regimes have been deeply threatened by political radicalism, the origins of which are partly explained by the failures of economic globalization to sustain the living conditions of the working class. Insofar as elites are global elites, resentment of elites has spilled over into resentment against cosmopolitanism. Without some solution to economic and political uncertainty, liberal cosmopolitanism may be short-lived. More deeply problematic and uncertain is the future of parliamentary democracy itself. Consequently, it would be a fateful delusion to believe that we are safe from nuclear conflict, communal and religious violence, authoritarian rule, and the persecution of minorities. Ethnic cleansing in Myanmar, driven by a mixture of ethnic and religious resentment and the guidance of a brutal military elite, is one tragic example of the contemporary failure of the international framework of human rights to protect minorities. It may also illustrate the paradox that, without citizenship, human rights are only a thin protection for the vulnerable. Cosmopolitanism, along with civilization and civility, if they survive at all, will require far more than constant vigilance. They will require grounding in new structures in law, politics, and religion. They will require a new Axial Age.

References

Biskupic, J. 2009. *American Original: The Life of Constitution Supreme Court Judge Antonin Scalia*. New York: Farrar, Straus, and Giroux.

Booth, J. and P. Baert. 2017. *The Dark Side of Podemos: Carl Schmitt's Shadow in Progressive Populism*. Cambridge, UK: Cambridge University Press.

Canovan, M. 1981. *Populism*. New York: Harcourt Brace Jovanovich.

Casanova, J. 1994. *Public Religions in the Modern World*. Chicago: University of Chicago Press.

Cesari, J. and J. Casanova (eds.). 2017. *Islam, Gender and Democracy: Comparative Perspectives*. Oxford: Oxford University Press.

Conway, G. 1997. *Islamophobia: A Challenge to Us All*. London: The Trust.

Gauchet, M. 1999. *The Disenchantment of the World*. Princeton, NJ: Princeton University Press.

Halton, E. 2014. *From the Axial Age to the Moral Revolution: John Stuart-Glennie, Karl Jaspers and a New Understanding of the Idea*. New York: Palgrave Macmillan.

Jaspers, K. 1953. *The Origin and Goal of History*. London: Routledge & Kegan Paul.

McDonnell, D. 2016. 'The Lega Nord: The New Savior of Northern Italy.' In *Saving the People: How Populists Hijack Religion*, edited by N. Marzouki, D. McDonnell, and O. Roy, 13–28. Oxford: Oxford University Press.

Mann, M. 2005. *The Dark Side of Democracy: Explaining Ethnic Cleansing*. Cambridge, UK: Cambridge University Press.

Marzouki, N., D. McDonnell, and O. Roy (eds.). 2016. *Saving the People: How Populists Hijack Religion*. Oxford: Oxford University Press.

Momigliano, A. 1975. *Alien Wisdom: The Limits of Helenization*. Cambridge, UK: Cambridge University Press.

Moyn, S. 2015. *Christian Human Rights*. University Park: University of Pennsylvania Press.

Mudde, C. 2007. *Populist Radical Right Parties in Europe*. Cambridge, UK: Cambridge University Press.

Nasr, V. 2006. *The Shia Revival: How Conflicts within Islam Shape the Future*. New York: W. W. Norton.

Podhoretz, N. 2007. *World War IV: The Long Struggle against Islamofascism*. New York: Doubleday.

Stamatov, P. 2013. *The Origins of Global Humanitarianism: Religion, Empires and Advocacy*. Cambridge, UK: Cambridge University Press.

Turner, B. S. 2006. *Vulnerability and Human Rights*. University Park: Pennsylvania State University Press.

CHAPTER 24

The Dialectic of Populism and Cosmopolitanism

Lauren Langman

>
> The question was put to Diogenes, what country he was from, and he replied, 'I am a citizen of the world.'

∴

1   Introduction

After the USSR collapsed, without alternatives to capitalism and/or liberal democratic political systems, Francis Fukuyama (1992) proclaimed 'end of history.' But neoliberal global capitalism had adverse consequences. Outsourcing, advanced technologies, financialization, and privatization of resources and services led to greater inequality and precarity, fostering discontent, anxiety, anger, and often resistance, with a plethora of conflicting cosmopolitanism and authoritarian populist mobilizations, social movements, and/or direct actions by workers, subordinate classes, or marginalized groups arising as a result. Cosmopolitans seek tolerant, inclusive, egalitarian societies while intolerant, authoritarian populist or ethno-nationalist movements see themselves as a distinct, aggrieved 'moral community' of the 'real' people angry toward existing political elites and/or mainstream political parties seen as self-serving, inept, corrupt, and, *opposed to the 'will of the people.'* 'Right' populisms would 'return' power to the 'real' people, neither corrupt elites nor intrusive Others, and restore a 'better' world now lost.

Neoliberal globalization has not well served the interests of the masses, whether they be left or right voters. This was clear in the progressive mobilizations of the Arab Spring, Southern Europe, or the Occupy movement, seeking more equitable economic and entitlement policies, recognition and dignity. However, even when they 'won' electoral victories, such as Syriza or Podemos, the 'victories' proved Pyrrhic—Brussels prevailed (Langman et al., 2013) Nonetheless, the cultural side of globalization, especially mass media and social media, spread universalistic, cosmopolitan values and post-national identities. Such fissures dispose populisms as compensatory reactions to the spread of cosmopolitan values and identities, leading to virulent 'clashes of identities' between various modern, better-educated, urban cosmopolitans and more traditional rural or ex-urban groups who embrace reactionary populisms in reaction to a rapidly changing world that challenges and undermines economic well-being as well as challenges traditional values, lifestyles, and heretofore 'privileged,' inclusive, identities of the 'real people' facing decline if not extinction, Hochschild (2017) described this as feeling left behind. This in turn has engendered fear, anxiety, anger, and *ressentiment* that triggers authoritarianism and intolerance leading to an embrace of powerful leaders and political parties with anti-democratic agendas that promise restoration of a 'more glorious' past that was typically more mythical than actual. While populisms *cannot simply be reduced to identities or underlying character*, these are essential factors mediating the impacts of both political economy and cosmopolitanism and thus impelling support for and participation in various right-wing populist social movements.

2   Cosmopolitanism

The idea that all human beings are equal fellow citizens of the world—the essence of cosmopolitanism—derived from the Greek word *kosmopolitês*, 'citizens of the world,' and emerged among 4th-century Greek philosophers (Appiah, 2007). Millennia later, bourgeois intellectuals offered critiques of dynastic rule that promoted the rise of capitalism and justifications for bourgeois claims to lead the 'people.' These included the social contract legacies of Locke, whereby governance was by the 'consent of the governed,' Rousseau's 'general will' (not particular will), and Kant extolling the Enlightenment in anticipation of a reason-based peaceful world of cosmopolitanism, democratic governance, the inclusion and recognition of all citizens, the toleration of differences, the overcoming of social boundaries, and the rise of prosperity.

The ascendant bourgeois classes embraced rational legal authority, constitutionally based, elected governments, limited-term leadership, and clear-cut delegations of authority; that is, rules, checks, balances, and guaranteed rights. Rationally (bureaucratically) administered governance displaced patrimonialism. The legacies of post-Westphalian territorial boundaries of sovereignty and a growing market society enabled the emergence of bourgeois 'public spheres,' where 'free-speech' situations created 'publics' as political forces to secure the legitimacy of leadership claims and construct inclusive, cosmopolitan 'civic nationalisms' with citizenship-based identities within modern nation-states (Habermas, 1962; Calhoun, 1999). With the American

Revolution, Constitution, and Bill of Rights, then the French Revolution and Decoration of the Rights of Man, cosmopolitanism joined with liberal democracy to express the 'general will' of the governed. Modern nations would incorporate and unite disparate groups living within national boundaries by forging hegemonic, inclusive, common, national identities of citizenship within socially constructed 'imagined communities' characterized by 'mediated ties' of belonging (Anderson, 1963). Thus, political liberalism joined cosmopolitism in creating and uniting diverse groups into a 'people' by systematically generating an identity, bestowing a national political community with a common language, and a shared history and meanings, mediated through schools, valorized by a 'national' culture (art, music, literature), and celebrated during national holidays (Calhoun, 1999). Moreover, citizens were granted various social, political, and economic rights that would mitigate capitalist inequality, secure the legitimacy of the system, generate loyalty, and dispel potential resistance (Marshall, 1950).

Following the Second World War and the Holocaust, there was a concerted effort to secure *universally inviolable human rights*, culminating in the 1948 United Nations (UN) Declaration of Human Rights, itself an updated version of the 'rights of man' promising universal equality and dignity. With globalization came a variety of progressive social and cultural changes, *but, dialectically understood, these very same changes, along with massive migrations, were seen as challenges and assaults to traditional identities and values, and thus initiated a number of reactionary responses and fundamental, indeed unresolvable,* conflicts between cosmopolitanism and populism.

3   Populism

Modern capitalist democracies have inherent contradictions and crises that migrate to the lifeworlds of identity and emotion, often leading to a withdrawal of support for the system of governance (Habermas, 1975). Electoral politics has also enabled 'democracy's bastards'—some adversely impacted groups embrace anti-democratic authoritarian populisms, often ethno-religious nationalisms celebrating the superior and specialness of the people. It is difficult to define populism, especially since it takes so many different forms, depending on history, class structures, and/or national differences, and so on; while fascist dictatorships may have inspired populisms, populisms are not dictatorships (Finchelstein, 2017). Nevertheless, most authoritarian populist movements and/or states have certain integral features in common that may or may not necessarily by themselves define populism.

Populisms are generally anti-pluralistic, anti-democratic, anti-elitist, intolerant, and authoritarian (Mueller, 2016). Populists typically feel that their moral community—'the real people'—have been victimized, their interests, values, and identities have been ignored, challenged, or subverted by self-serving, indifferent, inapt, and/or corrupt elites who use their wealth and power to support 'unpopular' economic, social, political, and cultural agendas (including by rigging elections to secure 'unpopular' and often cosmopolitan agendas). Almost a hundred years ago, Carl Schmitt (2007 [1932]) offered a trenchant critique of liberal democracy in mass societies, where ordinary people were left powerless, rather, only a strong powerful leader could represent the ordinary people, the 'authentic people' whose interests and will were ignored. Such leaders may use democratic elections to gain power, but once gained, uses that power to erode democratic principles from the rule of law to freedoms of speech, a free press etc. Think Trump, Orban, Modi, Erdoğan, Bolsonaro, etc. Moreover, such leader designate 'enemies' that must be opposed, if not eliminated, ab thus unifying the people through anger, hatred and aggression toward the enemy. Today, Big Brother uses social media and today, every day is 'hate day.'

Populists disdain equality, democracy, cultural, ethnic, or racial diversity, and, most of all, social/cultural changes that are seen as danger to the moral superiority and purity of the people. Populists are typically nativist, decrying foreigners—especially recent immigrants. Populisms are generally intolerant of 'democratically' elected governments—unless they are the victors—in which they attempt to implement reactionary policies and replace incumbent government workers, judges, and so on with loyal cronies. Populists create rigid, impermeable boundaries between themselves and various enemy 'Others,' be they liberal elites or despised subordinates who might differ by ethnicity, race, religion, and so on. Most populists tend to be patriarchal and misogynist, notwithstanding the fact there are many right-wing women who defend traditional versions of femininity—*Kinder, Küche, und Kirche*. There is a general disdain toward human rights, a free, critical mass media, and independent non-governmental organizations (NGOs) that might challenge reactionary populism. When gaining power, authoritarian populists often close or limit universities, especially philosophy and social sciences departments that might critique power—as seen in Erdoğan's Turkey.

Populism has a long history in early America, seen in the election of Andrew Jackson, who, while not part of the establishment, as a military hero who had defeated the British and removed Native Americans was seen as a representative of the 'common people' for whose sake he would democratize power (Kazin, 1995). These 'people' were mostly less-educated, rural *white people*; many were not only religious, but held that the colonization of this new land, as a 'city on the hill,' was an expression of God's will, and the 'success' of American colonization, expansion, capitalism, and independence was a sign of His blessing (Langman and Lundskow, 2016). In the years that would follow, various expressions of authoritarian populism, typically intertwined with nativism, reactionary nationalism, ethnocentrism, xenophobia, and racism, were held by politicians such as William Jennings Bryan, Huey Long, George Wallace, and Ross Perot. In Europe, similar movements, initially, fascist, were clearly evident with the rise of Benito Mussolini and Adolf Hitler.

One of the earliest analyses of populism was Marx's analysis of Bonapartism in which Louis Napoleon led a coup against the government. With the support of the peasantry and urban *lumpenproletariat*, he led a revolt against the French bourgeoisie parties to establish the Second Republic that, ironically enough, primarily benefited French capitalism. But several elements of that coup remain salient, beginning with the fact that Louis Napoleon, notwithstanding his illustrious uncle, was a political outsider, more a flamboyant fool than a leader. His primary support came from the rural petite bourgeoisie farmers who faced high taxes and mortgages while trying to survive on ever smaller plots of land as each generation divided the land. Moreover, their limited education and communication meant that the peasantry were like a 'sack of potatoes,' isolated with little understanding of the larger world. They, of course, looked back to restoring the glorious time when Napoleon Bonaparte first gave them the land—but two generations later the now divided plots were ever smaller. Most subsequent populisms seek to restore a lost, better world.

Marx's analysis provides us with several insights, beginning with the conflicting economic and cultural differences between the petit bourgeois merchants, artisans, and rural peasants and urban capitalist elites that subsequently informed theories of modernity such as Tönnies' analysis of *Gemeinschaft* and *Gesellschaft*, and Durkheim's distinction between traditional societies with mechanical solidarity and a relatively limited division of labor that were integrated by religious morality. Such societies were likely to embrace punitive repressive justice. Modern urban societies with a highly complex division of labor requiring specialized higher education were more likely to be held together by an 'organic solidarity' based on the interdependence of more specialized, individualized people. Such societies were likely to embrace restitutive forms of justice. Simmel's analysis of the 'objective culture' of the modern city referred to its diversity and cosmopolitanism. Modern urban life meant more individual freedom, *stadtluft macht frei*, expressed in a multitude of diverse social interactions and relationships, lifestyles, values, and cultural tastes—requiring toleration of differences. With modernity, there were growing bifurcations between the cosmopolitan social life and cultures of the more highly fragmented, pluralistic urban centers, and the more traditional cultures of the rural hinterlands that, more often than not, consisted of less-educated, less-affluent, and less-sophisticated people; among the latter, cosmopolitanism is rarely found.

Contemporary globalization has accelerated the differences between the economic, cultural, and psychological differences between cosmopolitan cities and the more traditional cultures, values, lifestyles, and identities of the hinterland. Neoliberal capitalism has radically transformed, incorporated, and colonized national economies in which a transnational billionaire class now owns most of the assets of the world. The centralization of finance, and the growth of tourism and cultural centers, have reconfigured urban life as 'global cities' have become nodes of global finance (Sassen, 2012). High-tech centers like Silicon Valley or Pittsburgh, with advanced technologies, including digital communication, have enabled a global diffusion of a globalized cosmopolitan culture that transcends national or ethnic differences. The rural hinterlands have 'fallen behind' economically and culturally. Consequently, heretofore traditional identities, based on privileges of race, gender, ethnicity, and/or religion, have been under cultural and demographic assault.

3.1 *Political Economy*
Globalization has produced vast, albeit unequally distributed, wealth, especially in financial and digital markets, including online merchandising like Amazon or Alibaba. A highly privileged transnational class has disproportionate influence over global economic practices though trade agreements (World Trade Organization (WTO), International Monetary Fund (IMF), or the World Bank). Neoliberalism and market fundamentalism encouraged the deregulation of businesses, the retrenchment of state benefits, and the privatization of services and resources. Thus, along with growing wealth we've seen growing economic inequality, with the increasing precarity of vast numbers of workers with fewer benefits now facing a great deal of anxiety. An essential part of global political economy has been the various aspects of advanced technologies, not least of which have been technologies of digital communication, which are now an essential part of contemporary commerce. Mass media and/or social media provide vast amounts of information—but much of that is misinformation that appeals to selected targets. Indeed, the Internet has created a variety of 'virtual public spheres' that have enabled a plurality of 'internetworked social movements,' both left and right, in response to these adversities (Langman, 2005).

3.2 Kulturkampf

Globalization has widely diffused cosmopolitanism values that are quite often socially progressive, but, conjoined with the economic factors noted, have engendered a number of economic and/or cultural hardships, if not assaults, prompting a variety of authoritarian populisms and reactionary nationalisms. Thus, the globalized 'culture industries' enabled the diffusion of cosmopolitan consumer tastes in music, fashion, and cuisine, as well as more liberal notions of sexuality across barriers of nation, time, space, culture, and language, which for many, especially younger generations, have *encouraged celebrations of difference, openness to a variety of ideas, pluralities of cultural tastes, and perhaps most important, greater toleration for diverse peoples, cultures, and values*. The underlying economic, political, and cultural aspects of globalization disposed the fundamental opposition between urban cosmopolitan and more rural, political mobilizations. Cosmopolitanism typically includes secularism, racial, ethnic, and gender equality, sexual freedom (itself dependent upon women's agency and rights to control their own bodies), and toleration for various aspects of LGBTQ (lesbian, gay, bisexual, transgender, or queer). Thus we have seen a growing politically based *Kulturkampf* fought on the terrains of race, class, gender, religion, and/or ethnicity, and so on. Ergo, explosions of virulent authoritarian populisms mobilize the more traditional, more rural, and often less-educated populations, who are impelled by a deep-seated *ressentiment* of practices and policies that have given them few economic benefits, and who feel that cosmopolitan, educated elites have challenged and undermined their cultures and values; thus certain groups embrace cosmopolitanism while others embrace various reactionary authoritarian positions.

4 Character and Social Change

The earliest attempts to explain the relationship between character and support for reactionary politics began with Frankfurt School studies of a sadomasochistic, authoritarian character type, with a rigid, punitive, superego emotionally disposed to submit to authority, dominate subordinates, and project his/her aggression and anger toward outgroups. At times of crises, such character types were predisposed to support authoritarian, indeed fascist mobilizations with leaders like Hitler or Mussolini (Adorno et al, 1950). Current neuroscience has similarly shown that less-educated, more culturally isolated, more homogeneous rural people tend to be less critical and more likely to embrace hierarchical, authoritarian relationships, submit to authority, and domination of subordinates. Furthermore, being more fearful, they are likely to project aggression to outsiders and/or non-conformists; they are also cognitively rigid, dogmatic, uncritical, intolerant of ambiguity, disdain novelty, and they are susceptible to mass media, especially partisan social media. There are many reasons why people internalize and/or develop values and political agendas, namely early socialization, social class and kinds of education, rural–urban environments, and so on. *To understand the dialectic of populism and cosmopolitanism, we need to consider character—psychodynamically understood as a constellation of conscious and underlying unconscious thoughts, feelings, and desires that provide the underlying motivational and normative bases for thoughts, feelings, and actions.* Typical patterns of socialized character mediate between the larger political economy, social contexts, and individual dispositions. To paraphrase Weber, character acts as the switchman on the tracks of history.

The adverse economic consequences of global capitalism, liberal democracy, urbanism, mass migrations, secularism, and the growing embrace of cosmopolitanism *have been anathema to the values and identities of many traditional groups, whose very identities and values—that have here heretofore provided them with meaning, dignity, status, power, privilege, and respect—have been challenged and undermined.* The result has been called 'extinction anxiety.' The fear of death is one of the most powerful human motives (Becker, 1973). Like caged animals facing existential threats, they violently seek to defend their very selves, cultures, and identities through social or political mobilizations and a willingness to use violence to fight whomever or whatever they regard as immoral, unnatural, and, indeed, evils that must be eradicated by whatever means are necessary. The expansion of democratic political rights has enabled a revolt of (right-wing) masses defending their identities, values, and/or lifestyles. Thus we have witnessed economic and cultural opposition in which various right-wing authoritarian populisms and ethno-religious nationalisms promise to restore the privileged identities of glorious past that never was.[1]

For such groups, factors of class position, location, character structure, and/or generation and reactions to economic uncertainty that are intertwined with cosmopolitan assaults upon their identities lead to fear, anxiety, anger, and a *ressentiment* toward blameworthy elites and aggression toward various different racial, ethnic, or religious groups seen as despicable interlopers—'enemies of the people.'

For Nietzsche (2006), *ressentiment* had a specific meaning, not simply disdaining or not liking something or someone, *but an intense visceral loathing and disgust toward the elites and the desire for revenge.* To summarize and

---

1 See Chapter 23 in this volume.

simplify, the conquerors of Israel—once powerful warriors—were themselves later conquered by Roman warriors, who personified and celebrated wealth, power, and free sexuality. The now subjugated Jewish priestly class—poor, powerless, and ascetic—then embraced a 'herd mentality' of subjugation that made a virtue of necessity, as they saw themselves as 'morally superior' to the wealthy, powerful, and hedonist Romans. This compensatory *ressentiment* provided an alternative 'status,' an elevated 'moral superiority' rooted in a desire for revenge and in a sense of envy responsible for the sadistic cruelty and denigration of others as compensatory forms of self-esteem. *Ressentiment* is intertwined with a desire to have that which is disdained; repressed feelings and desires generate certain values that might be understood as 'reaction formations.'

> Ressentiment is a self-poisoning of the mind which is caused by the systematic repression of certain emotions and affects. that leads to the constant tendency to indulge in certain kinds of value delusions and corresponding value judgments. The emotions and affects primarily concerned are revenge, hatred, malice, envy, the impulse to detract, and spite.
> SCHELER, 1972 45

> *Ressentiment* is a state of repressed feeling and desire which becomes generative of values. The condition of *ressentiment* is complex both in its internal structure and in its relations to various dimensions of human existence. While it infects the heart of the individual, it is rooted in our relatedness with others. On the one hand, *ressentiment* is a dark, personal secret, which most of us would never reveal to others even if we could acknowledge it ourselves. On the other hand, *ressentiment* has an undeniably public face. It can be creative of social practices, mores, and fashions; of scholarly attitudes, academic policies, and educational initiatives; of political ideologies, institutions, and revolutions; of forms of religiosity and ascetic practices. ... The account of the conflict between the Roman warrior class and the Jewish priestly class is reminiscent of Hegel's master/slave dialectic and prefigures Freud's use of mythological models of conflict. Scheler's phenomenological approach to *ressentiment* aims at an understanding of the condition as a whole and in its constitutive elements. Scheler was concerned with grounding an a priori axiological ethics through a phenomenological typology of the field of affectivity. The Jewish priests did not simply resign themselves in humility to their inferior social position. They had a deep sense of self-esteem and pride, and this fueled a simmering rage at their situation and hatred

toward their conquerors. An account of the heart would not be complete without an investigation of the corrosive condition of *ressentiment.*
MORELLI, 1998; original emphasis

This *ressentiment* fuels reactionary populisms' blame and wrath toward progressive, cosmopolitan politics and leaders; populists seek revenge, indeed sadistic punishment, of blameworthy elites and subaltern interlopers. Populism is a reaction to the demise of heretofore privileged identities, thus inspiring anger, vitriol, and disdain toward 'establishment' elites and or cosmopolitan values. The desire for revenge provides compensatory self-esteem for various (typically more rural/ex-urban, less-educated) populations who feel they are being 'left behind' and are losing their 'country' and formerly privileged 'esteemed' identities based on race, gender, and/or religion now facing challenges. Cosmopolitan values of universalism, equality, inclusion, and tolerance for difference are cast as evils. Reactionary politics defends and celebrates identities that provided 'superiority' and economic status; 'extinction anxieties' become transformed into compensatory forms of punitive aggression toward 'enemies' while providing new forms of solidarity based on common hatreds. Nietzsche strongly disdained equality and democracy, as especially evident in socialism and anarchism, which he saw as rooted in the spirit of revenge and hatred of the powerful, typical of subordinated slaves thwarted in their 'will to power.' Authoritarian populisms can be seen as 'slave revolts' that would displace the corrupt, weak elites with the strong, powerful, and superior identities of the 'real people.' *Ressentiment*—the hatred of the powerless—is an entirely negative sentiment, rejecting what is life-affirming, disdaining what is different, what is 'outside' or 'other.' It is, of course, ironic that authoritarianism populism in fact sustains a herd mentality that disdains expressions of nonconformity and individuality. But as Nietzsche foretold, nothing consumes a man more quickly than the passion of *ressentiment.*

4.1 *Cosmopolitanism and Character*
But there are also character structures that are disposed to empathy, toleration, inclusion of all people as equal humans, that valorize freedom, that support democratic movements and/or leaders. Given far less attention than the studies of authoritarian supporters of right-wing populisms, there is a great deal of evidence to suggest that the cosmopolitan, typically democratic, character is the diametrical opposite of the authoritarian. It is more egalitarian, inclusive, tolerant of diversity, less likely to be hostile, more likely to be nurturant, empathic, open-minded, and seek novelty. Why? Although a great deal of research has addressed this question, one answer can be found in the analysis

of socialization and politics by Lakoff (2008, 2011). Early family life influences later political orientations' resting notions of morality. The values, role models, and child-rearing practices of one's family may vary between 'nurturant parenting' that encourages empathy, curiosity, creative self-fulfillment, compassion, and empathy, versus the 'strict-father' orientation, instilling the necessity for toughness and independence in order to survive in a tough, competitive, and dangerous world. This latter fosters an intolerance, if not a punitive orientation, to those who appear to be weak and/or dependent. Such 'producerism' is an essential part of populisms in which the 'good and decent people' are the 'hard workers' who take care of themselves and their families while 'outsiders' are weak, dependent parasites, if not criminals. Conversely, the 'nurturant-parent' orientation fosters compassion, caring, and sharing, especially toward the poor, weak, old, and unfortunate.

Socialization styles become reflected in political orientations: Should governments be oriented toward securing equality, inclusion, and care for the poor and unfortunate, or should they stress political and/or economic hierarchy and power? As Lakoff (2011) has suggested, political values are not simply rational calculations of benefits and losses, but reflect deeper emotional dispositions. In his words, the most important aspect of the different socialization styles is empathy:

> Empathy is at the heart of progressive thought. It is the capacity to put oneself in the shoes of others—not just individuals, but whole categories of people: one's countrymen, those in other countries, other living beings, especially those who are in some way oppressed, threatened, or harmed. Empathy is the capacity to care, to feel what others feel, to understand what others are facing and what their lives are like. Empathy extends well beyond feeling to understanding, and it extends beyond individuals to groups, communities, peoples, even species. Empathy is at the heart of real rationality, because it goes to the heart of our values, which are the basis of our sense of justice. Progressives care about others as well as themselves. They have a moral obligation to act on their empathy—a social responsibility in addition to personal responsibility, a responsibility to make the world better by making themselves better. This leads to a view of a government that cares about its citizens and has a moral obligation to protect and empower them. Protection includes worker, consumer, and environmental protection as well as safety nets and health care. ... No one can earn anything at all in this country without protection and empowerment by the government. All progressive legislation is made on this basis.
> LAKOFF, 2011

Perhaps equally important, ideologies depend on normalizing power while restricting contradictory information, barring arguments, facts, evidence, and data that might undermine hegemonic ideologies. Insofar as an ideology is an essential part of one's identity, people use motivated reasoning to actively select confirmations or ward off challenges to their beliefs. Ideologies provide a variety of gratifications, not the least of which is to minimize anxiety by organizing reality and providing self-esteem and a sense of meaning to one's life.

4.2 *Ideology*

For Engels and Marx, the move from 'primitive communism,' hunting and gathering societies marked by caring, sharing, and the equality of all, to the personal ownership of property, horticulture and/or pastoralism, marked the decline of the status of women. A few millennia later, with the rise of civilizations, with literacy and priestly classes, came religious ideologies that privileged, if not sacralized the leadership, and differentiated the 'good and righteous' believers of the society from the evil, infidel others. With modern capitalism, alienated wage labor thwarted human agency, fragmented society, and left workers devoid of recognition, without dignity, ergo with truncated selfhood, estranged from 'species being'—the universality of humanity as aware of itself, as creative, social, and worthy of dignity:

> Man is a species-being, not only because he practically and theoretically makes the species—both his own and those of other things—his object, but also—and this is simply another way of saying the same thing—because he looks upon himself as the present, living species, because he looks upon himself as a universal and therefore free being.
>
>   MARX, 1978: 75

Marx's critical understanding of alienation as estrangement and objectification based on private property/wage labor, dehumanized workers, rendered them powerless, isolated and thwarted in their human potentials for creative self-realization and dignity. Such suppression of human fulfillment led Marx to see capitalist political economy as a negative ontology: although the social world subsists through and rests on human social practice, the human being obtains a mere character-mask of social objectivity. This understanding also contains the material basis for the emancipatory critique that all social relations have to be overthrown where humans exist as degraded, exploited, debased, forsaken, and enslaved beings. Such a society is not worthy of Man. It is a society without human dignity (Bonefeld, 2005).

To maintain their political-economic power, ruling classes controlled values and ideologies, hegemonic ideologies provided justifications for the 'superiority of capital,' its leaders, and its promises of wealth, as well as compensatory forms of 'dignity' based on gender, religion, and eventually race. Not only did these statuses secure hegemonic functions, but they provided material consequences as well. Women could be paid lower wages and nothing for the domestic work of reproduction. Racial/ethnic differences within segments of the working classes played each against one another rather than uniting to oppose the wealthy elite. Prayer was not just the wail of the oppressed, and religion an opiate of the people that promised better in the hereafter for those who submitted to authority, but provided elites with justifications for wars and imperialism, bringing the Christian God and civilization to the heathens. Finally, as noted, the bourgeoisie, extolling Reason, rendered capitalism the most 'reasonable' form of political economy, beneficial to all, especially when compared to the slave-based civilizations of antiquity or the general serfdom of feudalism.

For Marx, with freedom, agency, and universal recognition of the fundamental humanity of all, came the realization of human beings as 'species beings,' people could/should attain *universal* dignity, not tied to a particular nation, ethnicity, race, gender, or social class. *As noted, the UN call for universal human dignity is clearly apparent in a variety of cosmopolitan lifestyles, values, and identities, as well as being the implicit goal of a variety of progressive social movements—the very movements so despised and loathed by authoritarian populisms.* Given the critical theoretical traditions of the Marxist *Ideologiekritik*, Frankfurt School critiques of rationality and character, together with the recent work of social scientists like Lakoff (2008), Tompkins (1962), or Westin (2007), inform thinking about how different patterns of emotions and subjectivity undergird the polarity between humanistic versus authoritarian character that is reflected in the dialectic among cosmopolitan and populist identities, ideologies, and political agendas.

5 Conclusion: Mad Max or a Better World?

As Marx suggested, changing economic systems and changing class dynamics required discarding 'troublesome' class relationships and ideologies, to which we would add, necessitating changes in character and identity as well. Just as modernity replaced feudalism, we are again in a period of changing political economies, cultures, and identities that are moving from fixed and hierarchical, inflexible and inegalitarian notions of culture and identity to more flexible, pluralistic notions of selfhood disposed toward a more egalitarian cosmopolitan society (Langman, 2017). We are now in a transitional moment in which the dialectic of cosmopolitanism and populism is yet to unfold. For Durkheim, this is a period of anomie, normlessness, when old values and identities are no longer adaptive while new values and identities have not yet been established.[2] In the USA, Poland, or Turkey, the hinterlands are more religious, more nativist, xenophobic, and intolerant, and less open to change; they are thus more likely to support those authoritarian populist leaders, parties, and movements that promise to preserve traditional values and the heretofore privileged identities of 'the true people,' and arrest, if not reverse, the *inexorable* cosmopolitan social and cultural changes contesting these identities' values and lifestyles. For Gramsci, the period between the death of one society and birth of another was an 'interregnum,' a time marked by morbid symptoms, as is clearly evident in the explosions of authoritarian populisms, reactionary ethno-religious nationalisms, right-wing political agendas, and support for dictators who claim to not simply thwart social change but restore a desirable 'lost society.' The mobilizations of various authoritarian, reactionary movements, replete with various expressions of anger, bullying, violence, aggression, and punitive sadomasochism, shade into the love of death and destruction that Erich Fromm (1967) called 'necrophilia'—the reaction to thwarted creative self-realization that can be seen as the morbid symptoms of a transitionary period.

For cosmopolitans, the contemporary world looks fairly bleak, but even during the darkest moments of fascism, genocide, and the annihilation of cities, some of the Frankfurt School scholars, Jews who might have perished in Auschwitz had they not gone into exile, never forsook their messianic Utopianism. The contemporary world is in a period of transition, an interregnum, but at the same time, we do not yet have a vision of an alternative to the present. The promises of neoliberal capitalism have proven empty, much as the state capitalism of the USSSR that called itself 'communism.' What then does the future hold? While mass media provides distracting one-dimensional infotainment labeled news, *less noted is how younger generations are spearheading a more progressive, cosmopolitan world.*[3] *Thus, we see number of rapidly changing aspects of contemporary cultures in which traditional values, identities, and lifestyles have been discarded by many people, especially younger generations, who embrace the cosmopolitan values of inclusion, tolerance, freedom, democracy, and equality.*

---

2   See Chapter 20 in this volume.
3   See Chapter 19 in this volume.

While the progressive movements of the early 21st century may seemed to have disappeared, this is not in fact the case. In the face of growing populisms, heretofore submerged networks have flourished and become more politically engaged. Consider only the impact of young progressive cosmopolitans supporting Bernie Sanders or Jeremy Corbyn, feminist movements like Me Too, inclusionary movements like Black Lives Matter (BLM), or the environmentalist Extinction Revolution. Or note youth movements in Hong Kong, Chile, Lebanon, Will they succeed? Or will the reactionary nationalist/authoritarian populist movements lead to civil wars, and/or make national wars apocalyptic while climate change renders vast devastation inevitable? However, just as these populisms were reactions to cosmopolitanism, so too can the growing cosmopolitanism of the youth relegate authoritarian populisms to the dustbins of history. Let us hope so.

References

Adorno, T., E. Frenkel-Brunswik, D. Levinson, and N. J. Sanford. 1950. *The Authoritarian Personality*. New York: Harper & Row.

Anderson, B. 1963. *Imagined Communities*. London: Verso.

Appiah, A. 2007. *Cosmopolitanism: Ethics in a World of Ethics in a World of Strangers*. New York: W. W. Norton & Co.

Becker, E. 1973. *The Denial of Death*. New York: Simon and Schuster.

Bonefeld, W. 2005. 'Social Form, Critique and Human Dignity.' Libcom.org, July 31, https://libcom.org/library/social-form-critique-and-human-dignity.

Calhoun, C. 1999. *Nationalism*. Minneapolis: University of Minnesota Press.

Finchelstein, F. 2017. *From Fascism to Populism in History*. Berkeley: University of California Press.

Fromm, E. 1967. *The Anatomy of Human Destructiveness*. New York: Holt, Rinehart and Winston.

Fukuyama, F. 1992. *The End of History and the Last Man*. New York: Free Press.

Habermas, J. 1962. *The Structural Transformation of the Public Sphere*. Cambridge, MA: MIT Press.

Habermas, J. 1975. *Legitimation Crisis*. Boston, MA: Beacon Press.

Hochschild, A. 2017. *Strangers in their Own Land: Anger and Mourning on the American Right*. New York: New Press.

Kazin, M. 1995. *The Populist Persuasion*. New York: Basic Books.

Lakoff, G. 2008. *Moral Politics: How Liberals and Conservatives Think*. New York: Viking Press.

Lakoff, G. 2011. 'Empathy, Sotomayor, and Democracy: The Conservative Stealth Strategy.' *Huffpost,* https://www.huffpost.com/entry/empathy-sotomayor-and-democracy (accessed June 18, 2019).

Langman, L. 2005. 'From Virtual Public Spheres to Global Justice: A Critical Theory of Internetworked Social Movements.' *Sociological Theory* 23 (1): 42–74.

Langman, L. 2017. 'After Marcuse.' *Radical Philosophy Review* 20 (1): 75–105.

Langman, L., T. Benski, I. Perugorría, and B. Tejerina (eds.). 2013. 'From Indignation to Occupation: A New Wave of Global Mobilization.' *Current Sociology* 61 (4): 377–392.

Langman, L. and G. Lundskow. 2016. *God, Guns, Gold and Glory.* Leiden; Boston, MA: Brill.

Marshall, T. H. 1950. *Citizenship and Social Class and Other Essays.* Cambridge, UK: Cambridge University Press.

Marx, K. 1976. *Collected Works,* vol. 3: *Introduction to A Contribution to the Critique of Hegel's Philosophy of Right.* New York.

Marx, K. 1978. 'The Economic and Philosophical Manuscripts of 1844.' In *The Marx–Engels Reader,* edited by R. C. Tucker. New York: W. W. Norton & Co.

Morelli, E. M. 1998. '*Ressentiment* and Rationality.' Paper given at the Twentieth World Congress of Philosophy, Boston, MA, August 10–15, https://www.bu.edu/wcp/Papers/Anth/AnthMore.htm.

Mueller, J. W. 2016. *What is Populism?* Philadelphia: University of Pennsylvania Press.

Nietzsche, F. 2006. *The Genealogy of Morals.* Cambridge, UK: Cambridge University Press.

Sassen, S. 2012. *Cities in the World Economy.* Thousand Oaks, CA: Pine Forge Press.

Scheler, M. 1972. *Ressentiment.* New York: Schocken.

Schmitt, C. 2007 [1932]. *The Concept of the Political.* Chicago: University of Chicago Press.

Tompkins, S. 1962. *Affect Imagery and Consciousness.* New York: Springer.

Westin, Drew. 2007. *The Political Brain.* New York: Public Affairs, Perseus Group.

CHAPTER 25

Terrorism and Counterterrorism as Counter-cosmopolitanism

Clive Walker

1   Introduction

The concept of cosmopolitanism remains not just salient to contemporary debates about terrorism but might even be claimed to be of growing importance because of the post-1945 'New World Order' based on human rights discourse.[1] Cosmopolitanism retains enduring value through its normative emphasis on universal human value 'beyond ... the ties of kith and kin' (Appiah, 2006: xv), whether derived from family, local, or even national affiliation (Nussbaum, 1997: 9). Its institutional implications also promulgate the ideal of a shared community, as reflected in the emergence of post-1945 federations of nations, such as the United Nations (UN) and Council of Europe (COE).

Yet can these generous precepts of cosmopolitanism hold fast in the face of contemporary terrorism, especially after 9/11? Terrorism brings double trouble. One set of problems arises through terrorism itself, which often denies shared and equal worth and instead demands superiority or at least distinctiveness and separation by reference to nationality, culture, or religion. For instance, the title of the political wing of 20th-century Irish republicanism, Sinn Féin (alongside its slogan, *Sinn Féin Amháin*), tellingly translates as 'Ourselves' (and 'Ourselves Alone').[2] The second set of problems arises through the impacts, sometimes intended, sometimes unforeseen or unwanted, of counterterrorism. Thus, states are motivated to curtail cosmopolitan comity by adopting exceptionalism in foreign affairs, such as the US withdrawal from the International Criminal Court (ICC) (Pash, 2007; Ralph, 2011) and then from the 'hypocritical and self-serving' Human Rights Council,[3] and also irreconcilable

---

[1] See Anderson-Gold (2001); Tan (2004); Benhabib (2006); Appiah (2006); Fine (2007); Douzinas (2007).
[2] See Laffan (1999: 20). A film of the same name was banned in Northern Ireland in 1936: Hill (2010: 317).
[3] Secretary of State Michael R. Pompeo, https://www.state.gov/remarks-on-the-un-human-rights-council/, June 19, 2018.

forms of illiberal nationalism at home,[4] now compounded by the politics of populism (Ingram, 2017).

Despite this unpromising landscape, a 'weak' and 'moderate' version of cosmopolitanism (Tan, 2004: 10) will be applied in this chapter. The version is 'weak' in that it is not claimed that cosmopolitanism equates to wholly equal treatment without borders, but it does demand an equation of treatment at a sufficient level of enjoyment which satisfies international standards of treatment. The version is 'moderate' since it is not claimed that cosmopolitanism is the sole normative value of relevance. For present purposes, the core of the applicable morality within cosmopolitanism will remain the universality of human rights. However, the point of this chapter's regard for cosmopolitanism beyond human rights doctrine is to draw out the force of its restraint upon both political violence and state-centric security to demand mutual respect within and beyond jurisdictional boundaries. Another helpful feature of cosmopolitanism is to recognize that solidarity demands more than negative respect for universal rights, though allied agendas including mobilizing shared values (such as citizenship) and collective 'human security' transcend the scope of this chapter.[5]

The plan of the chapter will involve consideration of terrorism as contrary to cosmopolitanism and then the assessment of counterterrorism. It is not implied that both aspects are to be equated either in normative or practical terms. The errors of states must not to be endorsed or ignored, but those states labelled as liberal democracies can lay claim to underlying justifications and resources (including legislation and formal courts and inquiries) which are unavailable to, or even rejected by, non-state terrorist groups. Of course, not all states can conceivably be depicted as liberal democracies, and state terrorism has resulted in far more damage to cosmopolitanism than all revolutionary terrorism in history (Conquest, 2007). It is also intended to focus mainly on examples from within the United Kingdom. That focus may be justified by the country's prominent counterterrorism strategy and infrastructure (including laws), but at the same time an expressed official commitment to 'put respect for human rights at the centre of our response to the terrorist threat ...' (Cabinet Office, 2009: 5). Whether this mature polity can keep this promise provides

---

4 An illustration might be the exclusion from the USA of Muslims from selected countries: US Executive Order 13780 Protecting the nation from foreign terrorist entry into the United States; *Trump v International Refugee Assistance Project*, US Supreme Court, 582 US _ (2017), December 4, 2017.

5 See UN Commission on Human Security (2003); Annan (2005); MacFarlane (2007); Kaldor (2007); Tadjbakhsh and Chenoy (2007); Zwitter (2010).

a good test for the viability of cosmopolitanism in the context of counterterrorism. Ultimately, it must be asked whether terrorism and counterterrorism are inevitably forces of counter-cosmopolitanism or can reconciliation with high ideals be secured?

2   Terrorism as Counter-cosmopolitanism

The proposition that all terrorism represents counter-cosmopolitanism may be more readily resolved than the case of counterterrorism. Terrorism can be revolutionary, counterrevolutionary, sub-revolutionary, or statist (Walker, 2011b: ch. 1). The emphasis here will be on revolutionary terrorism. Revolutionary terrorism arises where a movement seeks to implement a change which can be counted as 'revolutionary'—a transformation in state allegiance or in fundamental constitutional arrangements. This tactic of terrorism may be adopted as an end in itself, for example, by anarchists or nihilists, but is more frequently undertaken as a tactic emanating from conditions of endemic political and military weakness. There are two contexts in which the weak commonly resort to revolutionary terrorism: as part of a campaign for ethnic separation or within independent states to assert political, cultural, or religious transformation (Wilkinson, 2011: ch. 1). Within the latter category, jihadi movements like Al-Qa'ida have been depicted as 'counter-cosmopolitans' by Appiah (2006: 143). As already argued, the ideology of terrorists often denies pluralist values, and their actions consist too often of brutal and catastrophic attacks in apparent denial of the shared humanity of their victims.

One can readily find indices of the detriments of counter-cosmopolitanism on human welfare caused by terrorism. An overall picture is provided by the Global Terrorism Database (GTD), which records information on terrorist events around the world from 1970 to 2017,[6] comprising over 180,000 terrorist attacks and involving 348,759 deaths. Reservations about the accuracy of the data returns from some countries and especially about the chosen boundaries of what counts as terrorism should be kept in mind.[7] Nevertheless, the scale

---

6   See https://www.start.umd.edu/gtd/.
7   According to the Global Terrorism Database (2019: 10–11), *Codebook: Inclusion Criteria and Variables*, a terrorist attack is defined as follows: 'The incident must be intentional—the result of a conscious calculation on the part of a perpetrator. The incident must entail some level of violence or immediate threat of violence—including property violence, as well as violence against people. The perpetrators of the incidents must be sub-national actors. The database does not include acts of state terrorism. In addition, at least two of the following three criteria must be present for an incident to be included in the GTD: Criterion 1: The act

and apparently indiscriminate nature of the imposed suffering, core characteristics of terrorism in pursuance of the generation of fear, cannot be doubted. Furthermore, any shortcomings in the GTD can be tested by studying more confined instances of terrorism. For example, since 1970, 3,395 deaths resulted from terrorism in the UK (mainly in Northern Ireland), the highest total in Western Europe (McKittrick et al., 1999; Kirk, 2017). Injuries, property damage, the costs of security measures, and ongoing political instability and communal divisions must also be taken into account,[8] though some would argue that Western societies have overreacted (Furedi, 2007; Wolfendale, 2007; Mueller and Stewart, 2014). The transgressions of the Islamic State in Iraq and the Levant (ISIL, also known as Da'esh) are even starker and may be indicated by the UN Security Council Resolution (UNSCR) 2379 of September 21, 2017 (setting up an investigation team)[9] in which ISIL is censured

> [as] a global threat to international peace and security through its terrorist acts, its violent extremist ideology, its continued gross, systematic and widespread attacks directed against civilians, its violations of international humanitarian law and abuses of human rights, particularly those committed against women and children, and including those motivated by religious or ethnic grounds, and its recruitment and training of foreign terrorist fighters …

---

must be aimed at attaining a political, economic, religious, or social goal. In terms of economic goals, the exclusive pursuit of profit does not satisfy this criterion. It must involve the pursuit of more profound, systemic economic change. Criterion 2: There must be evidence of an intention to coerce, intimidate, or convey some other message to a larger audience (or audiences) than the immediate victims. It is the act taken as a totality that is considered, irrespective if every individual involved in carrying out the act was aware of this intention. As long as any of the planners or decision-makers behind the attack intended to coerce, intimidate or publicize, the intentionality criterion is met. Criterion 3: The action must be outside the context of legitimate warfare activities. That is, the act must be outside the parameters permitted by international humanitarian law, insofar as it targets non-combatants.'

8   Those costs are ongoing in Northern Ireland, with political instability and thousands of unresolved killings: Northern Ireland Office (2018).
9   See also Sixth Report of the Secretary-General on the threat posed by ISIL (Da'esh) to international peace and security and the range of United Nations efforts in support of Member States in countering the threat, New York: S/2018/80, January 31, 2018; Letter dated July 16, 2018 from the Chair of the Security Council Committee pursuant to resolutions 1267 (1999), 1989 (2011) and 2253 (2015) concerning Islamic State in Iraq and the Levant (Da'esh), Al-Qaida and associated individuals, groups, undertakings and entities addressed to the President of the Security Council New York: S/2018/705, 27 July 2018; see Vlasic and DeSousa (2018) and El-Masri (2018: 1047).

... [for] the commission of acts ... involving murder, kidnapping, hostage-taking, suicide bombings, enslavement, sale into or otherwise forced marriage, trafficking in persons, rape, sexual slavery and other forms of sexual violence, recruitment and use of children, attacks on critical infrastructure, as well as its destruction of cultural heritage, including archaeological sites, and trafficking of cultural property,

... [for] war crimes, crimes against humanity or genocide ...

Deaths in Iraq and Syria caused by ISIL are estimated to amount to many thousands.[10]

In more abstract terms, the UN Secretary-General reported in 2018 on the effects of terrorism on the enjoyment of human rights,[11] noting that terrorism has been successively condemned by the UN General Assembly, ranging from Resolution 46/51 of December 9, 1991 to Resolution 246/72 of January 18, 2018. While recognizing also the impacts of state measures against terrorism (discussed later in the chapter), the document accepts that 'It is precisely to protect the rights to life, liberty and security of person that States have a duty to take effective measures to prevent and counter terrorism.'[12] In this way, populations controlled by terrorist groups, such as ISIL, suffer arbitrary detentions and 'a complete disregard for due process.'[13] The impacts of terrorism on economic, social, and cultural rights and the right to development are also highly negative because of the destruction of critical infrastructure and the exacerbation of unrest, insecurity, inequalities, poverty, poor governance, and decline.[14] Some terrorist groups directly attack human rights that are critical to development, such as Boko Haram's campaign against the right to education, especially of girls, as well as attacks on health and cultural assets.[15] Terrorist groups are also depicted as discriminatory by 'destroying the diverse fabric of communities, including through the systematic and intentional targeting of religious communities, women, children, political activists, journalists, human rights defenders and members of the lesbian, gay, bisexual, transgender and intersex community, who have been victims of abductions, torture and killings.'[16]

---

10   See https://www.iraqbodycount.org/; http://www.syriahr.com/en/; BBC (2018).
11   New York: A/73/347, August 28, 2018.
12   Ibid., para. 5.
13   Ibid., para. 9.
14   Ibid., para. 22.
15   Ibid., para. 23.
16   Ibid.

Can any variant of terrorism be redeemed from this stark indictment as counter-cosmopolitan? The commonplace mantra, indicating moral shading, is that 'one man's terrorist is another man's freedom fighter' (Ganor, 2002: 287). In that vein, the attempt has been made in 'just war' theory to stake a justification for terrorism in some circumstances or in some formats.[17] Perhaps the most promising claim in international law is where political violence is used within armed conflict, especially to secure the right of self-determination under Article 1 of the UN Charter and within 'armed conflicts in which peoples are fighting against colonial domination and alien occupation and against racist regimes in the exercise of their right of self-determination' under Article 1(4) of Protocol I Additional to the Geneva Conventions of August 12, 1949, and relating to the Protection of Victims of International Armed Conflicts.[18] Potential claims under these provisions by terrorist groups, such as the IRA,[19] and also Al-Qa'ida,[20] which often claim to be fighting against foreign occupation and other forms of unbearable oppression, will next be examined.

In reality, formidable obstacles face any group which claims the foregoing conflict privileges and immunities. First, some notable states (Israel, Iran, Pakistan, India, Turkey, and the USA) have not ratified Protocol I. Second, the claim to be fighting colonial or racist regimes may now be outdated. Though resistance to foreign invaders could still apply in, for example, Afghanistan, Iraq, and Syria, the essence of many conflicts is now to displace sovereign regimes. Third, 'armed conflict' is considered to require fighting at sustained and severe levels (Fleck, 2013: ch. 2), whereas most states depict their internal instabilities as falling below that level and therefore treat armed opponents, including those depicted as 'terrorists,' as criminals rather than combatants.[21]

---

17 See Honderich (2003); Nielsen (2003); Coady (2004: 37); Primoratz (2004); Waldron (2004: 5); Scheffler (2006: 1); Goodin (2006); Steinhoff (2007); Meisels (2008).

18 1125 United Nations Treaty Series (UNTS) 3, 1978. See Wilson (2003); Tilley (2011); Blank (2015).

19 The first public statement of the Provisional IRA, on December 28, 1969, was as follows: 'We declare our allegiance to the 32 county Irish republic, proclaimed at Easter 1916, established by the first Dáil Éireann in 1919, overthrown by forces of arms in 1922 and suppressed to this day by the existing British-imposed six-county and twenty-six-county partition states' (English, 2003: 106).

20 World Islamic Front (1998): 'for over seven years the United States has been occupying the lands of Islam in the holiest of places, the Arabian Peninsula, plundering its riches, dictating to its rulers, humiliating its people, terrorizing its neighbors, and turning its bases in the Peninsula into a spearhead through which to fight the neighboring Muslim peoples.'

21 See *Prosecutor v Limaj, Bala and Musliu* IT-03-66-T, Judgment (November 30, 2005); *Prosecutor v Boskoski and Tarculovski* IT-04-82-T, Trial Chamber Judgment (July 10, 2008); Duffy (2015: ch. 6).

The United Kingdom has followed this approach in Northern Ireland (Walker, 1984), and it is reflected in its domestic law whereby the definition of terrorism allows no exceptions for situations of armed conflict whether at home or abroad.[22] Finally, while the concept of rebellion may be depicted by some as wonderfully cathartic and even heroic, the lived experiences of revolution, whether during *La Terreur* of the French Revolution, the Russian Revolution, or the Algerian War of Independence, involved costs to cosmopolitan values which were substantial, unfairly distributed, and enduring (Trotsky, 1920; Zizek, 2007; Evans, 2012; Wahnicj, 2015). In the light of such experiences, international humanitarian law has taken care not to condone every manner of warfare. Thus, specific techniques of violence, including some which are emblematic of terrorism, such as the bombing of civilians, have become unpardonable wrongs in international law,[23] and in international humanitarian law.[24]

In conclusion, the prospects of delineating any progressive version of terrorism seem bleak. Violence in the mode of terrorism, indiscriminate and disproportionate, can be condemned as unrighteous. This stance can best be sustained in liberal democracies since any grievance harboured by terrorists cannot relate to the fundamental infringement of human rights, otherwise the liberal democracy would cease to be so, and because, for lapses from standards, alternative non-violent pathways are available for political change in ways which respect the humanity of others. So terrorism as 'counter-cosmopolitanism' seems a fair portrayal.

3   Counterterrorism as Counter-cosmopolitanism

Whether state counterterrorism should correspondingly be depicted as 'counter-cosmopolitanism' involves a more complex and nuanced debate. It has already been mentioned that extreme instances of state terrorism are the most severe of all. However, at the other extreme, international law demands rather than proscribes counterterrorism. The events of 9/11 represented a turning point in the global mobilization of sovereign counterterrorism. Before then, international law did specify a range of counterterrorism measures to

---

22 Terrorism Act 2000, s.1. See *R v Gul* [2013] UKSC 64; Walker (2014: ch. 1).
23 International Convention for the Suppression of Terrorist Bombings, adopted by the General Assembly of the United Nations on December 15, 1997, 37 I.L.M. 249.
24 Third Geneva Convention 1949 Art. 119; Fourth Geneva Convention 1949, Art. 33; Protocol I 1977 Art.51; Protocol II 1977 Arts. 4, 13.

be activated. However, beyond specialist sectors such as air transportation,[25] which could be enforced through the economic dominance of Western states rather than through the vapid diplomacy of international institutions, progress had been faltering. A stark indicator is that the UN Convention for the Suppression of the Financing of Terrorism 1999 had attracted just four nation signatories (Botswana, Sri Lanka, the United Kingdom, and Uzbekistan), but they were joined within two years after 9/11 by 128 others.[26] Furthermore, jurisdictions such as Bahrain, Iran, and Saudi Arabia, which still strive to carve out exceptions for 'national liberation movements' associated with Palestine, are subjected to denunciation and the threat of blacklisting by the Financial Action Task Force (FATF).[27]

The proliferation of counterterrorism codes since the events of 9/11 has occurred because those attacks were deemed to demonstrate to the world not only a heightened and to some extent novel risk of terrorism (Neumann, 2009), but also the need for imperative counteraction by all states (Wittes, 2008; Duffy, 2015). That message was promulgated immediately by the UN Security Council, which, by Resolution 1368 of September 12, 2001, 'Calls ... on the international community to redouble their efforts to prevent and suppress terrorist acts including by increase cooperation and full implementation of the relevant international anti-terrorist conventions ...' More concrete demands followed in Resolution 1373 of September 28, 2001 (Szasz, 2002: 901; Becker, 2006: 881; Bianchi, 2006: 881), which requires compliance with international laws against terrorism financing (including the Financing Convention of 1999 and economic sanctions against supporters of the Taliban and Al-Qa'ida),[28] the passage of domestic laws against recruitment and other forms of support, no safe havens, and the establishment of the Counter-Terrorism Committee (CTC) to chivvy national implementation. The international clamour for action has been unrelenting since 2001. Many extra demands have been issued, notably, in 2005, for laws against the incitement and

---

25   Convention on Offences and Certain Other Acts Committed on Board Aircraft 1963; Convention for the Suppression of Unlawful Seizure of Aircraft 1970; Convention for the Suppression of Unlawful Acts against the Safety of Civil Aviation 1971; Protocol for the Suppression of Unlawful Acts at Airports Serving International Civil Aviation 1988; Convention on the Suppression of Unlawful Acts Relating to International Civil Aviation 2010. See Abeyratne (2010).

26   See 2178 UNTS 197.

27   See FATF (2018a: 168; 2018b: 3; 2018c).

28   UNSCR 1267 of October 15, 1999, as amended by UNSCR 1333 of December 19, 2000 and UNSCR 1989 of June 17, 2011.

glorification of terrorism,[29] and in 2014, against the phenomenon of foreign terrorist fighters.[30]

Post-9/11, almost all governments have become willing to demonize those who reject their values (Thobani, 2007) and to proffer for their own security the 'lesser evil' of counterterrorism in order to combat the greater evil of terrorism (Ignatieff, 2004). The counterterrorism world order thus can readily compromise the 'Perpetual Peace' grounded in non-intervention and universal hospitality, as outlined by Kant (1795), and draws closer to an inhospitable 'war all the time' (Walker, 2005). The war rhetoric which arose in the aftermath of 9/11 has now diminished, and counterterrorism is usually distant from any 'state of exception'[31] and nothing like a 'zone of anomie in which all legal determinations are deactivated' (Agamben, 2005: 50). Instead, the official rhetoric, as represented at least by the then UK Foreign Secretary, David Miliband, is that 'We must respond to terrorism by championing the rule of law, not by subordinating it, for it is the cornerstone of the democratic society.'[32] A more ambitious elaboration of the trend back toward human security in counterterrorism is represented by the UN Global Counter Terrorism Strategy of 2006,[33] which, instead of 'total war on terror,' moves toward 'total counterterrorism' by addressing the conditions conducive to the spread of terrorism and state capacity-building, which must be implemented alongside military and policing measures to prevent and combat terrorism. Part IV crucially emphasizes 'Measures to ensure respect for human rights for all and the rule of law as the fundamental basis of the fight against terrorism.'

Whether the applications of counterterrorism match these fine words is debatable, but this promise of protection from naked state power surely reflects cosmopolitanism (Campbell and Connelly, 2006: 339; Marks, S. 2006: 339; Vaughan and Kilcommins, 2008: 13). Certainly, the strong international demand for state action against terrorism is compounded by domestic pressures to respond to terrorism which may result in disproportionate measures (Posner and Vermeule, 2006: 1091; Sunstein, 2007) and further dangers to cosmopolitan values. Mechanisms to temper the negative impacts have tended to take longer

---

29 See UNSCR 1624 of September 14, 2005.
30 See UNSCR 2170 of August 15, 2014 and 2178 of September 24, 2014. See further https://www.securitycouncilreport.org/un-documents/terrorism/.
31 Derogations were made in the UK from 2001 to 2005 and in France from 2015 to 2017. Derogation has also been proposed for external military interventions: Rooney (2016). Some authors see no dangers to cosmopolitanism and call for greater reliance on derogation: Fenwick and Fenwick (2018).
32 *The Guardian*, January 15, 2009: 29.
33 UNGA Res 60/288, 2006.

to install than the constant encouragement of new interferences with human values. For instance, it took until UNSCR 1456 of January 20, 2003 for human rights protection within counterterrorism to be placed firmly on the agenda, while tangible mechanisms of support did not appear until the UN Commission on Human Rights Resolution 2005/80 appointed the Special Rapporteur on the promotion and protection of human rights and fundamental freedoms while countering terrorism.[34] Within the financial sanctions regimes, the Office of the Ombudsperson was not established until UNSCR 1904 of December 17, 2009. and is still confined to the ISIL (Da'esh) and Al-Qa'ida Sanctions Lists (King et al., 2018: chs. 36–37). This hesitant recognition of human rights within counterterrorism has engendered temptations and condonations of dubious state countermeasures at the cost of cosmopolitanism.

Temptations can arise in at least two ways. One is that the public support for repression, in the expectation that the burden will fall upon minorities rather than the majority (Cole, 2005; Guild, 2015), encourages the disregard of fundamental values. As a result, human rights are no longer trump cards in the age of terror, even against torture, irregular detention, and extraordinary rendition.[35] Second, the quantity of international demands for sovereign action has often not been matched with quality in the design of required measures. In particular, no comprehensive international definition of terrorism has been promulgated, affording an opportunity to states to weaponize counterterrorism in order to repress political opponents who thus are branded as terrorists (Saul, 2015).

Condonations arise because many of the hallowed documents designed to protect cosmopolitanism, especially human rights covenants, are riddled with limits which can be exploited within counterterrorism. Taking the European Convention as a prime example, derogation under Article 15 was invoked after 9/11 by the United Kingdom (in 2001) and by France (in 2015) to cover aspects of counterterrorism which infringed Article 5's rights to liberty.[36] Beyond the direct invocation of emergency powers, many specific rights such as privacy (Lennon, 2015: 643), as well as other measures related to asylum, are subject to concessions to protect national security interests (Walker, 2007).

---

34 See https://www.ohchr.org/en/issues/terrorism/pages/srterrorismindex.aspx.
35 Compare Dershowitz (2002); Sands (2006); Senate Select Committee on Intelligence (2014).
36 See for example *Brogan v United Kingdom* App. nos. 11209, 11234, 11266/84, 11386/85, Ser. A 145-B (1988); *Brannigan and McBride v United Kingdom* App. nos. 14553/89, 14554/89, Ser. A 258-B (2001); Walker (2011a); Samaan and Jacobs (2020). Before 9/11, see *Ireland v United Kingdom*, App. no. 5310/71, Ser. A 25 (1978).

As expected, a complex and nuanced debate has emerged around the depiction of counterterrorism as 'counter-cosmopolitanism.' The analysis has noted the frantic enthusiasm in international institutions for the embrace of counterterrorism but has concluded with warnings about damage to human values whereby state security has been treated as a distinct and overriding policy. As a result, the previously cited UN Secretary-General's report on the 'Effects of Terrorism on the Enjoyment of Human Rights,'[37] says more about state abuses of counterterrorism than terrorist abuses. Its warnings to member states relate to torture, due process and fair trial rights, expressive rights, the rights to privacy and freedom of movement and to a nationality, economic, social, and cultural rights and the right to development, and equality and non-discrimination. The list of infractions by state counterterrorism is as grave and potentially longer than the indictment against terrorists.

4   Conclusions

If one adopted an optimistic outlook regarding respect for cosmopolitanism within counterterrorism, one might cling to the prospect that rights gain traction as terrorism and counterterrorism campaigns mature. One might speculate that the factors behind this effect arise from a growing public estimation of threat and an emboldening of the judiciary and legislature by a fuller grasp of facts, including the revelation of executive mistakes made in earliest phases of conflict (Walker, 2012). In the meantime, a balanced and realistic overview should equally highlight the dangers of 'counter-cosmopolitanism,' whether in terrorism or counterterrorism. Key to the insidious threat of the latter is not to depict state security and human security as conflicting considerations.[38] This point is reflected by the UN Secretary-General, who has argued that, 'In accordance with the first and fourth pillars of the Global Counter-Terrorism Strategy, an approach based on human rights and the rule of law is the only way to effectively counter terrorism.'[39] A broader theme along the same lines would emphasize the concept of constitutionalism (see Walker, 2011b: ch. 1), a concept which involves, first, an ongoing need for a rights audit (Marks, 2006), a special role for the courts as the prime deliberative forum for individual protection, 'accountability' which demands information provision, open and

---

37   New York: A/73/347, August 28, 2018.
38   See Eminent Jurists Panel (2009); Amnesty International (2017).
39   'Effects of Terrorism on the Enjoyment of Human Rights.' New York: A/73/347, August 28, 2018, para. 51.

independent debate, and an ability to participate in decision-making, and finally 'constitutional governance.' This latter aspect includes the subjection of governmental action to a lawfulness requirement that terrorism laws 'indicate with reasonable clarity the scope and manner of exercise of the relevant discretion conferred on the public authorities.'[40] Next, the 'constitutional' mode of governance demands respect for meta-norms—tenets of national constitutional law and also international law. Legal and constitutional techniques such as these cannot guarantee protection for cosmopolitan values, but they can trigger debate and challenge which give some hope that the higher ideals and values of cosmopolitanism will prevail over the counter-cosmopolitan clamour of the day created by the immediate wounds of terrorism.

References

Abeyratne, R. 2010. *Aviation Security Law*. Heidelberg: Springer.

Agamben, G. 2005. *The State of Exception*. Chicago: University of Chicago Press.

Amnesty International. 2017. 'Dangerously Disproportionate: The Ever-Expanding National Security State in Europe.' EUR 01/5342/2017, London.

Anderson-Gold, S. 2001. *Cosmopolitanism and Human Rights*. Cardiff: University of Wales Press.

Annan, K. 2005. *In Larger Freedom: Towards Development, Security and Human Rights for All*. New York: UN General Assembly A/59/2005/Add.3.

Appiah, A. K. 2006. *Cosmopolitanism: Ethics in a World of Strangers*. London: Allen Lane.

BBC. 2018. 'Islamic State and the Crisis in Iraq and Syria in Maps.' March 28, https://www.bbc.co.uk/news/world-middle-east-27838034.

Becker, T. 2006. *Terrorism and the State*. London: Bloomsbury.

Benhabib, S. 2006. *Another Cosmopolitanism*. New York: Oxford University Press.

Bianchi, A. 2006. 'Assessing the Effectiveness of the UN Security Council's Anti-Terrorism Measures.' *European Journal of International Law* 17 (5): 881–919.

Blank, L. R. 2015. 'What's in a Word?' In *Routledge Handbook of Law and Terrorism*, edited by G. Lennon and C. Walker, 52–67. Abingdon: Routledge.

Cabinet Office. 2009. 'Pursue, Prevent, Protect, Prepare.' Command Paper 7547. Stationery Office, London.

Campbell, C. and I. Connelly. 2006. 'Making War on Terror?' *Modern Law Review* 26: 935–939.

Coady, C. A. J. 2004. 'Terrorism and Innocence.' *Journal of Ethics* 8 (1): 37–58.

---

40 *Malone v United Kingdom*, App. no. 8691/79, Ser. A 82 (1984) para. 79.

Cole, D. 2005. *Enemy Aliens: Double Standards and Constitutional Freedoms in the War on Terrorism*. New York: New Press.
Conquest, R. 2007. *The Great Terror*. Oxford: Oxford University Press.
Dershowitz, A. 2002. *Why Terrorism Works*. New Haven, CT: Yale University Press.
Douzinas, C. 2007. *Human Rights and Empire*. London: Routledge-Cavendish.
Duffy, H. 2015. *The 'War on Terror' and the Framework of International Law*. Cambridge, UK: Cambridge University Press.
El-Masri, S. 2018. 'Prosecuting ISIS for the Sexual Slavery of the Yazidi Women and Girls.' *International Journal of Human Rights* 22 (8): 1047–1066.
Eminent Jurists Panel. 2009. 'Assessing Damage, Urging Action.' Report of the International Commission of Jurists, Geneva.
English, R. 2003. *Armed Struggle: The History of the IRA*. London: Macmillan.
Evans, M. 2012. *Algeria: France's Undeclared War*. Oxford: Oxford University Press.
FATF (Financial Action Task Force). 2018a. 'Mutual Evaluation Report: Kingdom of Saudi Arabia.' http://www.fatf-gafi.org/publications/mutualevaluations/documents/MER-Saudi-Arabia-2018.html.
FATF (Financial Action Task Force). 2018b. 'Mutual Evaluation Report of the Kingdom of Bahrain.' http://www.fatf-gafi.org/publications/mutualevaluations/documents/MER-Bahrain-2018.html.
FATF (Financial Action Task Force). 2018c. 'High-risk and other monitored jurisdictions Public Statement—October 2018.' http://www.fatf-gafi.org/publications/high-riskandnon-cooperativejurisdictions/documents/public-statement-october-2018.html.
Fenwick, H. and D. Fenwick. 2018. 'The Case for a More Ready Resort to Derogations from the ECHR in the Current "War on Terror."' *European Human Rights Law Review* 4: 303–310.
Fine, R. 2007. *Cosmopolitanism*. London: Routledge.
Fleck, D. 2013. *The Handbook of Humanitarian Law in Armed Conflicts*. Oxford: Oxford University Press.
Furedi, F. 2007. *Invitation to Terror*. London: Continuum.
Ganor, B. 2002. 'Defining Terrorism: Is One Man's Terrorist another Man's Freedom Fighter?' *Police Practice and Research* 3 (4): 287–304.
Global Terrorism Database. 2019, *Codebook: Inclusion Criteria and Variables*.
Goodin, R. 2006. *What's Wrong with Terrorism?* Cambridge, UK: Polity Press.
Guild, E. 2015. 'Aliens and Counter Terrorism.' In *Routledge Handbook of Law and Terrorism*, edited by G. Lennon and C. Walker, 251–265. Abingdon: Routledge.
Hill, J. 2010. '"Purely Sinn Fein Propaganda": The Banning of Ourselves Alone (1936).' *Historical Journal of Film, Radio and Television* 20 (3): 317–333.
Honderich, T. 2003. *After the Terror*. Montreal: McGill-Queen's University Press.
Ignatieff, M. 2004. *The Lesser Evil*. Edinburgh: Edinburgh University Press.

Ingram, J. D. 2017. 'Populism and Cosmopolitanism.' In *The Oxford Handbook of Populism*, edited by C. R. Kaltwasser, P. Taggart, P. O. Espejo, and P. Ostiguy, 644–660. Oxford: Oxford University Press.

Kaldor, M. 2007. *Human Security*. Cambridge, UK: Polity Press.

Kant, I. 1795. *Perpetual Peace: A Philosophical Sketch*. Königsburg: Nicolovius.

King, C., C. Walker, and J. Gurulé (eds.). 2018. *The Palgrave Handbook of Criminal and Terrorism Financing Law*. London: Palgrave Macmillan.

Kirk, A. 2017. 'How many people are killed by terrorist attacks in the UK?' *Daily Telegraph* https://www.telegraph.co.uk/news/0/many-people-killed-terrorist-attacks-uk/, October 17.

Laffan, M. 1999. *The Resurrection of Ireland: The Sinn Féin Party, 1916–1923*. Cambridge, UK: Cambridge University Press.

Lennon, G. 2015. 'Stop and Search Powers in UK Terrorism Investigations.' *International Journal of Human Rights* 20 (5): 634–648.

MacFarlane, S. 2007. *Human Security and the UN*. Bloomington: Indiana University Press.

Marks, J. H. 2006. '9/11 + 3/11 + 7/7 =? What Counts in Counterterrorism?' *Columbia Human Rights Law Review* 37: 559–626.

Marks, S. 2006. 'State Centrism, International Law and the Anxieties of Influence.' *Leiden Journal of International Law* 19 (2): 339–347.

McKittrick, D., C. Thornton, S. Kelters, and B. Feeney. 1999. *Lost Lives*. Edinburgh: Mainstream.

Meisels, T. 2008. *The Trouble with Terror*. Cambridge, UK: Cambridge University Press.

Mueller, J. and M. G. Stewart. 2014. 'Terrorism and Counterterrorism in the US: The Question of Responsible Policy-Making.' *International Journal of Human Rights* 18 (2): 228–240.

Neumann, P. 2009. *Old and New Terrorism*. London: Polity Press.

Nielsen, K. 2003. 'On the Moral Justifiability of Terrorism (State and Otherwise).' *Osgoode Hall Law Journal* 41 (2): 427–444.

Northern Ireland Office. 2018. 'Consultation Paper: Addressing the Legacy of Northern Ireland's Past.' Belfast.

Nussbaum, M. C. 1997. 'Kant and Stoic Cosmopolitanism.' *Journal of Political Philosophy* 5 (1): 1–25.

Pash, M. K. 2007. 'Human Security and Exceptionalism(s).' In *Protecting Human Security in the Post 9/11 World*, edited by G. Shani, M. Sato, and M. K. Pash, 177–182. Basingstoke: Palgrave Macmillan.

Posner, E. A. and A. Vermeule. 2006. 'Emergencies and Democratic Failure.' *Virginia Law Review* 92 (6): 1091–1146.

Primoratz, I. 2004. *Terrorism: The Philosophical Issues*. Basingstoke: Palgrave Macmillan.

Ralph, J. 2011. 'The International Criminal Court and the State of the American Exception.' In *International and Comparative Criminal Justice and Urban Governance*, edited by A. Crawford, 76–85. Cambridge, UK: Cambridge University Press.

Rooney, J. M. 2016. 'Extraterritorial Derogation from the European Convention on Human Rights in the United Kingdom.' *European Human Rights Law Review* 6: 656–663.

Samaan, J. L. and A. Jacobs. 2020. 'Countering Jihadist Terrorism: A Comparative Analysis of French and German Experiences.' *Terrorism and Political Violence*, 32(2): 401-415.

Sands, P. 2006. *Lawless World*. London: Penguin.

Saul, B. 2015. 'Terrorism as a Legal Concept.' In *Routledge Handbook of Law and Terrorism*, edited by G. Lennon and C. Walker, 19–37. Abingdon: Routledge.

Scheffler, S. 2006. 'Is Terrorism Morally Distinctive?' *Journal of Political Philosophy* 14 (1): 1–17.

Senate Select Committee on Intelligence. 2014. 'Committee Study of the Central Intelligence Agency's Detention and Interrogation Program.' SSCI Report, Washington, DC.

Steinhoff, U. 2007. *On the Ethics of War and Terrorism*. New York: Oxford University Press.

Sunstein, C. R. 2007. *Worst-Case Scenarios*. Cambridge, MA: Harvard University Press.

Szasz, P. C. 2002. 'The Security Council Starts Legislating.' *American Journal of International Law* 96 (4): 901–905.

Tadjbakhsh, S. and A. M. Chenoy. 2007. *Human Security: Concepts and Implications*. Abingdon: Routledge.

Tan, K.-C. 2004. *Justice without Borders*. Cambridge, UK: Cambridge University Press.

Thobani, S. 2007. 'Nationality in the Age of Global Terror.' In *Exalted Subjects: Studies in the Making of Race and Nation in Canada*, edited by S. Thobani, 217–247. Toronto: University of Toronto Press.

Tilley, V. (ed.). 2011. *Beyond Occupation: Apartheid, Colonialism and International Law in the Occupied Palestinian Territories*. Cambridge, UK: Pluto Press.

Trotsky, L. 1920. *Terrorism and Communism*. London: G. Allen & Unwin.

UN Commission on Human Security. 2003. *Human Security Now*. New York: Commission on Human Security.

Vaughan, B. and S. Kilcommins. 2008. *Terrorism, Rights and the Rule of Law*. Cullompton: Willan.

Vlasic, M. V. and J. P. DeSousa. 2018. 'The Illicit Antiquities Trade and Terrorism Financing.' In *The Palgrave Handbook of Criminal and Terrorism Financing Law*, edited by C. King C. Walker, and J. Gurulé., 1167–1191. London: Palgrave Macmillan.

Wahnicj, S. 2015. *In Defence of the Terror*. London: Verso.

Waldron, J. 2004. 'Terrorism and the Uses of Terror.' *Journal of Ethics* 8 (1): 5–35.

Walker, C. 1984. 'Irish Republican Prisoners: Political Detainees, Prisoners of War or Common Criminals?' *Irish Jurist* 19: 189–225.

Walker, C. 2005. 'Prisoners of "War All the Time."' *European Human Rights Law Review*: 50–74.

Walker, C. 2007. 'The Treatment of Foreign Terror Suspects.' *Modern Law Review* 70 (3): 427–457.

Walker, C. 2011a. 'Cosmopolitan Liberty in the Age of Terrorism.' In *International and Comparative Criminal Justice and Urban Governance*, edited by A. Crawford, 413–438. Cambridge, UK: Cambridge University Press.

Walker, C. 2011b. *Terrorism and the Law*. Oxford: Oxford University Press.

Walker, C. 2012. 'Counter-Terrorism and Human Rights in the UK.' In *The Ashgate Research Companion to Political Violence*, edited by M. Breen-Smyth, 443–463. Farnham: Ashgate Publishing.

Walker, C. 2014. *The Anti-Terrorism Legislation*. Oxford: Oxford University Press.

Wilkinson, P. 2011. *Terrorism versus Democracy*. Abingdon: Routledge.

Wilson, H. A. 2003. *International Law and the Use of Force by National Liberation Movements*. Oxford: Oxford University Press.

Wittes, B. 2008. *Law and the Long War*. New York: Penguin.

Wolfendale, J. 2007. 'Terrorism, Security and the Threat of Counter Terrorism.' *Studies in Conflict and Terrorism* 30 (1): 75–92.

World Islamic Front. 1998. 'Jihad against Jews and Crusaders.' World Islamic Front Statement, February 23, https://fas.org/irp/world/para/docs/980223-fatwa.htm.

Zizek, S. 2007. *Virtue and Terror*. London: Verso.

Zwitter, A. 2010. *Human Security, Law and the Prevention of Terrorism*. Abingdon: Routledge.

CHAPTER 26

Competition for Global Hegemony

Frédéric Ramel

'I speak … as a fellow citizen of the world' (Obama, 2008). These were the words used by Barack Obama in Berlin in July 2008 during his first presidential campaign. If he explicitly echoed another very well-known assertion, that of President Kennedy 'Ich bin ein Berliner,' Obama seems here a cosmopolitan candidate. This interpretation relies not only on his own life, which is, to a certain extent, cosmopolitan; his father was Kenyan and he spent part of his childhood in Indonesia. He also elaborates his speeches by referring to this cosmopolitan tradition of thought (Hammack, 2010). In fact, his election generated hope not only in the United States but also in the rest of the world. This first black man who accessed to the highest political responsibility of the country embodies a cosmopolitan president. Peoples felt that his presidency would be as beneficial to Americans as to the nationals of other countries. The Nobel Peace Prize he received shortly after his enthronement strengthened such feeling. Indeed, Barack Obama would be a Kantian in the Oval Office (Selzer, 2010).

This episode illustrates the link between hegemony and cosmopolitanism. The two do not seem antithetical. Such a link directly echoes the concept used for the first time in the history of political ideas. In the Peloponnesian War, Thucydides distinguishes between *arkhe* (control and domination) and *hegemonia* (legitimated leadership). While the first is based on instruments of coercion, the second means responsibility. In other words, hegemony differs from an imposed order or force but refers to the protection and recognition of others. The term is used to describe Sparta (and not Athens) by the Corinthians, who complain of being threatened by the Athenians. They call to the Spartans for help and, more fundamentally, ask them to secure their hegemony by protecting their allies. This idea of hegemony is applied at the individual level. For the Stoics, a hegemonic human being is a person responsible for himself. *Hegemonism* may be deformed and in this case, human beings deny themselves, deny others and their existence. The purpose of this chapter is to discuss this thesis and, more specifically, to show the limits of a virtuous link between hegemony (and *a fortiori* hegemonism) on one hand and cosmopolitanism on the other. The competition for hegemony specifically prevents a cosmopolitization of states. But this competition differs from the classic military struggle. We must point out that cosmopolitanisms are not uniform, but have different shades. They nonetheless refer to the same idea that the world relies on a legal or even political unification. In this chapter, I will use the Kantian model as the most important cosmopolitan source.

After having specified the nature of relations between hegemony and cosmopolitanism in the theory of international relations (both scientific and normative), I will analyze a double dimension of this competition in the contemporary context. The first is located on the strategic level, the second has a normative aspect.

1   Hegemony and Cosmopolitanism in International Relations Theories

Hegemony is one of the key concepts in international relations studies. As security, for instance, this concept of hegemony is highly disputed. Beyond controversies relating to its properties and its foundations, the nature of the links between hegemony and the cosmopolitan horizon generate a debate. This first section helps to clarify the three types of relationships provided by theories in this field. It also aims to mobilize a major tension between a Kantian moment and Machiavellian moment to understand the links between hegemony and cosmopolitanism.

1.1   *Three Theoretical Relations*

Relations between hegemony and a cosmopolitan horizon are analyzed in three different perspectives, according to incompatibility (realist approaches), corruption (neo-Marxist approaches), or even complementarity (neoliberal approaches).

1.1.1   The Incompatibility of Hegemony with the Cosmopolitan Project

The thesis of incompatibility is developed by the realist approaches (classical or neorealist). It is based first and foremost on a materialistic conception of hegemony. A state becomes a hegemon from the moment where it accumulates mainly military power resources. This superiority prevents the emergence of other rivals in the international system. Hegemony cannot be global in the sense that a state doesn't have the ability to control the whole international system. Hegemony remains geographically limited to key areas and, thus, to a regional dimension (Mearsheimer, 2001). This thesis insists upon the impossible convergence between the unity of the world and the struggle for hegemony. Unity of the world aims at changing behaviors of the states and even their forms. This perspective defines war as a residue of history. The pacification progress that results from this cosmopolitanism relies on an utopia for realists. They emphasize the anarchic structure of the international system, within which more or less robust power poles are born, increase, and decline or even die. The quest for hegemony calls into question this cosmopolitan unity of the world even though the existence of a hegemon can promote stability of the international system thanks to coercion (Gilpin, 1981, 1987). Therefore, the concept of 'world citizenship' is shown to be an illusion.

1.1.2   The Corruption of the Cosmopolitan Project

This second thesis is mainly provided by neo-Marxist theorists, more specifically by Richard Cox, inspired by the work of Gramsci.[1] By distancing the concept from the materialist conception of hegemony and its concrete forms of usage, Gramsci insists upon its ideological basis (Gramsci, 1971: 57). Hegemonic power does not solely mean the possession of material resources such as military or economic capacity, or technical innovations. Hegemony relies less on coercion than on ideological consensus or compliance. Cox transfers this approach at the international level by analyzing the ideological conditions that diffuse the values defended by the *hegemon*. Hegemony is then defined as a construction that aims at protecting a world order universal thanks to a general consent. This consent relies on 'universal norms, institutions and mechanisms which lay down general rules of behavior for stats and for those forces of civil society that act across national boundaries—rules which support the dominant mode of production' (Cox, 1983: 172). Cox insists in this specific process. A State becomes hegemonic when it 'would have to found and protect a world order which was universal in conception, that is, not an order in which one state directly exploits others but an order which most other states (or at least those within reach of the hegemony) could find compatible with their interests'(Cox, 1983: 171). Material capabilities are not sufficient for establishing hegemony. They are associated to ideas and institutions for making believe that the interests of States is compatible with the hegemonic state (Cox, 1981).

Hegemony goes beyond the accumulation of the material resources of power. It supposes the promotion of dominant norms and, especially, the action of the dominant class within the hegemon, which disseminates the values abroad thanks to the support of civil society. The dominant social forces shape the international order. The values promoted by the hegemon are confused with those of other actors in the international system and, more generally, with so-called universal interest. Gramsci sees a neoliberal transnational

---

1   Arrighi (1993: 150) will extend this perspective.

historic bloc as being in favor of the laws of the market economy. Nicos Poulantzas discusses the concept introduced by Gramsci by limiting its relevance to the center's states (capitalist and developed) and not of the peripheries, which are less affected by the mechanism of ideological consensus (Poulantzas, 1973). Thus, neo-Marxist critical approaches seek to show that hegemonic projects are only a way to dominate the weakest countries through a discourse based on the confusion between interests of the more powerful and the universal interest.

1.1.3 Complementarity with the Cosmopolitan Project

The idea that the hegemony can be built easily with a cosmopolitan horizon is mainly defended by liberal theory. International relations are not defined thanks to the balance of powers. They insist upon the development of complex interdependences between states, which require enhanced cooperation within international organizations. Liberals use the concept of hegemony by underlining the crucial influence of the hegemon in the international system. Robert O. Keohane considers that the presence of a hegemon has structural consequences, for instance by supporting the development of an open and global liberal economy (Keohane, 1980). The concept has a double dimension: hegemony is defined as an accumulation of essentially economic material resources (Keohane, 1984), but also by the skills and the will to use them in order to control the system. The concept differs from imperialism as it requires the consent of the other actors. The hegemon does not rely on brute force to ensure supremacy but rather on the ability to create rules accepted and recognized by all the players. Finally, the hegemony does not mean a lack of cooperation between states. Although American power has begun to erode since the 1970s, this cooperation has been renewed and has opened new opportunities, especially in the fields of commerce and finance. A hegemonic actor as the United States is expected to continue in its position; a position which, far from leading to conflicts, promotes a cooperative global order (Ikenberry, 2001, 2011), even in the long term. The argument is also used in a contrasting way, as Charles Kindleberger shows. The absence of a hegemonic actor explains the Great Depression during the interwar period (Kindleberger, 1973). These approaches rest *ultimately* on the need to preserve American power because its decline would entail dislocation of the liberal world order.

The thesis of compatibility is questionable. On the one hand, these hegemonic strategies intend less to develop a new political form than to reduce the competition between states in the global market. Moreover, this reduction may be interpreted as a power multiplier and not a factor of genuine cosmopolitization (Beck, 2007). On the other hand, well embedded in a liberal perspective, this thesis conceals a major tension between hegemony and cosmopolitanism, including Kantian ideas. It remains far from hegemonic peace.

1.2   *A Normative Tension: Machiavellian Moment v. Kantian Moment*
The normative theories reveal a divide between the search for hegemony and a cosmopolitan unity of the world. The first refers to a certain extent to a Machiavellian moment. The second Kantian inspiration aims to distance itself from a centralist conception of power on a global scale.

The notion of a Machiavellian moment not only refers to a historical period, the Renaissance, during which several authors, including Machiavelli, clarified the conditions of a stable republic. It also focuses on the existence of a tumultuous political unity at the heart of a historical contingency (Pocock, 1997: 563). In *Discourses on Livy*, Machiavelli (1980) distinguishes the destiny of Venice, Sparta, and Rome. The first two cities embody small republics that disappeared after having been conquered. The third was facing internal dissension between the Senate and the people. A policy of conquests allowed it to exceed this trend by arming the people. The territorial extension represented both a new basis for power and a way to control the external environment. This description entails a judgment of value. Machiavelli advises following the example of Rome seeking hegemony and the two small republics. He draws on two major arguments. First, a small republic cannot withdraw within its limits. Although their constitution is favorable to a strategic restraint, such a posture can only be temporary. Venice and Sparta were able to achieve inner peace, but this was not immutable. To arouse the fear of the other republics while refusing an offensive policy is an extremely precarious balancing act. Moreover, it is against nature. Second, the Roman example is the most honorable. Beyond domestic concerns, Rome became aware of impossible isolation. To reject a policy of expansion abroad exposed the city to the winds of fate (or opened it up to be invaded by another republic). This argument echoes the problem of the *Prince*, which deals with innovation in politics. Rome opted for expansion in order to anticipate the risks caused by this innovation. Therefore, the city became an empire, controlling the fallout of its own actions. Machiavelli leads on to the idea that the greatness of Rome is not the result of fortune but rather a *virtù* that forced its path (in particular the absence of two simultaneous wars). The path chosen by Rome is the glorious way despite the certainty, in the eyes of Machiavelli, of its provisional character, because final degeneration is irremediable. The quest for hegemony is thus articulated within the dynamics of preservation—always fragile—of the republics. Such a quest does not aim at setting up a single global republic or the idea of world citizenship.

Kant does not use the term of hegemony in his *Perpetual Peace* published in 1795 (Kant, 1991). But obviously his cosmopolitanism is highly opposed to the idea of a hegemonic peace. This type of peace is centralizing in favor of a single power (Arcidiacono, 2011). Therefore, it can switch at any time into an imperial construction, which comes with a paternalistic despotic state: a spectrum even more disturbing than that of monarchies based on absolute power within nation-states. Hegemony proves to be incompatible with the idea of perpetual peace: the civil constitution of every state should be republican (the nature of political regimes), there should be a confederation of free states (law of nations), and the universal hospitality (law of world citizenship) should abound. That's why Miller (2002), for instance, argues for a link only between imperialism and institutional cosmopolitanism and not moral cosmopolitanism, as conceived by Tan (2004).

This tension between the Kantian moment and the Machiavellian moment remains identifiable in the contemporary context. It is located between major powers, which continue their struggle for hegemony by other means.

2 Cosmopolitanism Prevented by the Competition for Hegemony

According to Gilpin, the history of international relations consists of different cycles of hegemony. Each cycle is punctuated by a war between great powers. Since 1945, no war for hegemony has happened. This fact seems to achieve empirically the Kantian thesis that the experience of the 20th century's total wars has promoted a cultural change toward the resort of force. This change encourages perpetual peace. However, the absence of such wars does not entail the end of all competitions for hegemony. The latter contradict the cosmopolitan perspective because they reveal the existence of a Machiavellian moment between major powers.

2.1 *The Obsolescence of Major Wars for Hegemony Since 1945*

To describe the statistical evolution of armed conflict is a delicate work both methodologically and conceptually. Several databases provide annual reports in the field. Although developed using different tools or even questionable definitions of what is a war,[2] general trends show a diminution of wars between major powers (Goldstein, 2011). None has occurred since 1945 for example, and

---

2   For example, it's often the threshold of a thousand deaths that allows one to talk of war or twenty-five deaths related to combat in one year to designate an armed conflict (this is the test of one of the main bases produced by Uppsala University).

interstate conflicts have decreased during the same period. In parallel, internationalized intrastate conflicts embody the main source of contemporary conflicts.[3] These data also show that food shortages, conditions of health, or, more generally, human insecurity cause more deaths than terrorist attacks, challenging the notion that since 9/11 more civilians have died from this kind of violence (Roche, 2017).

The obsolescence of war between major industrialized powers has generated a vast literature. This obsolescence may result from the force of international law which prohibits offensive warfare, from the nuclear weapon which would require restraint because of the logic of deterrence, or from a new cultural relationship to such war as an institution of the past (Mueller, 1996). Already in the second part of the 20th century, Raymond Aron pointed out a law concerning a reduction in the profitability of conquests. The power of the states would no longer come from predatory wars in order to access material or territorial resources. The financial and human costs of the use of the force between great powers would then make war futile and not useful. That's what Chris Brown highlights. for example: 'while in the past it was common for rising powers to believe that they had to set their new status by questioning the existence of the incumbent powers, building Empires or spheres of prosperity, […] this is no longer necessary and can become more counterproductive than previously' (Brown, 2010: 8). However, the competition for hegemony takes a more insidious form, which is one of the major contemporary strategic issues.

2.2 *Freedom of Navigation in the Global Commons: the Source of a New Competition*

A foundation of the hegemony nowadays is a free access and movement in the global commons: areas that are accessible to all and free from ownership by any one state. These areas are vital both for national economies that are increasingly interdependent (they are necessary for the flows of communication and the circulation of goods) and for the usage of military means. The global commons correspond to the high seas, the atmosphere, the international air space, and cyberspace. A principle of freedom of navigation is set up within these areas. Until the beginning of the 21st century, the United States had a virtual monopoly on these global commons (Posen, 2003). The situation is very different today, particularly because of emerging countries' foreign policies. They adopt strategies of denying access close to their areas of influence in order to challenge the United States. Tensions have appeared above or close to

---

3 See http://ucdp.uu.se/#/exploratory; http://www.correlatesofwar.org/.

exclusive economic zones in South China Sea. Russia has attempted to capture a part of the resources of the Arctic Ocean. More generally, the cyber world becomes an area in which offensive attacks are valued since the origin of the attacks is especially difficult to trace. This is called a *sub rosa cyber war* (Libicki, 2009). As for outer space, the Kessler syndrome, which inspired the movie *Gravity* (2013), must not be neglected. Collision—accidental or intentional, as the destruction by China of one of its weather satellites in 2007—of space debris is comparable to conventional weapons' effects (a microbead of 1 mm diameter corresponds to a hand grenade).

In other words, the competition for hegemony between great powers is less to conquer new territories for direct control, but rather to control access and freedom of movement within these global commons. This practice entails a new tragedy of the commons, more based on appropriation of these areas than to the indifference described by Hardin in the 1970s (Ramel, 2014).

The competition for hegemony between major powers may be more latent in the form of maneuvers to destabilize rivals. Strategic studies have developed the idea of hybrid war, which includes conventional (regular war) and unconventional means (irregular warfare). Among these instruments, campaigns of disinformation or influence, having targeted 'publics,' can undermine the morale of the opponent. These practices were adopted, for example, by Russia during the war in Ukraine. But they are also to be seen in the relationship between United States and Russia, as the 2016 presidential election illustrated.

The motivation of the major powers is therefore far from cosmopolitan imperatives. These powers are shaped by the reference of interest defined in exclusive national terms to preserve political unity. The reasons are both economic sustainability and strategic maneuvers.

3 Cosmopolitanism Disputed in the Competition for Hegemony

The cosmopolitan project is also subject to challenge by alternative norms. It can, paradoxically, lead to new wars while generating counter-narratives.

3.1 *Post-National Wars: toward a New Overlay*

Public international law has a liberal origin. It aims to ensure the coexistence of states and thus their freedom. Initially, this right is based on a double indifference with respect to the internal affairs of states and their political system. However, in the post-Cold War era, this formal right became more substantial. This double indifference was gradually altered under the influence of a humanitarian argument. The fate of individuals within the states and, more widely, the absence of protection of human rights can lead to military intervention. Some strong controversies, like the debates on the responsibility to protect (R2P), call into question the nature of international law. But these give new justifications for the use of armed force called *post-national wars* (Beck, 2006: 130f.). The security argument to preserve a state is not the sole argument mobilized for legitimating the resort of force. These wars are in tension with the principle of non-interference in the internal affairs of states on behalf of human rights. These so-called 'post-national' wars differ from those to which Kant gives legitimation. Namely, the states are fighting against an 'unfair enemy,' that is, those that do not act according to the obligations of perpetual peace (Hassner, 2013). Beyond this Kantian inscription of post-national wars, the main consequence of this justification is a new overlay among states that subscribe to this new conception of public international law and those against such a trend. Hegemony here has the traits of a liberal standard. It tries to shape international lines. But it causes reactions by emerging countries and, more generally, the states of Global South, that perceive a new form of Western domination behind the differentiated usage of human rights (Ramel, 2018).

3.2 *Opposition to 'Western Hegemony' through the Promotion of Alternative Values*

Beyond the contentious diplomatic positions adopted by emerging countries, one of the current alternative political projects to the hegemony exercised by Western values has been developed by the Islamic Caliphate. Certainly, the Islamic State has suffered defeats, especially when the proto-state was dissolved in October 2017. Although they have driven their practices underground, active members of the Islamic State promote another conception of the world. Based on a narrow reading of Islam's sacred texts, this conception was inspired by a theocracy that aims to carry on the Sharia in a new political entity beyond Middle East states' borders. This project shows the main transformation of the current international system. This change results not only from a consistent deletion of the American moment and therefore of unipolarity. It comes also from the heterogeneous nature of the system concerning political values. In this context, a plurality of spheres of authority that distance themselves from the idea of state sovereignty emerges. These spheres do not necessarily accommodate the territorial division of states. They are fluid and depend on the loyalty of their affiliated members (Rosenau, 2007). In the case of ISIL, they are clearly against a cosmopolitan project. Political unity is conceived by rejecting the Western philosophical categories characterized by the unity of the world.

This opposition to Western hegemony may be linked to a philosophical critique of the Kantian model itself. Although opposed to the idea of a global political centralization, does Kantian cosmopolitanism not nourish a moral hegemony through the promotion of values stemming from the Western trajectory and, more specifically, from European civilization? Moral cosmopolitanism would not then escape the throes of the hegemonism denounced in its time by Thucydides: to force the other to be the same. It leads us to 'recall the justifications, tacitly, and we would like to believe, unintentionally alleged by the Enlightenment, of colonialism as a *mission civilisatrice*' (Couture, 2010: 34).

4 Conclusion

Hegemony and cosmopolitan projects do not make good bedfellows. They echo, respectively, a Machiavellian moment and a Kantian moment, whose aims are in tension: the first guarantees the preservation of the state in a turbulent context, the second aims at establishing world political unity. Therefore, their horizons are different. At best, a hegemonic strategy can reduce competition between states by imposing the stability of an international system whereby different states accept the same principles (a separate and regional hegemony might say because no state can assure hegemony on the whole planet). But even in this case, hegemony generates illusion and contestation (Badie, 2019). It does not marry well with cosmopolitanism. Nevertheless, when the construction of common sense does not accept differences, hegemonism, and therefore imperialism, appears behind moral and all more institutional cosmopolitanisms. At that point, dealing with the relationship between hegemony and cosmopolitanism becomes a pivotal element of the universalization of the cosmopolitan project: How can the other be integrated within it without denying their singularity of otherness, from their ways of thinking to their manners of designing polities?

References

Arcidiacono, B. 2011. *Cinq types de paix. Une histoire des plans de pacification perpétuelle (XVIIe–XXe siècles)*. Paris: Presses universitaires de France.

Arrighi, C. 1993. 'The Three Hegemony of Historical Capitalism.' In *Gramsci, Historical Materialism and International Relations*, edited by S. Gill, 148–185. Cambridge, UK: Cambridge University Press.

Badie. B. 2019. *L'hégémonie contestée. Les nouvelles formes de domination internationale*. Paris : Odile Jacob.

Beck, U. 2006. *Cosmopolitan Vision*. Cambridge, UK: Polity Press.

Beck, U. 2007. *Power in the Global Age*. Cambridge, UK: Polity Press.

Brown, C. 2010. 'Rules and Norms in Post-Western World.' In *On Rules, Politics and Knowledge: Friedrich Kratochwil, International Relations, and Domestic Affairs*, edited by O. Kessler, R. B. Hall, C. Lynch, and N. Onuf, 213–225. New York: Palgrave Macmillan.

Couture, J. 2010. 'Qu'est-ce que le cosmopolitisme?' In *Le cosmopolitisme. Enjeux et débats contemporains*, edited by R. Chung and G. Nootens, 15–35. Montreal: Les Presses de l'Université de Montréal.

Cox, R. 1981. 'Social Forces, States and World Order: Beyond International Relations Theory.' *Millennium* 10 (2): 126–155.

Cox, R. 1983. 'Gramsci, Hegemony and International Relations: An Essay in Method.' *Millennium* 12 (2): 162–175.

Cox, R. 1987. *Production, Power and World Order: Social Forces in the Making of History*. New York: Columbia University Press.

Gilpin, R. 1981. *War and Change in World Politics*. Princeton, NJ: Princeton University Press.

Gilpin, R. 1987. *The Political Economy of International Relations*. Princeton, NJ: Princeton University Press.

Goldstein, J. S. 2011. *Winning the War on War: The Decline of Armed Conflict Worldwide*. New York: Penguin.

Gramsci, A. 1971. *Selections from the Prison Notebooks of Antonio Gramsci*. New York: International Publishers.

Hammack, P. L. 2010. 'The Political Psychology of Personal Narratives.' *Analyses of Social Issues and Public Policy* 10 (1): 182–206.

Hassner, P. 2013. 'Sovereignty, Morality, and History: The Problematic Legitimization of Force in Rousseau, Kant and Hegel.' In *Just and Unjust Military Intervention*, edited by S. Recchia and J. M. Welsh, 176–193. Cambridge, UK: Cambridge University Press.

Ikenberry, J. 2001. *After Victory: Institutions, Strategic Restraint, and the Rebuilding of the World Order*. Princeton, NJ: Princeton University Press.

Ikenberry, J. 2011. *Liberal Leviathan: The Origins, Crisis and Transformation of the American World Order*. Princeton, NJ: Princeton University Press.

Kant, E., 1991. *Vers la paix perpétuelle*. Paris: Flammarion.

Keohane, R. O. 1980. 'The Theory of Hegemonic Stability and Changes in International Relations.' In *Change in the International System*, edited by R. H. Ole, 131–162. Boulder, CO: Westview Press.

Keohane, R. O. 1984. *After Hegemony: Cooperation and Discord in the World Political Economy*. Princeton, NJ: Princeton University Press.

Kindleberger, C. 1973. *The World in Depression, 1929–1939*. Berkeley: California University Press.

Libicki, M. C. 2009. 'Sub Rosa Cyber War.' In *The Virtual Battlefield: Perspectives on Cyber Warfare*, edited by C. Czossek and K. Geers, 53–65. Amsterdam: IOS Press.

Machiavelli, N. 1980. *Discours sur la décade de Tite-Live*. Paris: Berger-Levrault.

Mearsheimer, J. 2001. *The Tragedy of Great Power Politics*. New York: Norton & Co.

Miller, D. 2002. 'Cosmopolitanism: A Critique.' *Critical Review of International Social and Political Philosophy* 5 (3): 80–85.

Mueller, J. 1996. *Retreat from Doomsday: The Obsolescence of Major Wars*. New York: Basic Books.

Obama, B. 2008. 'Obama's Speech in Berlin.' *New York Times*, July 24, http://www.nytimes.com/2008/07/24/us/politics/24text-obama.html.

Pocock, J. G. A. 1997. *Le moment Machiavélien*. Paris: Presses universitaires de France.

Posen, B. 2003. 'Command of the Commons: The Military Foundation of US Hegemony.' *International Security* 28 (1): 5–46.

Poulantzas, N. 1973. 'L'internationalisation des rapports capitalistes et l'Etat-nation.' *Les Temps Modernes* 319: 1456–1500.

Ramel, F. 2014. 'Accès aux espaces communs et grandes stratégies. Vers un nouveau jeu mondial.' *Etudes de l'Irsem* 30: 11–41.

Ramel, F. 2018. 'Contesting Sovereignty: Human Security as a New Justification for War?' In *The Ethics of War and Peace Revisited: Moral Challenges in the Era of Contested and Fragmented Sovereignty*, edited by D. Brunstetter and J.-V. Holeindre, 241–261. Washington, DC: Georgetown University Press.

Roche, J.-J. 2017. 'Chiffres.' In *Dictionnaire de la guerre et de la paix*, edited by B. Durieux, J.-B. J. Vilmer, and F. Ramel, 193–197. Paris: Presses universitaires de France.

Rosenau, J. 2007. 'Governing the Ungovernable: The Challenge of a Global Disaggregation of Authority.' *Regulation & Governance* 1: 88–97.

Selzer, O. F. 2010. 'Barack Obama, the 2008 Presidential Election, and the New Cosmopolitanism: Figuring the Black Body.' *MELUS* 35 (4): 115–137.

Tan, K. C. 2004. *Justice without Borders*. Cambridge, UK: Cambridge University Press.

CHAPTER 27

Capitalism and Cosmopolitanism

Robert Holton

1   Introduction

Is cosmopolitanism an emancipatory force capable of overcoming global inequalities associated with capitalism, racism, and ethno-nationalism? Has its time finally arrived in an epoch of globalization, now able to transcend narrow and particularistic boundaries of nation, race, patriarchy, and cultural distinction? Or is cosmopolitanism implicated in some fundamental way with inequality, privilege, and sectional interest? Is the apparent universalism of cosmopolitanism a robust unifying force for global justice in an unequal world? Or is its claim to universalism deeply flawed through connections with global capitalism, imperialism, inequality, and context-bound Western forms of moral and social philosophy?

Much debate about cosmopolitanism is rightly concerned with these general questions. Yet it is not at all clear that cosmopolitanism can be regarded as a unitary phenomenon about which general propositions can be sustained. The recent shift of perspective in cosmopolitan studies, from an exclusive emphasis on cosmopolitanism as philosophy to cosmopolitanism as social practice, has brought with it a pluralizing tendency, which sees multiple cosmopolitanisms rather than a single unitary cosmopolitanism (Holton, 2009; Glick Schiller and Irving, 2015). The recent proliferation of types of cosmopolitanisms has given us cosmopolitanism from above and from below, African, Middle Eastern, and Western variants, as well as liberal, subaltern, communist, Islamic, military, and spiritual types (Holton, 2009: 212–216). What, if anything, these cosmopolitanisms have in common is not easy to determine, beyond rather vague notions of openness to others (see Hannerz, 1990, 1996; Beck and Sznaider, 2006; Skrbiš and Woodward, 2007).

The relationship between cosmopolitanism, capitalism, and inequality is typically conducted within one of two intellectual idioms. The first asserts a general relationship between cosmopolitanism and inequality, whether positive or negative. The second abandons any kind of general or unitary theory for a middle-range plurality of cosmopolitanisms that relate in different and often conflicting ways with capitalism, globalization, inequality, and social justice.

There are two prominent arguments, which, from a simple normative viewpoint, see cosmopolitanism as either good/progressive or bad/regressive. In the positive version cosmopolitanism is an emancipatory force drawing on both ancient and modern philosophical traditions (Nussbaum, 1997), changes in institutions in the direction of cosmopolitan law (Berman, 2004), and new social movements oriented to social justice, human rights, and environmental sustainability (Cohen and Shirin, 2000; Koukouzelis, 2017). These developments, it is claimed, have been able to extend democracy—whether from the level of nation-states to transnational forms of governance (Held, 1995), or from nation-states to new reflexive social movements arising from civil society (Beck, 2000a).

The contrasting argument sees a strong connection between cross-border flows of capital, commodities, technology, and power on the one hand, and free-floating transnational cultural orientation on the other. The negative consequences of cosmopolitanism center on the undermining of national political and cultural institutions and practices by what are regarded as 'rootless' cosmopolitan forces. Cross-border economic transactions transcend the control of nation-states in the name of global capital. Transnational mobility symbolizes privilege, as in Calhoun's much-quoted formulation that cosmopolitanism is 'the class consciousness of frequent travellers' (2002). Local cultural repertoires, meanwhile, become distorted by intrusive, culturally privileged tourists.

Thinking of this kind is often less a matter of sustained theoretical analysis than suspicion, political resistance, and the assertion of particularistic cultural identities. These views may be advanced by a diverse set of critics: from outward-looking inclusive democrats, industrial workers suffering from offshoring of employment, or proud local communities seeking to protect their heritage, to inward-looking racists and anti-Semites. The most promising line of critical analysis capable of making sense of these diverse reactions against cosmopolitanism is that offered by Calhoun (2012). He maintains that most versions of cosmopolitanism are contained within liberalism, which, over time, has proved inadequate as a way of securing a sense of belonging and community. Yet liberalism is not a necessary feature of capitalism, so this powerful argument is not really designed to shore up negative general theories of cosmopolitanism and capitalism.

General theories of cosmopolitanism and capitalism are thus in retreat. Objection to simplistic discussions of cosmopolitanism, however, lead in two very different directions. One is to provide a more complex (dialectical) kind of general theory of cosmopolitanism capable of integrating cosmopolitanism as social justice and emancipation, with cosmopolitanism as global capitalism. Ulrich Beck is the most notable exponent of this approach. For him, cosmopolitanization is characteristic of a second stage of modernity, successor to 19th-century modernity linked with nation-states (2000a). Capitalism is an intrinsic element in both phases, shifting from national to global processes. A further key feature of the second phase is the centrality of socially generated risk arising in large measure from the negative impacts of global capitalism on the natural environment and social inequality. At the same time, new forms of reflexive anti-systemic resistance emerge, linking the cosmopolitan phase of modernity with new social movements seeking greater social justice and environmental sustainability (Beck, 2000b).

The other alternative to general theory of whatever kind is to argue that general theorizing of any kind has been pushed too far. It should therefore be abandoned in favor of a more nuanced middle-range analysis open to multiple connections among cosmopolitanism, capitalism, and social justice. This middle-range alternative deconstructs cosmopolitanism as a unitary category. The emphasis is on diverse and often politically contradictory versions of cosmopolitanism. Some may have positive connections with capitalism, others do not. Capitalist cosmopolitanism is only one out of a vast range of types of cosmopolitanism. Others may be centered on religion, music, or social reform.

Two implications follow. The first is that there is no necessary relationship, either between cosmopolitanism and capitalism, or cosmopolitanism and inequality. The second is that Beck's conception of cosmopolitan modernity oversimplifies the complex and diverse character of contemporary cosmopolitanisms.

I now look in more depth at the complex connections among cosmopolitanism, social justice, capitalism, and inequality.

2   Cosmopolitanism: Emancipatory Project or Ideology of Global Capitalism?

The linkage between cosmopolitanism and social justice relies first on a strong sense of continuity between cosmopolitan philosophy in the ancient Greek and Roman world, through Kant and the European Enlightenment, to contemporary self-styled manifestations of cosmopolitanism (Nussbaum, 1997). These are identified variously in law, political institutions and social movements. The continuity is represented in values to do with the interests of humanity as a whole, and with the transcendence of partial sectional interests. Cosmopolitanism as both thought and action is seen therefore as an evolving and ever widening social trend, subject to historical reversals but resilient across time and space.

In current circumstances this resilience is reflected in the turn back to universal cosmopolitan principles in global governance after the world wars, depression, and political traumas of fascism, authoritarian communism, racism, and ethno-nationalism. This is claimed to be evident in the influence of human rights, social justice, and environmental values and norms in institutions around the United Nations (UN) and European Union (EU) (Berman, 2004), animated by social movements and non-governmental organizations (NGOs) such as Amnesty International, Médecins Sans Frontières, and Greenpeace International.

There are, nonetheless, three major criticisms of this kind of optimistic thinking. The first is that cosmopolitan claims to universalism and concern for humanity as a whole have concealed particular sets of Western political and cultural norms. Rather than taking cosmopolitan universalism at face value as a self-evident form of universalism, it is always necessary to ask 'whose cosmopolitanism' is being asserted (Glick Schiller and Irving, 2015).

'Human rights,' in this view, have typically been articulated in terms of Western notions of individual rights, democracy, and the rule of law, rather than any transcendent trans-contextual universalism. They have emerged, in other words, from a particular context. To universalize globally across political and cultural borders, therefore, amounts to the imposition of specific norms and institutions through the exercise of Western forms of discursive and sovereign power over others.

A second argument deriving from various realist schools of international relations is that the global arena is dominated by powerful nation-states and organized political-economic interests. Movements of ideas, resources, and people across borders are generally articulated and controlled by nation-states, either individually or in alliance with each other. Meanwhile, global regulatory processes in economic life typically involve nation-states, international organizations, and corporations as major players in setting and implementing policy agenda. The influence of cosmopolitan norms of human rights and social justice—even in ostensibly global organizations such as the International Criminal Court (ICC) or World Bank—is very much subordinated to sectional political economic interests

The third remaining argument, with which this chapter is primarily concerned, is that cosmopolitanism as a worldview and way of acting in the world has a strong elective affinity with global capitalism. The clearest general connection between capitalism and cosmopolitanism occurs in the modern and contemporary epoch. Cross-border trade, technological transfer, and migration have a very long history over several millennia (Frank and Gills, 1993). Early versions of capitalism were, however, very much embedded within relations in which local political and cultural preoccupations dominated (Polanyi, 1957). What is most striking since the late 1860s is the increasing dominance of transnational economic processes over national economies and strong forms of external regulation.

To be sure, economic globalization is not a simple upward linear trend, as the de-globalization and the rise of nationalism between the two world wars indicates (James, 2001; Holton, 2011). Nonetheless, the resurgent global economic trends of the late 20th and early 21st centuries have been accompanied by a revival of apparently cosmopolitan cross-border trends, reaffirming the plausibility of strong connections between the two.

There are a number of possible links between modern capitalism and cosmopolitanism. I speak of modern capitalism to indicate that the focus here is not on age-old economic acquisitiveness nor on small-scale production for local markets. The emphasis, drawing on Marx and Weber, is rather on the predominance of capital accumulation involving the commodification of labor power, together with cultural orientations toward a rational goal-directed pursuit of profit as a way of life.

The first connection is structural in form. The argument is that capitalism has an intrinsic tendency to transcend both local and national limitations, and to secure autonomy from external political and cultural controls. In this respect it has a strong formal affinity with cosmopolitan openness and engagement across borders, transcending, where necessary, local and particularistic claims and affiliations. As is well known, this line of argument is pursued by Marx and Engels in the *Communist Manifesto* (1993). The bourgeoisie give a cosmopolitan character to production manifested in the emergence of a world market that sweeps away static local and parochial institutions, undermining national industries through radical economic and social transformation. Yet, as David Harvey (2015: 51) pointed out in a recent commentary, Marx and Engels were also keenly aware of further cosmopolitan trends, such as the emergence of a world literature. Cosmopolitanism is not then simply reducible to capitalism. Although not pursued further, there is a clear opening here for arguments that see the relationship between capitalism and cosmopolitanism not as one of structural necessity, but as a looser form of structural affinity.

From an early 21st-century viewpoint, this argument can be elaborated by two further observations. First, capitalism per se does not have an explicit interest in the substance of cosmopolitan norms to do with social justice, human rights, and cultural openness. Its relationship with political institutions and norms varies markedly between democratic and authoritarian, religious and secular. Liberal cosmopolitanism does have a close elective affinity with liberal capitalism, but this does not amount to a general structural necessity linking capitalism and cosmopolitanism.

Second, capitalism is not necessarily incompatible with local and national forms of organization. The large literature on national varieties of capitalism makes that clear (Hall and Soskice, 2001; Jacoby, 2005). Marx's general theories of capitalism evolution, extended by subsequent political economists, have rightly identified tendencies toward globalization, but these can and have been offset to a significant extent, both by national regulatory variations and by historic tendencies for phases of globalization to be succeeded by phases of de-globalization (James, 2001). Phases of de-globalization, like that between 1914 and 1945, also tend to see an erosion of cosmopolitanism, with the rise of nationalism and resort to war. This is not to say, however, that the dynamics and vicissitudes of cosmopolitanism and capitalism are totally entwined. The seeds of many post-1945 developments in global governance and of cosmopolitan social movements were sown in the previous de-globalizing phase (Holton, 2012).

A second structural argument linking global capitalism and cosmopolitanism is the relationship between global finance capital and cosmopolitanism. Recent developments in the evolution of global capitalism have seen the intensification of financialization (Epstein, 2005). This term may be broadly defined as 'the increasing role of financial motives, markets, financial actors, and financial institutions in the operation of the domestic and international economies' (Epstein, 2005: 30). Such financial processes have taken on a profoundly cross-border character, operating twenty-four hours a day, utilizing new communications technology. Trillions of dollars circulate across the globe each day, much of it managed by wealth managers and financial advisors acting for institutions and the world's superrich (Harrington, 2016). Large volumes also find their way into offshore tax havens, which shield wealth from global and national regulation (Palan, Murphy, and Chavagneux, 2010).

This financial world, increasingly detached from sites of production, clearly fits the concept of 'capital without borders' (Harrington, 2016). It is also intimately connected with increases in global inequality, especially inequalities of wealth. The 2017 Global Wealth Report, compiled by Credit Suisse, found that the top 10 percent of the world's population owned 88 percent of the wealth, and the top 1 percent around half, while the bottom 50 percent owned only 1 percent (Credit Suisse, 2017: 9). These levels also represent a continuing trend in wealth inequality that has intensified since the 1990s (Piketty, 2014; Holton, 2016). They depend not only on systemic tax avoidance organized through global tax havens (as already pointed out), but also on neoliberal tax regimes in many large capitalist nations such as the USA, recently strengthened by the Trump administration.

Inequalities of income are not rising as fast as inequalities of wealth (Holton, 2014: 76–91). There are also greater complexities in income patterns in the global arena, where it is too simplistic to attribute increased inequality to global capitalism alone (Milanovic, 2011: 153–154). Here mixed trends are observable in income inequalities, dependent in part on the impact of variations in public policy on the distribution of income (Holton, 2014). Nonetheless, inequalities in both wealth and income are very much connected with neoliberal deregulated capitalism, whether this applies to within-country or between-country inequality.

Yet how do these structural trends connect with the cross-border world of social actors? There are a range of questions that arise here. First, is there a global capitalist class, and how far is this cosmopolitan in orientation? Second, do sites of global production encourage or undermine cosmopolitanism, and how far is inequality implicated in these processes. Third, how far do sites of global consumption take on a cosmopolitan form in sectors like cross-border tourism? Answers to these questions have much to do with social action and the lifeworlds of actors who control, work within, or consume commodities in increasingly urbanized and digitally connected settings in the global economy.

I look first at the claim that cosmopolitanism is a worldview well fitted to the interests of dominant classes and elites. These interests not only promote and manage the deregulated flows of capital, commodities, and transformative forms of technological innovation across the world, but are implicated in political power and cultural influence.

Atossa Araxia Abrahamian (2015) makes a compelling though ironic case in support of this proposition. Case studies of powerful global billionaires show how multiple citizenships and passports can be bought, both to facilitate tax avoidance but also to move effortlessly across borders conducting political and economic ventures in support of other powerful interests. This may involve the organization of coups, provision of offshore services for rogue regimes, massive tax-free property developments, or the promotion of citizenship in tax havens to global banks and elite financial planners. This has been described as the 'flattening of borders for a price' (Surak, 2016: 39).

And yet this connection between ultra-mobile elites and cosmopolitanism is both ironic and paradoxical. The paradox is that those most able to flatten political borders and hold multiple citizenships are nonetheless committed to self-interest rather than to humanity as a whole. Global citizenship is an ironic social formation in that it is founded on the avoidance of responsibility for global challenges and human rights, even while operating in a profoundly cross-border manner. By contrast to the activist slogan 'think globally, act locally,' Abrahamian's cosmopolites 'think self-interestedly and act globally.' Put another way, while cosmopolitanism in its many historical variants involved a thick sociality, the ostensibly new global citizens practice a very thin sociality. They are indeed the new global sociopaths.

Other explorations of the possible existence of a global or transnational capitalist class emphasize shared normative and ideological dimensions of class. Sklair (2001: 255–294), for example, argues that corporate leaders increasingly think globally and pursue a 'consumer-oriented global vision for humanity.' Some kind of global vision is necessary, in his view, because corporations are denationalizing. This vision incorporates not merely entrepreneurs and senior managers, but also the mass media, advertising media, and neoliberal politicians. What is less clear is how far this set of actors form any kind of community, let alone a proto-cosmopolitan cultural formation.

Carroll (2010) looks not at ideological visions but at interlocking connections between global business actors that cross and, in some sense transcend, national and regional borders. Such connections are evident in global corporate boards and elite global policy meetings of bodies like the World Economic Forum and Bilderberg Group. His conclusion is that 'there has been no massive shift from nationally bound corporate elites to a transnational network detached from national moorings' (Carroll, 2010: 224). A less dramatic shift has nonetheless occurred since the mid-1990s, with transnational interlocking becoming stronger among the largest global firms, especially in Europe. Interestingly, the largest US firms are seen as sufficiently powerful to remain less well integrated into this network. However, Carroll's extensive research program remains dominated by structure, and says little about the lifeworld of this transnational network.

A more general implication of both these studies is that capitalism does not require a dominant ideology to function. This argument was proposed by Abercrombie, Hill, and Turner (1980), but has not been explored very far in the recent global context. Their argument helps to buttress the proposition that there is no strong or necessary connection between capitalism and cosmopolitanism.

A further set of analytical issues arise when considering capitalism, cosmopolitanism, and the world of work. In a very general sense, the relative share of income received by labor is currently in decline, while the share received by capital is increasing (Haldane, 2015). How far this is due to globalization, technological change, and the decline of trades unionism is a complex matter. What is more relevant to the present discussion are the political and cultural dimensions of this decline and dislocation. One major aspect to this is the rise of anti-globalization feeling and economic nationalism, especially among workers in older industries and regions. This was politically expressed in the election of Trump in the USA and the vote for Brexit in the UK. On the other hand, it is worth considering how far there are winners arising from global capitalism beyond the top 1 percent and what part cosmopolitanism plays in their lifeworlds.

Yeoh and Huang (2011) consider the case of so-called 'talent workers,' often migrants, whose marketable skills are in great demand. Both highly skilled and highly mobile, working in sectors like business management, law, and financial services, this group have often been regarded as nomads (Robbins, 1998), forever on the move and forever detached from particular contexts in the hypermobile cosmopolitan space of flows. Yet these assumptions turn out to be simplistic. Hypermobility does not necessarily undermine senses of belonging linked with kinship, past locations, and cultural identity. Nor does the economic logic of ultra-mobile global capitalism necessarily dominate lifeworlds. Expectations among some corporate human resource managers may once have been that the ideal professional or managerial would be a rootless individual free from family and national ties and committed to the company.

Research, however, shows that such elite workers both retain wider social ties and may have non-pecuniary reasons for taking on mobile migratory work (Ley and Kobayashi, 2005; Ho, 2011). These do not necessarily entail any strong kind of cosmopolitan affiliation in an economic or political sense. Nor do they amount to cultural openness in any fundamental sense. The nearest linkages to cosmopolitanism may be through what Conradson and Latham (2007) call 'self-fashioning' or 'self-conscious' cosmopolitanism. This may involve friendships across cultural boundaries and new consumption patterns for food in cities where talent workers are concentrated. But this rather narcissistic quasi-cosmopolitanism often maintains exclusive and sometimes racialized conceptions of difference rather than active intercultural sharing (Ho, 2011).

At other less elevated points in the employment structure, attributions of cosmopolitan orientations based on integration into global capitalist enterprises have also been explored. The 'call-center cosmopolitanism' associated with India-located global outsourcing services, for example, has generated research, but also been a theme in popular culture, notably film and in novels (Guttman, 2017). Some commentators see the intrinsically cross-border character of outsourced call services as a context where cosmopolitan affiliations can be promoted. Taking on new names and accents to disguise their Indian location to international callers might be supposed to stimulate a kind of cultural hybridity. Some representations of call centers in Indian novels feed such presumptions. However, Guttman sees a more complex hybrid process in which complicity in corporate cosmopolitan communicative worlds is accompanied by some sense of liberation from Indian cultural norms, especially among the female workforce. It is not only elite talent workers, then, whose lifeworld may in some sense connect globalization, capitalism, and cosmopolitanism. This somewhat speculative exploration of the worlds of globalized production and cosmopolitan yields a diverse and somewhat discordant proliferation of possible connections. These defy general characterization and leave debates about capitalism and cosmopolitanism with an unfinished character.

3 Conclusion

There is no convincing general theory of connections between capitalism and cosmopolitanism. Capitalism and cosmopolitanism have such a diverse range of manifestations that there is no singular relationship between the two. Global inequality is a major destabilizing feature of the contemporary world, and capitalist corporations, labor markets, and elite political and cultural formations pay a very significant part in promoting and reproducing economic inequalities. Yet cosmopolitanism does not appear either as an unambiguous promoter of social justice able to offset global inequality, nor as a cultural buttress to the operation of global capitalism. There are elective affinities between capitalism and cosmopolitanism, but no more than that. There is no general theory of capitalism and cosmopolitanism. This relationship is best explored through middle-range theory.

References

Abercrombie, N., S. Hill, and B. S. Turner. 1980. *The Dominant Ideology Thesis*. London: Routledge.

Abrahamian, A. A. 2015. *The Cosmopolites: The Coming of the Global Citizen*. New York: Columbia Global Reports.

Beck, U. 2000a. 'The Cosmopolitan Perspective: Sociology in the Second Age of Modernity.' *British Journal of Sociology* 51 (1): 79–105.

Beck, U. 2000b. *What is Globalization?* Oxford: Blackwell.

Beck, U. and N. Sznaider. 2006. 'Unpacking Cosmopolitanism for the Social Sciences: A Research Agenda.' *British Journal of Sociology* 57 (1): 1–23.

Berman, P. S. 2004. 'From International Law to Law and Globalization.' *Columbia Journal of Transnational Law* 43: 484–556.

Calhoun, C. 2002. 'The Class Consciousness of Frequent Travellers: Towards a Critique of Actually Existing Cosmopolitanism.' In *Conceiving Cosmopolitanism: Theory, Context, and Practice*, edited by S. Vertovec and R. Cohen, 86–109. Oxford: Oxford University Press.

Calhoun, C. 2012. 'Cosmopolitan Liberalism and its Limits.' In *European Cosmopolitanism in Question*, edited by R. Robertson and A. S. Krossa, 105–125. Basingstoke: Palgrave Macmillan.

Carroll, W. K. 2010. *The Making of a Transnational Capitalist Class: Corporate Power in the 21st Century*. London: Zed Books.

Cohen, R. and R. Shirin. 2000. 'Global Social Movements: Towards a Cosmopolitan Politics.' In *Global Social Movements*, edited by R. Cohen and R. Shirin, 1–17. London: Athlone Press.

Conradson, D. and A. Latham. 2007. 'The Affective Possibilities of London: Antipodean Transnationals and the Overseas Experience.' *Mobilities* 2 (2): 231–254.

Credit Suisse. 2017. *Global Wealth Report 2017*. Zurich: Credit Suisse Research Institute.

Epstein, G. (ed.). 2005. *Financialization and the World Economy*. Cheltenham: Edward Elgar.

Frank, A. G. and B. Gills. 1993. *The Modern World System: Five Hundred Years or Five Thousand*. London: Routledge.

Glick Schiller, N. and A. Irving (eds.). 2015. *Whose Cosmopolitanism: Critical Perspectives, Rationalities, and Discontents*. New York: Berghahn.

Guttman, A. M. 2017. 'Call-Centre Cosmopolitanism: Global Capitalism and Local Identity in Indian Fiction.' *Postcolonial Text* 12 (1): 1–17.

Haldane, A. 2015. 'Labour's Share.' Speech to TUC Conference, London, November 12, http://www.bankofengland.co.uk/-/media/boe/files/speech/2015/labours-share.pdf (accessed September 10, 2016).

Hall, P. and D. Soskice (eds.). 2001. *Varieties of Capitalism: The Institutional Foundations of Comparative Advantage*. Oxford: Oxford University Press.

Hannerz, U. 1990. 'Cosmopolitans and Locals in World Culture.' In *Global Culture*, edited by M. Featherstone, 237–251. London: Sage.

Hannerz, U. 1996. *Transnational Connections*. Abingdon: Routledge.

Harrington, B. 2016. *Capital without Borders: Wealth Managers and the One Percent*. Cambridge, MA: Harvard University Press.

Harvey, D. 2015. 'What Do We Do with Cosmopolitanism?' In *Whose Cosmopolitanism: Critical Perspectives, Rationalities, and Discontents*, edited by N. Glick Schiller and A. Irving, 49–56. New York: Berghahn.

Held, D. 1995. *Democracy and the Global Order*. Stanford, CA: Stanford University Press.

Ho, E. L. 2011. 'Identity Politics and Cultural Asymmetries: Singapore Transmigrants Fashioning Cosmopolitanism.' *Journal of Ethnic and Migration Studies* 37 (5): 729–746.

Holton, R. J. 2009. *Cosmopolitanisms: New Thinking and New Directions*. Basingstoke: Palgrave Macmillan.

Holton, R. J. 2011. *Globalization and the Nation-State*, 2nd rev. ed. Basingstoke: Palgrave Macmillan.

Holton, R. J. 2012. *Global Finance*. Abingdon: Routledge.

Holton, R. J. 2014. *Global Inequalities*. Basingstoke: Palgrave Macmillan.

Holton, R. J. 2016. 'Global Inequality.' In *Routledge International Handbook of Globalization Studies*, 2nd ed., edited by B. S. Turner and R. J. Holton, 60–77. Abingdon: Routledge.

Jacoby, S. 2005. *The Embedded Corporation: Corporate Governance and Employment Relations in Japan and the United States*. Princeton, NJ: Princeton University Press.

James, H. 2001. *The End of Globalization*. Cambridge, MA: Harvard University Press.

Koukouzelis, K. 2017. 'Climate Change, Social Movements and Cosmopolitanism.' *Globalizations* 14 (5): 746–761.

Ley, D. and A. Kobayashi. 2005. 'Back to Hong Kong: Return Migration or Transnational Sojourn.' *Global Networks* 5 (2): 111–127.

Marx, K. and F. Engels. 1993. *The Communist Manifesto*. New York: International Publishers.

Milanovic, B. 2011. *The Haves and the Have-Nots*. New York: Basic Books.

Nussbaum, M. 1997. 'Kant and Stoic Cosmopolitanism.' *Journal of Political Philosophy* 5 (1): 1–25.

Palan, R., R. Murphy, and C. Chavagneux. 2010. *Tax Havens: How Globalization Really Works*. Ithaca, NY: Cornell University Press.

Piketty, T. 2014. *Capital in the 21st Century*. Cambridge, MA: Harvard University Press.

Polanyi, K. 1957. *The Great Transformation*. Boston, MA: Beacon Press.

Robbins, B. 1998. 'Introduction Part 1: Actually Existing Cosmopolitanism.' In *Cosmopolitics: Thinking and Feeling beyond the Nation*, edited by P. Cheah and B. Robbins, 1–19. Minneapolis: University of Minnesota Press.

Sklair, L. 2001. *The Transnational Capitalist Class*. Oxford: Blackwell.

Skrbiš, Z. and I. Woodward. 2007. 'The Ambivalence of Ordinary Cosmopolitanism: Investigating the Limits of Cosmopolitan Openness.' *Sociological Review* 55 (4): 730–747.

Surak, K. 2016. 'Our Citizenship is Expensive.' *London Review of Books*, September 22: 39–40.

Yeoh, B. and S. Huang, S. 2011. 'Introduction: Fluidity and Friction in Talent Migration.' *Journal of Ethnicity and Migration* 37 (5): 681–690.

Index of Names and Notions

Abercrombie, Nicholas 390
Abrahamian, Atossa Araxia 389
Adorno, Theodor 99
Agier, Michel 258
Alatas, Syed Farid 121–122, 125
Alston, Philipps 164
Althusser, Louis 97–98
Amin, Ash 197
Anderson, Benedict 223–224
Anderson, Elijah 196–197, 255
Anti-Cosmopolitanism, Anti-cosmopolitan 10, 17, 18, 101–102, 317, 318–319, 320, 323
Anti-Enlightenment 292, 292n1, 298–299
Anti-European 198, 213–214n3, 312
Anti-Humanism 1–2, 97–98
Anti-Liberalism, Anti-liberal 181–182
Anti-Semitism 100, 221–222, 292, 384–385
Anti-Terrorism 163, 346, 376–377
Anti-Westernism 74–75
Apartheid 68, 157, 189
Appadurai, Arjun 71–74, 75–77, 83–84, 276, 277
Appiah, Kwame Anthony 2, 15, 61, 184, 186, 187, 189, 276, 357
Archibugi, Daniele 14
Arendt, Hannah 115
Aristotle 35–37, 38
Armed Conflicts 226, 233, 235, 238–240, 241, 242, 243, 294–295, 360, 376–377, 377n2
Aron, Raymond 377
Arrighi, Giovanni 385n1
Asylum Seekers 121–122, 178, 233, 331–332
Authoritarianism, Authoritarian 87–88, 101–102, 106, 129–130, 171, 173, 174, 200–201, 328–329, 337, 339–340, 341–343, 345–346, 348–349, 351–352, 353, 387–388
Axial 28–30,
  Age 17–18, 27, 28–29, 37–38, 332–334, 337
  Revolution 12, 27–30, 31, 35–36, 39

Bagguley, Paul 17
Balibar, Étienne 212–213
Bauman, Zygmunt 269, 270–271, 272, 325

Beck, Ulrich 9–10, 12, 17, 53–54, 58, 60, 71–72, 74, 75–76, 77, 82–83, 84, 86–90, 92, 93–94, 122, 126, 208, 221, 224, 227, 269–270, 317–319, 322, 384–385
Beitz, Charles 111–112n5
Belonging 3, 4–5, 6–7, 83–84, 277–278, 283–284, 292–293, 340–341, 384–385, 391
Benhabib, Seyla 186
Benjamin, Walter 99, 267
Benmakhlouf, Ali 188
Bentham, Jeremy 171
Berger, Peter 111n4
Bessone, Magali 187
Bhabha, Homi K. 121–122, 127–128
Bhambra, Gurminder K. 91–92, 122–123
Bhargava, Rajeev 76–77
Bielsa, Esperança 16
Boli, John 276
Boltanski, Luc 280–281
Bonnelli, Cristobal 122–123
Borders 4–5, 7–8, 18, 37–38, 58, 60, 63–64, 72–73, 175–176, 185, 205, 206–207, 208, 209, 213–214, 234, 240, 297–298, 305–307, 309–310, 312, 313–314, 330–332, 356, 379, 386, 387, 388–390
Bosco, Estêvão 12
Brandel, Andrew 122–123
Breckenridge, Carol 72–74
Brexit 170, 213–214n3, 268, 292, 313, 317, 318–319, 320, 323–325, 390–391
Brotherhood 33–34, 55–56, 114, 332
Brown, Chris 377
Buddha 27, 29, 332–333
Butler, Tim 255–256

Çağlar, Ayşe 197, 250–251
Calhoun, Craig 194, 256–257, 384
Capitalism 12, 53, 54, 56–57, 60, 64, 126–127, 129–130, 207, 276, 284–285, 289–290, 313–314, 339, 340, 342–343, 350, 351, 383, 384, 385, 387–388, 390, 391–392,
  Financial 1, 330–331
  Global 7–8, 18, 319, 339, 346, 383, 384–385, 386–387, 388, 389, 390–391, 392
  Neoliberal 344, 352

Carlin, John 272
Carroll, William K. 390
Casanova José 328–329
Chakrabarty, Dipesh 121–122
Chanda, Naya 7–8
Chang, Kyung-Sup 126
Chauvier, Stéphane 12, 50
Chen, Tao 131
Chernilo, Daniel 13, 54, 75–76, 91
Chiapello, Eve 280–281
Cicchelli, Vincenzo 16–17, 129, 276n1
Cicero 4
Citizen of the World 4–5, 40–41, 43, 48–51, 97, 178, 184–185, 299, 339, 371
Citizenship 10, 11, 39, 62, 184–185, 186, 187, 194–195, 200–201, 211–212, 235–236, 255–256, 337, 356, 389
   Cosmopolitan 1, 296
   Supranational 7
   Universal 38
Civil Society 46, 84, 194, 198, 242, 248, 309, 373–374, 384
Civilization (s) 28–29, 31, 37–39, 57, 210–211, 318, 330, 337, 350, 351
   Chinese 27, 28, 124–125
   Eurasian 12, 27, 28
   European 10, 318, 379–380
   Greek 27, 28
   Indian 27
   Western 328, 332–333
Clash (es)
   of Cosmopolitanisms 209
   of Identities 18
   of Memories 227–228, 227–228n1
Class(es) 7–8, 33, 35–36, 42, 58–59, 60, 72, 84–85, 196, 199–200, 212–213, 254, 289–290, 292–293, 307–308, 319, 334–335, 341–342, 344, 346–349, 350, 351–352, 373–374, 384–389,
   Capitalist 57, 390
   Working 2, 60, 253, 255–256, 258–259, 319–324, 337, 351
Climate Change 238, 313, 353
Cohen, Robin 251
Colonialism, Colonial 6–7, 49, 56, 57, 76–77, 78, 92, 97, 116–117, 116–117n15, 122–123, 125, 193–194, 198, 200, 230, 235–236, 305–307, 311–312, 325, 331, 360–361, 379–380

Colonization 183, 236, 342–343
Communitarian 116–117, 181–182, 320
Community 4–5, 9–10, 35–36, 37, 46, 50, 56, 68–70, 113–114, 126, 140, 176, 178, 183–184, 196, 197, 198, 221, 235–236, 237, 240–241, 253, 280–281, 283–284, 296–297, 320, 355, 359, 390
   Cosmopolitan 13–14, 47–48
   Cultural 140, 281–282
   International 13–14, 148–149, 153, 159, 160–161, 162, 173, 362–363
   Global 168, 299
   Moral 2, 56, 62, 113–114, 339, 341–342
   National 10
   Political 36–37, 38, 171, 172, 175–176, 184–185, 190, 340–341
   Religious 140, 360
   Transnational 177
Competition 8–9, 15, 30–31, 44–45, 132, 229–230, 277–280, 313–314, 317, 371–372, 374–375, 376, 377, 378, 380
   Economic 118, 291–292, 296–297
   International 229
   Global 194–195, 207
Comte, Auguste 12, 53, 60–61
Conflicts 9, 28–30, 36, 84, 86, 87–88, 124, 129, 132, 175, 200–201, 229, 320, 328, 335, 337, 347–348, 360–361, 365–366, 374
Confucianism 5–6, 31, 126
Confucius 27, 31–36, 37, 332–333
Conradson, David 391
Constitutional Law 314–315, 329, 348, 365–366
Conviviality 16, 198
Cooperation 45, 90–91, 155–156, 169, 173–174, 194, 198, 362–363, 374
Cosmopolis 9–10, 12, 40, 47, 48, 194–195, 199–200
Cosmopolitan
   Canopy 196–197, 255–256
   City (ies) 1–2, 192–193, 194–196, 197–198, 199–201, 202, 344
   Competence 16, 90–91, 248, 251–252, 253, 257–258
   Condition 55–56, 258
   Constitution 41–42, 43–44, 46, 54
   Culture 16–17, 292–293, 344
   Education 276, 284
   Experience 248–249, 290

INDEX OF NAMES AND NOTIONS 397

Ideal   97, 168, 212, 233–234, 236
Imagination   126, 132
Individual   291, 297, 299, 319
Openness   299, 387
Project   18, 372, 373, 374, 378, 379, 380
Sentiment   42–43, 46–47
Society   40–41n1, 41, 87, 126
Stranger (s)   16, 263, 264–265n1, 267, 268–269, 270–272, 273, 352
Studies   6–7, 12, 67–68, 78–79, 289–290
World   54–55, 56, 73–74, 352
Cosmopolitanism
  Aesthetico-Cultural   16, 251–252, 256, 276–277, 283, 284–286
  Banal (Ordinary)   16, 28n1, 197, 249, 251–253, 284–285, 297–298, 319–320
  Institutional   1, 13–14, 40, 43–44, 46–48, 168–169, 376, 380
  Kantian   40–41, 44, 45, 46–48, 49–50, 55, 379–380
  Legal   43–44, 45, 113–114, 116
  Liberal   337, 387–388
  Moral   46–47, 109–110, 113–114, 116, 140, 141–142, 144, 185, 376, 379–380
  Normative   2, 44, 67, 212–213, 214–215
  Political   9–10, 13–14, 62–63, 182, 190
  Rooted   185, 189, 214
  Studies   2–3, 293–294, 383
  Subaltern   77–78, 121, 122–123
Cosmopolitanization   17–18, 60, 83–84, 85n2, 86, 87, 88, 89, 91–92, 92n3, 126, 230, 236, 293–294, 325, 371–372, 384–385
Cosmopolitics   187, 189, 190
Costa, Sergio   91–92
Cotesta, Vittorio   11
Counter-Cosmopolitanism   355, 356–359, 361–362
Counter-Enlightenment   1–2, 10–11
Counterterrorism   317, 355–357, 359, 361–364, 365–366
Cox, Richar   373
Crane, Diana   277–278
Creolization   70–71, 183, 189, 280–281
Crisis   4, 17, 37–38, 83–84, 98–99, 101, 162, 213–214, 307–308, 313, 320, 323–324, 332–333, 335–336,
  Economic   7, 84, 87, 169–170, 212, 251–252
  Financial   87, 212–213

Cultural   2–3, 7–9, 10–11, 13–14, 18, 28–31, 37, 38, 43, 57, 59, 60, 64, 73, 99, 106, 111, 112–114, 116–117, 126–127, 156, 164, 181–182, 183–184, 185, 186–187, 195–196, 197, 198, 199–200, 205, 206–207, 210, 226–227, 237, 251–252, 253, 276–279, 280–282, 283–284, 291–293, 295, 296–298, 299, 306–307, 319, 325, 339–340, 341–342, 344, 345, 346, 351–352, 357, 359, 377, 383
  Assimilation   240
  Difference   14–15, 38, 183–184, 186, 187, 276–277, 289–290, 295–296, 297–298, 321, 343–344
  Diversity   2, 184–185, 196, 199, 279–280, 284, 293, 297–298
  Homogenization   72, 73–74, 124–125
  Hybridization   64
  Pluralism   195–196
Culturalism   116–117
Culture (s)   10, 15, 27–28, 30–31, 32, 37–38, 57, 60, 64, 70–72, 73, 84, 93–94, 105, 116–117, 172, 182, 185–187, 188, 196–197, 199, 202, 206–207, 211–212, 221, 224, 237, 240, 276–278, 281–283, 295–297, 319, 355–356

Das, Veena   122–123
Decency, Decent   139–140, 142, 143, 147, 151, 334
Decolonization   10–11, 157, 182, 198
Delanty, Gerard   68, 93–94n3
Democracy   1, 7, 11, 14, 87, 92, 99–102, 106, 182, 278–279, 308–309, 313–314, 329–330, 337, 384, 386
  Cosmopolitan   14–15, 167–168, 169, 170–171, 172, 173–174, 175, 177, 178
  Liberal   163, 242, 361
Democratic   10–11, 14, 109–110, 111n4, 112–113, 122–123, 153, 172, 173–174, 175–176, 177–178, 181, 192–193, 194, 209–210, 289–290, 308–309, 313, 314, 323–324, 329–330, 336–337, 339–340, 341–342, 346, 348–349, 384, 387–388,
  System (s)   14, 32, 116–117, 167, 172, 176, 193, 339
  State (s)   173–174, 176
Democratization   68, 110–111, 173, 194–195

Derrida, Jacques   97–98, 236–237, 238, 241, 268
Despotism, Despotic   167, 309, 310–312, 376
Dialogue   7, 9–10, 13, 105–106, 122–123, 128, 167, 173–174, 197, 210, 224, 230
Diaspora   1, 67, 71–74, 76, 199–200, 251
Dickens, Charles   1, 2
Differentialism   116, 183
Discrimination (s)   116, 121–122, 157, 187, 196, 336, 365
Domination   49, 77–78, 93, 116–117, 132, 183, 186, 187, 277–278, 345–346,
   Colonial   360
   Western   116–117, 375
Donnelly, Jack   110–111
Douglass, Mike   195
Driessen, Henk, C.   198
Dufoix, Stéphane   12
Dunant, Henri   154–155
Durkheim, Émile   12, 54, 60–62, 63–64, 68, 343–344, 351–352
Dworkin, Ronald   113–114, 140

Egalitarianism, Egalitarian   40, 43–44, 100–102, 104, 106, 129–130, 140, 145–146, 150, 339, 340, 351–352
Eisenstadt, Shmuel N.   28–29
Eldem, Edhel   199
Elites   18, 38–39, 60, 62, 110–111, 177, 193–194, 198, 200–202, 212, 309, 310, 311–324, 334–335, 337, 341–342, 343–344, 345, 346–348, 351, 389–390, 391–392,
   Cultural   38
   Global   7–8, 284, 337
   Political   38, 319–320, 329–330, 339
Elitism, Elitist   97, 99–100, 104–105, 106, 194–195
Empathy   102–103, 105–106, 298–299, 348–349
Empire (s)   5–7, 28–30, 38, 91, 116–117, 277–278, 305–306, 310, 377
   Austro-Hungarian   5, 155
   British   323–324
   Ottoman   5, 155, 193–197, 198, 199
   Persian   29–30
   Roman   4–5, 31, 305–306
Empowerment, Empowered   7–9, 129–130, 158, 167–168, 170–171, 174, 276, 291–292, 307–308, 349

Engels, Friedrich   57, 350, 387
Enlightenment   5–6, 17–18, 154–155, 194, 242, 337, 340, 379–380, 385
Equal Moral Standing   14, 139, 151
Equality   10, 18, 43–44, 74, 112–113, 115, 169, 170, 172, 175–176, 181–182, 183–184, 186, 194, 210, 211–212, 236, 336, 341, 342, 345, 348, 349, 350, 353, 365
Eriksen, Erik Oddvar   209–210
Ethnic   140, 155, 193–194, 197, 238, 240, 250–253, 254–255, 320, 322, 323–325, 344, 351, 357, 358
   Cleansing   109–110, 305, 308–309, 337
   Group (s)   177, 186, 195–197, 330, 346
   Diversity   192, 195, 197, 199–202, 342
Ethnicity   10, 72, 73–74, 196, 250–252, 254, 318, 344, 345, 351
Ethnicization   10
Ethnocentrism   116, 126, 342–343
Ethno-Nationalism, Ethno-national   280, 283–284, 292, 339, 375, 383, 386
Ethno-racial   187
Eurocentrism, Eurocentric   57, 77, 92, 97, 101–102, 105–106, 121–122
European   5–6, 8–9, 10, 13, 49–50, 56, 57, 65, 77, 91–93, 122, 124–125, 128–129, 130–131, 145–146, 197, 198, 199, 206, 207–208, 209, 211, 212–213, 214, 230, 235–236, 252–253, 279–280, 307, 308–309, 311–312, 331–333, 335–336, 364, 385
European Convention on Human Rights   210
European Countries   62, 124, 168, 169, 174, 206–207, 227, 236, 242
European Court of Human Rights   159–160
European Union, Europe   15, 16, 17, 28, 49, 56–57, 61, 91–92, 118, 121–122, 122n1, 125, 127–129, 159–160, 168–169, 171, 173, 174, 178, 205–212, 213–215, 233–234, 240, 292, 309–310, 313–314, 323, 325, 329–334, 339–340, 342–343, 355, 357–359, 386, 390
Exclusion   7–8, 122–123, 175–176, 210–211

Falk, Richard   167
Feagin, Joe R.   319–320
Feinberg, Joel   141–142
Ferrara, Alessandro   206
Finchelstein, Federico   207

INDEX OF NAMES AND NOTIONS

Fine, Robert 91
Foreigner(s) 48, 50, 60, 175–176n2, 194–195, 200–201, 202, 221, 235–236, 239, 342
Foucault, Michel 97–98, 328–329
Fraternity 57–58, 332
Freud, Sigmund 347–348
Fromm, Erich 351–352
Fukuyama, Francis 1–2, 339

Gadamer, Hans-Georg 82n5
Gaius 38
Genocide(s) 109–110, 153, 225–226, 305, 328, 334, 352, 359
Germain, Annick 255
German Molz, Jenny 257
Gilpin, Robert 376
Glick Schiller, Nina 197, 250–251
Glissant, Edouard 183
Global
 City(ies) 13–15, 193, 194–195, 197, 199–201, 254, 344
 Commons 371, 377, 378
 Culture 71–72, 227, 277–278, 279–280
 Economy 1, 155, 319, 374, 389
 Finance 344, 388
 Market 163, 374–375
 Order 139–140, 144, 146–147, 148, 149–151, 374
 Political Economy 344
 Political Theory 140–141, 147–148
 Politics 14, 141, 151, 167, 168
 Poverty 139, 144, 145, 146–147
 Risks 6–7, 9–10, 82–83, 84, 86–88
 Society 1, 9–10, 11, 14, 15, 30–31, 37–38, 41–42, 47, 62, 64, 170, 299
 Turn 2–3, 71–72
 South 122–123, 378–379
 Studies 9–10, 11, 296–297
Globalization 7–10, 11, 12, 13–14, 17–18, 44, 46–47, 49–50, 53–57, 62–63, 67, 71–72, 73–76, 77–78, 82, 89, 97, 153, 154–155, 163, 167, 169–170, 178, 221, 224–225, 229, 230, 276–277, 279–280, 281–282, 289–290, 291–294, 296–298, 329–330, 334–335, 339–340, 344–345, 383, 388, 390–392,
 Cultural 16, 170, 181, 192, 195, 197, 201–202, 277–278, 283, 284–285, 339–340

Economic 17–18, 169, 177–178, 195, 337, 387
 Financial 169
 Social 169–170, 177–178
 Studies 7, 248, 251, 256–257
Globopolis 194–195
Gouldner, Alvin 70
Governance 8–9, 83–84, 125–126, 153, 194–195, 214, 340–342, 359, 365–366,
 Cosmopolitan 9
 Global 85, 141, 170–171, 177–178, 295–296, 386, 388
 Post-national 9
 Supranational 11
Gramsci, Antonio 351–352, 373–374
Grande, Edgar 93, 122, 208
Guenancia, Pierre 189
Guttman, Anna Michal 391–392

Habermas, Jürgen 87–88, 212–213
Haldrup, Michael 256
Hall, Stuart 71–74, 75–77
Hall, Susann 197, 254
Halton, Eugène 332–333
Han, Sang-Jin 126
Hannerz, Ulf 70–71, 253, 257, 267n2
Hardin, Garrett 378
Harrington, Austin 318–319
Harris, Neil 93–94n3
Harvey, David 387
He, Yijin 125
Hegel, Wilhelm Fiedrich 56–57, 347–348
Hegemony 18, 76–77n2, 124, 126, 371–376, 377–380,
 American 8–9, 122–123, 312, 318–319
 Cultural 8–9, 10–11, 28–29, 277–278
 Western 76–77, 121, 124, 127–128, 379–380
Heidegger, Martin 13, 98, 99–101, 100–101n1–n3, 102, 103, 106
Held, David 9–10, 14, 72, 167
Herodotus 29–30
Higbee, Will 281–282
Hill, Stephen 390
Hobbes, Thomas 55–56
Hochschild, Arlie Russel 341–342
Hollinger, David 292–293
Holocaust 109–110, 206–207, 225–227, 228–229, 230, 328, 341

Holton, Robert 18
Hospitality 16, 97, 214, 233, 234–236, 237–238, 240–242, 243, 295–296, 297–299, 337, 363, 376
Houts-Picca, Leslie 319–320
Huang, Shirlena 383
Human 30–31, 32–35, 37, 43–46, 49, 50, 53–54, 101–102, 103, 106, 107, 340, 346, 347–349, 350
  Basic Needs 139, 143–144, 291–292, 296–297, 298–299
  Dignity 13, 109–111, 111n4, 116–117, 118, 141–142, 148–149, 151, 209, 210, 296–297, 328, 334, 335–336, 339–340, 341, 350–351
  Flourishing 143
  History 27–28, 31, 40, 58, 60–61, 333–334
  Interests 47–48, 142–143, 144, 147–148
  Nature 97–98, 103–104, 113–114
  Suffering 139–140, 145, 153, 337, 384
Human Rights 13, 18, 28–30, 38, 56, 97–98, 109, 147–148, 167, 169, 175, 177–178, 212–213, 227, 233, 306–307, 314–315, 328, 334, 337, 341, 342, 355–357, 359, 361, 363–364, 365–366, 378–379, 386, 387–388, 389–390,
  Basic 139, 141, 142–143, 148–149, 172
  Civil and political 156–157, 163
  Discourse 109–111, 118, 160, 224–225, 227–228, 229, 230, 355
  Economic and social 163, 156
  Institutions 154, 155, 157, 159–160, 161, 162, 164
  Norms 14, 154, 155, 159–160, 162, 163, 164–165
  Solidarity 159
  System (Regime) 14, 109–110, 153, 164, 175
  Violations 154, 155, 158–159, 165, 171
Humanism, Humanist 1–2, 13, 16, 97–103, 104–107, 210, 237, 239–240, 243, 284–285, 298–299, 328, 351
Humanitarian Law 155, 157, 158–159, 357–358, 360–361
Humanitarianism, Humanitarian 118, 157, 162–163, 233–234, 318–319, 378–379
Humanity, Humaneness 6–7, 11, 15, 17–18, 27, 32–33, 34–35, 38, 40–41, 42–43, 44, 45, 49, 49n8, 60–62, 98–99, 102, 103, 104, 110–111, 148–149, 150, 164, 177, 183, 189–190, 221, 224, 225, 226–227, 229, 239–240, 291, 293, 294–295, 296–298, 299, 308–309, 332–334, 337, 351, 361, 385, 386, 389–390
Hume, David 188
Hussain, Yasmin 17, 280, 280–281n3

Identitarian Closure 7–8, 109–110, 116–117
Identity 72, 73–74, 84, 85, 88–89, 112–113, 116–117, 126, 129–131, 176, 182–184, 186, 187, 188, 189–190, 202, 209, 210, 213–214, 221–222, 223, 226–227, 228–230, 249, 251, 292–293, 320, 341–350, 351–352,
  Collective 72, 187, 188, 189–190, 221
  Cosmopolitan 187, 209
  Cultural 188, 391
  National 1–2, 53–55, 199–200, 221, 321–322, 335
Ideology, Ideological 7–8, 57, 97–98, 102, 116–117, 156–157, 192–193, 322, 328–329, 350, 357, 358, 390
Ilbert, Robert 198
Illiouz, Eva 280–281
Immigration 195–196, 200–201, 213–214, 240, 242, 291–292, 295–296, 306–307, 317, 324–325
Imperialism, Imperialist 92, 325, 351, 374, 376, 380, 383
Inclusion 7–8, 194, 195–196, 208–209, 348–349, 352
Individualism 113–114, 126–127, 129, 140
Individualization 84–85, 85n2, 126–127
Inequality (ies) 131, 139, 150, 199, 258–259, 291–293, 334–335, 340–341, 383, 385, 389
  Economic 344
  Global 147, 148–150, 388–389, 392
  Social 84–85, 384–385
  Wealth 149, 150, 388–389
Inglis, David 12
Institution (s,) 3, 7–8, 9, 14, 30, 85, 87–88, 101–102, 154–155, 157–158, 159–161, 173, 175, 176, 178, 187, 317, 331–332, 347–348, 373, 376, 377, 384, 385–386, 387–388,
  Global 141, 154
  International 157, 160–161, 172, 361–362, 365

INDEX OF NAMES AND NOTIONS

National 3, 90–91, 384
Regional 154, 161
Integration 7–8, 88, 173, 174, 178, 181–182, 193, 200–201, 213–214, 234, 289–290, 321
Cosmopolitan 212–213
European 10
International 168
Transnational 87
Intercultural 82, 94, 94n4, 105–106, 194, 197, 254, 280, 297–298, 391
International 2–3, 16, 18, 46–47, 50–51, 60, 61–62, 63–64, 83, 109–111, 111–112n5, 127–129, 141, 144–145, 146–147, 154–155, 156, 157, 158–160, 195, 200–201, 238, 248–249, 280, 289–290, 293, 307–308, 312, 337, 344, 356, 357–358, 363–364, 372–373, 377–378, 379, 380, 388, 391–392,
Bodies 14, 237
Cooperation 155–156, 169–170, 177–178, 209–210
Court of Justice : 175
Covenants 110–111, 156–158, 159, 165, 177, 364
Criminal Court 153, 169, 355–356, 386
Human Rights Regime (System) 14, 109–110, 153, 154, 164, 175
Law 9, 45–46, 47, 48, 160–161, 237, 318–319, 336, 360–363, 365–366, 377, 378–379
Order 8–9, 46, 47, 156, 170, 236
Organizations 14, 163–164, 165, 167–169, 171, 173, 174–175, 176, 177, 178, 248–249, 306, 309–310, 313, 374, 386
Politics 111–112n5, 165, 318–319
Relations 154, 160, 167, 173, 175, 213–214, 305–306, 317, 372, 376, 386
Society 64, 153, 154, 161
Trade 169, 334, 344
Islamic Radicalization 234
Islamic State 206–207, 357–358, 379
Islamophobia 17, 323, 331, 335
Iwabuchi, Koichi 281–282

Jaspers, Karl 27, 28–29, 31, 39, 332–334
Jünger, Ernst 99
Justice 1, 30, 34, 37, 55–56, 116, 118, 154, 157, 182, 183–184, 187, 211–212, 230, 236, 239, 343–344, 349

Cosmopolitan 185
Global 139–140, 151, 190, 383
Social 14–15, 99, 112–113, 181, 242, 336, 383–386, 387–388, 389

Kaldor, Mary 167
Kang, Jung In 126
Kang, Youwei 125–126
Katagari, Masataka 126–127
Kant, Immanuel 4, 12, 27, 40–41, 40–41n1-n2, 42–43, 44–45, 46–50, 49–50n8, 53, 54–58, 60–63, 64, 68, 97, 171, 194, 214, 236, 238–239, 340, 363, 376, 378–379, 385
Keohane, Robert O. 374
Kim, Seung Kuk 124, 126
Kindleberger, Charles 374
Koleva, Svetla 124
Kwang-Yeong, Shin 126
Kymlicka, Will 185–186, 242

Laffer, Arthur 149
Lakoff, George 348–349, 351
Langman, Lauren 18
Latham, Alan 192, 391
Latour, Bruno 83
Law of Peoples 48, 49–50
League of Nations 91, 170, 171
Lechner, Frank 276
Levi Strauss, Claude 97–98
Levy, Daniel 221
Li, Peiling 124, 125
Li, Youmei 130
Liberalism 17–18, 178, 181–182, 242, 243, 329, 384
Economic 168–169
Political 168–169, 182, 183–184, 186, 340–341
Lim, Song Hee 281–282
Localism, Local 1–2, 4–5, 6–7, 15, 28–31, 35, 41–42, 57, 59, 68–71, 77–78, 83–84, 89–90, 93–94, 129–130, 132, 168, 170–171, 176, 178, 235, 242, 254, 279–280, 296–298, 299, 313–314, 320, 322, 384, 386–387
Locke, John 340, 387, 388
Lourme, Louis 184–185
Löwith, Karl 100–101n2
Luhmann, Niklas 97–98
Lukes, Stephen 181–182

Machiavelli 375
Maffettone, Pietro 14
Mann, Michael 309, 329–330
Manners, Ian 210
Margalit, Avishai 116n13
Market 57, 59, 74–75, 85–86, 145, 212–215, 234, 251–253, 313, 334–335, 340, 344, 385, 388, 392
Martell, Luke 318–319
Martin, Herminio 74
Martinotti, Guido 254
Marx, Karl 12, 53, 54, 56–58, 59, 60, 65, 340–341, 343–344, 350, 351, 383, 387, 388
Marxism, Marxist 328–329, 372, 373–374
Mazakazu, Yamasaki 126–127
Mbembe, Achille 190
McCrew, Anthony 72
Memory
　Collective 15, 82, 221–225, 226, 227–230
　Cosmopolitan 15–16, 221–222, 224–227, 228–230
　National 15, 221, 224–226, 227
　Transnational 224–225
Mengzi 33–34, 35–36, 37
Merton, Robert K. 68–71, 296–297
Mesure, Sylvie 13, 183
Methodological Cosmopolitanism 74, 77–78, 88, 89, 92, 126
Methodological Nationalism 53–54, 60–61, 74, 75–76, 82–83, 88–89, 91, 92, 283, 318
Metropolis 53, 59, 60, 64, 193, 195
Michels Robert 75–76
Mignolo, Walter 77–78
Migrant(s) 175–176, 193, 194, 195–197, 198, 200–201, 202, 233–234, 238, 240–241, 248–249, 250–252, 253, 254, 255–256, 258, 278–279, 331–332, 335–336, 391
Migration 7, 11, 16, 17, 50, 169, 172, 177–178, 195, 200, 248–252, 253–254, 258, 323, 325, 331–332, 346, 386–387
Migration Studies 192–193, 233, 236, 239, 241, 250–251
Miller, David 187, 376
Minority 155, 171, 176, 183, 187, 190, 198, 199, 200–201, 319–320, 336, 337
　Ethnic 175–176, 199, 323–325
　Groups 167–168, 175–176, 195–196, 202

Mobility 11, 16, 59, 83–85, 194–195, 248–250, 253, 254, 255–259, 277–278, 283–284, 291–292, 319, 391
Modernity 9–10, 17–18, 72–73, 76, 78, 88, 92, 99–100, 101, 103–104, 106, 111n4, 129–130, 206, 305, 328, 329, 332–333, 337, 343–344, 351–352, 384–385,
　First 88–89, 91, 92, 111n4, 122–123, 124, 129–130, 181, 195
　Reflexive 88, 318
　Second 92, 93
Modernization 83, 84–85, 88, 91–93, 126, 153, 154–155, 199, 328–329
Montale, Eugenio 142–143
Montesquieu 253–254
Moral Equality 115, 116–117, 140–141
Moral Obligations 35–36, 43, 234, 236–237, 238, 239–240, 349
Moyn, Samuel 110–111n3, 328
Mozi 33–34, 39
Multiconfessional 4–5, 11
Multiculturalism, Multicultural 4–5, 11, 14–15, 37–38, 176, 181–182, 183, 184–185, 186–187, 189, 190, 193–194, 196–197, 200–201, 202, 240–242, 289–290, 329–330
Multilateralism, Multilateral 50, 312
Munford, Lewis 332–333

Nash, Kate 236
Nations 8–9, 10, 49, 57, 59, 60–61, 72, 73, 101–102, 122–123, 140, 155–156, 167–169, 170–171, 173, 174, 181–182, 187, 192–193, 235–236, 306–307, 308–309, 310, 313–314, 330, 340–341, 355
Nation-State(s) 5–6, 7–8, 9, 13–14, 17, 53–54, 58, 61, 62, 73, 74–75, 76, 88–89, 91, 92, 126–127, 154, 172, 190, 193, 221, 238, 251, 291–292, 295, 299, 305, 308–309, 313–315, 318, 325, 330, 340–341, 376, 384–385, 386
National 8–9, 41–42, 45–46, 47, 48, 82, 83, 87, 88–89, 91, 93–94, 115, 148, 157, 159–160, 163–164, 165, 168, 172, 187, 189, 199–202, 212–213, 238, 280, 283, 286, 299, 308–309, 311–312, 313, 321–322, 355, 361–363, 364, 365–366, 371, 378, 384–385, 386–387, 388, 390, 391

INDEX OF NAMES AND NOTIONS   403

Borders   14, 15, 54, 58, 61–62, 190, 221, 224, 225–226, 229–230, 291–292, 293, 318, 340–341, 373
 Culture   277–278, 280, 340–341
 Society (ies)   9, 45–46, 47, 87
 State   4, 9, 14, 46, 49–50, 54, 213–214
Nationalism, Nationalist   1–2, 15, 17, 62, 65, 89, 90–91, 92, 109–110, 168–169, 170–171, 177, 178, 211–212, 213–214, 221–222, 223–224, 227–228, 229–230, 299, 313, 317, 318, 325, 328, 331–332, 334, 340–343, 345, 346, 351–352, 355–356, 387, 388, 390–391
Nativism, Nativist   78, 233–234, 240, 342–343
Nava Mica   276–277
Nazism, Nazi   106–107, 206–207, 292
Neoliberalism, Neoliberal   77–78, 194–195, 212–213, 339–340, 344, 372, 373–374, 388–389, 390
Nietzsche, Friedrich   339
Non-Governmental Organizations   109–110, 127, 160, 163–164, 171, 228–229, 342, 386
Non-Western   12, 15, 67, 74, 76–77, 116–117, 125, 126, 128, 193, 200–201
Norms   9, 13–14, 29–30, 56, 62, 141, 154, 155, 208, 233–234, 240–241, 278–279, 282, 289, 310, 312, 333–334, 365–366, 373–374, 378, 386, 391–392,
 Cosmopolitan   55, 386, 387–388
 International   171
 Universal   87–88, 373
Nowicka, Magdalena   16, 242
Nussbaum, Martha   55, 290–291
Nyamnjoh, Francis B   239
Nye, Joseph   278–279n2

Occidentalism   92, 116
Octobre, Sylvie   16–17
Orientalism   74–75, 122–123, 127–128
Otherness   3, 16, 18, 181, 182, 183, 184–185, 248, 283, 290, 291, 293, 294–295

Pagès-El Karoui, Delphine   15
Pareto, Vilfredo   75–76
Park, Robert E.   250–251
Parochialism, parochial   10, 74–75, 116, 298–299, 387–388

Parsons, Talcott   126–127
Particularism   10, 35, 74–75, 97, 291
Patel, Sujata   77
Patriotism   58–59, 61, 62
Peace   56, 116, 125–126, 155, 167, 171, 173–174, 211, 253–254, 374–375,
 International   155–156, 173–174, 358, 358n9
 Perpetual   46–47, 48, 68, 97, 214, 363, 376, 378–379
Pécoud, Antoine   253
Pendenza, Massimo   15
Penn, William   171
Philipps, Anne   183–184, 185
Plato   36–37, 183
Pogge, Thomas W   140–141
Policar, Alain   14–15
Populism, Populist   1–2, 18, 109–110, 163, 323, 325, 329–330, 331–332, 334–335, 339–340, 341–343, 345, 346, 348–349, 351–352, 353, 355–356
Postcolonialism, Postcolonial   74–75, 78, 91–92, 125, 127–128, 156–157, 328
Post-national   169, 227, 289–290, 339–340, 378–379
Post-Westphalian   213–214, 213–214n3, 340–341
Poulantzas, Nikos   373–374
Power   8–9, 16, 30–31, 32, 33–36, 51, 54, 55–56, 57, 89–90, 111, 118, 126, 129–130, 164, 187, 208–209, 210, 214–215, 237, 239–241, 242, 243, 255–256, 258–259, 294–295, 309–312, 318–319, 321, 339, 341–343, 346–348, 349, 351, 364, 372–375, 376–377, 378, 383, 384, 386
 Economic   109–110, 174, 208–209
 Nuclear   175–176, 336
 Political   109–110, 167, 168, 389
 State   85, 309, 363–364
Progress   10–11, 43–44, 49, 97–100, 162–163, 173–174, 181–182, 372–373
Public Opinion   59, 60, 154–155, 171, 210–211, 233–234

Qu, Jingdong   125–126

Race (s)   33–34, 42, 49, 49n8, 72, 115, 187, 258–259, 342, 344, 345, 348, 351, 383

Racism, Racist 17, 55, 100–101, 104, 168, 233–234, 240, 317, 319–320, 323, 324–325, 342–343, 383
Radice, Martha 255
Ramcharan, Bertrand 157
Ramel, Frederic 18
Randeria, Shalini 93, 122–123
Rationalization 27–29, 37, 39, 84
Rawls, John 113–114, 142–143
Reflexivity 27, 29–30, 38, 83, 88, 89–90
Refugees 16, 175–176, 177, 205, 240, 241–243, 257–258, 292, 313, 328, 331–332, 356n4
Regev, Motti 280
Regulation 13–14, 30–31, 207, 295–296, 310–311, 313–314, 336, 388–389
Religion 9–10, 17–18, 27–28, 55–56, 63, 64, 115, 155, 189, 240, 254, 318, 328–329, 331–333, 334, 335, 336, 337, 344, 345, 348, 355–356
Religious 27–28, 30, 32, 35–36, 97–98, 106, 112–114, 153, 155, 187, 210, 254, 321–322, 342–344, 346, 350, 351–352, 357, 357–359n7, 358–385, 387–388,
  Fundamentalism 4, 109–110, 329
  Traditionalism 328
Renaut, Alain 182, 183
Respect 2, 13–14, 106, 112–114, 115, 140, 336
Ressentiment 18, 339–340, 345, 346–348
Rhys-Taylor, Alex 254
Ricoeur, Paul 94n4, 130
Rights 13–14, 17–18, 38, 40–41, 49, 50, 131, 182, 185–186, 190, 205–207, 294–295, 305–306, 340–341, 345, 356
  Basic 14, 111, 172
  Civil Rights 10–11, 109–110, 156, 176
  Cultural 157–158, 186, 359, 365
  Political 109–110, 111, 156–157, 227, 340–341, 346
  Social 109–110, 111, 115–116, 129–130, 156–157, 207, 210–214, 340–341
  Solidarity 159
Rorty, Richard 111–112
Roudometof, Victor 296–297
Roulleau-Berger, Laurence 13
Rousseau, Jean-Jacques 340
Rule of Law 43–46, 47–48, 51, 100–101, 167, 169, 171, 234, 307, 308–309, 336–337, 341–342, 363, 365–366, 386
Rumford, Chris 265–266, 270, 271n3

Safier, Michel 194
Said, Edward 121–122, 270–271
Saint-Simon, Claude Henri de 12, 53–54, 60–61, 171
Saito, Hiro 15
Salazar, Noel B. 257–258
Sandercock, Leonie 194
Santos, Boaventura de Sousa 77–78, 122–123
Sartre, Jean-Paul 13, 98, 100–101, 102–107
Sassen, Saskia 195
Scanlon, Thomas 150
Scapes
  Ethnoscapes 73–74, 276
  Finanscapes 73–74
  Ideoscapes 73–74, 276
  Mediascape 73–74
  Technoscapes 73–74
Scheler, Max 347–348
Schmitt, Carl 99, 102, 330–331
Schmoll, Camille 16
Schütz, Alfred 269, 271
Secularism, Secular 10, 17–18, 97–98, 113–114n9, 115, 122–123, 328, 329, 331–332, 337, 345, 346
Secularization 17–18, 328–329
Security 9, 40–41, 87, 153, 154, 161–162, 174–175, 211, 308, 321, 323–324, 325, 356, 356–357n5, 357–358, 358n9, 359, 363, 365–366, 372, 378–379,
  Environmental 177
  Human 154, 356, 356n5, 363, 365–366
  National 154, 364
  State 365–366
Sen, Amartya 115–116
Sennett, Richard 194
Shi, Yunqing 130
Shin, Kwang-Yeong 126
Shue, Henry 141, 144
Shujiro, Yasawa 124, 126–127
Silverstone, Roger 34
Simmel, Georg 60, 249–251, 253–254, 263–266, 264–265n1, 268–32, 269, 270–271, 273, 343–344
Sklair, Leslie 390
Skrbiš, Zlatko 31n2
Sloterdijk, Peter 98–99, 100–101
Smith, Adam 56, 58
Smith, Anthony 227
Sociability 42, 45, 49–50, 55–56, 235

INDEX OF NAMES AND NOTIONS 405

Socialization   16–17, 240, 299, 345–346, 348–349
Society of Nations   46, 47, 50
Sociology
   American   70
   Asian   121, 124, 128–129
   Chinese   124–125, 129, 130–131, 132
   Classical   12, 53–54, 57–58, 60, 64–65, 74–76, 92, 125–126, 309
   Cosmopolitan   11, 53–55, 60, 74–76, 82–83, 90–91, 93–94
   European   121, 124, 128–129, 130
   Global   74–76, 122–123, 124, 128–129
   Post-Western   121, 122n1, 127, 128–129, 132
   Southern   74, 77
   Western   13, 70–71, 74, 126–127, 130, 132
Socrates   27, 29, 332–333
Soft Power   8–9, 278–279, 278–279n2
Solidarity   13–14, 53–54, 64, 122–123, 189, 194, 210–213, 214–215, 221, 229, 251–252, 298–299, 343–344, 348, 356
Sovereignty   14, 17, 74, 160–162, 169, 213–214, 237, 291–292, 305, 306–308, 309–312, 340–341,
   National   223–224, 328, 332
   State   223–224, 310–311, 314–315, 372
   Westphalian   305–306
Spinoza, Baruch   109–110
Spivak, Gayatari Chakravorty   121–122
Sternhell, Zeev   292n1
Stranger (s)   16, 100–101, 184, 190, 193–194, 196–197, 249–250, 253–254, 323, 324–325
Stuart-Glennie, John Stuart   332–333
Sun, Bewen   124–125
Sun, Feiyu   130
Supranational   3, 5–6, 7–8, 9, 13–14, 15, 74–75, 299, 309–310
Szerynski, Bronislaw   319
Sznaider, Nathan   221, 227

Takakura, Hiroki   127
Tan, Kok-Chor   376
Tarrius, Alain   251–252
Tassin, Etienne   190
Terrorism   7, 18, 87, 172, 200–201, 206–207, 234, 239, 321–322, 323–324, 331, 355–364, 365–366
Terzani, Tiziano   272

Thucydides   371–372
Tolstoy, Leo   306
Tompkins, Robert   351
Tönnies, Ferdinand   12, 53, 57–60, 343–344
Tourism   16, 172, 178, 248–249, 256–258, 292–293, 344, 389
Tradition   28, 35–36, 38, 48, 60, 73–74, 76–77, 94, 102, 113–114, 117–118, 129–130, 154, 176, 186–187, 211–212, 251, 291, 292–293, 328, 332–333, 334, 337
Translation   90–91, 126–127, 320
Transnational   7–8, 12, 15, 53–54, 58, 70–72, 76, 83, 84, 86, 87, 89, 121, 122–123, 128–129, 131, 132, 141, 165, 212–213, 227–229, 230, 250–251, 277–279, 280–282, 299, 344, 373–374, 384, 386–387, 390
Transnational Networks   70–71, 228–229, 390
Transnationalism   65, 76, 93–94, 93–94n3, 251
Turinsky, Theresia   188
Turner, Bryan S.   17–18, 54, 62, 74–76, 318, 390

United Nations   109, 111, 116–117n7, 155–156, 157–159, 164, 165, 168, 171, 175, 227, 279–280, 306, 341, 358n9, 360–361n1, 361–362n23, 386
Universal Declaration of Human Rights   13, 109–111, 113–114, 113–114n9, 115–117, 115n10, 116–117n17, 118, 153, 155, 156, 159, 165, 328
Universal State   46, 47
Universalism   10, 12, 13, 27, 63, 75–76, 77, 87–88, 116–117, 122, 183, 193–194, 291, 292n1, 294–295, 296, 348, 383, 386
Universality   18, 35, 38, 74, 105–106, 118, 140, 154, 251, 293, 296, 350, 356
Universalization   18, 27, 78, 284, 380
Utilitarianism   140, 212–213
Urry, John   319

Values   10, 14, 76, 100–101, 104, 161, 186, 208, 210, 211, 233–234, 240–241, 278–279, 282, 284, 321–322, 328, 331–332, 336, 337, 341–342, 343–344, 345–348, 349, 351, 352, 357, 363, 364, 365, 373–374, 379–380, 386
   Asian   116

Values (cont.)
  Christian 331–332
  Cosmopolitan 18, 167, 169, 171, 172, 176, 257–258, 329–330, 334, 339–340, 345, 348, 352, 360–361, 363–364, 365–366
  Cultural 77–78, 116–117, 281–282
  International 299
  Moderne 100–101, 336
  Political 349, 379
  Religious 233–234, 331–332
  Traditional 18, 37, 339–340, 351–352
  Universal 210, 332
  Western 331, 379
Vertovec, Steve 193–194, 254
Vicherat Mattar, Daniela 122–123
Violence 1–2, 109–110, 158, 230, 236, 237, 238–239, 331–332, 337, 356, 357–359n7, 359, 360–361, 376–377
Voltaire 56
Vulnerability 115–116, 153, 334

Wagnleitner, Reinhold 278–279
Waldron, Jeremy 110–111
Walker, Clive 18
War(s) 40, 55–56, 62–63, 105–106, 153, 162–163, 171, 173–175, 177–178, 206–207, 209–210, 223–224, 227–228, 227–228n1, 234–235, 298–299, 328, 330–331, 351, 353, 359, 360–361, 371–372, 374, 375, 376–377, 377n2, 378
  Cold War 13, 109–110, 154, 156–157, 160, 163, 168–169, 206–207, 228–229, 228–229n2, 378–379
  Colonial 206–207
  First World War 62, 155
  Second World War 13, 98, 102–103, 109–110, 124, 153, 167, 168–169, 206–207, 278–280, 332–333, 341, 388
  World Wars 97–98, 99, 161–162, 386, 387
  War on Terror 87, 163, 308, 363
Wasser, Frederick 281–282
Waters, Malcom 276–277

Weber, Max 28–29, 38, 39, 54, 221, 345–346, 383
Werbner, Pnina 72
Wessendorf, Susanne 196–197, 255
West 8–9, 49, 70–71, 72, 91–92, 121–123, 128, 156–157, 167, 168–169, 206, 317, 318–319, 329, 331, 334–336
Western 13, 15, 28, 39, 92, 93, 97, 116, 118, 121–123, 146, 148, 168–169, 174, 193–194, 199, 200–201, 230, 277, 281–282, 310, 318–319, 357–359, 361–362, 383, 386
  Countries 174, 200–201, 277, 318–319
  Culture 139, 240–241
  Societies 92
  Tradition 32–33, 35–36
Westin, Drew 351
Westphalian 13–14, 155, 305–306
Whelan, Daniel J 14
Wittgenstein, Ludwig 188
Woodward 267n2
World
  Bank 144–145, 146–147
  Citizenship 372–373, 375–376
  Culture 62, 70–71
  Economy 151, 313
  Moral Culture 56, 62–63, 70–71
  Patriotism 61–62
  Risk Society 82, 83, 84, 85–86, 126
  State 61
  Trade Organization 77–78, 169, 172, 312, 344

Xenophobia, Xenophobic 1–2, 17, 168, 170, 178, 212, 233–234, 240, 317, 325, 342–343, 351–352
Xie, Jiabiao 131
Xie, Lizhong 125
Xunzi 36

Yamasaki, Masakazu 126–127
Yanakakis, Ilios 198
Yatabe, Kazuhiko 126–127
Yazawa, Shujiro 124
Yeoh, Brenda S.A. 391

Printed in the United States
By Bookmasters